Lecture Notes in Computer Science 15058

Founding Editors

Gerhard Goos
Juris Hartmanis

Editorial Board Members

Elisa Bertino, *Purdue University, West Lafayette, IN, USA*
Wen Gao, *Peking University, Beijing, China*
Bernhard Steffen, *TU Dortmund University, Dortmund, Germany*
Moti Yung, *Columbia University, New York, NY, USA*

The series Lecture Notes in Computer Science (LNCS), including its subseries Lecture Notes in Artificial Intelligence (LNAI) and Lecture Notes in Bioinformatics (LNBI), has established itself as a medium for the publication of new developments in computer science and information technology research, teaching, and education.

LNCS enjoys close cooperation with the computer science R & D community, the series counts many renowned academics among its volume editors and paper authors, and collaborates with prestigious societies. Its mission is to serve this international community by providing an invaluable service, mainly focused on the publication of conference and workshop proceedings and postproceedings. LNCS commenced publication in 1973.

Michèle Weiland · Sarah Neuwirth ·
Carola Kruse · Tobias Weinzierl
Editors

High Performance Computing

ISC High Performance 2024 International Workshops

Hamburg, Germany, May 12–16, 2024
Revised Selected Papers

Editors
Michèle Weiland
University of Edinburgh
Edinburgh, UK

Sarah Neuwirth
Johannes Gutenberg University Mainz
Mainz, Germany

Carola Kruse
Cerfacs
Toulouse, France

Tobias Weinzierl
Durham University
Durham, UK

ISSN 0302-9743   ISSN 1611-3349 (electronic)
Lecture Notes in Computer Science
ISBN 978-3-031-73715-2   ISBN 978-3-031-73716-9 (eBook)
https://doi.org/10.1007/978-3-031-73716-9

© The Editor(s) (if applicable) and The Author(s), under exclusive license
to Springer Nature Switzerland AG 2025, corrected publication 2025
Chapter "Interactive in Situ Visualization" is licensed under the terms of the Creative Commons Attribution 4.0 International License (http://creativecommons.org/licenses/by/4.0/). For further details see license information in the chapter.

This work is subject to copyright. All rights are solely and exclusively licensed by the Publisher, whether the whole or part of the material is concerned, specifically the rights of translation, reprinting, reuse of illustrations, recitation, broadcasting, reproduction on microfilms or in any other physical way, and transmission or information storage and retrieval, electronic adaptation, computer software, or by similar or dissimilar methodology now known or hereafter developed.
The use of general descriptive names, registered names, trademarks, service marks, etc. in this publication does not imply, even in the absence of a specific statement, that such names are exempt from the relevant protective laws and regulations and therefore free for general use.
The publisher, the authors and the editors are safe to assume that the advice and information in this book are believed to be true and accurate at the date of publication. Neither the publisher nor the authors or the editors give a warranty, expressed or implied, with respect to the material contained herein or for any errors or omissions that may have been made. The publisher remains neutral with regard to jurisdictional claims in published maps and institutional affiliations.

This Springer imprint is published by the registered company Springer Nature Switzerland AG
The registered company address is: Gewerbestrasse 11, 6330 Cham, Switzerland

If disposing of this product, please recycle the paper.

Preface

The 39th edition of the ISC High Performance conference (ISC-HPC 2024) was held in Hamburg, Germany. The conference was held in-person during the period from May 12–16, 2024. As for the previous editions, the HPC community responded enthusiastically as manifested by over 3,000 attendees.

As in past years, ISC 2024 was accompanied by the ISC High Performance workshop series on the Thursday after the main event. In total, 10 workshops chose the option to contribute to this edition of proceedings: Compiler-Assisted Correctness Checking and Performance Optimization for HPC Workshop (C3PO 2024), HPC on Heterogeneous Hardware Workshop (H3 2024), Third Workshop on Communication, I/O, and Storage at Scale on Next-Generation Platforms – Scalable Infrastructures (ISC 2024 IXPUG), HPC I/O in the Data Center Workshop (HPC-IODC 2024), Third Combined Workshop on Interactive and Urgent Supercomputing (CW-IUS 2024), 5th ISC HPC International Workshop on Monitoring & Operational Data Analytics (MODA24), Fourth International Workshop on RISC-V for HPC, 2nd International Workshop on Sustainable Supercomputing, Second International Workshop on Converged Computing on Edge, Cloud, and HPC (WOCC'24), and 8th International Workshop on In Situ Visualization (WOIV'24). Also, 13 other workshops opted for a presentation-only format, i.e. workshops without proceedings.

In total, 50 full papers were submitted for review, of which 35 were accepted for publication. Each paper underwent a thorough review by their respective workshop's Program Committee. With on average three reviewers per paper, single-blind reviews, and the opportunity for the authors to revise their contribtion after the event, the 34 finally submitted papers in the present volume are of outstanding quality. Each chapter of this proceedings book contains the papers for one single workshop. For most of the workshops, an additional preface describes the review process and provides a summary of the outcomes.

We will gather next year in Hamburg, Germany, for another successful ISC High Performance workshops series. Until then, we want to thank our workshop committee members, workshop organizers, and all contributors and attendees of the ISC 2024 workshops, and we are proud to present the latest findings on the topics related to the research, development, and applications of large-scale, high-performance systems.

July 2024

Michèle Weiland
Sarah Neuwirth
Carola Kruse
Tobias Weinzierl

Organization

Workshop Committee

Michèle Weiland (Chair)	The University of Edinburgh, UK
Sarah Neuwirth (Deputy Chair)	Johannes Gutenberg University Mainz, Jülich Supercomputing Centre (JSC), Germany
Nick Brown	Edinburgh Parallel Computing Centre (EPCC), The University of Edinburgh, UK
Norbert Eicker	Jülich Supercomputing Centre, Bergische Universität Wuppertal, Germany
Norihisa Fujita	University of Tsukuba, Japan
Heike Jagode	University of Tennessee Knoxville, USA
Sandra Mendez	Barcelona Supercomputing Center, Spain
Arnab Paul	BITS Pilani, Goa Campus, India
Ivy Peng	KTH Royal Institute of Technology, Sweden
Eva Siegman	Stony Brook University, AHUG, USA
Julien Sindt	Edinburgh Parallel Computing Centre, UK
Miwako Tsuji	RIKEN, AHUG, Japan
Andy Turner	Edinburgh Parallel Computing Centre, UK
Lipeng Wan	Georgia State University, USA
Bing Xie	Microsoft, USA

Proceedings Chairs

Carola Kruse (Chair)	CERFACS, France
Tobias Weinzierl (Deputy)	Durham University, UK

Contents

Compiler-assisted Correctness Checking and Performance Optimization for HPC Workshop (C3PO'24)

Compiler-Based Precalculation of MPI Message Envelopes 5
   Tim Jammer, Tim Heldmann, Michael Blesel, Michael Kuhn, and Christian Bischof

Adaptive Parallelism in OpenMP Through Dynamic Variants 17
   Adrian Munera, Guerau Dasca, Eduardo Quiñones, and Sara Royuela

Augmentation of MPI Traces Using Selective Instrumentation 31
   Sebastian Kreutzer, Josep Pocurull Serra, Christan Iwainsky, Marta Garcia Gasulla, and Christian Bischof

Leveraging Static Analysis to Accelerate Dynamic Race Detection for Remote Memory Access Programs 45
   Simon Schwitanski, Yussur Mustafa Oraji, Cornelius Pätzold, Joachim Jenke, and Matthias S. Müller

Static-Dynamic Analysis for Performance and Accuracy of Data Race Detection in MPI One-Sided Programs 59
   Radjasouria Vinayagame, Van Man Nguyen, Marc Sergent, Samuel Thibault, and Emmanuelle Saillard

HPC on Heterogeneous Hardware Workshop (H3 2024)

Introducing SYCL to Accelerate a Fock Operator Calculation Library of the BigDFT Electronic Structure Code 79
   Christoph Bauinger and Luigi Genovese

Portable GPU Implementation of the WP-CCC Ion-Atom Collisions Code 102
   I. B. Abdurakhmanov, N. W. Antonio, M. Cytowski, and A. S. Kadyrov

Benchmarking of GPU Performance Saturation on Accelerated Cluster Nodes via Molecular Dynamics Software Packages 115
   Plamen Dobrev and Gerald Mathias

Accelerating Fusion Plasma Collision Operator Solves with Portable
Batched Iterative Solvers on GPUs 127
   Paul T. Lin, Pratik Nayak, Aditya Kashi, Dhruva Kulkarni,
   Aaron Scheinberg, and Hartwig Anzt

Optimizing GNN-Based Multiple Object Tracking on a Graphcore IPU 141
   Mustafa Orkun Acar, Fatma Güney, and Didem Unat

A Novel Mixed Precision Defect Correction Solver for Heterogeneous
Computing 154
   Yann T. Delorme, Mark Wasserman, Alon Zameret, and Zhaohui Ding

Third Workshop on Communication, I/O, and Storage at Scale on Next-Generation Platforms - Scalable Infrastructures (ISC 2024 IXPUG)

Investigating the Performance of LLVM-Based Intel Fortran Compiler (ifx) 173
   Dhani Ruhela

High Performance Fabric Support in DAOS 185
   Michael Hennecke, Alexander Oganezov, Jerome Soumagne,
   John Carrier, and Joseph Moore

HPC I/O in the Data Center Workshop (HPC-IODC 2024)

Secure Elasticsearch Clusters on HPC Systems for Sensitive Data 199
   Hendrik Nolte, Lars Quentin, and Julian Kunkel

Introducing the Metric Proxy for Holistic I/O Measurements 213
   Jean-Baptiste Besnard, Ahmad Tarraf, Alberto Cascajo,
   and Sameer Shende

Third Combined Workshop on Interactive and Urgent Supercomputing (CW-IUS 2024)

Challenges in Computing Resource Sharing Towards Next-Gen Interactive
Accelerated HPC 231
   Toshio Endo, Shohei Minami, Akihiro Nomura, Hiroki Ohtsuji,
   Jun Kato, Masahiro Miwa, Eiji Yoshida, Tomoya Yuki,
   and Ryuichi Sakamoto

Accelerating Time-to-Science by Streaming Detector Data Directly
into Perlmutter Compute Nodes 243
   *Samuel S. Welborn, Chris Harris, Peter Ercius, Deborah J. Bard,
and Bjoern Enders*

Use Cases for High Performance Research Desktops 257
   *Robert Henschel, Jonas Lindemann, Anders Follin, Bernd Dammann,
Cicada Dennis, and Abhinav Thota*

5th ISC HPC International Workshop on Monitoring and Operational Data Analytics (MODA24)

An Exascale Slurm Testing and Evaluation Environment Utilising
Generated DAG Workloads 273
   Laslo Hunhold and Stefan Wesner

Challenges for Monitoring and Data Analytics in a Leadership Public
Data Repository 287
   Patrick M. Widener, Alex May, Tatiyanna Singleton, and Olga Kuchar

Fourth International Workshop on RISC-V for HPC

Preparing to Hit the Ground Running: Adding RISC-V Support to EESSI 297
   *Julián Morillo, Caspar Van Leeuwen, Bob Dröge, Kenneth Hoste,
Lara Peeters, Thomas Röblitz, and Alan O'Cais*

Scaling an Augmented RISC-V Processor Design with High-Level
Synthesis 312
   Johannes Schoder and H. Martin Bücker

Performance Analysis of BERT on RISC-V Processors with SIMD Units 325
   *Héctor Martínez, Sandra Catalán, Carlos García,
Francisco D. Igual, Rafael Rodríguez-Sánchez, Adrián Castelló,
and Enrique S. Quintana-Ortí*

Integrating RISC-V SIMT and Scalar Cores: Loosely to Tightly Coupled 339
   *Sooraj Chetput, Anusuya Nallathambi, Spencer Bowles,
Justin Cambridge, Alex Chitsazzadeh, Gagan Gundala,
Zengxiang Han, Johnathan Hong, Guilliame Hu, Ronit Nallagatla,
Ansh Patel, Khoi Pham, Abinands Ramshanker, Htet Yan,
FangLing Zhang, Zach Lagpacan, Clay Hughes, Kevin Pedretti,
Mark Johnson, and Timothy G. Rogers*

Performance Characterisation of the 64-Core SG2042 RISC-V CPU
for HPC 354
   Nick Brown and Maurice Jamieson

2nd International Workshop on Sustainable Supercomputing

Impact of Computational Load Balance and Power Capping on Energy
Efficiency in HPC Centers 371
   Martin Rose, Jose Gracia, Christian Simmendinger, Andreas Ruopp,
   Ramil Nabiev, and Christoph Niethammer

**Second International Workshop on Converged Computing on Edge,
Cloud, and HPC (WOCC'24)**

Cluster in the Cloud—Scalable, Heterogeneous Compute Clusters
for HPC, HTC and AI in the Public Cloud or On-Premise 389
   Matt Williams, Chris Edsall, Christopher Woods, and Sadaf Alam

A User-Oriented Portable, Reproducible, and Scalable Software Ecosystem 402
   Alfio Lazzaro, Utz-Uwe Haus, Sandrine Charousset, and Nina Mujkanovic

Leveraging Private Container Networks for Increased User Isolation
and Flexibility on HPC Clusters 415
   Lise Jolicoeur, François Diakhaté, and Raymond Namyst

FLOTO: Beyond Bandwidth - A Framework for Adaptable, Multi-sensor
Data Collection in Scientific Research 427
   Alicia Esquivel Morel, Mark Powers, Kate Keahey, Zack Murry,
   Tomas Javier Sitzmann, Jianfeng Zhou, and Prasad Calyam

Understanding Layered Portability from HPC to Cloud in Containerized
Environments 439
   Daniel Medeiros, Gabin Schieffer, Jacob Wahlgren, and Ivy Peng

8th International Workshop on In Situ Visualization (WOIV'24)

Interactive in Situ Visualization 457
   Dennis Grieger

InsitUE - Enabling Hybrid In-situ Visualizations Through Unreal Engine
and Catalyst 469
   Marcel Krüger, Jan Frieder Milke, Torsten W. Kuhlen, and Tim Gerrits

In Situ in Transit Hybrid Analysis with Catalyst-ADIOS2 482
  François Mazen, Louis Gombert, Lucas Givord, and Charles Gueunet

Correction to: Interactive in Situ Visualization C1
  Dennis Grieger

Author Index 491

Compiler-assisted Correctness Checking and Performance Optimization for HPC Workshop (C3PO'24)

Preface to the Workshop on Compiler-assisted Correctness Checking and Performance Optimization for HPC (C3PO'24)

1 Objectives/Topics

The changing of HPC architecture and software stack create enormous challenges for HPC application developers that need to write performance portable code and keep existing applications up to speed. Purely manual solutions are cost prohibitive. Source-to-source translators are poised to address these challenges automatically or with user input semi-automatically. Practical compiler-enabled programming environments, applied analysis methodologies, and end-to-end tool- chains are crucial to performance portability in the exascale era.

C3PO is a workshop at the intersection of compilers/translators, HPC middleware, and HPC applications. The workshop brings together researchers with a shared interest in applying compilation and source-to-source translation method- ologies to enhance parallel programming, including explicit programming models such as MPI, OpenMP, and hybrid models.

2 Workshop Organization

Six papers were submitted, and after a double-blind review process, five papers were accepted. The workshop took place on May 16, 2024.

2.1 Organizers

Emmanuelle Saillard	Inria, France
Julien Jaeger	CEA, France
Anthony Skjellum	University of Tennessee at Chattanooga, USA
Purushotham Bangalore	University of Alabama at Birmingham, USA
Peter Pirkelbauer	Lawrence Livermore National Laboratory, USA
Peter Thoman	University of Innsbruck, Austria

2.2 Program Committee

Christian Bischof	TU Darmstadt, Germany
Patrick Carribault	CEA, France
Liao Chunhua	Lawrence Livermore National Laboratory, USA

Alexander Hueck	TU Darmstadt, Germany
Jan-Patrick Lehr	AMD, Germany
Pei-Hung Lin	Lawrence Livermore National Laboratory, USA
Dorian Leroy	CEA, France
Benson Muite	Kichakato Kizito, Kenya
Sara Royuela	BSC, Spain
Markus Schordan	Google, USA
Aravind Sukumaran Rajam	Meta, USA
Ali Tehrani	Iowa State University, USA
Philippe Virouleau	Inria, France
Amalee Wilson	Stanford University, USA

3 Outcome of the Workshop

The workshop content was built on three tracks: one invited talk and two sessions with research paper presentations.

Invited Talk

MLIR is a novel compiler technology that permits the user to take control of the compiler IR in an easy and flexible way: the Multi-Level Intermediate Representation can mix various IRs to (1) represent your input program and (2) control the compiler code generation, at a small development cost. MLIR outputs LLVM IR that can be adapted to the architectural needs for better performance, without having to write complex LLVM passes and insert them into the pass manager. This talk related an experience with MLIR in the MICROCARD European project (microcard.eu), to optimize the code for a real-life application: the electrophysiology kernels from the openCARP cardiac simulator (opencarp.org). The ionic currents crossing the membranes of the heart cells are described using mathematical modelizations written in a domain specific language (DSL). These DSL programs were originally converted into C code by a python script, and compiled by a standard compiler. This script was modified to generate MLIR code, and generate both very efficient parallel and vector CPU codes, and GPU codes (CUDA for Nvidia and ROCm for AMD GPUs). Vincent Loechner from the University of Strasbourg presented the MLIR dialects that he used for this, the MLIR transformation passes, and the performance results of the optimized code.

Research Papers

The first speaker was Simon Schwitanski from RWTH. He presented three static analysis approaches that detect irrelevant local memory accesses at compile time to avoid systematic instrumentation of local memory accesses. In the next presentation, Radjasouria Vinayagame from Eviden presented a method to efficiently detect errors in MPI-RMA programs. Then Tim Jammer from TU Darmstadt described a novel approach to optimize MPI communication overhead by precomputing the used message envelopes at the initialization of MPI. Sebastian Kreutzer from TU Darmstadt presented a method for augmenting MPI traces with call contexts using selective instrumentation based on static call graph analysis. Finally, Adrian Munera from BSC talked about work that extends OpenMP function variants to allow the parallel runtime system to gather metrics and use them to dynamically decide among the set of function specializations provided by the user.

The workshop program information is available under https://c3po-workshop.github.io/2024/program.

Compiler-Based Precalculation of MPI Message Envelopes

Tim Jammer[1]($\boxtimes$), Tim Heldmann[1], Michael Blesel[2], Michael Kuhn[2], and Christian Bischof[1]

[1] Department of Scientific Computing, Technical University Darmstadt, 64283 Darmstadt, Germany
{`tim.jammer,tim.heldmann,christian.bischof`}`@tu-darmstadt.de`
[2] Otto von Guericke University Magdeburg, 39106 Magdeburg, Germany
{`michael.blesel,michael.kuhn`}`@ovgu.de`

Abstract. In this paper, we propose a novel approach to optimize MPI communication overhead by precomputing the used message envelopes at the initialization of MPI. This allows for selective disabling of MPI message matching when no conflicts are present, which leads to an enhanced communication performance, while still ensuring correctness.

We developed an LLVM compiler pass that automatically inserts the precomputations of message envelopes into an application and is capable of handling advanced C++ language features like polymorphism and exceptions. We demonstrate the effectiveness of our approach using a complex C++ N-body simulation code, achieving performance gains despite the runtime-overhead of precomputation. In our experiments, the runtime overhead of envelope precomputation is negligible compared to the potential performance gain ($\leq 0.25\%$ of performance gain are lost to precompute overhead).

Our code is available at https://github.com/tudasc/MPI-precompute.

Keywords: MPI · static analysis · MPI persistent communication · message matching

1 Introduction

MPI stands as the cornerstone of distributed memory computing, serving as the de facto standard in facilitating large-scale distributed memory applications. Handling messages inside the MPI library is associated with a certain communication overhead. One major technique to reduce this overhead is the overlapping of communication with computation by using non-blocking MPI operations. For non-blocking operations, the network hardware can handle the message transfer, while the application continues its calculations. But even in the case of non-blocking operations, MPI still needs to perform matching based on the message envelopes. A message envelope, as defined by the MPI standard [9], consists of the MPI communicator used for communication, the target and destination processes (rank) as well as a user-defined integer (message tag).

In some cases, the message matching is superfluous, though. An example is the usage of persistent MPI operations. In a persistent MPI operation, one first defines a message envelope and then sends repeated messages with the **same** envelope. So if a persistent send and receive operation match once, they will also match in every other instance, making all operations spent to determine that those two operations will match again superfluous. However, the MPI standard does not mandate that a persistent send operation is matched by a persistent receive operation. Additionally, several different persistent operations may use the same envelope. In order to ensure a correct program execution, message matching is still required in those cases. Therefore, an MPI implementation is not allowed to just disable message matching for persistent MPI operations.

Here, we see a potential to further reduce the overhead of MPI communication by eliminating the superfluous message matching in cases where this is applicable. This is especially beneficial to the performance of message passing, as the operations needed to perform the matching can not be overlapped with computation without special hardware. Schonbein et al. identified the cost of message matching, especially in multi-threaded environments, as one component that adds the most overhead to MPI communication [10]. But the communication overhead does not only consist of envelope matching. Zambre et al. points out that for a non-blocking send operation, up to 90% of the overhead is spent within the MPI implementation whereas only less than 10% is spent in the lower levels of the software stack actually dealing with the network hardware [14]. Before actually engaging with the network hardware the MPI library may perform various other steps such as checking if the data is contiguous, computing which communication interface and protocol to use, etc. Similar to matching, these operations are also mostly superfluous if the same (persistent) MPI operation is executed repeatedly. Our approach also targets these superfluous operations.

Several techniques to reduce the cost of message matching have been proposed. Some are software-based, like Flajslik et al. who propose to "utilize a hash map that is extended with message ordering annotations" [3]. Their work complements ours, focusing on irregular communication patterns with matching wildcards, while ours concentrates on regular communication patterns.

Most studies explore hardware-based approaches, where specialized hardware is used to accelerate the message envelope matching instead of the CPU performing the required operations [2,4,8,11,13]. One drawback is their potential inability to adapt to future changes in MPI usage. For example, the current constraints of MPI message matching do not translate well to GPU architectures [7]. We argue that in the case of redundant matching operations, it is better to utilize such hardware to perform tasks relevant for the application, like in-network computing or reduction operations for example.

In terms of completely eliminating superfluous message matching operations, Jammer and Bischof demonstrated that in certain cases, the compiler can identify redundant matching [6]. The idea is that the compiler can in some cases prove that all envelopes sent out are different and therefore, no "matching conflict" can occur. In order to guarantee a correct execution one needs to prove that no matching conflict can occur **before** message matching is disabled. Therefore, speculatively disabling message matching is not a viable option.

The compiler-based approach by Jammer and Bischof is currently limited to MPI calls that occur within the same function [6]. Additionally, a purely static analysis may not always conclusively decide message envelopes to be different, even if they are so during execution.

Therefore, we propose to precompute all used MPI message envelopes before they are used to check for the presence of matching conflicts at runtime. The compiler does however also play a crucial role in our approach as it is used to automatically generate the instructions necessary to precompute the used MPI message envelopes. Consequently, no manual work by the programmer is needed in order to exploit the performance gain achieved by the optimization developed by Jammer and Bischof, where message matching is disabled [6].

This paper is structured as follows: First, we introduce how we utilize the compiler to compute all message envelopes in Sect. 2. In Sect. 3, we discuss in which cases our approach does not work optimally, while providing a case study on a complex application, the MUrB N-body simulation code, in Sect. 4. We summarize and conclude with an overview over possible avenues of future work in Sect. 5.

2 Analysis Approach

The general idea of our approach is to precompute all used message envelopes before the program starts right after MPI_Init. Then the MPI library can check all used envelopes for matching conflicts and disable message matching if applicable. The compiler will automatically determine how to compute the message envelope used and insert the necessary instruction after the call to MPI_Init. This is done by generating a copy of the original program's instructions containing only ones necessary for calculating the message tag and source (or destination) process. This is sufficient, as a difference in a subset of the envelope, as defined by the MPI standard, is already enough to tell different messages apart.

We do not consider the communicator as integral to the envelope as the tag and involved processes, as a significant portion of MPI communication operations directly use MPI_COMM_WORLD [5]. Nonetheless, the idea of precomputation can also be applied to the communicator.

We implemented a compiler transformation pass operating on the LLVM intermediate representation (IR). The analysis and transformation workflow is illustrated in Fig. 1. The compiler transformation will search for all MPI send/receive operations in LLVM IR and mark the rank and tag parameters as "necessary to precompute". Then, the values used to compute the values marked as "necessary to precompute" are also marked recursively, until we arrive at a value known to the compiler (e.g. a constant value) or a value derived from the execution environment (such as a command line argument or the number of MPI processes present). An example is shown in Listing 1.1, where the statements "necessary to precompute" are highlighted. In this example, first step, lines 5

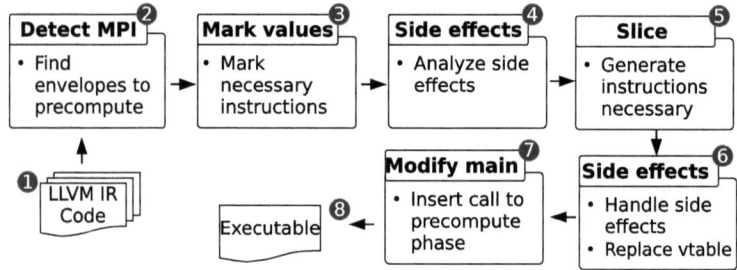

Fig. 1. Illustration of the analysis process. Starting from the LLVM IR (1), first the message envelopes that should be precomputed are detected (2). Then, all instructions necessary for calculation and control flow are marked (3) and their side effects analyzed (4). The pass then generates the part of the program necessary for precomputation (5) and adds the handling of side effects (6). Finally (7), a call to the precompute phase is injected into `main`, before the usual LLVM LTO optimizations pipeline is run (8) in order to produce a binary.

will be marked as "necessary to precompute", as the result of this calculation is used as the target rank argument.

When marking values as "necessary to precompute" the analysis also marks the instructions necessary for the control flow to reach the precomputed value as "necessary to precompute". This way, the generation of multiple envelopes inside a loop is also correctly handled. This also happens recursively until we reach the program entry. In the example in Listing 1.1, the call to `init_communication` is marked (line 18 in Listing 1.1), as some instructions in this function are considered "necessary to precompute". The for loop (lines 17–18 in Listing 1.1) is not "necessary to precompute", however, as its execution has no effect on the envelopes.

When the compiler analysis does not find any remaining value that is "necessary to precompute", it copies only those marked instructions. In this regard, this is an application of program slicing techniques [12], as we extract the part of the program that is necessary for the calculation of the message envelopes used.

The MPI calls used to define send/receive envelopes are then replaced with a callback to the precompute backend library, that keeps track of all the values precomputed. The information, which envelope belongs to which MPI operation, is based on order of execution, as the order of calls to the precompute backend will match the order of MPI calls in the "real" execution of the application. After the precalculation of all the message envelopes is finished, the compiler inserts instructions, to make sure the program is in the same[1] global state as it was in the beginning of the precomputation. Then, the normal execution of the program resumes. This execution process is illustrated in Fig. 2.

Our analysis does work even if the envelopes are spread across multiple translation units, as we run the compiler transformation pass at the Link Time

---

[1] The state of the precompute backend library is excluded in this consideration.

```
1   double *DATA;
2   int numprocs ;
3
4   void init_communication(int rank , int tag_to_use ) {
5     int other = ( rank + 1) % numprocs ; // next
6     MPI_Send_init(/*buf, size, dtype*/, other , tag_to_use , /*comm, req*/);
7     MPI_Recv_init(/*buf, size, dtype*/, other , tag_to_use , /*comm, req*/);
8   }
9
10  int main(int argc , char *argv[]) {
11    int rank ;
12    MPI_Init(&argc, &argv);
13    MPI_Comm_rank(MPI_COMM_WORLD, &rank );
14    MPI_Comm_size(MPI_COMM_WORLD, &numprocs );
15    DATA = malloc(sizeof(double) * 100);
16    for (int i = 0; i < 100; i++) {
17    DATA[i] = 42.0; }
18    init_communication( rank , argc );
19    // run some calculation
20  }
```

Listing 1.1: Example code with statements "necessary to recompute" highlighted.

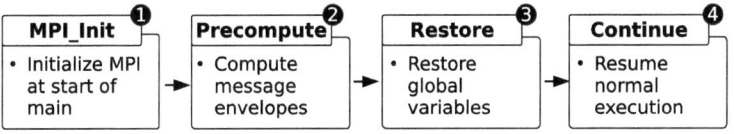

Fig. 2. Illustration of the execution of an application altered by our pass. First (1) MPI is initialized like normal. Then (2) the precomputation phase starts, where all message envelopes are computed and registered to the backend library. After the precomputation phase, the original global state is restored (3), before normal execution resumes (4).

Optimization (LTO) phase. If a function needs to be called that is not part of the information that is available at the LTO phase, our analysis will abort with an error, unless the user explicitly marked this function as "side-effect free if called during precompute phase" with an environment variable.

The following sections details how to handle complex control flows and side effects of the instructions necessary to precompute.

2.1 Global Side Effects

In our analysis, it is crucial to consider all side effects conveyed by envelope precomputation. We detail how we handle these effects to ensure they don't impact application execution in this section.

Pointer Aliasing. Pointer aliasing is a key concern for many static analysis approaches. When determining whether a memory read operation is "necessary to precompute", our analysis needs to mark any write operations to that location that might be executed before as "necessary to precompute". A key challenge in our analysis is that we need to determine all write operations in all functions that may be executed before. Therefore, our analysis does not only consider pointer usages "upwards" (in the LLVM def-use chain) to find the pointer origin (likely its allocation), but also its "downward" usages to find the write operations that are important. In Listing 1.1, this is important for the variables `numprocs` and `rank` (lines 2 and 11), as these variables are accessed via pointers by the MPI library (lines 13–14). If a pointer is passed to a function, our analysis will trace the pointer usages in this function. During this analysis, if we see that another pointer is derived and a new alias is created, we treat it the same as the original pointer. When determining the write operations that are important, our pass only considers those that can happen before the read of the value that was marked "necessary to precompute". In the case of two operations being in separate functions, their order is determined by the order of calls to the functions in question in their least common caller in the call hierarchy (at least `main`).

Memory Management. If the application allocates memory during the precomputation phase, the precompute library will intercept the allocation call in order to keep track of the allocated memory, so that it will be freed after the precomputation phase. Our implementation is limited in the allocation calls it currently supports (see Sect. 3).

Global Variables. For global variables, our pass will re-initialize them with their original value after the precomputation phase has finished, similar to checkpointing. This is necessary, if they could have been modified during the precomputation phase. This applies to `numprocs` in the example in Listing 1.1 (line 2).

MPI Library. For the state of the MPI library, there are no relevant side effects as our analysis is aware of the side effects of MPI operations. Usually, only side-effect free operations are necessary to compute the message envelopes, like reading the rank of the current process or the number of processes (lines 13–14 in the example of Listing 1.1). Our analysis would abort with an error if execution of other MPI operations was determined necessary for envelope computation. We did not encounter this case in our evaluation, though.

Execution Environment. The program may interact with its execution environment such as reading the command line arguments, environment variables or input files. For the execution environment, reading from the environment is considered "side effect free" for our purposes, as it does not modify the environment, therefore executing code interacting with the execution environment in a read-only way is not harmful in the precomputation phase, as the "real" execution of the application can read the execution environment again. Any writing to the execution environment is therefore not allowed. But modifying the execution environment should not be necessary in order to compute the message envelope used, as write operations have no "result" that can be used in order to derive a message envelope from it. We will discuss in which cases this presents a limit to our approach in Sect. 3.

2.2 Advanced C++

Our pass operates on LLVM IR and is therefore capable of handling C as well as C++ codes. For C++, there are some advanced language features, commonly challenging static analysis tools. Templates are already instantiated by the clang-fronted, but other language features require extra consideration at LLVM IR level, which we detail in this section.

Polymorphism. For control-flow and call-graph analysis, complex inheritance hierarchies with polymorphic objects does present a challenge.

Polymorphic objects are implemented with virtual tables (vtable). This results in indirect calls in the LLVM IR, where the function pointer to call is first loaded from the vtable and then called. The LLVM tool chain does already include a whole program de-virtualization pass that can be run during the LTO phase. We piggybacked on the analysis part of this pass to determine the possible call sites for indirect calls. If the de-virtualization does not yield a list of all possible call targets for a given call, we do consider all functions, whose pointer is captured, as possible call targets.

The load of a function pointer that can lead to a callee that is marked as "necessary to precompute" is therefore also marked. As explained above in Sect. 2, this leads to all relevant stores to also being marked. Our transformation then replaces the usage of the original function pointer with an altered one, so that instead of the original function, the altered one – containing only the instructions "necessary to precompute" – is called. This means that the pass will create an alternative vtable that is used in the precompute phase, while the original one is still used after the precompute phase.

Exceptions. Exceptions may alter the control flow of a program, therefore we need to analyze them. In most cases, our analysis actually ignores exceptions and aborts, as these are considered so harmful that the precomputation does not work correctly anyway. In these cases, for example when the process is out of memory, it is very likely that the original application will also crash. However, for the exceptions that are properly handled by the original application, this approach is not sufficient. Consider the example sketched in Listing 1.2: In this case, the envelope to precompute depends either on the input data or is based on the default input, if there was some exception during file I/O.

This case is correctly handled by our analysis as well. In the LLVM IR, exceptions are handled with a `landingpad` instruction. Our pass discovers that the `landingpad` (analogous to the `catch` statement in line 5 in Listing 1.2) is important, as the resulting value of `target_process` does depend on it. The analysis therefore marks all operations that can raise an exception caught by the `landingpad` as "necessary to precompute", so those are executed in the precompute phase to check if the exception is raised. This approach does also work if – in contrast to the code example in Listing 1.2 – the operation that raises the exception is not "necessary to precompute" in the exception-free case.

```
struct input_parameters;
try{
  input_parameters = Read_Input_File(); }
catch (const std::system_error& e) {
  // catch I/O errors like file not found
  input_parameters = default_input; }
target_process=depends_on_input(input_parameters);
```

Listing 1.2: Sketch of exception that is "necessary to precompute".

For optimization purposes, our analysis can ignore exceptions that result in diverging the control-flow completely away from the computations of message envelopes. Examples are exceptions that may be the result of writing to the execution environment (e.g. writing to stdout). The compiler can generate exception handling code when for example a write operation to stdout fails, as C++ semantics require that certain destructors are called in this case. We discuss in which cases ignoring certain exceptions limits our approach in Sect. 3.

3 Discussion

In this section we discuss the current shortcomings of our approach. First, we will discuss the general limitations of our approach, before detailing some limitations in our implementation that we do not consider a general shortcoming of the precomputation idea.

Limits of the Approach in General. In general, our approach only works with full LTO information, which can increase compile time. On the other hand, this also allows the application to reap the benefits obtained by LTO.

The current implementation does not include any heuristic to determine if precomputation is worth the effort. If e.g. the application termination depends on the input data (i.e. on convergence) and then some messages are sent at the end of the program, the precompute phase needs to actually run the whole computationally intensive part of the program, in order to arrive at the point where those final message envelopes are computed. In the future, we want to incorporate a heuristic that can find such cases and disable the precomputation if it does lead to too much runtime overhead.

Limits of the Current Proof of Concept Implementation. Additionally, there are some limitations in the current implementation, described in Sect. 2.

There is the possibility of a resource leak in the current implementation, for example when memory is allocated or files are read, as the corresponding free or file close is not part of the precompute phase. A solution for this problem could be the precomputation library intercepting all resource acquiring calls such as memory allocations. The precompute library can than keep track of all aquired resources and properly clean them up after the precompute phase.

Reading from stdin is currently not supported, as it may require interactive input by the user. Although we have not encountered a scenario where message envelopes depend on input form `stdin`, this capability could be added, by capturing `stdin` to an internal buffer for usage after the precompute phase. We did not consider programs that write to the execution environment and then later expect to read these written values for further usage, as any process could change the environment in between.

Where our implementation can currently lead to unexpected or even undefined behavior is the handling of exceptions. For example, consider an exception thrown while reading the input arguments, that cause the program to print a help message about its arguments. As discussed in Sect. 2.2, most exceptions are actually ignored. Therefore, our analysis will ignore the exception handling in that case, as no message envelope depends on it. This can lead to a program crash without the help message being printed, resulting in a different program behavior than without the precompute phase.

Furthermore, this can lead to undefined behavior (i.e. if the wrong arguments are later used), as no such exception will be raised during the precompute phase. We do consider this as a limitation of our implementation that needs further investigation, as we want to avoid executing all exception checking code during the precompute phase for performance reasons.

However, this isn't inherent to our precomputation approach, as in the worst case, the precompute library can catch any unhandled exception thrown during the precompute phase and abort the precomputation. In this case, we can just tell the MPI library that matching conflicts may be present and proper message matching mechanisms need to be used, in order to continue like normal. We elected to stay with the current implementation, as our assumption is that the user is capable of using the optimized program correctly and most programs do not handle exception in other ways than just aborting anyway. We regard this choice similar to assertions, which are not included in release code.

4 Evaluation

We demonstrate the capabilities of our analysis by showcasing it on an N-body Simulation code: MUrB (MoveUrBody). The code was developed by Adrien Cassagne to showcase different implementations of N-body simulations using his MIPP SIMD wrapper [1]. MUrB has roughly 42,000 lines of C++ code across ≈150 files. MUrB uses complex C++ features such as polymorphic inheritance and templates, making it very challenging to analyse with static analysis tools. Additionally, the communication scheme used does depend on the implementation selected. The user can choose the implementation to use via a command line parameter, the usage of one of the different implementations is then managed with polymorphic inheritance. Therefore, this code allows us to sufficiently showcase the capabilities of our analysis approach, as a purely static tool would not be able to decide which implementation will be selected by the user at runtime.

Table 1. Performance gain contrasted with the run time required for precalculation.

numProc	msg size	performance gain	cost of precompute	performance gain lost to precompute overhead
2	2.28 MB	0.11% (1701 ms)	3 ms	≈ 0.18%
4	1.14 MB	15.59% (6749 ms)	3 ms	≈ 0.04%
8	0.57 MB	5.75% (6788 ms)	3 ms	≈ 0.04%

In order to successfully apply our analysis to MUrB, we only needed to swap the used compiler with a compiler wrapper that passes the needed command line arguments to enable our transformation pass during the CMake build step.

Our compiler pass successfully transforms the application to include a precompute phase. This allows us to *automatically* apply the optimization developed by Jammer and Bischof [6] to the complex MUrB code. The application transformed by our pass behaves like the original one. The only exception is the wrong usage of command line arguments, where the altered application just crashes, while the original one prints a help message (see Sect. 2.2).

When knowing all message envelopes, one can see that MUrB uses distinct message tags for each pair of persistent send/receive operations, so that message matching is not observe a performance benefit, detailed in Table 1.

We measured the performance benefit on a system consisting of eight nodes, each equipped with one AMD Epyc 7443 CPU (2.85 GHz, 24 cores), 128 GB RAM and 100 Gbit Ethernet. The setup uses CentOS 8 Stream, LLVM 16.0.1 and our modified version of Open MPI 4.1.1. We executed MUrB with one MPI process with 24 threads per node.

As the optimization only targets the communication overhead, we do not expect to see a very high overall performance benefit, considering that a high computation-communication overlap is already present in MUrB. Still, there is a performance benefit that exceeds the runtime overhead of precomputation. As seen in Table 1, the relative performance gain increases with a growing communication overhead caused by more processes being used for the same problem size.

5 Conclusion

In this work, we demonstrated the feasibility of precomputing the used MPI message envelopes at MPI initialization. This does allow for disabling of proper message matching inside the MPI library, when no matching conflicts are present. Disabling message matching can increase communication performance, while retaining correctness according to the MPI standards semantics, due to the precomputed information.

We demonstrated the capability of our implementation to handle complex C++ codes, by successfully applying it to the N-body simulation code MUrB. In this example application, we were also able to achieve a speedup by *automatically* applying the optimization developed by Jammer and Bischof [6]. During our measurements, the cost of precomputing the message envelopes was offset by the increased communication performance as soon as the second iteration.

In the future, we want to further address the current shortcomings of our implementation discussed in Sect. 3 with a specific focus on efficient exception handling. Additionally, we want to include a heuristic to decide if precomputation of message envelopes is worth the runtime overhead. We also want to explore how further static analysis could be used to limit the amount of message envelopes necessary to precompute. We have already done some initial investigations into this approach by using a Clang plugin that creates a global control flow graph of the program and analyses it for MPI communication patterns. The main challenge with this static approach is the possible influence of runtime dependent parameters on the message envelopes, which is tackled by our precompute approach. Nevertheless, there are communication patterns that could be analyzed correctly at compile time. In that case the Clang plugin can annotate the affected persistent operations, where it was able to show the absence of matching conflicts. By incorporating such a static approach, we could reduce the amount of precomputations necessary. Furthermore, if one could determine different phases of the application, one could apply our approach to the main phase and enable message matching again for a later cleanup phase, in order to skip the precalculation of message envelopes for the cleanup phase.

Our code is available on GitHub: https://github.com/tudasc/MPI-precompute. To enhance reproducibility, the repository contains not only the developed compiler pass, but also the code of MUrB and the altered Open MPI with the performance adjustments developed in [6].

Acknowlegements. This work was in part supported by the Hessian Ministry for Higher Education, Research and the Arts through the Hessian Competence Center for High-Performance Computing and by the Federal Ministry of Education and Research (BMBF) and the states of Hesse as part of the NHR program. The N-Body Simulation Code MUrB was written by Adrien Cassagne and uses his MIPP SIMD wrapper [1].

References

1. Cassagne, A., Aumage, O., Barthou, D., Leroux, C., Jégo, C.: MIPP: a portable C++ SIMD Wrapper and its use for error correction coding in 5G standard. In: WPMVP'18: Proceedings of the 2018 4th Workshop on Programming Models for SIMD/Vector Processing. Association for Computing Machinery, New York, NY, USA (2018). https://doi.org/10.1145/3178433.3178435
2. Ferreira, K., Grant, R.E., Levenhagen, M.J., Levy, S., Groves, T.: Hardware MPI message matching: insights into MPI matching behavior to inform design. Concurrency Comput. Pract. Experience **32**(3), e5150 (2019). https://doi.org/10.1002/cpe.5150
3. Flajslik, M., Dinan, J., Underwood, K.D.: Mitigating MPI message matching misery. In: Kunkel, J.M., Balaji, P., Dongarra, J. (eds.) ISC High Performance 2016. LNCS, vol. 9697, pp. 281–299. Springer, Cham (2016). https://doi.org/10.1007/978-3-319-41321-1_15

4. Hemmert, K.S., Underwood, K.D., Rodrigues, A.: An architecture to perform NIC based MPI matching. In: 2007 IEEE International Conference on Cluster Computing. IEEE (2007). https://doi.org/10.1109/clustr.2007.4629234
5. Hück, A., Jammer, T., Jenke, J., Bischof, C.: Investigating the usage of MPI at argument-granularity in HPC codes. In: EUROMPI '23: Proceedings of the 30th European MPI Users' Group Meeting. ACM (2023). https://doi.org/10.1145/3615318.3615322
6. Jammer, T., Bischof, C.: Compiler-enabled optimization of persistent MPI operations. In: 2022 IEEE/ACM International Workshop on Exascale MPI (ExaMPI). IEEE (2022). https://doi.org/10.1109/exampi56604.2022.00006
7. Klenk, B., Froening, H., Eberle, H., Dennison, L.: Relaxations for high-performance message passing on massively parallel SIMT processors. In: 2017 IEEE International Parallel and Distributed Processing Symposium (IPDPS). IEEE (2017). https://doi.org/10.1109/ipdps.2017.94
8. Levy, S., Ferreira, K.B.: Evaluating tradeoffs between MPI message matching offload hardware capacity and performance. In: EuroMPI 2019: Proceedings of the 26th European MPI Users' Group Meeting. ACM (2019). https://doi.org/10.1145/3343211.3343223
9. Message Passing Interface Forum: MPI: a message-passing interface standard version 4.0. https://www.mpi-forum.org/docs/mpi-4.0/mpi40-report.pdf (2021)
10. Schonbein, W., Dosanjh, M.G.F., Grant, R.E., Bridges, P.G.: Measuring multithreaded message matching misery. In: Aldinucci, M., Padovani, L., Torquati, M. (eds.) Euro-Par 2018. LNCS, vol. 11014, pp. 480–491. Springer, Cham (2018). https://doi.org/10.1007/978-3-319-96983-1_34
11. Underwood, K., Hemmert, K., Rodrigues, A., Murphy, R., Brightwell, R.: A hardware acceleration unit for MPI queue processing. In: 19th IEEE International Parallel and Distributed Processing Symposium. IEEE (2005). https://doi.org/10.1109/ipdps.2005.30
12. Weiser, M.: Program slicing. IEEE Trans. Softw. Eng. **SE-10**(4), 352–357 (1984). https://doi.org/10.1109/tse.1984.5010248
13. Xiong, Q., Skjellum, A., Herbordt, M.C.: Accelerating MPI message matching through FPGA offload. In: 2018 28th International Conference on Field Programmable Logic and Applications (FPL). IEEE (2018). https://doi.org/10.1109/fpl.2018.00039
14. Zambre, R., Grodowitz, M., Chandramowlishwaran, A., Shamis, P.: Breaking band: a breakdown of high-performance communication. In: ICPP 2019: Proceedings of the 48th International Conference on Parallel Processing. ACM (2019). https://doi.org/10.1145/3337821.3337910

Adaptive Parallelism in OpenMP Through Dynamic Variants

Adrian Munera[1]([✉]), Guerau Dasca[2], Eduardo Quiñones[1], and Sara Royuela[1]

[1] Barcelona Supercomputing Center, Barcelona, Spain
{adrian.munera,eduardo.quinones,sara.royuela}@bsc.es
[2] Universitat Politècnica de Catalunya, Barcelona, Spain
guerau.dasca@estudiantat.upc.edu

Abstract. Performance portability is the holy grail in modern High-Performance Computing (HPC) systems due to the heterogeneity in the processor architectures and their rapid evolution. Efficiently utilizing diverse and ever-changing hardware is complex and limits domain experts not proficient in computer science and parallel programming.

High-level parallel programming models, like OpenMP and Kokkos, offer a good trade-off between performance, programmability and portability. Performance portability is the next target to enable portability through minimal or no changes in the source code. OpenMP is a great candidate to bring this quality due to its capabilities for exploiting various forms of parallelism across different hardware architectures, the huge community developing OpenMP applications, and the latest extensions towards performance portability based on function and directive variants.

This work extends OpenMP function variants to allow the parallel runtime system to gather metrics and use them to dynamically decide among the set of function specializations provided by the user. This allows taking into account dynamic conditions of the system, like the workload of a device at a given time and the memory consumption of a given implementation. This work includes an implementation of the proposal in LLVM and its evaluation using a number of benchmarks and configurations. This technique is evaluated in terms of CPU, GPU and memory usage against vanilla OpenMP variants, showing the significant gains it can obtain in different evolving scenarios.

Keywords: Performance portability · Adaptability · OpenMP · Function specialization

1 Introduction and Motivation

Modern High-Performance Computing (HPC) systems feature heterogeneous architectures that incorporate CPUs, GPUs, and other accelerators [1,5]. The complexity to efficiently exploit this diversity of hardware is exacerbated by their rapid evolution. Hence, achieving efficiency and productivity involves the same code attaining high performance across a variety of hardware configurations while reducing the need for manual optimization for each platform, and so enhancing code maintenance and usability, and reducing development costs. In other words, HPC applications pursue *performance portability*.

While low-level languages can achieve great levels of performance in specific hardware, e.g., CUDA in NVIDIA devices, several studies reveal that high-level models like OpenMP [2] and Kokkos [9] provide competitive performance while offering better programmability and portability. In this sense, previous studies show that OpenACC, OpenMP, Kokkos and RAJA have great levels of performance portability [4] that varies depending on the hardware (i.e., CPU and GPU) and the compiler (e.g., Cray and Clang). Based on these facts and given the large community developing and maintaining applications and tools that leverage OpenMP, this work focuses on this programming model.

OpenMP supports the exploitation of different types of parallelism and hardware architectures. Regarding the former, OpenMP includes a *thread-centric* prescriptive model suitable for loop-based kernels, and a *task-centric* descriptive model suitable for both loop-based and task-based kernels, that provides support for highly dynamic and unstructured parallelism. Furthermore, OpenMP includes an accelerator model coupled with the task-centric model, for task offloading, a thread-centric model, to define parallelism within the GPU.

OpenMP 5.0 [6] introduced the `metadirective` and `declare variant` directives, which enable the selection of directive variants and function variants at a call site, respectively, based on compile-time traits of the enclosing context. Later, OpenMP 5.1 [7] augmented this support to enable user-defined conditions that can be checked at run-time. Although these extensions clearly enhance the adaptability of the system to the target system or the semantics of the program, none of these options are suitable to allow responsiveness to the state of the system during execution, e.g., workload of a specific device, or to changing conditions of the architecture, e.g., increased amount of available memory.

Based on the usefulness of these mechanisms to achieve performance portability through adaptability, the robustness gained by exposing variants with OpenMP directives, and the limitations of the current OpenMP specification to adapt to system conditions, this work introduces the following contributions:

- A new concept of *dynamic variants* that moves the responsibility of variant selection to the run-time based on system conditions.
- A mechanism implemented in LLVM to instrument function variants to extract metrics, i.e., execution time, memory consumption, including heap and stack, and device (CPU/GPU) usage.
- A set of heuristics, based on the metrics previously gathered, implemented in the OpenMP runtime of LLVM to dynamically decide which specialization to execute, and therefore provide adaptability to changing conditions.
- An evaluation of the proposal and its implementation using different benchmarks, implementations, and configurations.

2 Function Specializations in OpenMP

Based on a proposal for enabling developers to specify different code paths based on compile-time conditions [8], OpenMP 5.0 [6] introduced support for the `metadirective` and the `declare variant` directives. These directives allow the selection of directive or function specializations based on traits evaluated at compile-time. While the former allows tuning specific aspects of the parallelization, e.g., the number of threads to be used in the device depending on the architecture, the latter provides further flexibility by enabling completely different strategies for implementing and parallelizing a given functionality. Consequently, this work focuses on function variants, although the proposal for dynamic selection of variants could be easily extended to metadirectives.

Function variants in OpenMP 5.0 are selected based on *traits* like the directive names in the calling context to be considered (i.e., *construct* selector) the characteristics of the targeted device (e.g., *kind* and *isa* selectors), implementation defined selectors and user-defined conditions. Figure 1 shows an example of the use of OpenMP variants for implementing the *Axpy* operation, which performs a scalar multiplication and vector addition. The code in Fig. 1b shows the parallel implementation for CPUs, whereas Fig. 1a shows implementation for GPUs. Then, Fig. 1c shows the default implementation augmented with the different variants and the traits to be used by the compiler during the selection process. In particular, the CPU version will be used when the construct is set to *parallel*, while the GPU version will be used with that trait is set to *target*. Finally, Fig. 1d shows the calling context for the three possible situations.

```
void axpy_gpu(int* x, int* y, int a) {
  #pragma omp teams distribute \
    map(to:x[:N]) map(tofrom:y[:N])
  for (int j=0; j<N; j+=BS)
    #pragma omp parallel for firstprivate(j)
    for (int k=0; k<BS; k++)
      y[k+j] = a * x[k+j] + y[k+j];
}
```

(a) Parallel version for GPU.

```
void axpy_par(int* x, int* y,
              int a) {
  #pragma omp for
  for (int j=0; j<N; j++)
    y[j] = a * x[j] + y[j];
}
```

(b) Parallel version for CPU.

```
#pragma omp declare variant(axpy_par) \
  match(construct={parallel})
#pragma omp declare variant(axpy_gpu) \
  match(construct={target})
void axpy(int* x, int* y, int a)
{
  for (int j=0; j<N; j++)
    y[j] = a * x[j] + y[j];
}
```

(c) Function definition with variants.

```
int main(void) {
  ...
  axpy(&x, &y, a);        // default
  #pragma omp parallel
  axpy(&x, &y, a);        // axpy_par
  #pragma omp target
  axpy(&x, &y, a);        // axpy_gpu
  ...
}
```

(d) Context selection of variants.

Fig. 1. OpenMP example of function variants for the *Axpy* operation.

Yan et al. [10] proposed an extension to the `metadirective` directive to allow runtime evaluation of user-defined conditions. This work transforms, at compile-time, user-defined conditions into if-else statements that follow the same order as that defined in the `metadirective`. Accordingly, at run-time, the first condition that evaluates to true decides the variant that is chosen. Figure 2 shows an example of the syntax (in Fig. 2a) and the lowering decided by the compiler (in Fig. 2b). The experiments performed with this extension show limited benefits on performance derived from choosing between the CPU and the GPU versions on an implementation of the Smith-Waterman application because data transfers between devices dominate the execution time. Based on this proposal, which enhances the adaptability of the system improving its sensitivity with regard to the semantics of the application, OpenMP v5.1 [7] extended its support for specializations with user-guided runtime adaptation.

```
1 #pragma omp metadirective
2   when(user={condition(nEle<MED)}) \
3   when(user={condition(nEle<LAR)}) \
4       parallel for \
5   default (target teams distribute \
6       parallel for map(to: ...) \
7       map(tofrom: ...))
8 for (j=0; j<nEle; ++j)
9   similarityScore(...);
```

(a) Syntax.

```
1 if (nEle < MED) {
2   for (j=0; j<nEle; ++j)
3       similarityScore(...);
4 } else if (nEle < LAR) {
5   #pragma omp parallel for
6   for (j=0; j<nEle; ++j)
7       similarityScore(...);
8 } else {
9   #pragma omp target teams \
10      distribute parallel for \
11      map(to: ...) map(tofrom: ...)
12  for (j=0; j<nEle; ++j)
13      similarityScore(...);
14 }
```

(b) Compiler lowering.

Fig. 2. Proposal to extend OpenMP `metadirective` directive with user-defined conditions evaluable at run-time on the Smith-Waterman application [10].

Along similar lines, Liao et al. [3] proposed an enhancement to dynamic user-directed directive variants that relieves users from the burden of defining the conditions. In this proposal, users define a series of aspects of the supervised machine learning (ML) method to be used and the relevant features (e.g., variables) to be analyzed. Then, a pipeline implemented on top of the ROSE source-to-source compiler, the Apollo runtime and the LLVM back-end compiler, generates executable code that adapts to the semantics of the program based on the behavior of the features specified. Figure 3 shows an example of the syntax (in Fig. 3a) and a snippet of the transformed code (in Fig. 3b) of the proposed feature for the same Smith-Waterman application shown before. The experiments performed with this extension show that the adaptive version chooses the variant that runs faster when changing the size of the problem. Furthermore, the accuracy of the model fluctuates between 75% and 93%, mainly due to inaccuracies during the instrumentation of the code.

The above solutions enable the dynamic adaptation of variants based on the behavior of the application, but system conditions are not considered in

```
1 #pragma omp declare adaptation
2   model_name(score) \
3   model(decision_tree) \
4   feature(nDiag)
5 #pragma omp metadirective \
6   when(:) \                    /*serial*/
7   when(:parallel for)          /*CPU par*/
8   default(target teams distribute \
9   parallel for map(...)        /*GPU*/
10 for (j=0; j<nEle; ++j)
11    similarityScore(...);
```

(a) Syntax.

```
1  Apollo::Region *region = Apollo::
2    instance->getRegion("score",...);
3  region->begin({nDiag});
4  switch (region->getPolicyIndex()) {
5    case 0:    ...    /*serial*/
6    case 1:           /*CPU par*/
7      #pragma omp parallel for
8      ...
9    case 2:           /*GPU*/
10     #pragma omp target teams \
11     distribute parallel for map(...)
12     ...
13   default:          /*error handling*/
14 }
15 region->end();
```

(b) ML-based lowering

Fig. 3. Proposal to augment OpenMP `metadirective` with user-directed ML-based conditions evaluable at run-time on the Smith-Waterman application [3].

any case. Based on this, the work proposed in this paper to augment function variants (and also applicable to directive variants) is a relevant contribution and a step forward for achieving performance portability, as it allows to adapt the application to changing system conditions, either because the load in specific components of the system changes, or because the system itself changes.

3 OpenMP Extensions for Dynamic Adaptability

This study introduces a new methodology for dynamic variant selection, based on the system's resources and their evolving state, to facilitate improve performance portability through adaptability. The approach includes two key contributions: (1) automatic instrumentation of variants to collect system metrics during a warm-up process, and (2) support for runtime heuristics designed to effectively choose the optimal variant, considering user inputs and system conditions.

The proposed technique operates transparently to the user and is integrated into the LLVM 17.0.0 compiler framework[1]. Upon enabling this technique, the compiler produces two distinct binaries: (1) an instrumented binary equipped with runtime calls that collect resource usage metrics from the variants, and (2) a binary that interprets the metrics gathered by the instrumented version to guide variant selection. The second binary generated once instrumented binary runs and collects the metrics. This behavior is represented in Fig. 4.

3.1 Compilation Phase: Variants Instrumentation

The instrumentation of function variants is integrated as an optimization pass in LLVM and is activated by a new compiler flag, named -dynamic-variant. Specifically, the optimization pass is responsible for:

---

[1] A public version of the extended LLVM framework is available at https://gitlab.bsc.es/ppc-bsc/research/c3po2024-dynamicvariants.

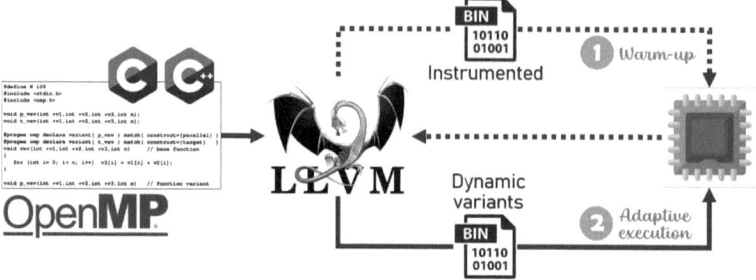

Fig. 4. Overview of the adaptations implemented on top of LLVM to support function variants adaptable to system conditions.

- Enclose the invocations of variant functions with *instrumentation start* and *instrumentation end* runtime calls to signal the runtime system when to begin and cease gathering metrics. (see Sect. 3.2).
- Replace all calls to functions with variants with a runtime call that (i) receives the list of names of all variants of the called function and (ii) returns the variant selected for execution. When executed in the instrumented code, it selects a different variant for each execution in a round-robin approach. When executed in the final code, it uses the default or user-defined heuristics and the results of the warm-up phase to drive the selection (see Sect. 3.3).
- Force the re-execution of the application to gather metrics for all possible variants by launching the application as many times as the maximum number of variants in any function of the program, ensuring that each variant is executed at least once. Note that static global variables may need to reinitialize their default values to ensure the correctness of each execution.

Figure 5a illustrates the syntax proposed, which does not require any condition for the variants, as the conditions will be defined through the heuristics at execution-time. Figure 5b shows a simplification of the Intermediate Representation (IR) when using the proposed compilation flag.

3.2 Warm-Up Phase: Recording System Metrics

The warmup phase involves running the instrumented binary to gather metrics. To ensure accuracy, this phase should ideally be conducted in isolation. It only needs to be performed once for each application and architecture, minimizing its impact when the application is executed multiple times thereafter. Typically, each variant is executed at least once by default. However, if a variant has a prohibitively long execution time, users have the option to disable its execution and manually provide estimated values for each metric.

The metrics captured for each variant include:

- **Average and peak CPU usage (%)**: These metrics are computed by a specific thread that monitors, using a configurable sampling interval, active and idle CPU clock cycles and computes its average and peak ratio.

(a) Proposed syntax.

```
1 void foo_omp();
2 void foo_cuda();
3
4 #pragma omp declare \
5       variant(foo_omp)
6 #pragma omp declare \
7       variant(foo_cuda)
8 void foo(){
9   ...
10 }
11
12 int main(){
13    foo();
14 }
```

(b) Code instrumented.

```
1 void foo_omp();
2 void foo_cuda();
3 void foo(){ ... }
4
5 int num_execs = 0;
6 int main() {
7    __kmpc_instrument_variant_start(...);
8    int selection= __kmpc_dynamic_variant("foo",
9       "foo_omp", "foo_cuda");
10   switch (selection){
11      ... // Select foo || foo_omp || foo_cuda
12   }
13   __kmpc_instrument_variant_end(...);
14   if (num_execs < __kmpc_get_executions()){
15      num_execs++;
16      main();
17   }
18 }
```

Fig. 5. Example of the proposed mechanism for dynamic variant instrumentation.

- **Average and peak GPU usage (%)**: These metrics capture GPU use employing manufacturer's libraries, e.g., NVIDIA's NVML, and AMD's ADL.
- **Thread Stack memory consumption (%)**: This metric represents the percentage of stack memory utilized by the primary thread[2]. Before executing a variant, a *stack painting* technique pre-fills the stack with a specific data pattern. After execution, the technique identifies the lowest stack memory address that still holds the pattern. The utilized stack size is then determined by calculating the difference between this address and the base address recorded prior to executing the variant.
- **Heap memory consumption (%)**: This metric calculates the volume of heap memory allocated by the variant via wrappers for *malloc* and *free* defined in the OpenMP runtime. *LD_PRELOAD* mechanism is used during execution to overwrite the original calls. Note that while all allocations are wrapped, only those occurring within the variant's context are considered.
- **GPU memory consumption (%)**: This metric measures the GPU memory utilized, using manufacturer's libraries, e.g., *nvmlDeviceGetMemoryInfo*.
- **Execution time (ms)**: This metric reflects the actual wall clock duration of the execution of the variant.

With the exception of execution time, all metrics are calculated as a percentage of the system's available resources in order to represent relative consumptions. To ensure the accuracy of these metrics, the warm-up process must be conducted for each type of input and on each target system where the application is intended to run.

Furthermore, due to the warm-up procedure, the same variant might be executed more than once. In that case, the metrics gathered are aggregated to

---

[2] A *primary thread* in OpenMP is a thread with thread number 0 [7].

obtain a more accurate result, e.g., for the execution time an arithmetic mean is computed as an average and for the use of memory the maximum value collected is the one retrieved.

To be able to adapt better to the system, those variants exploiting OpenMP (tagged during compilation) can be measured for different numbers of threads. This is tuned passing the OMP_VARIANTS_NUM_THREADS environment variable passed at execution time to the instrumented binary with the list of desired number of threads to be used.

The obtained metrics are stored in a C source file, with each variant represented by a struct. This source file is human-editable and is subsequently used to compile the final binary. It exist the possibility to bypass the warmup phase, to do so one can copy this file from a previous warmup execution of the same application on a different machine. However, this approach may result in a loss of accuracy due to differences in the architectures.

3.3 Execution Phase: Heuristic-Based Variant Scheduler

During the execution of the final binary, each time a function with variants is triggered the runtime receives the list of them through the *kmpc_dynamic_variant* function, and returns the identifier of the selected variant. The user can provide a list of metrics to guide variant selection, represented as a set of comma separated triplets of the form of metric:threshold:weight, where:

- metric: the metric to optimize. Possible values are: *cpu, gpu, mem, stack, heap*. Notice that *mem* represents the sum of *stack* and *heap*. Performance (time) is always optimized by default.
- threshold: optional value indicating a system threshold in the form of a percentage. It states when the metric should be optimized, i.e., when the system's usage for the metric reaches the threshold the scheduler will select the variant with less usage of that metric. If not specified, the threshold is 0 and the metric is always optimized.
- weight: optional value indicating the weight this metric has in the variant selection, as an integer. The default value is 1.

Triplets are defined by the user as a list in the METRIC_OPTIMIZATION environment variable. When multiple metrics are present, a multi-criteria optimization algorithm is employed to select the most appropriate variant.

The runtime criteria optimize the variant selection based on current system resource usage (CPU, GPU, and memory). Initially, a score is assigned to each metric of each variant by normalizing the resource usage according to system specifications. It then checks if the current usage, combined with the variant's average usage, exceeds predefined thresholds for each metric. The algorithm selects the variant with the highest score among those reaching the fewest thresholds. If no thresholds are met, it chooses the variant with the shortest execution time. This approach ensures that the chosen variant is resource-efficient and well-suited to the current system conditions.

Usually, thresholds are established at 100% to prevent system saturation, but setting a lower threshold can be beneficial for reserving resources for future processes.

4 Evaluation

The evaluation analyzes the benefits of the proposed technique using applications with variants in scenarios with different system conditions. The applications are evaluated in terms of CPU, GPU, memory usage and performance.

4.1 Experimental Setup

Hardware Platform. The experiments are performed in two different systems: (1) a node of the MareNostrum 4 (MN) supercomputer, equipped with 2 sockets Intel Xeon Platinum 8160 CPU with 24 cores each at 2.10 GHz and 96 GB of main memory; and (2) a workstation equipped with an Intel i7-12700 processor containing 12 cores and 20 threads, 32 GB of main memory, and a RTX NVIDIA GeForce RTX 4080 GPU.

Applications. The analysis uses three well-known applications from the HPC domain: (1) **Multisort**, which implements different integer array sorting algorithms, including parallel and sequential variants of *mergesort* and *quicksort*; (2) **Cholesky**, which performs a matrix decomposition implemented with parallel *blocked* and *in-place* variants, and a GPU version using cuBLAS; and (3) **Heat**, which performs a 2D heat propagation simulation given a list of heat sources using parallel versions of the *Gauss-Seidel* algorithm for the CPU and the GPU. Furthermore, a dummy application is used to set the use of memory, CPU and GPU of the system to a given value.

4.2 Optimization of CPU Usage

This section evaluates the impact on the execution time of an application that leverages the parallelism of the CPU using both the vanilla LLVM OpenMP runtime, and our modified toolchain. The experiment is conducted on a single socket of MN, which includes 24 cores. This evaluation analyzes the multisort application, with an input vector of 100 million elements. The heuristic set is `cpu:100`, meaning that the runtime will avoid to surpass 100% of CPU usage.

Table 1. Performance recorded on warm-up for the parallel mergesort variant.

	Sequential	2 Thr	4 Thr	8 Thr	12 Thr	14 Thr	16 Thr	20 Thr	24 Thr
Time(s)	24,3	12,3	6,2	3,8	2,5	**2,1**	2,3	2,9	4,7

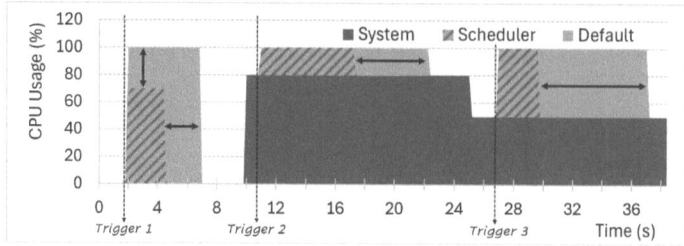

Fig. 6. System CPU usage and performance of parallel mergesort variant, for both default execution and our variant scheduler in three executions.

Table 1 presents the performance metrics recorded during warm-up for the parallel mergesort variant executed in isolation. Optimal results are obtained with 14 threads for the selected input data. This data is fed to the runtime for the evaluation shown in Fig. 6. This chart illustrates the CPU usage of the system over a span of 40 s, capturing the instances when multisort is executed (triggers). The blue area depicts the varying baseline system CPU usage simulated through the dummy application. The line pattern shows the CPU utilization (vertical) and time (horizontal) taken by the application using the variant selected by the proposed dynamic scheduler. The yellow area denotes the CPU and time needed with the default execution. Horizontal arrows indicate the performance gain, while vertical arrows represent the gain in CPU usage.

The variant scheduler strategically selects the parallel mergesort variant with 14 threads for the initial trigger, as it is the most efficient version according to the recorded metrics. For the subsequent triggers, it opts for variants employing 4 and 12 threads, respectively, adapting to the prevailing CPU usage of the system. The vanilla scheduler consistently employs 24 threads in all triggers, matching the total core count. Notably, the variant scheduler achieves performance speedups of x2, x1.8, and x4, respectively, demonstrating its effectiveness in optimizing CPU utilization and enhancing overall performance. For systems with rapidly changing states, the responsiveness of the technique can be improved by breaking down the variants into smaller, more frequent calls.

4.3 Optimization of Memory Usage

This section evaluates the impact of the proposed scheduler on the memory and the performance using two Cholesky implementations on a 30Kx30K matrix: the *blocked* variant, which allows efficient parallelization but requires extra memory allocations, and the *in-place* variant, which offers slower computation without needing extra allocations. The platform used is the workstation (featuring 32 GB of main memory) because it allows to customize swap memory. The heuristic set is mem:100 to limit the memory usage at 100% and so avoid errors or slowdowns.

During warm-up, the *blocked* version uses 21% (7 GB) of main memory and executes in 138 s, while the *in place* version does not use extra memory but executes in 216 s. Figure 7a and 7b illustrate the use of memory over a span of 400 s. Again, the blue area indicates the baseline system memory usage simulated through the dummy application, the line pattern represents the usage of the variant selected by the scheduler and the yellow area shows the default execution. While Fig. 7a represents the case when there is no swap memory, Fig. 7b represents a system with 8 GB for swapping.

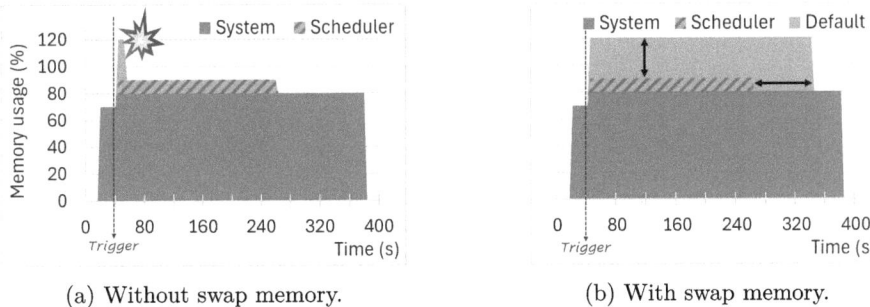

(a) Without swap memory.

(b) With swap memory.

Fig. 7. System memory usage and performance for Cholesky with both vanilla runtime and the proposed variant scheduler.

Figure 7a shows that the default execution causes a crash in the system, attempting to allocate more memory than available. However, the scheduler is able to inspect the system state and therefore select the *in place* variant instead, which is less efficient but allows the execution. Furthermore, in Fig. 7b extra swap memory is configured, so applications may be able to run using disk space (swap memory) but affecting performance. In this scenario, the default execution avoids the crash but inccurs in a high slowdown penalty, meanwhile the variant scheduler selects the *in place* variant obtaining better performance.

4.4 Optimization of GPU Usage

This section evaluates the impact on the execution time when optimizing for GPU usage with the heat application implementing GPU and parallel CPU *Gauss-Seidel* variants, with an image of 2K resolution. The application is divided in variants of 50 iterations to allow the scheduler select a different variants through the whole execution. This division does not add any noticeable overhead to the application. The experiment is performed in the workstation featuring a RTX NVIDIA GeForce RTX 4080 GPU. The heuristic set is gpu:100, meaning that runtime will avoid to execute GPU variants when it is used at 100%.

For this system, the warm-up phase records an execution time of 6 ms for the GPU variant and 40 ms for the parallel CPU variant, each one using a 100% of the GPU and CPU respectively. Figure 8 illustrates the execution of 300 iterations of heat using the vanilla and the variant schedulers. It shows the CPU and GPU utilization during the execution, as well as the performance obtained.

The system GPU usage represents the GPU utilization caused by other system process, and is simulated through the dummy application.

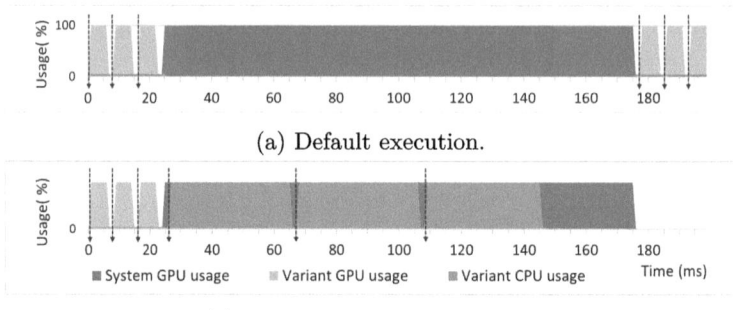

(a) Default execution.

(b) Variant scheduler execution.

Fig. 8. System and variant resources usage for the heat application.

Results show how the vanilla execution only uses the GPU version because it has better performance. However, when the GPU is occupied by other process, the execution of heat is stalled until the GPU is free. In this scenario, the stalled time is 150 ms, and hence heat needs a total of 200 ms to complete. On the other hand, the proposed scheduler is aware of the evolving GPU utilization and selects the parallel CPU variant when the GPU is in use. The scheduler obtains a speedup of approximately x1.37 compared to the vanilla one, showing the benefit provided by the adaptability of our technique. Notice that the amount of loop iterations per variant can be tuned to improve responsiveness. For the given input, the data copy to/from the GPU takes approximately 7 ms, so the technique will still provide benefits for every other process kernel that occupies the GPU for more than 8 ms.

5 Conclusions and Future Work

HPC systems consist of diverse hardware, including CPUs, GPUs, FPGAs, and advanced accelerators, like neuromorphic hardware, each with unique compute capabilities. This variety requires applications to be finely tuned for each target platform to leverage its specific strengths.

The adaptive scheduler based on function variants proposed in this work fosters performance portability across varied HPC environments by ensuring applications leverage platform capabilities effectively without requiring manual tuning from users. The technique evaluates function variants during a warm-up phase to gather key performance indicators that later will guide runtime decisions together with the evolving system status.

The results from the evaluation clearly demonstrate the effectiveness and advantages of the technique. It successfully adapts parallel CPU variants to determine the best thread count based on the current state of the system. Furthermore, it adapts to systems with limited memory, effectively preventing errors or slowdowns. Lastly, the technique adjusts to the current GPU usage, seamlessly switching between CPU and GPU variants. However, in environments where the system's state fluctuates rapidly, the technique could introduce overhead, with decisions potentially becoming outdated quickly. Nonetheless, this can be mitigated by dividing the variants into smaller segments or by creating more granular variants, which allows for quicker adaptation to changing conditions.

For future work, there's an opportunity to fine-tune the decision-making algorithm for better efficiency in environments where conditions evolve quickly. This improvement might encompass deploying more refined predictive models that can foresee changes in the system's state. Additionally, metrics for power consumption can easily be included in systems that allow this measure, like the NVIDIA Jetson series, to optimize this key aspect of the execution.

Acknowledgments. This work has been funded by the European Space Agency LIONESS project, contract no. I-2022-05399, and the MSCA-RISE Rising STARS project, contract no. 873120.

References

1. Cardwell, S.G., et al.: Truly heterogeneous HPC: co-design to achieve what science needs from HPC. In: Nichols, J., Verastegui, B., Maccabe, A.B., Hernandez, O., Parete-Koon, S., Ahearn, T. (eds.) SMC 2020. CCIS, vol. 1315, pp. 349–365. Springer, Cham (2020). https://doi.org/10.1007/978-3-030-63393-6_23
2. Gayatri, R., Yang, C., Kurth, T., Deslippe, J.: A case study for performance portability using OpenMP 4.5. In: Chandrasekaran, S., Juckeland, G., Wienke, S. (eds.) WACCPD 2018. LNCS, vol. 11381, pp. 75–95. Springer, Cham (2019). https://doi.org/10.1007/978-3-030-12274-4_4
3. Liao, C., et al.: Extending OpenMP for machine learning-driven adaptation. In: Bhalachandra, S., Daley, C., Melesse Vergara, V. (eds.) International Workshop on Accelerator Programming Using Directives, pp. 49–69. Springer, Cham (2021). https://doi.org/10.1007/978-3-030-97759-7_3
4. Marowka, A.: On the performance portability of OpenACC, OpenMP, Kokkos and RAJA. In: International Conference on High Performance Computing in Asia-Pacific Region, pp. 103–114 (2022)
5. Milojicic, D., Faraboschi, P., Dube, N., Roweth, D.: Future of HPC: diversifying heterogeneity. In: Design, Automation & Test in Europe Conference & Exhibition, pp. 276–281. IEEE (2021)
6. OpenMP Architecture Review Board (ARB): OpenMP application programming interface version 5.0 (2018). https://www.openmp.org/wp-content/uploads/OpenMP-API-Specification-5.0.pdf
7. OpenMP Architecture Review Board (ARB): OpenMP application programming interface version 5.1 (2020). https://www.openmp.org/wp-content/uploads/OpenMP-API-Specification-5-1.pdf
8. Pennycook, S.J., Sewall, J.D., Duran, A.: Supporting function variants in OpenMP. In: de Supinski, B.R., Valero-Lara, P., Martorell, X., Mateo Bellido, S., Labarta, J. (eds.) IWOMP 2018. LNCS, vol. 11128, pp. 128–142. Springer, Cham (2018). https://doi.org/10.1007/978-3-319-98521-3_9

9. Trott, C., et al.: The Kokkos ecosystem: comprehensive performance portability for high performance computing. Comput. Sci. Eng. **23**(5), 10–18 (2021)
10. Yan, Y., Wang, A., Liao, C., Scogland, T.R.W., de Supinski, B.R.: Extending OpenMP Metadirective semantics for runtime adaptation. In: Fan, X., de Supinski, B.R., Sinnen, O., Giacaman, N. (eds.) IWOMP 2019. LNCS, vol. 11718, pp. 201–214. Springer, Cham (2019). https://doi.org/10.1007/978-3-030-28596-8_14

Augmentation of MPI Traces Using Selective Instrumentation

Sebastian Kreutzer[1](✉)[iD], Josep Pocurull Serra[2][iD], Christan Iwainsky[3][iD], Marta Garcia Gasulla[2][iD], and Christian Bischof[1][iD]

[1] Scientific Computing, Technische Universität Darmstadt, Darmstadt, Germany
`{sebastian.kreutzer,christian.iwainsky}@tu-darmstadt.de`
[2] Barcelona Supercomputing Center, Barcelona, Spain
`{josep.pocurull,marta.garcia}@bsc.es`
[3] Hessian Competence Center for High Performance Computing, Technische Universität Darmstadt, Darmstadt, Germany
`christian.bischof@tu-darmstadt.de`

Abstract. Tracing tools provide detailed program execution timelines, aiding the identification of subtle performance issues. MPI-based tracing, as employed by Extrae, focuses on recording communication events, thus keeping the trace size manageable. However, analyzing the cause of detected issues can be difficult, as the limited information in the trace does not allow direct correlation to source code. In order to get this information, stack unwinding to a high depth may be required, which increases overhead and trace size. In this work, we present an alternative instrumentation-based approach relying on static call graph analysis. This approach identifies the functions correlating to the critical region in the trace based on the direct callers of the surrounding MPI events. The relevant call paths are then instrumented using LLVM's dynamic instrumentation feature, enabling them to be recorded in the trace. The presented method is evaluated on test cases of the OpenFOAM computational fluid dynamics solver. Results show that our approach is applicable for very large call-graphs with over 400,000 functions, while displaying moderate runtime and trace size overheads.

Keywords: Instrumentation · Profiling Tools · Static analysis

1 Introduction

Tracing tools, such as Extrae [22] and Score-P [11], are an invaluable part of the performance analysis toolbox on HPC systems. They enable the visualization of detailed timelines of the program's parallel execution, which can help in identifying issues that may not be directly apparent in call profiles. However, traces require significantly more storage space and typically produce higher measurement overheads. Extrae addresses this concern by focusing on MPI communication and tracing only these operations by default. This allows for detailed analysis of highly-parallel runs, while keeping the generated trace sizes manageable. The drawback of this approach is that the trace provides limited information about the context of the recorded operations, apart from the communication type and involved processes. This can lead to difficulties when analyzing such traces. Consider a scenario, in which the analysts discovers a possible performance issue located in between two MPI calls, e.g. load imbalance between ranks. The next step for the analyst is then to identify the origin of the two calls, i.e. the first common function in the two call stacks at the time of the MPI call, and find the corresponding source code region. The typical approach is to enable stack unwinding to record the call stack at each MPI event up to a certain depth. However, the minimum unwinding depth required to identify the common function cannot be determined statically and full unwinding to high depths is costly [8]. Moreover, unwinding is limited to identifying the location of the call sites only, and cannot be used to determine exact call information, such as the time at entry and exit or the value of performance counters. This information, however, may be critical to pinpoint the root of the investigated performance issue.

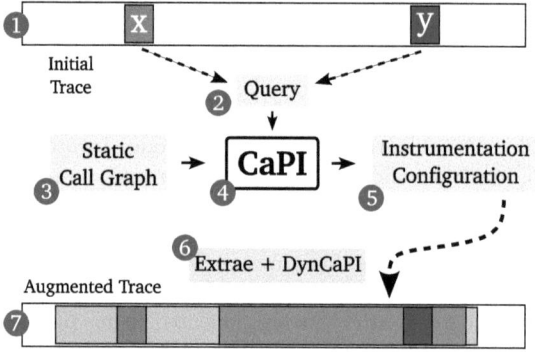

Fig. 1. Trace augmentation workflow.

This work aims to aid the analyst in this task by augmenting the trace with additional call information without incurring the overhead of full instrumentation. To this end, the *Compiler-assisted Performance Instrumentation* tool (CaPI) [12,13] was extended with a dedicated selection strategy for Extrae. Based on the static call graph of the investigated program, this strategy identifies relevant call paths originating from possible common callers of the critical MPI calls. These call paths are then instrumented using the XRay instrumentation feature [2] of the LLVM compiler infrastructure [14] to supplement the Extrae trace with detailed call context information. An illustration of the proposed analysis workflow is shown in Fig. 1:

- The analyst starts with a generic low overhead trace (**1**) that contains all MPI calls and information about their direct caller.
- Detecting a performance issue, the analyst identifies the direct callers x and y of the surrounding MPI calls.

- The analyst passes a query (**2**) to the CaPI selective instrumentation tool (**4**) executing a common ancestor analysis on the static call graph (**3**) to obtain a tailored instrumentation configuration (**5**).
- The analyst re-runs the program with Extrae and the CaPI runtime library (DynCaPI) (**6**), generating the augmented trace (**7**).

Our approach has several advantages over a generic unwinding approach. First, additional data is only collected for the regions of the trace relevant to the current measurement objective, thus reducing overhead and trace size. Secondly, the common origin of the investigated MPI calls is directly captured in the trace, avoiding the manual analysis of unwound call stacks. Finally, the instrumentation offers well placed hooks to capture performance counters for the relevant region, supporting the analyst in pinpointing the investigated issue. We make the following contributions:

1. A novel approach to identify relevant common ancestors of function pairs from static whole-program call graphs.
2. An implementation of the presented static selection method within the CaPI tool, in conjunction with a dynamic filtering approach.
3. An extension of the CaPI runtime library interfacing with Extrae to trace functions instrumented via LLVM-XRay.

2 Background and Related Work

2.1 Extrae and Paraver

Extrae and Paraver [20] have been developed for performance analysis and visualization of parallel and multithreaded high-performance computing applications. They aid to understand the behavior of parallel programs to identify bottlenecks and optimize performance. Extrae is a performance profiling tool that helps capture and analyze the runtime behavior of parallel applications. It collects various types of runtime information, such as function calls, memory accesses, communication events, and synchronization points. This information is stored in trace files used for further analysis. Complementing the capabilities of Extrae, Paraver transforms the trace files generated by Extrae and provides an interactive graphical representation of the program's execution.

2.2 CaPI

Code instrumentation is a standard technique for collecting detailed performance data from programs, used by tools such as Score-P [11] and TAU [23]. A common side effect when working with fully instrumented code is the introduction of large runtime overheads, which may affect the observed performance characteristics. Therefore, the analyst must typically create a reduced *instrumentation configuration* (IC) that filters out functions deemed irrelevant w.r.t. the current measurement objective.

The *Compiler-assisted Performance Instrumentation* tool (CaPI) was created to aid in the creation of low-overhead instrumentation configurations by incorporating static analysis based on a whole-program call graph. CaPI enables the creation of tailored ICs using a custom domain-specific language (DSL). This DSL enables the analyst to combine modular *selectors* into a adjustable pipeline to fit the measurement objective and target application.

The performance analysis workflow with CaPI is comprised of the following steps:

- MetaCG [16] is used to create a whole-program static call graph of the target application.
- The analyst specifies a CaPI query, according to the measurement objective.
- The query and call graph are passed to CaPI, which runs the analysis and produces the desired IC.
- The IC is used for the selective instrumentation of the target function (statically or dynamically).
- The instrumented program is executed, collecting performance data via the chosen measurement interface.

CaPI's preferred instrumentation workflow employs dynamic instrumentation based on LLVM's *XRay* feature [2]. Compared to a static instrumentation approach requiring recompilation after each change to the IC, the use of XRay greatly facilitates iterative adjustments and switching between ICs for different use cases. CaPI itself has no built-in profiling or tracing capabilities but offers a runtime library that serves as an interface between XRay and an external measurement tool. At the time of writing, CaPI provides interfaces for Score-P, TALP [17] and a generic profiling interface compatible with GCC's `-finstrument-functions` option.

2.3 Related Work

Various selection approaches have been investigated to lower instrumentation overhead. Instrumentation based profiling tools typically allow the user to manually specify filter files [11,23]. In addition, some tools, such as Score-P [11], provide the option to automatically create low-overhead filter files based on a previously collected profile. An alternative approach is to select code regions based on static analysis. Previous research in this category considers function-local properties, such as lines of node, cyclomatic complexity and number of call sites [18]. Other approaches incorporate a static whole-program call graph analysis, e.g. to compute aggregated statement counts [7]. The PIRA project [15] refines this static statement aggregation selection over multiple program executions, adjusting the instrumentation according to the collected profile.

Research specific to traces has largely focused on reducing storage requirements. CAPEK [4] is a clustering approach that applies in-situ analysis to identify groups of processes with similar performance behavior. ScalaTrace [19] applies a lossless run-time compression technique that greedily matches and combines MPI event sequences. More recently, Pilgrim [24] combines near lossless compression of MPI traces with detection of regular communication pattern. Cypress [25] incorporates static analysis, by constructing a communication structure tree at compile-time in order to improve the effectiveness of the dynamic trace compression. There is little work regarding the use of instrumentation to augment existing traces. Folding [21] maps similar computation regions, e.g. solver iterations, into new synthetic regions. Metrics collected via coarse sampling are aggregated in this region, mimicking the results of high-frequency sampling. Ilsche et al. [6] investigate combining instrumentation and sampling approaches with MPI-based tracing. We are not aware of any previous work that attempts to augment specific regions of an existing trace based on the requirements of a specific analysis approach.

3 Motivating Example

This section introduces a case from OpenFOAM [9] to illustrate the problem of correlating regions in the MPI trace with the corresponding source code locations. We examine a microbenchmark developed under the exaFOAM project[1], simulating a rotating car wheel [3]. Performance analysis of the case revealed a region displaying load imbalance between ranks, shown in Fig. 2. The primary issue is that certain ranks have excessively long execution times outside of MPI, causing all other ranks to idle at the `MPI_Bcast` call. To investigate this issue, the performance analyst needs to identify the code location corresponding to this outside MPI state. With the current state of the art, this can be achieved by enabling stack unwinding in Extrae and manually identifying the lowest common caller in the call stack of the encapsulating `MPI_Waitall` and `MPI_Gather` calls. In this case, the common caller is in the tenth level of the `MPI_Waitall` call stack and in the sixth level of the `MPI_Gather` call stack, as shown in Fig. 3. However, unwinding to this depth increased the runtime by 19% and trace size by 133%. The aim of this work is to improve this process by directly tracing relevant call events, thereby eliminating the need for manual examination of the call stack and providing additional performance data within the selected region.

4 Static Selection and Instrumentation

This section describes the problem of identifying the common caller and outlines our novel static selection approach.

4.1 Graph Definitions

Different graph representations of the call hierarchy are used at different points of the program's lifetime. We use the following definitions:

---

[1] https://exafoam.eu.

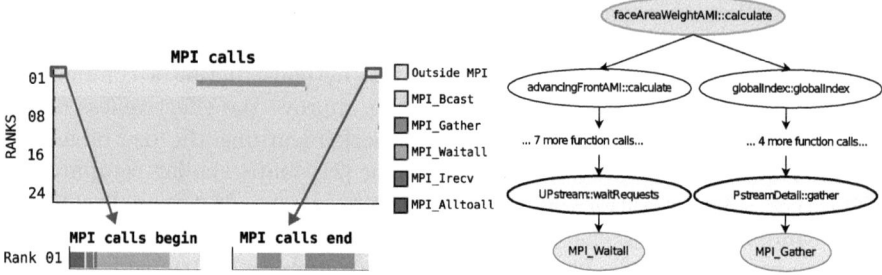

Fig. 2. Region of the Paraver trace showing MPI calls

Fig. 3. Call paths corresponding to the critical trace region

Static call graph: The static call graph G_s is determined analytically from the source or other code representation. It contains all function calls that are statically present in the code. Since it does not take program inputs into account, it may contain edges that are never taken during execution.

Dynamic call graph: The dynamic call graph G_d represents the call hierarchy of the program over the runtime of a specific execution. It is a subgraph of the static call graph for a given set of input parameters.

Dynamic call path: The dynamic call path to a function v_n is given by the vertex sequence $p = (v_1, ..., v_n)$, where v_1 is a vertex with in-degree zero (e.g. the main function). It is equivalent to the call stack at the time of function entry.

4.2 Lowest Common Ancestor Problem

Given the dynamic call paths p_x and p_y of two function calls to x and y, the wanted function is the lowest common ancestor [1] of the union of the two call paths. We refer to this node as the *dynamic lowest common ancestor $dLCA(p_x, p_y)$*. Figure 4 provides an example. However, p_x and p_y are not available in the original trace. Hence, our objective for the trace augmentation is the following: Given only the delimiting target functions x and y, identify the $dLCA$ for a region in the trace corresponding to call paths p_x and p_y. By instrumenting the $dLCA$ and the subjacent call paths, the analyst can subsequently identify the corresponding source code regions.

4.3 Static Analysis Approach

In our approach, we rely on the static call graph to determine potential candidates for the $dLCA$. There is generally more than one possible $dLCA$, as illustrated in Fig. 5. Our aim is therefore to identify a subset of nodes, called candidates, that comprise the set of possible dLCAs for all paths to x and y. More formally, we define candidates as follows:

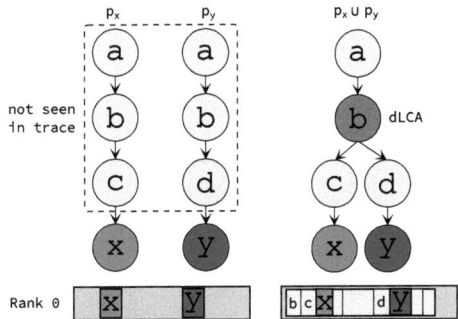

Fig. 4. Visualization of the dLCA of two call paths. The left side shows the two call paths p_x and p_y, where x and y correspond to the two MPI calls observed in the trace (shown below). The right side shows the union of these paths, with b as the resulting $dLCA$. By instrumenting b and the callees in the subtree, the trace can be augmented as shown.

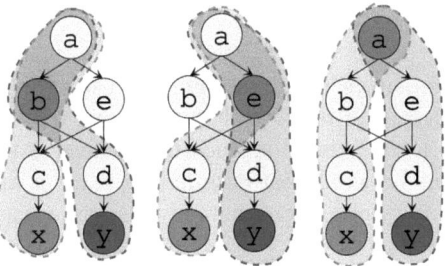

Fig. 5. This figure shows a possible static call graph corresponding to the previous call path example. Due to the additional call edges, multiple paths to x and y with different dLCAs are feasible. Here, a, b and e are all possible candidates.

Definition 1 (Candidate). *Node $v \in CA(x,y)$ is a candidate in the static call graph, if there are paths p_x and p_y such that $v = dLCA(p_x, p_y)$.*

For complex codes with many candidates, instrumenting all possible candidates is too costly. Thus, we heuristically (see 4.5) select a subset of candidates and corresponding call paths for instrumentation.

4.4 Identifying Candidates

We use *postdominance* to identify candidates: Node v is said to *post-dominate* u w.r.t. exit node e if all paths from u to e must pass through v. It can be shown that $v \in CA(x,y)$ is a *candidate* in the static call graph iff there is no node $w \neq v$ that post-dominates v w.r.t. x and y.

Hence, candidates can be identified using the following steps (illustrated in Fig. 6):

1. Perform a breadth-first search to find the common ancestors of x and y.

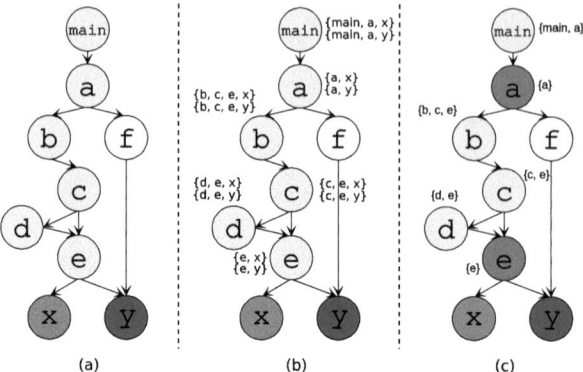

Fig. 6. Example for the candidate selection process. In (a), the common ancestors of x and y are highlighted in yellow. In (b), the post-dominators w.r.t. x (orange) and y (blue) are computed for each common ancestor, displayed next to the nodes. Finally, (c) depicts the resulting candidates a and e. (Color figure online)

2. Compute post-dominators of all common ancestors w.r.t. x and y, e.g. by using a worklist algorithm to solve the underlying data flow problem [5].
3. Starting with the lowest common ancestors, traverse the graph bottom-up to find intersections between post-dominators w.r.t. x and y. Mark nodes as candidates if the intersection contains only the node itself.

4.5 Heuristic Filtering

To reduce the number of candidates, we focus on candidates that are structurally closest to the two target functions. To this end, we examine the possible paths from the candidate node to x and y. We call candidates *distinct*, if there are paths to x and y that do not pass through another candidate. We call them *partially distinct* if this criterion is fulfilled for only one of the target functions. In Fig. 6, for example, e is a distinct candidate and a is partially distinct. We explore two selection heuristics: a *minimal selection* that considers only distinct candidates and an *extended selection* that includes partially distinct candidates as well. *Minimal selection* results in a smaller IC and fewer recorded events, but might fail to capture some calls to x and y. In Fig. 6, for example, the call path $p_y = (main, a, f, y)$ is not recorded with *minimal selection*. *Extended selection* ensures that for each call to x and y, the preceding call path is at least partially recorded, even if the dLCA itself is not instrumented.

4.6 Handling Cycles

The presented selection mechanism was designed for DAGs. In general, the static call graph of a program cannot be assumed to be acyclic, e.g. due to recursion or over-approximation. This issue can be circumvented by using a technique called *condensation*, turning a directed graph G into a DAG by combining the nodes of each *strongly connected component* (SCC) into a supervertex. The nodes of the resulting graph G_{SCC} are the SCCs of G, and (C_1, C_2) is an edge, iff $\exists u \in C_1, v \in C_2$ such that (u,v) is an edge in G. The presented algorithm can then be applied to this cycle-free condensation graph, instrumenting all subvertices of selected SCCs.

5 CaPI Extension for Extrae

The CaPI runtime library (*DynCaPI*) was extended to record instrumented functions in the Extrae trace.

Extrae Interface: To use CaPI in conjunction with Extrae, the new Extrae variant of the DynCaPI library is statically linked into the target binary. If DynCaPI detects the Extrae API, the available XRay sleds are collected and cross-checked with the user-specified IC file. Included functions are then patched via XRay and registered with Extrae. We are currently using a "flat" tracing mode that records nested calls on a single timeline, always displaying the function on top of the call stack. The runtime library maintains a simple shadow stack to correctly reset the current function in the trace on exit events.

Scoped Instrumentation: The common ancestor IC includes not only each selected candidate dLCA, but also all functions on call paths below it to any of the two target functions. These functions may also be called in different, unrelated, parts of the program, potentially leading to a lot of unwanted trace events. To combat this, CaPI was extended with the notion of *scope triggers*. Function events are only recorded in the trace, if a scope trigger is part of the current call stack. By marking candidates as scope triggers, we are able to filter out instrumented function invocations from unrelated program parts.

6 Evaluation

The presented selection mechanism is evaluated on the `lulesh` proxy application [10], as well as two much larger OpenFOAM benchmarks using the `icoFoam` and `pimpleFoam` solvers. The `pimpleFoam` setup corresponds to the benchmark initially presented in Sect. 3. For each of the benchmarks, we first generated an MPI-based trace with Extrae. We then identified interesting regions in the trace, alongside the direct callers x and y of the surrounding MPI calls. The corresponding dLCA was then manually located from the call paths collected via stack unwinding. Details for the setups are shown in Table 1. Measurements were conducted on the CLAIX-2018 cluster[2], running on Intel Xeon Platinum 8160 CPUs.

---

[2] https://help.itc.rwth-aachen.de/en/service/rhr4fjjutttf/article/fbd107191cf14c4b8307f44f545cf68a/.

Table 1. Benchmark details. `#f` is the number of functions in the static call graph. The `depth` is the call-depth distance to reach x and y from `dLCA`.

Benchmark	#f	x	y	dLCA	depth
lulesh	3,360	CommRecv	CommSend	LagrangeLeapFrog	1
icoFoam	496,959	waitRequests	allReduce<bool>	main	5
pimpleFoam	496,964	waitRequests	gather	calculate	10

6.1 Building the Call Graph

The whole-program call graph is generated with MetaCG, by first building individual call graphs for each translation unit and then merging them together. The call graph for `pimpleFoam` consists of 496,964 function nodes. The call graph for `icoFoam` is of similar size as it uses the same library set. CaPI's SCC analysis shows that 99.94% of the contained SCCs are acyclic, i.e. of size 1. The remaining 276 cyclic SCCs contain a total of 1984 functions, of which 562 make up the largest SCC. A manual examination of this SCC showed that the concerned functions are mostly related to error handling and logging. Such cycles in the static call graph are likely a result of over-approximation of potential callers and therefore not expected to materialize during execution. The `lulesh` call graph is cycle-free.

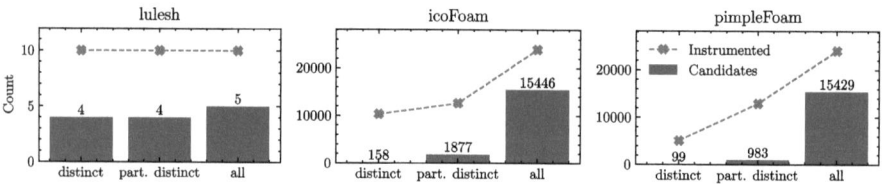

Fig. 7. Number of selected candidates and corresponding instrumented functions.

6.2 Selection

For each setup, CaPI queries were run to find candidates for the target functions. Figure 7 shows the number of candidates and resulting number of instrumented functions. For `lulesh`, the target functions are called in a single code location. This results in a very small number of candidates as well as instrumented functions. There is no difference between the minimal and extended selection heuristics. The OpenFOAM code base is much more complex and uses the target functions in different contexts, resulting in a much higher number of candidates. One observation can be made regarding the change in number of instrumented function when increasing the number of selected candidates. There are approx. 10 times as many partially distinct compared to distinct candidates

Table 2. Trace results comparing the two selection heuristics with base Extrae and stack unwinding to a depth of 10. T_{init} is CaPI initialization and XRay patching time, T_{main} the run time excluding initialization in seconds. Trace size is measured in MB. *dLCA coverage* states whether the configuration recorded events for the investigated region.

Benchmark	Variant	T_{init}	T_{main}		Trace Size		dLCA coverage
lulesh	extrae		104		97		–
	unwind_10		105	(+1%)	178	(+92%)	–
	capi_min/ext	1.7	104	(+0%)	105	(+8%)	✓
icoFoam	extrae		95		285		–
	unwind_10		125	(+31%)	615	(+118%)	–
	capi_min	4	98	(+3%)	287	(+2%)	✗
	capi_ext	4	109	(+15%)	315	(+10%)	✓
pimpleFoam	extrae		283		9,227		–
	unwind_10		337	(+19%)	21,507	(+133%)	–
	capi_min	10	300	(+6%)	9,729	(+5%)	✓
	capi_ext	12	364	(+28%)	13,425	(+38%)	✓

for `pimpleFoam`. However, the number of instrumented functions is only twice as high. This is due to large parts of the instrumented call paths already being covered by the distinct candidate instrumentation. A similar effect can be observed when going from partially distinct to all candidates.

6.3 Tracing

We executed the benchmarks in different configurations, comparing the standard Extrae trace with and without unwinding to the *minimal* and *extended* variants of our instrumentation approach. The results are shown in Table 2. We also considered a purely dynamic augmentation mode, in which full instrumentation is turned on between calls to x and y. This, however, increased the runtime too much to be feasible, and is therefore not included here. Augmenting the trace using the *minimal* heuristic was sufficient to cover the investigated trace regions in all but one cases and kept both runtime and trace size overheads below 8%. The `icoFoam` case was the only one requiring the *extended* heuristic, increasing runtime by 15% and trace size by 10%. The traditional unwinding approach introduced comparable runtime overheads to the *extended* heuristic but yielded much larger traces.

7 Conclusion

We present a method for augmenting MPI traces with call contexts using selective instrumentation based on static call graph analysis. Evaluation on two Open-FOAM test cases shows that our static selection method is viable even for very large applications with call graphs consisting of hundreds of thousands function nodes. The regions of interest were successfully instrumented, extending the trace with detailed function call information and simplifying the process of mapping detected performance issues back to the responsible source code locations. The extended selection heuristic in particular was able to cover the region of interest in all cases, making it a viable alternative to stack unwinding, which yielded comparable runtime overheads but much larger traces, while providing less detailed information to the analyst. Improvements can be made by streamlining the process of generating the whole-program static call graph, which currently requires some initial configuration effort. Furthermore, the accuracy of the selection may be improved by reducing the amount of over-approximated edges in the call graph, e.g. by incorporating analysis of the intermediate representation during compilation.

CaPI is available at https://github.com/tudasc/CaPI under the BSD 3-Clause license.

Acknowledgments. This research has been conducted as part of the exaFOAM Project https://www.exafoam.eu, which has received funding from the European High-Performance Computing Joint Undertaking Joint Undertaking (JU) under grant agreement No 956416. The JU receives support from the European Union's Horizon 2020 research and innovation programme and France, Germany, Italy, Croatia, Spain, Greece and Portugal. Furthermore, this work was funded by the Bundesministeriums für Bildung und Forschung (BMBF) - 16HPC023.

The authors gratefully acknowledge the computing time provided to them at the NHR Centers NHR4CES at RWTH Aachen University (project number p0021597) and TU Darmstadt. This is funded by the Federal Ministry of Education and Research, and the state governments participating on the basis of the resolutions of the GWK for national high performance computing at universities (www.nhr-verein.de/unsere-partner).

Disclosure of Interests. The authors have no competing interests to declare that are relevant to the content of this article.

References

1. Bender, M.A., Farach-Colton, M., Pemmasani, G., Skiena, S., Sumazin, P.: Lowest common ancestors in trees and directed acyclic graphs. J. Algorithms **57**(2), 75–94 (2005). https://doi.org/10.1016/j.jalgor.2005.08.001
2. Berris, D.M., Veitch, A., Heintze, N., Anderson, E., Wang, N.: XRay: a function call tracing system (2016). https://static.googleusercontent.com/media/research.google.com/en//pubs/archive/45287.pdf
3. Galeazzo, F.C.C., et al.: Performance comparison of CFD microbenchmarks on diverse HPC architectures. Computers **13**(5), 115 (2024). https://doi.org/10.3390/computers13050115
4. Gamblin, T., de Supinski, B.R., Schulz, M., Fowler, R., Reed, D.A.: Clustering performance data efficiently at massive scales. In: ICS '10: Proceedings of the

24th ACM International Conference on Supercomputing, pp. 243–252. Association for Computing Machinery, New York, NY, USA (2010). https://doi.org/10.1145/1810085.1810119
5. Hecht, M.S., Ullman, J.D.: A simple algorithm for global data flow analysis problems. SIAM J. Comput. **4**(4), 519–532 (1975). https://doi.org/10.1137/0204044
6. Ilsche, T., Schuchart, J., Schöne, R., Hackenberg, D.: Combining instrumentation and sampling for trace-based application performance analysis. In: Niethammer, C., Gracia, J., Knüpfer, A., Resch, M.M., Nagel, W.E. (eds.) Tools for High Performance Computing 2014, pp. 123–136. Springer International Publishing, Cham (2015). https://doi.org/10.1007/978-3-319-16012-2_6
7. Iwainsky, C., Bischof, C.: Calltree-controlled instrumentation for low-overhead survey measurements. In: Proceedings - 2016 IEEE 30th International Parallel and Distributed Processing Symposium, IPDPS 2016, pp. 1668–1677. Institute of Electrical and Electronics Engineers Inc. (2016). https://doi.org/10.1109/IPDPSW.2016.54
8. Iwainsky, C., Lehr, J.P., Bischof, C.: Compiler supported sampling through minimalistic instrumentation. In: 2014 43rd International Conference on Parallel Processing Workshops, pp. 166–175 (2014). https://doi.org/10.1109/ICPPW.2014.33
9. Jasak, H., Jemcov, A., Tukovic, Z.: OpenFOAM: a C++ library for complex physics simulations. In: International Workshop on Coupled Methods in Numerical Dynamics, vol. 1000, pp. 1–20. IUC Dubrovnik Croatia (2007)
10. Karlin, I., et al.: Exploring traditional and emerging parallel programming models using a proxy application. In: 2013 IEEE 27th International Symposium on Parallel and Distributed Processing, pp. 919–932 (2013). https://doi.org/10.1109/IPDPS.2013.115
11. Knüpfer, A., et al.: Score-P: a joint performance measurement run-time infrastructure for Periscope, Scalasca, TAU, and Vampir. In: Proceedings of the 5th International Workshop on Parallel Tools for High Performance Computing 2011, pp. 79–91 (2012). https://doi.org/10.1007/978-3-642-31476-6_7
12. Kreutzer, S., Iwainsky, C., Garcia-Gasulla, M., Lopez, V., Bischof, C.: Runtime-adaptable selective performance instrumentation. In: 2023 IEEE International Parallel and Distributed Processing Symposium Workshops (IPDPSW), pp. 423–432. IEEE Computer Society, Los Alamitos, CA, USA (2023). https://doi.org/10.1109/IPDPSW59300.2023.00073
13. Kreutzer, S., Iwainsky, C., Lehr, J.P., Bischof, C.: Compiler-assisted instrumentation selection for large-scale C++ codes. In: Anzt, H., Bienz, A., Luszczek, P., Baboulin, M. (eds.) High Performance Computing. ISC High Performance 2022 International Workshops, pp. 5–19. Springer, Cham (2022). https://doi.org/10.1007/978-3-031-23220-6_1
14. Lattner, C., Adve, V.: LLVM: a compilation framework for lifelong program analysis amp; transformation. In: International Symposium on Code Generation and Optimization, 2004. CGO 2004, pp. 75–86 (2004). https://doi.org/10.1109/CGO.2004.1281665
15. Lehr, J.P., Hück, A., Bischof, C.: PIRA: performance instrumentation refinement automation. In: AI-SEPS 2018 - Proceedings of the 5th ACM SIGPLAN International Workshop on Artificial Intelligence and Empirical Methods for Software Engineering and Parallel Computing Systems, Co-located with SPLASH 2018, pp. 1–10. Association for Computing Machinery, Inc, New York, NY, USA (2018). https://doi.org/10.1145/3281070.3281071

16. Lehr, J.P., Hück, A., Fischler, Y., Bischof, C.: MetaCG: annotated call-graphs to facilitate whole-program analysis. In: TAPAS 2020 - Proceedings of the 11th ACM SIGPLAN International Workshop on Tools for Automatic Program Analysis, Co-located with SPLASH 2020, pp. 3–9. ACM, New York, NY, USA (2020). https://doi.org/10.1145/3427764.3428320
17. Lopez, V., Ramirez Miranda, G., Garcia-Gasulla, M.: Talp: a lightweight tool to unveil parallel efficiency of large-scale executions. In: PERMAVOST '21: Proceedings of the 2021 on Performance EngineeRing, Modelling, Analysis, and VisualizatiOn STrategy, pp. 3–10. Association for Computing Machinery, New York, NY, USA (2021). https://doi.org/10.1145/3452412.3462753
18. Mußler, J., Lorenz, D., Wolf, F.: Reducing the overhead of direct application instrumentation using prior static analysis. In: Jeannot, E., Namyst, R., Roman, J. (eds.) Euro-Par 2011. LNCS, vol. 6852, pp. 65–76. Springer, Heidelberg (2011). https://doi.org/10.1007/978-3-642-23400-2_7
19. Noeth, M., Ratn, P., Mueller, F., Schulz, M., de Supinski, B.R.: ScalaTrace: scalable compression and replay of communication traces for high-performance computing. J. Parallel Distrib. Comput. **69**(8), 696–710 (2009). https://doi.org/10.1016/j.jpdc.2008.09.001
20. Pillet, V., Labarta, J., Cortes, T., Girona, S.: Paraver: a tool to visualize and analyze parallel code. In: Proceedings of WoTUG-18: Transputer and OCCAM Developments, vol. 44, pp. 17–31 (1995)
21. Servat, H., Llort, G., Giménez, J., Huck, K., Labarta, J.: Folding: detailed analysis with coarse sampling. In: Brunst, H., Müller, M.S., Nagel, W.E., Resch, M.M. (eds.) Tools for High Performance Computing 2011, pp. 105–118. Springer, Berlin, Heidelberg (2012). https://doi.org/10.1007/978-3-642-31476-6_9
22. Servat, H., Llort, G., Huck, K., Giménez, J., Labarta, J.: Framework for a productive performance optimization. Parallel Comput. **39**(8), 336–353 (2013). https://doi.org/10.1016/j.parco.2013.05.004
23. Shende, S.S., Malony, A.D.: The tau parallel performance system. Int. J. High Perform. Comput. Appl. **20**(2), 287–311 (2006). https://doi.org/10.1177/1094342006064482
24. Wang, C., Balaji, P., Snir, M.: Pilgrim: scalable and (near) lossless MPI tracing. In: SC '21: Proceedings of the International Conference for High Performance Computing, Networking, Storage and Analysis. Association for Computing Machinery, New York, NY, USA (2021). https://doi.org/10.1145/3458817.3476151
25. Zhai, J., Hu, J., Tang, X., Ma, X., Chen, W.: Cypress: combining static and dynamic analysis for top-down communication trace compression. In: SC '14: Proceedings of the International Conference for High Performance Computing, Networking, Storage and Analysis, pp. 143–153 (2014). https://doi.org/10.1109/SC.2014.17

Leveraging Static Analysis to Accelerate Dynamic Race Detection for Remote Memory Access Programs

Simon Schwitanski[✉][iD], Yussur Mustafa Oraji[iD], Cornelius Pätzold[iD], Joachim Jenke[iD], and Matthias S. Müller[iD]

Chair for High Performance Computing, RWTH Aachen University, Aachen, Germany
{schwitanski,oraji,c.paetzold,jenke,mueller}@itc.rwth-aachen.de

Abstract. MPI Remote Memory Access (RMA) allows processes to modify the memory of other processes directly. Due to its complexity, however, data races may occur when concurrent conflicting remote or local memory accesses are synchronized incorrectly. Dynamic race detectors for MPI RMA detect those races at runtime. They rely on compile-time instrumentation of all remote and all local memory accesses and subsequently analyze them during program execution. Not all the local memory accesses are relevant for RMA race detection, but their instrumentation leads to unnecessary tool overhead. This paper presents three static analysis approaches that detect irrelevant local memory accesses at compile time to avoid their instrumentation. The analyses are implemented as compiler passes working on LLVM IR. An evaluation using six RMA proxy applications shows that, depending on the application, the static analysis filters reduce the race detection overhead by a factor of 1.3 to 10.

Keywords: Race Detection · RMA · MPI · Memory Access Filtering

1 Introduction

One-sided communication models, for example MPI Remote Memory Access (RMA) [7], provide a mechanism to directly modify the memory of remote processes in distributed-memory environments. Compared to the traditional two-sided message-passing model, this enables efficient implementations of irregular communication patterns [6]. Further, RMA communication can be directly translated to Remote Direct Memory Access (RDMA) calls to the network [5].

Since in MPI RMA, processes can directly read from and write to the memory of other processes, programmers have to be careful in the case of concurrent conflicting accesses to the same memory location: Without proper synchronization, data races might occur, resulting in undefined behavior [7, §12]. Since the consistency model of MPI RMA is complex, different race detection approaches have been proposed, such as static tools [9], on-the-fly dynamic tools [1,11,13], and post-mortem dynamic tools [2,3]. Dynamic race detection requires the instrumentation of remote accesses as well as the instrumentation of plain local load and store accesses. For the latter, the dynamic tools rely on compile-time instrumentation. Not all local memory accesses are relevant for RMA race detection: Instrumenting and analyzing a local memory access to a memory location that will never be a target of an RMA routine produces unnecessary overheads. However, existing dynamic RMA race detection tools either instrument *all* local memory accesses, use ineffective methods to detect relevant accesses, or are limited to C/C++ programs.

This paper presents static analysis techniques that filter out irrelevant local memory accesses to accelerate dynamic race detection in RMA programs. In particular, we make the following contributions:

- We discuss three static analysis filters relying on data-flow analyses to detect and ignore irrelevant local memory accesses for RMA race detection.
- We present how we implemented those filters as LLVM-IR passes and integrated them into the dynamic RMA race detector MUST-RMA [11].
- We analyze the effects of our filters on the race detection accuracy with the classification quality benchmark suite RMARaceBench [10] which we have expanded to include codes that are challenging for static analyses.
- We evaluate how the filters speed up the race detection of MUST-RMA on six RMA applications.

The paper is structured as follows: Sect. 2 provides background information on MPI RMA race detection and Sect. 3 discusses related work. Section 4 describes our static analysis filters and Sect. 5 their implementation. In Sect. 6, we evaluate the effects on detection accuracy and tool slowdown and conclude in Sect. 7.

2 MPI RMA Race Detection

The following subsections discuss the basic concepts of MPI RMA [7, §12], the different kinds of races that may occur, and provide an overview of race detection approaches and relevant memory access instrumentation.

2.1 RMA Concepts

Before any communication in MPI RMA, remotely accessible memory regions have to be exposed. The routines `MPI_Win_allocate` and `MPI_Win_create` allocate a new memory region or expose existing memory, respectively. Subsequently, the exposed regions are addressed in RMA routines using an opaque *window* handle. The underlying local memory region is called *window buffer*.

For the actual communication, MPI RMA defines three kinds of routines: A *remote read* such as `MPI_Get` reads a value from a remote location and writes the result to a provided local buffer, while a *remote write* such as `MPI_Put` reads a value from a provided local buffer and writes it to a remote location. Lastly,

```
1   void compute_1d_stencil(double *U, double *Unew) {
2     for (int i = 1; i < N-1; i++)
3       Unew[i] = 0.5 * (U[i-1] + U[i+1]);
4   }
5
6   void halo_exchange(double* bufOut, MPI_Win win, int myrank, int nranks) {
7     MPI_Win_fence(win);  // synchronize
8     MPI_Put(&bufOut[0], 1, MPI_DOUBLE, (myrank-1+nranks) % nranks, ..., win); // left neighbor
9     MPI_Put(&bufOut[1], 1, MPI_DOUBLE, (myrank+1) % nranks, ..., win); // right neighbor
10    MPI_Win_fence(win);  // synchronize
11  }
12
13  int main() { // N: number of elements per process
14    double *U = malloc(N*sizeof(double)), *Unew = malloc(N*sizeof(double));
15    double *tmp, *bufIn, *bufOut = malloc(2*sizeof(double)); MPI_Win win;
16    // init MPI and data (omitted here)
17    MPI_Win_allocate(2 * sizeof(double), ..., &bufIn, &win); // for halo exchange
18    // stencil loop
19    for (int iter = 0; iter < num_iters; iter++) {
20      bufOut[0] = U[1]; bufOut[1] = U[N-2]; // copy to buffer for halo exchange
21      halo_exchange(bufOut, win, myrank, nranks);
22      U[0] = bufIn[0]; U[N-1] = bufIn[1]; // copy from buffer in halo cells
23      compute_1d_stencil(U, Unew);
24      tmp = U; U = Unew; Unew = tmp; // pointer swap
25    } // ...
26  }
```

Fig. 1. 1D-stencil exchange in MPI RMA using `MPI_Put` and fences. The relevant local memory accesses for RMA race detection are underlined, and the associated MPI RMA calls are in boldface. The example is based on a 2D-stencil code adapted from [14].

remote update routines atomically update a remote memory location, e.g., increment a value. The process performing the communication routine is named *origin*, while the process whose memory is accessed is named *target*.

Due to the one-sided nature of communication in RMA, the user has to ensure that remote memory modifications performed at the origin are visible to the target by using completion routines: The active target *fence* completion is a collective call that provides barrier synchronization and guarantees completion of all previously issued RMA communication calls. For more fine-grained consistency, *post-start-complete-wait* ensures completion between individual process groups. Further, MPI RMA provides passive target completion where only the origin calls completion routines without the target being involved at all. This, however, still requires synchronization with the target at some point, e.g., through an MPI barrier. Figure 1 shows a 1D-stencil calculation that uses MPI RMA fences for the halo exchange of the ghost cells with left and right neighbors. Each process writes its halo data into the local buffer bufOut and puts it into the corresponding window buffer bufIn of the left and right neighbor.

2.2 RMA Races

Concurrent access to the same memory location with at least one write access without proper synchronization is a data race leading to undefined behavior [7, §12.7]. RMA races can be classified into two categories [10]: In a *local buffer race*, the origin accesses the locally provided buffer of an RMA communication routine before completion is ensured. Figure 2a shows such a code where the result of

```
 1  int res;
 2  MPI_Win_fence(win);
 3  if (rank == 0) {
 4    // reads from remote,
 5    // writes result to 'res'
 6    MPI_Get(&res, 1, MPI_INT, ...);
 7
 8    // undefined
 9    printf("result is %d\n", res);
10  }
11  MPI_Win_fence(win);
```

(a) Local buffer race example

```
 1  int target, value;
 2  MPI_Win_fence(win);
 3  if (rank == 0) {
 4    target = 1; value = 42;
 5    // writes to winbuf[0] at rank 1
 6    MPI_Put(&value, 1, MPI_INT, target,
 7            0, 1, MPI_INT, win);
 8  } else if (rank == 1) {
 9    printf("%d", winbuf[0]); // undefined
10  }
11  MPI_Win_fence(win);
```

(b) Remote race example

Fig. 2. MPI RMA usage examples with a local buffer race and a remote race.

an MPI_Get call is read by *printf* before completion. The MPI_Get routine is non-blocking, and only after the call to MPI_Win_fence the value of res should be read. In a *remote race*, the origin accesses a remote memory location at the target that is not properly synchronized with the accesses from another process. In Fig. 2b, rank 0 writes to a remote memory location, while the target rank 1 reads and prints out the value of the same memory location. There is no synchronization between the accesses, so the output of rank 1 is undefined.

2.3 Race Detection

The high complexity of MPI RMA synchronization led to the development of different RMA race detection tools: MC-Checker [2] and MC-CChecker [3] first collect all RMA calls and memory accesses at runtime and traverse post-mortem a DAG to detect RMA races. MUST-RMA [11] and PARCOACH [1,13] analyze RMA and local memory accesses during execution to provide immediate feedback on races. While MUST-RMA relies on shadow memory to track the status of memory accesses, PARCOACH uses a binary-search tree to find conflicts. Besides dynamic analysis, the static analysis approach presented in [9] traverses the program CFG to detect local buffer races.

2.4 Relevant Local Memory Accesses

Dynamic race detection in MPI RMA programs requires the instrumentation of all remote memory accesses and all MPI routines that affect synchronization and completion. Further, all local memory accesses that might be in conflict with the remote memory accesses must be recorded. Not all such local memory accesses are relevant for RMA race detection: Revisiting the stencil code in Fig. 1, only the accesses to the underlined buffers bufOut and bufIn need to be instrumented to detect potential RMA races. In particular, U and Unew are neither part of any window buffer nor used as any local buffer passed to an RMA routine. Thus, the accesses to U and Unew in the main stencil loop in compute_1d_stencil do not need to be instrumented. Considering that this loop is responsible for a significant amount of memory accesses and thus execution time, ignoring such memory accesses may significantly reduce the tool slowdown.

3 Related Work

Previous works on dynamic RMA race detection rely on local memory access instrumentation at compile time. For each memory access, additional code is added to the program that records the access in an analysis infrastructure. MC-Checker [2] uses the Clang frontend for local memory access instrumentation. To only instrument relevant accesses, it labels all variables that are part of a local buffer or a window segment. The labels are propagated by traversing pointer assignments, and function calls with pointers as parameters. Finally, only labeled memory accesses are then instrumented. This method may miss relevant memory accesses hidden by pointer aliasing, e.g., through memory copies. Further, relying on the Clang frontend means that the method is limited to C/C++ programs, while Fortran programs cannot be instrumented.

PARCOACH [13] instruments memory accesses at the LLVM intermediate representation (IR) level. Its instrumentation method only looks isolated at each function: If it contains at least one call to a relevant RMA routine, then subsequent local memory accesses in *that* function are instrumented, otherwise not. Interprocedural dependencies are not considered and may lead to missed races.

MUST-RMA [11] instruments all local memory accesses without any filtering. This avoids missed races but leads to a high overhead. For example, on a simple 2D-stencil kernel, the slowdown only due to local memory access instrumentation is in the order of 10x [11], independent of the number of processes.

4 Static Memory Access Filtering

Detecting and instrumenting only relevant local memory accesses may significantly reduce the overhead of dynamic RMA race detectors. In the following, we present three static analysis ideas that detect those memory accesses: The *buffer dependence analysis* recursively traverses pointer assignments and function calls of local and window buffers used in RMA calls. This idea is similar to that of MC-Checker [2], but our approach is designed to work on LLVM IR. The *remote access type analysis* further optimizes the result in case an RMA program only uses either remote reads or remote writes exclusively. Finally, the *cluster analysis* detects some superfluous instrumentations at the basic-block level. All approaches assume that the code has been transformed to a static single-assignment (SSA) form analogous to LLVM IR.

4.1 Buffer Dependence Analysis

Whenever an MPI RMA communication routine or a window allocation routine is called, the accesses to memory locations passed (as pointers) to those routines need to be instrumented, as shown in the 1D-stencil example in Fig. 1. In the following, we call such RMA communication and window allocation routines *generator routines*. The source code in Fig. 3 shows an example of an `MPI_Put` call that reads from the memory location of the `localbuf` pointer. All other

Source Code	LLVM IR
assume: int* otherbuf, int* <u>localbuf</u>	assume: %0 = otherbuf, <u>%1</u> = localbuf
otherbuf[0] = 42;	%2 = getelementptr i32, ptr %0, i64 0
	store i32 42, ptr %2
<u>localbuf</u>[1] = 1337;	<u>%3</u> = getelementptr i32, ptr <u>%1</u>, i64 1
	store i32 1337, ptr <u>%3</u>
MPI_Put(&<u>localbuf</u>[1], ..., win)	%4 = load i32, ptr @win
	%5 = **call** i32 MPI_Put(ptr <u>%3</u>, ..., i32 %4)
printf("%d", <u>localbuf</u>[1]);	<u>%6</u> = **load** i32, ptr <u>%3</u>
	%7 = call @printf(ptr @.str, i32 <u>%6</u>)
<u>localbuf</u>[1] = 0;	store i32 0, ptr <u>%3</u>
my_func(<u>localbuf</u>, otherbuf);	<u>%8</u> = **load** ptr, ptr <u>%1</u>
	%9 = load ptr, ptr %0
	call void @my_func(ptr <u>%8</u>, ptr %9)

Fig. 3. LLVM-IR example with local buffer access of MPI_Put. Variables relevant to race detection are underlined. The bold load/store instructions are relevant accesses.

local memory accesses relying on localbuf are therefore relevant for race detection. The instrumentation must consider any aliasing introduced by assignment statements or function calls to avoid missing relevant memory accesses.

The *buffer dependence analysis* systematically flags all pointer variables relevant for RMA race detection in the LLVM IR and puts them into an allowlist for later instrumentation. For any pointer p passed as a buffer to a generator routine, it finds all pointer assignments and function calls that *use* p. All other pointers that p itself *uses* in its definition also have to be flagged.

The pseudocode in Fig. 4 shows the basic idea of the analysis: First, it scans the IR for any generator routine that expects a local or window buffer. For any relevant buffer pointer variable p, a worklist algorithm recursively traverses the use-def and def-use chains to find pointer assignments and function calls resulting in aliasing pointer variables. In an upward pass, it checks whether the definition of p *uses* another pointer o and adds it to the worklist. In a downward pass, it checks all pointers and parameters of function calls that *use* the buffer pointer variable p and also adds them to the worklist. Then, the process repeats with the next item on the worklist. All variables discovered during those worklist traversals are put into an allowlist.

In Fig. 3, the value represented by %3 in the LLVM IR is identified as a local buffer of the MPI_Put call. The upward pass detects that %3 depends on %1 due to "%3 = getelementptr %1, 1" and puts %1 into the worklist. The downward pass detects that %3 itself is used in a load instruction to define %6, thus putting %6 into the worklist. Then, the algorithm continues with %1 and detects in the downward pass that %1 is used in a load instruction to define %8 which is also put into the worklist. Continuing like that, all relevant pointer variables are detected. With the allowlist containing all relevant pointer variables, the memory instrumentation only instruments loads and stores using those pointer variables.

Our implementation of the worklist algorithm also works across borders of function calls: Whenever a relevant pointer variable is used as a parameter for

```
 1: procedure BufferDependenceAnalysis(code)
 2:     allowlist = ∅
 3:     for Instruction I in code do
 4:         if IsGeneratorCall(I) then                    ▷ MPI_Get, MPI_Put, MPI_Win_allocate, ...
 5:             Value buf = getRelevantBufferParameter(I)
 6:             allowlist.add(findAliasingVariables(buf))  ▷ Add buf and aliases to list
 7:     return allowlist
 8:
 9: procedure findAliasingVariables(Value buf)
10:     worklist = [buf], aliaslist = ∅
11:     while worklist != ∅ do
12:         Value cur = worklist.pop()
13:         if cur in aliaslist then continue              ▷ If value is already in aliaslist, skip
14:         aliaslist.add(cur)
15:         for Operand o of getPtrOperands(cur) do        ▷ Check if cur depends on other pointers o
16:             worklist.add(o)
17:         for Use u of getPtrUses(cur) do                ▷ Check if cur is used by other pointers u
18:             worklist.add(u)
19:     return aliaslist
```

Fig. 4. Worklist algorithm to find relevant pointer variables.

a call to a function, the corresponding parameter in the callee's definition will also be flagged and traversed. Similarly, when the relevant pointer variable is a function parameter, then the corresponding parameter of all call sites of that function will also be flagged and traversed.

The buffer dependence analysis is conservative in the sense that it might instrument memory accesses that are not of relevance. For example, it does not differentiate between accessed array elements: If an RMA routine only accesses a single element of an array, then *any* access to that array will also be marked and instrumented. Further, a buffer considered relevant might be an alias to many other variables that are irrelevant for RMA race detection and used in entirely different contexts. For the latter case, we decided to add a configurable maximum aliasing depth D: Since accesses leading to RMA races are often close to the generator routines in terms of the aliasing chain, it is often enough to look at the next D aliases in the chain and ignore any aliases further away. However, this may lead to false negatives if D is chosen too small. We will analyze the effect of that optimization in the evaluation in Sect. 6.

In rare cases such as external functions generating pointer aliases, e.g., calls to memcpy, or in the case of calls to function pointers where it is unknown at compile time which function is actually called, relevant memory accesses might not be detected and thus not be instrumented leading to non-detected races.

4.2 Remote Access Type Analysis

RMA communication sometimes uses remote reads or writes exclusively to exchange data. Then, some instrumentation of local memory reads might be omitted: If a program exclusively performs remote reads (MPI_Get), the corresponding *window buffers* at all target processes will only be read from the remote. Thus, any local load access to the window buffers cannot lead to a data race and does not have to be instrumented. For the reverse case, where a program exclusively performs remote writes (MPI_Put, MPI_Accumulate), the *local buffer* at the origin will only be read. Thus, any local load access to the local buffer cannot lead to a data race and can be ignored. Considering the example of Fig. 3 and assuming MPI_Put is the only kind of remote memory access performed in the program, the local load access of the printf statement to localbuf would not have to be instrumented. If a local buffer and the window buffer overlap or even refer to the same memory location, this optimization has no effect and is not applied.

The *remote access type analysis* is incorporated into the buffer dependence analysis: The worklist algorithm additionally saves and propagates for each pointer variable or its found aliases the type *read-buf* or *write-buf* depending on the usage of that pointer, or *dirty* if it could not be determined. Based on a scan of the program source whether it uses remote read or remote write routines exclusively, the optimizations as described before can be applied.

Because the current approach requires the whole program source to include only remote reads or writes, it is rather coarse-grained. This analysis could be applied to smaller code segments by using flow analysis techniques such as dominator trees to separate different epochs of remote accesses.

4.3 Cluster Analysis

Multiple local memory accesses to the same memory location might occur within a basic block. Since a basic block has only a single entry and exit, only one access has to be instrumented: For multiple reads to the same memory location, it is sufficient to instrument a single read, while for mixed access with reads and writes to the same memory location, only a single write has to be instrumented. The *cluster analysis* finds such redundant accesses and keeps a single representative.

Special care is required for MPI routines called within a basic block, especially calls to RMA routines: Local memory accesses occurring *before* the call might have a different effect than those occurring *after* the call. The same is true if the basic block contains a call to a function that itself calls MPI functions. Each of those calls splits the basic block into subblocks. Those subblocks are then analyzed regarding access to the same memory location.

In Fig. 3, the shown code is a single basic block. Since the MPI routine MPI_Put is called, the basic block is split into instructions before and after the MPI routine. For the instructions after MPI_Put, there is both a load and store access to %3, so only the store instruction needs to be instrumented.

This analysis has no impact on the detection accuracy, except that only one representative conflicting memory access is found in the case of a race, not all of them. The cluster analysis could then be turned off to detect all such conflicts.

5 Implementation

The described analyses to detect relevant local memory accesses for RMA race detection have been implemented in LLVM as standalone passes. They are publicly available at https://github.com/RWTH-HPC/static-filter-rma-c3po24 and https://doi.org/10.5281/zenodo.11651638. In the following, we describe the instrumentation workflow and analysis passes.

5.1 Instrumentation Workflow

The instrumentation workflow is shown in Fig. 5. The source code written in C, C++, or Fortran is first translated to language-agnostic LLVM IR. Then, our implemented LLVM analysis passes are applied to find and instrument relevant memory accesses in the LLVM IR. The instrumented IR is finally compiled into a binary, which can be used with a dynamic RMA race detector, in our case MUST-RMA, that processes the instrumented memory accesses at runtime.

5.2 LLVM Passes

The static analyses are split into three different LLVM passes: The buffer dependence and remote access type analysis module pass implements the worklist algorithm described in Sect. 4.1 together with its extensions described in Sect. 4.2. The resulting list of variables relevant for race detection is handed over to a pass for memory access instrumentation. For that, we modified the already existing ThreadSanitizer [12] pass: The original pass iterates over all local memory accesses and inserts calls to the callback routines tsan_read and tsan_write in the LLVM IR with the address and size of the memory access. In our modified variant, the pass considers the computed allowlist and only instruments the corresponding memory accesses. Lastly, the cluster analysis function pass removes redundant instrumentations as described in Sect. 4.3.

The passes are configurable so that all three analyses (buffer dependence, remote access type, cluster) can be turned on or off. Optionally, the buffer dependence analysis can be configured with the maximum aliasing depth to consider a reduced set of memory accesses.

The module passes only work on single translation units (source files), but the buffer dependence analysis requires a view on the whole program source to capture all dependencies. To achieve that, all source files are first translated to IR files and merged with llvm-link in a monolithic IR file. The passes are then applied to that monolithic IR file. The implementation also provides a compiler wrapper script that simplifies the adaptation of existing build processes.

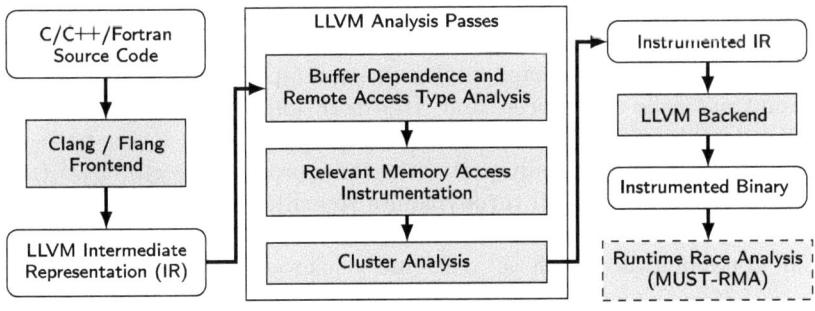

Fig. 5. Instrumentation workflow using the static analysis filters.

6 Evaluation

To evaluate our filter approaches, we analyzed the effect on classification quality with the RMARaceBench suite [10] and performed an overhead evaluation on six RMA proxy applications for the filter combinations. In our setup, we used Clang 16 for C/C++ and Classic-Flang 16 for Fortran programs to translate them to LLVM IR and further process them with our LLVM passes. We combined our filter approaches with MUST-RMA [11] for this evaluation. An artifact with the results is available at https://github.com/RWTH-HPC/static-filter-rma-c3po24 and https://doi.org/10.5281/zenodo.11651638.

6.1 Effects on Classification Quality

All presented filter approaches try to detect irrelevant memory accesses to avoid their instrumentation. However, if they unintentionally remove relevant memory accesses, an RMA race might be missed (false negative). Therefore, we checked whether applying the filters changes the classification quality of MUST-RMA on the RMARaceBench test cases. RMARaceBench [10] contains different small codes covering different race scenarios in RMA programs.

For the original test cases of RMARaceBench, we did not see any change in the detection accuracy of MUST-RMA with any filter applied. However, since we know by the construction of our analyses that there are restrictions that might lead to false negatives, we added additional test cases: As discussed in Sect. 4.1, any kind of aliasing not considered in the buffer dependence analysis might lead to missed relevant memory accesses. Aliasing via function pointers or external function calls such as memcpy is currently undetected, so we added corresponding test cases leading to a false negative. Further, when using a maximum aliasing depth D, we constructed a test case where the pointer aliases are deeply nested D times, and the relevant memory access is D aliases away, also leading to a false negative. We incorporated those new test cases as an additional test set in RMARaceBench, the new tests and results are available in the artifact.

6.2 Performance Evaluation

We evaluated the effectiveness of the filters on six RMA applications: We chose two simple RMA kernels, *Stencil* implementing a 5-point stencil on a 2D square grid using *put* calls and fences, and *Transpose* implementing a transposition of a distributed square matrix using *put* calls and RMA locks, both taken from [14]. Further, we manually ported the three proxy codes *miniMD*[1] (molecular dynamics), *LULESH*[2] (hydrodynamics stencil), and *NPB BT*[3] (block tridiagonal solver) to MPI RMA. For miniMD and LULESH, we replaced the point-to-point communication with *get* calls and synchronization via RMA locks for

---

[1] https://github.com/Mantevo/miniMD.
[2] https://github.com/LLNL/LULESH.
[3] https://www.nas.nasa.gov/software/npb.html.

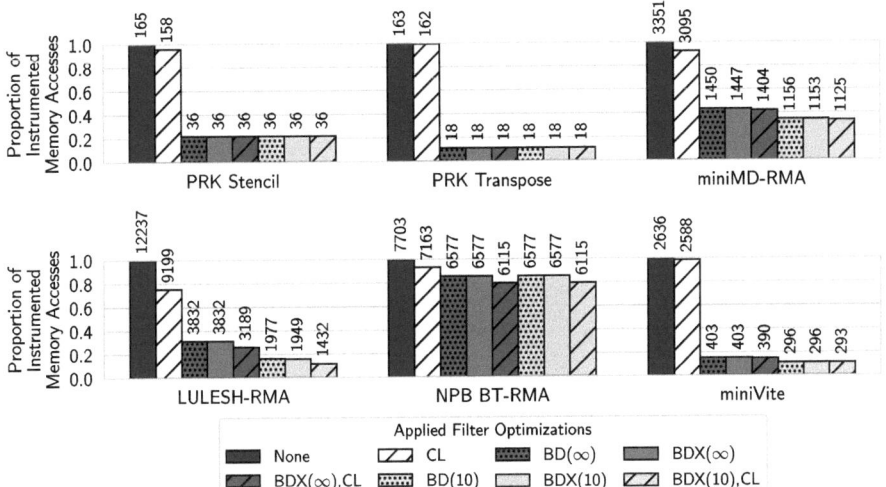

Fig. 6. Relative amount of instrumented memory accesses with the filter optimizations applied. The bar labels show the absolute number of instrumented memory accesses.

miniMD and fences for LULESH. For NPB BT, we replaced the point-to-point communication with *put* calls and fences. Lastly, we tested *miniVite* [4], a proxy application for a graph community detection algorithm using *put* calls with RMA locks. All codes are written in C/C++ besides NPB BT, which is a Fortran code.

The experiments were performed on a single node with 96 cores (two Intel 8468 Sapphire Rapids) using Intel MPI 2021.9. Since the evaluation focuses on reduced instrumentation of memory accesses per process, we only show the measurements on a single node; the results for large-scale measurements look similar. MUST-RMA requires an additional core for the race analysis for each MPI process. Thus, the maximum number of MPI processes used in the experiments is 48 or lower in case of restrictions on the benchmarks' process numbers.

First, we evaluated the number of instrumented memory accesses at compile time for the different filter optimizations, shown in Fig. 6. The cluster analysis (CL) filters out a few hundred to thousand load accesses for miniMD, LULESH, and NPB BT but has no significant effect on the others. Its effectiveness strongly depends on the number of repeated reads and writes in a basic block.

The buffer dependence analysis (BD) was performed without any maximum aliasing depth in BD(∞) and with a depth of 10 in BD(10). We chose a depth of 10 because from our RMA programming experience, this is the typical area around RMA calls where data races occur. Still, this may lead to false negatives in detection, so the depth should be set to ∞ if the highest accuracy is required. For Stencil, Transpose, LULESH, and miniVite, BD(∞) and BD(10) lead to many filtered memory accesses. For those codes, the RMA communication parts, along with their buffers, are clearly separated from the computation. In NPB BT, many aliases are introduced due to frequent use of global variables, leading

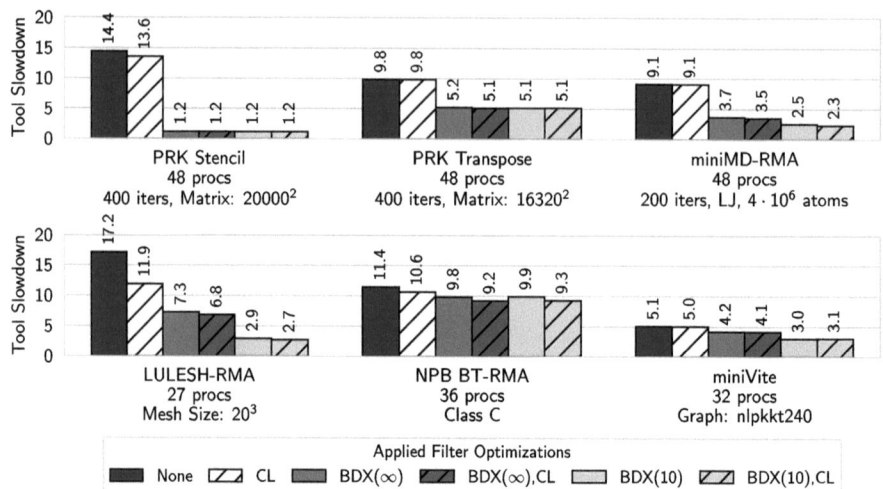

Fig. 7. Tool slowdown of MUST-RMA with the different filter optimizations applied, compared to an execution without tool. Average of 5 runs for each configuration.

to a high number of instrumented accesses. For Stencil, Transpose, and NPB BT, BD(∞) equals BD(10), so an aliasing depth of 10 is sufficient to find all relevant memory accesses. The remote access type analysis (BDX), which extends BD, has only negligible effects, although all the benchmarks exclusively use either remote write or remote read RMA calls. But since most benchmarks also use the window buffers as local buffers for RMA in other program sections, the analysis classifies most buffers as dirty. Separating RMA epochs as discussed in Sect. 4.2 might help to increase its effectiveness.

We also evaluated how the compile time changes due to the static analyses: With all filters applied, the compile time increases roughly by 1.5x to 3x for all benchmarks, which should be reasonable also for larger code bases.

Second, we analyzed how the filtered memory accesses reduce the execution overhead with MUST-RMA. Figure 7 shows the tool slowdown with the different filter optimizations applied for the benchmarks. The run configurations are shown below the benchmarks. The benchmark inputs were chosen such that the runtime of the execution without any tool is in the order of one minute. There were no performance differences between BD and BDX, so we just show the measurements of BDX for readability. CL reduces the slowdown significantly from 17.2x to 11.9x for LULESH and slightly for Stencil and NPB BT. BDX reduces the tool slowdowns for all benchmarks. In particular, BDX(∞) could reduce the slowdown for PRK Stencil from 14.4x to 1.2x since the RMA halo exchange is performed using separate buffers independent of the stencil kernel, similar as shown in Fig. 1. On the other hand, the tool slowdown is only reduced from 11.4x to 9.8x for NPB BT and from 5.1x to 3.0x for miniVite, due to stronger coupling of communication and computation. Combining BDX with CL reduces the overhead for some benchmarks, but sometimes also nullifies its effect, since some memory accesses filtered by CL are already filtered by BDX.

In summary, the results indicate that the cluster and buffer dependence analysis are promising approaches to reduce the amount of instrumented memory accesses for RMA race detection, resulting in reduced tool overhead. Using CL+BDX(∞) is the best choice for better performance without affecting accuracy. If a higher performance with a loss of detection accuracy is acceptable, then CL+BDX(10) or a similar depth choice might be reasonable.

7 Conclusions

The complexity of MPI RMA programming requires appropriate tool support to avoid RMA races with undefined behavior. To reduce the overhead of existing dynamic race detection tools, we presented three static analyses detecting local memory accesses that are irrelevant for RMA race detection and avoid their instrumentation at compile time. The analyses were implemented as compiler passes on LLVM-IR level. The evaluation of six RMA applications shows that the effectiveness of the filters strongly depends on the code: The speedup ranges from 1.3x to 10x and does not affect detection accuracy in most cases; aliasing via function pointers or external library functions might lead to false negatives.

For future work, we plan to incorporate further semantic knowledge to improve the accuracy of our filters. Isolating RMA epochs with data-flow analyses could help to improve the buffer dependence and remote access type analysis. Combining existing static race detection analysis tools with our filters could help to detect race-free code regions that do not have to be instrumented at all.

Acknowledgments. Parts of this work were done in the bachelor thesis of Yussur Mustafa Oraji [8] under supervision of Simon Schwitanski. The authors gratefully acknowledge the German Federal Ministry of Education and Research (BMBF) and the state of North Rhine-Westphalia for supporting this work as part of the NHR funding.

Disclosure of Interests. The authors have no competing interests to declare that are relevant to the content of this article.

References

1. Aitkaci, T.C., Sergent, M., Saillard, E., Barthou, D., Papauré, G.: Dynamic data race detection for MPI-RMA programs. In: EuroMPI '21: European MPI Users' Group Meeting (2021). https://hal.science/hal-03374614
2. Chen, Z., et al.: MC-Checker: detecting memory consistency errors in MPI one-sided applications. In: International Conference for High Performance Computing, Networking, Storage and Analysis, SC 2014, New Orleans, LA, USA, November 16–21, 2014, pp. 499–510. IEEE (2014). https://doi.org/10.1109/SC.2014.46

3. Diep, T., Fürlinger, K., Thoai, N.: MC-CChecker: a clock-based approach to detect memory consistency errors in MPI one-sided applications. In: EuroMPI'18: European MPI Users' Group Meeting, Barcelona, Spain, September 23–26, 2018, pp. 9:1–9:11. ACM (2018). https://doi.org/10.1145/3236367.3236369
4. Ghosh, S., Halappanavar, M., Tumeo, A., Kalyanaraman, A., Gebremedhin, A.H.: MiniVite: a graph analytics benchmarking tool for massively parallel systems. In: 2018 IEEE/ACM Performance Modeling, Benchmarking and Simulation of High Performance Computer Systems (PMBS), pp. 51–56. IEEE (2018). https://doi.org/10.1109/PMBS.2018.8641631
5. Hoefler, T., et al.: Remote memory access programming in MPI-3. ACM Trans. Parallel Comput. **2**(2), 1–26 (2015). https://doi.org/10.1145/2780584
6. Li, M., et al.: Scalable graph500 design with MPI-3 RMA. In: 2014 IEEE International Conference on Cluster Computing, CLUSTER 2014, Madrid, Spain, September 22–26, 2014, pp. 230–238. IEEE (2014). https://doi.org/10.1109/CLUSTER.2014.6968755
7. Message Passing Interface Forum: MPI: a message-passing interface standard version 4.1 (2023). http://mpi-forum.org/docs/mpi-4.1/mpi41-report.pdf. Accessed 14 Jun 2024
8. Oraji, Y.M.: Evaluating static analysis techniques to accelerate data race detection for MPI RMA. Bachelor Thesis, RWTH Aachen University, Aachen (2023). https://doi.org/10.18154/RWTH-2023-05106
9. Saillard, E., Sergent, M., Kaci, C.T.A., Barthou, D.: Static local concurrency errors detection in MPI-RMA programs. In: Sixth IEEE/ACM International Workshop on Software Correctness for HPC Applications, Correctness@SC 2022, Dallas, TX, USA, November 13–18, 2022, pp. 18–26. IEEE (2022). https://doi.org/10.1109/CORRECTNESS56720.2022.00008
10. Schwitanski, S., Jenke, J., Klotz, S., Müller, M.S.: RMARaceBench: a microbenchmark suite to evaluate race detection tools for RMA programs. In: Proceedings of the SC '23 Workshops of the International Conference on High Performance Computing, Network, Storage, and Analysis, SC-W 2023, Denver, CO, USA, November 12–17, 2023, pp. 205–214. ACM (2023). https://doi.org/10.1145/3624062.3624087
11. Schwitanski, S., Jenke, J., Tomski, F., Terboven, C., Müller, M.S.: On-the-fly data race detection for MPI RMA programs with MUST. In: Sixth IEEE/ACM International Workshop on Software Correctness for HPC Applications, Correctness@SC 2022, Dallas, TX, USA, November 13–18, 2022, pp. 27–36. IEEE (2022). https://doi.org/10.1109/CORRECTNESS56720.2022.00009
12. Serebryany, K., Potapenko, A., Iskhodzhanov, T., Vyukov, D.: Dynamic race detection with LLVM compiler. In: Khurshid, S., Sen, K. (eds.) RV 2011. LNCS, vol. 7186, pp. 110–114. Springer, Heidelberg (2012). https://doi.org/10.1007/978-3-642-29860-8_9
13. Vinayagame, R., Saillard, E., Thibault, S., Nguyen, V.M., Sergent, M.: Rethinking data race detection in MPI-RMA programs. In: Proceedings of the SC '23 Workshops of the International Conference on High Performance Computing, Network, Storage, and Analysis, SC-W 2023, Denver, CO, USA, November 12–17, 2023, pp. 196–204. ACM (2023). https://doi.org/10.1145/3624062.3624086
14. Van der Wijngaart, R.F., Mattson, T.G.: The parallel research kernels. In: IEEE High Performance Extreme Computing Conference, HPEC 2014, Waltham, MA, USA, September 9–11, 2014, pp. 1–6. IEEE (2014). https://doi.org/10.1109/HPEC.2014.7040972

Static-Dynamic Analysis for Performance and Accuracy of Data Race Detection in MPI One-Sided Programs

Radjasouria Vinayagame[1(✉)], Van Man Nguyen[1], Marc Sergent[1], Samuel Thibault[2], and Emmanuelle Saillard[3]

[1] Eviden, Echirolles, France
radjasouria.vinayagame@eviden.com
[2] University of Bordeaux, Bordeaux, France
[3] Inria, Bordeaux, France

Abstract. To take advantage of asynchronous communication mechanisms provided by the recent platforms, the Message Passing Interface (MPI) proposes operations based on one-sided communications. These operations enable a better overlap of communications with computations. However, programmers must manage data consistency and synchronization to avoid data races, which may be a daunting task. In this paper, we propose three solutions to improve the performance and the accuracy of the data race detection in MPI one-sided programs. First, we extend the node-merging algorithm based of a Binary Search Tree (BST) presented in a previous work that keeps track of memory accesses during execution to take into account non-adjacent memory accesses. Then, we use an alias analysis to reduce the number of load/store instrumented. Finally, we extend our analyses to manage synchronization routines. Our solutions have been implemented in PARCOACH, a MPI verification tool. Experiments on real-life applications show that our contributions lead to a better accuracy, a reduction of the memory usage by a factor up to 4 of the dynamic analysis and a reduction of the overhead at runtime at larger scale.

Keywords: MPI One-Sided Communications · Verification · Data Race · Non-adjacent Memory Accesses

1 Introduction

The Message Passing Interface (MPI) standard provides one-sided communications, also known as Remote Memory Access (RMA). It enables a rank to remotely access and manipulate memory located on a target rank without requiring an explicit coordination from the latter. In comparison to traditional MPI point-to-point two-sided communication, such as `MPI_Send` and `MPI_Recv`, one-sided communications decouple data transfers and synchronizations. Therefore, MPI one-sided communications have shown good performance in several applications like in [2] where Ghosh et al. compare the performance of a program that implements an approximate weighted graph matching algorithm when using one-sided and two-sided communications. As one-sided communications enable direct memory access and reduce communication overhead, their use can improve the performance of applications, especially those with irregular communication pattern.

Nonetheless, developers still use two-sided communications in their programs because one-sided communications are difficult to use. Indeed, with one-sided communications, developers are exposed to data races if they do not ensure memory consistency, which can be a challenging task. Some approaches exist to detect data races in MPI one-sided applications and help developers write correct and efficient programs. However, these approaches come with restrictions (they do not consider all the features presented in the MPI standard) and most of them imply a significant overhead at runtime. This paper proposes new methods to improve the performance and the accuracy of the data race detection in PARCOACH. We improve the work presented in [10] with the following contributions:

- A new algorithm to merge non-adjacent accesses in the Binary Search Tree (BST) during the execution of programs
- The use of an alias analysis to reduce load/store instrumentations at compile time
- Considering flush synchronizations in the data race detection algorithm to avoid false positives

The paper is organized as follows: Sect. 2 provides background elements, the key concepts this work relies on and related work. Section 3 describes our contributions to enhance the existing PARCOACH static and on-the-fly data race detection analyses in order to improve the accuracy, and reduce the memory usage during execution. Section 4 shows results on two applications and compares our contributions against the previous version of PARCOACH and MUST-RMA, the only other active state-of-the-art tool that can detect data races in MPI one-sided programs. Finally, Sect. 5 concludes this work.

2 Background and Related Work

2.1 MPI-RMA

When using MPI one-sided communications, each process exposes a *distributed shared memory* that can be accessed by all MPI processes. These memory regions are called *windows*. To perform remote memory accesses to these windows, developers must define an *epoch*. Within an epoch, MPI-RMA proposes several communication operations which involve two processes: *origin* and *target*. Process *origin* issues the MPI-RMA communication while the *target* process window is accessed via the communication. In this paper, we only consider programs that use MPI_Fence and MPI_(un)lock_all to create an epoch. We support the two major one-sided communication operations: MPI_Put and MPI_Get.

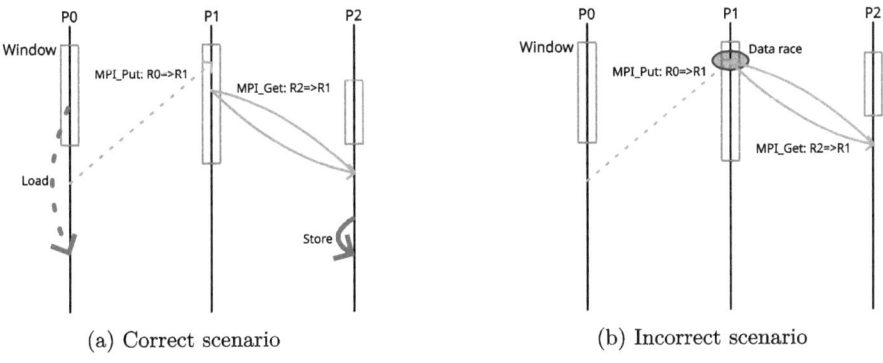

Fig. 1. Examples of correct and incorrect use of Put/Get operations with three MPI processes. From the *origin* process perspective, plain lines represent *WRITE* operations and dashed lines represent *READ* operations. Thin and thick lines respectively represent remote and local operations.

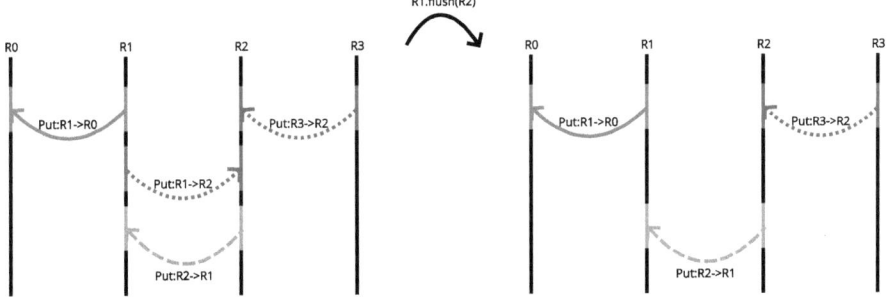

Fig. 2. Behavior of the MPI_Win_flush routine. The coloured lines represent ongoing communications. The line type characterizes the target of the communication. The call to MPI_Win_flush by R1 toward R2 completes all the communications initiated by R1 for which R2 is the target.

Figure 1 shows examples of these operations. In both subfigures, MPI_Put writes a value owned by the *origin* process R0 to the window of the *target* process R1, and MPI_Get allows the *origin* process R2 to locally retrieve a value from the window of the *target* process R1. It should be mentioned that a process can also access its own window through local memory accesses (LOAD and STORE).

MPI-RMA programs expose memory through an abstraction that allows to read from and write to distant memory at any time, which can lead to data races. In such programs, it is the developer's responsibility to ensure memory consistency to avoid data races. A data race occurs in a MPI-RMA program if (1) two operations access the same data, (2) at least one operation is a one-sided communication operation, and (3) at least one operation is a WRITE operation. Figure 1b shows an example of a data race. Both processes R0 and R2 access the same memory space of R1 (in purple on the figure) with one-sided operations including the Put operation that writes on the memory space. The value read by the Get operation is thus undefined.

To avoid data races and ensure the completion of communications within an epoch, the MPI-3 standard proposes sychronization routines such as MPI_Win_flush and MPI_Win_flush_all that can only be used with the passive target synchronization mode. According to the MPI standard, MPI_Win_flush completes all outstanding RMA operations initiated by the calling process to the target rank on the specified window. The operations are completed both at the origin and at the target. An example of how the routine works is depicted in Fig. 2. Given four ranks initiating communications toward other ranks, when R1 calls MPI_Win_flush on R2, only communications initiated by R1 and targeted to R2 are completed after the function returns. Completion of communications from R2 to R1 is however not guaranteed. It is crucial to consider these synchronizations when looking for data races.

2.2 Related Work

Several approaches exist to detect data races in MPI one-sided programs. In [5], Park et al. developed an approach that creates a mirror window that stores all one-sided communications. Upon execution of a communication, the tool checks if a data race can occur with a previous communication in the mirror window. This approach does not consider local memory accesses and can miss errors. *MC-CChecker* [1] uses a post-mortem analysis based on the encoded vector clock to detect data races. It is only compatible with the MPI-2 standard and thus does not support newer MPI one-sided features such as the MPI_Win_lock_all/MPI_Win_unlock_all functions.

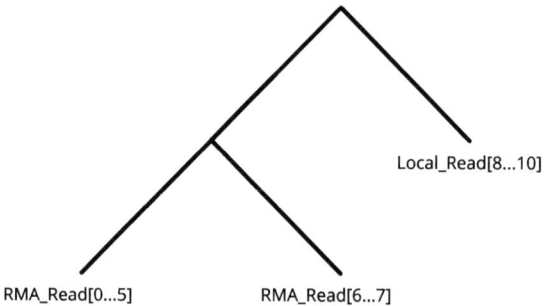

Fig. 3. Example of a Binary Search Tree in PARCOACH.

To the best of our knowledge, MUST-RMA [7] and PARCOACH [6,10,11] are the only two active tools capable of detecting errors in MPI-RMA programs. MUST-RMA combines MUST [4], a dynamic MPI verification tool and

ThreadSanitizer, a shared-memory data race detector [8]. It constructs concurrent regions based on the happens-before relation and forwards them to ThreadSanitizer that checks for data races.

PARCOACH combines static and dynamic analyses to detect data races caused by one-sided communications. The static analysis performs a traversal of the Control Flow Graph to report errors at origin side and instrument memory accesses. The dynamic analysis builds a Binary Search Tree (BST) of memory addresses during execution. A node in the BST is called an *Access*. It represents one memory access and contains the following relevant information about it:

- An interval representing the limits of the memory access. All accessed addresses are contained in this interval.
- The access type: local or remote (*Local_** or *RMA_**) and read or write operation (**_READ* or **_WRITE*). Note that a one-sided operation implies two memory accesses: one for origin rank and one for the targeted rank.
- Debug information for error reporting (e.g., line in the source code).

In the BST, nodes are ordered by the lower bound of the memory addresses. An example of a BST containing three nodes is shown in Fig. 3.

In [10], Vinayagame et al. enhance this approach with a node-split algorithm that splits nodes of the BST to ensure no intervals overlap and a node-merging algorithm that reduces the size of the BST. The resulting algorithm that insert a node in the BST is presented in Algorithm 1. This algorithm first checks if a new access *NewAcc* can lead to a data race with a previous memory access by identifying the conflicting intersections of memory access intervals (line 2). If no data race is possible, a BST node representing this new access is created. The algorithm identifies the intervals intersecting with *NewAcc* (line 4). These intersections do not cause a data race because they have compatible access types. Based on these intersections, new nodes are created, called fragments, that are not overlapping (line 5). All of these nodes are then merged when possible and especially when they represent adjacent addresses (line 6). Finally, the merged nodes replace the previous nodes (line 7). For example, in Fig. 3, nodes $RMA\_READ[0...5]$ and $RMA\_READ[6...7]$ can be merged, and replaced by the node $RMA\_READ[0...7]$. Despite good results on different benchmarks, this approach has several limitations. First, non-adjacent memory accesses are not considered in the node-merging algorithm. This limits the speedup the analysis could achieve on such applications like *MiniVite* [3] that are making equidistant memory accesses. Additionally, PARCOACH does not consider synchronizations with `flush` operations in its analyses. The tool can then report false positives. Indeed, in the CFD-Proxy [9] application, PARCOACH returns an error because of an uncaught `MPI_Win_flush`.

In this paper, we propose an extension of the node-merging algorithm that takes into account non-adjacent memory accesses to reduce the size of the BST. We also improve the memory accesses instrumentation described in [6]. This also reduces the number of nodes in the BST. Finally, we extend the dynamic analysis presented in [10] to support `flush` synchronizations during the detection of data races to avoid false positives.

Algorithm 1. Insertion of a memory access in the BST

1: **function** INSERT_BST(NewAcc, BST)
2:     $HasError \leftarrow$ dataRaceDetection($NewAcc, BST$) ▷ report an error in case of a data race
3:     **if** !$HasError$ **then**
4:         $InterAcc \leftarrow$ get_intersecting_accesses($NewAcc, BST$)
5:         $FragAcc \leftarrow$ create_accesses($InterAcc, NewAcc$)
6:         $MergedAcc \leftarrow$ merge_accesses($FragAcc$)
7:         finish_insertion($InterAcc, MergedAcc, BST$)

3 Contributions

In this section, we present three contributions that aim at reducing the memory usage of the analysis and at improving its accuracy. Section 3.1 explains how equidistant memory accesses can be merged in the BST to reduce the number of nodes. Section 3.2 proposes a solution to reduce the number of instrumentations to relieve the dynamic analysis. Finally, Sect. 3.3 presents a way to consider synchronizations in the analysis of data races to increase its accuracy.

3.1 Merging Non-adjacent Accesses in the BST

The goal of this section is to reduce the size of the BST by merging nodes in the BST that represent equidistant memory accesses. Thus, as shown in Fig. 4b, instead of storing nine nodes in the BST, only one, representing the nine memory accesses, should be inserted. Thus, the BST induced by the program presented in Fig. 4a should contain one node instead of the number of iterations as it was the case with PARCOACH.

In order to take into account non-adjacent memory accesses, we propose a new representation of a node that now describes equidistant sub-intervals instead of a single interval. To this end, two new pieces of information are added in the *Access* structure: a *Size* attribute representing the size of each sub-interval, and a *Distance* attribute representing the constant distance of the sub-intervals.

```
struct data A {
    char buffer1[MAX_BUFFER_SIZE];
    char buffer2[MAX_BUFFER_SIZE];
}
struct data A[MAX_TAB_SIZE];
for(int i = 0; i < MAX_TAB_SIZE; i++)
    MPI_Put(A[i].buffer2,MAX_BUFFER_SIZE,1,...)
```

(a) Example of code with non-adjacent memory accesses.

(b) Merging of equidistant memory accesses in the BST.

Fig. 4. Example of a code making non-adjacent memory accesses and how the latter should be represented in the BST.

These new attributes are represented in Fig. 4b. Nonetheless, the analysis still has to ensure that no sub-intervals are intersecting in the BST. Additionally, the analysis should represent the memory access issued in a code such as the one presented in Fig. 5a as two nodes represented in Fig. 5b. As a consequence, the functions of the insertion algorithm presented in Algorithm 1 have been amended to improve the analysis. These changes are explained in the following paragraphs.

```
struct data {
  char buffer1[MAX_BUFFER_SIZE];
  char buffer2[MAX_BUFFER_SIZE];
}
struct data A[MAX_TAB_SIZE];
for(int i = 0; i < MAX_TAB_SIZE; i++)
  MPI_Put(A[i].buffer1,MAX_BUFFER_SIZE,1,...)
[some computations]
for(int i = 0; i < MAX_TAB_SIZE; i++)
  MPI_Put(A[i].buffer2,MAX_BUFFER_SIZE,1,...)
```

(a) Example of code with equidistant memory accesses that are interlacing.

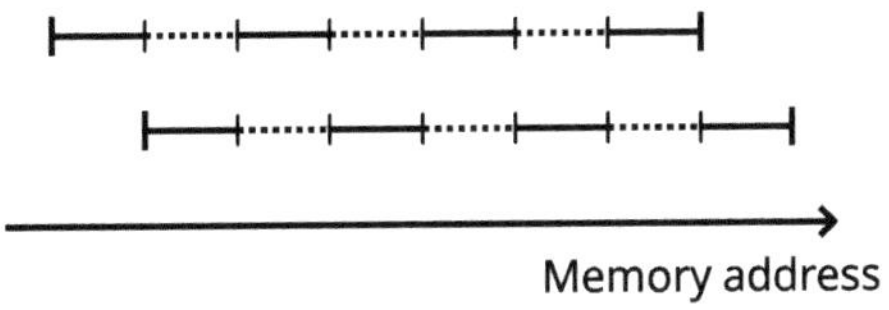

(b) Merging the memory accesses into two nodes

Fig. 5. Example of desired representation of interlaced non-adjacent accesses.

`get_intersecting_intervals` The purpose of this function is to find all nodes intersecting with *NewAcc*. It now considers two extra non-intersecting nodes on the right of the rightmost inserted node, and two extra nodes on the left of the leftmost inserted node. These extra nodes may be useful for the merging of the nodes in the case where they can be merged with the new created node. Additionally, in order to not miss any intersecting interval, this function must check if the nodes that contain the smallest and largest intervals inserted so far are intersecting with *NewAcc*. An example of its execution is shown in Fig. 6. We can distinguish four types of nodes with `get_intersecting_intervals`:

– Nodes intersecting with *NewAcc* returned by the function during the traversal of the BST. These node are referred as "*Intersecting*", and are the only nodes reported by the original `get_intersecting_intervals` of PARCOACH.
– Nodes that are not intersecting *NewAcc* but are returned because they might be mergeable. These nodes are tagged "*ExtraTwo*".
– Nodes intersecting with *NewAcc* but not returned during the traversal because a non-intersecting node separates them from the rest of the intersecting nodes. These nodes are referred as "*Included in*". These nodes (which can be arbitrarily far in the BST) will be reached from a returned node through interval-inclusion pointers represented as vertical arrows tagged "*Is included in*" (maintained hierarchically).
– Nodes that are not returned by the function, which are called "*Not returned*" in the Fig. 6.

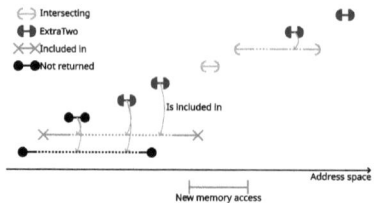 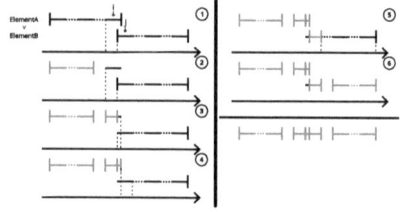

Fig. 6. Determining which intervals are intersecting with the new access.

Fig. 7. Fragmentation process of two intersecting intervals.

create_accesses. Consider a set X of $Access$ objects, that are now composed of several sub-intervals, and the memory access $NewAcc$ that is being inserted in the BST. If $NewAcc$ intersects with a sub-interval of any element of X, then this function creates new $Access$ objects representing disjoint memory accesses. For each memory access $m \in X$, if $NewAcc$ is intersecting with at least one sub-interval of m, then both m and $NewAcc$ are divided into fragments. An example of how the fragments are computed is depicted in Fig. 7. Given nodes $ElementA \in X$ and $ElementB \in X$ such as there is a sub-interval of $ElementA$ that intersects with a sub-interval of $ElementB$, step ① gets the two aforementioned sub-intervals. Step ② then creates a node representing the first sub-intervals that are not intersecting with the sub-intervals of the other node. Steps ③, ④, and ⑤ create disjoint fragment nodes until the function reaches the end of one of the nodes. Finally, step ⑥ tries to create a node representing the remaining sub-intervals.

merge_accesses. Given a set of ordered and disjoint memory accesses, this function merges the elements of this set when possible. It looks per batch of three nodes if they can be merged. They have to be equidistant, with the same debug information, and have the same access type and size. If the batch of three nodes can be merged, the function looks for the next nodes in the set and adds them in the merged node. If the three nodes cannot be merged, the function creates one or two nodes depending on whether the first two nodes can be merged.

3.2 Reducing Memory Accesses Instrumentations for the Dynamic Analysis

The original dynamic analysis is implemented by instrumenting, at compile time, all memory accesses within an epoch, whether they are local or remote accesses. This is concerning since the instrumentation of those instructions adds an overhead to the execution time of the analysis, which slows down the execution of the whole application.

The goal of this section is to reduce the number of instrumentations for the dynamic analysis by removing at compile time the instrumentation of operations that are not subject to data races.

Table 1 summarizes all the possible combinations of operations, with the colored cells representing the ones subject to data races. Depending on which ranks are initiating the operations and toward which rank, we discern three types of data race:

R0 (Origin)	R1 (Target)
Win_lock_all	Win_lock_all
Get(buf, 1, X)	
printf(buf)	
Win_unlock_all	Win_unlock_all

(a) Local concurrency errors detected by the static analysis.

R0 (Origin)	R1 (Target)
Win_lock_all	Win_lock_all
Put(buf, 1, X)	**X = 0**
Win_unlock_all	Win_unlock_all

(b) *target* rank accesses its window while a communication has been initiated at it.

R0 (Origin 1)	R1 (Target)	R2 (Origin 2)
Win_lock_all	Win_lock_all	Win_lock_all
Put(buf, 1, X)		**Put(buf, 1, X)**
Win_unlock_all	Win_unlock_all	Win_unlock_all

(c) Two ranks are making a remote access toward the same target rank.

R0 (Origin)	R1 (Target)
Win_lock_all	Win_lock_all
Get(buf, 1, X)	
Flush(1)	
printf(buf)	
Win_unlock_all	Win_unlock_all

(d) **Flush** makes the operations safe.

Fig. 8. Examples of the different types of data races. **X** represents the window of R1.

- *Local-Local* data races, also known as local concurrency errors, involve two operations that are called by the same rank. Table 1a presents combinations of operations that can lead to this type of data race and Fig. 8a presents an example of this type of data race.
- *Remote-Local* data races may occur when an origin rank initiates a communication toward a target rank while the latter also makes an operation. Table 1b describes these cases and Fig. 8b presents one of them.
- *Remote-Remote* data races are induced by two origin ranks operating a remote access toward the same target rank. Table 1b depicts these cases and Fig. 8c highlights one of them.

The static analysis presented by Saillard et al. [6] enables the detection of local concurrency errors. Thus, the analysis can detect the data races presented in blue and green cells in Table 1a. Remote-Local data races can only occur in the window of a rank: an origin performs a remote access to the window of the target rank while the latter also accesses its own window. Remote-Remote data races cannot be predicted at compile time, especially when the target of the communication is not known at compile time, which is the case in most applications. That is why all remote operations have to be instrumented.

By combining these three observations, we present a new instrumentation algorithm that instruments operations in three cases:

- MPI One-Sided Communications. This is done by instrumenting all `MPI_Put` and `MPI_Get` instructions.

- Local concurrency errors. This is done by first performing the static analysis proposed in [6] and then instrumenting the instructions flagged by the static analysis.
- Load/Store instructions that access the window. To that end, an alias analysis is used to check if a Load/Store operation is accessing a part of the window.

It should be mentioned that in the cases that are in the scope of the static analysis, there is no false negative. Indeed, the pointer analysis used in the approach is conservative, and flags any undecidable situations as a danger that has to be checked at runtime. As a consequence, we are not missing any instrumentation of operations that might lead to a data race.

Table 1. Pair of instructions that are instrumented. X cells are not instrumented because they are not subject to data race. Hatched cells (in grey) are instrumented because they involve two remote operations. Dotted cells (in blue) are instrumented if a data race is reported by the static analysis. Filled cells (in red) are instrumented if the local memory access accesses the window of a rank.

	Get	Put	Load	Store
Get				
Put			x	
Load	x	x	x	x
Store	x	x	x	x

(a) Local-Local table: an origin rank first calls an instruction given in row and a second instruction given in column.

	Get	Put	Load	Store
Get			x	
Put				
Load	x		x	x
Store			x	x

(b) Remote-Local table: an origin rank calls an instruction given in row and a target calls an instruc- tion given in column.

	Get	Put
Get		
Put		

(c) Remote-Remote table: two origin ranks are remotely accessing the window of the same target rank.

Thereby, the new instrumentation algorithm instruments all the relevant instructions for the dynamic data race analysis while ensuring to not instrument instructions marked as X in Table 1 that represent safe memory accesses.

3.3 Considering Synchronizations in the Analysis

In this section, we present a solution to support synchronization routines such as MPI_Win_flush and MPI_Win_flush_all. Being able to properly analyse the behavior of codes using these calls improves the accuracy of data race detection tools.

MPI one-sided programs decouple data movements and synchronizations. Indeed, to allow a process the reuse of data involved in a remote operation, synchronization functions such as MPI_Win_flush can be called to ensure that a remote operation is completed. For example, to resolve the data race depicted in

Fig. 8a, a `MPI_Win_flush` can be inserted between the two accesses to *buf* as shown in Fig. 8d. This synchronization ensures that the *buf* variable can be reused by the second access, since it waits for the completion of the communication.

To instrument the `MPI_Win_flush` routine, in addition to the BST of *Access* objects, a 2D communication array is created for each MPI process to store all the communications in which it is involved. This implies that each time a remote operation is initiated, the *target* MPI process is also notified so the latter can update its communication array. Thus, when `MPI_Win_flush` is called by a rank A for a rank B, A looks in its communication array for communications for which A is the origin and where B is the target. The nodes in its BST that are associated with this communication, which are the related memory accesses, are then removed. The same process is made for rank B. As a consequence, any new memory access that would have been conflicting with a node in the BST, without the `MPI_Win_flush` operation, will not raise a data race since the aforementioned node is not in the BST anymore.

4 Experimental Results

In this section, we compare the impact of the different contributions presented in this paper to the two state-of-the-art approaches that are MUST-RMA [7] and PARCOACH [10]. We compare these approaches on two-real life applications: CFD-Proxy [9] and Mini-Vite [3]. We performed our experiments on an Eviden cluster that belongs to the Eviden R&D department, located at Echirolles, France. Each node has 2 x AMD ome 24 core (AMD EPYC 7402) with 128GB of RAM. The nodes are connected using the InfiniBand HDR interconnection. All the nodes run an RHEL 8.8 system. Our software stack is built with LLVM-15 and we used an Eviden fork of OpenMPI, in version 4.1.6.

4.1 Implementation Details

Our contributions have been implemented on top of the analyses of PARCOACH[1], which is itself based on the LLVM compiler. Relevant instructions are instrumented at compile time. The BST is implemented using the *multiset* containers provided by the C++ standard.

In the following, in addition to the base version of the applications which is running without any analysis (referred as *None*), we compare the performance of five combinations:

- *PARCOACH* is the base version of the application using the algorithm presented in [10]. This version can be found on the commit tagged `Merge-adjacent`.
- *PARCOACH+Merge* represents the implementation of the new node-merging algorithm presented in Sect. 3.1 (commit tagged `Merge-non-adjacent`).

---
[1] https://gitlab.inria.fr/parcoach/parcoach.

- *PARCOACH+Instr* is the implementation of the reduction of instrumentations solution presented in Sect. 3.2 (commit tagged `Instru`).
- *PARCOACH+Both* gathers the two previous implementations (commit tagged `Merge-nonadjacent+Instru`).
- *PARCOACH+Flush* is the implementation considering the synchronizations as presented in Sect. 3.3 (commit tagged `Flush`).
- *MUST-RMA* is the state-of-the-art approach for data race detection in MPI-RMA programs presented in Sect. 2.2. The performance analysis is done with MUST-RMA v1.9.0[2]

4.2 Method Validation

We added 18 test codes using `MPI_Win_flush` to the PARCOACH test suite in order to illustrate the accuracy of our approach. This new test suite includes the code presented in Fig. 8d. *PARCOACH+Flush* does not report a data race anymore while the previous version of *PARCOACH* reports a false positive.

We run the different approaches on CFD-Proxy [9] a proxy-application for computational fluid dynamics. In the application, each rank operates two `MPI_Put` communications that are separated by a `MPI_Win_flush` synchronization. The application is correct and *PARCOACH+Flush* is the only approach that does not detect a data race between the two `MPI_Put` operations.

Table 2. Number of Load/Store instrumentations for Mini-Vite

	# Load+Store instr. (/total)
PARCOACH	20 (/102)
PARCOACH+Merge	20 (/102)
PARCOACH+Instr	10 (/59)
PARCOACH+Both	10 (/59)

Table 3. Number of nodes in the BST when running on MiniVite with a problem size of 1,280,000, depending on the number of processes (in column)

Number of procs	32	64	128	256
PARCOACH	176,460	96,762	51,691	28,671
PARCOACH+Merge	40,531	23,006	12,081	7,041
PARCOACH+Instr	176,460	96,523	51,247	27,785
PARCOACH+Both	40,503	22,815	11,993	6,980

Table 4. Size in MB of the BST when running on MiniVite with a problem size of 1,280,000, depending on the number of processes (in column)

Number of procs	32	64	128	256
PARCOACH	11.29	6.19	3.31	1.84
PARCOACH+Merge	3.24	1.84	0.97	0.56
PARCOACH+Instr	11.29	6.18	3.28	1.78
PARCOACH+Both	3.24	1.83	0.96	0.56

---

[2] https://github.com/RWTH-HPC/must-rma-correctness22-supplemental.

4.3 Performance Analysis

To evaluate the overhead introduced by the different approaches, this section presents a performance analysis on MiniVite [3] which is a proxy-application that implements a single phase of Louvain method for graph community detection.

Table 2 summarizes the number of LOAD/STORE instructions instrumented. As expected, the *PARCOACH+Instr* and *PARCOACH+Both* approaches reduce the number of instrumentations by a factor up to 2. It is noteworthy that the approach instruments less files because it considers that the instructions in some files are not relevant for instrumentation, because it was able to ascertain that no data race is possible.

Table 3 gives the number of nodes in the BST when running the different PARCOACH approaches on Mini-Vite with a problem size of 1,280,000. On the one hand, the number of nodes is reduced by the *PARCOACH-Instr* approach since it instruments less memory accesses. The reduction of nodes is small because the reduction of instructions did not remove instructions called several times and also because the alias analysis used for the approach is conservative and wrongly considers that a lot of memory accesses are aliasing the window. On the other hand, *PARCOACH-Merge* considerably reduces the number of nodes by a factor up to 4. This is thanks to the equidistant memory accesses that are merged into one node in the BST. Finally, *PARCOACH-Both* is the best approach in terms of memory usage since it reduces the number of instrumentations and merges the remaining memory accesses. Figure 4 shows the size used by the BST in memory. Since each node stores more information in *PARCOACH-merge* and *PARCOACH-Both*, the size of a single node is increased by 16 bytes in memory, and is now equal to 80 bytes. Nonetheless, these two approaches compensate this overhead with the reduction of nodes and reduce the size of the BST by a factor greater than 3.

Figure 9 presents a comparison of the time spent in epochs when running MiniVite from 32 processes on 2 nodes to 256 processes on 16 nodes. Each point represents the average over 50 runs. When comparing *PARCOACH* to the approaches presented in this paper, *PARCOACH-Instr* slightly reduces the runtime overhead. This is due to the reduction of instrumentations which implies that fewer instructions are analyzed by our approach. This speedup is small for the same reason as why the number of nodes is not reduced by the approach. *PARCOACH-Merge* requires more operations when inserting a new node which has a cost. This cost is not compensated by the reduction of the size of the BST. For the same reason, *PARCOACH-Both* has more overhead than *PARCOACH* because of the cost of the merging algorithm. Nevertheless, for users that have memory usage limitations, these approaches have a good trade off between performance and memory usage. Moreover, these two approaches have better performance when running at larger scale as the number of analyzed instructions is reduced and so is the cost of the insertion algorithm.

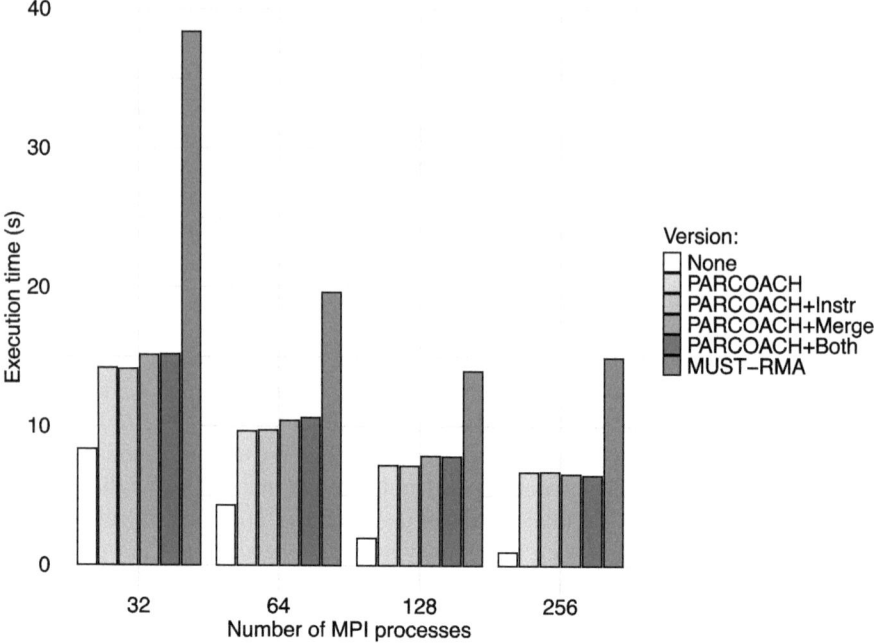

Fig. 9. Execution time of MiniVite with a problem size of 1,280,000, depending on the number of processes and the approach used.

MUST-RMA has a notable overhead compared to the PARCOACH approaches. The reason is that ThreadSanitizer instruments all the memory accesses of the application.

5 Conclusion

This paper proposes an extension of PARCOACH analyses to take advantage of the static analysis to reduce the number of memory accesses instrumentation, reduce the overhead of the analysis at runtime, and support synchronizations in the data race detection and avoid false positives. Experiments have shown that these contributions lead to a better accuracy, and a reduction of the memory usage which may be useful for users that have memory boundaries. Therefore, a reduction of the execution time can be noticed at larger scale. We leave for future work an in-depth study on the behaviour of our contributions on applications with different memory access patterns. We plan to make an interprocedural analysis for the new instrumentation analysis since the latter does not instrument instructions within a function call which may lead to false negatives. We also plan to propose an other way to promote the use of MPI one-sided communications with a code transformation solution that finds regions in the code where one-sided communication may be beneficial, and transforms MPI two-sided communications into one-sided communications.

References

1. Diep, T.D., Fürlinger, K., Thoai, N.: MC-CChecker: a clock-based approach to detect memory consistency errors in MPI one-sided applications. In: EuroMPI'18: Proceedings of the 25th European MPI Users' Group Meeting. Association for Computing Machinery, New York, NY, USA (2018)
2. Ghosh, S., Halappanavar, M., Kalyanaraman, A., Khan, A., Gebremedhin, A.H.: Exploring MPI communication models for graph applications using graph matching as a case study. In: 2019 IEEE International Parallel and Distributed Processing Symposium (IPDPS), pp. 761–770 (2019)
3. Ghosh, S., et al.: Distributed Louvain algorithm for graph community detection. In: 2018 IEEE International Parallel and Distributed Processing Symposium (IPDPS), pp. 885–895 (2018)
4. Hilbrich, T., Schulz, M., de Supinski, B.R., Müller, M.S.: MUST: a scalable approach to runtime error detection in MPI programs. In: Tools for High Performance Computing 2009, pp. 53–66 (2010)
5. Park, M.Y., Chung, S.H.: Detecting race conditions in one-sided communication of MPI programs. In: 2009 Eighth IEEE/ACIS International Conference on Computer and Information Science (2009)
6. Saillard, E., Sergent, M., Aitkaci, T.C., Barthou, D.: Static local concurrency errors detection in MPI-RMA programs. In: Correctness 2022 - Sixth International Workshop on Software Correctness for HPC Applications. Dallas, United States (2022). https://hal.inria.fr/hal-03882459
7. Schwitanski, S., Jenke, J., Tomski, F., Terboven, C., Müller, M.S.: On-the-fly data race detection for MPI RMA programs with MUST. In: 2022 IEEE/ACM Sixth International Workshop on Software Correctness for HPC Applications (Correctness), pp. 27–36 (2022)
8. Serebryany, K., Potapenko, A., Iskhodzhanov, T., Vyukov, D.: Dynamic race detection with LLVM compiler. In: Khurshid, S., Sen, K. (eds.) Runtime Verification, pp. 110–114 (2012)
9. Simmendinger, C.: PGAS community benchmarks CFD-proxy version 1.0.1 (2014). https://github.com/PGAS-community-benchmarks/CFD-Proxy
10. Vinayagame, R., Saillard, E., Thibault, S., Nguyen, V.M., Sergent, M.: Rethinking data race detection in MPI-RMA programs. In: SC-W '23: Proceedings of the SC '23 Workshops of the International Conference on High Performance Computing, Network, Storage, and Analysis (2023)
11. Virouleau, P., Saillard, E., Sergent, M., Lemarinier, P.: Highlighting PARCOACH improvements on MBI. In: SC-W 2023: Workshops of the International Conference on High Performance Computing, Network, Storage, and Analysis (2023)

HPC on Heterogeneous Hardware Workshop (H3 2024)

Preface to the Workshop HPC on Heterogeneous Hardware (H3 2024)

1 H3 Workshop's Main Objectives

The HPC on Heterogeneous Hardware (H3) Workshop was an in-person event in Hamburg, Germany. It provided a platform for pioneering work on algorithmic research, software library design, programming models, and workflow development for increasingly heterogeneous hardware. In the workshop context, such hardware includes mainstream processors featuring long-vector extensions, GPU-accelerated systems, and also architecture platforms deploying special function units, FPGAs, or deep learning engines. The workshop content was a well-balanced mix of invited talks, peer-reviewed contributions, and audience interactions with experts in heterogeneous computing.

2 Topics of Interest and Thematic Scope of the Event

More specific topics of interest focused the submissions and drew specific speakers and invited broad participation of attendees discussing the following:

1. Heterogeneous algorithms that scale not just in terms of the system size but across diverse hardware kinds.
2. Heterogeneity in data approaches that incorporate mixed-precision storage and compute including data compression as well as hierarchical and randomized projections.
3. Software environments and libraries that support heterogeneous compute hardware and networking.
4. Programming models and tools that incorporate heterogeneity of both on-node compute and cross-node networking.

Perhaps the most challenging aspect was to limit the workshop's contributions to the very few thematic areas that currently dominate the efforts of the community. This year, these broad aspects of modern HPC were represented:

- Heterogeneity in programming approaches including language solutions and DSL-friendly (domain specific languages) middleware libraries.
- Heterogeneous workloads that rely on convergence of scientific modeling, data analytics, and scientific AI/ML data models.
- Heterogeneity in data representation, including hierarchical, randomized, compressive, and mixed-precision methods.

3 H3 Workshop Organization

Out of the 9 submitted papers, the reviewers selected 6 for in-person presentation. The review process was single-anonymous with an average of 3.8 reviews per paper and each program committee member reviewing 2.4 papers from their relevant area of expertise.

One of the authors of each of the accepted papers presented a talk with initial highlights of their manuscripts and also including the latest updates on their specific research contributions.

The workshop opened with an invited talk that aligned very well with the major themes of the workshop. See below for further details of the talks and presenters.

3.1 Steering Committee

Hartwig Anzt	University of Tennessee, USA
Bilel Hadri	King Abdullah University of Science and Technology, Saudi Arabia
Hatem Ltaief	King Abdullah University of Science and Technology, Saudi Arabia
Piotr Luszczek	MIT Lincoln Lab, USA

3.2 Program Committee

Andrey Alekseenko	KTH Royal Institute of Technology, Sweden
Pedro Diniz	University of Porto, Portugal
Alfredo Goldman	São Paulo University, Brazil
Mehdi Goli	Codeplay, UK
Ravi Reddy Manumachu	University College Dublin, Ireland

4 Outcome of the Workshop

The workshop was attended by about 30 participants who engaged the speakers in discussion on the presented research topics. The presented talks followed the schedule:

Keynote talk: *Democratizing of computing innovation via a CHIPS-enabled Renaissance in Co-design* by James Ang, Chief Scientist for Computing at Pacific Northwest National Laboratory, USA

Talk 1: *Accelerating Fusion Plasma Collision Operator Solves with Portable Batched Iterative Solvers on GPUs* by Paul Lin from Lawrence Berkeley National Lab, USA

Talk 2: *Benchmarking of GPU Performance Saturation on Accelerated Cluster Nodes via Molecular Dynamics Software Packages* by Plamen Dobrev from Leibniz Supercomputing Centre, Germany

Talk 3: *Introducing SYCL to accelerate a Fock operator calculation library of the BigDFT electronic structure code* by Christoph Bauinger from Intel, USA

Talk 4: *A Novel Mixed Precision Defect Correction Solver for Heterogeneous Computing* by Yann Delorme from Huawei

Talk 5: *Portable GPU implementation of the WP-CCC ion-atom collisions code* by Ilkhom Abdurakhmanov from Pawsey Supercomputing Centre, Australia

Talk 6: *Optimizing GNN-based Multiple Object Tracking on a Graphcore IPU* by Mustafa Acar from Koç University, Turkey

Based on the presented research findings, we can clearly conclude that the prevalence of heterogeneity in both hardware and software is an increasingly important aspect of running modern workloads: be it high-performance computing, AI/ML, and even quantum computing simulations. The community continues to face a variety of challenges of productively obtaining a large fraction of the peak performance. Fortunately, the presented advances in programming models and software libraries help with lowering the barrier to obtaining high levels of efficiency thus fully exploiting the performance gains that heterogeneity affords the modern high-performance computing designs.

Introducing SYCL to Accelerate a Fock Operator Calculation Library of the BigDFT Electronic Structure Code

Christoph Bauinger[1(✉)] and Luigi Genovese[2]

[1] Intel Corporation, Santa Clara, CA, USA
christoph.bauinger@intel.com
[2] CEA-MEM-L_Sim, Grenoble, France
luigi.genovese@cea.fr

Abstract. We present our experience porting the Fock operator application, which is a key operation of highly accurate computational methods in Electronic Structure Calculations, implemented in the BigDFT code, to SYCL, to enable the code for computer systems accelerated by Intel GPUs. We investigate the performance of the new SYCL code on Intel CPUs and GPUs and compare the results to the existing OpenMP CPU implementation and the CUDA implementation on Nvidia hardware. We show that the SYCL implementation is highly competitive, outperforming the alternatives. We additionally investigate the intra- and inter-node strong scaling properties of the SYCL code to multiple Intel GPUs with a focus on the communication overhead imposed by the SYCL implementation and derive readiness for larger computer systems.

Keywords: BigDFT · SYCL · GPU acceleration · MPI · Intel GPU

1 Introduction

Density-functional theory (DFT) [1] is the most widespread quantum mechanical simulation method in physics, chemistry and materials science [2]. It allows the calculation of the electronic structure as well as a large number of derived quantities of any condensed matter system such as atoms, molecules, and bulk structures. Kohn-Sham (KS) DFT [3] avoids the explicit solution of the intractable many-electron Schrödinger equation by solving instead a much simpler system of non-interacting electrons. This reduces the complexity of the approach tremendously, and thereby the calculation time, allowing large systems, up to few thousand atoms, to be routinely handled [4]. In principle, the DFT approach is exact, and should produce the exact ground-state energy and density, but in practice, the crucial contribution, called the exchange-correlation (XC) energy functional, although proved to exist [1], is unknown and must be approximated. The quality of the results depends on the quality of this approximation. Many approximate functionals have been proposed which vary in numerical cost and in accuracy.

Some examples relevant to this contribution are briefly presented in the following.

John Perdew [5] introduced the widely used metaphor of a Jacob's ladder (see e.g. [6]) to describe the search for high accuracy functionals. The lowest rung in this metaphor is the local density approximation (LDA), in which the XC energy can be calculated by a local function on the electronic density. On the next rung are the generalized gradient approximations (GGAs), such as the Perdew Burke Erzerhof (PBE) functional [7], that use both the density and its spatial derivatives at each point. One of the highest rungs of the standard functionals contains the hybrid functionals, which mix some exact exchange (EXX), calculated by mixing the same approach used in the Hartree-Fock Equation, with a portion of the GGA functionals. These hybrid functionals reach an accuracy that is rather close to the desired chemical accuracy of 1 kcal/mol, which represents in this metaphor the "heaven". Some of these hybrid functionals are very popular in the community nowadays; B3LYP [8,9], PBE0 [10] and HSE06 [11] are among the most common. In Solid State Physics, such hybrid functional treatments are especially needed for investigating the electronic structure of systems where the description of the electronic interactions provided by XC approximations of lower "rungs" is not accurate enough to meet the accuracy requirements of Quantum Chemistry calculations, which utilize computational methods that are still much more expensive than DFT calculations. This approach has been implemented in the BigDFT code [12], a highly precise wavelet-based implementation of Kohn-Sham DFT, which has been efficiently parallelized to allow calculations on much larger computational domains than have previously been accessible using hybrid functionals and Nvidia GPU accelerators [13], by the usage of CUDA language. Such implementation based on CUDA has shown unprecedented capabilities for systems which were belived to be untractable not one decade ago [14].

In this paper, we show that by using a highly efficient accelerated implementation of EXX we speed up considerably the implementation of hybrid functionals within DFT codes employing real-space or plane waves approaches. This is achieved by performing all operations of the numerically expensive EXX part, including the data communication, on the accelerator platform.

There are several cross-platform alternatives to CUDA for the development of heterogeneous codes [15–17]. In the present contribution, we focus on porting BigDFT to SYCL [18]. SYCL is an open standard developed by the Khronos group which was released in 2014 to enable the development of cross-platform code for heterogeneous processors in C++ and which has been implemented in several compilers [19–22]. Our focus lies on Intel's oneAPI DPC++ compiler. SYCL code may be executed with various backends. Of particular interest in the present contribution, aside from the performance on Intel GPUs, is the SYCL performance on CPUs to show the viability of removing the default OpenMP-parallelized Fortran code in favor of the SYCL code.

In the present contribution we show that the approach in [14] has enabled the effective and straightforward implementation of a SYCL-based version of such EXX calculations, which can be ported onto other computational platforms.

Moreover, an approach based on localized functions makes it possible to explicitly control the nature of the boundaries of the simulation domain, allowing complex environments like mixed boundary conditions and/or systems with a net charge.

The Summary of the Paper is as Follows. We first present the main operation we have implemented and the algorithm employed for its efficient parallelisation. Then we illustrate the way in which we have ported this operation to the SYCL programming paradigm, and the libraries which have been employed. We then present our performance results in two ways, first by focusing on a mini-app which illustrates the importance of our accelerations in the actual EXX algorithm, then by inspecting the behavior of the full BigDFT application, in use-case showing different behavior.

2 The Fock Operator Calculation

According to the Hartree-Fock model, the calculation of the exact exchange energy E_X requires a double summation over all the N occupied orbitals ψ_i, $i = 1, \cdots, N$.

$$E_X = -\frac{1}{2} \sum_{i=1}^{N} \sum_{j=1}^{N} \int \int d\mathbf{r}\, d\mathbf{r}'\, \frac{\psi_i^*(\mathbf{r})\, \psi_j(\mathbf{r})\, \psi_j^*(\mathbf{r}')\, \psi_i(\mathbf{r}')}{|\mathbf{r} - \mathbf{r}'|}. \quad (1)$$

Each orbital contributes to the one-particle density matrix of the DFT problem, which is related to the eigenproblem of the Kohn-Sham Hamiltonian operator, of which the ψ_i are the eigenstates. In the EXX functionals the Hamiltonian contains the so called Fock operator $\hat{D}_X$, whose action onto a KS orbital reads:

$$\left[\hat{D}_X \psi_i\right](\mathbf{r}) = \sum_j \int d\mathbf{r}'\, \frac{\psi_j^*(\mathbf{r}')\psi_i(\mathbf{r}')}{|\mathbf{r} - \mathbf{r}'|} \psi_j(\mathbf{r}). \quad (2)$$

The numerical evaluation of this quantity has a computational cost which might constitute a severe limitation for calculations with highly precise basis sets. Systematic approaches like plane-wave and wavelet basis set density-functional codes evaluate the exact exchange in a similar way. They form all the $N(N+1)/2$ charge densities $\rho_{i,j}(\mathbf{r}) = \psi_j^*(\mathbf{r})\,\psi_i(\mathbf{r})$ – also named co-densities – and then solve the Poisson equation (PEq) for each of them. The Poisson equation can be solved in this basis with a $M\log(M)$ scaling for all boundary conditions, where M here indicates the number of points of the (uniform) grid of the direct space simulation domain. The same scaling can be obtained in a plane wave program for periodic boundary conditions. Thus, the number of operations behaves as $N^2 M\log(M)$ for sufficiently large M and N. The underlying convolutions require $M\log(M)$ operations, utilizing Fourier techniques, essentially based on zero-padded FFTs [23].

To better understand the way in which our method is conceived, we present the main steps employed for the evaluation of the Fock operator of (2) and the exact exchange energy (1). Essentially, the main point for evaluating the exact exchange terms is related to the evaluation of the electrostatic potential originated from the co-densities, for each pair of orbitals $i = 1, \ldots, N$ and $j = 1, \ldots, N$. Therefore, a communication mechanism has to be implemented such that the $\rho_{i,j}(\mathbf{r})$ can be calculated. Each MPI process owns permanently a subset of orbitals $\psi_i(\mathbf{r})$, which are sent around by MPI communication routines such that any orbital i can be paired with all the orbitals j. Since the orbitals represent substantial data packets, the communication cost of this step is important. To hide the cost of this communication, the communication scheduling is overlapped with the calculation procedure and, in the GPU case, GPU-direct capabilities of Intel MPI are exploited. This approach, named Overlapped Point-to-Point (OP2P) communication, is illustrated in Algorithm 1, with a pseudocode of the overlap between communication and calculations. Calculations are performed on a single MPI task with data that are simultaneously sent/received to/from the neighboring processes. The neighboring tasks are associated on the basis of the MPI rank on a round-robin scheme.

Algorithm 1. OP2P Communication Scheduling

1: iter = OP2P.iterator(data, res)   ▷ Instantiate iterator
2: **while** true **do**
3:     P2P_COMM(iter) ▷ ISend data to proc $i+1$ and/or IRecv data from proc $i-1$
4:     **if** iter.event == OP2P_EXIT **then return** ▷ Exit when last data are received
5:     **end if**
6:     FOCK_KERNELS(iter.psi_i, iter.psi_j)   ▷ Calculate sequentially with local data on ψ_j
7: **end while**

The calculations do not make use of distributed memory paradigms. Instead, they are decomposed into the subprograms (kernels), as indicated in Algorithm 2.

Algorithm 2. Fock Kernels

1: $\rho_{i,j}(\mathbf{r}) \leftarrow \psi_j^*(\mathbf{r})\,\psi_i(\mathbf{r})$ ▷ On a real space grid
2: $V_{i,j}(\mathbf{r}) \leftarrow \nabla^2 V_{i,j}(\mathbf{r}) = \rho_{i,j}(\mathbf{r})$ ▷ Solve the Poisson Equation
3: $\left[\hat{D}_X \psi_i\right](\mathbf{r}) \leftarrow V_{i,j}(\mathbf{r})\psi_j(\mathbf{r})$ ▷ On a real space grid
---

Most of the numerical work is performed in the solution of the PEq in kernel 2. We use our recent approach based on interpolating scaling functions [24], that has also been ported to Nvidia GPUs [14,25]. This approach has proven to have excellent parallel scaling, and has enabled the usage of thousands of heterogeneous compute nodes for large problems (up to 17,000 KS orbitals [26]). One of the advantages of our approach is that the result is obtained with high precision, via a direct solution of the PEq by applying to the co-densities, via suitably zero-padded fast Fourier transforms (FFTs), the discretization of the Green's function of the Laplacian operator. Such a Green's function can be exactly and explicitly discretized for the most common types of boundary conditions encountered in electronic structure calculations, namely free, slab, wire and periodic boundary conditions. In addition, the kernel is executed on a single MPI task thereby not suffering of specific parallelization schemes. This approach can therefore be straightforwardly used in all DFT codes that are able to express the densities ρ_{ij} on uniform real-space grids. This is not a significant restriction since uniform real-space grids are the standard discretization scheme for XC potentials. Our solver is already integrated in various DFT codes like ABINIT, CP2K, OCTOPUS and CONQUEST. It was shown in [27] that the parallel CPU implementation of this Poisson Solver (not employed in this study) outperforms alternative approaches in most workloads, due to the Green's function approach to solve the PEq.

3 SYCL in BigDFT

To increase the performance and enable the solution of increasingly large problems, BigDFT has been GPU enabled since 2009 [13] utilizing Nvidia's CUDA language [28]. CUDA has been employed in the acceleration of the Fock operator calculations (2) with the intensive usage of CuFFT [29] calls in the Interpolating Scaling Function Poisson Solver of the code. In particular, as alluded to above in Sect. 2 and as was shown in [14], the expensive evaluation of the EXX required in the cubic-scaling PBE0 approximation can be offloaded to GPUs to decrease the computing time and, consequently, to achieve computing times which are competitive to the less accurate PBE approximation. Relying solely on CUDA for the GPU acceleration is no longer sufficient—it only allows to offload to Nvidia GPUs—considering the recent usage of other companies' GPGPUs (e.g. AMD's instinct series [30] and Intel's Max series [31]) in several of the fastest supercomputers in the world [32,33]. Moreover, CUDA and SYCL are in many ways similar, which permits a swift migration from CUDA code to SYCL. To illustrate the commonalities and differences between SYCL and CUDA, Fig. 1 shows the same kernel written in the two language models. To further simplify the code migration from CUDA, Intel provides the DPC++ compatibility tool (dpct) [34]. It performs the code migration automatically. In fact, the SYCL code shown in Fig. 1 was automatically generated with this tool. The downside of this automatized approach is that an additional dpct interface layer may be added to the generated code, which may increase code complexity and impact the performance. The SYCL implementation presented in this contribution is based on the automatically generated code from the dpct tool[1] which was manually cleaned and optimized to achieve the performance demonstrated in Sect. 4.

As indicated in Sect. 2, the GPU-accelerated computations in BigDFT are three-dimensional FFT-based Poisson equation solvers, which are part of the Fock operator evaluation. As presented in [25], instead of using two large zero-padded three-dimensional FFTs (one forward and one backward transform) per iteration, the implementation utilized in BigDFT is based on multiple batched

---

[1] Intel DPC++ Compatibility Tool version 2023.1.0. Codebase:(89a0192e122 343c2a13cec7dc6d57cab899c7b64).

one-dimensional FFTs in the three spatial dimensions. The CUDA implementation utilizes the CuFFT library [29] for these FFTs. The SYCL implementation, in contrast, utilizes the double-batched FFT (dbfft) library [35]. For the SYCL implementation, an alternative approach would be to use FFT algorithms provided by the Intel oneMKL [36], due to the straight-forward availability as part of Intel's oneAPI suite [37]. However, the FFTs of oneMKL have several disadvantages compared to dbfft. First, due to the double-batching feature inherent in dbfft, explicit data transpositions (cf. Section 3 in [25]) are avoided. Additionally, dbfft includes features to define "callback functions" for the load and store operations. These callback functions enable on-the-fly zero-padding instead of explicit zero-padding, which is required when solving problems with free boundary conditions (cf. Section 3 in [25]). Figure 2 shows two pseudo-codes outlining the two different algorithms.

Thus, with the dbfft library, the GPU memory requirements are approximately halved compared to the CUDA implementation based on CuFFT or an alternative implementation based oneMKL FFTs and the required memory bandwidth is reduced since the data transpositions are avoided. This results in significant performance gains, especially on the CPU.

The downside of utilizing dbfft is that the BigDFT-SYCL implementation cannot be executed on Nvidia or AMD GPUs, due to the lack of support from dbfft. Extending the SYCL code to fully support various non-Intel backends and to take advantage of the cross-platform capabilities of SYCL is left for future work.

4 Numerical Results

This section presents numerical results generated with the SYCL implementation of BigDFT. First, Sect. 4.1 summarizes the hardware and software used for these experiments. A special focus is put on the recently released Intel Data Center GPU Max 1550 [31], which is an Intel accelerator similar to the device used in the Aurora supercomputer [33] and which is thus predominantly used in the subsequent experiments. Further, Sect. 4.2 compares the performance of the new SYCL implementation on the Intel GPU and the CPU to the existing CUDA and CPU (OpenMP) implementations on the basis of the "Fock miniapp". The Fock miniapp is a small test program to evaluate the performance of the computation of the Fock operator (2) in a way which is representative for the Fock operator evaluation performed in the execution of the full BigDFT suite. The Fock miniapp is part of the psolver library in the BigDFT suite [38]. Finally, Sect. 4.3 presents similar comparisons between different code versions, but for the full BigDFT suite. As part of these tests on the full suite, we show strong scaling results on up to 8 nodes (32 GPUs) of relevant real-world problems and analyze the MPI communications to show that the SYCL implementation does not infer higher communication times—even when running on the GPU—thus showing readiness of the SYCL code for large computer systems.

```
1  //CUDA
2  __global__ void kernel(int nx, int ny, int nz,
3  double *rho, double *data1, int shift1,
4  double *data2, int shift2, double hfac) {
5
6    int tj = threadIdx.x;
7    int td = blockDim.x;
8    int blockData = (nx*ny*nz)/(gridDim.x*gridDim.y);
9    int jj = (blockIdx.y*gridDim.x + blockIdx.x)*
10     blockData;
11
12   for (int k=0; k<blockData/td; k++) {
13     int idx = jj + tj + k*td;
14     data1[idx+shift1] = data1[idx+shift1] +
15       hfac*rho[idx]*data2[idx+shift2];
16   }
17 }
18
19 //SYCL
20 void kernel(int nx, int ny, int nz,
21   double *rho, double *data1, int shift1,
22   double *data2, int shift2, double hfac,
23   const sycl::nd_item<3> &item) {
24
25   int tj = item.get_local_id(2);
26   int td = item.get_local_range(2);
27   int blockData = (nx*ny*nz) /
28     (item.get_group_range(2)*
29      item.get_group_range(1));
30   int jj = (item.get_group(1)*
31     item.get_group_range(2) +
32     item.get_group(2))*blockData;
33
34   for (int k=0; k<blockData/td; k++) {
35     int idx = jj + tj + k*td;
36     data1[idx+shift1] = data1[idx+shift1] +
37       hfac*rho[idx]*data2[idx+shift2];
38   }
39 }
```

Fig. 1. Example of one of the BigDFT CUDA kernels compared to the SYCL equivalent to demonstrate the commonalities between SYCL and CUDA. The SYCL code was automatically generated using the Intel DPC++ Compatibility Tool version 2023.1.0. Note that there is a manually translated version of the above SYCL code, which is simpler and which is used in the latest version of BigDFT.

4.1 Hardware and Software Details

The numerical experiments focus on executing the SYCL implementation of BigDFT version 1.9.4 [38] on the Intel Data Center GPU Max 1550 [31], which is introduced briefly in what follows.

Each Intel Data Center GPU Max 1550 includes 128 gigabyte (GB) of high-bandwidth memory (HBM) delivering a theoretical peak memory bandwidth of 3276.8 GB per second (GB/s). The Intel Data Center GPU Max 1550 is not

```
1   if (<Boundary condition in x is free>)
2     <zero-pad in x direction>
3   1DFFT_X(Ny*Nz, Sx) //real-to-complex FFT
4   if (<Boundary condition in y is free>)
5     <zero-pad in y direction>
6   <transpose data>
7   1DFFT_Y((Sx/2+1)*Nz, Sy)
8   if (<Boundary condition in z is free>)
9     <zero-pad in z direction>
10  <transpose data>
11  1DFFT_Z((Sx/2+1)*Sy, Sz)
12
13  <Convolution kernel multiplication>
14
15  inverse_1DFFT_Z((Sx/2+1)*Sy, Sz)
16  if (<Boundary condition in z is free>)
17    <remove padding in z direction>
18  <inverse transpose>
19  inverse_1DFFT_Y((Sx/2+1)*Nz, Sy)
20  if (<Boundary condition in y is free>)
21    <remove padding in y direction>
22  <inverse transpose>
23  inverse_1DFFT_X(Ny*Nz, Sx) //complex-to-real
24  if (<Boundary condition in z is free>)
25    <remove padding in x direction>
```

(a) CuFFT version of the Poisson solver, as presented in [25].

```
1   if (<Boundary condition in x is free>)
2     <set callback to add zeros>
3   1DFFT_X(Ny*Nz, Sx) //real-to-complex FFT
4   if (<Boundary condition in y is free>)
5     <set callback to add zeros>
6   1DFFT_Y((Sx/2+1)*Nz, Sy)
7   if (<Boundary condition in z is free>)
8     <set callback to add zeros>
9   1DFFT_Z((Sx/2+1)*Sy, Sz)
10
11  <Convolution kernel multiplication>
12
13  inverse_1DFFT_Z((Sx/2+1)*Sy, Sz)
14  inverse_1DFFT_Y((Sx/2+1)*Nz, Sy)
15  inverse_1DFFT_X(Ny*Nz, Sx) //complex-to-real
```

(b) New dbfft Poisson equation solver implementation. Due to the double-batching, no transpositions are required and the callbacks zero-pad on-the-fly. The callback only needs to be set once for all subsequent Poisson solver calls and requires $\mathcal{O}(1)$ memory and time.

Fig. 2. Pseudocode to demonstrate the simplification yielded by utilizing the double-batched FFT library. Removing the transpose operations and the explicit zero-padding also increases the performance. The first arguments in the FFT calls above are the batch size, the second argument the size of each FFT. The variables Nx, Ny, and Nz denote the domain size in x, y, and z directions, respectively. The variables Sx, Sy, and Sz denote the padded problem size and is either equal to the domain size Nx, Ny or Nz, (in case of boundary conditions differing from free boundary conditions) or twice the domain size in the respective direction.

a monolithic device but consists of two sub-devices, so-called "Xe stacks" [39]. When referring to half an Intel GPU, we refer to one of the stacks.

The SYCL results in this contribution were generated on the largest available cluster with Intel GPUs, i.e., a small eight-node computer system where each node consists of two 4th Generation Intel Xeon Scalable Processors (Intel Xeon Platinum 8480+ [40]) and four Intel Data Center GPUs Max 1550 [31] which are interconnected with Xe-Links [39]. Each node in the cluster includes 512GB of DDR5 random-access memory (RAM) and the nodes are interconnected with an InfiniBand HDR fabric. In all tests performed on Intel GPUs, the processes are pinned such that each MPI rank executes on a different GPU stack. E.g., two-GPU-tests correspond to four MPI ranks, eight-GPU-tests on Intel hardware correspond to two nodes and sixteen MPI ranks. All the CPU tests were performed on the same Intel nodes with 16 MPI ranks per node and 7 OpenMP threads per MPI rank to saturate the available 112 physical CPU cores. Thus, we do not use hyper-threading in our CPU tests. When displaying CPU and Intel-GPU results in the same plot, we follow the convention that 4 GPUs correspond to a full node, i.e., all 112 physical cores.

The CUDA tests, on the other hand, were performed on dual-socket dual-GPU nodes with two Intel Xeon Platinum 8360Y Processors [41], 256GB RAM, two Nvidia A100 40GB accelerators [42], without NVLink [43]. The nodes are connected through an HDR InfiniBand fabric. To enable a fair comparison, especially in Sect. 4.2, two MPI ranks per GPU are also used in the Nvidia case. To maximize the performance with two ranks on the A100 GPU, Nvidia's MPS [44] was enabled. Unfortunately, we were not able to source sufficiently large systems with matching CPUs. Due to the differing CPUs, we avoid competitive benchmarking on the full BigDFT suite—since it includes computations on the CPU which impact the walltime—and limit the competitive benchmarking to Sect. 4.2.

In all tests, host code was compiled with Intel's LLVM compilers [45], namely, ifx for Fortran code, icx for C code, and icpx for C++ code, versions 2023.1 (for the Nvidia tests) and 2023.2 (for the SYCL tests), which are part of Intel oneAPI 2023.1 and 2023.2.1, respectively [37]. The differing host compilers are due to differing software stacks on the test systems at the time of testing. The SYCL code was compiled with icpx, the CUDA code with Nvidia's nvcc [46], version 12.1. The MPI version used in all cases is Intel MPI version 2021.9 [47].

4.2 Performance Comparison Fock Miniapp

The present section compares the performance of the different implementations on the basis of the Fock miniapp. The results in this section are highly representative for the performance of the full suite in many situations, since the Fock operator evaluation constitutes the most time-consuming computations in the CPU code version of the full suite when using the PBE0 approximation. In addition, when utilizing the SYCL or CUDA versions of the miniapp on GPUs, the work performed on the CPU is minimal. It is therefore a better code for competitive benchmarking between different GPU vendors than the full BigDFT suite.

Note that the Fock miniapp requires the number of MPI ranks to be a divisor of the number of orbitals, which prohibits some of the configurations. The full suite does not suffer from this limitation, although the performance typically degrades in cases where the number of orbitals is not divisible by the number of MPI ranks due to load-imbalance. We choose to study in this example three different use-cases, a "medium", "large" and a "small" workload.

The first "medium" workload is presented in Fig. 3, which shows the time required for a single Fock operator evaluation for a grid size of 256 points in each of the three dimensions (for a total of 256^3 points), 64 orbitals, and free boundary conditions (which results in a grid size for the Poisson solver of 512^3 points). The tests were performed in the system described above in Sect. 4.1. The results of three different code versions, namely, the original CPU implementation, the SYCL implementation on the CPU and the SYCL implementation on Intel Data Center GPUs Max 1550, are shown in red, green, and blue, respectively. One can observe that, i) the SYCL implementation is significantly faster on the CPU than the original CPU implementation by approximately a factor two. This is due to the usage of the highly optimized double-batched FFT library, as discussed in Sect. 3, ii) the SYCL implementation on the Intel GPU significantly outperforms the other implementations, and iii) The scaling of the GPU implementation levels off from 1 to 8 nodes (i.e. 4 to 32 GPUs) due to the increasingly small computing times which fail to hide the communications. The CUDA version was not tested since the workload requires approximately 60 GB of GPU memory and therefore does not fit in the memory of a single Nvidia A100 40GB GPU. In addition, since the algorithms differ between the SYCL and the CUDA implementations (see Sect. 3; SYCL uses callbacks to implicitly perform the zero-padding required for free boundary conditions), competitive data would not be that meaningful.

The results of the "small" workload are presented in Fig. 4. It shows a Fock operator evaluation for a grid size of 96 points in each of the three dimensions (for a total of 96^3 points), 128 orbitals, and periodic boundary conditions (which does not require zero-padding and thus maintains a grid size of 96^3 points for the Poisson solver). This workload is particularly interesting since it coincides with the Fock operator evaluation occurring during the full BigDFT suite computation of thirty-two H2O molecules shown in the following Sect. 4.3. In addition to the previous three configurations, the graph also shows results achieved on A100 GPUs with the existing CUDA implementation. One can observe that the SYCL implementation on the Intel Max GPU is highly competitive in terms of computing times, outperforming the CUDA implementation. This increase in performance, especially for the small computing times on many GPUs, may be attributed to the minor differences in the fabric and the lack of NVLink for the Nvidia GPUs.

Similarly to the workload shown above, the scaling in the SYCL GPU case degrades significantly for more than a single node due to relative increase of the time required for the communication. The different CPUs in the SYCL-GPU and CUDA cases have minimal impact on the presented execution times since the majority of the timed code is executed on the GPUs. To confirm that there

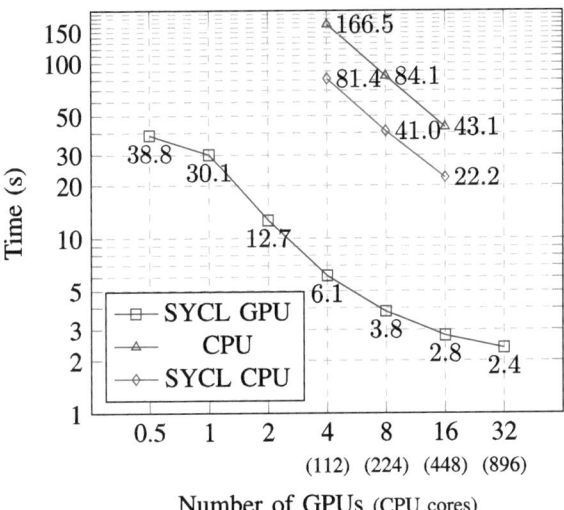

Fig. 3. Wall time to solution (y-axis) as a function of the number of GPUs or nodes (x-axis) of the Fock miniapp for free boundary conditions, a grid size of $n = 256^3$ and $o = 64$ orbitals. The CPU tests on 8 nodes are missing since the number of MPI ranks cannot exceed the number of orbitals. The first data point was performed on one stack of the two stacks of the Intel GPU. The SYCL implementation was run on the CPU (SYCL CPU) or on Intel GPUs (SYCL GPU).

Table 1. Comparison of the average read and write L3- and HBM-bandwidths achieved by the Fock miniapp on a single stack of the Intel GPU. The "small" case ($n = 96^3$, $o = 128$) fits in L3 cache and therefore hardly utilizes HBM. The "medium" case ($n = 256^3$, $o = 64$) does not fit in L3 and induces heavy HBM traffic. Data measured with oneprof [48].

Case	Read (GB/s)		Write (GB/s)		Read+Write	
	L3	HBM	L3	HBM	L3	HBM
$n = 256^3$, $o = 64$	0.02	468	336	315	336	783
$n = 96^3$, $o = 128$	1172	66	1744	48	3516	114

is only a minimal impact of the CPU on the GPU timings, we tested running the SYCL-GPU version on a single stack in a computer with the same Intel Xeon Platinum 8360Y Processor as the Nvidia node—the measured execution times match with the presented data from the Intel GPU system outlined in Sect. 4.1.

Table 1 compares the average HBM and L3 bandwidths during the single-stack executions on the Intel GPU of the workloads shown in Fig. 3 and 4. From the table it is evident that the "small" workload ($n = 96^3$) fits into L3 cache and thus induces minimal HBM traffic. The "medium" workload, in contrast,

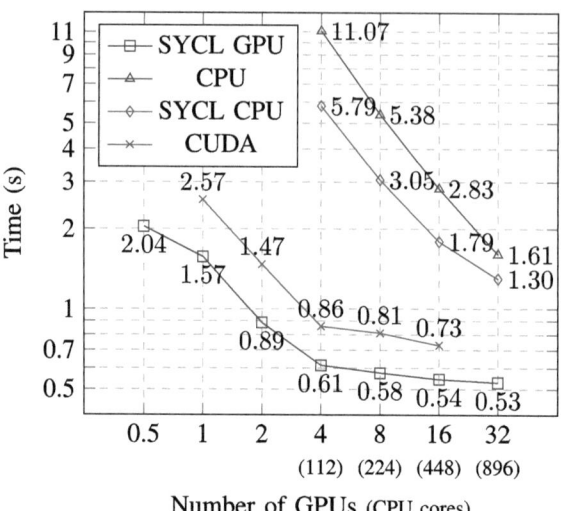

Fig. 4. Wall time to solution (y-axis) as a function of the number of GPUs or nodes (x-axis) of the Fock miniapp for periodic boundary conditions, a grid size of $n = 96^3$ and $o = 128$ orbitals. This workload coincides with the exact exchange computation performed during a full solve of the H2O-32 case presented in Fig. 6. The last CUDA data point could not be measured on the available hardware due to stability issues of the nodes. The CUDA implementation was run on Nvidia A100 40GB GPUs. The SYCL implementation was run on CPU (SYCL CPU) or on Intel GPUs (SYCL GPU).

does not fit in L3 and induces heavy HBM traffic. In the case of the "medium" workload, the code utilizes on average 783 GB/s of HBM bandwidth, which represents approximately 48% of the theoretical peak bandwidth of a single stack. A roofline analysis shows that the arithmetic intensity of the "medium" workload is approximately 0.47 flops per byte loaded from HBM, confirming that the code is highly memory bandwidth bound. The "small" workload, on the other hand, shows a higher arithmetic intensity of approximately 14.8 flops per byte loaded from HBM.

Finally, Fig. 5 shows the "large" workloads which consists of a grid size of 108^3 points, 1472 orbitals and periodic boundary conditions. It is an approximation of the Fock operator evaluation performed during the full BigDFT suite workload shown in Fig. 8. The only difference is that the number of orbitals was increased to the next multiple of 64 due to the restrictions imposed by the Fock miniapp that the number of ranks has to be a divisor of the number of orbitals, which is also the reason the 8-node CPU cases are missing. As before, the results show that the SYCL CPU version is faster than the original CPU version by approximately a factor 2. In addition, the SYCL GPU version is approximately another 13–15 times faster. As indicated by the results shown in Figs. 3 and 4, the

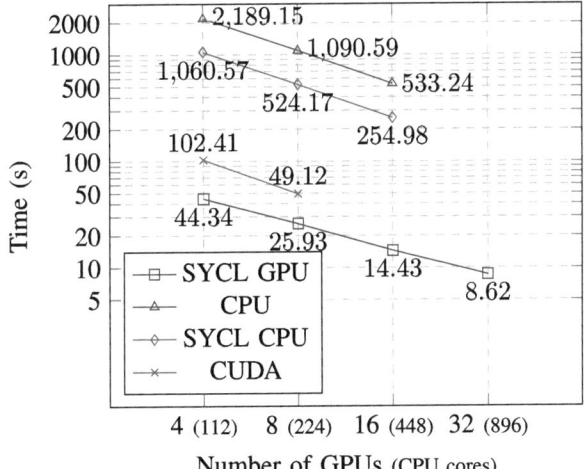

Fig. 5. Wall time to solution (y-axis) as a function of the number of GPUs or nodes (x-axis) of the Fock miniapp for periodic boundary conditions, a grid size of $n = 108^3$ and $o = 1472$ orbitals. The missing CUDA data points could not be measured on the available hardware. The CUDA implementation was run on Nvidia A100 40GB GPUs. The SYCL implementation was run on CPU (SYCL CPU) or on Intel GPUs (SYCL GPU).

scaling of the GPU improves with a larger number of orbitals and the workload achieves a strong parallel scaling efficiency of approximately 64.3% (compared to the 32% shown in Fig. 3) from 1 node to 8 nodes. Based on the data, it is evident that the GPU acceleration is preferable for large numbers of orbitals. It is interesting to note that the performance of the SYCL implementation on Intel's GPU relative to the CUDA implementation on the Nvidia A100 40GB increases significantly for this larger problems. This may be due to the missing NVLink interconnect between GPUs, the differing CPUs, or differences in the cluster configuration. Due to the lack of suitable hardware, further investigations are left for future work.

4.3 Performance Comparison—BigDFT Suite

As described in Sect. 2, the full BigDFT suite requires multiple iterations of Fock operator evaluations, which constitute the most time consuming calculations in the original OpenMP-Fortran CPU code. It is thus reasonable to expect that the full suite shows similar scaling properties to the Fock miniapp shown the previous Sect. 4.2. To confirm this, in what follows, we have chosen to analyze the full BigDFT suite on the basis of two different molecular systems, exhibiting different numerical behaviors. Those two systems are extracted from previous production data presented in the literature [14,26].

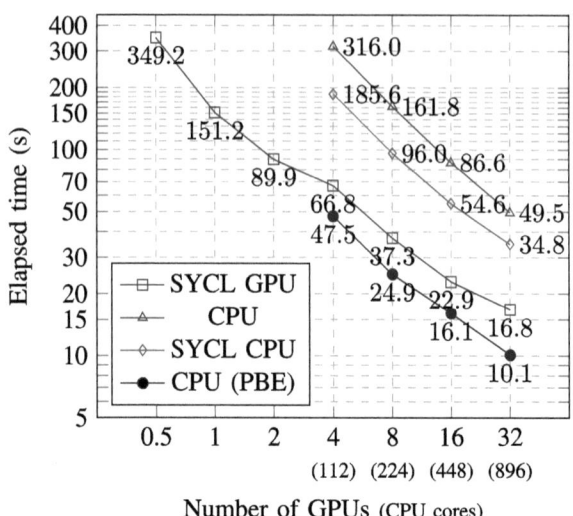

Fig. 6. Comparison of the wall time to solution (y-axis) for the different implementations as a function of the number of GPUs or nodes (x-axis). Lower wall time is better. The graph includes a comparison to the cheaper (yet less accurate) PBE approximation—which is not accelerated—for the same number of iterations (12). The first data point was generated on one of the two stacks of the Intel GPU. The SYCL implementation was run on CPU (SYCL CPU) or on Intel GPUs (SYCL GPU).

For both systems we show the strong scaling properties of the original CPU, the SYCL CPU and the SYCL GPU version. We also show a breakdown of the wall time spent in different parts of the DFT optimization cycle (which is not the full app). In addition to the strong scaling properties, a focus of the analysis is put on the impact represented by the communications to the overall behavior and wall time to ensure that SYCL and the Intel GPUs do not introduce additional communication overhead and to conclude the suitability of the SYCL code for larger computer clusters accelerated by Intel GPUs (e.g. Aurora [33]). Note that by "communications" we here indicate the time actually spent in *waiting* for the communications to finish, and not the full time spent by the interconnect, which is overlapped with the calculations. The measurements were conducted with tools built-in to the BigDFT code and confirmed with Intel's APS tool [49].

The first workload under investigation is a system consisting of 32 H2O molecules, which has been employed as a reference calculation for the initial porting to GPU of the exact exchange operator [14]. Note that the requisite Fock operator evaluation (a grid size of 96^3 points, 128 orbitals and periodic boundary conditions) was investigated in the previous section in Fig. 4. The computing times of the full BigDFT suite of these thirty-two water molecules are visualized in Fig. 6. As expected from the results shown in Fig. 4, the SYCL GPU version outperforms the SYCL CPU version which, in turn, outperforms the original CPU version. In contrast to the results shown in Fig. 4, the GPU version continues to scale all the way to 32 GPUs (8 nodes). This is due to the scaling of the host code.

Aside from the various results of the cubic-scaling PBE0 approximation, Fig. 6 also shows the computing time required when utilizing the PBE approximation instead (in pink), which does not make use of the Fock operator and it is therefore a much cheaper – albeit less accurate – DFT approximation. While the PBE approximation requires one more iteration for convergence than the PBE0 approximation (13 instead of 12), the elapsed time shown for the PBE0 approximation is also for 12 iterations. This proves that the GPU acceleration of the code makes affordable calculations which would rapidly become prohibitive with traditional platforms.

Figure 7 shows several breakdowns of the time spent in different parts of the H2O benchmark for the different implementations. Figure 7a, in particular, displays an overall breakdown of the time spent in the different parts of the code and shows, unsurprisingly, that the main contribution to the wall time is provided by the computations. The communication time has a minimal impact on the wall time, except for the GPU runs on more than one node, where the relative time spent in the communication increases up to approximately 30% (8 nodes) of the overall time. This is expected from the results shown in Fig. 4, which indicate that the communication dominates the Fock operator evaluation. The communication is further broken down and visualized in Fig. 7b. It is clear that the CPU and the SYCL CPU version show similar communication behavior whereas the time spent in the communication is slightly reduced for the SYCL GPU version. This behavior coincides with our expectation: as soon as the time for computations lowers, the communication time increases as the time spent in the OP2P message passing cannot be efficiently overlapped. Moreover, the SYCL GPU version uses only half the MPI ranks compared to the CPU versions and thus a reduced number of communications. Finally, Fig. 7b also shows that most of the communication time is spent in the Fock operator evaluation for the many-GPU results.

The second workload under consideration consists of of 96 Uranium dioxide (UO2) molecules, resulting in 1432 orbitals. The workload is taken from [26], where the different wave function minima of a Uranium dioxide crystals are studied. The "large" Fock miniapp workload shown in Fig. 5 is inspired by this full workload. The two main differences of this example compared to the H2O molecules are i) a higher computational cost provided by the larger number of KS orbitals (we recall that the scaling of the method is proportional to the square of this quantity), and ii) the presence of MPI load imbalance in the calculations, due to the fact that the number of MPI processes is not a divisor of the number of KS orbitals. In production calculations, this is a common situation as the user can hardly modify the number of orbitals of a system, which is dictated by the chemical properties of the atoms involved in the calculation. Therefore, it is important that the algorithm is able to exhibit some level of resiliency with respect to load-imbalanced workloads.

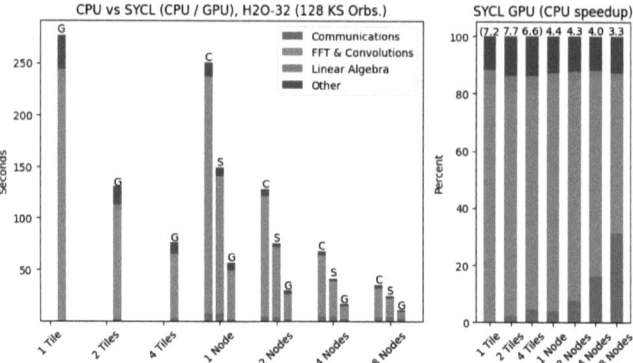

(a) Breakdown of the time spent in the DFT optimization cycle into various categories for the H2O workload. The CPU, SYCL CPU and SYCL GPU runs are labeled C, S, and G, respectively. The left panel shows the overall wall time. The right panel shows the relative time of all the different calculation categories for the SYCL GPU case. The overall speedup of the accelerated version with respect to the reference CPU implementation is presented on top of the right panel. The numbers in brackets are estimations since there are no reasonable CPU reference results corresponding to, e.g., "1 Tile".

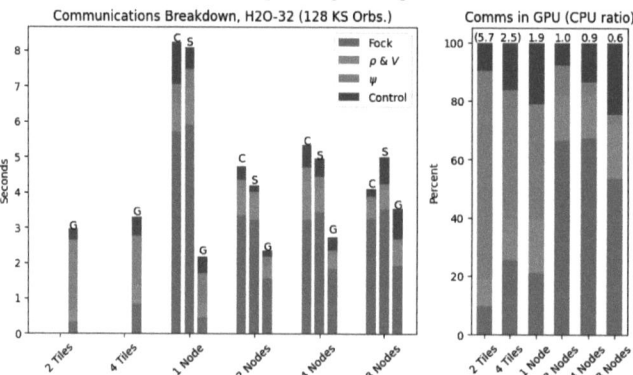

(b) Breakdown of the time spent in communication for the H2O workload. The left panel shows absolute time for the three implementations: CPU (C), SYCL CPU (S), and SYCL GPU (G). The right panel shows the relative time for the SYCL GPU implementation. The Fock communication time is mainly time spent in waiting for the P2P communication to finish, whereas all the other categories are related to blocking collective MPI operations. The numbers on top of the percent bar chart indicate the ratio between the time spent in communication of the SYCL GPU runs with respect to the same quantity of the CPU runs, normalized by the number of MPI tasks. The 1 Tile result is not shown due to the absence of communication.

Fig. 7. Analysis of the full DFT calculation of a thirty-two H2O molecules case, with $o = 128$ orbitals, and a grid size of $n = 96^3$.

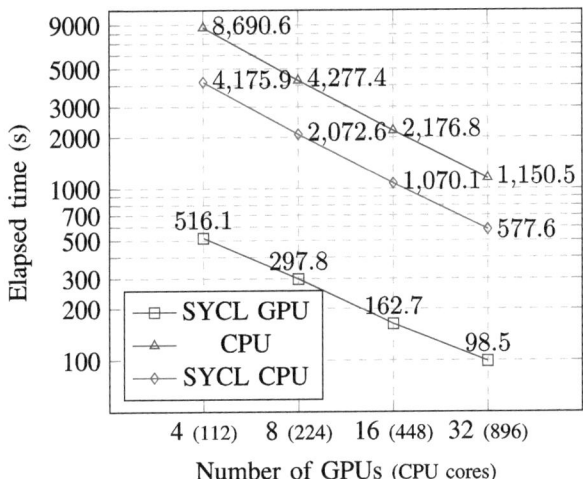

Fig. 8. Comparison of the wall time for 3 iterations of the UO2 workload, which consists of $o = 1432$ orbitals and a grid size of $n = 108^3$.

The wall time to solution required for the full BigDFT suite for the UO2 workload, on an increasing number of GPUs and nodes, is shown in Fig. 8. It shows that the inter-node strong scaling efficiency from 1 node to 8 nodes is 65.5%, which coincides well with the Fock miniapp results shown in Fig. 5. Due to the higher number of orbitals and the resulting higher number of calculations, which lead to a better hiding of the necessary communications, the GPU speedup is considerably higher compared to the H2O workload. In fact, the SYCL GPU case is more than one order of magnitude faster than the reference CPU implementation.

Figure 9, in turn, shows breakdowns of the time spent on the DFT optimization cycle. Figure 9a shows that the Fock operator evaluation (orange) and the communication (blue) dominate the computing time. Interestingly, the graph indicates that the communication time is dependent on the execution time, i.e., the communication for the CPU version takes approximately twice as long as the communication for the SYCL CPU version, which is in contrast to the H2O test from above. Further investigations show that this workload suffers from load-imbalance and, consequently, from long MPI waiting times, which is measured as part of the communication category. Thus, the faster computations also minimize the communication time by minimizing the waiting time induced by load-imbalance. Despite this load-imbalance, the relative communication time is significantly less compared to the H2O case, which shows the aforementioned resiliency with respect to the reference CPU implementation. Note that the "1 Node" GPU is not imbalanced since it uses only 8 MPI ranks which allow an equi-partition of the 1432 orbitals.

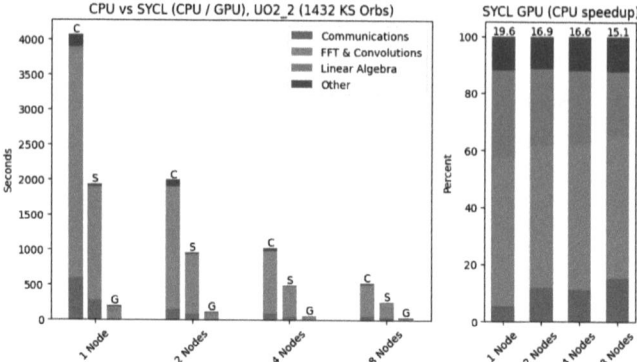

(a) Breakdown of the time spent in the DFT optimization cycle into various categories for the UO2 workload. The CPU, SYCL CPU and SYCL GPU runs are labeled C, S, and G, respectively. The left panel shows the overall wall time. The right panel shows the relative time of all the different calculation categories for the SYCL GPU case. The overall speedup of the accelerated version with respect to the reference CPU implementation is presented on top of the right panel.

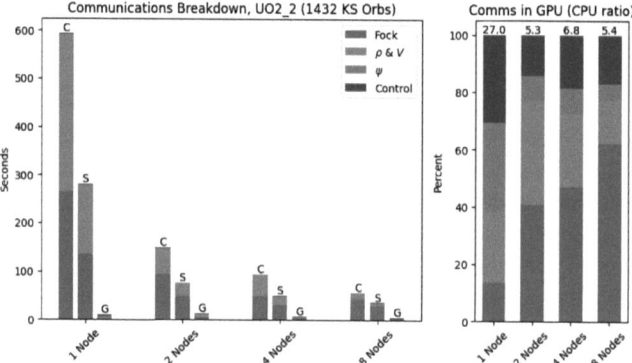

(b) Breakdown of the time spent in communication for the UO2 workload. The left panel shows absolute time for the three implementations: OpenMP CPU (C), SYCL implementation on the CPU (S), and SYCL implementation on the Intel GPU (G). The right panel shows the relative time for the SYCL GPU implementation. The Fock communication time is mainly time spent in waiting for the P2P communication to finish, whereas all the other categories are related to blocking collective MPI operations. The numbers on top of the percent bar chart indicate the ratio between the time spent in communication of the SYCL GPU runs with respect to the same quantity of the CPU runs, normalized by the number of MPI tasks. The 1 Tile result is not shown due to the absence of communication.

Fig. 9. Analysis of the full DFT calculation of 96 UO2 molecules, with $o = 1432$ orbitals, and a grid size of $n = 108^3$.

Introducing SYCL to Accelerate a Fock Operator Calculation Library

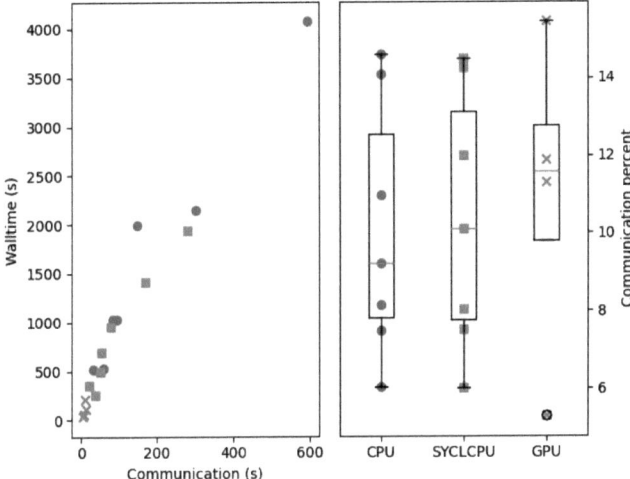

Fig. 10. Average behaviour of the communication time for the different runs performed in the campaign. In the left panel the total wave function optimization wall time (y-axis) is plotted against the communication wall time (x-axis), showing that the trends are similar for all the various implementations (blue dots, yellow squares and green cross indicating the OpenMP CPU implementation, the SYCL implementation on the CPU and the SYCL implementation on the Intel GPU, respectively). The box plots in the right panel show the distribution of the percent of the wall time dedicated in the communications. Data for the H2O runs are not shown for the GPU implementation because of the too fine granularity of the calculation (in other terms, such test-case is too small for a multi-node GPU platform) (Color figure online)

Finally, Fig. 10 shows the relative time spent in communication for the two workloads presented in this section for all implementations. We removed the H2O data points from the GPU data since their granularity is too fine and in this case communication clearly bounds the performance (as it can be seen from cf. Fig. 4). Overall, the left panel of Fig. 10 shows that all three implementations show a similar relation between the wall time and communication time. The right panel shows a box plot which indicates that the average relative communication time is slightly higher in the SYCL GPU case than in the SYCL CPU case which, in turn, shows a minimal increase in the relative communication time compared to the reference CPU implementation. The increases are within expectations.

To summarize, our tests indicate that i) load-imbalance is not a problem and can be mitigated by faster calculations, and ii) the communication time in the SYCL versions behaves similar to the reference implementation, i.e., no significant or unexpected overhead is introduced. Thus, good scaling properties to larger node and GPU counts are expected.

5 Conclusion and Future Work

The presented SYCL implementation of the expensive Fock operator evaluation is highly competitive to the existing CUDA-GPU and OpenMP-CPU implementations in all tested workloads, mostly due to the highly optimized nature of the utilized double-batched FFT library. The SYCL version exhibits good parallel scaling properties indicating readiness for large scale workloads on, e.g., the Aurora cluster, which represents the next step in the BigDFT effort. This fact has a number of important consequences. First, hardware accelerators, when effectively utilized, enable the simulation of more complex workloads made by more accurate approximations or larger systems without the need to design new algorithmic approaches. The user can therefore tackle more challenging calculations without changing the scientific approach, which would unlock low-hanging-fruit opportunities that such investigations would enable. It is also worth mentioning, that including mixed precision, like starting the calculations in simple precision in the DFT iterations, can further represent one source of optimization. In addition, we have proven with this work that efficient acceleration, once achieved on one platform, already paves the way to a likewise (or even better, as illustrated here) efficient code on another platform. Leveraging usage of NVidia accelerators with CUDA language enabled us to singled out some abstraction layers in the original host implementation. We have experienced in this work that such code factorizations made easier our work in the low-level libraries of Fock operator calculation, which would further increasing code portability in other architectures. The extension of the SYCL implementation to work with various backends while maintaining or increasing the performance and the consolidation of the different code paths are left for future work.

Acknowledgments. We acknowledge the support from EUPEX and MaX EU projects.

Disclosure of Interests. Performance varies by use, configuration and other factors. Learn more on the Performance Index site.

Performance results are based on testing as of dates shown and may not reflect all publicly available updates. No product or component can be absolutely secure.

Your costs and results may vary.

Intel technologies may require enabled hardware, software or service activation.

©Intel Corporation. Intel, the Intel logo, and other Intel marks are trademarks of Intel Corporation or its subsidiaries. Other names and brands may be claimed as the property of others.

References

1. Hohenberg, P., Kohn, W.: Inhomogeneous electron gas. Phys. Rev. **136**, B864–B871 (1964). https://doi.org/10.1103/PhysRev.136.B864
2. Lejaeghere, K.: Reproducibility in density functional theory calculations of solids. Science **351**(6280) (2016). http://science.sciencemag.org/content/351/6280/aad3000

3. Kohn, W., Sham, L.J.: Self-consistent equations including exchange and correlation effects. Phys. Rev. **140**, A1133–A1138 (1965). https://doi.org/10.1103/PhysRev.140.A1133
4. Ratcliff, L.E., Mohr, S., Huhs, G., Deutsch, T., Masella, M., Genovese, L.: Challenges in large scale quantum mechanical calculations. WIREs Comput. Mol. Sci. **7**(1), e1290 (2017). https://wires.onlinelibrary.wiley.com/doi/abs/10.1002/wcms.1290
5. Perdew, J.P., Schmidt, K.: Jacob's ladder of density functional approximations for the exchange-correlation energy. In: AIP Conference Proceedings, pp. 1–20 (2001)
6. Zhang, I.Y., Xu, X.: On the top rung of Jacob's ladder of density functional theory: toward resolving the dilemma of SIE and NCE. WIREs Comput. Mol. Sci. **11**(1), e1490 (2021). https://wires.onlinelibrary.wiley.com/doi/abs/10.1002/wcms.1490
7. Perdew, J.P., Burke, K., Ernzerhof, M.: Generalized gradient approximation made simple. Phys. Rev. Lett. **77**, 3865–3868 (1996). https://doi.org/10.1103/PhysRevLett.77.3865
8. Becke, A.D.: Density-functional thermochemistry. III. The role of exact exchange. J. Chem. Phys. **98**(7), 5648–5652 (1993)
9. Lee, C., Yang, W., Parr, R.G.: Development of the Colle-Salvetti correlation-energy formula into a functional of the electron density. Phys. Rev. B **37**(2), 785 (1988)
10. Adamo, C., Barone, V.: Toward reliable density functional methods without adjustable parameters: the PBE0 model. J. Chem. Phys. **110**(13), 6158–6170 (1999)
11. Heyd, J., Scuseria, G.E., Ernzerhof, M.: Erratum: "hybrid functionals based on a screened coulomb potential" [j. chem. phys. 118, 8207 (2003)]. J. Chem. Phys. **124**(21), 219906 (2006)
12. Ratcliff, L.E., et al.: Flexibilities of wavelets as a computational basis set for large-scale electronic structure calculations. J. Chem. Phys. **152**(19), 194110 (2020). https://doi.org/10.1063/5.0004792
13. Genovese, L., Ospici, M., Deutsch, T., Méhaut, J.-F., Neelov, A., Goedecker, S.: Density functional theory calculation on many-cores hybrid central processing unit-graphic processing unit architectures. J. Chem. Phys. **131**(3), 034103 (2009). https://doi.org/10.1063/1.3166140
14. Ratcliff, L.E., Degomme, A., Flores-Livas, J.A., Goedecker, S., Genovese, L.: Affordable and accurate large-scale hybrid-functional calculations on GPU-accelerated supercomputers. J. Phys. Condensed Matter **30**(9), 095901 (2018). https://doi.org/10.1088/1361-648X/aaa8c9
15. OpenMP: OpenMP Compilers (2023). https://www.openmp.org/resources/openmp-compilers-tools/
16. OpenACC-standard.org. OpenACC (2023). https://www.opcnacc.org
17. Khronos Group. OpenCL (2023). https://www.khronos.org/opencl/
18. Khronos Group. SYCL (2023). https://www.khronos.org/sycl/
19. Codeplay Software Ltd.: Codeplay ComputeCpp (2023). https://developer.codeplay.com/
20. Intel Corporation: Intel oneAPI DPC++ (2023). https://www.intel.com/content/www/us/en/developer/tools/oneapi/data-parallel-c-plus-plus.html
21. Alpay, A., Soproni, B., Wünsche, H., Heuveline, V.: Exploring the possibility of a hipSYCL-based implementation of oneAPI. In: International Workshop on OpenCL, ser. IWOCL 2022. Association for Computing Machinery, New York (2022). https://doi.org/10.1145/3529538.3530005
22. Alpay, A.: OpenSYCL Github (2023). https://github.com/OpenSYCL/OpenSYCL

23. Genovese, L., Deutsch, T., Neelov, A., Goedecker, S., Beylkin, G.: Efficient solution of Poisson's equation with free boundary conditions. J. Chem. Phys. **125**(7), 074105 (2006)
24. Cerioni, A., Genovese, L., Mirone, A., Sole, V.A.: Efficient and accurate solver of the three-dimensional screened and unscreened Poisson's equation with generic boundary conditions. J. Chem. Phys. **137**(13) (2012). http://scitation.aip.org/content/aip/journal/jcp/137/13/10.1063/1.4755349
25. Dugan, N., Genovese, L., Goedecker, S.: A customized 3D GPU Poisson solver for free boundary conditions. Comput. Phys. Commun. **184**(8), 1815–1820 (2013). https://www.sciencedirect.com/science/article/pii/S0010465513000817
26. Ratcliff, L.E., Genovese, L., Park, H., Littlewood, P.B., Lopez-Bezanilla, A.: Exploring metastable states in UO2 using hybrid functionals and dynamical mean field theory. J. Phys. Condensed Matter **34**(9), 094003 (2021). https://doi.org/10.1088/1361-648X/ac3cf1
27. García-Risueño, P., et al.: A survey of the parallel performance and accuracy of Poisson solvers for electronic structure calculations. J. Comput. Chem. **35**(6), 427–444 (2014)
28. NVIDIA Corporation: CUDA toolkit (2023). https://developer.nvidia.com/cuda-toolkit
29. NVIDIA Corporation: cuFFT (2023). https://docs.nvidia.com/cuda/cufft/index.html
30. Advanced Micro Devices, Inc.: AMD Instinct GPUs (2023). https://www.amd.com/en/graphics/instinct-server-accelerators
31. Intel Corporation: Intel Max Series GPUs (2023). https://www.intel.com/content/www/us/en/products/details/discrete-gpus/data-center-gpu/max-series.html
32. Oak Ridge National Laboratory: Frontier Supercomputer (2023). https://www.olcf.ornl.gov/frontier/
33. Argonne Leadership Computing Facility: Aurora Supercomputer (2023). https://www.alcf.anl.gov/aurora
34. Intel Corporation: DPC++ compatibility tool (2023). https://www.intel.com/content/www/us/en/developer/tools/oneapi/dpc-compatibility-tool.html
35. Carsten Uphoff: double-batched FFT library (2023). https://github.com/intel/double-batched-fft-library
36. Intel Corporation: Intel oneAPI Math Kernel Library (2023). https://www.intel.com/content/www/us/en/docs/oneapi/programming-guide/2023-2/intel-oneapi-math-kernel-library-onemkl.html
37. Intel Corporation: Intel oneAPI (2023). https://www.intel.com/content/www/us/en/developer/tools/oneapi/overview.html
38. Luigi Genovese: BigDFT 1.9.4 (2023). https://gitlab.com/l_sim/bigdft-suite/-/tree/7a01d4de79bdd834243e707954d5c4bfa1f61362
39. Intel Corporation: Intel Xe GPU Architecture (2023). https://www.intel.com/content/www/us/en/docs/oneapi/optimization-guide-gpu/2023-2/intel-xe-gpu-architecture.html
40. Intel Corporation: Intel Xeon Platinum 8480+ Processor (2023). https://www.intel.com/content/www/us/en/products/sku/231746/intel-xeon-platinum-8480-processor-105m-cache-2-00-ghz/specifications.html
41. Intel Corporation: Intel Xeon Platinum 8360Y Processor (2023). https://www.intel.com/content/www/us/en/products/sku/212459/intel-xeon-platinum-8360y-processor-54m-cache-2-40-ghz/specifications.html
42. NVIDIA Corporation: NVIDIA A100 40 GB (2023). https://www.nvidia.com/de-de/data-center/a100/

43. Nvidia Corporation: Nvidia NVLink (2023). https://www.nvidia.com/en-us/design-visualization/nvlink-bridges/
44. NVIDIA Corporation: NVIDIA Multi-Process Service (2023). https://docs.nvidia.com/deploy/mps/index.html
45. Intel Corporation: Intel oneAPI Compiler (2023). https://www.intel.com/content/www/us/en/developer/articles/technical/getting-to-know-llvm-based-oneapi-compilers.html
46. NVIDIA Corporation: NVIDIA CUDA Compiler Driver NVCC (2023). https://docs.nvidia.com/cuda/cuda-compiler-driver-nvcc/index.html
47. Intel Corporation: Intel MPI (2023). https://www.intel.com/content/www/us/en/developer/tools/oneapi/mpi-library.html
48. Intel Corporation: PTI-GPU repository (2024). https://github.com/intel/pti-gpu
49. Intel Corporation: Intel APS (2023). https://www.intel.com/content/www/us/en/docs/vtune-profiler/get-started-application-snapshot/2024-0/overview.html

Portable GPU Implementation of the WP-CCC Ion-Atom Collisions Code

I. B. Abdurakhmanov[1]([✉]), N. W. Antonio[2], M. Cytowski[1], and A. S. Kadyrov[2,3]

[1] Pawsey Supercomputing Research Centre, 1 Bryce Avenue, Kensington, WA 6151, Australia
ilkhom.abdurakhmanov@csiro.au
[2] Department of Physics and Astronomy, Curtin University, GPO Box U1987, Perth 6845, Australia
[3] Institute of Nuclear Physics, Ulugbek, Tashkent 100214, Uzbekistan

Abstract. In this manuscript we present our experience of porting the code used in the wave-packet convergent-close-coupling (WP-CCC) approach to NVIDIA V100 and AMD MI250X GPUs. The WP-CCC approach is used in the field of ion-atom collision physics to describe various processes such as elastic scattering, target excitation and electron-capture by the projectile. It effectively models collisions between proton or bare ion projectiles and various atomic and molecular targets, particularly those resembling one or two-electron systems. These calculations are used in computational atomic physics, fusion plasma modeling, and hadron therapy for cancer treatment. The main computational cost of the method is solving a set of coupled first-order differential equations. This involves implementing the standard Runge-Kutta method while varying the projectile position along multiple straight-line paths. At each projectile position several millions of matrix elements need to be calculated which is accomplished using the OpenACC programming model. After computing these matrix elements, the next steps involve matrix inversion and multiplication with another matrix. To expedite these operations, a GPU-accelerated LAPACK routine, specialised for solving systems of linear equations, is employed. For AMD GPUs, this routine is accessible through the hipSOLVER library, while for NVIDIA GPUs, it can be obtained from the cuSOLVER library. The portability, performance and energy efficiency of the CPU-only code have been compared with the GPU-accelerated version running on AMD and NVIDIA GPUs. The implementation of GPU-accelerated WP-CCC code opens up avenues for exploring more sophisticated collision processes involving complex projectile and target structures, which were previously considered infeasible.

Keywords: GPU acceleration · NVIDIA V100 GPU · AMD MI250X GPU · OpenACC · Cuda · HIP

1 Introduction

GPUs offer several advantages over CPUs for computational tasks due to their highly parallel architecture, featuring thousands of cores capable of executing tasks concurrently. This parallel processing power enables GPUs to handle large-scale computations with exceptional speed and efficiency, making them particularly well-suited for tasks such as graphics rendering, scientific simulations, and machine learning algorithms. Additionally, GPUs boast high memory bandwidth, enabling rapid data access and transfer, crucial for memory-intensive applications. Their energy efficiency, ability to offload tasks from CPUs, scalability with multiple GPUs, and cost-effectiveness further contribute to their appeal as powerful accelerators for a wide range of computational workloads.

Programming for GPUs used to be a complex task, requiring developers to write codes using low-level languages such as CUDA or OpenCL. These languages demanded a deep understanding of the underlying hardware architecture and intricate memory management techniques, making GPU programming inaccessible to many developers. Furthermore, optimizing code for GPUs often involved manual tuning and experimentation, which could be time-consuming and error-prone. As a result, the adoption of GPU acceleration in scientific computing was limited to a relatively small community of experts with specialized knowledge in parallel programming.

However, the invention of directive-based GPU offloading models such as OpenACC [1] and OpenMP [2] provided a significant boost for scientific computing by offering a simpler approach. It simplifies the process of GPU programming, without requiring extensive restructuring of the original CPU code. Additionally, directive-based models provide portability across different GPU architectures and vendors, allowing code to run efficiently on a number of diverse hardware platforms without major modifications.

While GPUs are highly effective in many computational tasks, they may demonstrate inefficiencies in certain scenarios. One notable limitation is their performance for tasks with irregular or sequential data dependencies, where parallelism is challenging to be exploited fully. In these cases, the overhead of coordinating threads and managing memory can outweigh the benefits of parallelism, leading to suboptimal performances compared to CPUs. Additionally, GPUs may struggle with tasks that involve frequent branching or conditional operations, as divergent thread execution can hinder parallel efficiency. Furthermore, GPU programming requires careful optimization and tuning to leverage the hardware effectively, and not all algorithms are easily parallelizable or well-suited for GPU acceleration. As a result, while GPUs offer significant advantages for many computational tasks, their efficiency may vary depending on the nature of the workload and the effectiveness of parallelization techniques employed.

In this work we present our experience and challenges encountered during the process of GPU acceleration of the WP-CCC code. The CPU-based WP-CCC code, written in Fortran, employs MPI for parallelization across multiple nodes and OpenMP within each node [3,4]. The acronym WP-CCC stands for Wave-Packet Convergent Close-Coupling (WP-CCC) approach which is utilized to simulate ion-atom collisions. The WP-CCC method offers a highly accurate and computationally efficient framework for simulating ion-atom collisions by coupling bound states and wave-packet pseudostates and iteratively refining the scattering solutions until convergence is achieved. This method allows researchers to study the dynamics of ion-atom interactions, including elastic scattering, excitation and electron capture processes, with high precision, making it a valuable tool for understanding fundamental atomic and molecular physics phenomena. Apart from the fundamental interest it is also useful in the modelling of fusion plasmas [5] and in hadron therapy for cancer treatment [6]. It has demonstrated its effectiveness in studying collisions involving proton or bare ion projectiles with various atomic and molecular targets, especially those which can effectively be considered as one or two-electron systems [7–10]. However, the existing CPU-only code used for these computations experiences notable slowdowns as the complexity of the projectile and target increases. To address this limitation and extend the applicability of the method to more sophisticated collision processes, there is a pressing need to migrate the computations to GPUs. GPUs, consisting of thousands of cores, can significantly enhance the computational efficiency and accelerate the calculations performed using the WP-CCC method.

The primary computational burden of the WP-CCC method lies in solving the resulting set of coupled first-order differential equations. This involves implementing the standard Runge-Kutta method while varying the projectile position along multiple straight-line paths. In typical collision calculations, each path involves consideration of several thousand projectile positions, with the total number of paths typically ranging from 30 to 50. At each projectile position, the computation involves evaluating several millions of matrix elements. This task is handled using the OpenACC programming model, as the expression for matrix elements involves multiple summation operations, making it an excellent candidate for highly parallel execution. Once these matrix elements are computed, the subsequent steps involve matrix inversion and multiplication with another matrix. To speed up these operations, a GPU-accelerated LAPACK routine, specialized for solving systems of linear equations, is employed. This library capitalizes on the parallel architecture of GPUs, enabling rapid and efficient computation of the necessary matrix transformations within the WP-CCC method. For AMD GPUs, this routine is accessible through the hipSOLVER library [11], while for NVIDIA GPUs, it can be obtained from the cuSOLVER library [12].

Thorough performance evaluation of the GPU-accelerated version of the code, executed on both AMD MI250X and NVIDIA V100 GPUs in comparison with the CPU-only code has been carried out. Through rigorous benchmarking and analysis, the computational efficiency gains achieved by migrating the calculations to GPUs have been quantified. The comparison covers various metrics such as execution time and scalability across different problem sizes. Notably, the GPU-accelerated implementation shows significant speedup, particularly pronounced when dealing with a case where the total scattering wave function is expanded in terms of a larger number of bound states and wave-packet pseudostates.

The paper is set out as follows. Section 2 details the algorithms used in the WP-CCC code and their GPU implementation. The results of performance comparisons are presented in Sect. 3. Finally in Sect. 4 we draw conclusions.

2 Brief Description of the Method and the GPU Implementation

The formalism for the WP-CCC approach has been outlined in Refs. [3,4]. Here, we only focus on the computational aspects of the method. The WP-CCC method involves expanding the total scattering wave function of the collision system as a linear combination of basis functions. The basis functions consist of bound eigenstates and wave-packet pseudostates describing the projectile and the target atom. By increasing the number of these basis functions we are able to find convergence in the results obtained for observables such as the cross sections and transition probabilities for each of the collision processes.

Skipping the mathematical derivations, we will transition directly to outlining the most time-consuming part of the code. It involves solving the following set of coupled first-order differential equations to determine the time-dependent coefficients, **F** and **G**, which represent direct scattering and electron transfer transitions, respectively:

$$iv \begin{bmatrix} \mathbf{I} & \mathbf{K} \\ \mathbf{K}^\dagger & \mathbf{I} \end{bmatrix} \times \frac{d}{dz} \begin{bmatrix} \mathbf{F} \\ \mathbf{G} \end{bmatrix} = \begin{bmatrix} \mathbf{D}_T & \mathbf{Q} \\ \mathbf{Q}^\dagger & \mathbf{D}_P \end{bmatrix} \times \begin{bmatrix} \mathbf{F} \\ \mathbf{G} \end{bmatrix}, \qquad (1)$$

where $\dagger$ denotes a complex conjugate operator and **I** is the identity matrix, v is the speed of the projectile and z is its position along the z-axis. Submatrices **K**, $\mathbf{D}_T$, $\mathbf{D}_P$ and **Q** represent the overlap between the target and projectile states, direct target-target scattering, direct projectile-projectile scattering and electron-transfer, respectively. Based on profiling of the CPU-based code, this part of the WP-CCC code proven to take more than 98% of the total execution time in production runs.

In order to proceed with solving this system of equations we transform it to the following form:

$$\frac{d}{dz} \mathbf{X} = \mathbf{M} \times \mathbf{X}, \qquad (2)$$

where a newly denoted solution vector **X** joins subvectors **F** and **G**

$$\mathbf{X} = \begin{bmatrix} \mathbf{F} \\ \mathbf{G} \end{bmatrix}, \qquad (3)$$

and

$$\mathbf{M} = -\frac{i}{v} \begin{bmatrix} \mathbf{I} & \mathbf{K} \\ \mathbf{K}^\dagger & \mathbf{I} \end{bmatrix}^{-1} \times \begin{bmatrix} \mathbf{D}_T & \mathbf{Q} \\ \mathbf{Q}^\dagger & \mathbf{D}_P \end{bmatrix}. \qquad (4)$$

A straightforward approach to calculating the matrix **M** based on matrix inversion and subsequent scalar matrix-matrix multiplication is prone to numerical errors. Instead, we rely on the highly accurate ZGESV routine of LAPACK library [13] and find the matrix M by solving the system of linear equations. The GPU-accelerated version of ZGESV is also available. For AMD GPUs, it can be accessed via the hipSOLVER library, whereas for NVIDIA GPUs, it is available through the cuSOLVER library.

It is worth noting that much of the computational complexities disappear when the projectile is negatively charged. In this case, the projectile is unable to capture the target electron. Consequently, the matrix **M** reduces to:

$$\mathbf{M} = \mathbf{D}_\mathrm{T}. \tag{5}$$

The set of differential equations (2) has parametrical dependence on the impact parameter, b, which is the perpendicular distance between the path of a projectile and the center of mass of the target. Therefore, it needs to be solved while varying the projectile position along multiple straight-line paths characterised by the z-coordinate of the projectile and the impact parameter. The solution vector **X** is advanced along the predefined z-grid, by employing the standard fourth-order Runge-Kutta method [14]. When selecting the z-grid, we take into account the dynamics of the collision process. We aim for a denser distribution of points in the region where the projectile is closest to the target, ensuring greater accuracy in areas where the interaction between the particles is strongest. Conversely, we adopt a sparser distribution in the region where the projectile is furthest from the target, optimizing computational efficiency without compromising accuracy. To achieve this objective, the z-grid is constructed according to zgrid$[i] = z_\mathrm{min}(z_\mathrm{max}/z_\mathrm{min})^{i/n_z}$, zgrid$[0] = 0$ and zgrid$[-i] = -$zgrid$[i]$, with i ranging from 1 to n_z. Here, the parameter z_min is utilized to adjust the density of the z-grid. In typical calculations, z_min is set to 10^{-3}, n_z is set to 500, and z_max is set to 100 atomic units.

Algorithm 1 presents the pseudo code for the differential equation solver. Lines 1 and 2 ensure that the initial boundary conditions are satisfied, meaning that the target atom is in the ground state before the collision occurs. At each step, the **for** loop implements the fourth-order Runge-Kutta method to advance the solution vector to the next z-position, z_new. This process involves computing four slopes, $\mathbf{K}_1$, $\mathbf{K}_2$, $\mathbf{K}_3$ and $\mathbf{K}_4$, which represent the derivative of the solution vector at different points within the step. That is achieved by evaluating the matrix **M** at two z-positions, z_mid and z_new. During the overall cycle the matrix **M** gets evaluated $4n_z + 1$ times. At the end of the i loop the solution vector is evaluated at the position z_max which is used to calculate observables such as cross sections for various reaction processes. In typical collision calculations, multiple paths characterized by various impact parameters b need to be computed, with the total number typically ranging from 30 to 50. Each path involves the consideration of several thousand projectile positions and is handled by a separate MPI process. Consequently, communication between MPI processes is minimal, rendering the calculation embarrassingly parallel in terms of CPU cores.

Algorithm 1: Algorithm for solving Eq. (2)

```
1   X[:] = 0
2   X[1] = 1
3   Computing M at zgrid[−n_z]
4   M_new = M(zgrid[−n_z])
5   for i=−n_z to n_z − 1 do
6       z = zgrid[i]
7       z_new = zgrid[i + 1]
8       z_mid = (z + z_new)/2
9       h = z_new − z
10      h_2 = h/2
11      h_6 = h/6
12      M_z = M_new
13      Computing M at z_mid and z_new
14      M_mid = M(z_mid)
15      M_new = M(z_new)
16      K_1 = M_z × X
17      K_2 = M_mid × X + h_2 M_mid × K_1
18      K_3 = M_mid × X + h_2 M_mid × K_2
19      K_4 = M_new × X + h M_new × K_3
20      X_new = X + h_6(K_1 + 2K_2 + 2K_3 + K_4)
21      X = X_new
22  end
```

The computation of the matrix $\mathbf{M}$ involves evaluating two structurally distinct types of matrix elements: direct matrix elements and overlap matrix elements. The electron-transfer matrix elements resemble overlap matrix elements and can be computed using a similar technique. The final expression for the direct matrix elements, which constitute matrix $\mathbf{D}_T$ is as follows:

$$D_{\alpha'\alpha} = -\sum_{\lambda\mu} \frac{\sqrt{(2l_\alpha + 1)(\lambda - \mu)}}{\sqrt{(2l_{\alpha'} + 1)(\lambda + \mu)}} C^{l_{\alpha'}0}_{\lambda 0 l_\alpha 0} C^{l_{\alpha'}m_{\alpha'}}_{\lambda\mu l_\alpha m_\alpha}$$
$$\times P^{\mu}_{\lambda}\left(\frac{z}{\sqrt{b^2 + z^2}}\right) F_{n_{\alpha'}l_{\alpha'}n_\alpha l_\alpha \lambda}\left(\sqrt{b^2 + z^2}\right), \quad (6)$$

where n_α, l_α and m_α are principal, orbital and magnetic quantum numbers of state α, $C^{l_{\alpha'}m_{\alpha'}}_{\lambda\mu l_\alpha m_\alpha}$ are Clebsch-Gordan coefficients, P^{μ}_{λ} are Legendre polynomials and

$$F_{n_{\alpha'}l_{\alpha'}n_\alpha l_\alpha \lambda}(R) = \int_0^\infty dr\, r^2 f_{n_{\alpha'}l_{\alpha'}}(r) f_{n_\alpha l_\alpha}(r)$$
$$\times \frac{\min(r,R)^\lambda}{\max(r,R)^{\lambda+1}}, \quad (7)$$

where $f_{n_\alpha l_\alpha}(r)$ is the radial function of the state α.

The computation of another type of matrix elements, namely overlap matrix elements, relies on the following expression:

$$K_{\beta\alpha} = \sum_{q'q} d^{l_\beta}_{m_\beta q'}(\theta) d^{l_\alpha}_{m_\alpha q'}(\theta) S_{n_\beta l_\beta q', n_\beta l_\beta q}(z). \tag{8}$$

The Wigner rotation operator, $d^{l_\alpha}_{m_\alpha q'}(\theta)$, is employed to rotate the target frame to an angle of $\theta = \arccos(z/\sqrt{z^2 + b^2})$ in order to transition to the collision frame. The matrix elements in the target frame, $S_{n_\beta l_\beta q', n_\beta l_\beta q}(z)$, are defined as:

$$S_{n_\beta l_\beta q', n_\beta l_\beta q}(z) = \frac{i^{q-q'}(z^2+b^2)^{3/2}\sqrt{2l_\alpha+1}\sqrt{2l+1}}{16}$$

$$\times \sqrt{\frac{(l_\beta - q')!(l_\alpha - q)!}{(l_\beta + q')!(l_\alpha + q)!}}$$

$$\times \int_1^\infty d\eta \int_{-1}^1 d\tau (\eta^2 - \tau^2) \exp\left(i\frac{vz}{2}\eta\tau\right)$$

$$\times f_{n_\beta l_\beta}\left(\frac{R(\eta+\tau)}{2}\right) f_{n_\alpha l_\alpha}\left(\frac{R(\eta-\tau)}{2}\right)$$

$$\times P^{q'}_{l_\beta}\left(\frac{\eta\tau+1}{\eta+\tau}\right) P^q_{l_\alpha}\left(\frac{\eta\tau-1}{\eta-\tau}\right)$$

$$\times J_{q-q'}\left(\frac{vb}{2}\sqrt{(\eta^2-1)(1-\tau^2)}\right), \tag{9}$$

where $J_{q-q'}$ is the Bessel function of the first kind.

The computations of the $D_{\alpha'\alpha}$ and $K_{\beta\alpha}$ matrix elements are offloaded to the GPU using the OpenACC programming model. To ensure optimal performance, we adhere to the OpenACC best practices by breaking down computations into smaller kernels rather than relying on a single large kernel. This approach enhances parallelism and load balancing, optimizes the memory access patterns, enables finer-grained parallelism, creates opportunities for targeted optimizations, and simplifies error isolation and debugging processes. Furthermore, based on our experience, this approach can also help reduce register pressure within the kernels.

Before computing the actual matrix elements, we first compute the necessary components in separate OpenACC kernels. These components include the quantities and functions $\sqrt{2l+1}$, $\sqrt{\lambda-\mu}$, $\sqrt{\lambda+\mu}$, $C^{l_{\alpha'}m_{\alpha'}}_{\lambda\mu l_\alpha m_\alpha}$, $P^\mu_\lambda\left(\frac{z}{\sqrt{b^2+z^2}}\right)$, $P^{q'}_{l_\beta}\left(\frac{\eta\tau+1}{\eta+\tau}\right)$, $P^q_{l_\alpha}\left(\frac{\eta\tau-1}{\eta-\tau}\right)$, $\exp\left(i\frac{vz}{2}\eta\tau\right)$, $J_{q-q'}\left(\frac{vb}{2}\sqrt{(\eta^2-1)(1-\tau^2)}\right)$, $f_{n_\alpha l_\alpha}(r)$ and $F_{n_{\alpha'}l_{\alpha'}n_\alpha l_\alpha \lambda}(R)$ for all possible index and argument values. To enhance parallelism, multi-dimensional indices, such as the six-dimensional $n_{\alpha'}l_{\alpha'}n_\alpha l_\alpha \lambda$ in $F_{n_{\alpha'}l_{\alpha'}n_\alpha l_\alpha \lambda}(R)$, are converted into one dimension. This process is equivalent to implementing the **collapse** directive, which combines a specified number of indices into a single dimension. However, we have observed that our manual approach yields faster code execution and enables the storage of arrays in a more compact form with better memory access. Whenever feasible, we implement gang + vector levels of parallelism for these unified indices. Moreover, the following components are precomputed and stored in the GPU global memory prior to proceeding with the equation solver: $\sqrt{2l+1}$, $\sqrt{\lambda-\mu}$, $\sqrt{\lambda+\mu}$, $C_{\lambda\mu l_\alpha m_\alpha}^{l_{\alpha'} m_{\alpha'}}$, $f_{n_\alpha l_\alpha}(r)$ and $F_{n_{\alpha'} l_{\alpha'} n_\alpha l_\alpha \lambda}(R)$, as they are independent of either z or b characterising the projectile path. The arguments R and r are discretized into a predefined radial grid, r-grid, spanning the range from 0 to 100 atomic units, typically comprising up to 10,000 points. The grid is denser around the origin to capture finer details in that region. The same grid is also used in the computation of the integral in Eq. (7). The integrals over η and τ in Eq. (9) are computed using the Gauss-Laguerre and Gauss-Legendre quadrature points. When computing the radial wave function $f_{n_\alpha l_\alpha}$ or the integral $F_{n_{\alpha'} l_{\alpha'} n_\alpha l_\alpha \lambda}$ at arguments beyond the r-grid point, such as at $\sqrt{b^2 + z^2}$ as shown in Eq. (6), we employ a five-point polynomial interpolation method. With all necessary components stored in a global GPU memory the last step is to compute matrix $\mathbf{D}_T$ and $\mathbf{K}$, where the pair of indices $\alpha'\alpha$ and $\alpha\beta$ are converted into the unifying index which ranges from one to several millions in production calculations. This index is utilized within the gang + vector levels of OpenACC parallelism. The computations of other submatrices, namely $\mathbf{D}_P$ and $\mathbf{Q}$, are carried out using a similar approach.

3 Performance Analysis

For our performance analysis, we utilise the prototype system of proton collisions with atomic hydrogen. This system represents the simplest collision scenario, comprising of only three particles: two protons and an electron. Despite its simplicity, it encompasses a wide range of reaction channels that are typical of ion-atom collisions. We consider two types of calculations, the so called one-centre (1C) and two-centre (2C) calculations. The 1C calculations are simpler in nature, requiring computations of only one type of matrix elements: direct matrix elements. They are particularly relevant for collisions where the projectile is negatively charged, where electron capture is impossible. While also applicable to collisions involving positively charged projectiles, they are limited to determining total electron-loss cross sections and lack the capability to distinguish between the electron-capture and ionization processes. The 2C calculations utilize the entire codebase and possess significantly broader applications.

We select an impact energy of 100 keV for the projectile. That is the energy where all reaction channels are approximately equally significant. The z-grid describing the projectile path spans from -300 to 300 atomic units, containing 6001 points. To accommodate the number of all available GPUs within the Setonix GPU node, each calculation simultaneously considers eight values of the impact parameter, or in other words, eight paths.

We execute our GPU-accelerated code on two different systems: the Setonix GPU node, which comprises 64 AMD EPYC 7A53 CPU "Trento" cores and 8 AMD MI250X GCDs [15], and the Gadi NCI GPU node, which consists of 48 Intel Xeon Scalable 'Cascade Lake' CPUs and 4 NVIDIA V100 GPUs. However,

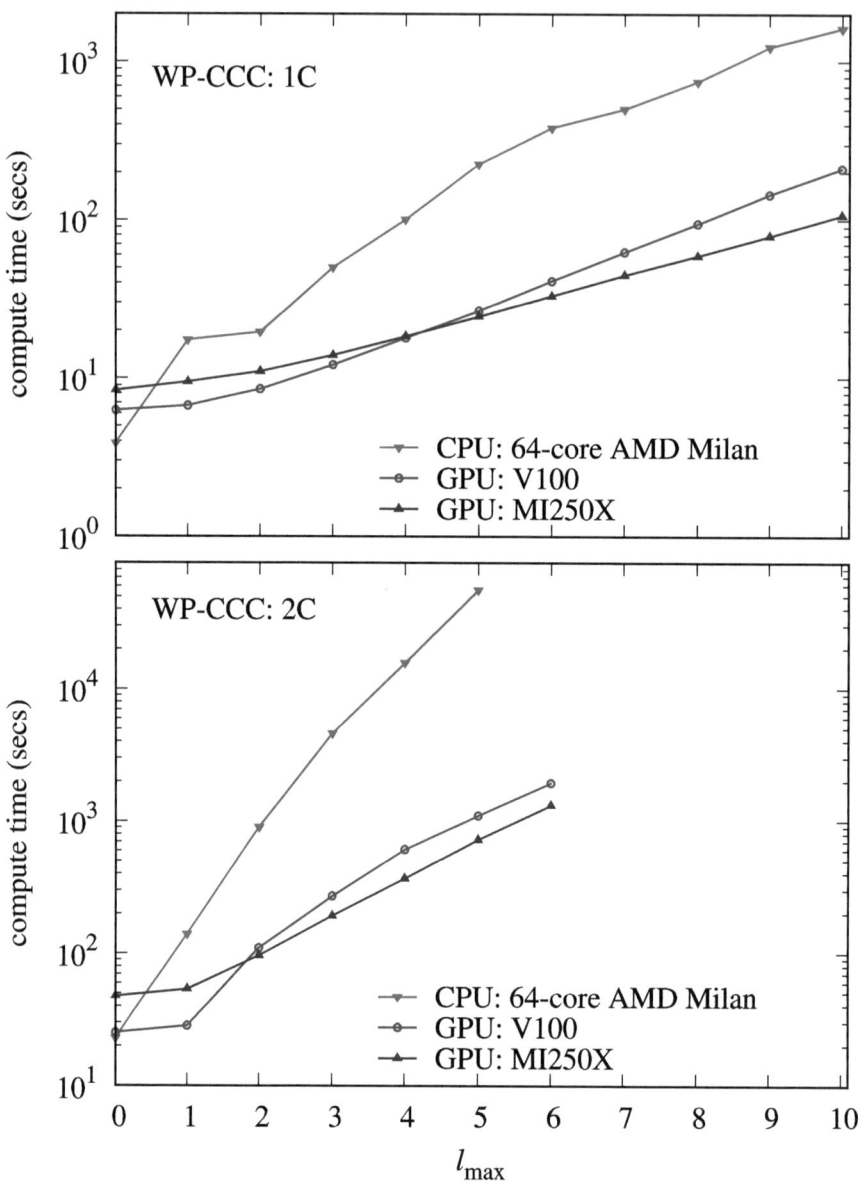

Fig. 1. The compute time of the WP-CCC code in both 1C and 2C modes is depicted as a function of the maximum allowed angular momentum, l_{max}, a parameter that governs the size of the set of differential equations (Eq. (2)). The performance of the CPU-only code has been compared with that of the GPU-accelerated version, executed respectively on the V100 NVIDIA GPU and the MI250X AMD GPU.

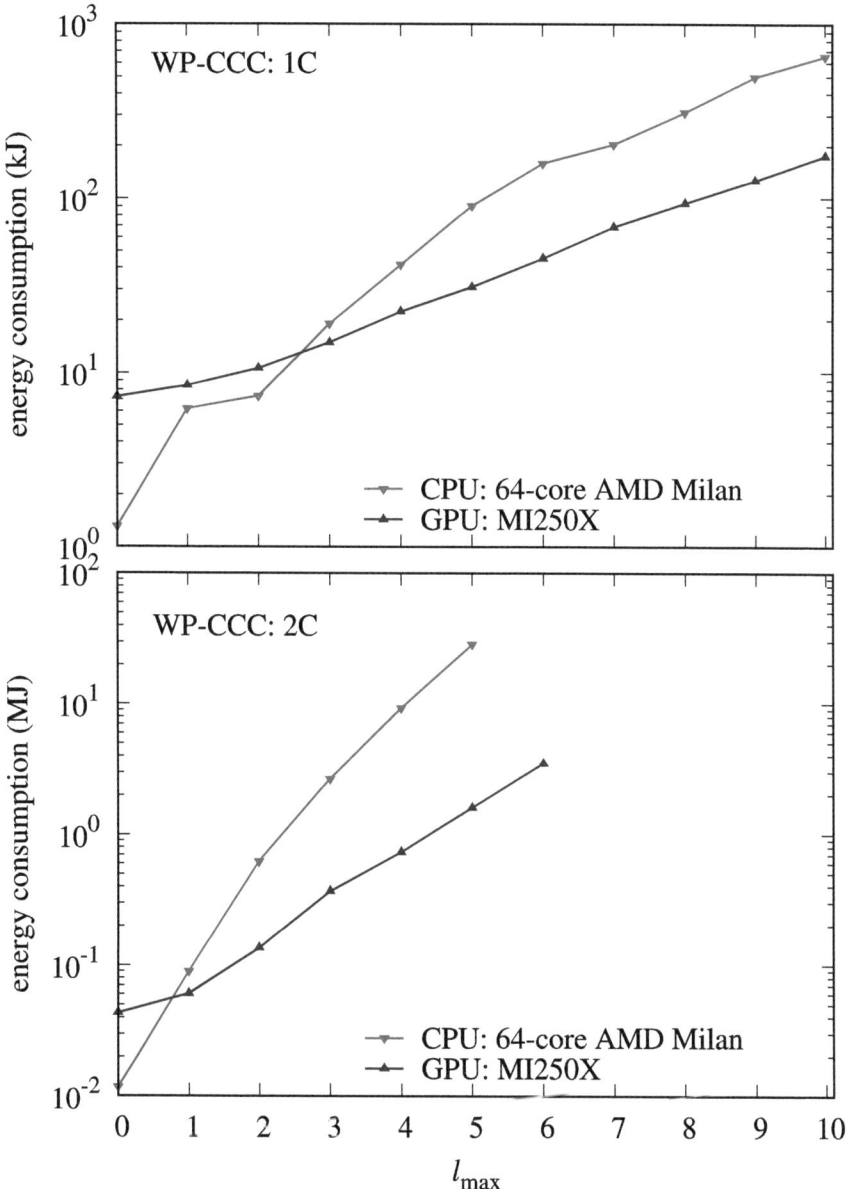

Fig. 2. The energy consumption of the WP-CCC code in both 1C and 2C modes is depicted as a function of the maximum allowed angular momentum, l_{max}, a parameter that governs the size of the set of differential equations (Eq. (2)). The energy efficiency of the CPU-only code has been compared with that of the GPU-accelerated version, executed respectively on the V100 NVIDIA GPU and the MI250X AMD GPU.

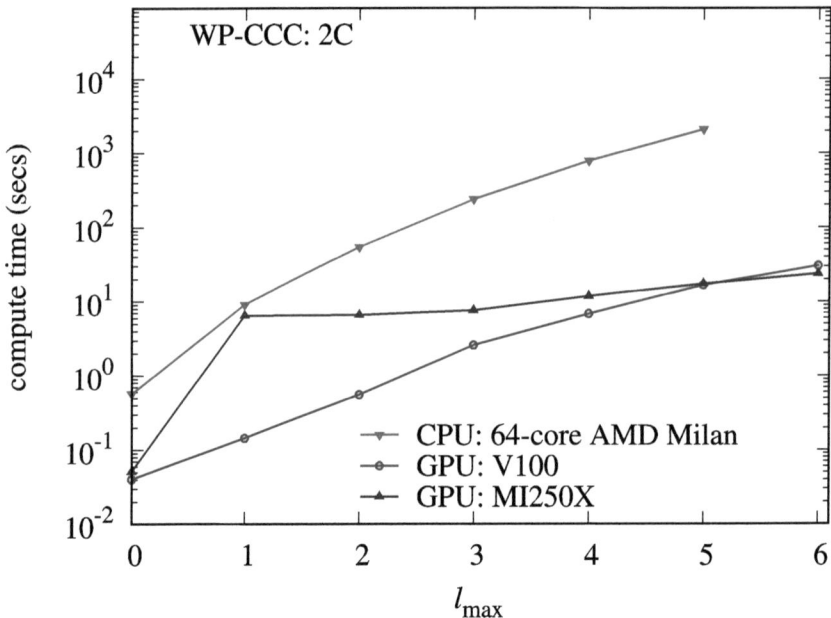

Fig. 3. (color online) The compute time of linear equation solver within WP-CCC code in 2C mode is depicted as a function of the maximum allowed angular momentum, l_{max}, a parameter that governs the size of the set of differential equations (Eq. (2)). The performance of the CPU-version of LAPACK ZGESV has been compared with the GPU-accelerated versions of ZGESV from cuSOLVER and hipSOLVER libraries.

during the GPU job execution, only the number of CPU cores equal to the number of GPUs is utilized. The remaining CPU cores remain idle. The GPU-accelerated code running on Setonix MI250X GPUs is compiled using the Cray Fortran compiler provided with the CPE 23.03, while on NVIDIA V100 GPUs, it is compiled using NVFortran from the PGI 19.7 suite.

For CPU-only jobs based on the MPI + OpenMP parallelism model, we utilize the Setonix CPU node, which has 128 AMD EPYC 7763 CPU "Milan" cores. Each of these nodes contain 2 CPU sockets, enabling a maximum of 64 OpenMP cores. Consequently, the CPU-based WP-CCC code can utilize up to 64 CPU cores concurrently to compute results for a single impact parameter.

Figure 1 illustrates the performance and scalability of the WP-CCC CPU and GPU codes as the size of the problem increases by incrementing the maximum allowed angular momentum quantum numbers from 0 to 10. In the 1C case, the size of the underlying set of first-order differential equations gradually grows from 42 at $l_{max} = 0$ to 4257 at $l_{max} = 10$. In the 2C case, it increases from 60 at $l_{max} = 0$ to 1910 at $l_{max} = 5$. We compare the total compute time of the WP-CCC code required to obtain results for one impact parameter when executed on 64 CPU "Milan" cores, 1 NVIDIA V100 GPU, and 1 AMD MI250X GCD. In both 1C and 2C cases, we do not observe significant acceleration of the code when the problem size is small. However, as the problem size increases, the GPU versions of the code demonstrate increasingly faster performance compared to the CPU code. Specifically, in the 1C case, when $l_{\max} = 10$, the GPU code executed on the V100 GPU is 7.6 times faster, while on the MI250X GPU, it is 15.17 times faster compared to the computational performance achieved using the 64 "Milan" cores of a single CPU socket within the 128-core Setonix CPU node. In the 2C case, when $l_{\max} = 5$, the speedup factors are even larger, reaching 77 for the AMD GPU and 51 for the V100 GPU. At $l_{\max} = 6$, our 2C CPU job exceeds the 24-h walltime limit and does not finish.

The significant speedups achieved by the GPU code also translate into reduced energy consumption. This comparison was achieved by using HPE Cray EX Application Task Orchestration and Management (ATOM) energy reports which are integrated with SLURM workload manager on Setonix. In Fig. 2, we examine the energy consumption of the calculations depicted in Fig. 1. For the largest calculations shown in the 1C case ($l_{\max} = 10$), the MI250X GPU consumed 3.7 times less energy than the 64-core CPU node. In the 2C case ($l_{\max} = 5$), the MI250X GPU is even more efficient, consuming 17 times less energy. Furthermore, it is important to note that a single 128-core CPU node can only process 2 impact parameters at a time, while the AMD MI250X GPU can process 8 impact parameters simultaneously. This factor alone makes the 1C GPU code 15 times more energy efficient and the 2C GPU code 68 times more energy efficient.

Lastly, Fig. 3 presents a comparison of the total time spent on the linear equation solver within the WP-CCC code in the 2C case. It is evident that the GPU-accelerated linear equation solvers from the hipSOLVER and cuSOLVER libraries outperform the CPU-based multithreaded equation solver from the LAPACK library by two orders of magnitude. When comparing the performance of cuSOLVER and hipSOLVER, it becomes apparent that cusolver's performance is more stable for smaller problem sizes.

4 Conclusion

In conclusion, this manuscript has detailed our experience in porting the WP-CCC code to run efficiently on both NVIDIA V100 and AMD MI250X GPUs.

Our comparisons have shown significant performance improvements and energy efficiencies with GPU acceleration. For the largest performed calculations, in the 1C case, the GPU code executed on the V100 GPU was 7.6 times faster, while on the MI250X GPU, it was 15.17 times faster than on the 64-core CPU node. In the 2C case, speedup factors were even larger, reaching 77 for the AMD GPU and 51 for the V100 GPU.

Moreover, our energy consumption evaluations revealed significant gains. For identical computational tasks, the MI250X GPU consumed 15 times less energy in the 1C case and a remarkable 68 times less energy in the 2C case compared to CPU-only executions. Overall, our findings demonstrate substantial benefits of GPU acceleration in improving both performance and energy efficiency in WP-CCC calculations.

Furthermore, the implementation of GPU-accelerated WP-CCC code paves the way for exploring more intricate collision processes involving complex projectile and target structures that were previously impossible. This progress holds the potential to further advance research in ion-atom collision physics and related disciplines.

Acknowledgments. This work was supported by the Australian Research Council, the National Computing Infrastructure and the resources provided by the Pawsey Supercomputing Research Centre with funding from the Australian Government and the Government of Western Australia and the Pawsey Centre for Extreme Scale Readiness (PaCER). N.W.A. acknowledges support through an Australian Government Research Training Program Scholarship.

References

1. Chandrasekaran, S., Juckeland, G.: OpenACC for Programmers: Concepts and Strategies. Addison-Wesley Professional, Boston (2017)
2. Deakin, T., Mattson, T.G.: Programming Your GPU with OpenMP: Performance Portability for GPUs. MIT Press, Cambridge (2023)
3. Abdurakhmanov, I.B., Kadyrov, A.S., Bray, I.: Phys. Rev. A **94**, 022703 (2016). https://doi.org/10.1103/PhysRevA.94.022703
4. Abdurakhmanov, I.B., Bailey, J.J., Kadyrov, A.S., Bray, I.: Phys. Rev. A **97**, 032707 (2018). https://doi.org/10.1103/PhysRevA.97.032707
5. Hemsworth, R., et al.: Nucl. Fusion **49**, 045006 (2009). https://doi.org/10.1088/0029-5515/49/4/045006
6. Abril, I., Garcia-Molina, R., de Vera, P., Kyriakou, I., Emfietzoglou, D.: Adv. Quantum Chem. **65**, 129 (2013). https://doi.org/10.1016/B978-0-12-396455-7.00006-6
7. Antonio, N.W., Plowman, C.T., Abdurakhmanov, I.B., Kadyrov, A.S.: Phys. Rev. A **109**, 012817 (2024). https://doi.org/10.1103/PhysRevA.109.012817
8. Plowman, C.T., Abdurakhmanov, I.B., Bray, I., Kadyrov, A.S.: Phys. Rev. A **107**, 032824 (2023). https://doi.org/10.1103/PhysRevA.107.032824
9. Alladustov, S.U., Plowman, C.T., Abdurakhmanov, I.B., Bray, I., Kadyrov, A.S.: Phys. Rev. A **106**, 062819 (2022). https://doi.org/10.1103/PhysRevA.106.062819
10. Abdurakhmanov, I.B., Kadyrov, A.S., Fursa, D.V., Bray, I.: Phys. Rev. Lett. **111**, 173201 (2013). https://doi.org/10.1103/PhysRevLett.111.173201
11. hisolver: a GPU-accelerated library for dense and batched linear algebra subroutines. https://github.com/ROCmSoftwarePlatform/hipsolver
12. cusolver: a GPU-accelerated library for dense and batched linear algebra subroutines. https://developer.nvidia.com/cusolver
13. Anderson, E., et al.: LAPACK Users's Guide. Society for Industrial and Applied Mathematics, Philadelphia (1992)
14. Press, W.H., Teukolsky, S.A., Vetterling, W.T., Flannery, B.P.: Numerical Recipes: The Art of Scientific Computing, 3rd edn. Cambridge University Press, Cambridge (2007)
15. Setonix supercomputing research centre. https://doi.org/10.48569/18sb-8s43

Benchmarking of GPU Performance Saturation on Accelerated Cluster Nodes via Molecular Dynamics Software Packages

Plamen Dobrev and Gerald Mathias[✉]

Leibniz Supercomputing Centre of the Bavarian Academy of Sciences and Humanities, Boltzmannstraße 1, Garching, Germany
{Plamen.Dobrev,Gerald.Mathias}@lrz.de

Abstract. The fast development of Graphics processing units (GPUs) and the software libraries needed for their usage in scientific computing allows highly efficient calculations using not only a single but also multiple GPUs per task. One of the fields in which graphic cards are widely used is molecular dynamics (MD). By including a large number of GPUs in a single MD simulation, systems with the size of several millions of atoms can be simulated. However, the most common sizes of systems studied via MD rarely exceed 300 k atoms. The computational resources of a single GPU might not be fully occupied by such systems, making the use of further graphic cards inefficient. To estimate at which system size the resources of a given GPU are saturated, in this work, we studied the performance of data center-class graphic cards from different vendors as a function of the number of atoms in the simulated system.

We found out that for all graphic cards, the resource saturation is reached at system sizes of approximately 250 k atoms, confirming the initial assumption that the computational capabilities of a single GPU are sufficient for the most commonly studied system sizes.

Keywords: GPU · performance saturation · molecular dynamics · benchmarking · GROMACS · Amber

1 Introduction

The constant development of Graphics processing units (GPUs) and scientific algorithms that are executed on them require frequent benchmarking to estimate the best performance of a given software for specific hardware. As highly performing, parallel codes, molecular dynamics (MD) packages are widely used for benchmarking newly available GPUs. Moreover, in recent years multiple developments have been made in MD allowing the offload of almost the entire calculation required for MD step on the GPU [1], leaving only scheduling on the CPU, thus ensuring better graphic card performance estimation.

A significant step toward multiple GPU utilization for a single simulation has been made by introducing libraries that can split Particle Mesh Ewald (PME)

calculation (essential for the electrostatic calculation during MD) over several GPUs [2]. Such developments are crucial for simulating extremely large molecular systems in the range of several million atoms, e.g. viral particles, collagen fibers, or ribosomes. However, for most users, systems with the size of 100 to 250 k atoms are most relevant. Splitting systems of that size over multiple GPUs will lead to a loss of performance due to the inability of the system to saturate the computational resources of the GPU. Therefore, in most cases, a single GPU will be used per simulation, and for that reason, it is essential to estimate the system size at which the resources of a single graphic card are fully occupied.

Numerous manufacturers offer GPUs with different specifications and performance. To estimate the saturation of a single GPU resources from a given brand and model, in this work, we evaluated the performance of data center-class GPUs from AMD, Intel, and Nvidia as a function of system size, using Amber 22 [3–6] and GROMACS 2023 [7–14] software packages.

Because we would like to estimate the GPUs performance in the context of their usage on a computer cluster, with multiple ensemble simulations occupying each GPU on a compute node, we carried out the benchmarks using multiple MD simulations, one for each logical or physical GPUs on the node which was benchmarked. Thus we took into account the load on the CPU of the node due to competing for other node resources (e.g. memory bandwidth).

To estimate how multiple simulations running on a single node affect different GPU models, we compared the GPU performance between a case where all available graphic cards were occupied to a case where only a single GPU on a node was used. That was done for Nvidia A100 and Intel PVC GPUs, running GROMACS.

Due to the large computational resources of a computer node equipped with several data center-class GPUs, the benchmarks were carried out on a single node (no Infiniband utilization).

2 Methods

For a just comparison of GPU performance details of the hardware used need to be specified. Furthermore, details of the source code and software builds of Amber and Gromacs are required. Finally, details of the benchmarked systems and input sets are given.

2.1 Hardware and Software

The four hardware configurations benchmarked in the present study are shown in Table 1.

Both models AMD MI250X and Intel Ponte Vecchio (PVC) have two separate tiles acting as individual GPUs. Two separate simulations, one for each tile, were carried out on those graphic cards. In the case of the Nvidia GPUs, there are 8 GPUs per node while for the AMD and PVC, there are 4 (8 tiles). There are two CPU sockets per node for nodes equipped with AMD EPYC 7713 and Intel

Table 1. CPU/GPU combinations

CPU	GPU
AMD EPYC 7713	Nvidia A100
AMD EPYC 7713	Nvidia A40
AMD EPYC 7A53	AMD MI250X
Intel Xeon Platinum 8480+ (Intel Sapphire Rapids)	Intel Data Center GPU Max 1550 (Intel Ponte Vecchio)

Sapphire Rapids and one socket per node for nodes equipped with AMD EPYC 7A53 CPUs. The Intel Sapphire Rapids CPUs have 56 physical cores all other CPU models 64. For all hardware combinations, the GPU-CPU communication in the benchmarked nodes is carried out via PCIe interconnect.

The highest ratio between performance and CPU core numbers per GPU was estimated at 8 for GROMACS 2023 so all benchmarks for that software were carried out with 1 MPI rank and 8 openMP threads. One CPU core and one GPU were used for Amber 22. Because in our experience GROMACS performs equally on both the 80 and 40 GB memory versions of the Nvidia A100 GPUs were carried out the GROMACS benchmarks on the 40 GB and the Amber benchmarks on 80GB versions of the GPUs.

Amber 22 was compiled with CUDA support and used for benchmarking Nvidia GPUs only, while GROMACS was built with HIP, SYCL, and CUDA support for benchmarking the AMD, Intel, and Nvidia GPUs respectively. The C/C++ compilers used for the builds were the ones supported in ROCm and oneAPI for the AMD and Intel GPUs and GCC 11.2 for Nvidia A100 and A40, respectively. The used FFT libraries with GPU support for the builds on the AMD, Intel, and Nvidia GPUs were hipFFT, Intel MKL and cuFFTmp respectively.

2.2 Test Systems

The atomic position propagation of water molecules is calculated faster than that of other molecules in modern molecular dynamics packages such as GROMACS. To optimize performance most such codes divide the simulation cell into larger (rigid) water and smaller non-water domains. To evaluate hardware performance for a challenging case, we used a test system previously suggested by another research group [15]. The system consisted of 15 atomic percent (the approx. amount of protein atoms in a simulation) ethanol solution in water (Fig. 1).

Starting at ca. 8K atoms each system doubled the size of the previous up to ca. 11M atoms (Fig. 2).

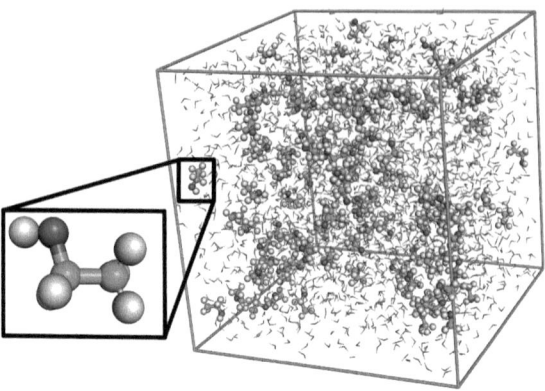

Fig. 1. System composition. 15% ethanol-water solution in the smallest system of ca. 8000 atoms.

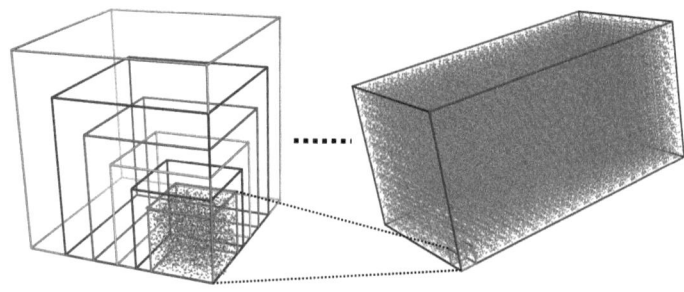

ca. 8k 16k 32k 64k 128k 256k............ca. 11 M atoms

Fig. 2. System size increment. On the left, the smallest system of ca. 8k atoms is shown in a green box. The simulation boxes for the next system sizes are shown with different colors and overlaid with the smallest. Each doubles the size of the previous, as the size of 250 k atoms is the largest one depicted. On the right is shown the largest system of 11 M atoms, overlaid with the simulation box of the smallest one.

GROMACS 2023 with OPLS [16] + tip3p [17] water model and Amber22 with GAFF 1.81 [18] + tip3p water model were used for the benchmarking. Performance was estimated from statistics over 100,000 steps with 2 fs time step. All simulations were carried out using PME [19,20] electrostatics and cut-off scheme for the Lennard-Jones interactions. A temperature of 300 K was maintained using Berendsen thermostat [21] in Amber and V-rescale [22] in GROMACS. In Amber, all hydrogen atom bond lengths were constrained using the SHAKE [23] algorithm, while in GROMACS the bond lengths of the hydrogen atoms of the ethanol molecules were constrained using LINCS [24] and the ones of water using SETTLE [25] algorithms. All bonded and non-bonded interactions, as well as the particle position update, were offloaded to the GPUs. Parameters that can affect performance, such as time step length and cut-off radius for non-bonded interactions, were kept identical for GROMACS and AMBER.

3 Results and Discussion

The main goal of the present study is to evaluate the performance of different GPUs as a function of system size in MD simulations and estimate at which size the computational resources of the hardware become saturated. We choose trajectory length in ns/day times number of atoms as our performance measure. This takes into account that for a fixed real space cutoff the direct particle – particle interactions scale linearly with the system size. Typically, this is the computationally dominant part of an MD Simulation. However, if system sizes are too small, not all streaming multiprocessors (NVIDIA), Xe core (Intel), or compute units (AMD) can be fully occupied with the workloads and computational power is wasted. We therefore expect to reach a maximal performance level for sufficiently large systems. For easy comparison with other performance assessments, the plain performance in ns/day is given in the Appendix. In Fig. 3 are shown the performances of the four benchmarked graphic cards vs. system size in number of atoms for a fully occupied node (parallel simulations carried out on all of the 8 GPUs for Nvidia and 8 tiles for AMD/Intel GPUs). The performance averages of the parallel simulations are plotted together with their standard errors. Due to the homogeneity of the hardware, the error bars are small.

As it can be seen from the leveling out of the curves, the saturation of the GPUs for almost all models is between approximately 128 k and 256 k atoms. It must be noted that both AMD and PVC reach a significant fraction of the Nvidia GPU performance, despite only a single tile, or in other words, only half of the computational resources, being used for one simulation. The scale of the out-performance of MI250X and PVC with respect to the Nvidia GPUs can be seen from the dashed lines which represent the performance of the Intel and AMD cards multiplied by two to account for the doubled number of simulations one can carry out on those GPUs compared to A100 and A40.

With respect to software performance, Amber22 and GROMACS 2023 show almost identical performance on GPUs that have fast memory, namely the HBM2 memory available in Nvidia A100 but the performance of Amber drops significantly on A40 which has slower memory. That effect is most probably due to the topology description of the systems in Amber and the large amounts of memory required for that. Memory problems were observed also during the test systems construction which was the reason systems with only up to 4M atoms could be benchmarked with Amber.

Because most of the time all GPUs are occupied during their normal operational mode in a computer center, it is important to estimate the GPU performance in fully vs partially occupied computer nodes. In Fig. 4 is shown the performance of GROMACS on PVC and Nvidia A100 for all-GPU vs single-GPU occupied nodes.

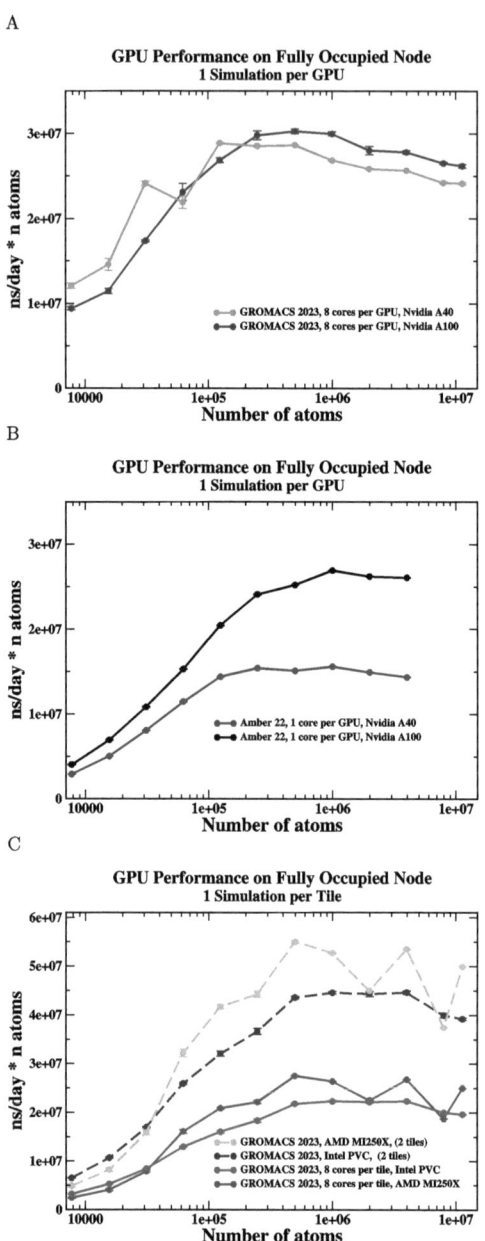

Fig. 3. **GPU performance vs. system size.** The benchmarking results of the Nvidia A100 and Nvidia A40 GPUs are shown in panels A and B and the ones from AMD and PVC in panel C. Different GPU models and MD software are shown in different color series in the panels. Because MI 250 X and PVC GPUs have two tiles with separate simulations running on each, the projected performance of an entire GPU (simulation length generated from both tiles) is represented in dash lines for a comparison

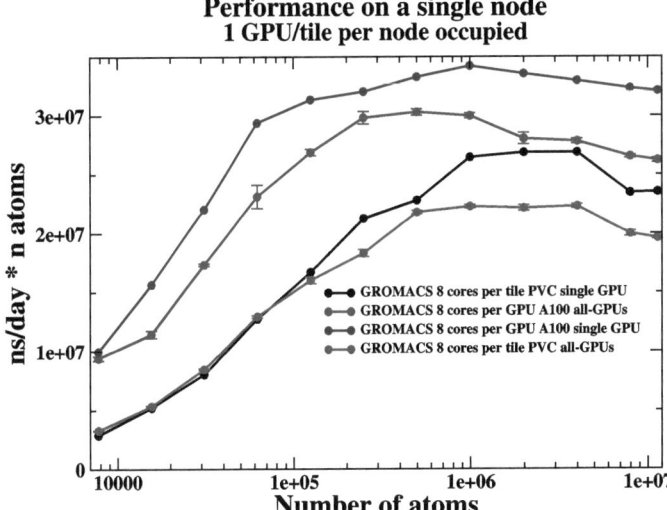

Fig. 4. Full- vs single GPU occupied node performance. The color series depicts the performance of two model GPUs, Intel PVC and Nvidia A100 in two cases, a fully occupied node, simulation running on each GPU and only a single GPU on the node being used.

In both models of graphic cards, there is a similar difference between the performance of single- and all- GPU occupied nodes. Because each simulation runs on a separate GPU/tile, there is no communication among the latter. Therefore, it can be concluded that the bandwidth competition for CPU (which still carries out the task scheduling for the GPUs) communication among the individual GPUs is what causes the slowdown when multiple simulations are running simultaneously.

4 Conclusions

The fast development of graphics cards in recent years allows simulating large molecular systems in MD setups. However, the most common system sizes simulated today are between 100 k and 200 k atoms. To estimate the system size at which the GPU resources become completely occupied, in the present study we carried out simulations of systems with increasing sizes and evaluated the performance of the respective GPUs.

What we see from our results is that even though the performance differs among the different GPU models, the complete saturation of the resources of a single GPU for almost all makes and models is reached no earlier than approximately 250 k atoms. Therefore it can be concluded that the original assumption, that the computational acceleration gained by a single graphic card is the optimal for most common cases, is indeed correct.

The difference in the performance of certain brands between fully and partially occupied nodes, suggests a competition for node resources between the individual GPUs, such as bandwidth of the PCI bus or the available power, similar to competing cores in a pure CPU computation. However, the leveling of the performance curves is at a similar number of atoms and it again leads to the conclusion that splitting simulations with the most common system size among more than one GPUs will not be beneficial irrespective of whether a computational node is fully occupied or not.

Acknowledgment. The authors would like to thank the Gauss Centre for Supercomputing e.V. (www.gauss-centre.eu) for funding this project as part of an innovation partnership aimed at a next-generation GCS supercomputer at the Leibniz Supercomputing Centre (www.lrz.de).

We also thank Erlangen National High-Performance Computing Center for the provided computer time at the NHR FAU's Alex cluster for the benchmarking of Nvidia GPUs.

We further acknowledge AMD and Intel for the help with compiling and installing GROMACS on MI250X and Intel PVC accelerated nodes, respectively.

Appendix

(See Table 2).

Table 2. Hardware/Software performance (ns/day)

System size (number of atoms)	Amber		Gromacs			
	Nvidia A100	Nvidia A40	Nvidia A100	Nvidia A40	Intel PVC	AMD MI250X
7782	522.34	377.99	1209.35	1552.63	421.63	318.83
15558	447.44	324.88	736.77	937.1	343.28	265.26
31110	348.56	260.04	557.89	776.26	272.46	255.25
62214	245.77	184.30	371.97	352.49	208.06	258.76
124422	164.60	115.71	216.05	232.21	128.81	167.55
248838	96.91	61.93	119.79	114.73	73.66	88.91
497670	50.71	30.35	60.87	57.60	43.80	55.25
995334	27.06	15.68	30.13	27.00	22.40	26.48
1990662	13.18	7.5	14.09	13.00	11.14	11.31
3981318	6.55	3.61	6.99	6.45	5.61	6.72
7962630			3.33	3.05	2.51	2.35
11337409			2.31	2.13	1.73	2.20

Answers to Reviewers

We thank the reviewers for their feedback and suggestions and for the time they spent on our paper. Below we address their questions and we implement their suggestions in the main text of the publication.

Reviewer 1

Q: From a standpoint of an MD user, "ns/day" is a more relevant quantity than "ns/day * atoms". If space permits, such a plot could be a valuable addition to make the paper relevant for a broader audience (outside the workshop).

A: The choice of ns/day*atoms was chosen so that we can identify the plateau of GPU resources saturation. However, we agree with the reviewer that the performance data given in ns/day could be useful information for many MD users and therefore we provide it as in an appendix to the main text of the publication. We have added the explanation of our choice to the first paragraph of the Results section.

Q: Figure 1 is quite hard to read due to many lines, even when viewed in color. Suggest splitting in two (perhaps NVIDIA A40 and NVIDIA A100 on one, and Intel PVC and AMD MI250 on the other, to get 4 lines per figure)?

A: We thank the reviewer for pointing the problem with the readability of Fig. 1. We split the figure into 3 subfigures making it much easier to recognize the different lines in the plots.

Q: There are two versions of GROMACS for running on AMD GPUs: the mainline GROMACS using SYCL layer (https://www.gromacs.org/; https://dl.acm.org/doi/abs/10.1145/3585341.3585350) and the AMD fork of GROMACS using ROCm directly (https://github.com/ROCm/Gromacs). It would be helpful to clarify which one was used.

A: We include additional information of the GROMACS builts in Subsect. 2.1 (Benchmarked Hardware) which includes the information of the SYCL and ROCm support used on the different GPUs.

Reviewer 2

Q: Multiple GPUs per node were mentioned in the introduction, but Table 1 does not give GPU counts. The Intel CPUs and GPUs are not detailed with model numbers. The variant of the Nvidia A100 is not given. CPUs per node are not given.

A: We thank the reviewer for noticing the missing information. We now include the missing details in Subsect. 2.1 (Benchmarked hardware) and Table 1.

Q: There is no detail regarding GROMACS build parameters, compilers and libraries, or mdrun invocation.

A: The additional information required by the reviewer is now included 2.1 (Benchmarked hardware)

Q: In Fig. 3, it is not clear whether the data presented is for multiple simulation occupying a single compute node, or for a node with a single GPU in use.

A: That information was provided in Sect. 1, but for clarification, we add that information also when introducing Fig. 3.

Q: Figure 3 gives performance against system size, and draws the main conclusion of the paper regarding the saturation point of GPUs. The authors do not go into more detail regarding why saturation is reached, which could have been an interesting topic. Which part of the MD solver's implementation becomes the bottleneck, and how does that interact with the GPU hardware?

A: The increase of the system size results in increased number of interactions to be calculated. All bonded interactions (potentials among atoms with chemical bonds) as well as near electrostatic (within cut-off radius) and Lennard-Jones interactions scale linearly with number of atoms for fixed cut-off radius. Since PME was used for calculating long-range electrostatic interactions, which scales with N log(N), where N is the number of particles, we expect (near) liner scaling of the GPU utilization with increasing system size. Because GPU has limited resources, eventually they are saturated and the performance levels out. All interaction calculations and the particle propagation were offloaded to the GPUs, so we don't expect a bottleneck due to large data transfer. The latter information has been added to Sect. 2.2 "Test systems". We added some explanation to the beginning of the "results" section. A more detailed analysis is beyond the scope of this work, but we will look deeper into it in the future.

Q: Figure 4 shows how multiple simulations occupying a single node reduces performance. This slow-down is attributed to "increased communication between GPUs and CPUs which causes a slowdown of the data transfer through the node infrastructure". It isn't clear that increased communication must be the cause, but this conclusion is not further substantiated.

A: Indeed, we do not provide evidence for this claim. We changed the manuscript such that we generally talk about node resources, such as communication bandwidth and power the discussion of the Fig. 4. In view of the vastly different architectures of the three GPU providers, we do not look deeper into this matter. Particularly, since letting the remaining GPUs or tiles run idle, is a prohibitive mode of operation.

Reviewer 3

Q: There was no comment on the statistical significance of the experiments.

A: Each data point in the plots presenting the results is averaged over all simulations carried out the node. The standard error is shown for each data point, however, due to the homogeneity of the hardware the error bars are very small, and can overlap with the data points themselves. We add clarification in the text discussing the figure.

Reviewer 4

Q: According to Sec. II, the simulation configurations are managed with external packages but there is little detail given for the importance for these constraints from the point of scientific fidelity and/or performance metrics. These include fixed-temperature, bond length limitations, etc.

A: Only tools within the GROMACS and AMBER packages we used for setting the parameters of the simulations and only the MD codes of both packages were used in the simulations. Parameters, such as time step, non-bonded cut-off radius etc., which can affect performance were kept identical for both packages. We add that information now in Sect. 2.2, "Test systems". Prompted by the reviewer question, we performed additional check of the default non-bonded cut-off radius in AMBER and a discrepancy with the GROMACS value was discovered. Therefore, the AMBER simulations were carried out again and the performance plots in Fig. 3 have been updated.

Q: The hardware configuration should be explicit whether a single or multi-node configuration was used and whether node-to-node communication affected the results. In case of single-node results, it should be noted what was the CPU-GPU connection to give proper context to discussion in Sect. 3.

A: The benchmarks were carried out on a single node, so no Infiniband was utilized. We add clarification now in the introduction of the paper. The change doesn't affect the Discussion or the Conclusions of the publication.

PCIe was used for CPU-GPU communication in all hardware combinations and we now add that information in Sect. 2.1 "Benchmarked Hardware".

References

1. Gray, A.: Creating faster molecular dynamics simulations with GROMACS 2020 (2020). https://developer.nvidia.com/blog/creating-faster-molecular-dynamics-simulations-with-gromacs-2020
2. Gray, A., Garg, G., Páll, S.: Massively improved multi-node NVIDIA GPU scalability with GROMACS (2023). https://developer.nvidia.com/blog/massively-improved-multi-node-nvidia-gpu-scalability-with-gromacs/
3. Salomon-Ferrer, R., Goetz, A.W., Poole, D., Le Grand, S., Walker, R.C.: Routine microsecond molecular dynamics simulations with AMBER - part II: particle mesh Ewald. J. Chem. Theory Comput. **9**(9), 3878–3888 (2013)
4. Goetz, A.W., Williamson, M.J., Xu, D., Poole, D., Le Grand, S., Walker, R.C.: Routine microsecond molecular dynamics simulations with AMBER - part I: generalized born. J. Chem. Theory Comput. **8**(5), 1542–1555 (2012)
5. Le Grand, S., Goetz, A.W., Walker, R.C.: SPFP: speed without compromise - a mixed precision model for GPU accelerated molecular dynamics simulations. Comput. Phys. Commun. **184**, 374–380 (2013)
6. Case, D.A., et al.: Amber 2023. University of California, San Francisco (2023)
7. Abraham, M.J., et al.: GROMACS: high performance molecular simulations through multi-level parallelism from laptops to supercomputers. SoftwareX **1**, 19–25 (2015)
8. Páll, S., Abraham, M.J., Kutzner, C., Hess, B., Lindahl, E.: Tackling exascale software challenges in molecular dynamics simulations with GROMACS. In: Markidis, S., Laure, E. (eds.) EASC 2014. LNCS, vol. 8759, pp. 3–27. Springer, Cham (2015). https://doi.org/10.1007/978-3-319-15976-8_1
9. Pronk, S., et al.: GROMACS 4.5: a high-throughput and highly parallel open source molecular simulation toolkit. Bioinformatics **29**, 845–854 (2013)
10. Hess, B., Kutzner, C., van der Spoel, D., Lindahl, E.: GROMACS 4: algorithms for highly efficient, load-balanced, and scalable molecular simulation. J. Chem. Theory Comput. **4**, 435–447 (2008)
11. van der Spoel, D., Lindahl, E., Hess, B., Groenhof, G., Mark, A.E., Berendsen, H.J.C.: GROMACS: fast, flexible and free. J. Comp. Chem. **26**, 1701–1719 (2005)
12. Lindahl, E., Hess, B., van der Spoel, D.: GROMACS 3.0: a package for molecular simulation and trajectory analysis. J. Mol. Mod. **7**, 306–317 (2001)
13. Berendsen, H.J.C., van der Spoel, D., van Drunen, R.: GROMACS: a message-passing parallel molecular dynamics implementation. Comput. Phys. Commun. **91**, 43–56 (1995)
14. https://doi.org/10.5281/zenodo.7588619

15. https://hpc.icc.ru/software/pdf/gromacs-5.0-benchmarks.pdf
16. Kaminski, G.A., Friesner, R.A., Tirado-Rives, J., Jorgensen, W.L.: Evaluation and reparametrization of the OPLS-AA force field for proteins via comparison with accurate quantum chemical calculations on peptides. J. Phys. Chem. B **105**, 28 (2001)
17. Mark, P., Nilsson, L.: Structure and dynamics of the TIP3P, SPC, and SPC/E water models at 298 K. J. Phys. Chem. A **105**(43), 9954–9960 (2001)
18. Wang, J., Wolf, R.M., Caldwell, J.W., Kollman, P.A., Case, D.A.: Development and testing of a general amber force field. J. Comput. Chem. **25**, 1157–1174 (2004)
19. Darden, T., York, D., Pedersen, L.: Particle mesh Ewald: an N·log(N) method for Ewald sums in large systems. J. Chem. Phys. **98**, 10089–10092 (1993)
20. Essmann, U., Perera, L., Berkowitz, M., Darden, T., Lee, H., Pedersen, L.: A smooth particle mesh Ewald method. J. Chem. Phys. **103**, 8577–8592 (1995)
21. Berendsen, H.J.C., Postma, J.P.M., van Gunsteren, W.F., Di Nola, A., Haak, J.R.: Molecular dynamics with coupling to an external bath. J. Chem. Phys. **81**, 3684–3690 (1984)
22. Bussi, G., Donadio, D., Parrinello, M.: Canonical sampling through velocity rescaling. J. Chem. Phys. **126**, 014101 (2007)
23. Ryckaert, J.P., Ciccotti, G., Berendsen, H.J.C.: Numerical integration of the cartesian equations of motion of a system with constraints; molecular dynamics of n-alkanes. J. Comp. Phys. **23**, 327–341 (1977)
24. Hess, B., Bekker, H., Berendsen, H.J., Fraaije, J.G.E.M.: LINCS: a linear constraint solver for molecular simulations. J. Comput. Chem. **18**, 1463–1472 (1997)
25. Miyamoto, S., Kollman, P.: SETTLE: an analytical version of the SHAKE and RATTLE algorithm for rigid water models. J. Comput. Chem. **13**, 952–962 (1992)

Accelerating Fusion Plasma Collision Operator Solves with Portable Batched Iterative Solvers on GPUs

Paul T. Lin[1](✉)[iD], Pratik Nayak[2][iD], Aditya Kashi[3][iD], Dhruva Kulkarni[1], Aaron Scheinberg[4], and Hartwig Anzt[5,6][iD]

[1] Lawrence Berkeley National Laboratory, Berkeley, CA, USA
paullin@lbl.gov
[2] Karlsruhe Institute of Technology, Karlsruhe, Germany
[3] Oak Ridge National Laboratory, Oak Ridge, TN, USA
[4] Jubilee Development, Arlington, MA, USA
[5] Technical University of Munich, Munich, Germany
[6] University of Tennessee, Knoxville, TN, USA

Abstract. High-fidelity numerical simulations are necessary to drive design choices for future fusion devices, e.g. the ITER tokamak. XGC is a gyrokinetic Particle-in-Cell (PIC) application optimized for modeling the edge region plasma. The Coulomb collision operator is one of the more computationally expensive components of XGC. It requires linear solutions for a large number of small matrices with an identical sparsity pattern. These are still performed on the CPU, a major bottleneck given that exascale-class machines have over 95% of their compute performance on the GPUs. As the collision operator matrices are sparse, well-conditioned, and of medium size, batched iterative solvers utilizing sparse data structures are an attractive option.

We showcase the acceleration of XGC with an integration of the GINKGO batched iterative solvers with realistic test cases from ITER and DIII-D. We build on our previous work, which focused on integration into a collision kernel proxy application, showing the substantial promise of GINKGO's solvers. We present results obtained from three platforms: NVIDIA A100 GPUs (NERSC Perlmutter), AMD MI250X GPUs (OLCF Frontier) and Intel Max 1550 GPUs (ALCF Aurora) and show the reduction in time provided by the GINKGO solver compared with the CPU solver. We present a weak scaling study to almost full-scale on the NVIDIA platform. The results show that GINKGO's batched sparse iterative solvers enable efficient utilization of the GPU for this problem. The performance portability of GINKGO in conjunction with Kokkos (used within XGC as the heterogeneous programming model) allows seamless execution on exascale-oriented heterogeneous architectures.

Keywords: Batched solvers · Large application use-cases · GPU computing · Plasma physics · Performance portability

1 Introduction

Research on magnetically confined fusion plasma devices, e.g. ITER tokamak, operates in a parameter space that is currently inaccessible to experiments. Design choices are therefore driven by high-fidelity numerical simulations that require exascale computing capabilities. Oak Ridge Leadership Computing Facility (OLCF)'s Frontier, the first computer to surpass the 1 exaflop HPL benchmark threshold, as well as the next two US Department of Energy (DOE) exascale computers are heterogeneous and incorporate both CPUs and GPUs. As most of the peak performance (over 95%) is in the GPUs, it is critical to efficiently exploit the GPUs to accelerate computationally intensive portions in simulation codes. The X-point included Gyrokinetic Code (XGC) [8] is part of the Whole Device Model Application (WDMApp) project, which aims to model the plasma in the entire fusion device. The Coulomb collision operator is one of the more computationally expensive components of XGC. As more and more of XGC has been ported to the GPUs, the collision operator CPU linear solver was rapidly becoming a bottleneck. Replacing this CPU solver with a GPU solver was becoming critical.

Batched linear solvers, which solve many related, but independent small linear systems, are important for highly parallel processors such as graphics processing units (GPUs). GPUs need a substantial amount of work to operate efficiently, and solving smaller problems sequentially is highly inefficient. Because of the small size of each problem, the task of implementing a parallel partitioning scheme and mapping the problem to hardware is not trivial. As the XGC collision operator matrices are sparse and well-conditioned, batched sparse iterative solvers are an attractive strategy.

We showcase our efforts to replace the LAPACK CPU banded solver `dgbsv` for the XGC collision operator with a batched sparse iterative GPU solver. In our previous works, we described the first two stages of this effort. The first study [6] described the development of batched iterative solver and SpMV kernels for NVIDIA and AMD GPUs. Results were presented for the batched BiCGSTAB Krylov subspace solver [12] with a Jacobi preconditioner using different batched sparse matrix formats.

In our previous work [6,7], we showcased the performance of our GPU-based batched iterative solvers in a proxy-app for the collision operator. In this work, building on the observations from our previous studies, we perform a full-integration study with the XGC application. We emphasize that the proxy-app was a simplified version of one component (collisions) of XGC: no time-integrator, smooth input distribution functions, and not MPI-enabled.

The key contributions of this work are:

1. A full integration of Ginkgo's batched solvers into XGC.
2. A detailed evaluation of the performance of Ginkgo batched solvers for production runs of XGC for two test cases: ITER and DIII-D tokamaks.
3. A detailed study of the linear and non-linear solver tolerances and iterations.

4. A demonstration that showcases the benefits of GINKGO batched solvers: a significant reduction in collision operator time and a reduction in total time for XGC on large supercomputers with NVIDIA, AMD or Intel GPUs.

We note that this full integration of the batched solvers into XGC, including two real-world test cases, represents a significant step from our previous work [7] with small-scale runs. In this work, we perform detailed studies of XGC with GINKGO for large-scale runs, i.e. up to 1536 nodes of the National Energy Research Scientific Computing Center (NERSC)'s Perlmutter (almost the entire GPU partition), on supercomputers with accelerators from the three major GPU vendors: Perlmutter (NVIDIA A100), the OLCF's Frontier (AMD MI250X) and the Argonne Leadership Computing Facility (ALCF)'s Aurora (Intel Max 1550).

In Sect. 2, we provide a brief summary of XGC and describe the factors that demonstrate the need for a high-performance batched linear solver for the XGC collision operator. Existing literature and work on batched solvers and batched routines are explored in Sect. 3. A brief overview of GINKGO's batched capabilities, with algorithmic and other optimizations to improve its performance on the collision operator, are described in Sect. 4. The integration with Kokkos and XGC is also discussed. Comparisons for the batched solve times on GPUs from three vendors are presented in Sect. 5.

2 Motivation and Background

XGC [8] is a 5D gyrokinetic particle-in-cell (PIC) code that numerically simulates fusion plasma for realistic geometries, and is optimized for boundary plasma. The electrostatic (ES) version solves the 5D gyrokinetic Boltzmann equation:

$$\frac{\partial f}{\partial t} + \dot{\mathbf{X}} \cdot \frac{\partial f}{\partial \mathbf{X}} + \dot{v}_\| \cdot \frac{\partial f}{\partial v_\|} = S(f) \qquad (1)$$

$$\dot{\mathbf{X}} = \frac{1}{G} \left[v_\| \hat{b} + \frac{m v_\|^2}{q B^2} \nabla \times \hat{b} + \frac{1}{q B^2} \mathbf{B} \times (\mu \nabla B - q \bar{\mathbf{E}}) \right]$$

$$\dot{v}_\| = -\frac{1}{mG} \left(\hat{b} + \frac{m v_\|}{qB} \nabla \times \hat{b} \right) \cdot (\mu \nabla B - q\bar{\mathbf{E}}), G = 1 + \frac{m v_\|}{qB} \hat{b} \cdot (\nabla \times \hat{b})$$

where f denotes the distribution function of gyrokinetic particles, $\mathbf{X}$ is the gyro-center position in the configuration space, $S(f)$ represents the dissipative terms (such as Coulomb collisions, heating/cooling sources, and atomic interactions with neutral particles), $v_\|$ is the velocity of the gyro-center parallel to the local magnetic field $\mathbf{B}$, $\hat{b} = \mathbf{B}/B$, $\mu = m v_\perp^2 / 2B$ is the magnetic moment, $v_\perp$ is the perpendicular velocity to the local magnetic field vector, $\bar{\mathbf{E}}$ is the gyro-averaged electric field, m is the mass, and q is the particle charge [8].

A nonlinear collision operator for the Coulomb collisions is required to accurately model edge plasma. XGC employs a nonlinear Fokker-Planck-Landau

(FPL) operator in the 2D guiding-center velocity space for multiple particle species. The evolution in time of the distribution functions is performed with a backward Euler time discretization [5,13]:

$$\frac{df_a}{dt} = \frac{f_{a,i+1}^{(k)} - f_{a,i}}{\Delta t} = \sum_b C_{ab}(f_{a,i+1}^{(k)} - f_{b,i+1}^{(k-1)}) \qquad (2)$$

where i is the time index and k is the Picard iteration index, which describes the evolution for the species a, and the collision operator C_{ab} models the collision between the species a and b. f_a and f_b denote the plasma particle probability distribution function for species a and b, respectively. The nonlinear solve is linearized using a Picard method. With each time step evolution requiring multiple nonlinear steps and each nonlinear step requiring multiple linear solves, a fast and efficient linear solve is important for XGC performance. Production simulations employ the LAPACK banded solver dgbsv CPU linear solver. However, as more of XGC is ported to GPU, the CPU solver time becomes a bottleneck, necessitating a fast GPU solver, particularly as these CPU solves involve expensive memory transfers between the host and GPU. XGC employs a 2D unstructured triangular (finite element) grid for poloidal planes and evenly spaced planes in the toroidal direction with a structured grid between them.

GINKGO is a performance portable numerical linear algebra library aiming to provide high performance numerical linear algebra algorithms with a focus on sparse data structures and algorithms. Execution across various hardware platforms is handled with a low-overhead runtime polymorphism strategy. GINKGO currently supports multiple GPU backends with CUDA, HIP, and Intel SYCL, as well as multicore CPU architectures with OpenMP [2].

3 Related Work

There have been efforts aiming to develop data-parallel algorithms that provide BLAS and LAPACK functionality in batched fashion [4]. Development for batched functionality for sparse and iterative linear algebra has not received as much attention as for their dense counterparts.

For batched sparse direct solvers, tridiagonal and pentadiagonal systems [11] have received some attention. While direct methods are robust, they do not provide the best performance when a highly accurate solution is not required and the problem is relatively well-conditioned. For general sparse matrices in compressed sparse row (CSR) format, a batched sparse QR factorization and solve is available in NVIDIA's cuSOLVER library [10].

Recently, a batched sparse iterative linear solver was developed for combustion simulations [1]. While significantly better performance compared to dense direct solvers was shown, it was not suitable for the medium-sized structured matrices of interest in the XGC collision operator. In further work [6,7], the flexibility and performance of these solvers were further enhanced to handle these larger cases and showcased through a proxy-app. A different batched solver design has also been explored [9] for the solution of batched linear systems from combustion simulations and has shown good performance for these problems.

4 Integrating Batched Solvers into XGC

The batched iterative solver design aims to utilize the embarrassing parallelism inherent in a batched algorithm and make good use of the fine-grained parallelism that is necessary to maximize the performance of GPU kernels. Batched solvers are particularly favorable in cases where the linear systems to be solved are relatively small, but one needs to solve large numbers of these small systems. There are important differences between batched sparse iterative solvers and their traditional large monolithic (non-batched) equivalents that warrant careful, specialized implementation of the former on GPUs. These have been discussed in previous work by the authors [6,7]. In this work, we focus on the integration of these batched iterative solvers into XGC, the challenges involved and the necessary optimizations required for the large-scale runs of XGC.

4.1 Interface Co-design

Within the XGC application, we focus on the collision operator, which models the Coulomb collisions of different species (different ions and electrons). As XGC targets the edge region plasma, a nonlinear Fokker-Planck-Landau collision operator is necessary. The evolution in time is performed with the backward Euler time discretization (Eq. 2) and a Picard iteration [5]. For each mesh vertex, a Picard method is employed to linearize the nonlinear operator, requiring a solution of a linear system for each species for each iteration. This requires (independent) linear solutions of N systems, where N is equal to the product of the number of mesh vertices and the number of species. Figure 1 shows the profile of one such Picard iteration loop, with the linear systems being solved on the CPU (in black) with the LAPACK banded solver, dgbsv. We aim to replace this CPU solver with a batched GPU solver to reduce the CPU-GPU memory traffic in addition to accelerating the Picard iteration loop. XGC uses Kokkos, a platform portability layer, to allocate and manage memory and implement physics kernels for different computing platforms in a single codebase.

To reduce memory usage, allocation overheads, and repeated transfers between host and device, the GINKGO integration wrappers **do not** allocate any additional memory in XGC, but instead only "view" the data, with read-/write access (for solution vector) or read-only access (matrix and right-hand side vector). When GINKGO's solve routine is concluded, the solution is written into the data already allocated and managed by Kokkos. The GINKGO layer is a plugin into the Picard iteration loop and is able to seamlessly provide high-performance batched sparse linear solvers to XGC, with minimal overhead. We created an abstraction layer that enables XGC to seamlessly switch between different linear solver backends and matrix formats. This layer requires that for each backend, some auxiliary functions such as subtract_from_identity,

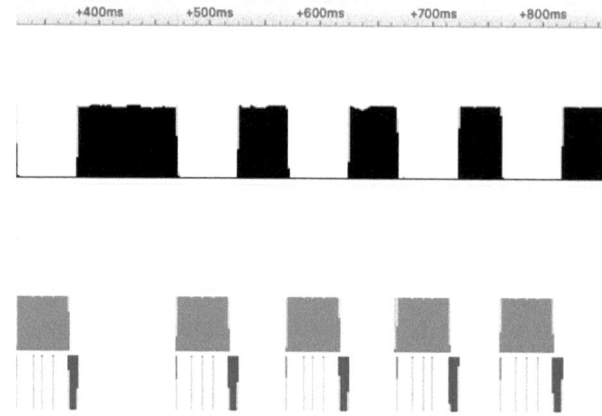

Fig. 1. Profile of one Picard iteration loop of the collision kernel proxy app showing time spent on CPU (black), GPU (blue), and memory transfer (red: Device to Host, green: Host to Device). The heights of the bars refer to the utilization of the relevant hardware - CPU, GPU, or PCIe bus for host-device transfers, while the x-axis is application run time. For this example, the host-device transfers took 9% of the time. (Color figure online)

add_identity_multiply, etc., are implemented. GINKGO provides this functionality for the batched iterative solvers (for all GPU backends), while for the CPU LAPACK backend, these are written using Kokkos. We refer the reader to our previous work [7] for details on this abstraction layer and to [3] for a comparison between the GINKGO and LAPACK interfaces.

4.2 Designing Iterative Solvers in a Batched Setting

The matrices involved in XGC originate from a 2D nine-point stencil discretization and have nine diagonal bands grouped by three. The matrices have a fairly uniform number of non-zeros per row, making BatchEll matrix format a natural candidate for this problem. The implementation of BatchCsr and BatchEll matrices in GINKGO, along with a discussion of how BatchEll maximizes resource utilization for collisions matrices, has been previously described [7].

In contrast to direct solvers, iterative solvers provide tunable accuracy, which is particularly useful when the linear solves are part of an outer nonlinear loop and hence an "exact" or machine epsilon solution is usually unnecessary. Additionally, iterative solvers can benefit from a good initial guess, which reduces the number of iterations and hence the time to solution. Within a nonlinear solver loop, such as a Picard iteration, we use the previous iteration's solution, which serves as a good initial guess for the iterative linear solves. To ensure flexibility without sacrificing performance, we design our implementation aiming to:

1. Reduce the number of kernel launches and enable the compiler to optimize the composite kernel,
2. Minimize the data movement from the global memory and maximize the cache utilization,
3. Maximize the occupancy of the GPU by utilizing as many warps as possible.

Different systems of a batch, being independent, can have different iteration counts. We use one workgroup of the GPU to solve one linear system which avoids cross-workgroup communication due to the independent convergence of the systems. This strategy maximizes the overall efficiency of the GPU due to reduced synchronization resulting in higher occupancy.

We implement batched versions of several iterative solvers. The problems we target here have relatively low condition numbers and relatively well-behaved eigenvalue distributions. Empirically, we observed that the batched version of the BiCGSTAB [12] solver was the most efficient, and hence we show all our results with the batched BiCGSTAB solver.

5 Experimental Evaluation

We showcase the performance of XGC with GINKGO to accelerate the collision operator linear solve for two different test cases: an electrostatic (ES) case from the ITER tokamak and an electromagnetic (EM) case from the DIII-D tokamak. These cases are accurate representations of the production runs used for XGC. We report performance and scaling on three machines, the pre-exascale machine Perlmutter, and the exascale machines Frontier and Aurora. All are Cray EX with Slingshot 11 dragonfly topology network with 25 GB/s network interface controllers (NICs).

- NERSC Perlmutter: 1792 GPU nodes (64-core AMD EPYC 7763, 4 NVIDIA 40 GB A100 GPUs, 256 GB DDR4, 4 NICs), NVHPC 22.7, CUDA 11.7.
- OLCF Frontier: 9408 nodes (64-core AMD EPYC 7A53 CPU, 4 AMD MI250X GPUs, 512 GB DDR4 RAM, 4 NICs); AMD 14.0.0, ROCm 5.2.0. Each MI250X consists of two GPU compute dies (GCDs) and appear as two discrete GPUs to the OS. Each GCD has 64 GB HBM2e (aggregate of 512 GB).
- ALCF Aurora:10,624 nodes, each with two 52-core Intel Xeon CPU Max 9470C Sapphire Rapids (SPR) with 512 GB DDR5 and 64 GB HBM2e (node total 1TB DDR5 and 128 HBM2e), 6 Intel Data Center Max 1550 Ponte Vecchio (PVC) GPUs, two "tiles" per GPU, each tile with 64 GB HBM2e (aggregate 768 GB GPU HBM2e/node), 8 NICs; OneAPI 2023.12.15.002.

5.1 Electrostatic (ES) ITER Test Case

The baseline run has two poloidal planes (1 million mesh vertices/plane) and is run on 64 Perlmutter nodes (605 million particles/node). XGC is run with one MPI process per GPU, and 32 OpenMP threads per MPI. The collision operator employs 32×31 velocity grids, producing matrices of size 992×992.

Every mesh vertex requires a Picard solve for every time step, and each Picard iteration requires two linear solves, one for electrons and the other for ions (deuterium). XGC decomposes the 2 million vertices into a set of batches each of "batch size" that are processed consecutively. Larger batch sizes result in fewer batches and fewer kernel invocations. The batches contain the same number of electron and ion species matrices. XGC simulations were performed for both 10 and 100 time steps. As the average times per step were similar, results for 10 steps are presented.

Whenever iterative methods are used for both an outer nonlinear solver and an inner linear solver, the convergence tolerance for the linear solve needs to be sufficiently tight so that the nonlinear solver iteration count does not increase. While a tolerance of 10^{-10} was sufficient for the proxy app, XGC required 10^{-16}. Table 1 presents the maximum, minimum, mean, and standard deviation for Picard iterations. For 10^{-10} and 10^{-14}, many nonlinear solves failed to converge, with many reaching the user-specified maximum value of 20 iterations. All the nonlinear solves converged with linear solver tolerance of 10^{-16}. Table 2 presents the maximum, minimum, mean and standard deviation for Picard iterations and BiCGSTAB (no preconditioner) iterations for both electron and ion linear solves. The typical number of Picard iterations is 4–6. Ion and electron solves require roughly 2–6 and 10–40 iterations, respectively. As the system matrix is not diagonally dominant, preconditioners such as point Jacobi were not effective in reducing the iterations.

Table 1. GINKGO absolute residual tolerance 10^{-16} needed for sufficient accuracy.

step	abs. res. tol.=10^{-10}				abs. res. tol.=10^{-14}				abs. res. tol.=10^{-16}			
	Picard iterations				Picard iterations				Picard iterations			
	max	min	mean	std dev	max	min	mean	std dev	max	min	mean	std dev
2	20	2	19.28	3.21	20	2	5.65	1.58	9	2	5.49	0.59
4	20	2	18.79	4.05	20	2	5.24	0.60	9	2	5.23	0.50
6	20	2	17.59	5.45	20	2	5.14	0.46	10	2	5.14	0.44
8	20	2	15.82	6.66	20	2	5.08	0.45	9	2	5.08	0.44
10	20	2	13.92	7.35	20	2	4.99	0.48	9	2	4.99	0.48

Table 2. Statistics for Picard iterations and electron/ion BiCGSTAB iterations for the 10 time steps (collision operator computed every second time step).

step	Picard iterations				electron linear solve iterations				ion linear solve iterations			
	max	min	mean	std dev	max	min	mean	std dev	max	min	mean	std dev
2	9	2	5.49	0.59	84	0	19.51	8.95	8	1	2.73	1.06
4	9	2	5.23	0.50	76	1	22.72	8.39	8	1	3.21	1.07
6	10	2	5.14	0.44	77	2	24.28	7.96	8	1	3.42	1.05
8	9	2	5.08	0.44	77	2	25.10	7.74	8	1	3.53	1.03
10	9	2	4.99	0.48	76	3	25.64	7.59	8	1	3.60	1.01

Figure 2a shows the time reduction for the collision operator using GINKGO vs. dgbsv on 64 nodes of Perlmutter. For each stacked column, the sum of the red (solver) and blue (rest of collisions time) regions denote the time for the collision operator. A different solver should not impact the blue region. Table 3 provides the raw timings. dgbsv requires an additional format conversion from CSC to banded format, and this time is included in the "linear solve" time. dgbsv takes 34% of the collision operator's time, which takes 15% of the XGC total time. The majority of the blue region is the time to assemble the matrix (calculate the elements in the matrix), which is performed on the GPU. GINKGO reduces the linear solve time by 92% compared with dgbsv, and reduces the time for the collision operator by 29%. While the reduction in the total time is about 4.3% (~2% reduction per species), the XGC team expects GINKGO to provide a substantial reduction in total run time for future multiple species (~10) runs, possibly up to a ~20% reduction.

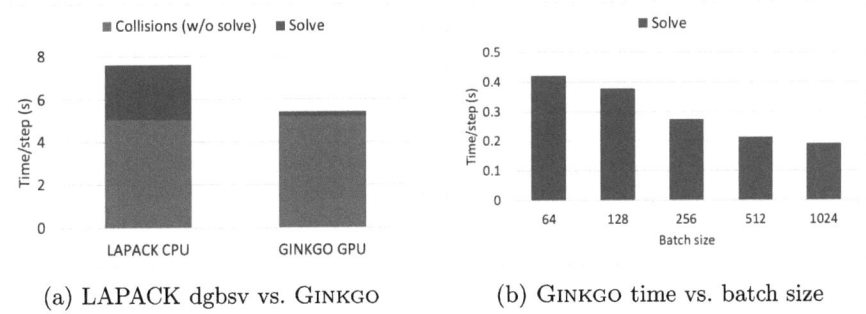

(a) LAPACK dgbsv vs. GINKGO   (b) GINKGO time vs. batch size

Fig. 2. (a) Collision operator (b) solve time decreases as batch size is increased. (Color figure online)

Table 3. Reduction in time (s) per step provided by GINKGO over dgbsv

	LAPACK dgbsv	GINKGO	% time reduction
Solve	2.56	0.21	92%
Collisions	7.61	5.43	29%
Total	50.8	48.7	4.3%

Our previous results from the collision kernel proxy app showed that GINKGO solve time decreased with an increase in batch size (larger batch sizes reduce the kernel invocation count), and Fig. 2b shows the same trend for XGC. Larger batch size requires more memory; memory was insufficient for batch size of 2048.

Figure 3a presents a weak scaling study for 64 to 1536 nodes on Perlmutter. 1536 nodes represents 86% of Perlmutter's GPU partition (almost the full scale) GINKGO provides a 5–7% reduction in total XGC runtime compared to dgbsv.

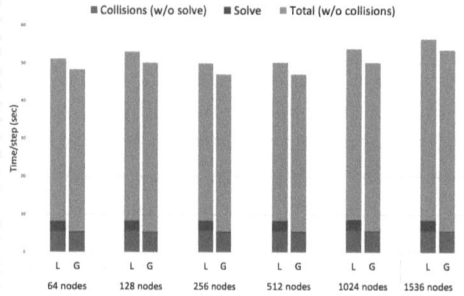
(a) Perlmutter weak scaling to 1536 nodes

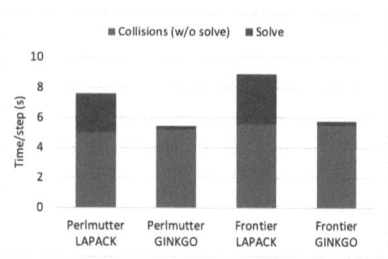
(b) collision operator time

Fig. 3. (a) Weak scaling to 1536 nodes: LAPACK (L) vs. GINKGO (G) (b) 64 nodes (256 MPI Perlmutter, 512 MPI Frontier): while collisions time is higher for Frontier, total time for Frontier was 38% less than Perlmutter with GINKGO

Figure 3b presents the reduction in solve time for GINKGO vs. dgbsv for Perlmutter vs. Frontier. The two columns on the left side of Fig. 3b are the same as in Fig. 2a. While the same batch size (512) is employed for both computers, one could use a larger batch size on Frontier (512 GB aggregate device memory vs. 160 GB). Alternatively, 3.2× more memory means 3.2× fewer Frontier nodes can be used to increase throughput. The dgbsv time is lower on Perlmutter because its CPU has higher clock frequency (2.45 GHz vs. 2.0 GHz). The larger amount of shared memory 192KB per CU on A100 vs. 80KB (16+64) on MI250X is a potential reason why the collisions time is not faster on Frontier.

5.2 Electromagnetic (EM) DIII-D Tokamak Test Case

The baseline EM turbulence DIII-D National Fusion Facility tokamak run had two poloidal planes (216,000 mesh vertices/plane) and 717 million particles/node (179 million/GPU), run on 8 Perlmutter nodes for 20 time steps. The collision operator employed a 33×39 velocity grid (1287-row matrices) with linear system batch size of 512. GINKGO used the batched BiCGSTAB (no preconditioner).

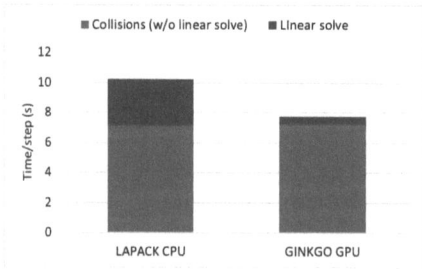
(a) LAPACK dgbsv vs. GINKGO

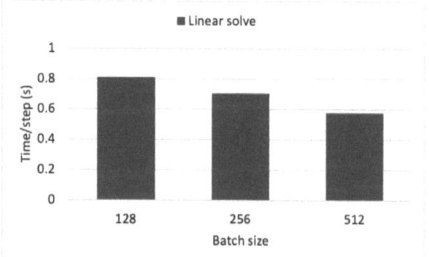
(b) GINKGO time vs. batch size

Fig. 4. (a) Collision operator (b) solve time decreases as batch size is increased. (Color figure online)

Table 4. Reduction in time (s) per step provided by GINKGO over `dgbsv`

	LAPACK dgbsv	GINKGO	% time reduction
linear solve	3.10	0.57	82%
collision	9.59	7.10	26%
total	57.0	54.5	4.4%

Figure 4a shows the reduction in collision time for GINKGO compared with `dgbsv`. We maintained the same color code from the ES test case, i.e. the sum of the red and blue regions denote the time for the collision operator, with the red region denoting the linear solve time and the blue region the rest of the time for the collision operator. The time required for the additional format conversion from CSC to banded for `dgbsv` is included in the "linear solve" time. Table 4 provides the raw timings. For this specific test case, when `dgbsv` is employed for the collision operator, it requires 32% of the collision operator's time, which requires 17% of the total time. The use of GINKGO reduced the linear solve time by 82% compared with `dgbsv`, and reduced the time for the collision operator by 26%. Similar to the ES case, we have only a single ion species giving us an overall reduction in total time of 4.4%, i.e. ~2% per species. Future simulations with more species (~10) can be expected to have significant reductions for both the collision solve and total time.

Figure 4b shows the reduction in GINKGO solve time with increase in batch size. More device memory is required as the batch size is increased; the amount of device memory is insufficient for batch size of 1024.

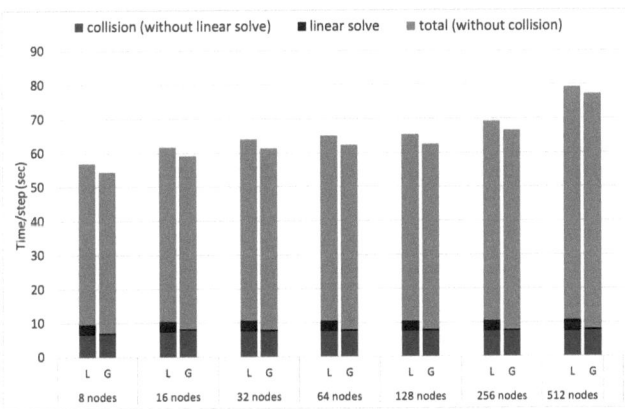

Fig. 5. EM test case on Perlmutter: weak scaling study for 8 to 512 compute nodes comparing LAPACK `dgbsv` (L) with GINKGO (G). Red denotes the LAPACK vs. GINKGO collision operator linear solve time, blue the collision operator time minus the solve time, and gray the total time minus the collision time. The sum of the three times is the total time. (Color figure online)

Figure 5 presents a weak scaling study for 8 to 512 GPU nodes on Perlmutter. No deterioration of scaling was observed. GINKGO reduced total time by ~4% compared with dgbsv.

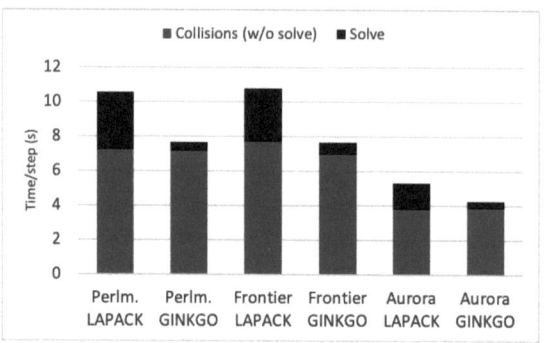

Fig. 6. Collision operator time comparing 8 nodes Perlmutter, Frontier and Aurora. Aurora disclaimer: This work was done on a pre-production supercomputer with early versions of the Aurora software development kit.

Figure 6 presents a comparison for 8 nodes for Perlmutter, Frontier and Aurora. XGC had 4 MPI ranks per Perlmutter node, 8 MPI ranks per Frontier node (1 per GCD) and 12 MPI ranks per Aurora node (1 per tile). GINKGO reduced the collision operator solve time by 84%, 77% and 71% on Perlmutter, Frontier and Aurora respectively, and XGC total time by ~4% for all three computers. While the same batch size (512) is employed for all systems, due to the larger aggregate device memory per node on Frontier vs. Perlmutter, a larger batch size could be employed. Alternatively, 3.2× fewer Frontier nodes to be used and still maintain the same aggregate device memory as Perlmutter nodes, in order to increase throughput. We note that results from Aurora are preliminary as the software stack is in an early stage of development. The GINKGO team aims to further tune the batched solvers to maximize the performance on the Intel Max 1550 GPU.

An equal number of nodes comparison among the three platforms is clearly not a fair comparison. But finding a fair comparison is challenging. Aurora nodes (2 CPUs, 6 GPUs and 8 NICs) are considerably more powerful (and consume a lot more power) than Perlmutter and Frontier nodes (1 CPU, 4 GPUs and 4 NICs for both). The fairest comparison is probably the same power, but obtaining the actual power consumption will not be easy. A crude approximation would involve summing TDP numbers for the components, but TDP numbers are only an approximation of the max power. Sum of TDP/node for CPU+GPU (majority of power): Perlmutter ~1880 W, Frontier ~2500 W and Aurora ~4300 W. An Aurora node has aggregate TDP that is ~2.5× that of a Perlmutter node.

For both the ES and EM test cases, GINKGO provided a ~2% reduction in total time per species.

6 Conclusion and Future Work

We have integrated the GINKGO batched sparse iterative solver capability into XGC to accelerate the collision operator solve. We have evaluated the batched iterative solver functionality for both electrostatic and electromagnetic test cases on compute platforms with A100, MI250X and Intel Max 1550 GPUs and compared them against CPU batched banded solvers. The MI250X platform is the first system to exceed the HPL 1 exaflop FP64 threshold. Weak scaling experiments and performance evaluations using up to 1,536 GPU nodes (6,144 A100 GPUs) demonstrate that the batched sparse iterative solvers in GINKGO are effective, efficient, and well-suited for the XGC application on exascale-class heterogeneous architectures providing reductions in time for the collision operator solve of up to 85%, 80% and 70% on Perlmutter, Frontier and Aurora respectively.

For both the ES and EM test cases, GINKGO provided a ∼2% reduction in total time per species. The XGC team is planning simulations with ∼10 species, and GINKGO is expected to provide up to a ∼20% reduction in total time.

Future work will focus on several areas, including, a more detailed analysis to determine how different test cases and different physics impacts the condition number of the matrices, more optimization work for Frontier and Aurora, multispecies test cases, etc.

Acknowledgments. We thank Dr. Seung-Hoe Ku (PPPL) for providing the EM test case and Dr. Timothy Williams (ANL) for porting XGC to Aurora. This research was supported by the Exascale Computing Project (17-SC-20-SC), a collaborative effort of the U.S. Department of Energy Office of Science and the National Nuclear Security Administration. It used resources of the Oak Ridge Leadership Computing Facility, which is a DOE Office of Science User Facility supported under Contract DE-AC05-00OR22725. This research used resources of the Argonne Leadership Computing Facility, a U.S. Department of Energy (DOE) Office of Science user facility at Argonne National Laboratory and is based on research supported by the U.S. DOE Office of Science-Advanced Scientific Computing Research Program, under Contract No. DE-AC02-06CH11357. This research used resources of the National Energy Research Scientific Computing Center (NERSC), a U.S. Department of Energy Office of Science User Facility located at Lawrence Berkeley National Laboratory, operated under Contract No. DE-AC02-05CH11231.

References

1. Aggarwal, I., Kashi, A., Nayak, P., Balos, C.J., Woodward, C.S., Anzt, H.: Batched sparse iterative solvers for computational chemistry simulations on GPUs. In: 2021 12th Workshop on Latest Advances in Scalable Algorithms for Large-Scale Systems (ScalA), pp. 35–43 (2021). https://doi.org/10.1109/ScalA54577.2021.00010
2. Anzt, H., et al.: Ginkgo: a modern linear operator algebra framework for high performance computing. ACM Trans. Math. Softw. **48**(1), 2:1–2:33 (2022). https://doi.org/10.1145/348093

3. Anzt, H., Luszczek, P.: Batched sparse linear algebra (final report for subcontract B648960) (2023). https://doi.org/10.2172/2228565. https://www.osti.gov/biblio/2228565
4. Dongarra, J., et al.: A proposed API for batched basic linear algebra subprograms (2016). http://eprints.ma.man.ac.uk/2464/
5. Hager, R., Yoon, E., Ku, S., D'Azevedo, E., Worley, P., Chang, C.: A fully non-linear multi-species Fokker-Planck-Landau collision operator for simulation of fusion plasma. J. Comput. Phys. **315**, 644–660 (2016)
6. Kashi, A., Nayak, P., Kulkarni, D., Scheinberg, A., Lin, P., Anzt, H.: Batched sparse iterative solvers on GPU for the collision operator for fusion plasma simulations. In: 2022 IEEE International Parallel and Distributed Processing Symposium (IPDPS), pp. 157–167 (2022). https://doi.org/10.1109/IPDPS53621.2022.00024
7. Kashi, A., Nayak, P., Kulkarni, D., Scheinberg, A., Lin, P., Anzt, H.: Integrating batched sparse iterative solvers for the collision operator in fusion plasma simulations on GPUs. J. Parallel Distrib. Comput. **178**, 69–81 (2023). https://doi.org/10.1016/j.jpdc.2023.03.012
8. Ku, S., et al.: A fast low-to-high confinement mode bifurcation dynamics in the boundary-plasma gyrokinetic code XGC1. Phys. Plasmas **25**(5), 056107 (2018)
9. Liegeois, K., Rajamanickam, S., Berger-Vergiat, L.: Performance portable batched sparse linear solvers. IEEE Trans. Parallel Distrib. Syst. **34**(5), 1524–1535 (2023). https://doi.org/10.1109/TPDS.2023.3249110
10. NVIDIA: cuSOLVER - GPU accelerated library for decompositions and linear system solutions on NVIDIA GPUs. https://docs.nvidia.com/cuda/cusolver/index.html. Accessed 24 Aug 2021
11. Valero-Lara, P., Martínez-Pérez, I., Sirvent, R., Martorell, X., Peña, A.J.: cuThomasBatch and cuThomasVBatch, CUDA routines to compute batch of tridiagonal systems on NVIDIA GPUs. Concurr. Comput. Pract. Exp. **30**, e4909 (2018)
12. van der Vorst, H.A.: Bi-CGSTAB: a fast and smoothly converging variant of Bi-CG for the solution of nonsymmetric linear systems. SIAM J. Sci. Stat. Comput. **13**(2), 631–644 (1992). https://doi.org/10.1137/0913035
13. Yoon, E.S., Chang, C.S.: A Fokker-Planck-Landau collision equation solver on two-dimensional velocity grid and its application to particle-in-cell simulation. Phys. Plasmas **21**, 032503 (2014). https://doi.org/10.1063/1.4867359

Optimizing GNN-Based Multiple Object Tracking on a Graphcore IPU

Mustafa Orkun Acar(✉), Fatma Güney, and Didem Unat

Koç University, Istanbul, Turkey
{macar20,fguney,dunat}@ku.edu.tr

Abstract. This paper improves multi-object tracking (MOT) efficiency using Graphcore's IPUs with GNNs. GNNs are crucial in real-time applications like autonomous driving and robotics for modeling complex object interactions, yet their computational demands, especially in key message passing operations, hinder performance. We discuss adapting a PyTorch model to TensorFlow for IPU execution and compare IPU and GPU performance. Baseline metrics such as average training and inference time per epoch are assessed, providing insights into each platform's strengths and limitations. We then focus on optimizing message passing operations for GNN efficiency on IPUs, evaluating the effects of these optimizations and adjustments to IPU-specific configurations.

Keywords: GNNs · Multiple object tracking · Graphcore IPU

1 Introduction

The ability to track multiple objects simultaneously in real-time is crucial for various applications, including autonomous driving, robotics, and surveillance. Graph Neural Networks (GNN) have shown promising results in Multiple Object Tracking (MOT) applications due to their ability to model complex relationships between objects. However, the high computational complexity of GNNs and their dependence on message-passing operations can lead to performance issues when applied to large-scale MOT systems. This is especially true for scatter and gather operations, which are essential components of GNN-based MOT algorithms but can be computationally expensive and challenging to optimize due to inefficient memory accesses, significant communication overhead, irregular data access patterns, and load imbalance among processing units. A recent study by Dong et al. [3], focusing on GPU architectures, found that General Matrix Multiplication (GEMM) operations typically achieve GFLOPS rates three times that of scatter and gather operations. This observation, as reported by the authors, suggests a considerable underutilization of GPU hardware overall. Given the potential dominance of these operations in execution time, the authors highlight the importance for both hardware and software developers to prioritize enhancing the performance of these operations. Another work [8] highlights the critical role of scatter and gather operations in training GNNs, where approximately

25% of the execution time for a single training step is directly spent on evaluating these operations, underscoring the critical role of efficient execution of these operations in determining the overall performance of GNN models.

Computation graphs are commonly used to represent the structure and flow of computations of deep learning (DL) models. These graphs enable efficient computation by organizing the computation and its order, allowing for parallelism and reducing the memory footprint. However, the traditional design of GPUs, optimized primarily for 2D matrix operations, may pose limitations for certain tasks, necessitating the use of large data batches to attain peak performance, which is a practice that may not always be suitable and could potentially contribute to overfitting, while it is worth noting that small batches can offer a regularizing effect [19]. In contrast to the CPUs and GPUs, IPUs (Intelligence Processing Units) are emerged as an alternative accelerator for deep learning workloads. They offer a distinctive architectural design that facilitates efficient massive compute parallelism, working cohesively with a large memory bandwidth. IPUs facilitate the gather-scatter process of information exchange between nodes, a critical aspect of GNN operations involving numerous small data pieces. Additionally, IPUs excel at handling the smaller matrix multiplications prevalent in GNNs, which are challenging to parallelize efficiently on GPUs optimized for larger matrix multiplications [6].

The primary aim of this work is twofold: i) to conduct a comprehensive comparative analysis between current-generation GPUs and IPUs with respect to their training and inference performance for MOT applications and ii) to enhance the efficiency of message-passing operations when executing a GNN-based MOT application on a Graphcore IPU, with a specific emphasis on optimizing scatter and gather operations. We migrated an existing PyTorch implementation [2] to TensorFlow for IPU execution. Our findings demonstrate the superior performance of IPUs over GPUs, particularly in scenarios with smaller batch sizes. Graphcore's optimized scatter and gather functions demonstrated a significant speed improvement (approximately 4× faster) compared to default TensorFlow implementations. However, due to focusing on a single IPU, experiments were limited to smaller input graph sizes. Future research could explore multi-IPU training for larger-scale applications.

2 Background and Related Work

2.1 Background on GNNs

GNNs were first introduced in 2009 [14], on a directed graph where nodes and edges have associated static feature vectors. Each node has a state vector that is recursively updated using information from neighboring nodes and edges, and a parametric output function computes the final output for a node. GNN-based approaches have demonstrated great success in the task of multiple-object tracking [18].

In Message Passing Networks (MPNs), proposed in [4], each node aggregates feature vectors from its neighbors to compute its new feature vector. The work by Braso et al. [2] presents a novel approach to solving the MOT problem using MPNs. They argue that existing learning-based MOT methods have primarily focused on enhancing feature extraction rather than directly addressing the data association challenge, a critical aspect of MOT. Their approach combines learning features for MOT with global reasoning over detections. Using a differentiable MPN framework, they predict graph partitions into trajectories without relying on traditional solvers or pairwise costs. By integrating deep features across the graph, their method captures global interactions among detections effectively within the MOT domain. Experimental results on three benchmarks show significant improvements in both MOTA and IDF1 metrics, highlighting the potential of learning-based approaches for the data association step. Additionally, the authors provide their code as open source, facilitating further research and application in the field.

As GNNs become more widely adopted in scientific machine learning, the significance of optimizing their training and inference efficiency is gaining greater attention. As deep learning communities continue to adopt deeper networks and work with larger datasets, hardware limitations have become more prevalent. Fortunately, the advent of specialized hardware platforms, such as GPUs and TPUs, offers a promising solution to address these challenges. Numerous techniques have been proposed to optimize GNN training on GPUs for efficient performance [17,20].

2.2 Intelligence Processing Units (IPUs)

Graphcore's IPU utilizes a MIMD (Multiple Instructions Multiple Data) architecture, diverging from the conventional SIMT design found in GPUs. This architecture incorporates ultra-high bandwidth memory located closely to the processor cores, making it highly efficient for handling irregular and sparse data access. This architectural choice is particularly advantageous for graph algorithms, which often involve unpredictable and irregular memory access patterns. Traditional processors relying on caching mechanisms often face performance bottlenecks with such characteristics. The IPU is composed of individual tiles, each containing a multi-threaded core and a limited amount of private SRAM. In its MK2 version, the IPU comes with 1472 processor cores, capable of concurrently executing nearly 9000 independent program threads.

As the pioneering study on IPUs, Mohan et al. [12] conducted a comprehensive comparison of the performance on IPUs, GPUs and CPUs across various neural network architectures and parameters. Their findings highlighted the significance of batch size as a critical variable. Their study revealed that IPU and GPU, both outperformed CPU, with IPU demonstrated superior performance over the GPU for batch sizes that are accessible to both processors. Furthermore, despite GPUs being able to handle larger batch sizes compared to IPUs, IPUs exhibited superior performance in terms of event generation speed, even when utilizing smaller batch sizes.

Recently Moe et al. [11] implemented a Spatio-Temporal Graph Neural Network (STGCN) on the IPU and its performance was thoroughly compared with the conventional GPU implementations of STGCN. Their findings proved the claims that the IPU effectively delivers the promised performance improvements for STGCN. The key finding of this study is a substantial performance increase of approximately 4 times when using the IPU in comparison to the Nvidia V100 SCM3 for training of GNNs.

In a subsequent study, Sumeet et al. [16] conducted a performance comparison between IPU and GPU for a compute-intensive text region detection application. Based on compute precision, number of IPUs used, and batch size, they evaluated the IPU's throughput, power consumption, and accuracy capabilities. Overall, the IPU demonstrated superior throughput than CPU and NVIDIA A100 GPU across all batch sizes, particularly with FP16 implementations. As compared to larger batches, the IPU demonstrated significant gains in throughput over other hardware, particularly with small batch sizes. In contrast, this study evaluates the suitability of IPUs for GNNs and contrasts their performance with GPUs specifically in the context of multi-object tracking.

The IPU architecture incorporates two key attributes that enhance performance in GNN workloads: [10]: Firstly, it keeps memory as close to the compute as possible by utilizing on-chip SRAM instead of off-chip DRAM, thereby maximizing bandwidth while adhering to a nominal power budget. Secondly, compute is divided into numerous small and independent arithmetic units to enable optimal utilization of available parallelism. This configuration is particularly advantageous for sparse communication operations, such as gather and scatter.

3 Methodology

The authors in [2] introduce a fully differentiable framework utilizing MPNs, capable of leveraging the inherent graph structure of the problem to conduct both feature learning and prediction. Formulating the MOT problem on a graph is advantageous as it facilitates the representation of complex relationships between objects over time. In practice, MPNs demonstrate successful association learning in tracking within this framework. Consequently, we have selected the method proposed in [2] as the foundation for our IPU implementation and experimental investigations.

The initial stage in constructing the graph dataset for the GNN model is detecting objects within the frames of the video segments. Subsequently, a frame window is selected to generate a single graph by converting each detection into a node. These nodes have initial node embeddings as feature tensors and are linked together to form a complete graph. Edge features are determined based on the attributes of connected nodes and geometric information such as the relative positions of detections. To reduce computational complexity, edges are pruned by removing those that connect nodes not found within their most similar 50-node list. In this study, we created graph datasets directly from [2] to generate training graphs for the experiments.

Despite the original implementation being developed in PyTorch, we opted for TensorFlow in our implementation due to the availability of more practical

GNN examples on TensorFlow for IPU at the time of development. When using TensorFlow for IPU, TensorFlow models are compiled into Poplar programs for execution on IPU. Fixed-size tensors are crucial for enabling static compilation, as varying sizes would result in multiple programs. For instance, separate programs are needed for training and inference due to their differing computations. In a MOT video segment, the number of detections varies across frames, leading to graph objects with differing node and edge counts. To enable static compilation, we standardized the node and edge counts of graphs in the dataset by applying truncation and padding to ensure a consistent number of nodes and edges. Moreover, within each graph, a dedicated loss mask tensor is included to identify padded placeholder edges, ensuring precise loss calculation for accurate model training and evaluation.

3.1 Model Structure

MPNN framework consists of four distinct networks for updating embeddings: three for nodes and one for edges. By employing a time-aware node model that processes messages separately from past and future nodes, the network inherently adheres to the flow conservation constraint, with each node maintaining at most one active edge linking it to a node in past frames and one in upcoming frames in 99% of cases. These networks incorporate time-awareness into the node model by leveraging two node models ($\mathcal{N}_v^{fut}$ and $\mathcal{N}_v^{past}$), facilitated by separate MLPs. They differentiate between the impacts of future and past interactions, enhancing the model's capacity to capture temporal dynamics in graph data. The final node embedding is updated by a third MLP, $\mathcal{N}_v$, which utilizes the computed future and past embeddings as inputs. Additionally, a fourth MLP ($\mathcal{N}_e$) calculates edge embeddings by considering node embeddings and the current edge embedding to calculate the edge embedding in the next time step.

Before execution, TensorFlow models are compiled into Poplar programs for the IPU. Utilizing fixed-size tensors ensures consistent program use, avoiding the inefficiency of compiling and executing different programs for each data point. Consequently, standardizing the number of nodes and edges across our graph dataset is essential. To optimize training speed while maintaining accuracy, we standardized node counts by padding smaller counts to match the maximum node count, typically below 500. For edges, given the significant computational costs associated with large edge counts exceeding 10000, and considering we conducted experiments in a single IPU setting, we limited the edge count to 6000. Some graphs have fewer edges, requiring padding, while others have more, necessitating truncating. This involves removing nodes with the highest IDs, corresponding to the latest detections in the time axis, to adjust the segment length for processing. We truncate edges to ensure a consistent edge count across the dataset. As illustrated in Fig. 1, the original dataset exhibits a significant variance in edge counts across graphs. As a result, standardizing edge counts across the entire dataset would lead to excessive padding and data loss due to high variability. Therefore, we selected a subset of 5000 graphs, each containing approximately 6000 edges, for standardization as seen in Fig. 1b (Tables 1 and 2).

Table 1. Message Passing Network

Past Update (N_v^{past})		
0	Input	80
1	FC+ReLU	56
2	FC+ReLU	32
Future Update (N_v^{fut})		
0	Input	80
1	FC+ReLU	56
2	FC+ReLU	32
Node Update (N_v)		
0	Input	64
1	FC+ReLU	32
Edge Update (N_e)		
0	Input	160
1	FC+ReLU	80
2	FC+ReLU	16

Table 2. Classifier

Edges (N_e^{class})		
0	Input	160
1	FC+ReLU	80
2	FC+Sigmoid	1

3.2 Optimization of the GNN Message Passing Process

Message-passing is the core component of MPNs. It involves iteratively propagating messages across the graph's nodes, updating their feature vectors based on received messages. The computational aspect relies on scatter and gather operations. Through analysis using the Graphcore's PopVision tool, we discovered that IPU cycles spent on these operations dominate execution time. Hence, optimizing their execution on the IPU is crucial for optimal performance.

During the transition from PyTorch to TensorFlow, the PyTorch indexing operator was replaced with `tf.gather()` as a substitution. However, it's important to note that not all standard TensorFlow library functions have been optimized for IPUs. Using `tf.gather()` resulted in longer execution times compared to efficient gather implementations, leading to higher inter-tile communication within the IPU.

Thankfully, Graphcore provides a specialized implementation for grouped gather and scatter operations, outperforming conventional TensorFlow operations [5]. This solution, implemented in C++, utilizes custom methods from Graphcore's tensor operation library, such as `popops::groupedMultiSlice` and `popops::groupedMultiUpdateMax`. Comparative evaluations show that these custom operations significantly outperform their TensorFlow counterparts, specifically `tf.gather` and `tf.scatter_max`. This optimized solution has been integrated into the MOT solver, providing a substantial boost in performance for gather and scatter operations.

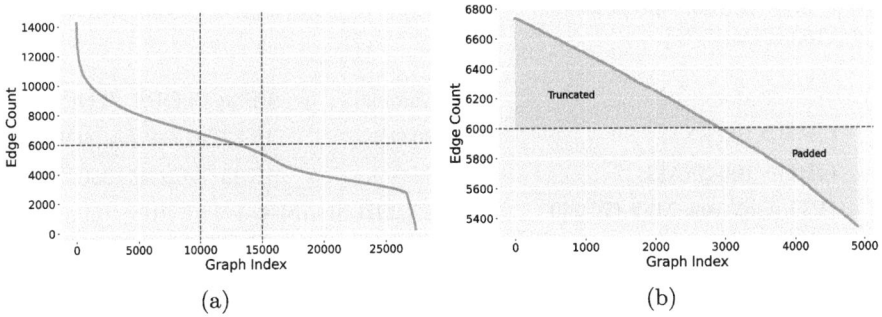

Fig. 1. (a) Number of edges per graph in the augmented dataset (b) Number of edges per graph in the selected training dataset before padding and truncation operations

3.3 Training

For the training phase, the Adam optimizer was utilized with hyperparameters $\beta_1 = 0.9$, $\beta_2 = 0.999$, and $\epsilon = 3 \times 10^{-4}$. The identical loss configuration as the original model was employed. Due to highly imbalanced labels, with positive edges constituting less than 4% of the total, Weighted Binary Cross-Entropy was utilized to account for the imbalance. In each batch, the loss function dynamically computed the ratio of negative to positive edges, which was then supplied as the pos_weight parameter to the tf.nn.weighted_cross_entropy_with_logits function. The resulting loss was further refined by multiplying it with a loss mask tensor, eliminating the influence of padded edges on the training process.

4 Experiments and Results

4.1 Dataset and Testbed

In the conducted experiments, 15 frames per graph were used to create a graph object. Each input graph is represented by four tensors: the edge list representing graph connectivity, node features encoding node data (2048 floats), edge features representing edge data (6 floats), and labels indicating ground-truth binary values for active/inactive edges.

We conducted our experiments on Simula Research Laboratory's high-performance computing cluster, eX3, accessible at [9]. The experiments were run on CPU, GPU and IPU nodes to compare performance of the models on different hardware. Specifications of the compute resources are as follows:

Each device represents a distinct trade-off in compute power, memory capacity, and power efficiency. Notably, the A100 SXM GPU stands out for its expansive memory capacity and high compute performance, while the Tesla V100-SXM3 GPU offers a balance between performance and power efficiency. In contrast, the Colossus Mk2 GC200 IPU prioritizes exceptional compute performance and lower power consumption. Meanwhile, the Intel Xeon Platinum 8168 CPU offers high system memory capacity (Table 3).

Table 3. Processor specifications of Graphcore GC200, NVIDIA Tesla V100-SXM3 and A100 SXM [7,15].

	Name	Cores	Memory	FP32 FLOPS	TDP
GPU	A100 SXM	6912	80 GB	19.5 TFLOPS	400 W
GPU	V100-SXM3	5120	32 GB	16.35 TFLOPS	350 W
IPU	Colossus Mk2 GC200	1472	900 MB SRAM	62.5 TFLOPS	150 W
CPU	Intel Xeon Platinum 8168	24	754 GB	–	205 W

4.2 Train and Validation Losses

The MOT17-09-SDP sequence dataset was used for both IPU and GPU experiments. Parameters max_detects = 500 and frames_per_graph = 15 were applied with data augmentation. After generating graphs, 5000 graphs were sampled for training and 100 graphs for validation, each containing 6000 edges, as explained previously.

The experimental setup was optimized for a batch size of 4, determined as the most efficient for the IPU. Larger sizes caused out-of-memory errors, while smaller sizes slowed training. Batch sizes of 8 and 16 resulted in decreased model accuracy. Thus, a batch size of 4 struck the optimal balance between efficiency and performance, minimizing memory issues and maintaining accuracy.

Table 4. Model ML Performance Comparison after 100 epochs on validation set

Metric	MOT Model on IPU	MOT Neural Solver
Precision	0.58	0.698
Recall	0.51	0.655

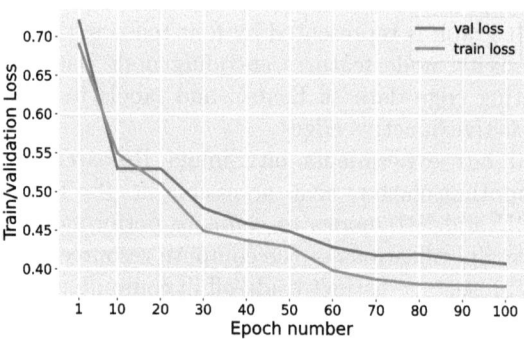

Fig. 2. Train and validation(val) loss graphs IPU (batch size = 4)

In Table 4, the training precision and recall of the original GPU model are compared against our IPU model after 100 epochs. Our model shows lower performance at the 100th epoch using the same learning rate 3×10^4. This aligns with expectations, as our implementation utilizes fixed-size graphs, necessitating the removal of edges from certain input graphs. Despite slower learning, our model displays the capability to train and learn from input data.

Figure 2 illustrates the training and validation losses across 100 epochs during MOT model training on the IPU. Training loss reflects model performance on learned data, while validation loss indicates error on unseen data. Initially, there's a notable enhancement in both metrics, signifying rapid learning from the data. However, as epochs progress, the rate of improvement diminishes, suggesting the model approaches a stable state with limited further insights. This trend suggests convergence towards an optimal solution, where additional cycles yield only marginal improvements.

4.3 Performance Comparison: MOT Neural Solver vs Our Model

In the experiments, a comparative analysis assessed the performance of an NVIDIA V100 and A100 against a Graphcore IPU MK2. Training sessions used batch sizes ranging from 1, 2, 4, 8, and 16 over 100 epochs. To mitigate device warm-up effects, the initial ten epochs were excluded from calculations, following the methodology in [13].

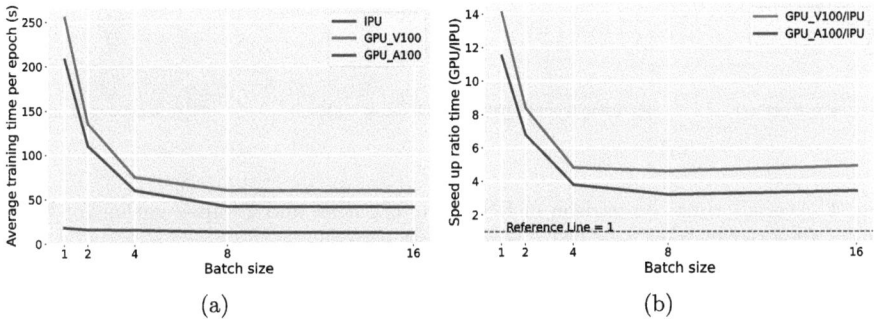

Fig. 3. (a) Comparison of average training times between IPU and GPUs as a function of batch size. (b) Speed up ratio of GPUs and IPU as a function of batch size. The red horizontal line represents a reference value of 1.

In Fig. 3, a comparative analysis is conducted between a TensorFlow model on an IPU and the original PyTorch model on GPU. Both models share identical layer architectures and parameters. The comparison maintains consistency using the same dataset across experiments [2].

Figure 3a depicts the average training time per epoch versus batch size for both IPU and GPUs. Initially, with small batch sizes, there's a notable decrease in the time per epoch for training. This indicates GPU under utilization, where computational work setup for each batch isn't distributed efficiently across data points. Essentially, this means GPU processing units are often idle, leading to extended training durations. As batch size increases, training time decreases for both processors, indicating efficient resource utilization due to increased parallel processing. Notably, the IPU consistently outperforms the GPU across all batch sizes, especially evident with smaller batches.

Figure 3b illustrates the speed-up ratio of GPU to IPU training times across various batch sizes. Initially, the IPU exhibits a significant speed advantage, notably prominent with a batch size of 1, where it outperforms the A100 and V100 by around 11 and 14 times, respectively. However, as the batch size increases, this advantage diminishes, stabilizing at approximately 3 and 5 times faster for A100 and V100, respectively, for batch sizes exceeding 4. The convergence towards a ratio of 4 suggests that as the batch size grows, the performance gap between IPUs and GPUs narrows, consistent with the findings in [1]. These findings reveal a significant trend: GPU performance decreases with smaller batch sizes, while larger batches enhance GPU competitiveness due to increased parallel execution, reduced kernel overhead, and improved memory bandwidth utilization.

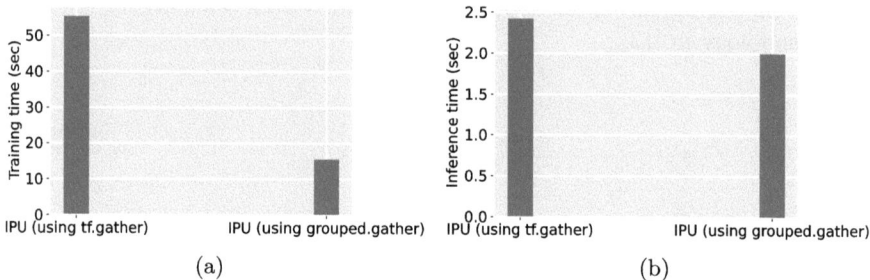

Fig. 4. Average time comparison of IPU using tf.gather and grouped gather for batch size = 4 for (**a**) training and (**b**) inference, respectively.

Figure 4 compares the average training and inference times on an IPU using standard TensorFlow tf.gather versus the optimized *grouped_gather*. The train and validation sets have an equal number of graphs in these experiments. The optimized gather function is crucial due to the inefficiency of standard tf.gather, which lacks specialized kernels for the IPU, resulting in excessive communication between compute tiles and longer run times.

The left side of the figure, utilizing tf.gather, exhibits significantly longer durations for training, emphasizing the necessity for hardware-optimized operations. Standard functions may underutilize hardware capabilities. Conversely, the right side, employing the *grouped_gather* which utilizes operations from Graphcore's popops library, showcases notable improvements. This function significantly reduces execution time for both training and inference.

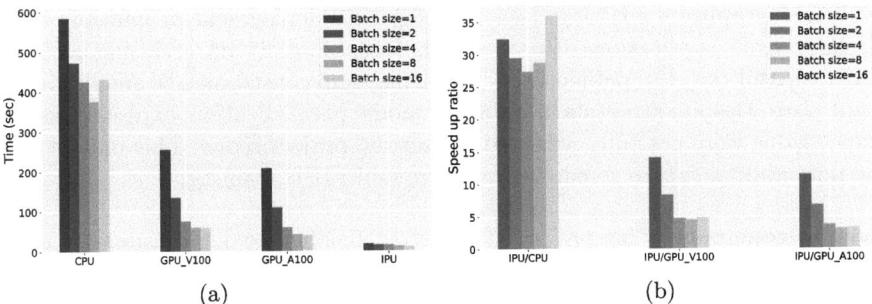

Fig. 5. Comparison of average training time across CPU, GPU, and IPU for varying batch sizes (1, 2, 4, 8, 16). **(b)** Speed up of IPU relative to the CPU and GPU for varying batch sizes (1, 2, 4, 8, 16).

The graph in Fig. 5a illustrates the average training times across three types of hardware: CPU, GPUs, and IPU. Starting with the CPU, it takes significantly longer to train compared to GPUs and IPUs due to its general-purpose design. Moving to the GPU, there's a clear decrease in training time due to its parallel processing capabilities. The IPU demonstrates the most efficient training time, attributed to its specialized architecture tailored for efficiency with smaller batch sizes, as noted in [12], contrasting with GPUs requiring larger batch sizes to fully utilize parallel processing capabilities. The graph in Fig. 5b indicates a significant 30-fold speed improvement of the IPU over the CPU. The IPU speedup over GPU is smaller yet notable, suggesting the IPU's superiority over GPUs, albeit to a lesser extent than over CPUs. Notably, the most substantial speedup, approximately 15-fold, occurs at a batch size of 1, diminishing to around 5-fold for larger batch sizes. This suggests the IPU's efficiency compared to GPUs diminishes with larger batch sizes while maintaining a substantial advantage over both CPUs and GPUs across all batch sizes.

5 Conclusion

The paper evaluated a multiple object tracking model, particularly comparing Graphcore's IPUs to traditional GPUs for training a GNN. By migrating an existing PyTorch implementation to TensorFlow and optimizing it for IPU execution, the study provided detailed insights into performance disparities between these computing architectures. The findings corroborate existing literature [1,12,13], emphasizing IPUs' superior performance over GPUs with smaller batch sizes. This advantage stems from IPUs' efficient resource utilization compared to GPUs' limitations in fully harnessing parallel processing capabilities with smaller batch sizes. Graphcore's optimized scatter and gather functions showed a substantial speed improvement (approximately 4× faster) compared to default TensorFlow implementations. Additionally, IPU-specific settings such as I/O tiles and prefetch depth were found to significantly influence performance.

While Graphcore's IPU architecture supports deployment of multiple units for large-scale applications, this research focused solely on assessing a single IPU's capabilities. Consequently, experiments were constrained to smaller input graph sizes. Despite attempts at data and model parallelization, expected performance gains were not fully achieved within the project scope. This underscores the potential for future research to explore multi-IPU training.

Acknowledgement. This project has received funding from the European High-Performance Computing Joint Undertaking under grant agreement No 956213 and from the Turkish Science and Technology Research Centre Grant No 120N003.

References

1. Arcelin, B.: Comparison of graphcore IPUs and Nvidia GPUs for cosmology applications. arXiv preprint arXiv:2106.02465 (2021)
2. Brasó, G., Leal-Taixé, L.: Learning a neural solver for multiple object tracking. In: Proceedings of the IEEE/CVF Conference on Computer Vision and Pattern Recognition, pp. 6247–6257 (2020)
3. Baruah, T., et al.: GNNMark: a benchmark suite to characterize graph neural network training on GPUs (2021)
4. Gilmer, J., Schoenholz, S.S., Riley, P.F., Vinyals, O., Dahl, G.E.: Neural message passing for quantum chemistry. In: International Conference on Machine Learning, pp. 1263–1272. PMLR (2017)
5. Graphcore: Custom grouped gather scatter (2022). https://github.com/graphcore/ogb-lsc-pcqm4mv2/tree/main/static_ops
6. Graphcore: What GNNs are great at - and why graphcore IPUs are great at GNNs (2023). https://www.graphcore.ai/posts/what-gnns-are-great-at-and-why-graphcore-ipus-are-great-at-gnns. Accessed 22 Feb 2024
7. Graphcore: Accelerating machine learning in the cloud (n.d.). https://www.graphcore.ai/. Accessed 1 June 2023
8. Helal, H., et al.: Acceleration of graph neural network-based prediction models in chemistry via co-design optimization on intelligence processing units. J. Chem. Inf. Model. **64**(5), 1568–1580 (2024)
9. Simula Research Laboratory: ex3 (2024). https://www.ex3.simula.no/. Accessed 16 Jan 2024
10. Masters, D., et al.: GPS++: an optimised hybrid MPNN/transformer for molecular property prediction. arXiv preprint arXiv:2212.02229 (2022)
11. Moe, J., Pogorelov, K., Schroeder, D.T., Langguth, J.: Implementing spatio-temporal graph convolutional networks on graphcore IPUs. In: 2022 IEEE International Parallel and Distributed Processing Symposium Workshops (IPDPSW), pp. 45–54. IEEE (2022)
12. Mohan, L.R.M., et al.: Studying the potential of graphcore IPUs for applications in particle physics. arXiv preprint arXiv:2008.09210 (2020)
13. Nasari, A., et al.: Benchmarking the performance of accelerators on national cyber-infrastructure resources for artificial intelligence/machine learning workloads. In: Practice and Experience in Advanced Research Computing, pp. 1–9 (2022)
14. Scarselli, F., Gori, M., Tsoi, A.C., Hagenbuchner, M., Monfardini, G.: The graph neural network model. IEEE Trans. Neural Netw. **20**(1), 61–80 (2008)

15. Shekofteh, S.-K., Alles, C., Fröning, H.: Reducing memory requirements for the IPU using butterfly factorizations. In: Proceedings of the SC 2023 Workshops of The International Conference on High Performance Computing, Network, Storage, and Analysis, pp. 1255–1263 (2023)
16. Sumeet, N., Rawat, K., Nambiar, M.: Performance evaluation of graphcore IPU-M2000 accelerator for text detection application. In: Companion of the 2022 ACM/SPEC International Conference on Performance Engineering, pp. 145–152 (2022)
17. Wang, Y., Murnane, D., Choma, N., Farrell, S., Calafiura, P., et al.: Benchmarking GPU and TPU performance with graph neural networks. arXiv preprint arXiv:2210.12247 (2022)
18. Wang, Y., Weng, X., Kitani, K.: Joint detection and multi-object tracking with graph neural networks. arXiv preprint arXiv:2006.13164 (2020)
19. Wilson, D.R., Martinez, T.R.: The general inefficiency of batch training for gradient descent learning. Neural Netw. **16**(10), 1429–1451 (2003)
20. Wu, W., Shi, X., He, L., Jin, H.: TurboMGNN: improving concurrent GNN training tasks on GPU with fine-grained kernel fusion. IEEE Trans. Parallel Distrib. Syst. **34**(6), 1968–1981 (2023)

A Novel Mixed Precision Defect Correction Solver for Heterogeneous Computing

Yann T. Delorme[1(✉)], Mark Wasserman[1], Alon Zameret[1], and Zhaohui Ding[2]

[1] Toga Networks, a Huawei Company, Tel-Aviv, Israel
{yann.delorme,mark.wasserman}@huawei.com
[2] Huawei Technologies Co. Ltd., Beijing, China
dingzhaohui@huawei.com

Abstract. Modern HPC architecture combines the use of CPUs with accelerators to obtained better performance and shorter time-to-solution. But in most cases, accelerators such as GPUs or NPUs benefit from low precision computations, to obtain faster arithmetic, and also reduce the overall memory footprint by reducing the total amount of data to be stored. In order to effectively offload as much of the computational workload to low-precision devices, it is important to use an algorithm that would ensure convergence of the final results to a level of accuracy that is acceptable by the user. Mixed-precision algorithms allow for recovery of high precision arithmetic while offloading most of the computation to low-precision arithmetic. Most available mixed-precision algorithm are based on iterative refinement approaches in which a correction is computed and added to the latest estimate of the solution in an iterative manner. In this study, we propose a defect correction approach that allows for recovery of high precision accuracy for linear and non-linear iterative solvers. The results are tested using an in-house solver, and then implemented within the OpenFOAM solver using the Ginkgo library. Current results are showing up to 40% acceleration while recovering accuracy close to double precision computation.

Keywords: Mixed-Precision · Iterative solver · Heterogeneous computing

1 Introduction

In the last decade, accelerators such as GPUs or NPUs became more and more popular in the HPC world. Most modern clusters today offer a heterogeneous architecture, combining CPUs and GPUs and/or other accelerators (NPUs, etc.) to reach and overcome the exa-scale barrier. Due to these recent advances, mixed precision solvers are becoming more and more important. The idea is that part of the workload can be offloaded to the accelerators, and be done using low precision floating point operations. By doing so, we tackle several important HPC bottlenecks:

1. Less communication: by reducing the memory traffic between the memory and the processor, and by reducing the network traffic from node to node
2. Less memory footprint: by reducing the total amount of data to store in memory and in storage
3. Faster arithmetic: by utilizing the faster low precision arithmetic, either from the CPU itself, or from the available accelerator

The main issue is that, for most modern scientific applications, high precision is required to obtain practically usable and meaningful results. This usually requires the use of high precision floating point operations such as FP64. Example of critical applications are any solver dealing with turbulent flows, combustion, weather forecast, etc. Because of this, it is impossible in most cases to utilize the maximum potential of modern accelerators for industrial applications. The objective of this project is to develop a mixed precision algorithm to solve for elliptic partial differential equations, allowing for overall high precision accuracy of the final solution (FP64) while offloading as much of the computation as possible to low precision hardware (FP32 and FP16). In the first section, the defect correction approach that we developed is presented. Some of the results that were obtained using manufactured solution are shown, as well as initial limitations at very low precision. In the second section, the extension of the defect correction approach to allow for better convergence to high accuracy, especially for FP16 operations is presented in details. Then, application to Navier-Stokes equations, both for implicit and explicit formulations are shown, with corresponding validating simulations. Finally, in the last section, extension of the defect correction approach to Ginkgo and its coupling to OpenFOAM is presented, as well as results using the simpleFoam solver for a 3D Lid-Driven cavity test case and the 3D DrivAer test case.

2 Mixed Precision Linear Solver for Elliptic Partial Differential Equations

As mentioned in the introduction, the goal of this study is to offload as much computational work as possible to low precision hardware while maintaining the overall accuracy of the converged solution. By doing so, the overall computational time can be drastically reduced while maintaining the accuracy at the same desired level.

2.1 Defect Correction Approach for General Linear Solver

The defect correction term is defined as the difference between the residual computed at high precision with the residual computed using low precision arithmetic. Define $\hat{}$ the operator and the variables estimated using low precision floating point. The defect correction term can then be written as:

$$D = (Au - f) - (\hat{A}\hat{u} - \hat{f}) \tag{1}$$

A can be a linear or non-linear operator. Based on this definition, the algorithm can be written as:

1. Relax several times using high precision, obtaining $\tilde{u}^k$ with a smooth corresponding error
2. Compute the defect correction term $D = (A\tilde{u} - f) - (\hat{A}\hat{u} - \hat{f})$
3. Solve, using low precision, the approximate equation $\hat{A}\hat{u} = \hat{f} - D$
4. After some low-precision iterations, we obtain $\hat{\tilde{u}}$, which is an approximate solution for u. We can then update the solution $\tilde{u}$ on high precision
5. Restart from step 1. and iterates

2.2 Convergence Results of the Mixed Precision Defect Correction Algorithm for a Manufactured Non-Linear Elliptic Partial Differential Equation

To study the convergence of the defect correction approach, the method of manufacturing solution was used. The following non-linear PDE is considered:

$$\frac{\partial^2 u}{\partial x^2} + \frac{\partial^2 u}{\partial y^2} + u^3 = f \qquad (2)$$

For validation purpose, the following manufactured solution was chosen:

$$u(x,y) = sin(\pi x) sin(\pi y) \qquad (3)$$

This results in the following source term:

$$f(x,y) = sin^3(\pi x) sin^3(2\pi y) - 5\pi^2 sin(\pi x) sin(2\pi y) \qquad (4)$$

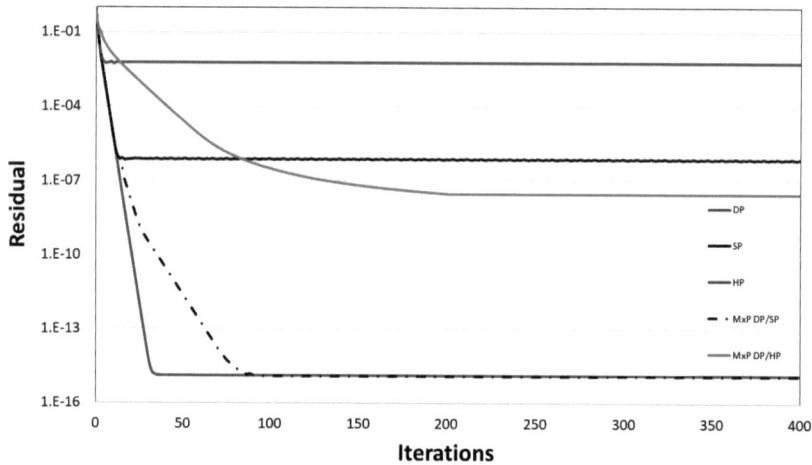

Fig. 1. Defect correction mixed precision residual convergence for the synthetic benchmark.

This problem is solved on a 2D square domain with 128 grid points in each direction. Figure 1 shows the results obtained with mixed precision FP64/FP32 and FP64/FP16 algorithms. The red line shows the results obtained using double precision floating point operations only, the black line shows the results obtained using single precision floating point operations only and the blue line shows the results obtained using half precision floating point operations only. Two more residual convergence can be seen, in green and dotted black. The dotted line shows the convergence of the solution using a combination of FP64 and FP32 operations. It can be seen that, using the defect correction approach, we manage to obtain a level of convergence similar to the one obtained using only FP64. This is an improvement of about 6 order of magnitude when compared to the convergence obtained using only FP32, for which the residual reached a plateau near the value 10^{-6}. The green line shows the convergence of the defect correction approach when using a combination of FP64 with FP16 floating point operations. In this case, it can be seen that the same level of convergence as the one obtained with pure double precision operation is not recovered. Instead, a plateau is reached at around 10^{-7}. This is an improvement of about 4 order of magnitude when compared to the convergence results obtained using only half precision floating point operations. But this is still not enough to be practically usable in the HPC scientific application community. The next section describes improvement brought to the algorithm.

2.3 Improvement of the Defect Correction Approach for Very Low Precision Offload

Recall that the defect correction term is computed as different between the non-linear operator evaluated using double precision and the non-linear operator evaluated using low precision (either single or half precision). This defect correction is then used with low precision. Because the defect correction term D represents the overall round-off error induced by the use of the low precision hardware, this term is usually very small, in the order of magnitude of the cut-off accuracy of the low precision hardware. Because of this, the term $\hat{f} - D$ might not be accurately represented on the low precision device, making the correction less and less dominant as the algorithm starts to converge. This explains the plateau seen on the light blue curve in Fig. 1. In order to remove this issue, it was decided to, once the limit convergence is reached, linearize the equations using Newton method, to obtain the following system:

$$\hat{L}\hat{u} = \hat{f}' - D \tag{5}$$

where f' contains the linearization term arising on the right-hand-side of the equation. Once the system is linearized, splitting of the source terms on the right-hand side can be done, and solve the contribution of each one separately, without losing the effect of any of them due to low precision accuracy. The equations now become

$$\begin{cases} \hat{L}\hat{u}' = \hat{f}' \\ \hat{L}\hat{u}'' = -D \end{cases} \tag{6}$$

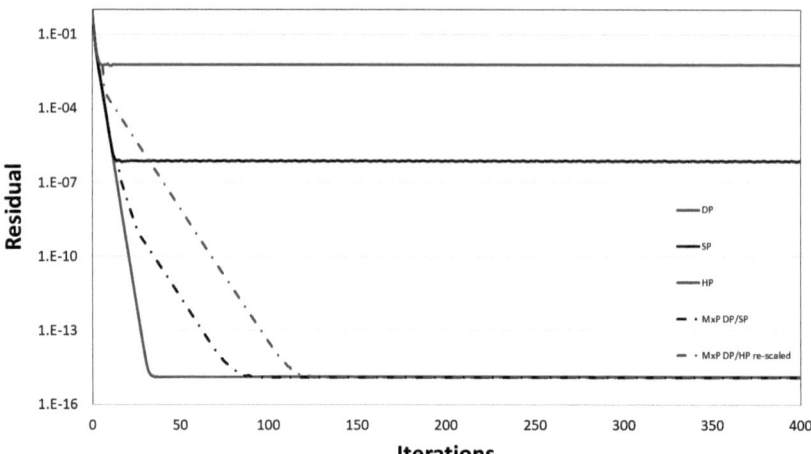

Fig. 2. Defect correction mixed precision residual convergence for the synthetic benchmark, after re-scaling strategy.

With the final solution being:

$$\hat{\hat{u}} = \hat{\hat{u}}' + \hat{\hat{u}}'' \tag{7}$$

By doing so, it is now possible to decouple the effects of the original source term from the defect correction term, removing the problems induced when large differences in order of magnitude is seen between these terms. There is still a second issue that needs to be taken care of: as the algorithm converges, the defect correction term becomes smaller and smaller as it is an indication of the error in the solution introduced by the use of the low precision arithmetic. As this error becomes very small, it becomes impossible to represent it on very low precision device, like our FP16 example. To solve this problem, after linearization and splitting is done, we implemented a re-scaling technique to make sure that all the source terms remain within the acceptable range for the targeted device.

Figure 2 shows the latest results obtained using the combination of all the mentioned improvement to the overall algorithm. For this test, a multi-grid linear iterative solver was implemented. The red line shows the convergence of the multi-grid approach using only FP64 operations. Similarly, the black and blue line show the multi-grid approach when using only FP32 and FP16 operations respectively. The black dotted line shows the convergence of the solution for the mixed FP64/FP32 algorithm, and the blue dotted line shows the convergence of the solution for the mixed FP64/FP16 algorithm. First of all, it can be seen that both simulations resulted in convergence of the solution similar to the pure double precision simulation, which means that the plateau that we had in Sect. 3.3 is now removed. It is important to notice that the x-axis represents the number of work units needed for the residual to drop. This is not the total simulation time. Indeed, in the case of the mixed precision simulation, most of the iterations (between 65 and 80%) are done on the low precision device, which can be several times faster than the high precision device. So, even though the total number of iterations to reach convergence increased, the total simulation time is reduced significantly.

3 Explicit Time Marching, Finite Difference Incompressible Navier-Stokes Solver

To show the capability of the recently developed solver for non-linear PDEs, a couple of 2D Incompressible Navier-Stokes solvers were developed. The first one is an explicit time-marching solver, based on high order finite difference numerical schemes, and with a segregated predictor/corrector approach. This approach mimics the OpenFOAM simpleFOAM solver.

3.1 Formulation

The incompressible Navier-Stokes equations can be written with Einstein notation as followed:

$$\begin{cases} \frac{\partial u_i}{\partial x_i} = 0 \\ \frac{\partial u_i}{\partial t} + u_j \frac{\partial u_i}{\partial x_j} = -\frac{\partial p}{\partial x_i} + \frac{1}{Re} \frac{\partial^2 u_i}{\partial x_j \partial x_j} \end{cases} \quad (8)$$

With the segregated prediction/correction approach, these equations are solved in two stages (simple Euler time integration is used here for simplicity):

1. First, the changes of velocity is predicted due to the convection and diffusion only (no pressure gradient)
$$u_i^* = u_i^n + \Delta t \left(-u_j^n \left(\frac{\partial u_i}{\partial x_j} \right)^n + \frac{1}{Re} \left(\frac{\partial^2 u_i}{\partial x_j \partial x_j} \right)^n \right)$$
2. In a second step, the equation for pressure is solved:
$$\frac{\partial^2 p^{n+1}}{\partial x_i \partial x_i} = \frac{1}{\Delta t} \frac{\partial u_i^*}{\partial x_i}$$
3. Finally, the velocity is corrected as followed:
$$u_i^{n+1} = u_i^* - \Delta t \frac{\partial p^{n+1}}{\partial x_i}$$

In this solver, fourth order energy conservative finite difference schemes are used to discretize the equations, with 4th order Runge-Kutta scheme for the time integration. The mixed precision multi-grid solver was used to solve the elliptic equation for pressure in the second stage.

3.2 Validation

In order to validate the implementation and accuracy of the mixed precision solver as part of the segregated incompressible solver, the case of the 2D double shear layer is considered. This case is great to estimate numerical dissipation coming from either numerical schemes or round-off errors coming from the use of low-precision arithmetic. The initial conditions are:

$$\begin{cases} u(x,y) = \tanh(80 \times (y - 0.25)) & (y <= 0.5) \\ u(x,y) = \tanh(80 \times (0.75 - y)) & (y > 0.5) \\ v(x,y) = 0.05 \times \sin(2\pi(x + 0.25)) \end{cases} \quad (9)$$

The computational domain is a $[0, 1]^2$ square periodic domain and Re=10000. Typically for this case, high numerical round-off errors produce spurious secondary braid vortices which result in an early breakdown of the shear layer. Figure 3a shows a typical example of a "clean" result taken from the literature [12]. In the following results, a 64^2 grid was used. High order finite difference schemes were used to compute all derivatives, and only the pressure solver used mixed precision. The rest of the solver was run using double precision accuracy. By employing high-order finite difference, we ensured that numerical dissipation could only arise from the use of low precision arithmetic, and not from additional numerical errors. Figure 3a shows the results obtained when using pure double precision (FP64). Figure 3b shows the results when using half precision for the pressure Poisson solver (FP16). It can be clearly seen that, when using high precision operations, the shear layer is thin and smooth, but using half precision operations for the pressure, dissipation is added to the solver, resulting in much thicker shear layer, far from the desired accuracy.

Figure 3c shows the results obtain for the simulation with double precision arithmetic for the prediction step, and mixed-precision multi-grid algorithm to solve for the elliptic PDE for the pressure. It can be seen that, using the mixed precision FP64/FP16 algorithm, the overall accuracy of the simulation came back to the accuracy obtained using FP64 only.

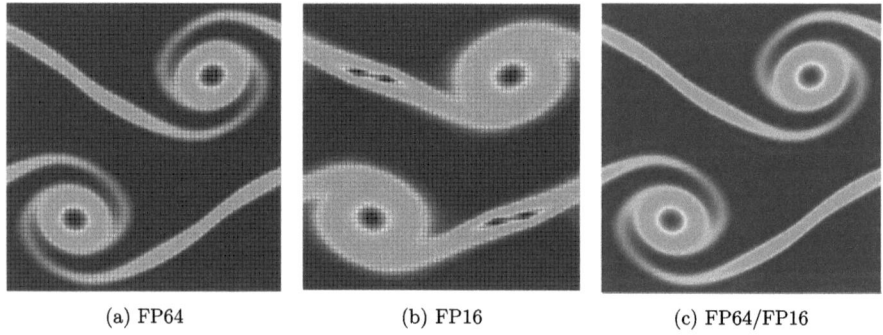

(a) FP64   (b) FP16   (c) FP64/FP16

Fig. 3. 2D double shear layer case at Re = 10000

4 Implicit, Finite Volume, Incompressible Navier-Stokes Solver

To test the multi-grid solver for a full system of equations, a 2D implicit incompressible Navier-Stokes solver was developed, based on the work of Candler et al. [13]. Details are added here for completion.

4.1 Formulation

The fully implicit form of the 2D Navier-Stokes equations can be written as:

$$\frac{U^{n+1} - U^n}{\Delta t} + \frac{\partial F^{n+1}}{\partial x} + \frac{\partial G^{n+1}}{\partial y} = 0 \tag{10}$$

where F and G are the flux vectors in the x and y directions respectively. We can linearize the flux vector using

$$F^{n+1} = F^n + \left(\frac{\partial F}{\partial U}\right)^n (U^{n+1} - U^n) = F^n + A^n \delta U^n \tag{11}$$

We can split the fluxes according to the sign of the eigenvalues of the Jacobians

$$F = A_+ U + A_- U = F_+ + F_- \tag{12}$$

The following upwind finite volume representation can then be obtained:

$$\begin{aligned}\delta U^n_{ij} + \frac{\Delta t}{V_{ij}}((A_{+_{i+1/2}} S_{i+1/2} \delta U_{ij} - A_{+_{i-1/2}} S_{i-1/2} \delta U_{i-1,j}) + \\ (A_{-_{i+1/2}} S_{i+1/2} \delta U_{i+1,j} - A_{-_{i-1/2}} S_{i-1/2} \delta U_{i,j}) + \\ (B_{+_{j+1/2}} S_{j+1/2} \delta U_{i,j+1} - B_{+_{j-1/2}} S_{j-1/2} \delta U_{i,j-1}) + \\ (B_{-_{j+1/2}} S_{j+1/2} \delta U_{i,j+1} - B_{-_{j-1/2}} S_{j-1/2} \delta U_{i,j})) = \Delta t R^n_{ij}\end{aligned} \tag{13}$$

The implicit Jacobians can be approximated as:

$$A_\mp = \frac{1}{2}(A \mp \rho_A I) \tag{14}$$

where ρ_A is the spectral radius of the Jacobian A, given by the magnitude of the largest eigenvalue. We can then rewrite the resulting implicit equation:

$$\begin{aligned}(1 + \Gamma_A I + \Gamma_B I)^n_{ij} \delta U^n_{ij} = \\ \Delta t R^n_{ij} + \frac{\Delta t}{V_{ij}} (A^n_{+_{i-1/2}} S_{i-1/2} \delta U^n_{i-1,j} - A^n_{-_{i+1/2}} S_{i+1/2} \delta U^n_{i+1,j} + \\ B^n_{+_{j-1/2}} S_{j-1/2} \delta U^n_{i,j-1} - B^n_{-_{j+1/2}} S_{j+1/2} \delta U^n_{i,j+1})\end{aligned} \tag{15}$$

where $\Gamma_A = \frac{\Delta t S}{V} \rho_A$. This set of equations use the in-house mixed precision multi-grid solver until convergence is reached

4.2 Validation

To validate the implementation of the implicit solver, we considered the classic 2D lid-driven cavity problem studied here for two different Reynolds numbers: 3200 and 5000. For both cases, the computational domain is a unit square and a 256 × 256 uniformly spaced grid was used. The simulations were run until steady state was reached. In all simulations, the mixed precision FP64/FP32 solver was used, and the solution was compared to the classic numerical solution set of Ghia et al. [14].

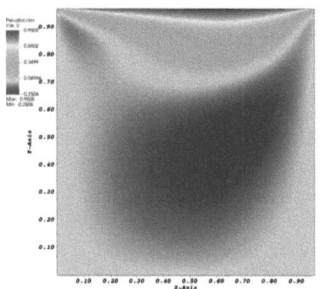 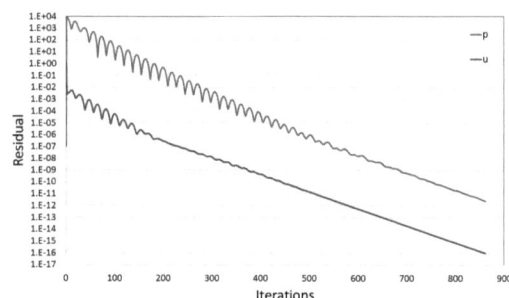

(a) contour of u-velocity at convergence
(b) Convergence history of the pressure (blue) and u-velocity (red)

Fig. 4. 2D lid driven cavity at Re = 3200

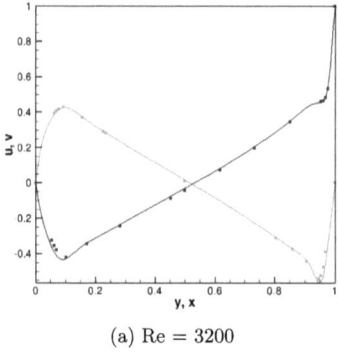 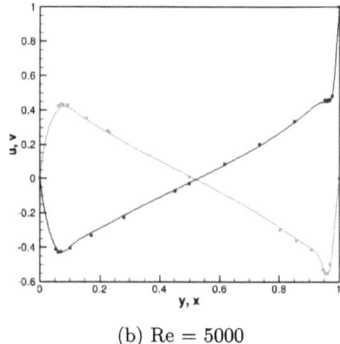

(a) Re = 3200 (b) Re = 5000

Fig. 5. 2D lid driven cavity at Re = 3200 and 5000: u and v velocity profiles compared to data from Ghia et al. [14].

Figure 4 shows on the left the convergence history of both the pressure and the u-component of the velocity using the mixed FP64/FP32 precision algorithm. It can be seen that double precision convergence is obtained with residual dropping near 10^{-12}. On the right, the contour of the u-component of the velocity after convergence of the solution is shown inside the computational domain. In order to fully validate the implementation of the method, as well as the accuracy of the mixed precision algorithm, velocity profiles were extracted for both simulations, and compared to the results from Ghia et al. [14]. The results are shown in Fig. 5a and 5b. In both cases, it can be seen that the results are in perfect agreement with the numerical reference data, showing that the mixed precision algorithm is suited for practical scientific applications.

5 Application of the Developed Solver Within OpenFOAM Using OGL

5.1 Coupling of Defect Correction Approach Within OpenFOAM Using the Ginkgo Framework

In order to test the defect correction approach on more practical applications, the developed algorithm was implemented and coupled to the OpenFOAM solver. OpenFOAM is a free, open source CFD software used widely in industry and academia to solve problems ranging from complex fluid flows, chemically reacting flows, turbulence and heat transfer, or even acoustic problems [16]. To facilitate the coupling of our in-house algorithm to the existing OpenFOAM application, the Ginkgo library [17] is used. Ginkgo is a high-performance linear algebra library for many-core systems, with a focus on solution of sparse linear systems. It offers a set of iterative solvers and preconditioners such as GMRES, AMG, Batched, BiCGSTAB... It has optimized support for OpenMP, CUDA, HIC, and SYCL. Ginkgo was used as a bridge between OpenFOAM and the developed solver thanks to its OGL layer [18] that allows for simple coupling of external libraries with OpenFOAM.

In the following simulations, the SIMPLE (Semi Implicit Method for Pressure Linked Equations) algorithm was targeted. With this approach, velocity components, pressure and turbulent variables are solved sequentially and the solution of the preceding equations is inserted in the subsequent equations. Each set of variables requires the use of linear solvers. Accelerating the linear solvers within Ginkgo will directly impact the overall computational time of the OpenFOAM simulations. For the purpose of this study, the Conjugate Gradient solver was targeted to be accelerated with the mixed precision algorithm.

5.2 Validation: 3D Lid Driven Cavity

To validate the accuracy and efficiency of the approach, the 3D lid-driven cavity case was simulated with OpenFOAM. The computational domain is $[0;1] \times [0;1] \times [0;1]$, with the lid of the cubic cavity moving parallel to the positive x-axis with the steady velocity of 1. The initial conditions is 0 everywhere. Two different Reynolds numbers were simulated: 100 and 400 based on the characteristic length of the cavity, lid velocity and kinematic viscosity. All the simulations were run on a 150^3 uniform grid to machine precision convergence, and steady state results are compared to the results of Wong et al. [15].

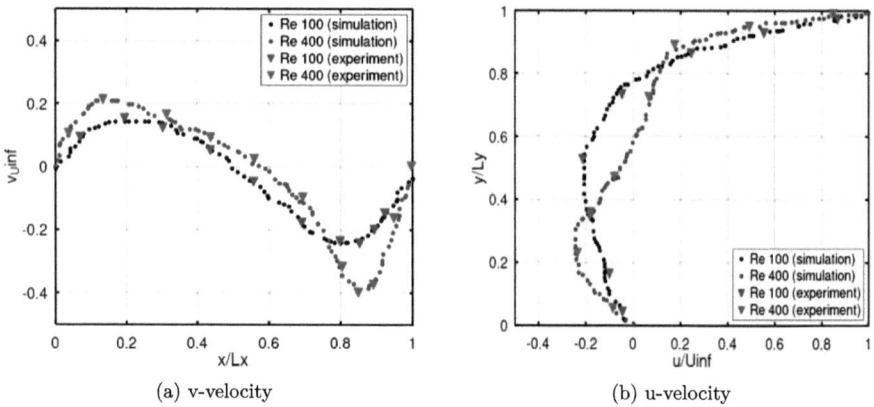

(a) v-velocity

(b) u-velocity

Fig. 6. 3D lid driven cavity at Re = 100 and 400: u and v velocity profiles compared to data from Wong et al. [15].

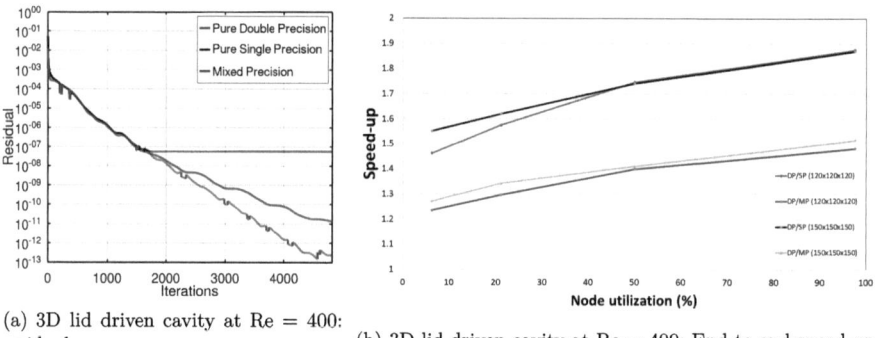

(a) 3D lid driven cavity at Re = 400: residual convergence

(b) 3D lid driven cavity at Re = 400: End-to-end speed-up

Fig. 7. 3D lid driven cavity at Re = 400: Accuracy and Efficiency of the mixed-precision algorithm within OpenFOAM.

Figure 6 shows the steady-state results obtained for both Reynolds numbers, compared to the reference results from Wong et al. [15]. It can be seen that, at convergence, the results are in very good agreement with the reference data. This showed the capability of the method to recover high accuracy for a 3D practical applications. At both Reynolds numbers, the solver is capable of capturing the differences in the mean flow-velocity profiles, especially as we get closer to the top moving lid. Figure 7 shows the convergence history and the solver efficiency for the LDC case at Reynolds number 400. Figure 7a shows the convergence history of simpleFOAM in the case of pure single precision computation (black line), pure double precision computation (red line) and mixed-precision implementation (blue line). It can be seen that, even though the mixed-precision does not fully converge to the same double-precision error, it provides 4 order of magnitude convergence when compared to the single-precision solver. It was important to also look at the overall efficiency gain obtained by using the mixed-precision approach. Figure 7b shows the acceleration obtained using pure single-precision computation and mixed-precision computation when compared to the end-to-end simulation time in double-precision. It can be seen the mixed-precision in-house solver allows for up to 1.5x speed-up of the openFoam application. This represents about 80% of the theoretical maximum acceleration that is obtained when running the code fully in low-precision, without the loss of the accuracy that would be obtained in high-precision.

5.3 Validation: DrivAer Test Case

The final test case to study accuracy and efficiency of the solver is the DrivAer validation case [20–22]. This is an automotive case that has extensive experimental data and that is part of the Automotive CFD Prediction Workshop [19]. The simulation is steady, incompressible, and fully turbulent with a $k-\omega-SST$ model with wall functions. The overall Reynolds number is $Re = 8.7 \times 10^6$ and 50 million cells were used. The case was simulated using a single Kunpeng 920 node, using 128 cores.

Figure 8 shows the results obtained using OpenFOAM using double precision computation, and mixed double-single precision computation. Figure 8a shows the residual convergence, as well as the drag coefficient convergence for a pure double precision simulation, pure single precision simulation and for the mixed double-single precision simulation. It can be seen that there is a perfect agreement between the double and the mixed precision simulations for the global convergence (blue and red lines). The green line shows the local convergence of the Conjugate Gradient solver in single precision, and as expected a plateau is reached near 10^{-8}. But the local convergence of both the FP64 and FP64/FP32 solvers are identical (black and yellow lines). Similarly, it can be seen that the convergence of the drag coefficient is very similar between double and mixed precision simulations, with an initial transient behavior before reaching a converged value near 0.28, which is in agreement with [20–22].

Figure 8b shows the overall acceleration obtained between the double precision simulation and the mixed precision simulation. To obtain convergence of the drag coefficient, it took 20.1 hours to run the 5000 iterations in double precision, while it took 14.4 hours to run the same amount of iterations with the mixed precision version of the solver. This represents an overall 1.4× speed-up. These results are very promising, showing the potential to obtain acceleration without losing overall accuracy of the numerical predictions.

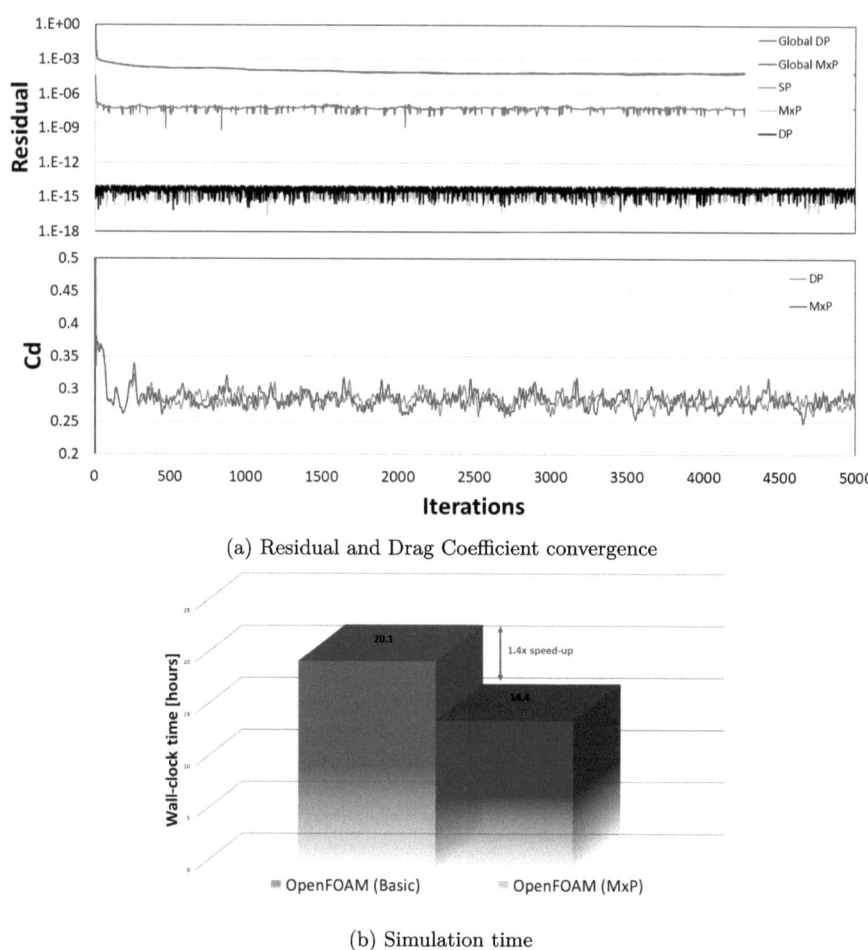

Fig. 8. 3D DrivAer: Accuracy and Efficiency of the mixed-precision algorithm within OpenFOAM.

6 Conclusion

In this study, a novel defect correction approach was presented, to allow for mixed-precision computation in the context of iterative solvers. The novelty of the approach is that it applies to both linear and non linear set of equations. The method was first tested for an analytical non linear problem, allowing to show the convergence of the overall approach when using FP64/FP32 and FP64/FP16 combinations in an in-house multi-grid solver. The approach was then extended and applied to the OpenFOAM CFD solver, using the OGL layer provided by the Ginkgo library to couple both solvers. It was tested for the 3D lid-driven cavity test case at two Reynolds numbers, and showed the approach allowed to recover an accuracy close to the one that would be obtained in high precision, while accelerating the application up to 1.5X. It was also tested for the DrivAer test case, a turbulent automotive test case for which 1.4X speed-up were obtained thanks to the mixed precision algorithm, while predicting a drag coefficient similar to the double precision simulation.

References

1. Stuben, K.: A review of algebraic multi-grid. J. Comput. Appl. Math. **128**, 281–309 (2001)
2. Mccormick, S., Benzaken, J., Tamstorf, R.: Algebraic error analysis for mixed precision multi-grid solvers. SCIAM J. Sci. Comput. **43**, S392–S419 (2021)
3. Emmans, M., Meer, A.: mixed-precision AMG as linear equation solver for definite systems. Procedia Comput. Sci. **1**, 175–183 (2012)
4. Tamstorf, R., Benzaken, J., Mccormick, S.: Discretization error accurate mixed precision multi-grid solvers. SCIAM J. Sci. Comput. **22**, S4420–S447 (2008)
5. Glimberg, S.L., Engsig-Karup, A.P., Madsen, M.G.: A fast GPU-accelerated mixed-precision strategy for fully nonlinear water wave computations. In: ENUMATH (2011)
6. Higham, N., Mary, T.: Mixed precision algorithms in numerical linear algebra. In: MIMS (2021)
7. Brune, P., Knepley, M., Smith, B., Tu, X.: Composing scalable nonlinear algebraic solver. arXiv arXiv:1607.04254 (2016)
8. Grant, Z.: Perturbed Runge-Kutta methods for mixed precision applications. J. Sci. Comput. **92**, 6 (2022)
9. Hida, Y., Li, X., Bailey, D.: Quad-double arithmetic: algorithms, implementation and application. Technical Report LBNL-46996 (2000)
10. Wasserman, M., Mor-Yossef, Y., Yavneh, I., Greenberg, B.: A robust implicit multi-grid method for RANS equations with two-equation turbulence models. J. Comput. Phys. **229**, 5820–5842 (2010)
11. Wasserman, M., Mor-Yossef, Y., Greenberg, B.: A positivity preserving, implicit defect-correction multi-grid method for turbulent combustion. J. Comput. Phys. **316**, 303–337 (2016)
12. Delorme, Y., Puri, K., Nordstrom, J., Linders, V.: A simple and efficient incompressible Navier-Stokes solver for unsteady complex geometry flows on truncated domains. Comput. Fluids **150**, 84–94 (2017)
13. Wright, M., Candler, G., Prampolini, M.: Data parallel lower-upper relaxation method for the Navier-Stokes equations. AIAA J. **34**, 1371–1377 (1997)
14. Ghia, U., Ghia, K., Shin, C.: High Reynolds solutions for incompressible flow using Navier-Stokes equations and a multi-grid method. J. Comput. Phys. **48**, 387–411 (1982)
15. Wong, K.L., Baker, A.J.: A 3D incompressible Navier-Stokes velocity-vorticity weak form finite element algorithm. Int. J. Numer. Meth. Fluids **38**(9), 9–23 (2002)
16. https://develop.openfoam.com/Development/openfoam
17. https://github.com/ginkgo-project
18. https://github.com/hpsim/OGL

19. http://www.wolfdynamics.com/tutorials.html?id=152
20. https://www.epc.ed.tum.de/en/aer/research-groups/automotive/drivaer/
21. Yazdani, R.: Steady and unsteady numerical analysis of the DrivAer model. Master Thesis, Chalmers University of Technology (2015)
22. Wieser, D., Schmidt, H.J., Mueller, S., Strangfeld, C., Nayeri, C., Paschereit, C.: Experimental comparison of the aerodynamic behavior of fastback and notchback DrivAer models. SAE Int. J. Passeng. Cars Mech. Syst. **7**, 682–91 (2014)

Third Workshop on Communication, I/O, and Storage at Scale on Next-Generation Platforms - Scalable Infrastructures (ISC 2024 IXPUG)

Preface to the Third Workshop on Communication, I/O, and Storage at Scale on Next-Generation Platforms - Scalable Infrastructures (ISC 2024 IXPUG)

1 Objectives

Next-generation HPC platforms must deal with increasing heterogeneity in their subsystems, including the following: multiple, internal, high-speed fabrics for inter-node communication; storage systems integrated with programmable data processing units (DPUs) or infrastructure processing units (IPUs) to support software-defined networks; traditional storage infrastructures with global, parallel, POSIX-based filesystems complemented by scalable object stores; and heterogeneous compute nodes configured with a diverse spectrum of CPUs and accelerators (e.g., GPU, FPGA, or AI processors) having complex intra-node communication. To assist the community in planning for and transitioning to such platforms, this workshop pursues the following objectives: (1) develop and provide a holistic overview of next-generation platforms with an emphasis on communication, I/O, and storage at scale, (2) showcase application-driven performance analysis with various HPC fabrics, (3) present early experiences with emerging storage concepts such as object stores using next-generation HPC fabrics, (4) share experience with performance tuning on heterogeneous platforms from multiple vendors, and (5) provide a forum for sharing best practices for performance tuning of communication, I/O, and storage to improve application performance at scale.

2 Workshop Organization

The organization of this workshop was driven by the Intel eXtreme Performance Users Group (IXPUG) with additional support provided by the leaders of the oneAPI Users Group. It was promoted via its own marketing channels: the IXPUG website (www.ixpug.org), IXPUG newsletters, IXPUG member mailing lists, and across IXPUG's social media channels like LinkedIn and Twitter. In addition to the IXPUG channels, the IXPUG members (such as Intel and several high-impact international research centers) announced the event through their own channels. The Program Committee invited two keynote speakers and encouraged participation by several internationally recognized research groups. Two papers were submitted, which were reviewed using a single-blind review process and accepted by the Program Committee.

2.1 Organizers

Amit Ruhela	Texas Advanced Computing Center, USA
David Martin	Argonne National Laboratory, USA
Hatem Ltaief	King Abdullah University of Science & Technology, Saudi Arabia

2.2 Program Committee

Aksel Alpay	Heidelberg University, Germany
Glenn Brook	Cornelis Networks, USA
Steffen Christgau	Zuse Institute Berlin, Germany
Toshihiro Hanawa	University of Tokyo, Japan
Clayton Hughes	Sandia National Laboratories, USA
Nalini Kumar	Intel Corporation, USA
James Lin	Shanghai Jiao Tong University, China
Hatem Ltaief	King Abdullah University of Science & Technology, Saudi Arabia
David Martin	Argonne National Laboratory, USA
Christopher Mauney	Los Alamos National Laboratory, USA
Amit Ruhela	Texas Advanced Computing Center, USA

3 Outcomes

The workshop provided a well-attended forum for presenting and discussing next-generation architectures and software approaches to leverage them properly. The keynote presentations focused on optimizing applications on the Aurora supercomputer by efficiently utilizing DAOS storage and aspects of forecasting application performance at different scales and objectives. The keynotes were complemented by invited talks on performance evaluation and optimization of seismic imaging applications on HBM-Enabled CPUs, leveraging SYCL to develop performance-portable libraries targeting different hardware targets, and experiences with Intel GPU Max for Deep Learning at Scale. The two accepted publications focused on the performance aspects of running DAOS over those high-performance fabrics and the performance of the LLVM-based Intel Fortran Compiler (ifx) on distinct Intel architectures. Collectively, the workshop presentations did an excellent job of highlighting emerging architectures for various sub-systems of next-generation computing platforms, along with strategies and approaches to harness their performance potential. The workshop presentations are available on the IXPUG website (https://www.ixpug.org/events/isc24-ixpug-workshop).

Investigating the Performance of LLVM-Based Intel Fortran Compiler (ifx)

Dhani Ruhela[✉]

Westwood High School, Austin, TX, USA
dhaniruhela@gmail.com

Abstract. LLVM is a free, open-source compiler framework for programmatically generating machine-native code. Developers nowadays are increasingly embracing LLVM to develop new languages or modify existing ones. LLVM-based compilers enable shorter build of compilers that are portable across various platforms, easy to maintain, and extensively optimized for the target systems. Intel oneAPI moved to an LLVM infrastructure with C (icx) and C++ (icpx) compilers in the 2021.3 release and a Fortran compiler (ifx) in the 2023.0 release. According to Intel, the LLVM-based compilers are packed with advanced language features and deliver the absolute best performance for various applications on Intel architectures. The LLVM-based Intel compilers have been extensively tuned for the 4th Gen Intel Xeon Scalable processors (code-named Sapphire Rapids) and Intel Xeon CPU Max Series (code-named Sapphire Rapids HBM) and the Intel Data Center GPU Max Series (code-named Ponte Vecchio). In this work, I aim to explore the features and performance of LLVM-based compilers compared with legacy compilers on three machine architectures, i.e. Sapphire Rapids with DDR5, Sapphire Rapids with HBM, and Intel Cascade Lake. To my best belief, this is the first extensive study that uncovers the potential of LLVM-based Intel compilers with eight scientific representative codes and demonstrates up to 17% performance improvements with Inter Fortran compiler (ifx) on Intel architectures.

Keywords: HPC · LLVM · Fortran · Intel Sapphire Rapids · HBM

1 Introduction

Over the last two decades, "Low-Level Virtual Machine" (LLVM) [1] compilers have gained massive popularity in software development. LLVM is an open-source compiler infrastructure project that started in 2000 as a research project at the University of Illinois to provide a set of production-quality modular and reusable libraries compatible with existing tools typically used on Unix systems. Today, LLVM has become an umbrella project consisting of several subprojects (LLVM Core, Clang, LLDB, libc++, compiler-rt, MLIR, OpenMP, poly, libclc, klee, LLD, BOLT), many of which are being used in production by a wide variety of commercial and open-source projects as well as in academic research.

Every developer comes across compilers in day-to-day program development. Simply put, a compiler is a software library that converts a high-level language code into a machine executable format. However, during this conversion, a code undergoes a series of complex transformations and is optimized to run on target systems. At the start of the LLVM project, existing open-source language implementations (GCC, Perl, Python, Ruby and Java) were designed as special-purpose tools, which were challenging to learn, hard to change, not reusable for other applications, and had monolithic executables that keep getting slower with every release. They did not have support for cross-file optimization and JIT codegen. LLVM addresses these issues by creating a set of modular and reusable compiler and toolchain technologies that expose well-defined interfaces that programmers can use to develop new compilers and language-oriented software and modify existing ones.

Modern scientific, cloud, and artificial intelligence applications are becoming incredibly complex and run on multiple processing cores for several hours or days. Compilers play a pivotal role in fulfilling the never-ending performance need by leveraging the full capabilities of modern multi-core processing and accelerator architectures to build and optimize the application binaries.

Intel oneAPI has moved to an LLVM infrastructure with the release of C (icx) and C++ (icpx) compilers in 2021.3 and a Fortran compiler (ifx) in 2023.0. According to Intel, the newer compilers provide advanced language features and deliver the absolute best performance for various applications on Intel architectures. These compilers have been extensively tuned for 4th Gen Intel Xeon Scalable processors (Sapphire Rapids), Intel Xeon CPU Max Series (Sapphire Rapids HBM), and the Intel Data Center GPU Max Series (Ponte Vecchio).

In this work, I aim to comprehensively investigate the features and performance of the recently released Fortran compiler against Intel legacy compilers on Sapphire Rapids with DDR5, Sapphire Rapids with HBM, and Intel Cascade Lake system. To my knowledge, this is the first large study investigating the performance of Intel LLVM-based Fortran compilers on various representative scientific codes.

1.1 Contributions

The main contributions of this paper are:

- present the key features of the Intel LLVM-based Fortran compiler.
- establish the performance of legacy and LLVM-based Fortran compiler on three architectures and compare it with State-of-the-art GNU Fortran compiler (gfortran).
- demonstrate up to 17% improvement in running time with eight popular SPEC OpenMP 2012 Fortran applications.
- present up to 60% improvement in running time of the benchmarks on architectures HBM memory compared to DDR5 memory.

– present potential of Intel compilers outperforming GNU Fortran compiler by up to seven times on Sapphire Rapids and four times on Cascade Lake architecture. The trend is more apparent in newer than previous-generation Intel architectures, indicating the necessity for further tuning the GNU Fortran compiler.

The rest of the paper is organized as follows: Sect. 2 explains Open MP, SPEC OMP 2012 benchmarks and the key features of the Intel Fortran compiler. Section 3.1 presents the experimental setup and software configuration details. Section 4 provides the performance evaluations with eight Spec OpenMP 2012 Fortran codes on three machine architectures. Finally, the conclusions are presented in Sect. 6.

2 Background

This section presents information about the Open MP programming model used in this study, SPEC OMP 2012 benchmarks, and a brief introduction to recently released Intel Fortran compilers.

2.1 Open MP

OpenMP is a portable and scalable model for developing parallel applications in C, C++, and Fortran languages that runs effectively on platforms ranging from embedded systems and accelerator devices to multicore systems and shared-memory systems. OpenMP implements parallelization using a multithreading approach in which a primary thread forks a defined number of sub-threads that run on cores/cpu threads, and the operating system schedules the tasks on sub-threads. The threads then run concurrently to complete the assigned tasks and join with the main threads at some point in the execution time before the application finishes.

OpenMP has been implemented in commercial compilers like Visual C++, Intel Parallel Studio, Oracle Solaris Studio, the Portland Group (now merged with NVIDIA), and GNU. This paper focuses on GNU [2] and Intel compilers [3].

2.2 SPEC OMP 2012 Benchmarks

The SPEC OMP 2012 suite is developed by the Standard Performance Evaluation Corporation (SPEC) [4] for measuring performance using applications based on the OpenMP 3.1 standard for shared-memory parallel processing. The benchmark includes 14 scientific and engineering application codes, covering domains from computational fluid dynamics (CFD) to molecular modelling to image manipulation. Eight out of fourteen benchmarks are written in Fortran language and are analyzed in this study. These benchmarks are "**Physics: Molecular Dynamics**"(350.md [5,6]), "**Physics: Computational Fluid Dynamics (CFD)**" (351.bwaves [7], 357.bt331 [8], 370.mgrid331 [9], 371.applu331 [9]), "**Lattic Boltzmann**"(360.ilbdc [10–12]), "**Mechanical Response Simulation**"(362.fma3d [13]), and "**Weather Prediction**"(363.swim [14,15]).

2.3 Intel LLVM-Based Fortran Compiler

Intel publicly released an LLVM-based Fortran compiler, 'ifx', in the OneAPI 2023.0 software suite. Ifx is based on the classic Intel Fortran compiler (ifort) frontend and runtime libraries but uses LLVM backend compiler technology. Ifx fully implements FORTRAN 77, Fortran 90/95, Fortran 2003, Fortran 2008 and Fortran 2018 language standards and most of OpenMP 4.5 and OpenMP 5.0/5.1 directives and offloading features. The previous release of the Intel Fortran compiler (ifort) has been deprecated in 2023 and will be "discontinued" in late 2024 [16].

Ifx is binary (.o/.obj) and module file (.mod) compatible with ifort. Binaries and libraries generated with ifort can be linked with binaries and libraries built with ifx, and .mod files generated with one compiler can be used by the other (64-bit targets only). Both compilers use the same runtime libraries, but Intel states that ifx may not match the performance of ifort compiled applications.

Users can leverage ifx compiler features to offload onto Intel GPUs via OpenMP TARGET directives. Ifx can only create 64-bit binaries for Windows or Linux and does not support IA-32. To leverage OpenMP TARGET directives, users must specify flag '-fiopenmp' and '-qopenmp'. The flag '-fopenmp' is deprecated and subject to removal in future releases.

As per Intel [17], ifx enables faster compilation times of applications and is optimized for the latest Intel processors. Ifx has the ability to accelerate application code with Intel GPUs.

3 Results

This section describes the experimental setup used in this paper and presents the performance results of experiments. The experiments are performed on three Intel architectures to establish the generality of performance analysis.

3.1 Experimental Setup

Cluster Configurations:

Intel Cascade Lake [18]: The dual-socket node contains Intel Xeon Platinum 8280 processors having 28 cores per socket and cores operate at 2.70 GHz base frequency and contains 192GB of DDR4 memory. The operating system is CentOS Linux release 7.8.2003 (kernel version Linux 3.10.0-1127.19.1.el7.x86_64).

Intel Saphire Rapids (SPR-D): The dual-socket SPR-D node contains a 4th-generation Intel Xeon Scalable 9480 processor having 56 cores where cores operate at a 1.9 GHz base frequency. Each core supports two hardware threads, resulting in 224 CPU threads per node. The node has 251 GB of DDR5 memory.

The operating system is Rocky Linux 8.6 with Kernel version as Linux 4.18.0-372.26.1.el8_6.x86_64.

Intel Sapphire Rapids with HBM (SPR-H): The SPR-H node is similar in architecture to the SPR-D node except that it has 125 GB of HBM memory and does not contain optional DDR5 memory.

Software Configurations: All test runs of this study are executed on one node of each machine architecture with SPEC OMP 2012 benchmarks. Legacy Intel Fortran compiler from oneAPI 2023.0 software suite is compared with new Intel Fortran compiler from oneAPI 2024.0 software suite and also contrasted in performance with GNU Gfortran 12.2 compiler.

The following configurations are set in the configuration files of the compilers.

ifort Compiler Settings
OPTIMIZE = -O3 -qopenmp -ipo1 -xCORE-AVX512 -qopt-zmm-usage=high -shared-intel

ifx Compiler Settings
OPTIMIZE = -O3 -qopenmp -ipo1 -xCORE-AVX512 -mprefer-vector-width=512 -shared-intel -axSAPPHIRERAPIDS

gfortran Compiler Settings
OPTIMIZE = -Ofast -fopenmp -mfpmath=sse -funroll-loops -march=native -mtune=native

Global Settings in All Three Compilers
FOPTIMIZE = -align array64byte
ENV_KMP_AFFINITY = compact,0
ENV_KMP_LIBRARY = turnaround
ENV_OMP_SCHEDULE = static
ENV_KMP_BLOCKTIME = infinite
ENV_KMP_STACKSIZE = 128M
ENV_OMP_DYNAMIC = FALSE
ENV_OMP_NESTED = FALSE

4 Performance Evaluation

A series of experiments are thoughtfully conducted to answer following questions.

1. Do the performance of the binaries generated by the different compilers scale with OMP threads?

2. How do Intel Fortran compilers perform with SPEC OMP benchmarks, and how do their performance compare with GNU Fortran compiler?
3. How does each compiler perform at nodes with HBM memory?

Goal 1: Performance of Intel Fortran Compilers with OMP Threads

Each Fortran SPEC OMP benchmark is run at OMP threads ranging between 28 and 224 threads. Each test is repeated three times, and a median value is reported in these results.

Figure 1 shows the performance of ifort and ifx compilers on a SPR-D node. It is observed that:

- Most of the SPEC OMP 2012 benchmarks run faster with increased OMP threads. The improvements in each benchmark's running time scales proportionally with increasing threads.
- In exceptions, the benchmark "**Mechanical Response Simulation (362.FMA-3D)**" takes more time at 224 threads compared to 112 threads. This behaviour might be the result of increased context switches at higher application threads. I plan to investigate this behavior by leveraging performance analysis tools and looking at latency and bandwidth characteristics and verifying the placement of application threads on CPU threads.
- The "**weather prediction benchmark 363.Swim**" and Computational Fluid Dynamics Code "**370.MGRID331**" shows no change in running time at 112 hardware threads compared with 56 hardware threads. The trend persists for both ifx and ifort compilers.

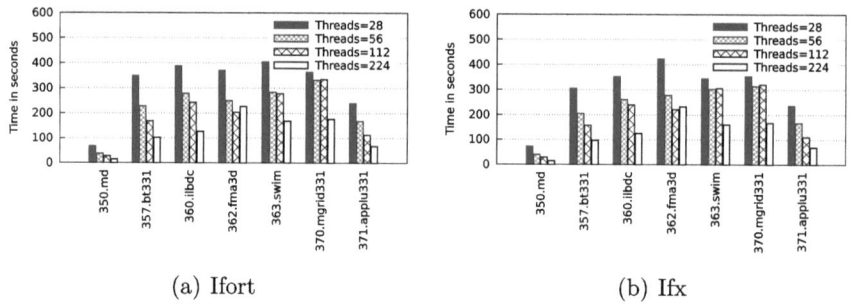

(a) Ifort   (b) Ifx

Fig. 1. Performance of Intel Fortran compilers at increasing hardware threads

Goal 2: Performance of Ifx, Ifort, and GFortran Compilers

In the next set of experiments, the performance of ifort, ifx, and gfortran compilers are compared at Sapphire Rapids and Cascade Lake nodes while fixing the OMP threads count to 224 and 56 respectively.

Figure 2 indicates the following observations.

1. Sapphire Rapids with DDR5 (224 threads):

    (a) Ifx shows up to 13% improved running time over ifort. The noteworthy performance gain was observed in "**Mechanical Response Simulation (FMA-3D)**" benchmark which is 13% "**Physics: Computational Fluid Dynamics (CFD) (bt331)**" benchmark which is 8% and "**Computational Fluid Dynamics Code MGRID: mgrid331**" benchmark which is 5%.
    (b) The benchmark "**Physics: Molecular Dynamics: 350.md** runs 7.3 times slower with Gfortran than ifort. For all other benchmarks, except **362.fma3d**, Gfortran shows up to 30% increased running time.

2. Sapphire Rapids with HBM (224 threads):
    (a) Ifx delivers up to 17% improved performance than ifort. Substantial performance gains were observed in **363.swim** (17%), **357.bt331** (13%), **360.ilbdc** (12%), and **351.waves** (7%) benchmarks.
    (b) The benchmarks **350.md, 362.fma3d, 371.applu331** when compiled with ifx compiler run 3% slower than ifort compiler. This behaviour is likely due to the higher memory latency of the SPR-H node (130ns) compared to the SPR-D node (110 ns).
    (c) The benchmark "**Physics: Molecular Dynamics: 350.md** run 7.6 times slower with GNU Fortran in comparison to ifort. For all other benchmarks except 362.fma3d, gfortran results in up to 1.5 times higher running time.

3. Intel Cascade Lake (56 threads):
    (a) The performance trend on Intel Cade Lake architecture stands contrary to the Sapphire Rapids architecture. Since the hardware threads were disabled on Intel Cascade Lake nodes, this experiment was conducted at 56 OMP threads which is equal to maximum available cores on this node. Figure 2c indicates that "**Lattic Boltzmann 360.ilbdc** runs 95% slower when compiled with ifx than ifort compiler. Similarly, **350.md** code shows 21%, **362.fma3d** shows 9%, and **363.swim** shows 8% running time overheads by ifx compared to ifort. The only benchmark that shows improved performance (9%) for the ifx compiler was "**Physics: Computational Fluid Dynamics (CFD) 371.applu331**. These observations indicate that ifort compiler is extensively optimized for the Intel Cascade Lake system in a series of software releases. However, ifx is relatively new and displays excellent performance for the new Sapphire Rapids architectures, but demands the through tunings/patches for the previous-generation Intel CPU architectures.
    (b) Gfortran performs much more satisfactorily on Cascade Lake architecture than Sapphire Rapids. Gfortran delivered 3.8 times reduced performance overheads with the "**Physics: Molecular Dynamics: 350.md** benchmark compared to Intel Sapphire Rapids. The overheads of GFortran was decreased to less than 17% for **357.bt331, 360.ilbdc, 351.bwaves**,

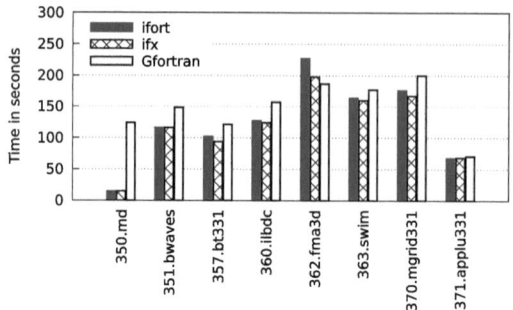

(a) Sapphire Rapids with DDR5

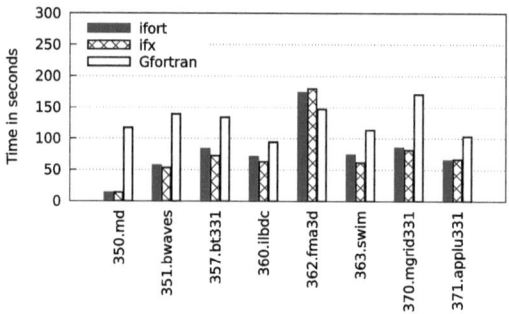

(b) Sapphire Rapids with HBM

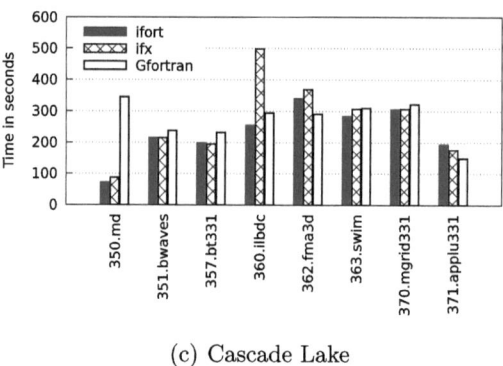

(c) Cascade Lake

Fig. 2. Performance of Ifort, Ifx, and Gfortran at 224 hardware threads

363.swim, and **370.mgrid331** benchmarks. Further surprisingly, Gfortran outperforms Intel compilers for **371.applu331** code by 23% and **362.fma3d** code by 14%.

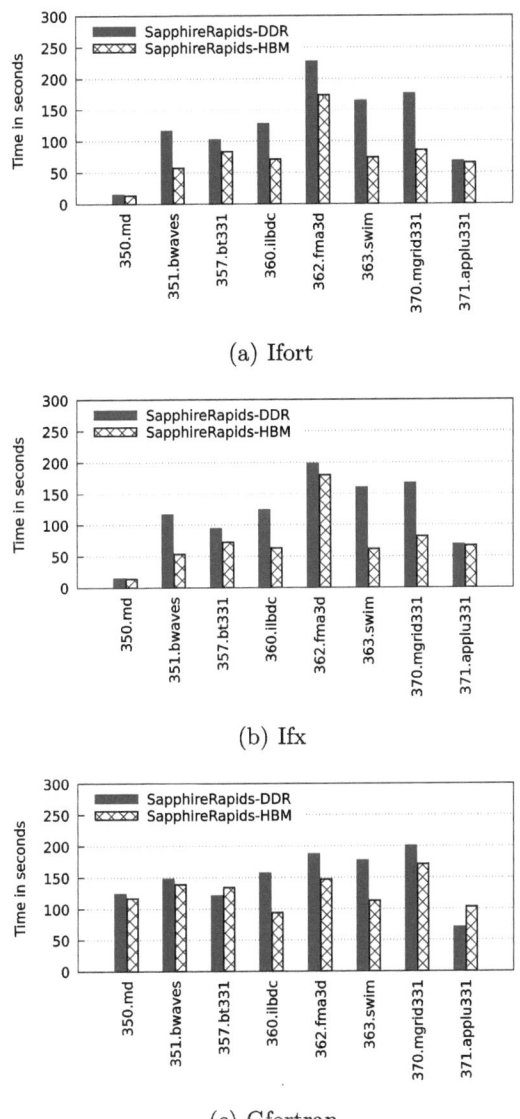

Fig. 3. Compilers performance across Sapphire Rapid Variants

Goal 3: Performance of ifx and ifort Compilers on Sapphire Rapids Architectures

These experiments are corollary of previous experiments and indicate the benefits of HBM memory at Intel Sapphire Rapids node. Figure 3) indicates that SPEC OMP benchmarks perform up to 60% better at SPR-H node than SPR-D node.

Previous research by John McCalpin [19] exhibited that the Sapphire Rapid node with HBM memory possess three times higher memory bandwidth than DDR5 memory. Therefore, these bandwidth sensitive benchmarks run faster due to additional data accessible to their processor in a given time unit. The performance gain is more significant for Intel compilers than GNU Fortran compilers.

5 Discussion

The experiments with eight representative scientific application codes in the SPEC OMP 2012 suite indicated that LLVM compilers could potentially speed up application performance. The performance gain differs with application characteristics and relies upon hardware capabilities, like processor and memory types. Though ifx showed up to 17% improved performance over ifort at Sapphire Rapids architecture, ifx do incurs noticeable performance overheads on prior generation processor architectures, e.g. Intel Cascade Lake. The current Fortran compiler, ifx, must be thoroughly investigated and tuned for the State-of-the-art Intel architectures. The experiments in this work demonstrate that GFortran is underperforming up to seven times that of Intel Fortran compilers. I plan to investigate this further uncovering the cause of such extensive degradation.

6 Conclusion

The quest for performance will always persist for modern scientific and machine-learning applications. Developers leverage efficient, reusable, and modular toolkits, e.g. LLVM, to develop new compilers that not only build and execute applications faster but are also portable to various target architectures and easy to maintain for several years. This research investigated the performance of the Intel LLVM-based Fortran compiler (ifx) compared to the Intel legacy compiler (ifort) on three machine architectures. To my best belief, this is the first more extensive study with eight scientific applications that uncover the potential of LLVM-based Intel Compiler. This work demonstrates up to 17% performance improvements for SPEC OMP 2012 scientific codes. I plan to extend this research to comprehend the performance difference on other state-of-the-art architectures and investigate the performance of the GPU offload feature of the ifx compiler on Ponte Vecchio.

Acknowledgment. I would like to thanks Texas Advanced Computing Center and its researchers for providing valuable feedback, and resources to run various experiments on the HPC systems.

References

1. Lattner, C., Adve, V.: LLVM: a compilation framework for lifelong program analysis & transformation. In: CGO '04: Proceedings of the International Symposium on Code Generation and Optimization: Feedback-Directed and Runtime Optimization, p. 75. IEEE Computer Society, USA (2004)
2. Gnu gfortran. https://gcc.gnu.org/wiki/GFortran
3. Intel oneapi. https://www.intel.com/content/www/us/en/developer/tools/oneapi/overview.html
4. SPEC OMP 2012 (2019). https://www.spec.org/omp2012/Docs/index.html
5. Caballero, O.L., Horowitz, C.J., Berry, D.K.: Neutrino scattering in heterogeneous supernova plasmas. Phys. Rev. C **74**, 065801 (2006). https://doi.org/10.1103/PhysRevC.74.065801
6. Horowitz, C.J., Berry, D.K., Brown, E.F.: Phase separation in the crust of accreting neutron stars. Phys. Rev. E **75**, 066101 (2007). https://doi.org/10.1103/PhysRevE.75.066101
7. Kremenetsky, M., Raefsky, A., Reinhardt, S.: Poor scalability of parallel shared memory model: myth or reality? In: Sloot, P.M.A., Abramson, D., Bogdanov, A.V., Gorbachev, Y.E., Dongarra, J.J., Zomaya, A.Y. (eds.) ICCS 2003. LNCS, vol. 2660, pp. 657–666. Springer, Heidelberg (2003). https://doi.org/10.1007/3-540-44864-0_68
8. Jin, H., Frumkin, M.A., Yan, J.C.: The OpenMP implementation of NAS parallel benchmarks and its performance (2013). https://api.semanticscholar.org/CorpusID:15837754
9. NAS Parallel Benchmarks. https://www.nas.nasa.gov/software/npb.html
10. Wellein, G., Zeiser, T., Hager, G., Donath, S.: On the single processor performance of simple lattice Boltzmann kernels. Comput. Fluids **35**(8), 910–919 (2006)
11. Axner, L., Bernsdorf, J., Zeiser, T., Lammers, P., Linxweiler, J., Hoekstra, A.: Performance evaluation of a parallel sparse lattice Boltzmann solver. J. Comput. Phys. **227**(10), 4895–4911 (2008). https://www.sciencedirect.com/science/article/pii/S002199910800051X
12. Zeiser, T., Hager, G., Wellein, G.: Benchmark analysis and application results for lattice Boltzmann simulations on NEC SX vector and intel Nehalem systems. Parallel Process. Lett. **19**(04), 491–511 (2009)
13. Key, S.W., Hoff, C.C.: An improved constant membrane and bending stress shell element for explicit transient dynamics. Comput. Methods Appl. Mech. Eng. **124**(1), 33–47 (1995). https://www.sciencedirect.com/science/article/pii/004578259500785Y
14. Sadourny, R.: The dynamics of finite-difference models of the shallow-water equations. J. Atmos. Sci. **32**(4), 680 – 689 (1975). https://journals.ametsoc.org/view/journals/atsc/32/4/1520-0469_1975_032_0680_tdofdm_2_0_co_2.xml
15. Hoffmann, G.R., Swarztrauber, P.N., Sweet, R.A.: Aspects of using multiprocessors for meteorological modelling. In: Hoffmann, G.R., Snelling, D.F. (eds.) Multiprocessing in Meteorological Models, pp. 125–196. Springer, Heidelberg (1988)
16. ifort deprecation notice. https://community.intel.com/t5/Blogs/Tech-Innovation/Tools/Deprecation-of-The-Intel-Fortran-Compiler-Classic-ifort/post/1541699
17. Ron Green (2022). https://community.intel.com/t5/Blogs/Tech-Innovation/Tools/The-Next-Chapter-for-the-Intel-Fortran-Compiler/post/1439297. Accessed 09 Nov 2024

18. Stanzione, D., West, J., Evans, R.T., Minyard, T., Ghattas, O., Panda, D.K.: Frontera: the evolution of leadership computing at the national science foundation. In: PEARC '20: Practice and Experience in Advanced Research Computing, pp. 106–111. Association for Computing Machinery, New York, NY, USA (2020). https://doi.org/10.1145/3311790.3396656
19. McCalpin, J.D.: Bandwidth limits in the intel Xeon max (sapphire rapids with HBM) processors. In: High Performance Computing: ISC High Performance 2023 International Workshops, Hamburg, Germany, May 21–25, 2023, Revised Selected Papers, pp. 403–413. Springer-Verlag, Berlin, Heidelberg (2023). https://doi.org/10.1007/978-3-031-40843-4_30

High Performance Fabric Support in DAOS

Michael Hennecke[✉] [ID], Alexander Oganezov [ID], Jerome Soumagne [ID], John Carrier [ID], and Joseph Moore [ID]

Intel Corporation, 2200 Mission College Blvd., Santa Clara, CA 95054-1549, USA
{michael.hennecke,alexander.a.oganezov,jerome.soumagne,
john.carrier,joseph.moore}@intel.com

Abstract. The Distributed Asynchronous Object Storage (DAOS) is an open source scale-out storage system that is designed from the ground up to support NVMe storage in user space. DAOS can run over any TCP network, but it can also take advantage of high performance fabrics like 100/200/400 Gbps Ethernet, InfiniBand, Slingshot, or Omni-Path. This paper describes the networking architecture of DAOS and discusses scaling and performance aspects of running DAOS over those high performance fabrics.

Keywords: DAOS · High-performance fabrics · Scalable object stores as HPC storage subsystems · InfiniBand · Slingshot · Omni-Path

1 Introduction

The Distributed Asynchronous Object Storage (DAOS) [1–3] is an open source software-defined object store designed from the ground up for massively distributed Non-Volatile Memory (NVM). It presents a key-value storage interface and provides features such as transactional non-blocking I/O, a versioned data model, and global snapshots – all completely in user space. Its design eliminates many of the bottlenecks of traditional parallel filesystems, as demonstrated by leadership performance rankings in HPC storage benchmarks like the IO500 [4].

As shown in Fig. 1, there are three distinct node roles in a DAOS environment:

1. The DAOS *Storage Nodes* contain the physical storage media (SCM and NVMe), and one or more high-performance fabric adapter(s) to connect to the DAOS Client Nodes. Each Storage Node runs one `daos_server` process, which implements the DAOS control plane. The daos_server process spawns and controls one or more `daos_engine` process(es), which implement the DAOS data plane.
2. The DAOS *Client Nodes* do not contain physical storage media. DAOS storage pools that are provisioned on the Storage Nodes are accessed by the client through the `libdaos` user space library, which connects to the `daos_engine` processes through the high-performance fabric. Each client node runs one `daos_agent` process, which is responsible for discovering the DAOS storage nodes, performing authentication, and informing client processes on that node about the available high performance fabric interface(s).

3. DAOS *Admin Nodes* run the dmg management command and/or other applications that use the DAOS management API. Those nodes only need network connectivity to the DAOS control plane, but not to the high performance fabric that is used by the DAOS data plane.

The three DAOS node roles can run on separate cluster nodes, but multiple node roles can also be co-located on the same cluster node. For example, the *Admin Node* role can also be assigned to a storage server which has the *Storage Node* role, to enable a storage administrator who is logged in to that storage server to manage the DAOS server cluster from there. The *Admin Node* role could also be assigned to the compute nodes (that have the *Client Node* role). A typical use case would be the creation and destruction of ephemeral DAOS storage pools as part of a batch system's prolog and epilog scripts. Those scripts run on the compute nodes and need the ability to run the dmg command for those storage provisioning steps.

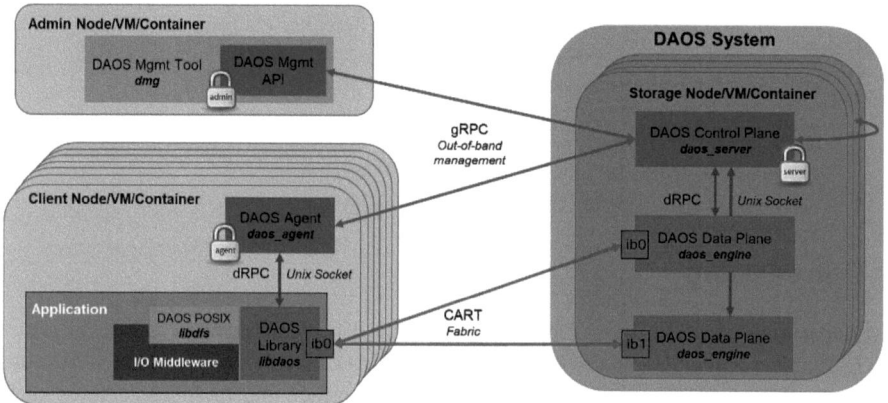

Fig. 1. DAOS Software Components and Network Connections.

The DAOS *control plane* uses the gRPC framework [5] for communication between the daos_server daemons, the daos_agent daemons, and the DAOS management API (including the dmg command). This control plane communication can run over a cluster management LAN (like a 25 Gbps Ethernet network), or it can be run over the high-performance fabric (for example using IP-over-IB on an InfiniBand fabric).

DAOS communication within a node uses local Unix domain sockets and the dRPC framework [6]. On each DAOS Storage Node, dRPC is used for communication between the daos_server and daos_engine processes. On each DAOS Client Node, dRPC is used by the libdaos library to communicate with the daos_agent.

The remainder of this paper focuses on the DAOS *data plane*, which uses the high performance fabric.

2 The DAOS High Performance Fabric Stack

The I/O flow in the DAOS data plane, from the user application on a client node to the storage media on a storage node, is show in Fig. 2.

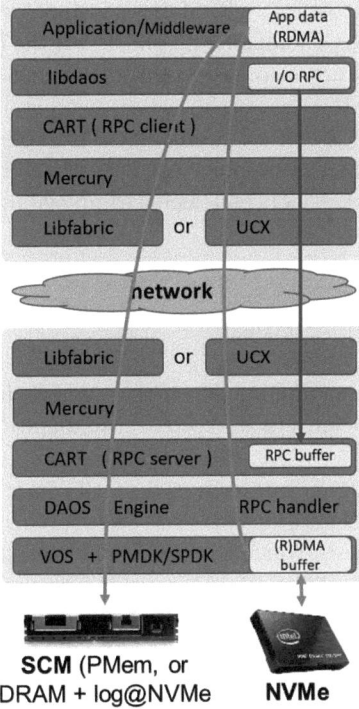

Fig. 2. DAOS I/O Flow.

Several layers of networking software provide the functionality that the DAOS data plane needs to perform efficiently on highly scalable, high performance fabrics:

- The OFI *libfabric* [7] layer provides point-to-point messaging capabilities in user space. Libfabric implements a simple, thin send/receive messaging layer but it does not provide RPCs. Not all the core fabric providers that are supported by libfabric (see fi_provider [8]) are supported by DAOS; this is discussed in more detail in the next section. Libfabric generally provides connection-less, Reliable Datagram (RD) communication. Some providers may be connection-ful, and the libfabric rxm utility provider (see fi_rxm [9]) can emulate a reliable datagram endpoint over a messaging endpoint of such core providers.
- On InfiniBand fabrics, the *UCX* [10] framework (maintained by the Unified Communication Framework (UCF) consortium) can be used as an alternative to libfabric to provide send/receive messaging. UCX supports Reliable Connection (RC), Dynamically Connected (DC) and Unreliable Datagram (UD) communication over InfiniBand. See below for more information.
- The *Mercury* framework [11–13], maintained by Argonne National Laboratory, Intel and the HDF Group, provides an RPC interface specifically designed for HPC on top of the point-to-point communication framework. Mercury's Network Abstraction (NA) layer supports multiple backend implementations; both OFI/libfabric and

UCX are supported. The `mercury` RPM that is included in the DAOS RPM distribution already includes the OFI/libfabric plugin. To use the UCX plugin in InfiniBand environments, the `mercury-ucx` RPM must be manually installed in addition to the base `mercury` RPM.
- The *Collective and RPC Transport (CaRT)* layer is a component of the DAOS core software. It provides both point-to-point and collective RPC capabilities on top of the Mercury RPC framework. CaRT implements additional functionality that is used by DAOS, including:

  – Timeouts for RPCs
  – Collective operations like broadcast
  – Distributed caching
  – Flow control (managing/limiting the number of in-flight RPCs)
  – Detection of server failures (gossip protocol similar to SWIM)

On a DAOS Client Node, `libdaos` uses the CaRT layer as the RPC client to send I/O requests to the Storage Nodes. On the DAOS Storage Nodes, CaRT is the RPC server that accepts client I/O requests, which are then handled by the `daos_engines`.

In DAOS environments with an RDMA-capable fabric and an RDMA-capable fabric provider, no memory copy is required: The application data is directly transferred from the application to an (R)DMA buffer in the DAOS *Versioning Object Store (VOS)* component. The `daos_engine` uses a pool of pre-registered buffers (allocated from huge pages) for these (R)DMA transfers.

3 Supported High Performance Fabrics

With the high performance fabric stack described in Sect. 2, the DAOS data plane supports all relevant high performance fabrics. The fabric provider is selected through the `provider:` statement in the `daos_server.yml` configuration file on the DAOS Storage Nodes. DAOS Client Nodes automatically discover the fabric provider through the `daos_agent`; they need no explicit configuration for the data plane.

- **Ethernet:** With the OFI/libfabric TCP provider, DAOS supports TCP/IP networks including high performance Ethernet fabrics. DAOS versions before v2.4 automatically appended the RXM utility provider to a `provider: ofi+tcp` statement in the `daos_server.yml` configuration file. Starting with DAOS v2.4 this is no longer the case; use `provider: ofi+tcp;ofi_rxm` to enable RXM with TCP.
- **Ethernet with RoCE v2:** To enable RDMA transport over an Ethernet network that is configured for RoCE v2, the OFI/libfabric VERBS provider can be used. DAOS will automatically append the RXM utility provider if it is not explicitly specified; for clarity it is recommended to specify `provider: ofi+verbs;ofi_rxm`.
- NVIDIA/Mellanox **InfiniBand** [14] fabrics are supported by DAOS with two alternative mechanisms:

a. The OFI/libfabric layer can be used with the VERBS provider to enable RDMA transport over InfiniBand. In this case the RXM utility provider is automatically added as described for RoCE v2 above; for clarity it is recommended to explicitly specify `provider: ofi+ verbs;ofi_rxm`. On large InfiniBand fabrics, using the VERBS provider may limit scalability because InfiniBand adapters provide a limited number of queue pair resources. This issue is discussed in Sect. 5.
b. Alternatively, DAOS can use UCX as its point-to-point messaging framework. The scaling behaviour of the RC and DC modes of UCX is similar to the libfabric VERBS provider. But using UCX in Unreliable Datagram (UD) mode requires much less resources on the InfiniBand adapters, and therefore scales to much larger InfiniBand fabrics. The recommended provider for large InfiniBand fabrics is therefore `provider: ucx+ ud_x`. Note that UD does not use RDMA transport so it may exhibit lower per-task bandwidth than VERBS in some scenarios, but aggregate performance of UCX + UD is comparable to VERBS.

- HPE **Slingshot** [15] fabrics are supported through the OFI/libfabric CXI provider that is implemented in an HPE-provided version of libfabric (CXI provider support is not yet upstreamed to the main libfabric repository). Because DAOS ships with an RPM build of libfabric that gets installed in the default library location `/usr/lib64`, in HPE Slingshot environments the library search path needs to be adjusted to ensure that the HPE-provided libfabric library (which includes the CXI support) is loaded first. The DAOS server configuration file should specify `provider: ofi+ cxi`.
- Cornelis **Omni-Path** [16]: With DAOS v2.4 and earlier, the only supported fabric provider on Omni-Path fabrics is the OFI/libfabric TCP provider. The PSM2 provider which is available in libfabric is not supported by DAOS, as it lacks some functionality that is required by DAOS. Cornelis has upstreamed a new Omni-Path Express (OPX) provider to OFI/libfabric, and all necessary code changes in Mercury and CaRT to enable the new OPX provider have been implemented. Unfortunately, testing of the OPX provider could not be completed in time for the DAOS v2.4 release. It is expected that OPX support will be enabled in a future DAOS release.

In terms of Scalability, the DAOS environment in the ANL Aurora supercomputer is by far the largest DAOS installation worldwide, with 1024 DAOS servers and over ten thousand compute nodes [17]. Aurora uses an HPE Slingshot 11 (200 Gbps) interconnect in a Dragonfly topology with adaptive routing. Aurora's DAOS storage system is ranked #1 on the IO500-SC23 production systems list [4], using 642 of the 1024 DAOS servers and 300 Aurora compute nodes. A small-scale investigation of DAOS performance scaling on an HDR InfiniBand network has been reported in Ref. [18].

4 Understanding Multiple Fabric Interfaces per Host

DAOS servers often use multiple high performance fabric adapters to balance their network bandwidth and the bandwidth of their internal NVMe storage media. This is typical for dual-socket DAOS servers, but even DAOS server with a single CPU socket can utilize multiple network interfaces (or dual-socket DAOS servers can use four fabric links to maximize bandwidth [19]). On the client side, traditional CPU-only

HPC compute nodes typically use a single high performance fabric link. But as both HPC and AI workloads are using more and more GPUs, it is now also very common to install multiple network interfaces in the DAOS clients to match this increased computational capability. Figure 3 shows an example configuration where both the DAOS servers and the compute nodes have two single-port InfiniBand HDR adapters.

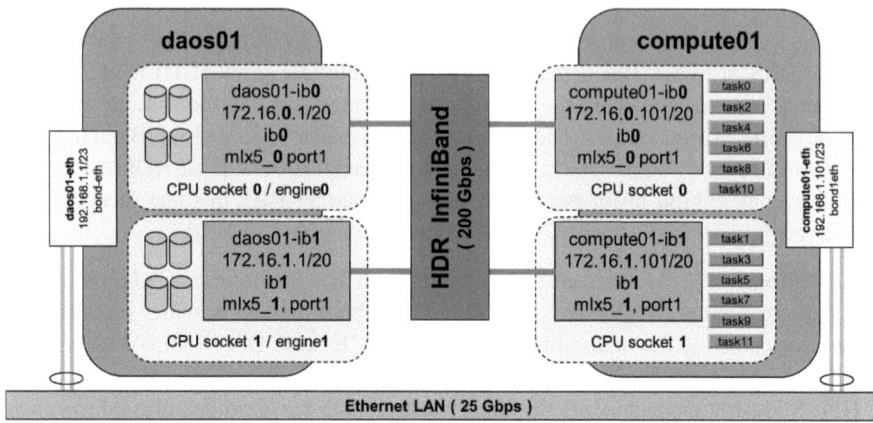

Fig. 3. Multiple HPC Fabric Ports in DAOS Servers and DAOS Clients.

The TCP/IP configuration in Fig. 3 shows the easiest way to set up such an environment, where all InfiniBand interfaces of the DAOS servers and the DAOS clients have IP addresses from the same large subnet (netmask /20). To make this work, some Linux sysctl settings need to be changed to ensure that responses to ARP requests are sent over the correct interface. Figure 4 shows the details.

```
/etc/sysctl.d # cat 95-daos-net.conf
net.ipv4.conf.all.accept_local = 1
net.ipv4.conf.all.arp_ignore = 2
net.ipv4.conf.ib0.rp_filter = 2
net.ipv4.conf.ib1.rp_filter = 2
...
```

Fig. 4. DAOS sysctl settings for multiple interfaces per host (same subnet).

4.1 Multiple Fabric Interfaces on DAOS Servers

On the DAOS servers, the daos_engine cannot stripe over multiple network interfaces in the data plane. With DAOS, every network interface must be controlled by a separate daos_engine process. The typical case shown in Fig. 3 is a dual-socket DAOS server that uses one InfiniBand interface on each of the two CPU sockets. The corresponding configuration entries for the data plane in the daos_server.yml configuration file is shown in Fig. 5.

```
/etc/daos # grep -E "provider|engines|^-|numa|fabric_iface" daos_server.yml
provider: ucx+ud_x
engines:
-
  pinned_numa_node: 0
  fabric_iface: ib0
  fabric_iface_port: 31416
-
  pinned_numa_node: 1
  fabric_iface: ib1
  fabric_iface_port: 32416
```

Fig. 5. Data plane configuration in daos_server.yml.

For a balanced configuration, the total number of NVMe disks of the server must also be evenly split between the two daos_engine processes (here: four NVMe disks per engine). The details of the storage configuration are not shown in Fig. 5, as this paper focuses on the fabric aspects.

One aspect of the storage configuration that is very important from the fabric perspective is the number of `targets` per engine that are set in the `daos_server.yml` configuration file. A target is a user-level thread that runs on one physical core within the engine. At least one target per NVMe disk is required to manage the storage. For performance reasons, it is often advisable to use multiple targets per NVMe disk. In that case, each target manages a fraction of a single NVMe disks' capacity. For the configuration in Fig. 3 with four NVMe disks per engine, the minimum number of targets per engine is four. But using 8, 16, 20 or 24 targets per engine (limited by the number of physical cores of the CPU socket) will provide better performance, in particular metadata rates and small I/O operations. Client processes communicate directly with *each* target (not with the engine as a whole), so the number of targets impacts scalability. This will be discussed further in Sect. 5.

4.2 Multiple Fabric Interfaces on DAOS Clients

On the DAOS client nodes, the `daos_agent.yml` configuration file should contain the same list of `access_points` that the DAOS servers use (those nodes run the DAOS management service). Through control plane connections to those DAOS storage nodes, the `daos_agent` daemon receives the list of all DAOS engines in the DAOS system as well as the fabric provider.

The `daos_agent` daemon then uses `hwloc` [20] to discover the NUMA structure of the node. In most environments this happens automatically; in special circumstances (for example, nodes with additional fabric adapters that are not used by DAOS) it is possible to overrule the `hwloc` discovery by explicitly specifying the fabric interfaces in the `daos_agent.yml` configuration file.

Processes that use `libdaos` will connect to the `daos_agent` through a local Unix domain socket, and the agent will assign *one* of the available fabric interfaces to each process. The agent will normally assign the fabric port that is "closest" to the NUMA node on which the process is running. This mechanism implies that:

- A single client process will only be able to utilize a single high performance fabric port, even if it is internally multi-threaded. Work is under way to enhance the CaRT layer so it can return a list of fabric interfaces instead of only a single fabric interface. When this is implemented, a future DAOS release will allow a single process to use multiple fabric interfaces.
- For MPI applications with many tasks per node, in which each MPI task constitutes a separate process, all the available fabric interfaces will be used (assuming that the MPI tasks are equally distributed across all NUMA domains).
- To prevent MPI tasks to move from one NUMA domain to another (which would break the locality to the assigned fabric interface), in configurations like Fig. 3 it is recommended to bind the MPI tasks to the NUMA domain (here, the CPU socket).

After the fabric context has been initialized the DAOS agent is no longer involved, and each user process communicates directly with each of the storage targets on the DAOS servers.

5 The InfiniBand Queue Pair Predicament

DAOS has been designed to run completely in user space, and this has an important implication for the number of communication paths that will be used: Contrary to other filesystems where a system-level daemon on the client nodes is communicating with a system-level daemon on the storage servers, in DAOS each user process will directly communicate with all targets on all DAOS engines.

For connection-based fabric providers, each connection requires some resources. On InfiniBand fabrics, the libfabric VERBS provider (which uses the Reliable Connection (RC) mode) will allocate a queue pair for each communication path. Each InfiniBand port can only support a limited number of queue pairs (128k for NVIDIA ConnectX-6 and earlier generations, see Fig. 6), and this physical adapter limitation imposes an upper limit on the scalability of RC based communication. UCX is affected by the same limitation *when using RC mode* – but not when using Unreliable Datagram (UD) mode.

```
# ibv_devinfo -v | egrep "^hca_id|max_qp:"
hca_id: mlx5_0
        max_qp:                         131072
hca_id: mlx5_1
        max_qp:                         131072
```

Fig. 6. InfiniBand queue pair resources (per port).

On each `daos_engine` of a DAOS server, each storage target communicates to all MPI tasks on all client nodes. As mentioned in Sect. 4.1 the engine needs to configure one or more storage targets for each of its NVMe disks, and because clients need to communicate with all targets, a low number of targets improves scalability. On the other hand, using more storage targets provides better performance. This can be clearly seen in Fig. 7 (from [14]), which shows IO500 mdtest [4] metadata rates for four NVMe disks per engine and 1 to 8 storage targets per NVMe disk (4 to 32 targets per engine).

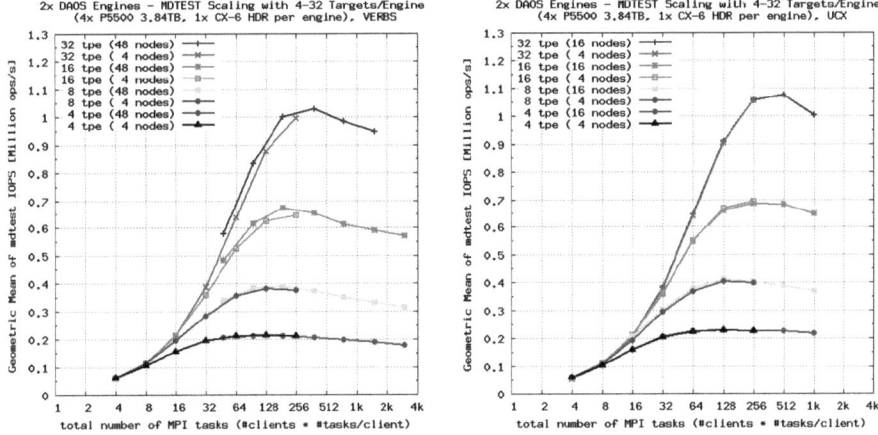

Fig. 7. Metadata performance scaling with the number of storage targets (from [14]).

With a maximum of 128k queue pairs per InfiniBand port, and the minimum of 4 targets per engine with 4 NVMe disks, the number of client-side MPI tasks doing I/O is already limited to 32k when using RC. Using 16 targets per engine reduces the number of possible client-side MPI tasks to 8k, and 24 targets per engine (a typical value for DAOS servers with ~32 cores per CPU socket) supports less than 6k MPI tasks. For this reason, we recommend using the connection-less UCX+UD mode for large InfiniBand fabrics, which does not suffer from the resource requirements that RC has.

Note that there is an additional I/O flow that needs to be accommodated within the same server-side 128k queue pair limit: DAOS background activities like rebuild operations also require that each target on each DAOS engine communicates with all other targets on all DAOS engines. This is normally a much smaller number (as most environments have more compute nodes than storage nodes), but it must be considered when deciding to configure a DAOS InfiniBand environment for RC or UD.

On the DAOS client side, each MPI task needs to communicate with all storage targets on all daos_engine instances. In scenarios like Fig. 3 with four NVMe disks per engine and one InfiniBand port per client CPU socket, and assuming 56 cores/socket, the 128k queue pair limit imposes the following restrictions:

- With 4 targets per engine (one per NVMe disk), the number of DAOS engines is limited to about 500 (or 250 two-socket DAOS servers) when running with one MPI task per physical CPU core. This is large enough for most environments.
- With 24 targets per engine (6 per NVMe disk), the number of DAOS engines that can be supported in RC mode drops to about 80 (or 40 two-socket DAOS servers). This is already too small even for moderately sized DAOS environments.
- For client nodes that only have a single fabric links, the above numbers are cut in half as a single fabric link needs to support twice the number of client CPU cores.

While the resource consumption on the DAOS servers is higher than on the clients, the estimations above show that even the client side may be limited in scalability and the move to UCX+UD on large scale InfiniBand fabrics is recommended or even required for scalability.

6 Summary and Conclusions

The DAOS high performance fabric stack is built on several open source frameworks (OFI/libfabric or UCX, Mercury, and the DAOS CaRT layer) and supports all popular HPC fabrics including 100/200/400 Gbps Ethernet, InfiniBand, Slingshot, and Omni-Path. We have described the software architecture and provider choices and have explained how DAOS uses multiple fabric interfaces per host. The scalability limitations of connection-based communication like InfiniBand verbs have been highlighted, which lead to the recommendation to use UCX in UD mode for large InfiniBand fabrics.

Future work includes the extension of CaRT to allow a single client process to use multiple network links, further studies with UCX in Dynamically Connected (DC) mode for potential scalability improvements over RC, and the continuation of scalability testing in the ANL "Aurora" and LRZ "SuperMUC-NG2" DAOS environments as these systems are brought fully online.

References

1. Liang, Z., Lombardi, J., Chaarawi, M., Hennecke, M.: DAOS: a scale-out high performance storage stack for storage class memory. In: Panda, D. (ed.) SCFA 2020. LNCS, vol. 12082, pp. 40–54. Springer, Cham (2020). https://doi.org/10.1007/978-3-030-48842-0_3
2. Zhen, L., Yong, F., Wang, D., Lombardi, J.: Distributed transactions and self-healing system of DAOS. In: Nichols, J., et al. (eds.) SMC 2022. CCIS, vol. 1315, pp. 334–348. Springer, Cham (2020). https://doi.org/10.1007/978-3-030-63393-6_22
3. Scot Breitenfeld, M., et al.: DAOS for extreme-scale systems in scientific applications (2017). https://arxiv.org/pdf/1712.00423.pdf
4. IO500 Homepage. https://io500.org/
5. gRPC: A high performance, open source universal RPC framework. https://grpc.io/about/
6. dRPC: A lightweight, drop-in, protocol-buffer based gRPC replacement. https://storj.github.io/drpc/
7. OFI libfabric. https://github.com/ofiwg/libfabric/releases/tag/v1.19.0
8. fi_provider(7) man page. https://ofiwg.github.io/libfabric/main/man/fi_provider.7.html
9. fi_rxm(7) man page. https://ofiwg.github.io/libfabric/main/man/fi_rxm.7.html
10. Unified Communication Framework (UCF) consortium. UCX. https://openucx.org/
11. The Mercury Remote Procedure Call (RPC) framework. https://mercury-hpc.github.io/user/overview/
12. Soumagne, J., et al.: Mercury: enabling remote procedure call for high-performance computing. In: IEEE International Conference on Cluster Computing (2013). https://doi.org/10.1109/CLUSTER.2013.6702617
13. Soumagne, J., Carns, P., Ross, R.: Advancing RPC for data services at exascale. IEEE Data Eng. Bull. **43**(1), 23–34 (2020). http://sites.computer.org/debull/A20mar/p23.pdf
14. NVIDIA InfiniBand fabric stack: Mellanox OFED. https://www.mellanox.com/products/infiniband-drivers/linux/mlnx_ofed
15. HPE Slingshot interconnect solutions for HPC networking. https://www.hpe.com/us/en/compute/hpc/slingshot-interconnect.html

16. Cornelis Omni-Path Express Fabric Software v10.14.1 (2024). http://www.cornelisnetworks.com/support
17. Argonne Leadership Computing Facility. Aurora. https://www.alcf.anl.gov/aurora
18. Hennecke, M.: Understanding DAOS storage performance scalability. In: International Conference on High Performance Computing in Asia-Pacific Region Workshops (HPCASIA-WORKSHOP 2023), 27 February–2 March 2023. Raffles Blvd, Singapore (2023). https://doi.org/10.1145/3581576.3581577
19. Hennecke, M.: Performance Evolution of DAOS Servers (2023). https://www.intel.com/content/www/us/en/high-performance-computing/performance-evolution-of-daos-servers.html
20. OpenMPI Portable Hardware Locality (hwloc). https://www.open-mpi.org/projects/hwloc/

HPC I/O in the Data Center Workshop
(HPC-IODC 2024)

Secure Elasticsearch Clusters on HPC Systems for Sensitive Data

Hendrik Nolte[1](✉)[iD], Lars Quentin[1], and Julian Kunkel[1,2][iD]

[1] Gesellschaft für wissenschaftliche Datenverarbeitung mbH Göttingen, Göttingen, Germany
{hendrik.nolte,julian.kunkel}@gwdg.de
[2] University of Göttingen, Göttingen, Germany

Abstract. Data catalogs are an established tool to integrate heterogeneous data, enrich raw data with semantic meaningful metadata, and make data easily searchable, maintainable, and shareable. This helps, for instance, data scientists to manage large data sets, which are often required for state-of-the-art artificial intelligence research. Driven by the increasing computing demand of these data-intensive projects, High-performance Computing (HPC) providers have to address the specific demands of these projects to attract this new user group to HPC systems. One particularly challenging domain are the life sciences working with highly-regulated, sensitive health data. This paper presents a workflow to deploy on-demand Elasticsearch (ES) clusters in user space on HPC systems, providing a backend for direct usage or user-defined, higher-order data catalog functionalities. Therewith, it augments the capabilities of a parallel file system by allowing processing of user-defined metadata. Two different encryption techniques are presented and used in two different use cases to systematically benchmark the developed setup, show its general scalability, and highlight important considerations when adapting it to a new use case. It is shown, that scaling out ES clusters has to be done using thorough data and workload modeling since larger clusters can be either beneficial or harmful to different workloads.

Keywords: Elasticsearch · High-Performance Computing · Data Catalog · Sensitive Data · Encryption · Benchmarking

1 Introduction

Driven by the increasing availability of data and by ever-cheaper sensors generating new datasets, data-driven methods were successfully utilized in many scientific domains and are being continuously adapted in new domains. The basic idea and advantages of data mining, i.e., using established or new statistical methods on diverse data, have been long discussed [6]. Life sciences working with health data are research areas of particular interest [10], as motivated by their potential impact for improved patient care as it is for instance showcased in [11]. With the increase in available data, there is a demand for similar powerful compute infrastructure. However, the theoretical promise of discovering hidden patterns and correlations in large data sets and revolutionizing a field with novel insights is often prevented in practice by insufficient data management, in particular on HPC systems. That is, because data-driven projects often rely on complicated workflows, where data is first extracted from diverse sources, and then needs to be integrated on a suitable storage system from where it can be pre-processed, analyzed, and post-processed. In addition, to the problem of bookkeeping about the data location, the general overview of the available data becomes challenging with growing data sets. That is because semantic information about the data is often encoded in the file names and paths.

The general solution to this problem is to index all data with their domain-specific semantic information in a data catalog, which then links to the location of the data. Therefore, such a data catalog can be used by users to explore the available data sets and to concisely select a subset of the data that caters best to their individual interests based on meaningful information, not on overly complex paths. However, when dealing with health data, data privacy and general data security become a large concern, as these data are commonly subjected to laws. Generally, regulations do not only apply to the data itself but also, or rather especially to the describing metadata, which can potentially contain person-identifiable attributes like, e.g. a name, or a rare disease.

In this paper a workflow is presented, with which an Elasticsearch (ES) cluster can be spawned on-demand in user space. This allows the provisioning of scalable ES clusters on supercomputers using mainstream resource managers like Slurm. This workflow can extended by incorporating different encryption methods which can be optionally used to provide the highest data privacy and full data sovereignty to users and therefore allow the processing of sensitive health data on shared HPC systems. In order to systematically benchmark this setup and the additional encryption cost, a throughput-focused benchmark is designed and utilized to demonstrate the scalability of this approach on the Top500 system Emmy by using a standard and a custom dataset based on Magnetic Resonance Imaging (MRI). The main contributions of this paper are:

- Design of a workflow for on-demand ES clusters in userspace for HPC systems that is suitable for sensitive metadata
- Design of a new throughput-oriented benchmark and a blueprint to use case-specific benchmarking to find an optimal server configuration
- Demonstrate the applicability and scalability of the developed workflow and benchmark on a standard and a specially designed MRI-based dataset

The remainder of the paper has the following structure: First, the related work is discussed in Sect. 2, the design of the ES spawner and benchmark in Sect. 3, the description of the experimental setup in Sect. 4, the discussion of the results in Sect. 5 and a conclusion in Sect. 6.

2 Related Work

In hospitals, medical images are typically stored in a *Picture Archiving and Communication System* (PACS) using the *Digital Imaging and Communications in Medicine* (DICOM) standard. There has been an increasing interest, in utilizing NoSQL databases in a PACS for indexing and retrieval [4,8,12]. There are different advantages compared to the state-of-the-art relational database systems, like the schemaless documents which allow to easily index all metadata of a DICOM file, or the horizontal scalability [1]. In parallel, researchers are exploiting big data in medicine in probably all domains [2,5].

Tagging and indexing data on HPC storage systems has become increasingly popular. Examples of this are VAST Data, which offers a tagging mechanism based on an SQL engine, or the Ngenea Hub which uses ES on top of a General Parallel File System (GPFS) to provide unstructured data management. These systems generally share the characteristic that they rely on a fixed number of dedicated servers to support their query engine. In contrast, in this paper, a workflow is proposed to spawn on-demand ES clusters in user space using standard Slurm job allocations, thus re-using existing resources and offering dynamically, use-case optimized scaled clusters.

In [7] an isolated partition can be used with encrypted data and a second factor to provide a secure compute environment on a shared HPC system. A different approach by *BioMedIT* [3], part of the Swiss Personalized Health Network, provides GPU-based cloud computing resources. Here, virtualization within the federated network is used to isolate compute environments and provide secure, and scalable compute resources. Also relying on cloud services, the *Private Cloud on a Compute Cluster* (PCOCC) was used in [9]. It offers a Slurm integration, enabling the use of HPC systems. Data privacy is conserved by using a dedicated Lustre filesystem.

The canonical tool for ES benchmarking is Rally[1], the official macrobenchmarking tool from *Elastic*. It runs distributed benchmarks with standard and user-defined datasets. Different benchmarking scenarios are defined as so-called *tracks*. Every track contains one or more *corpora*, which contain all JSON documents to be ingested into the according indices. Furthermore, every track contains many *operations* such as the ingestion or specific queries, which are then structured into a *challenge's schedule* in a fork-join model. This benchmark is sensitive to latency increases, therefore limiting its usefulness in high-load and high-throughput workloads.

3 Design

In this section, the design of the proposed on-demand cluster spawner and the throughput benchmarker is presented.

---
[1] https://github.com/elastic/rally.

3.1 On-Demand Cluster Spawner

The on-demand cluster spawner uses the Message Passing Interface (MPI) to automatically discover the available hardware nodes of an HPC job, by using the pre-configured MPI-environment of a batch job. This means that no previous configuration by the users is required, like the hostnames or IPs of the involved nodes. This dynamic host configuration is also capable of managing changing hostnames from one batch job to another. This also implies that the cluster can be dynamically sized, basically supporting any cluster size. To increase portability and reproducibility, ES is packaged into a controlled Singularity container, which is fully node-transparent and runs using the `--cleanenv` option. Additionally, it supports *statefulness* between jobs, which removes the need for reingesting on every job spawn. The container is based on the Ubuntu 22.04 official docker image. ES itself can be optionally included in the image, requiring that each user builds the container image themselves to ensure the correct uid/gid settings. Alternatively, it can be bind-mounted at runtime. For this, a `tar.gz` shipped with the spawner from which ES is extracted, and the uid/gid are set to the correct user. In this way ES can be deployed fully in userspace without any need to reconfigure anything on the HPC-server side. To achieve statefulness the data path where the ingested data, i.e., indexes are stored. In addition, by bind-mounting also the configuration and logging paths, the dynamic movement between different nodes, IPs, and even network interfaces, is achieved. Since the hostnames and IPs are not persistent from run to run, these are abstracted by the MPI ranks of the spawner. For this, using an `MPI_GATHER`, all hostnames and their ranks are sent to the root rank. Then, the root creates or updates the Elasticsearch configs while the other nodes are waiting at a barrier. The MPI root then updates the ES configs for all nodes with their new IP addresses. This does not effect the mapping of nodes, i.e., MPI ranks to the individual indexes stored on the shared filesystem. The first ranks are master-eligible nodes, from which only one node can be the active master. All nodes are active data nodes. Due to the abstraction of the hostnames by the MPI rank, any arbitrary permutation of hostnames will work, without the users realizing it. After creating the configs, each host starts the Singularity container with its config and the previously created ES configs bind-mounted in. The only change that is required on the nodes of Emmy is a higher-than-default number of memory-mapped areas per process, i.e., `vm.max_map_count` of 262144, where the default value is 65530. This is needed because ES uses a `mmapfs` directory to store its indices.

3.2 Distributed Thoughput Benchmarker

The proposed benchmarker is currently split into two tools. A write-focused benchmark measuring the ingestion throughput of a new index as well as a read-focused benchmark measuring the query performance of a previously ingested index. The benchmarker itself is inspired by Rally, and is in many parts compatible with it. Therefore, it can be even used alongside Rally to provide a more comprehensive picture.

Ingestion Benchmarker. The ingestion benchmarker measures the ingestion throughput into a new index for each configuration. It uses the Newline Delimited JSON (NDJSON) format which allows for trivial dataset creation and scaling. Furthermore, it allows for the usage of all Rally corpora which facilitates the aforementioned interoperability. Using MPI, the ingestion benchmarker can be arbitrarily scaled across nodes.

Before the ingestion can be measured, the root node creates the index. For this a configuration file containing all field mappings can be provided, i.e., each type of each attribute of the dataset is strictly defined at index creation time. Although ES allows for dynamic schemas, the benchmarker uses strict type mappings for reproducibility. The type definitions use the same ES Domain Specific Language (DSL) as Rally. The ES index is per default configured with one shard per node, but can be overwritten using a command line argument. After index creation, the offsets of the globally shared NDJSON file containing the dataset are calculated and shared across all processes which use offset *lseek* to start at the specified place for each rank. Then, all worker nodes parallelly ingest the data using the Bulk API. For this, the number of documents per request can be freely configured as a command line argument. All worker processes are simultaneously starting to ingest data and are then independently recording the individual timings of each single request. In the end, all measurements are gathered on the root rank and are streamed into a JSON file for further analysis. Lastly, in order to isolate the ES performance, caching is explicitly disabled for the index.

Query Benchmarker. The query benchmarker is also MPI-based and measures the documents per second as well as the latency of each individual request. Inspired by Rally, the benchmarks are structured into multiple steps using a fork-join model. The query benchmarker has a custom, JSON-based DSL for the benchmark design. The DSL embeds the ES query language internally, allowing for easy development for ES users as well as trivial portability to Rally tracks. Each request explicitly bypasses the cache, resulting in more realistic measurements. Lastly, it supports multiple alternating queries in a single fork-join task to create a mixed usage load.

For each of the fully disjunct benchmark steps the following workflow is executed: First, the root node waits until the ES cluster's health is green, to ensure the ES cluster has fully formed. If multiple queries are defined for a given task, each rank chooses a random permutation. This is done to maximize the randomness of the request pattern sent to the ES cluster. After that, if configured in the benchmark definition, warmup requests are done to fill the page caches and optimize the Java Virtual Machine (JVM) Just-In-Time (JIT) compiler. If this is not done, the query performance would increase over time, overshadowing other effects. Once the warmup is done, each worker starts the benchmark until the configured execution time is reached. The cache is explicitly disabled using the `request_cache` parameter. Per default *Session Objects* are used to facilitate persistent connections and reuse the underlying Transmission Control Protocol (TCP) connections. Thereby, additional HTTP overhead is limited which could otherwise taint the measured data, since handshaking and authentication are embarrassingly parallel tasks. If a request is successful, the latency and number of received documents are saved, otherwise the error HTTP code is recorded. A sleep between each request can be optionally configured. Lastly, all measurements get aggregated in the root rank and dumped into a JSON file.

4 Experimental Setup

In the following, the general experimental setup is described.

4.1 Datasets and Queries

Two different datasets are used for the benchmarks. The NYC Taxis dataset, based on the nyc_taxis Rally track provided by Rally as well as a custom use case-driven MRI benchmark that was developed based on extensive requirement engineering with the involved doctors and researchers.

NYC Taxis. The *NYC Taxis* dataset contains all rides that have been performed in yellow taxis in 2015. It is comprised of 165 million entries, resulting in an uncompressed size of 74.3 GiB, which makes it the largest corpus of all tracks provided by Elastic. Moreover, its Rally track is one of the canonical benchmarks commonly used for benchmarking ES, making the results comparable to previous work. Furthermore, while most Rally tracks are used for tail latency performance regression analysis, NYC taxis is designed for maximum throughput, making it a realistic use case for HPC computing.

Custom MRI. The goal of creating a custom dataset is to simulate the anticipated workload as precisely as possible. For this, each key from the DICOM headers of the MRI use case is used in the corpus in each document. The corresponding values and their distribution are determined and modeled. For instance, the *brain age* of a patient is modeled as a normal distribution around the patient's real age with a variance of 5 years. Other examples are the *KSpace* resolution, the magnetic field strength, the Larmor frequency, or the vendor-dependent measurement protocols, which are all chosen from a range of valid values of the existing scanners. Compared to the previous NYC taxis documents, these documents are rather large, with at least 61 different keys, although the overall corpus with 1 million documents is rather small, but realistic considering that each document represents an MRI scan.

4.2 Encryption Methods

In order to ensure full data privacy on an untrusted HPC system, the sensitive metadata within the ES indices has to be encrypted. That is because the data will be stored on a globally available filesystem where any attacker with administrative privileges has access to. For this, the following two methods have been implemented and benchmarked.

GoCryptFS. *GoCryptFS*[2] is a Filesystem in Userspace (FUSE)-based stacked cryptographic filesystem which provides filesystem-level encryption. In order to balance efficient file access while still offering the security of a block cipher even on large files, a single file is split into independent 4 kB-sized blocks, also known as extents. The block cipher is then only applied within these fixed-sized chunks. This enables performant random access to a file, since de- and encryption for write and read access only have to be computed per block, not per file. To deploy this, the data path of the dynamically generated ES configurations points to a directory, which has been mounted with GoCryptFS.

Attribute-Based-Encryption (ABE). GocryptFS has two limitations. First, it does need a secure environment to be executed in, i.e. it can't be deployed in any managed hosting. In addition, to spawn a new ES instance, the entire storage path has to be encryptable by the user. This means a user has either full access or none at all. Both of these limitations can be mitigated using an Attribute-Based Encryption (ABE) scheme, where each key-value pair gets individually encrypted. The developed method will be presented in an extended version.

5 Results

The discussed benchmark runs are done in a grid search manner, scaling the cluster size by increasing the node count from three, over seven to 15, and for each cluster size increasing the number of ingestion or query workers from 1, 2, 4, 8 to 16. This exhaustive approach resulted in a large dataset of which only a limited subset can be presented and discussed to highlight interesting caveats. The benchmarks are performed on Emmy[3], using double socket nodes with 2 Xeon Platinum 9242 CLX-AP, with 368 GiB of available RAM. The used storage was a Lustre consisting of 2 ES14KX with 500 12TB SAS HDD each and an SFA7700X with 16 1TB SAS SSD connected to 4 metadata servers. The compute nodes are running CentOS 7, and Singularity 3.11.0 and ES 8.6.0 are used. In all cases `xpack.security` is disabled, there is one shard per ES instance without any replica, and before each individual benchmark run, the cache is cleared, and the caching of the index within ES is disabled.

5.1 Rally Benchmarks

The first benchmarks are executed with Rally on a single node cluster using the NYC taxis corpus. On all three setups, i.e., the baseline, the GoCryptFS, and

---

[2] https://github.com/rfjakob/gocryptfs
[3] A German 6 PFLOP CPU-based system.

the ABE scenario the same throughput of three operations is recorded, which corresponds to a total maximum of 30,000 documents per second for a simple *match_all* query, which has a filter that is always true, i.e., just returns any document. The observed problem is, that Rally throttles itself when the latency starts to increase too much, or even timeouts occur. This limitation could not be circumvented by configuring Rally differently. However, it can be assumed that real-world use cases utilize less sensitive client/user workloads. To also simulate these and see, what an ES cluster is really capable of through putting, a new benchmark is needed.

5.2 Throughput Benchmarking

In this section, the proposed throughput benchmarking tool is presented.

Ingestion. To benchmark the performance and scalability of the ingestion process the two corpora, i.e., NYC taxis and the custom MRI dataset, are once fully ingested. To facilitate the different numbers of workers, or ingestors, the used corpus is split into equally long parts and each worker is solely responsible for ingesting one unique part of the corpus. Each of these calls ingests 10,000 documents at once, for which the time is measured and stored within an array in each worker process. When the entire corpus is successfully ingested, all unique timing arrays from all workers are streamed into a single result file.

Analyzing Single Runs. A single benchmark run is evaluated by summing up all individual timings of a single worker. This yields the total waiting time of a worker for an ES response. The measured times include the network latency, as well as the time ES requires to calculate the response. From the calculated timings the geometric mean and the geometric standard deviation of all workers are calculated. The results are shown for two examples in Fig. 1 for a three-node ES cluster with varying workers per node for both the MRI and the NYC datasets using an ethernet interface. One can see, that the much larger NYC dataset leads to a much better averaging effect of the measured ingestion times, therefore the error is minimal compared to the overall runtimes. Overall, the ingestion time is reduced from (48 ± 1) s to (14 ± 1) s when going from a single worker per node to 16 workers per node for the MRI use case, while only showing a diminishing return when going from four workers per node to 16. Similarly, the ingestion time of the NYC benchmark is reduced from (3273 ± 1) s to (590 ± 1) s, however exhibiting a larger benefit of more workers considering the runtime drop from (1237 ± 1) s for four workers to (591 ± 1) s for 16 workers. The scaling factors are 3.6 for the MRI dataset and 5.5 for the NYC dataset when scaling from 1 worker to 16.

Analyzing Different Cluster Sizes. To determine the influence of the cluster size, the chosen network interconnect, i.e., OPA or Ethernet, and the cost of the encryption, the single run analysis is done for all possible configurations. This

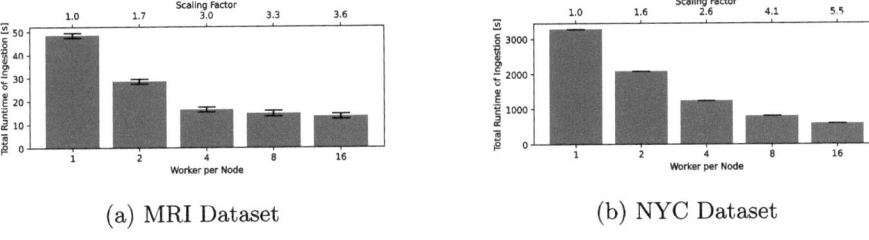

(a) MRI Dataset (b) NYC Dataset

Fig. 1. Geometric mean of the ingestion times on a 3 node cluster via ethernet without encryption.

gives a total of 180 independent measurements. To ease the representation, the number of considered measurements is reduced to 36 by only considering the fastest run depending on the number of workers. This would mean, that for the measurements shown in Fig. 1 only the run with 16 workers is used.

The results are shown in Fig. 2. The first observation is that in all cases the Ethernet performance is much better than the OPA used via Internet Protocol over Infiniband (IPoIB). The second observation is that generally, GoCryptFS exhibits the worst performance. This is expected since every operation has to go through the additional FUSE layer and needs to be transparently encrypted. The developed ABE is preliminary demonstrated in Fig. 2b and demonstrates a much faster ingestion time, which can be further analyzed in an extended Version. The increased ingestion time of ABE compared to the baseline can be explained by the overall larger dataset, where the one million documents in the MRI use case have a cumulated size of 1.5 GB whereas the ABE-MRI dataset has a size of 4.3 GB. Similarly, the size of the approximately 168 million documents for the NYC taxis data set is 75 GB for the unencrypted dataset and 184 GB for the encrypted. The resulting speedups are largest for the MRI use case and the Ethernet interface ranging between five to three times and for the OPA interface between two and three. For the larger NYC dataset speedups for the Ethernet interface are in the range of one to three and for the OPA interface very homogenously three.

Match All Queries. To establish a baseline, the *Match_All* query was used. This query just matches all documents. In theory, no complicated logic has to be done by ES and it can just stream the requested documents as soon as it gets the request for it. However, in practice, other effects can outweigh this simple model. For instance, ES dynamically allocates threads to execute and manage requests. On an unoptimized index with a high segment number the overhead of creating too many tasks to be executed on these segments can diminish the advantage of applying no logic within the filtering of documents. Thus, the Match_All query is not necessarily the very baseline query, but it is useful for either server configuration fine-tuning or network overhead optimizations.

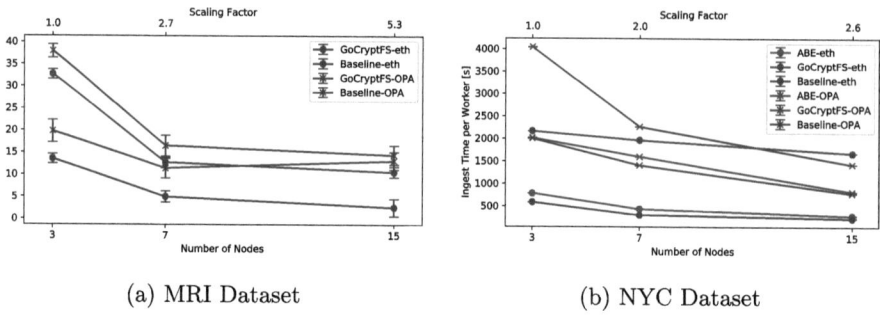

(a) MRI Dataset (b) NYC Dataset

Fig. 2. Ingestion times on varying cluster sizes interconnects.

Since the distribution of the measured latencies for the individual requests follows an exponential decay the geometric mean is used to calculate the average latency per single response. However, since there are for some measurements outliers which largely expand the geometric error and overshadow the actual measurement the standard deviation is used to indicate the spread. Dividing the number of documents per request by this averaged latency yields the averaged documents per second, as can be seen in Fig. 3 for the seven-node cluster running the NYC baseline benchmark. One can see, that by increasing the number of documents per response the overall throughput increases as well. Similarly, the overall throughput is increased by utilizing more workers to increase the number of parallel requests. In order to determine the encryption cost and the advantages of larger clusters, similar to the analysis of the ingestion, also here are only the best-performing values taken into account. The result is shown in Fig. 4. One can see that with increasing cluster sizes the throughput decreases. The reason for this behavior can be that in order to create the response, the requested ES node needs to communicate with the other nodes which are also holding an active data shard within the index. Since this benchmark is configured in such a way, that every ES node is an active data node, every node has to communicate with every other node. This adds a lot of overhead but yields no parallelization advantage since the request does not contain much logic that has to be processed.

NYC Aggregations. Analyzing the Match_All queries has demonstrated potential drawbacks to the performance when scaling out. However, it can be expected that positive effects can be observed when the workload required on the node to fulfill the request is increased. Such a more compute-bound query is a histogram aggregation within the NYC data set, where first all trips with a distance of greater than zero and smaller than 50 (miles) are selected and then aggregated into histograms according to their trip distance and cost. The result is shown in Table 1. One can see, that for the baseline as well as for the GoCryptFS scenario the latency drops from around 8 s per request for a three-node ES cluster, to 3 s for a seven-node cluster and to 1.6 s for a 15-node

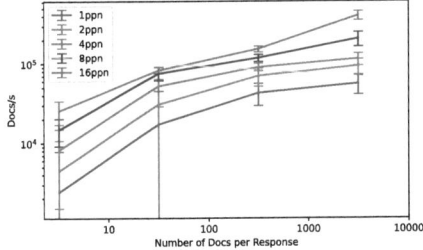
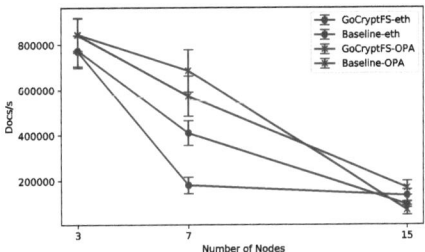

Fig. 3. Document-retrieval rate for varying response sizes and number of parallel workers for the seven-node cluster running the NYC baseline benchmark.

Fig. 4. Geometric mean of the documents per second for the best-performing worker configuration for a match_all query. (More is better)

cluster. For the three-node cluster, some large latencies were measured, causing the large error bars. The observed performance benefit of GoCryptFS could be due to additional page-caching introduced by the FUSE layer or it could be due to measurement uncertainties since the variation would also allow the

Table 1. Geometric means of the latencies of a histogram aggregation.

Cluster-Size	Baseline [s]		GoCryptFS [s]	
	Ethernet	OPA	Ethernet	OPA
3	7.4 ± 10	7 ± 3	7.1 ± 2	7.1 ± 1.4
7	3 ± 0.1	3.4 ± 0.1	2.9 ± 0.2	3.0 ± 0.2
15	1.6 ± 0.1	1.6 ± 0.1	1.4 ± 0.2	1.6 ± 0.2
Speedup	4.6	4.6	5.1	4.4

actual performance of GoCryptFS to be slightly lower than the baseline. Therefore, the additional encryption cost when doing compute-intensive operations is negligible.

MRI Custom Benchmark. Based on previously made experience with the Stanard NYC dataset, the presented benchmarking tool is used to run a custom MRI use case. For this, the following set of queries is defined together with researchers who want to use the data catalog in the future:

- **Body Part:** A *term* query for a body part, in this case, the head. Corresponds to "return all MRI scans of the head".
- **Systemvendor:** A *match_phrase* query for the Systemvendor, e.g. Siemens, Philips, or General Electric. Corresponds to "return all MRI scans form a specific system vendor".
- **Age:** A *range* query to select an age range of patients. Corresponds to "return all MRI scans of patients with an age between 50 and 60 years".
- **Body Part and Resolution:** Boolean-chained *term* queries selecting a body part and two resolution parameters. Corresponds to "return all MRI scans of the head with a resolution, i.e., *KspacePhaseEnc* of 256 times 256".
- **Brain-Age:** A *filter* which is based on a script included in the query which determines if the brain-age is larger than 5 years older than the real patient age.

- **Vendor and Body Part:** Boolean-chained *term* and *match* queries to query a body part and then match it against a specific system-vendor and protocol. Corresponds to "return all MRI scans of heads done on either a Siemens scanner with an MP2RAGE or a General Electric scanner with a BRAVO sequence".
- **Age-Weight Distribution:** A chained *match* query fpr the patient gender, followed by a *range* query of the age with an ending histogram aggregation. Corresponds to "select all men with an age lower than 70 and do a histogram of the patient weight with a binning size of 5".

To further determine the ideal setup, the same grid search as for the NYC dataset is done. In Table 2 the maximum throughput for documents per second is determined for each cluster size and query. For this, each run was individually analyzed similarly as shown in Fig. 3 to determine the ideal setup for each cluster size and query. One can see in Table 2 that for the baseline scenario, a seven-node cluster performs best for most cases, with only the Age and the Body Part and Resolution query peaking for the three-node cluster. For the Body Part, Body Part and Resolution, and the Brain-Age queries, the results lie within the error, so no direct conclusion is possible.

While for the GoCryptFS the three-node cluster performs best, except for the Age-Weight Distribution query which peaks for the seven-node cluster. Generally, all queries performed slightly worse in the GoCryptFS setup compared to the baseline, for individual performance drops ranging from a 5% to 13%, when comparing the two three-node setups. The observation, that the Brain-Age and the Vendor and Body Part are faster on the GoCryptFS setup is not clear beyond any doubt but could be explained by a temporary noisy-neighbor effect. The very limited effect of scaling from three to seven nodes can be explained by the smaller dataset size compared to the NYC corpus. Here, only a million documents, each representing a single MRI scan, are used, while the NYC taxis dataset has more than 165 million documents. Therefore, the additional network overhead of the intra ES cluster communication and thread management can not be outweighed by large parallelization gains.

To further analyze the advantages or disadvantages of scaling out, the latencies for single requests are analyzed in Table 3. One can see that for all queries except the Age-Weight Distribution the latencies increase or stay at least constant for larger cluster sizes. The Age-Weight Distribution seems to profit from a larger parallelization for the decrease of a single request latency. The reason, that the overall latency of the Age-Weight Distribution is very small compared to the others, excluding the Body Part and Resolution query, is that generally 10.000 documents are returned per response. Thus the overall payload of the response of the Age-Weight Distribution is three orders of magnitude smaller compared to the others, drastically reducing the network overhead which is included in all presented benchmarks.

Table 2. Documents per second for the MRI use case with the Ethernet interface.

Setup	Cluster-Size	Body Part	System-vendor	Age	Body Part Resolution	Brain-Age	Vendor+ Body P.	Age-W. Distr.
Baseline	3 Node	190k±15k	180k±13k	190k±15k	124k±6k	94k±5k	96k±5k	4k±160
	7 Node	212k±10k	244k±4k	103k±5k	114k±6k	101k±4k	166k±4k	12k±700
	15 Node	39k±9k	37k±4k	49k±4k	48k±34k	37k±4k	72k±5k	5k±2k
GoCryptFS	3 Node	180k±13k	157k±10k	176k±13k	119k±4k	170k±13k	153k±5k	5k±100
	7 Node	71k±9k	100k±12k	51k±4k	89k±7k	50k±5k	103k±4k	6k±480
	15 Node	29k±6k	33k±3k	49k±3k	41k±19k	39k±3k	60k±4k	4k±670

Table 3. Latencies for the MRI custom use case with the Ethernet interface.

Setup	Cluster-Size	Body Part	System vendor	Age	Body Part Resolution	Brain-Age	Vendor and Body Part	Age-Weight Distribution
Baseline	3	0.6±0.1	0.7±0.2	0.6±0.1	0.02±0.02	0.6±0.1	0.7±0.1	0.020±0.005
	7	0.7±0.1	0.7±0.1	0.7±0.1	0.02±0.02	0.7±0.1	0.5±0.1	0.013±0.003
	15	0.9±0.3	0.9±0.2	0.7±0.2	0.03±0.05	0.9±0.2	0.5±0.1	0.009±0.004
GoCryptFS	3	0.6±0.1	0.6±0.1	0.6±0.1	0.02±0.01	0.6±0.1	0.5±0.1	0.022±0.004
	7	0.7±0.1	0.7±0.1	0.7±0.1	0.02±0.02	0.7±0.1	0.5±0.1	0.013±0.003
	15	1.0±0.3	0.9±0.3	0.8±0.2	0.03±0.05	0.9±0.3	0.5±0.1	0.010±0.005

6 Conclusion

In conclusion, a workflow to deploy on-demand ES clusters for sensitive data on HPC systems is presented. Two different encryption techniques are implemented and are systematically benchmarked with a novel tool that can be used to create very aggressive throughput-oriented workloads, as well as latency-sensitive benchmarks. It is shown, that the achieved throughputs are significantly larger compared to the available Rally benchmark. Using two different data sets, a standard benchmark NYC taxis dataset as well as a custom MRI dataset, thorough testing is done to determine a suitable cluster configuration. The importance of accurate data and workload modeling is demonstrated, showing that for simple queries even on large datasets consisting of more than 165 million documents, larger ES cluster can decrease performance due to additional network and thread management overhead, while more compute-intensive operations can largely benefit from larger clusters, as is demonstrated for the histogram aggregations. For this scaling tests from three to 15 node-sized clusters are done. Due to the thorough requirement analysis, one of the discussed encryption techniques is excluded from the MRI use case. In addition, these benchmarks serve as a powerful foundation for further requirement engineering, to determine the needed throughput and latency of the histogram aggregations. It is shown that in this scenario these workloads behave inverse, therefore, a balanced server configuration needs to be chosen. This can be done guided by the presented benchmark and through the thorough methodology. For future work an extended version to discuss the developed ABE method is planned, as well as to extend the weak scaling to strong scaling on larger ES clusters.

Acknowledgments. We gratefully acknowledge funding by "Nationales Hochleistungsrechnen" and BMBF under 01|S22093A.

Disclosure of Interests. The authors have no competing interests to declare that are relevant to the content of this article.

References

1. Almeida, A., Oliveira, F., Lebre, R., Costa, C.: NoSQL distributed database for DICOM objects. In: 2020 IEEE International Conference on Bioinformatics and Biomedicine (BIBM), pp. 1882–1885. IEEE (2020)
2. Cirillo, D., Valencia, A.: Big data analytics for personalized medicine. Curr. Opin. Biotechnol. **58**, 161–167 (2019)
3. Coman Schmid, D., Crameri, K., Oesterle, S., Rinn, B., Sengstag, T., Stockinger, H.: SPHN-the BioMedIt network: a secure it platform for research with sensitive human data. Digit. Pers. Health Med. **270**, 1170–1174 (2020)
4. Costa, C., Ferreira, C., Bastião, L., Ribeiro, L., Silva, A., Oliveira, J.L.: Dicoogle-an open source peer-to-peer PACS. J. Digit. Imaging **24**, 848–856 (2011)
5. Hulsen, T., et al.: From big data to precision medicine. Front. Med. **6**, 34 (2019)
6. Michalski, R.S., Kaufman, K.A.: Data mining and knowledge discovery: a review of issues and a multistrategy approach (1997)
7. Nolte, H., et al.: Secure HPC: a workflow providing a secure partition on an HPC system. Futur. Gener. Comput. Syst. **141**, 677–691 (2023)
8. Rascovsky, S.J., Delgado, J.A., Sanz, A., Calvo, V.D., Castrillón, G.: Informatics in radiology: use of CouchDB for document-based storage of DICOM objects. Radiographics **32**(3), 913–927 (2012)
9. Scheerman, M., et al.: Secure platform for processing sensitive data on shared HPC systems. arXiv preprint arXiv:2103.14679 (2021)
10. Shilo, S., Rossman, H., Segal, E.: Axes of a revolution: challenges and promises of big data in healthcare. Nat. Med. **26**(1), 29–38 (2020)
11. Shimabukuro, D.W., Barton, C.W., Feldman, M.D., Mataraso, S.J., Das, R.: Effect of a machine learning-based severe sepsis prediction algorithm on patient survival and hospital length of stay: a randomised clinical trial. BMJ Open Respir. Res. **4**(1), e000234 (2017)
12. Silva, L.A.B., Beroud, L., Costa, C., Oliveira, J.L.: Medical imaging archiving: a comparison between several NoSQL solutions. In: IEEE-EMBS International Conference on Biomedical and Health Informatics (BHI), pp. 65–68. IEEE (2014)

Introducing the Metric Proxy for Holistic I/O Measurements

Jean-Baptiste Besnard[1]($\boxtimes$), Ahmad Tarraf[2], Alberto Cascajo[3], and Sameer Shende[1]

[1] ParaTools SAS, Bruyères-le-Châtel, France
jbbesnard@paratools.fr
[2] Department of Computer Science, Technical University of Darmstadt, Darmstadt, Germany
[3] Computer Science and Engineering Department, University Carlos III of Madrid, Madrid, Spain

Abstract. High-Performance Computing (HPC) systems face a wide spectrum of I/O patterns from various sources including workflows, in-Situ data operations, or from Ad-hoc file storages. However, accurately monitoring these workloads at scale is challenging due to multiple layers' interference on system performance metrics. The metric proxy addresses this by providing real-time insights into system states, reducing overhead and storage constraints. By utilizing a Tree-Based Overlay Network (TBON) topology, it efficiently collects metrics across nodes in HPC systems. This paper explores the conceptual foundation of the metric proxy, its architecture design, and how it can be used to improve I/O performance modelling and detection of periodic I/O workload patterns, ultimately aiding in more informed system optimization strategies.

Keywords: Profiling · I/O · modelling · Prometheus

1 Introduction

In High-Performance Computing, we are observing a growing diversity in I/O patterns since workloads evolve towards being more horizontal. This expanding array of I/O workloads presents challenges in accurately assessing overall system throughput, as I/O operations are susceptible to various factors and interferences from multiple layers of the system. Therefore, the capability to monitor and track the system state in real-time at the scale of supercomputers becomes crucial for effectively characterizing I/O workloads at scale.

Such characterization not only aids in understanding the system's behavior but also informs the development of active I/O layers capable of dynamically adjusting themselves in response to load variations or resource availability. To achieve this, we have developed a specialized monitoring and modelling framework designed to track the entire system at scale. This tool, known as the *metric proxy*, can monitor per-node, per-job, and global states in near real-time, with low overhead and within limited storage constraints, owing to its Tree-Based Overlay Network topology.

In this paper, we begin by outlining the rationale behind the real-time availability of both global and per-job system metrics. Following this, we delve into the architecture of the metric proxy. Subsequently, we showcase practical applications that harness its monitoring capabilities. Firstly, we explore a traditional integration with a Grafana dashboard. Secondly, we examine the generation of performance models combined with the detection of I/O periodicity using FTIO. Finally, we provide our conclusion and future work.

2 Motivation: Holistic I/O Measurement

As parallel machines continue to incorporate an increasing number of cores per node, the challenge of efficiently utilizing these computational units grows exponentially. Consequently, addressing the burgeoning demand for data access has become crucial for maximizing performance. One critical aspect in achieving this optimization lies in effectively managing input/output operations (I/Os). The entire memory hierarchy presents an opportunity for enhancing I/O throughput. For instance, leveraging node-local memory for Ad-Hoc storage [44] can significantly boost I/O performance. Moreover, I/O bottlenecks extend beyond backend file systems; they also manifest at the network level due to the shared network substrate. In this complex environment, initiatives such as the ADMIRE project [15] explore holistic optimization of I/O by utilizing the global system state to balance I/O resources among concurrent jobs. The optimization process involves fine-tuning various parameters, including configuring I/O subsystems such as burst-buffer dimensioning, as well as adapting application behavior through moldability. Additionally, employing malleable applications to reshape job characteristics further enhances flexibility in resource utilization. By intelligently adjusting these tuning knobs, our goal is to achieve more efficient I/O management and to improve overall system performance.

To facilitate the reconfiguration of heuristics, we have developed the *metric proxy*. Its primary objective is to collect data at scale, offering various levels of granularity ranging from system-wide to individual nodes and specific jobs. This proxy continuously generates a stream of performance metrics, providing insights into all ongoing tasks, all while adhering to storage constraints per job through the utilization of sampled traces. With hundreds of metrics spanning both the machine and its associated jobs, the proxy doubles as a *model server*, capable of generating predictive analyses concerning scaling and temporal behavior. Scaling predictions are derived by consistently monitoring past job statistics and iteratively constructing a performance model. This process is facilitated by the seamless integration of the proxy with the Extra-P [14], which enables the generation and evaluation of performance models. Temporal analysis is another critical aspect, particularly relevant for I/O operations. The proxy characterizes metrics within the frequency domain, leveraging FTIO [43], which is designed explicitly for phase prediction. By integrating the results within the proxy environment, these insights are readily accessible to inform reconfiguration decisions and aid different system components.

3 Related-Work

Aggregating metrics in a distributed environment has become common for system administrators. To monitor the state of the entire infrastructure, various tools have been designed to collect and persist metrics over time for later consumption. Prometheus [5] is one such tool. It is a Time-Series Database (TSDB) known for its ability to compose and persist measurements from various data sources. Prometheus data can then be visualized using Grafana [24], as an interactive dashboard. However, this data forwarding operation is not unique to Prometheus; other databases like InfluxDB [2], Graphite [1], OpenTSDB [4], Nagios [3] or Sensu [6] also offer similar capabilities. While these tools differ in their alerting features, query languages, and storage methods, they all collect and persist metrics over time for later consumption. The proxy described in this paper has been specifically designed to handle short-lived jobs and spatial and temporal aggregation while remaining compatible with existing monitoring tools such as Prometheus.

In the realm of high-performance computing, there are two main tools with goals similar to our proxy: aggregating both application and system-level resources in a coherent manner. The first one is Caliper [12], which presents application metrics using a blackboard architecture for analysis. The second one is DCDB [34,35], aiming to collect a wide range of metrics while persisting them as time series using a tree of pushers and collector agents feeding a Cassandra DB backend. Both are advanced and mature tools for performing Operational Data Analytics (ODA) [35] at scale. Other tools are more targeted at global system monitoring, including LDMS [25], TACC Stats [20], JobDigest [36], Ganglia [31], ClusterCockpit [18], and LLVIEW [21], which are dedicated to visualizing the global state of a supercomputer. Although they share several aspects in terms of design with our metric proxy, our tool focuses on being self-sufficient through a static binary that uses the file system for storage. Its sole focus is on efficiently collecting and persisting metrics and associated models in various scopes at a machine scale while seamlessly integrating with existing tools.

Another class of HPC performance tools is application-focused [7,23,27,40], aiming to collect data from a specific job in a precise manner. Our approach differs fundamentally because its goal is to portray a realistic global state of the system while maintaining a job-specific view. Specifically, for I/O there are several approaches that have been devised to improve monitoring [10,28]. Darshan [22] is a common way of capturing I/O behavior. Additionally, the proxy is designed to be always on, acting as a monitoring tool; whereas some analyses are too expensive or verbose to be constantly enabled. Therefore, these tools serve a different purpose than passive monitoring and logging, as they are more intended for performance optimization and analysis.

4 Overview of the Metric Proxy

In this section, we introduce our main contribution in the form of a monitoring daemon called the *metric proxy*. This daemon is versatile and capable of providing several outputs for arbitrary metrics it aggregates. We first present an overview of its overall architecture, deployment, and data forwarding mechanisms. Subsequently, we focus on its monitoring capabilities, listing the various data sources we currently support and their underlying transport layers. Finally, we will discuss its interfaces and APIs, demonstrating briefly how it enables both later consumption and storage of performance data.

4.1 Architecture

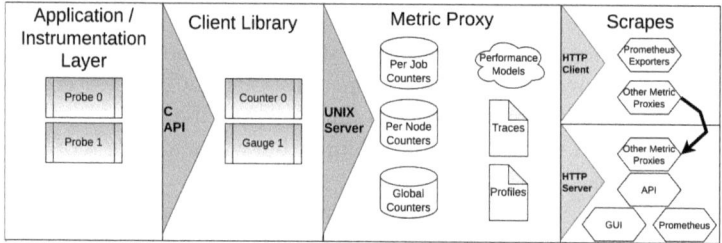

Fig. 1. Overview of the *metric proxy* architecture.

Figure 1 presents an overview of the metric proxy[1], outlining how it is to be deployed on each node as a daemon. This architecture allows the (1) collection and (2) forwarding of arbitrary data at various granularities, enabling both global and per-job state tracking. Each proxy instantiates two servers and can act as an HTTP client to collect and dispatch performance data as follows:

Metric Server: A Unix server is created on each node, which can collect metrics from short-lived jobs more efficiently than traditional methods such as HTTP. Additionally, the client remains connected, avoiding unnecessary handshakes for each job that requires tracking. This persistent connection protocol also enables the monitoring of when a job terminates. To achieve this, the tool provides a client library. The library allows developers to register arbitrary counters and gauges with names and documentation in the local proxy, enabling them to update these values over time for each counter. Implementation-wise, each counter has its own lock that protects its value during updates, and only one lock is used when updating the local value of a counter. Meanwhile, a polling thread regularly checks all known counters in random order and sends snapshots of their values over the Unix socket.

---
[1] https://github.com/besnardjb/proxy_v2.

HTTP Server: The HTTP server in each proxy plays a dual role: (1) it provides an API that enables users to query and set data using various endpoints, and (2) it also exposes a graphical user interface as a dynamic website that utilizes the previously mentioned API endpoints. These proxies are interconnected in a Tree-Based Ordered Network fashion, facilitating easy connectivity between them via this HTTP API, which provides structured data endpoints in JSON format. Furthermore, each proxy features a /metrics endpoint, which outputs all metrics in Prometheus-compatible format.

HTTP Client: Multiple proxies can collaborate effectively for large-scale data gathering and aggregation purposes. These proxies act as mediators, capable of handling API requests to collect and aggregate metrics over the TBON. The proxy is equipped with Prometheus exporter scraping capabilities, enabling it to manage its metrics dynamically. Scrape intervals can be configured on demand, and new scrapes can also be added as needed.

The metric proxy and all its components are implemented in Rust, including the C interface. Rust [32] is a language allowing memory safety at compile time [45] while preserving performance, it also has a rich set of libraries (crates) thanks to the Cargo build system. Metric proxies are to be used by building a hierarchy to monitor multiple nodes in a distributed fashion.

4.2 Measurement Scopes

As illustrated in Fig. 1, the proxy maintains measurements at three levels defined as follows:

Job Level: Each job, when connecting using the client library, sends a unique *jobid*, which is used to maintain a job table in the proxy memory. Similarly, jobs are propagated across the TBON towards the root, providing a global view of all jobs. In practice, when a metric proxy scrapes another metric proxy, it consumes a JSON array of all jobs and metrics. When all references to a job are removed (i.e., disconnected clients and no longer in scrapes), the job is considered finished; at this point, the proxy saves and closes the respective counters, potentially generating artifacts such as profiles or traces. This process progressively propagates the start and termination of jobs across the TBON towards the root proxy, including distributed jobs spawned by a batch manager like slurm.

Node Level: All metrics accumulated on a node are summarized in a node-level array, which is then sent up the Tree-Based Object Network to allow the root proxy to expose counters from all nodes under a single collection point. This root exporter can be scraped using Prometheus, thus enabling monitoring of the state of an entire machine within a single exporter, aggregating data sources including other Prometheus exporters across space. As a result, the Prometheus Time-Series Database only needs to scrape a single exporter rather than querying successively from all nodes, hence improving monitoring scalability.

Global Level: The last level summarizes all jobs at the current time, providing visibility into the overall load of various applications. This holistic overview allows for tracking metrics such as application-level call rates, for example, MPI, across different tooling systems, a characteristic that sets our approach apart from others in this regard.

In practice, the Tree-Based Overlay Network [16,29,39] aggregates job states to generate the overall state at its root. This means that data with complete spatial visibility is only available in the root proxy. In this central hub, individual jobs can be listed and queried for detailed information. JSON and Prometheus exporter endpoints are also made available for all measurement scopes if needed, simplifying data-scraping when compared to other systems that often rely on their own storage format. This allows users or additional tools to directly access data from the system using basic 'curl' requests.

4.3 Spatial Aggregation

One of the main goals of the proxy is to gather metrics from multiple nodes and jobs over time to create a comprehensive view of a distributed system state. This process is facilitated through the TBON topology, which defines a reduction tree among the servers. To implement this hierarchy, defining operations for counter and gauge-type metrics is necessary.

From the data model perspective, the proxy shares many similarities with Prometheus since we require it to act as an aggregating push gateway. As such, the proxy currently supports two main types of metrics: counters and gauges. Counters are incremented indefinitely, while gauges fluctuate over time, storing their data along with a name and documentation string in a 64-bit floating point value format. Please note that Prometheus's metric types include *Histogram* and *Summary*, which track statistical properties of values. These aren't currently implemented within the TBON, as they are dropped when scraped – their support is currently future work.

The summation of counters is relatively straightforward because of their monotonic nature - it simply involves accumulating all incoming values. When a client sends a value to the proxy, it resets its local accumulator; starting from zero again. This means that values are summed up in various profiles. Similarly, when proxies scrape each other, they keep track of the previous value to forward any increments. As such, the total counter value is progressively aggregated at the root. The aggregation process for gauges is slightly more complex than that for counters because, at the node level, when considering 200 MPI processes contributing to the same *jobid*, we would like their gauge values to be averaged. Furthermore, it is not straightforward to determine how much each subtree contributes to the total value as we ascend the tree. Therefore, gauges are represented by four floating-point numbers: minimum, maximum, number of hits, and total sum. This simple process allows the root proxy to monitor both the average (as $\frac{total}{hits}$) and dynamics of a gauge over time across different scopes in a space-independent manner using the tree to perform the reduction for the individual jobs and scopes.

4.4 Data-Sources

Each proxy can aggregate data from multiple endpoints, including existing Prometheus exporters that can already cover a broad range of services. We have also implemented an exporter for BeeGFS[2] to enhance our monitoring infrastructure, (Bytes written and read, and total number of operations). In addition, the proxy monitors several node-local metrics, including temperature, load, and disk usage. Furthermore, on the client side, using UNIX sockets, our tool currently supports the instrumentation of the whole MPI interface using LD_PRELOAD and optional wrapping of the process with a modified strace to capture all system calls. Overall, the proxy typically captures hundreds of counters, and this measurement capability can be readily expanded to accommodate more specific needs.

Finally, all these measurement results are represented as counters and gauges in the proxy, and are forwarded indiscriminately to the root. Multiple components of various types (Prometheus exporters and Unix clients) can be associated with a given job, as long as they share the same label. This allows gathering performance data per-job. By default, if a scrape is not tied to a specific job, all jobs are updated with its values. For example, this enables capturing the overall file-system load within individual jobs.

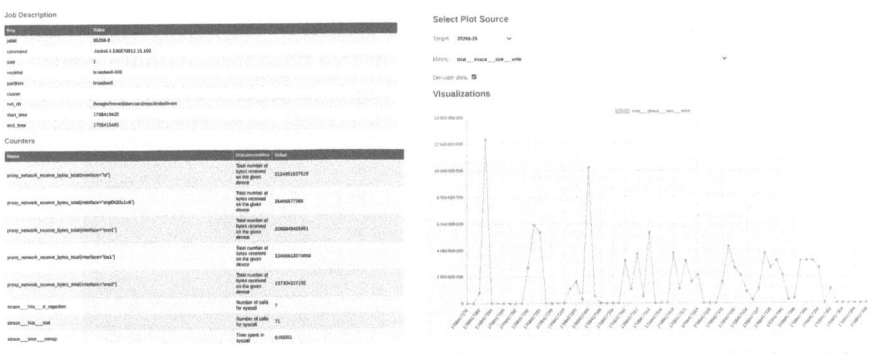

(a) Profile excerpt for IMB-IO.   (b) Real-time write bandwidth for a job.

Fig. 2. Screenshots from the interactive HTML GUI.

4.5 State Preservation

Until now, we have been meticulous in detailing the architecture of the metric proxy, which was noteworthy because it clarified our primary goal: making performance data actionable. The proxy provides multiple ways to consume measurement data: (1) all instantaneous measurements can be accessed via JSON endpoints for every measurement scope. (2) After a job is completed, a profile

---
[2] https://github.com/besnardjb/beegfs-exporter.

with the final value of its counters is stored in the file system along with metadata about the job, including but not limited to its execution scale extracted from Slurm environment variables. The proxy enables you to access previous profiles through an API by either JobID or command-line interface. (3) The proxy generates traces for all jobs. These traces can be described as a series of profile snapshots over time [33]; this is precisely how they were created. One advantage of this process is that profiles retain their summative nature, just as in the TBON, enabling us to reduce profiles within the trace. The proxy is configured with a maximum trace size of 32 MB per job. When this limit is reached, the trace folds over itself, reducing temporal resolution by half; concurrently, the profile snapshot frequency is halved, causing the trace to fill up more slowly. The proxy offers an interface to explore and visualize traces both in the graphical user interface (GUI) (Fig. 2) and using JSON endpoints. A side tool also exports traces directly from the file system in JSON format.

5 Use-Cases and Evaluation

This section presents two simple use cases that demonstrate the use of the metric proxy. First, we connect it to a Prometheus time-series database and expose its values in Grafana to illustrate the compatibility of the proxy with state-of-the-art tools. Second, we utilize a modeling feature provided by the proxy, which enables us to perform regressions on points in various profiles and compute equations that infer the behavior of metrics as a function of execution scale.

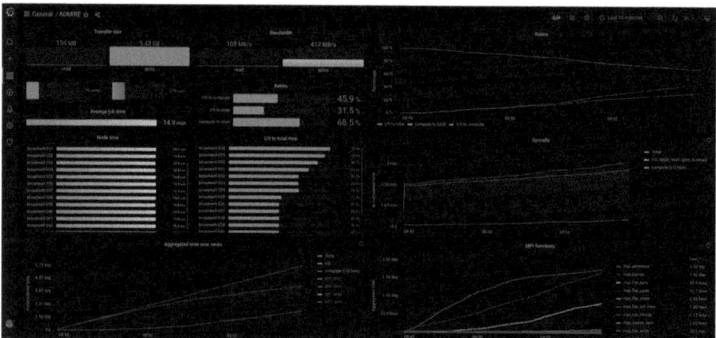

Fig. 3. Grafana dashboard showing the queried metrics during the execution of IMB-IO with 576 processes.

5.1 Sample Output: Grafana

One way to visualize data captured by the always-on measurement approach is through Grafana, an open-source analytics and interactive visualization web application. We simply scrape the root proxy using a Prometheus TSDB instance and then point Grafana toward this database to achieve this. The visualization approach is straightforward and easy to set up as the data are now projected in widely used formats. For our approach, we query the data from the Prometheus database every 5 s to illustrate metrics such as bandwidth, total transferred size, and elapsed time of different functions. Many other metrics can also be queried, for instance, the runtime of the job, visits per function call, number of nodes, and processes. The primary speciality of this dashboard lies in its ability to combine both machine-wide metrics with application-level metrics.

Grafana allows you to perform arithmetic with traces, such as aggregating the total time or calculating rates over a specific interval. It also allows you to filter by matching patterns and aggregate the results. This way, ratios like the I/O to total time ratio can be calculated, demonstrating how much an application is I/O intensive during its runtime. Moreover, Grafana helps visualize the individual times of MPI functions per node by aggregating them at the application level. By aggregating all I/O functions, we can see the total I/O time or the total number of bytes read or written. Note that no root access is required since all data gathering is done in the user space. This lets users visualize performance traces online - a task often reserved for system administrators.

To demonstrate the approach, we executed Intel MPI Benchmarks IMB-IO on the HPC4AI cluster [9] Haswell partition. We ran the benchmark suite with default settings, except for the iteration flag, which was set to 10. The experiment was run with 576 MPI ranks. Each benchmark run is repeated for a different number of processes up to 576, following an iterative pattern typical to IMB-IO. The results during the execution of the experiments are visualized in the Grafana dashboard (refer to Fig. 3). As seen in the figure, the I/O to total ratio varies among the compute nodes, which can be traced back to the iterative nature of the benchmark suite as described previously. Moreover, the accumulated runtime of various functions can be observed.

5.2 Multi-level Behavioral Projection

Depending on the use case, high-level profiles or low-level traces may be required. For performance modeling, for example, profiles are essential. On the other hand, while performance models can be seen as an abstract representation obtained from several runs, profiles, which are at a lower abstraction level, describe application behavior at a higher granularity but only for a single run. However, aggregated profiles often fail to properly represent the *temporal* behavior of applications [46]. This becomes especially relevant if the use case is to perform optimizations during the execution of an application. In this case, traces and predictions built on traces may be more favorable than profiles. To adapt to different scenarios, our metric proxy can deliver behavioral projections at different levels, as described below.

From Profiles to Performance Models: A performance model is a formula that expresses a performance metric of interest, such as execution time or energy consumption, as a function of one or more execution parameters (e.g., the size of the input problem or the number of processors). Performance models can be generated to characterize the scalability of a single function call up to the entire application behavior. Performance modeling has a long research history [8,11,14,19,30,37,38,41,42] in HPC. The proxy can leverage Extra-P [14] to model the scalability of the application's computing, communication, and I/O functions. As such, when a job finishes, the proxy invokes Extra-P to regenerate the performance models. These models are then available for consumption in the proxy interface. Practically, it means metrics from a given proxy can be evaluated at other scales using Extra-P models, as illustrated in Fig. 4b which shows the predicted total I/O in function of the number of MPI processes.

From Traces to Temporal Predictions: While performance models are great for predicting the scaling behavior of an application, online projection might be required, for example, by an I/O scheduler to decrease contention. In fact, recent studies on I/O scheduling showed that knowledge of periodic I/O patterns, even when not *perfectly precise*, leads to good contention avoidance [13,17,26]. FTIO [43], which stands for frequency techniques for I/O and is publicly available on GitHub[3], is a tool that can predict the period of the I/O phases. The tool simply needs the bandwidth over time. FTIO supports an online prediction mode in which the period is predicted at runtime. For that, however, the tool requires online traces. Furthermore, the higher the accuracy of the traces, the more reliable the predictions from FTIO are. With such use cases in mind, we developed the metric proxy to provide FTIO with this information. Besides, FTIO is not limited to I/O, but can also predict any of the metrics which are traced. This is, for example, shown in Fig. 4a, where the total MPI bytes of an application are illustrated: the figure shows the amount of information exchanged between the processes of an application during certain phases, while in other phases, the processes barely communicate. This pattern can be found in many applications, such as when they perform periodic checkpointing. For this example, FTIO found with an 87.06% confidence that the frequency of the phases is 4.57710^{-3} Hz, corresponding to a period of 218.5 s.

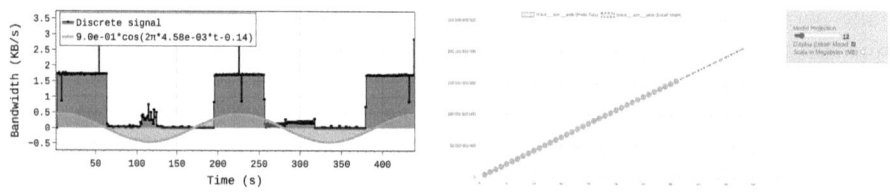

(a) FTIO prediction for MPI Bandwidth.   (b) I/O size projection with Extra-P.

Fig. 4. Sample models generated by the metric proxy.

---

[3] https://github.com/tuda-parallel/FTIO.

6 Conclusion

In this paper, we introduce *metric proxy*, a monitoring system designed for HPC systems that collects a wide range of metrics at scale. The proxy is built to store profiles and traces for each job executed, facilitating real-time system reconfiguration. It does this through a tree-based overlay network architecture, which allows it to provide measurement data in close to real-time. Combining these functionalities makes the metric proxy a model server that can interact with Extra-P and FTIO for performance projections and frequency predictions, respectively. By integrating multiple tiers of data (global, node, and per-job), the system constantly leverages the most pertinent information at any given moment, improving the decision-making for optimal performance.

The design of the *metric proxy* is flexible enough to be adapted or integrated with existing systems. It is available in open-source form and can offer its users scalable and comprehensive monitoring capabilities. The combination of a robust tracking system and real-time prediction tools opens up new possibilities for optimizing HPC workloads, from fine-tuning I/O subsystem parameters to modifying job execution, ultimately improving system efficiency. In addition, as far as the proxy is concerned, our current work is on assessing the system response at scale by studying new topologies for the TBON to maximize the temporal accuracy of the root proxy.

Acknowledgment. We acknowledge the support of the European Commission and the German Federal Ministry of Education and Research (BMBF) under the EuroHPC Programmes ADMIRE (GA no. 956748, BMBF funding no. 16HPC006K) which receive support from the European Union's Horizon 2020 program and DE, FR, ES, IT, PL, SE. This work was also funded by the Deutsche Forschungsgemeinschaft (DFG, German Research Foundation) - Project No. 449683531 (ExtraNoise). Moreover, the authors gratefully acknowledge the computing time provided to them on the high-performance computer at the University of Turin from the laboratory on High-Performance Computing for Artificial Intelligence [9].

References

1. Graphite. https://graphiteapp.org/. Accessed 27 Feb 2024
2. InfluxData. https://www.influxdata.com/. Accessed 27 Feb 2024
3. Nagios. https://www.nagios.org/. Accessed 27 Feb 2024
4. OpenTSDB. http://opentsdb.net/. Accessed 27 Feb 2024
5. Prometheus time series database. https://prometheus.io/. Accessed 27 Feb 2024
6. Sensu. https://sensu.io/. Accessed 27 Feb 2024
7. Adhianto, L., et al.: HPCTOOLKIT: tools for performance analysis of optimized parallel programs. Concurrency Comput. Pract. Experience **6**, 685–701 (2010)
8. Aggarwal, V., Yoon, C., George, A., Lam, H., Stitt, G.: Performance modeling for multilevel communication in shmem+. In: PGAS '10: Proceedings of the Fourth Conference on Partitioned Global Address Space Programming Model. Association for Computing Machinery, New York, NY, USA (2010). https://doi.org/10.1145/2020373.2020380

9. Aldinucci, M., et al.: HPC4AI, an AI-on-demand federated platform endeavour. In: ACM Computing Frontiers. Ischia, Italy (2018). https://doi.org/10.1145/3203217.3205340
10. Betke, E., Kunkel, J.: Footprinting parallel i/o–machine learning to classify application's i/o behavior. In: High Performance Computing: ISC High Performance 2019 International Workshops, Frankfurt, Germany, June 16–20, 2019, Revised Selected Papers 34, pp. 214–226. Springer (2019)
11. Bhattacharyya, A., Hoefler, T.: PEMOGEN: automatic adaptive performance modeling during program runtime. In: Proceedings of the 23rd International Conference on Parallel Architectures and Compilation (PACT'14), pp. 393–404. ACM (2014)
12. Boehme, D., et al.: Caliper: performance introspection for HPC software stacks. In: SC'16: Proceedings of the International Conference for High Performance Computing, Networking, Storage and Analysis, pp. 550–560. IEEE (2016)
13. Boito, F., Pallez, G., Teylo, L., Vidal, N.: IO-sets: simple and efficient approaches for I/O bandwidth management. IEEE Trans. Parallel Distrib. Syst. **34**(10), 2783–2796 (2023)
14. Calotoiu, A., Hoefler, T., Poke, M., Wolf, F.: Using automated performance modeling to find scalability bugs in complex codes. In: Proceedings of the ACM/IEEE Conference on Supercomputing (SC13), Denver, CO, USA. pp. 1–12. ACM (2013). https://doi.org/10.1145/2503210.2503277
15. Carretero, J., et al.: Adaptive multi-tier intelligent data manager for exascale. In: Proceedings of the 20th ACM International Conference on Computing Frontiers, pp. 285–290 (2023)
16. Cascajo, A., Singh, D.E., Carretero, J.: Limitless-light-weight monitoring tool for large scale systems. Microprocess. Microsyst. **93**, 104586 (2022)
17. Dorier, M., Antoniu, G., Ross, R., Kimpe, D., Ibrahim, S.: CALCioM: mitigating I/O interference in HPC systems through cross-application coordination. In: IPDPS'14, pp. 155–164. IEEE (2014)
18. Eitzinger, J., Gruber, T., Afzal, A., Zeiser, T., Wellein, G.: Clustercockpit-a web application for job-specific performance monitoring. In: 2019 IEEE International Conference on Cluster Computing (CLUSTER), pp. 1–7. IEEE (2019)
19. Eller, P.R., Hoefler, T., Gropp, W.: Using performance models to understand scalable krylov solver performance at scale for structured grid problems. In: ICS '19: Proceedings of the ACM International Conference on Supercomputing, pp. 138–149. Association for Computing Machinery, New York, NY, USA (2019). https://doi.org/10.1145/3330345.3330358
20. Evans, T., et al.: Comprehensive resource use monitoring for HPC systems with TACC stats. In: 2014 First International Workshop on HPC User Support Tools, pp. 13–21. IEEE (2014)
21. Forschungszentrum Jülich, J.S.C.: LLview. https://github.com/FZJ-JSC/LLview. Accessed 30 Apr 2024
22. Gabriel Jr, D.J.: I/O throughput prediction for HPC applications using darshan logs. Ph.D. thesis, University of Nevada, Reno (2022)
23. Geimer, M., Wolf, F., Wylie, B.J.N., Ábrahám, E., Becker, D., Mohr, B.: The Scalasca performance toolset architecture. Concurrency Comput. Pract. Experience **22**(6), 702–719 (2010)
24. Grafana (2023). https://github.com/grafana/grafana
25. Izadpanah, R., Naksinehaboon, N., Brandt, J., Gentile, A., Dechev, D.: Integrating low-latency analysis into HPC system monitoring. In: Proceedings of the 47th International Conference on Parallel Processing, pp. 1–10 (2018)

26. Jeannot, E., Pallez, G., Vidal, N.: Scheduling periodic I/O access with bi-colored chains: models and algorithms. J. Sched. **24**(5), 469–481 (2021)
27. Knüpfer, A., et al.: Score-P: a joint performance measurement run-time infrastructure for Periscope,Scalasca, TAU, and Vampir. In: Brunst, H., Müller, M.S., Nagel, W.E., Resch, M.M. (eds.) Tools for High Performance Computing 2011, pp. 79–91. Springer, Berlin, Heidelberg (2012). https://doi.org/10.1007/978-3-642-31476-6_7
28. Kunkel, J.M., et al.: Tools for analyzing parallel I/O. In: High Performance Computing: ISC High Performance 2018 International Workshops, Frankfurt/Main, Germany, June 28, 2018, Revised Selected Papers 33, pp. 49–70. Springer (2018)
29. Lee, C.W., Malony, A.D., Morris, A.: Taumon: scalable online performance data analysis in tau. In: Euro-Par 2010 Parallel Processing Workshops: HeteroPar, HPCC, HiBB, CoreGrid, UCHPC, HPCF, PROPER, CCPI, VHPC, Ischia, Italy, August 31–September 3, 2010, Revised Selected Papers 16, pp. 493–499. Springer (2011)
30. Marathe, A., et al.: Performance modeling under resource constraints using deep transfer learning. In: SC '17: Proceedings of the International Conference for High Performance Computing, Networking, Storage and Analysis. Association for Computing Machinery, New York, NY, USA (2017). https://doi.org/10.1145/3126908.3126969
31. Massie, M.L., Chun, B.N., Culler, D.E.: The ganglia distributed monitoring system: design, implementation, and experience. Parallel Comput. **30**(7), 817–840 (2004)
32. Matsakis, N.D., Klock II, F.S.: The rust language. In: ACM SIGAda Ada Letters, vol. 34, pp. 103–104. ACM (2014)
33. Morris, A., Spear, W., Malony, A.D., Shende, S.: Observing performance dynamics using parallel profile snapshots. In: Euro-Par 2008–Parallel Processing: 14th International Euro-Par Conference, Las Palmas de Gran Canaria, Spain, August 26–29, 2008. Proceedings 14, pp. 162–171. Springer (2008)
34. Netti, A., et al.: From facility to application sensor data: modular, continuous and holistic monitoring with DCDB. In: Proceedings of the International Conference for High Performance Computing, Networking, Storage and Analysis, pp. 1–27 (2019)
35. Netti, A., et al.: DCDB wintermute: enabling online and holistic operational data analytics on HPC systems. In: Proceedings of the 29th International Symposium on High-Performance Parallel and Distributed Computing, pp. 101–112 (2020)
36. Nikitenko, D., et al.: Jobdigest–detailed system monitoring-based supercomputer application behavior analysis. In: Russian Supercomputing Days, pp. 516–529. Springer (2017)
37. Obaida, M.A., Liu, J., Chennupati, G., Santhi, N., Eidenbenz, S.: Parallel application performance prediction using analysis based models and HPC simulations. In: SIGSIM-PADS '18: Proceedings of the 2018 ACM SIGSIM Conference on Principles of Advanced Discrete Simulation, pp. 49–59. Association for Computing Machinery, New York, NY, USA (2018). https://doi.org/10.1145/3200921.3200937
38. Price, J., McIntosh-Smith, S.: Improving auto-tuning convergence times with dynamically generated predictive performance models. In: MCSOC '15: Proceedings of the 2015 IEEE 9th International Symposium on Embedded Multicore/Many-Core Systems-on-Chip, pp. 211–218. IEEE Computer Society, USA (2015).https://doi.org/10.1109/MCSoC.2015.31
39. Roth, P.C., Arnold, D.C., Miller, B.P.: MRNet: a software-based multicast/reduction network for scalable tools. In: Proceedings of the 2003 ACM/IEEE Conference on Supercomputing, p. 21 (2003)

40. Shende, S.S., Malony, A.D.: The tau parallel performance system. Int. J. High Perform. Comput. Appl. **20**(2), 287–311 (2006). https://doi.org/10.1177/1094342006064482
41. Sodhi, S., Subhlok, J., Xu, Q.: Performance prediction with skeletons. Cluster Comput. **11**(2), 151–165 (2008). https://doi.org/10.1007/s10586-007-0039-2
42. Sun, J., Sun, G., Zhan, S., Zhang, J., Chen, Y.: Automated performance modeling of HPC applications using machine learning. IEEE Trans. Comput. **5**, 749–763 (2020). https://doi.org/10.1109/TC.2020.2964767
43. Tarraf, A., Bandet, A., Boito, F., Pallez, G., Wolf, F.: Capturing periodic I/O using frequency techniques. In: Proceedings of the 38th IEEE International Parallel and Distributed Processing Symposium (IPDPS), San Francisco, CA, USA, pp. 1–14. IEEE (2024)
44. Vef, M.A., et al.: Gekkofs - a temporary distributed file system for HPC applications. In: 2018 IEEE International Conference on Cluster Computing (CLUSTER), pp. 319–324 (2018). https://doi.org/10.1109/CLUSTER.2018.00049
45. Weiss, A., Gierczak, O., Patterson, D., Ahmed, A.: Oxide: the essence of rust. arXiv preprint arXiv:1903.00982 (2019)
46. Yang, W., Liao, X., Dong, D., Yu, J.: A quantitative study of the spatiotemporal I/O burstiness of HPC application. In: 2022 IEEE International Parallel and Distributed Processing Symposium (IPDPS), pp. 1349–1359 (2022). https://doi.org/10.1109/IPDPS53621.2022.00133

Third Combined Workshop on Interactive and Urgent Supercomputing (CW-IUS 2024)

Preface to the Third Combined Workshop on Interactive and Urgent Supercomputing (CW-IUS 2024)

1 Background and Objectives

Traditionally, high-performance computing system resources have been managed using a batch queuing scheduler, which maintains a queue of pending jobs while other, previously submitted jobs are executing. While batch queuing usually keeps the utilization percentage of all of the HPC resources high, it makes interactive debugging, rapid prototyping, real-time visualization, and urgent workloads very difficult to accommodate. In all of these workflows, HPC users are in the loop during job execution where a human is monitoring a job, steering experiments, or visualizing results to make immediate decisions that influence the current or subsequent interactive jobs.

This workshop series brings together researchers, developers, computational scientists, HPC system users, system managers, and system engineers to present and discuss the leading edge of research and engineering to enable interactive and urgent HPC capabilities. The topics include organizational and system policies; effective scheduling; technologies and tools; data management; user education and training; and case studies.

2 Workshop Organization

Five research papers were submitted to this workshop, and three of the five were selected to appear in the proceedings and were presented during the workshop. The papers were reviewed by members of the organizing committee and program committee in a single blind-manner. The workshop also included a keynote talk, two work-in-progress lightning talks, and a panel session. All of the presenters (keynote, paper presentations, and lightning presentations) were invited to serve as panelists to further the discussion of the presentations and answer other pertinent questions.

2.1 Organizers

Albert Reuther	MIT LL Supercomputing Center, USA
Nick Brown	EPCC, UK
William Arndt	National Energy Research Scientific Computing Center, USA

2.2 Program Committee

Johannes Blaschke	Lawrence Berkeley National Laboratory, USA
Antony Chazapis	FORTH, Greece
Silvina Grad-Freilich	MathWorks, USA

Robert Henschel	Indiana University, USA
Marshall McDonald	Oak Ridge National Laboratory, USA
Mike Ringenburg	Microsoft, USA
Karsten Siller	University of Virginia, USA
Rollin Thomas	National Energy Research Scientific Computing Center, USA

3 Outcome of the Workshop

The workshop took place on the afternoon of Thursday, May 16, 2024. After a brief welcome and introduction from the organizers, Prof. Julian Kunkel (GWDG and Univ. of Göttingen) gave the keynote talk. He explained how interactive and urgent HPC workflows have increased dramatically at GWDG over the past several years, and how they are addressing this increase in terms of scheduling, I/O, and tools. The three accepted papers were presented next. Sam Welborn (NERSC) presented how he and his team are able to stream and accelerate detector data analysis jobs on Perlmutter compute nodes using interactive and urgent scheduling techniques. Robert Henschel (Indiana University) presented how he and his team have integrated high-performance research desktops into their HPC ecosystem and how this improves the adoption and utilization of high-performance computing capabilities across many research teams and classes across campus. And Toshio Endo presented a new scheduling model for enabling interactive jobs on their clusters, which includes preemption methods, that he and his team have integrate on their clusters.

The workshop also included two lightning talks. The first was from Björn Enders (NERSC), who presented the successful results of an interactive scheduling prototype study on a computing sidecar cluster. And Glenn Lockwood (Microsoft) shared how similar executing searches and matching memes to user profiles were used to enable urgent HPC capabilities. The workshop concluded with a lively panel discussion with all of the presenters and audience participating.

Challenges in Computing Resource Sharing Towards Next-Gen Interactive Accelerated HPC

Toshio Endo[1(✉)], Shohei Minami[1], Akihiro Nomura[1], Hiroki Ohtsuji[2], Jun Kato[2], Masahiro Miwa[2], Eiji Yoshida[2], Tomoya Yuki[1], and Ryuichi Sakamoto[1]

[1] Tokyo Institute of Technology, 4259-Nagatsutacho, Midori-ku, Yokohama 226-8501, Japan
endo@is.titech.ac.jp
[2] Fujitsu Limited, 4-1-1 Kamikodanaka, Nakahara-ku, Kawasaki 211-8588, Japan

Abstract. As interactive usage of high performance computing (HPC) resources become major, HPC systems require new resource management strategy to support both traditional jobs and interactive usages. Our direction for next generational interactive HPC systems is introduce a job scheduling method both with space-sharing and time-sharing. This paper describes observation and issues of a current production supercomputer when it accepts interactive usages. And then we provide our scheduling model and ongoing work mainly related to choices of preemption methods toward realistic interactive HPC systems.

Keywords: supercomputer · interactive · job scheduling · gang scheduling

1 Introduction

Usage of high performance computing (HPC) systems and supercomputers are crucial in advance of science, manufacturing, realization of safe society, and so on. The demand for computing resources even accelerates in the era of generative AI. For example, it is unrealistic for a single research group to possess huge scale of computing resources for pre-training of large language models (LLMs), thus sharing of computing resources among multiple users/groups/institutes is essential in HPC. Since the dawn of supercomputers, computing resources, such as computing nodes, CPU cores and memory, have been shared by using batch job schedulers [1,3]. Users' jobs are submitted to the scheduler, and start of a job may be delayed if sufficient resources are unavailable. When the scheduler successfully finds the sufficient resources, they are typically dedicated to the job.

This method, however, separates the time when a user requests job execution and the time when it is actually executed, losing realtimeness. On the other hand, demand for interactive/realtime usage of HPC resources is increasing, such as visualization of simulations, debugging of highly parallel software. For simulation jobs such as weather simulation and traffic simulation, data assimilation technology using realtime sensor data can improve the accuracy. In machine learning area, inference jobs tend to be realtime compared with learning jobs. Widespread of web based remote interface, including JupyterLab [5], supports this trend. Several production HPC systems have been supported interactive usage by preparing the "interactive queue", with which a limited fraction of nodes are dedicated for interactive usage while the rest major parts are for batch queues. This method is still inflexible and tends to limit effective usage of the entire resource as shown in Sect. 2.

Therefore overall operation and design of HPC systems should be reconsidered towards interactive HPC [13]. This paper focuses on resource sharing or job scheduling; it reports current status of TSUBAME supercomputer in Tokyo Institute of Technology [6] with GPU accelerators, which can lead to additional issues compared with CPU-only systems. And then this paper introduces our several research directions for improved resource sharing towards the interactive HPC era.

2 Current Status: Case of TSUBAME Supercomputer

2.1 Overview of TSUBAME

TSUBAME3.0 is a supercomputer system, which was operated in Tokyo Institute of Technology [6]. The system has 540 computing nodes, each of which is equipped with heterogeneous processors: two x86 CPUs and four GPUs. More details of node specification is shown in Table 1. The table also shows a node of TSUBAME4.0, a new system in operation from April 2024. This paper mainly describes TSUBAME3.0, on which our data has been collected.

Table 1. Specification of a computing node in TSUBAME3.0/4.0 supercomputers. TSUBAME3.0 had 540 nodes while TSUBAME4.0 has 240 nodes.

	TSUBAME3.0 node	TSUBAME4.0 node
CPU	2 × Intel Xeon E5-2680v4 (Broadwell)	2 × AMD EPYC 9654 (Genoa)
# of cores/CPU	14	96
Clock (base)	2.4 GHz	2.4 GHz
Host Memory	DDR4 256 GiB	DDR5 768 GiB
GPU	4 × NVIDIA Tesla P100 SXM	4 × NVIDIA H100 SXM (memory customized)
# of SMs/GPU	56	132
Device Memory/GPU	HBM2 16GB	HBM2e 94 GB
Network Interface	4 × OmniPath 100Gb/s	4 × InfiniBand NDR200 200Gb/s

2.2 Resource Sharing in TSUBAME3.0

Computing nodes in TSUBAME3.0 are shared by multiple users/jobs via the Grid Engine batch job scheduler. In order to support both of batch jobs and interactive jobs, two separated batch queues are provided. The interactive queue contains only 4 nodes out of 540 nodes and the batch queue contains the rest nodes, which are more than 99% of the system.

Each queue is designed so that resource sharing among users/jobs is promoted in a different way [10]. The designs are based on the observation that the amounts of required resources per job have large variation. For instance, large scale simulations or learning jobs may involve multiple jobs. Some inference jobs may be designed for a single GPU. Also there are CPU only jobs, some of which use a few or a single CPU core.

For efficient resource usage, the batch queue adopts dynamic node partition. In each job submission, the user specifies a "resource instance type" and the number of instances that should be allocated for the job. The instance types are listed in Table 2. The batch scheduler assigns the requested instances to idle computing resources, thus *space-sharing* of each physical node is achieved, where multiple instances for different jobs may share a node. On the other hand, *time-sharing* is not used as dedicated CPU cores and/or GPUs as allocated for each instance. While this space-sharing enables efficient resource usage, submitted jobs still wait for available resources.

Table 2. Resource instance types defined in TSUBAME3.0.

Name	# of CPU cores (# of HW threads)	Memory (GiB)	# of GPUs
f_node	28 (56)	235	4
h_node	14 (28)	120	2
q_node	7 (14)	60	1
s_gpu	2 (4)	15	1
q_core	4 (8)	30	0
s_core	1 (2)	7.5	0

Another queue, the interactive queue is provided for interactive and real-time usage. Each user requests invocation of an interactive job, the resource is basically allocated at once. For simplicity, each interactive job must have a shape of q_node instance with 7 cores and one GPU. To reduce chances of allocation failure, we allow not only space-sharing but *time-sharing* of resources; multiple (up to 7) jobs may share the set of 7 cores and one GPU. In the job scheduler level, it is achieved by *oversubscribing* configuration. After invoked, the collocating jobs/processes are not managed explicitly, and we simply rely on OS context switch. Thus each job may suffer from speed down by CPU/GPU usage by other collocating jobs.

This configuration with the separated queues is not new and has been adopted other production systems [12]. In case of TSUBAME, we enable oversubscribing only on the interactive queue. This is based on expectation that interactive jobs tend to have lower resource usage than batch jobs, since such jobs including debugging jobs or usage via JupyterLab frequently wait users actions. Intuitively, if CPU/GPU usage of each job is not higher, the effect of slowdown caused by collocating processes would be mitigated. In the next section, we discuss the feasibility of the above expectation based on statistics measured on TSUBAME.

2.3 Observations and Issues

This section discusses resource usage of TSUBAME3.0 and its potential effects on users' experience. Table 3 shows the usage from October to December 2023. Basically information on the resource usage is obtained from TSUBAME3 web portal[1]. In the table, "node allocation" shows percentage of nodes, on which some instances are allocated for user jobs (Thus when we could see "vacant" resources in CPU core-wise or GPU-wise). While all the values in the table include both of batch nodes and interactive nodes, they mainly show tendency of batch nodes, which dominate >99% of the system.

Batch users suffer from waiting times in job submissions, which tends to be longer with higher node usage. They are 68.3 to 81.6% in the table, while it has reached 97% in December 2022, which burden users with longer waiting times. Although we observe high node allocation rates, we see actual resource usage has a gap and CPU usages are only 17.8 to 23.8%. GPU usages are even lower. We consider this is due to the following factors.

– Even in a well-parallelized job, it consists of multiple phases, initialization, main computation and finalization, and so on. The initialization sometimes may not be parallelized or dominated by file I/O, which degrades the entire CPU usage.
– By similar reasons, even a job that allocates GPU instances, may not use GPUs continuously.
– Users may choose resource instance type, whose counts of core or GPUs are larger than necessity, in order to allocate sufficient memory capacity.

Next, we focus eyes on interactive jobs. In order to verify the assumption that interactive jobs tend to have lower resource utilization, we have collected information on changes of CPU utilization during execution of interactive jobs [8]. Figure 1 shows data of four interactive jobs out of the collected data of 193 jobs. X-axis and Y-axis corresponds to the time and the CPU utilization rate at that time. In TSUBAME3.0 configuration, an interactive job is assigned to 14 hardware threads (7 CPU cores), thus the maximum value of Y is 1400%.

In the graphs, we see utilization in the case (b) reaches almost 1400%, while others are lower. In (a), (b) and (c), we observe large fluctuation of utilization; the periods when cores are utilized are sandwiched by idle periods, which are

---

[1] https://www.t3.gsic.titech.ac.jp/monitoring.

Table 3. Resource usage of TSUBAME3.0 in three months.

	Oct 2023	Nov 2023	Dec 2023
Node allocation	68.3%	74.3%	81.6%
CPU	17.8%	20.1%	23.8%
Memory	13.9%	11.9%	15.0%
GPU	5.8%	5.2%	6.2%

considered to be duration to wait for users' actions. The exception is case (d), where the utilization is always in the range of 700% to 800%. From this observation, we can say some users use the interactive queue to execute batch-like jobs.

So far we have investigated resource utilization of TSUBAME3.0 supercomputer and observed:

– Jobs in the batch queue may have lower resource utilization
– Jobs in the interactive queue may have higher utilization

And these can be incompatible with the assumption in the design of the separated queues on TSUBAME3.0 and can introduce inefficiency of system resource utilization. Also the policy that assign a fixed number of nodes to the interactive queue may cause an issue of inflexibility; when the amounts of interactive jobs increase suddenly, the system is hard to accommodate them with fixed configuration.

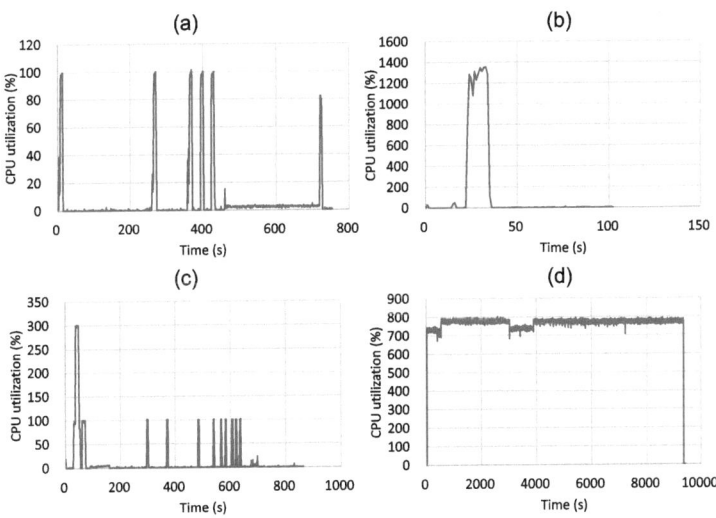

Fig. 1. Changes of CPU usage during execution of interactive jobs on TSUBAME3.0. Four instances are picked up. These figures have been shown in [8]

3 Ongoing Projects Towards Resource Sharing for Interactive HPC

3.1 Scheduling Model

In the previous section, we have pointed out issues of system configurations with fixed separated queues/nodes for interactive jobs from those for batch jobs. Instead we introduce alternative system configurations to improve both realtimeness for individual users and effectiveness of system resource usage. First we describe a scheduling model based on our previous work [8,9] and then mention some variations.

In the simple model, all the compute nodes in the system participate in a single queue, which accept all types of jobs, regardless batch jobs or interactive jobs. When a user submit or request a job, the user specifies:

- Information of amounts of CPU cores for the job, specified as a pair of "number of nodes" and "number of cores per node".
- Largest memory amount per job.
- Number of GPUs per node for the job.

Basically information for job types (batch or interactive) is not necessary. Also information on the longest job time is not mandatory in the simple model.

The job scheduler maintain allocation status of the entire system. The following information are maintained.

- The number of collocating jobs per core. These numbers may exceed 1 since we allow oversubscribing.
- Allocated memory amount per node.
- The number of collocating jobs per GPU.

When the scheduler receives the job request, it traverses status information to find a set of nodes/cores that have enough memory amount. If there are multiple candidates, the scheduler determines nodes/cores so that the maximum number of collocating jobs on any cores or GPUs are mitigated [9]. When the resource set is determined, the job is immediately started there, which may collocate with existing job processes. Note that even with this scheduling model that allows oversubscribing, a requested job may be suspended until its start, regardless the job type. This situation is critical for interactive usage and should be avoided.

After the job execution is started, one of technical key points is how job processes collocates on the same cores/GPUs are preempted. This issue is discussed in Sect. 3.2.

3.2 Discussion on Context Switch

After the job execution is started, its speed performance is largely affected by how the job processes time-share resources such as CPU cores with others. The most naivest way is "do nothing explicitly", and processes/threads are managed by OS context switch. Another method is adopting *gang scheduling* [4], which schedules processes/threads in a single job synchronously. This section discusses pros and cons of those methods.

Relying on OS Context Switch. Using OS context switch is simple, however, also well known that it tremendously degrades execution speeds, especially for parallel jobs. This issue is explained by Table 4 that compares the performance of single executions of NAS Parallel benchmarks [2] with executions with collocation; "Speed with sharing" show when two same benchmark executions share the same set of CPU cores, relying on OS context switch. The intuitive behaviour is that the single execution speed is halved and shared by two executions. It is the case in the sequential executions with 1 process, while we observe significant degradation with multi-process executions. Also degree of the degradation largely depends on software. While the speed of parallel "is.C" is degraded to less than 1/10, that of parallel "ep.B" is not sacrificed. The degradation of parallel performance is considered to be due to effects of application level synchronization among processes/threads. More results and discussion are found in [7].

Table 4. Effects of resource collocation on performance of NPB jobs. The table includes speeds of single execution and speed of execution when two same type of jobs share CPU cores. NPB3.4-MPI is used on a q_node instance of TSUBAME3.0.

Benchmark	# of processes	single speed	Speed with sharing	Performance degradation
is.C	1	87.1	43.5+43.5	0.03%
	4	321	12.3+11.5	92.6%
ep.B	1	54.1	27.1+27.1	−0.3%
	7	367	188+193	−4.0%
cg.B	1	485	247+220	3.6%
	4	2166	267+259	75.7%
bt.B	1	2956	1480+1481	−1.6%
	4	10669	3687+3701	30.8%

Gang Scheduling and its Scalability. In order to keep performance of parallel jobs with time-sharing scheduling, gang scheduling has a long history and is implemented on major job scheduler including Slurm. When jobs are sharing the same CPU cores, the scheduler assigns time slots to each job. During a time slot for one of jobs, all processes/threads in the job are awaken simultaneously and proceeded. After the slot finishes, processes/threads are preempted and other jobs are awaken.

Gang scheduling has tuning knobs including:

Time slot length: The length of each slot, which is 30 s in Slurm default, is configured by the system administrator. The longer slots mitigate costs for context switch, while it reduces realtimeness of each job.

Memory swapping: When it is important for the system to save the total memory consumption, the scheduler may force each job to evict its memory contents to storage after the time slot. The memory contents are resumed at the beginning of the next slot. Such memory swapping introduces time costs.

In the context of interactive HPC short time slots required, since it is desirable for each interactive job to have its successive time slots at sub-second intervals to react to users' interactions. For the same reason, it is unrealistic to employ memory swapping, and memory contents used by each job are resident on memory during its execution.

Although Slurm has a support of gang scheduling, we found that its context switch mechanism is not scalable. When a job consists of large number of (such as >1000) processes or threads, we require a method to send signals efficiently to suspend all of them nearly simultaneously. For this purpose, we have proposed a synchronization mechanism harnessing unreliable broadcast [11]. Figure 2 shows job performance with gang scheduling of 0.5 s time slots. Here two GROMACS parallel jobs share the same 128 nodes. Compared with the case with Slurm's default signal propagation mechanism, 2.7 times speedup is achieved with the proposed mechanism.

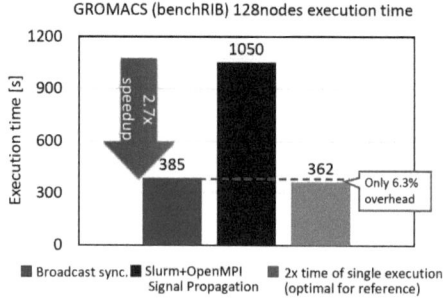

Fig. 2. Gang scheduling performance with unreliable broadcast synchronization mechanism. Each GROMACS job uses 128 Fujitsu FX700 nodes, each has a A64fx (48-core) CPU. This figure has been shown in [11].

Towards More Effective Scheduling. The previous section demonstrated that gang scheduling can be scalable with sub second time slots. On the other hand, it has still rooms for more improvement when we consider resource usage in the entire system.

In Sect. 2.3 we have observed that CPU/GPU utilization could be low not only in interactive jobs but in batch jobs, thus there are idle periods during job execution. The scheduler with gang scheduling allocates a time slot for a job even in idle periods, degrading the entire resource usage. In this aspect, using OS context switching may be preferable since busy processes can monopolize CPU cores if others are idle.

Thus one of our future research topics is development of context switching with advantages of both methods; simultaneous scheduling of processes in the same process and yielding of resources in idle periods.

3.3 Simulation Evaluation of Interactive HPC Scheduling

We have evaluated our scheduling model for interactive HPC via simulation [8]. For this purpose, our simulation takes the following factors into account.

- Collective data of realistic workload on a HPC system that supports both batch jobs and interactive jobs. For this purpose, we adopted workload trace data of The University of Luxemburg Gaia Cluster [12] with 51,987 jobs. The dataset contains the submission time, the execution time, the number of allocated processors, etc., per job.
- The above dataset does not contain information CPU core utilization during execution. To fill this missing information, we artificially produced fluctuation patterns of utilization. To make our evaluation realistic, the patterns are generated based on the actual interactive jobs observed on TSUBAME3.0 supercomputer (Sect. 2.3). While a job is in idle periods, it does not affect performance of collating jobs.
- For batch jobs, we have a simple assumption that all allocated cores are busy.
- Currently jobs use CPU cores and GPUs are out of scope here.
- The context switching method that is simulated is OS context switching method, which is expected to improve the entire resource utilization. On the other hand, it is hard to simulate performance degradation preciously, since it largely depends on process characteristics (Sect. 3.2). Instead, we have an assumption that performance degradation ratio when busy processes/threads are sharing cores is 20%.

Since we did not find a simulator that supports the above factors, we have developed new one named *node conscious oversubscribing scheduler simulator* (NCS). The simulator takes workload trace and processor utilization patterns for interactive jobs as input, and executes simulation.

Among the results obtained through the simulation, Fig. 3 suggests the impact of scheduling method on turnaround time of jobs. During simulation with different scheduling methods, we recorded turnaround time for each job. The turnaround time was divided by its single execution time. The relative turnaround (or sometimes called *slowdown*) is 1 in the ideal case, and gets larger by job waiting time and obstacles by collocating jobs. In the figure, Y-axis shows the maximum relative turnaround among the simulated jobs.

"Traditional" corresponds to the simplest scheduling with a unique queue that accepts both batch jobs and interactive jobs, without allowing time-sharing. Here the turnaround is very long, losing realtimeness.

"Separate queue" is similar to scheduling of TSUBAME3.0. Some (2%) nodes are dedicated for interactive jobs, allowing time-sharing. In this case, turnaround time is largely shorten and 3.7 at the worst interactive job. Also we have observed that all interactive jobs are started without waiting after their submissions. While this method is much better than the above method in realtimeness, it still has issues of inflexibility described in Sect. 2.3.

"OSub schedule" shows results with our scheduling model with time-sharing on a single queue. This method again achieves realtimeness for interactive jobs. We also observe that it largely improves relative turnaround of batch jobs, reducing waiting times.

For more observations, please refer to the paper [8].

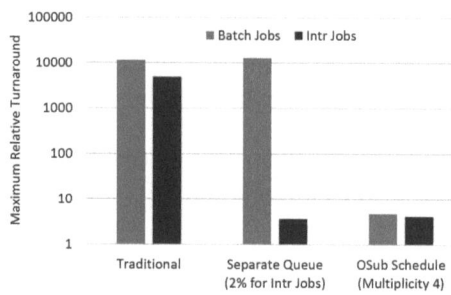

Fig. 3. Results of job simulation with time-sharing. UniLu workload traces are used and the largest slowdown among the jobs is shown.

3.4 Directions for Improvement

In the previous sections we have introduced a simple and rather aggressive job scheduling model. Some users, however, may be dissatisfied with this model. The followings are candidates of improvements to alleviate them.

– With the model, even batch jobs can time-share resources with other jobs. While Sect. 3.2 discusses methods to alleviate costs for collocation, some users still dislike it for speed measurement and so on. The system may provide job classes for jobs that do not time-share resources with others.
– Even interactive jobs may be suspended until the requested resource (currently memory resource) becomes available. To improve realtimeness, the system may provide job classes that can be aborted when the system is too crowded. They work like spot instances in Amazon EC2 and usage fee for such jobs should be cheaper than others.

4 Summary

This paper presented ongoing work on a scheduling model towards realistic and efficient interactive HPC systems, where batch jobs and interactive jobs share computing resources. Our scheduling model introduces time-sharing of resources with preemption, regardless of job types. While this direction is simple, current production systems tend to avoid it. We have pointed out several issues in scheduling with time-sharing and described that one of key factors is design method of context switching. This paper introduced improvement of gang scheduling, for lower switching costs and better scalability. Also we have conducted the entire system simulation to show impacts of our scheduling model on the system and responsiveness of each job.

Many investigations are still needed towards interactive scheduling on production HPC systems. Gang scheduling should be improved for higher resource utilization under existence of jobs with lower resource utilization, by importing advantages of OS context switching. Also effective sharing of GPU resources is necessary. Comparison of gang scheduling and OS context switching including GPU jobs is needed. Also we consider GPU supports of gang scheduling are required; one of issues is lack of signal-like mechanism to suspend running GPU kernels from outside. Finally, in the current model, the lack of memory capacity may cause suspension of jobs before their start. To alleviate this issue, introducing high performance memory pool by CXL can be promising.

Acknowledgements. This research is supported by Fujitsu Next-Generation Computing Infrastructure Collaborative Research Cluster. This research is carried out using the TSUBAME supercomputer at Tokyo Institute of Technology.

References

1. Altair Engineering Inc.: Grid Engine. https://altair.com/grid-engine
2. Bailey, D.H., et al.: The NAS parallel benchmarks. Int. J. High Perform. Comput. Appl. **6**(3), 63–73 (1991)
3. Jette, M., Grondona, M.: Slurm: Simple Linux utility for resource management. In: ClusterWorld Conference and Expo (2003)
4. Jette, M.A.: Performance characteristics of gang scheduling in multiprogrammed environments. In: Proceedings of the 1997 ACM/IEEE Conference on Supercomputing (SC 1997) (1997)
5. Kluyver, T., et al.: Jupyter notebooks – a publishing format for reproducible computational workflows. In: Loizides, F., Schmidt, B. (eds.) Positioning and Power in Academic Publishing: Players, Agents and Agendas, pp. 87 – 90. IOS Press (2016)
6. Matsuoka, S., et al.: Overview of TSUBAME3.0, green cloud supercomputer for convergence of HPC, AI and big-data. e-Sci. J. GSIC Tokyo Inst. Technol. **16**, 2–9 (2017)
7. , Minami, S., Endo, T., Nomura, A.: Measurement and modeling of performance of HPC applications towards overcommitting scheduling systems. In: Proceedings of Workshop on Job Scheduling Strategies for Parallel Processing (JSSPP 2021), in Conjunction with IPDPS, pp. 59–79 (2021)
8. Minami, S., Endo, T., Nomura, A.: The aggressive oversubscribing scheduling for interactive jobs on a supercomputing system. In: proceedings of IEEE High Performance Extreme Computing Conference (HPEC 2023), p. 7p. (2023)
9. Minami, S., Endo, T., Nomura, A.: Effectiveness of the oversubscribing scheduling on supercomputer systems. In: Proceedings of High Performance Computing in the Asia-Pacific Region (HPC ASIA), pp. 18–28 (2023)

10. Nomura, A.: Introducing container technology to TSUBAME3.0 supercomputer. ISC2019 High Performance, Invited Talk (2019)
11. Ohtsuji, H., Hayashi, E., Kinoshita, R., Miwa, M., Yoshida, E.: Scalable fine-grained gang scheduling for HPC systems with unreliable broadcast synchronization mechanisms. In: The International Conference for High Performance Computing, Networking, Storage, and Analysis (SC23), Poster Session (2023)
12. Parallel Workloads Archive: The University of Luxemburg Gaia Cluster log. https://www.cs.huji.ac.il/labs/parallel/workload/l_unilu_gaia/index.html
13. Reuther, A., et al.: Interactive and urgent HPC: challenges and opportunities. arXiv:2401.14550 [cs.DC] (2024)

Accelerating Time-to-Science by Streaming Detector Data Directly into Perlmutter Compute Nodes

Samuel S. Welborn⬤, Chris Harris⬤, Peter Ercius⬤, Deborah J. Bard⬤, and Bjoern Enders(✉)⬤

Lawrence Berkeley National Laboratory, Berkeley, CA 94720, USA
{swelborn,cjh,percius,djbard,benders}@lbl.gov

Abstract. Recent advancements in detector technology have significantly increased the size and complexity of experimental data, and high-performance computing (HPC) provides a path towards more efficient and timely data processing. However, movement of large data sets from acquisition systems to HPC centers introduces bottlenecks owing to storage I/O at both ends. This manuscript introduces a streaming workflow designed for an high data rate electron detector that streams data directly to compute node memory at the National Energy Research Scientific Computing Center (NERSC), thereby avoiding storage I/O. The new workflow deploys *ZeroMQ*-based services for data production, aggregation, and distribution for on-the-fly processing, all coordinated through a distributed key-value store. The system is integrated with the detector's science gateway and utilizes the NERSC Superfacility API to initiate streaming jobs through a web-based frontend. Our approach achieves up to a 14-fold increase in data throughput and enhances predictability and reliability compared to a I/O-heavy file-based transfer workflow. Our work highlights the transformative potential of streaming workflows to expedite data analysis for time-sensitive experiments.

Keywords: streaming · 4D-STEM · high-performance computing · real-time processing

1 Introduction

The transition from analog to digital data acquisitions and processing has greatly accelerated scientific discovery, but it also introduced the challenge of managing, processing, and interpreting an ever-expanding volume of data. In recent years, this challenge has intensified, with modern microscope detectors now achieving data generation rates five orders of magnitude greater than in the 1920s [1,2].

The National Energy Research Scientific Computing Center (NERSC) at Lawrence Berkeley National Laboratory (LBNL) responded to these challenges with the Superfacility Project [3,4]. The project was designed to integrate experimental and observational science (EOS) facilities, many of which are incorporating high framerate detectors into their instruments, with state-of-the-art high-performance computing (HPC) resources. One of its notable achievements was a semi-automated file transfer and data reduction workflow developed for users of the National Center for Electron Microscopy (NCEM) facility of The Molecular Foundry (TMF), also at LBNL. Powered by NERSC's Superfacility API [3,4] and the *Distiller* web application [5], this workflow enables microscopists at NCEM to offload and process data from the 4D Camera [6]—an advanced detector that generates data at 480 Gb/s—on NERSC compute nodes. Compared to processing at the edge on a single node, the NERSC workflow improved throughput by a factor of two.

Despite its impact, this workflow suffers from a large file I/O bottleneck. For example, a 695 GB dataset (~1 million detector frames) transferred by bbcp [7] from NCEM's local NFS buffer to NERSC scratch incurs delays of six or more minutes. These delays impact the microscopists' ability to make timely experimental decisions and impede real-time data analysis, highlighting the need for enhanced data management strategies that can support the high throughput demands of fast detectors.

This manuscript presents an approach to circumvent traditional file-based operations through data streaming. Utilizing *ZeroMQ*, our new workflow facilitates direct data transfer from NCEM server RAM to NERSC compute node RAM for on-the-fly processing. This solution involves deploying several services to facilitate the transfer, including a data production service on the detector's data receiving servers, a data aggregation and fair-queuing distribution service at NCEM, and data consumption services at NERSC. We developed a *ZeroMQ*-based distributed key-value store to connect and coordinate these services. Finally, to facilitate adoption of this new workflow, we extended enabled the creation of streaming sessions (compute jobs) from a web frontend.

2 Background

TMF is a shared experimental facility that attracts researchers from many scientific disciplines to fabricate and analyze nanomaterials with state-of-the-art tools. The NCEM facility houses several advanced electron microscopes. Among these is the TEAM 0.5 [6], a scanning transmission electron microscope (STEM) outfitted with the 4D Camera (Fig. 1b) designed to rapidly capture large numbers of electron diffraction patterns. During data acquisition, a focused electron probe rasters across a sample in a 2D grid, pausing at each grid point for a predefined interval, the dwell time, to generate electron scattering events from the probe-sample interactions. The 4D Camera captures these events at 87 kHz on a 576 by 576 pixel array [6], resulting in a 4D dataset consisting of two sample (x, y) and two detector coordinates (q_x, q_y) leading to the name 4D-STEM. These complex datasets enable analytical methods like electron ptychography, which has gained traction in recent years for its ability to image atomic structure of a sample with high resolution [8,9].

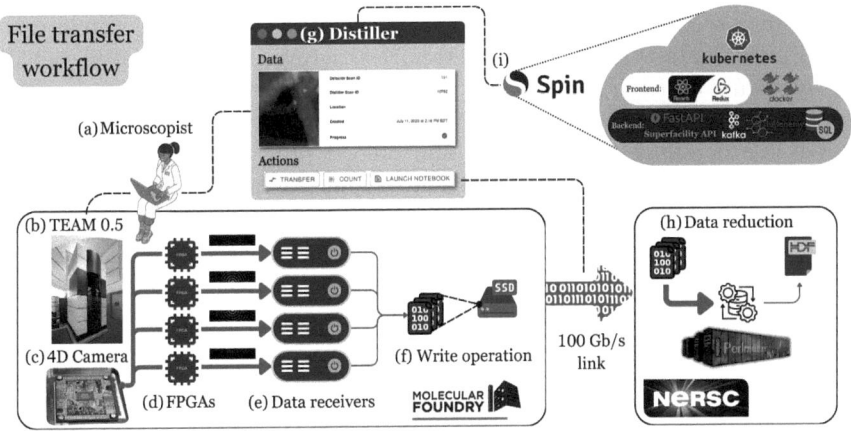

Fig. 1. Schematic of the conventional file transfer workflow at The Molecular Foundry (TMF). A microscopist (a) takes an acquisition on the TEAM 0.5 microscope (b) with the 4D Camera (c). The data is read out from the detector by FPGAs (d) and sent upstream over UDP to data receiver servers (e) at 120 Gb/s per link. The receivers descramble the UDP packets and write files to a network file system (NFS) buffer. The microscopist can then interact with *Distiller* (g) to transfer this data to NERSC for data reduction (h). *Distiller* runs on Spin, NERSC's cloud-inspired infrastructure (i).

4D Camera acquisitions produce relatively large data volumes—approximately 695 GB for an acquisition of ~1 million frames—in the same time as compared to traditional STEM imaging (megabytes per image). The data can be considered sparse, comprised of individual electron strike events, and can be compressed by an order of magnitude using a thresholding and peak finding algorithm (called "electron counting"). *stempy* [10] implements a highly parallelized version of this algorithm; however, the NCEM 10-core edge compute processing machine necessitates 10–12 min for a full dataset. During this time, new scans cannot be taken, thus imposing a 10–12 min interval between acquisitions.

These wait times led to the development of a file transfer workflow (Fig. 1) that offloads the processing onto NERSC compute nodes. In this workflow, a microscopist (Fig. 1a) initiates an acquisition (Fig. 1b) and the 4D Camera collects the scattered electrons (Fig. 1c). During data capture, FPGAs (Fig. 1d) facilitate readout from the detector, transmitting the data at 120 Gb/s per FPGA (480 Gb/s aggregate) to four data receiving servers (Fig. 1e) utilizing the User Datagram Protocol (UDP). On these servers, a process is deployed that preallocates a significant fraction (~85%) of the server's 256 GB RAM with an array of data structures. These structures contain both header information and a 144 × 576 `uint16` array representing pixels from a single detector sector. Each detector frame is therefore initially dispersed across the four data receiving servers and can not be processed until they are recombined. The arrays are then flushed to multiple binary files on an 8 TB network file system (NFS) flash buffer (Fig. 1f).

The microscopist tracks the write operation via the *Distiller* [5] web interface (Fig. 1g), hosted on NERSC's *Spin* [11] infrastructure (Fig. 1i). *Distiller's* backend, leveraging *FastAPI* [12], *Apache Kafka* [13], and a *postgreSQL* database [14], processes acquisition metadata in real time. Concurrently with data writing, a JSON file detailing the scan's ID and offload progress is used to update a *FastAPI* database with a new scan record. Upon completion, users can launch data transfer and reduction jobs from the *Distiller* frontend ("count" in Fig. 1g). Orchestrated by *FastAPI*, *Kafka*, and an event-triggered job worker, this action will create a *Slurm* [15] batch script using *Jinja* [16] templates and submit it to NERSC's realtime queue using the Superfacility API [4]. The job moves the raw files to NERSC scratch storage over a 100 Gb/s connection and sparsifies them according to the electron counting algorithm with *stempy* [10] (see also Sect. 3.1).

While the workflow depicted in Fig. 1 effectively offloads data processing to NERSC and offers a user-friendly frontend for initiating data transfers, it incurs a notable performance cost due to four file I/O operations: initial writing to NFS at NCEM, reading and transferring data to NERSC, writing to NERSC's scratch system, and loading data from scratch into batch nodes. Our streaming workflow, detailed in the following section, completely bypasses this I/O bottleneck and significantly reduces the processing time.

3 Methods

Our streaming workflow extends the tooling discussed in Sect. 2 by integrating *ZeroMQ* sockets over a wide-area-network (WAN) that facilitates data streaming from NCEM to NERSC. This setup employs two *ZeroMQ* patterns: (1) the pipeline pattern, a work queue pattern where messages are fair-queued to downstream connections distributing messages evenly across workers, and (2) the clone pattern, which enables effective communication of system state through a distributed key-value store across the nodes. Additionally, we have extended *Distiller* to provide NCEM users with access to the streaming workflow.

3.1 Pipeline Pattern

Described in Chapter 2 of the *ZeroMQ* guide [17], the pipeline pattern fairly distributes messages from a push socket to all connected pull sockets. Microscope data is sensitive to dropped messages (i.e., data loss), and push sockets block instead of dropping messages when they reach their high water mark (HWM). This also ensures equitable data distribution across NERSC compute nodes. In our pipeline, the Data Receiving Servers use push sockets to send messages to an aggregator at NCEM (Fig. 3b–c). The aggregator then relays these messages to the appropriate NERSC node (Fig. 3d) for frame assembly and data reduction, Fig. 3e. The pipeline includes two distinct messaging channels: the info channel informs downstream processes about the number of messages they can expect to receive and the data channel transmits the detector data. Color coding in Fig. 2 signifies the origin and route of data from specific detector sectors to NERSC.

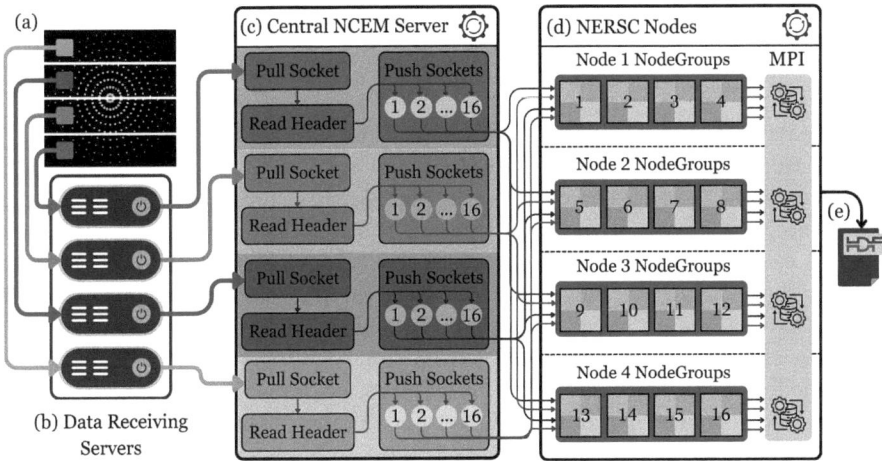

Fig. 2. Schematic representation of the *ZeroMQ* pipeline from NCEM to NERSC. (a) A 4D camera is partitioned into four 144 × 576 sectors, each connected to a dedicated receiving server via FPGAs. (b) During data acquisition, the RAM of the data receiving servers is populated with sector data. The Producer objects on these servers push this data to a central aggregator service at NCEM. (c) Aggregators, denoted by varying colors, manage incoming messages by sequentially receiving them, extracting frame numbers from message headers, and forwarding the messages to the correct NodeGroup at NERSC. (d) On the compute nodes at NERSC, each node is subdivided into one or more NodeGroups (four per node depicted here). Each NodeGroup receives data from all NCEM Aggregators and forwards this data over the inproc protocol to stempy consumer threads. (e) The data is processed and aggregated using *stempy*'s electron counting methods with Message Passing Interface (MPI), consolidating the events in an HDF5 file.

Producers: Data Receiving Servers. As mentioned in our description of the file transfer workflow (Sect. 2), identical services running on each of the four data receiving servers ingest UDP packets from the detector (Fig. 3a–b) and then flush data to disk. In our streaming workflow, the servers run similar application logic up until the data flushing stage. Each thread now uses push sockets to send data downstream to a central aggregator at NCEM (Fig. 3b–c).

The threads first extract unique identifiers (UIDs) of the NodeGroups (Sect. 3.1) from the distributed key-value store (Sect. 3.2) and create a map of UID ↦ n_expected_messages. For example, if a thread receives 100 sectors from the FPGA and ten NodeGroups are available, it apportions ten sectors to each UID. This map, sent through the info channel, informs downstream processes of expected message volume.

The threads then continuously send two-part messages to the central server on the data channel. Each message is composed of a *MsgPack* [18]-serialized header (part 1) and a 144 × 576 uint16 data array (part 2), representing a single frame sector. It is important to note that *ZeroMQ* guarantees that all parts of a multi-part message are received, preventing message interleaving.

Aggregator: Central NCEM Server. The central aggregator server at NCEM runs four threads as depicted by the colored blocks in Fig. 2c. Each thread receives messages from all producer threads running on an individual Data Receiving Server (Fig. 2b–c) through the info channel. The threads then forward these messages to `NodeGroups` (see Sect. 3.1) based on each received sector's frame number. This approach ensures that the `Aggregator` threads divide the sector data evenly amongst the `NodeGroups`, and that all four sectors of a single frame will end up on the same `NodeGroup`. Each thread executes the following procedure: First, it receives a UID $\mapsto$ n_expected_messages map for each connected producer thread and combines them. If a Data Receiving Server process has five threads each with UID $\mapsto$ n_expected_messages, for example, we expect five maps to be received and the combined map to be UID $\mapsto$ 5*n_expected_messages. After combining, the thread pushes a message containing n_expected_messages to the appropriate downstream `NodeGroup` based on its UID. The thread then enters a tight pull-deserialize-push loop, illustrated in Fig. 2c. During each iteration, it receives two-part header/data message and deserializes the header to identify the sector's frame number. A push socket is selected based on the value of frame_number modulo n_NodeGroups, and the two-part message is forwarded on this socket. These push sockets are connected one-to-one to downstream `NodeGroups`, which we have illustrated in Fig. 2c–d.

Consumers: NERSC Nodes. At NERSC, `NodeGroups` receive the messages routed to them by `Aggregator` threads. Each `NodeGroup` contains of four threads, as depicted by the four colored squares in Fig. 2d, that are connected one-to-one to an `Aggregator` thread. Each of these threads receives an info message to inform it of the expected message volume. Then, it enters a pull-push loop to receive header/data messages and send them over inproc to *stempy* consumer threads.

We extended a *stempy* Reader class, which normally reads from disk, to read from *ZeroMQ* messages. As consumer threads pull two-part header/data messages from the `NodeGroups`, the header is deserialized to extract the frame number and sector number, and data is stored in a map of frame number $\mapsto$ sector number $\mapsto$ data. Once the outer frame number map entry is populated with four sectors, the frame is complete and data reduction on that frame begins.

The electron counting algorithm employed for data reduction comprises several steps [19]. First, a subset of frames is chosen to establish thresholds for X-ray and background levels, utilizing binning techniques and Gaussian distribution fitting to the histogram generated from these samples. The Gaussian fit's initial parameters are derived from the sample mean and standard deviation. Specifically, the x-ray threshold is calculated as $(mean + M \times stddev)$, where $M = 10$, while the background threshold is given by $mean + N \times stddev$, where N is a tunable parameter (usually 4 or 4.5) set at runtime. After threshold determination, each frame undergoes a series of transformations. This includes subtracting a dark reference frame, if available, and applying the established X-ray and background thresholds. Following threshold application, local maxima are identified in relation to the nearest neighboring pixels; these maxima are interpreted as electron strike events.

As discussed in Sect. 3.1, data transmission in our pipeline begins with UDP-based communication from the FPGAs, a method that lacks guaranteed packet delivery. For very large scans, approximately 0.1% of sectors are lost before the data enters our *ZeroMQ* pipeline. To account for this, we only count complete frames until all expected messages are received and then count any incomplete frames. Eventually, all counted data is gathered on the first MPI rank. This aggregated dataset is then stored as a single HDF5 file on NERSC's scratch filesystem and asynchronously transferred to a long-term storage filesystem for later analysis.

3.2 Clone

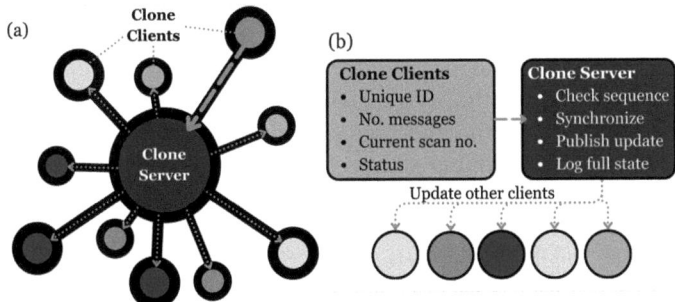

Fig. 3. Network clients (producers, routers, and consumers) relay state updates through the central server, as schematized in (a). These updates include client-specific details like ID, sequence number, expected message count, scan number, and status (streaming, idle, etc.), as shown in (b). These updates are processed by the central server to adjust the network state and broadcast to all other clients.

Alongside the pipeline, we use the Clone messaging pattern, a reliable publish-subscribe architecture detailed in Chapter 5 of the *ZeroMQ* Guide [17]. This pattern enables state synchronization across network nodes through a distributed key-value store. This pattern pushes the network state to a central server, which then disseminates these updates network-wide (Fig. 3). Our adaptation introduces shared state objects to bridge client and pipeline threads, capturing and broadcasting essential details such as message count expectations, current scan numbers, and operational status (idle or streaming), as illustrated in Fig. 3b. Further, we serialize the shared state objects with *MsgPack* [18] for efficient transmission.

A key feature of the Clone pattern is dynamic network membership, enabling nodes to seamlessly join or exit. This flexibility is crucial for managing the lifecycle of streaming jobs at NERSC. Specifically, when we initiate a streaming job through *Distiller*, the Producers and Aggregators are informed that new nodes have been added to the network, and consequently, they can begin to stream data to NERSC. When a job concludes, the Producers and Aggregators recognize that there are no available nodes, prompting a switch back to disk-based raw data storage.

This dynamic model serves several purposes: (1) It eliminates the necessity for an external notification system to inform Producers and Aggregators about node availability for streaming, thus removing the need for users to manually toggle between streaming and disk writing modes through a signaling mechanism. (2) It enables flexible node allocation for streaming jobs, ensuring the network can smoothly adjust to varying job sizes, whether they involve 2, 4, or more nodes. (3) It improves resiliency by defaulting to traditional disk writing as a reliable backup method when streaming nodes are not available.

3.3 Initiating Consumers at NERSC Through *Distiller*

In developing the components in Sects. 3.1 and 3.2, we recognized the necessity to accommodate end-users (the microsopists) who might not be familiar with high-performance computing (HPC) systems. Integrating the streaming workflow into an application familiar to the end-user is critical for adoption, so we upgraded *Distiller* to include a streaming session manager. Initiating a session in many ways mirrors the user action event flow described in Sect. 2, but now the event-triggered job worker can create *Slurm* scripts that launch consumer services (Sect. 3.1). Once available (as detailed in Sect. 3.2), microscope acquisitions stream into Consumers. After an acquisition is transferred to long-term storage, `MPI rank 0` sends an asynchronous request to *Distiller*'s FastAPI to update its location and session association in the database. The user is informed in *Distiller*'s frontend when this acquisition is ready.

4 Results

The streaming workflow demonstrates a faster and more consistent distribution of data transfer and processing times when compared to the file transfer approach based on our comparative analysis described below. This has two critical implications: (1) *Acceleration*. The streaming pipeline significantly enhances data throughput, demonstrating approximately 14-fold and 5-fold increases for smaller and larger datasets, respectively. For larger datasets (i.e., 1024×1024), data transfer and processing occur more quickly than the initial file write operation from RAM to disk in the traditional file transfer method—the file-writing performance is approximately 4.6 GB/s, whereas the streaming pipeline achieves 7.2 GB/s. (2) *Reliability*. The narrower time distribution indicates a more reliable and predictable system. This robustness is particularly advantageous for scheduling time-sensitive experiments and paves the way for future integration with automated systems. For example, the 695 GB streaming transfer has a standard deviation of ±4.9 s (σ_s) compared to the file transfer method with ±53.5 s (σ_{ft}).

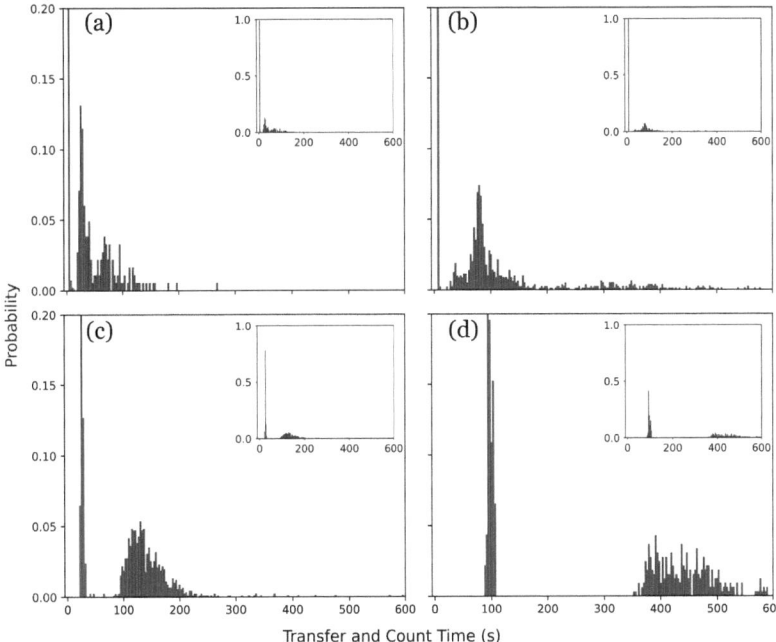

Fig. 4. Histograms demonstrating superior performance of streaming (blue) compared with file transfer (red). (a–d) correspond to real space data dimensions 128×128, 256×256, 512×512, and 1024×1024, respectively. It is evident that the distribution of streaming times is both much narrower, and much faster than the distribution of file transfer times.

We assessed the performance metrics for both pipelines on four standard real-space pixel dimensions (i.e., 2D array of probe positions) commonly used at NCEM: 128×128 (10 GB), 256×256 (43 GB), 512×512 (173 GB), and 1024×1024 (695 GB). To measure the streaming performance, we triggered the 4D Camera to send data at regular intervals while the electron beam was not active, so that the data collected did not contain electron events. Consequently, the metrics outlined here represent the optimal throughput for the current streaming architecture, as there is overhead on the NERSC consumer processes when events are present in the data. As we show in the accompanying repository, this overhead comes primarily from the only file I/O operation in the streaming pipeline—the disk write operation of counted data at NERSC. This non-parallelized write operation occurs at around 340 MB/s. Both the sample area and pixel dimensions influence the number of events, and therefore the write time can be variable. For instance, for the sample used in the accompanying repository, the overhead for saving data from a 128 × 128 acquisition is roughly 0.25 s, and extends to about 16 s for a 1024 × 1024 acquisition covering the same sample area.

Metrics for the file transfer pipeline were sourced from the *Distiller* database, which stores acquisition metadata and facilitates cross-referencing information with *Slurm* such as queue time (the duration between job submission and job start times) and elapsed time (the time required for job execution). Aside from transfer and count times, another bottleneck in the file transfer workflow is the file write time (RAM to disk) at NCEM. To quantify this, we executed a series of 'offload time' experiments for different common dataset sizes. 30 datasets were acquired for each configuration, and the average interval between initial file creation and final modification timestamps were calculated. These averages were added to the *Slurm* elapsed times to encompass all steps of the file transfer pipeline. Finally, we take into account the overhead from writing the counted data at NERSC, discussed in the preceding paragraph. Since this overhead is variable, we conservatively subtract double the average write time for each data dimension (see accompanying repository for details) from the file transfer times. Metrics for the streaming pipeline were obtained through a similar analysis of timestamps, derived from NCEM logs and last modification times at NERSC.

Table 1. Comparison of file transfer and streaming times for various data dimensions.

Data Dimension	Data Size (GB)	File Transfer (s) ($\mu_{ft} \pm \sigma_{ft}$)	Streaming (s) ($\mu_s \pm \sigma_s$)	Enhancement (μ_{ft}/μ_s)
128 × 128 × 576 × 576	10 GB	52.0 ± 30.6	4.0 ± 0.0	13.0
256 × 256 × 576 × 576	43 GB	92.3 ± 38.6	6.8 ± 0.6	13.6
512 × 512 × 576 × 576	173 GB	138.5 ± 28.2	25.1 ± 1.3	5.5
1024 × 1024 × 576 × 576	695 GB	442.6 ± 53.5	97.2 ± 4.1	4.6

Outliers were identified and removed in accordance with standard practices before summarizing the data in Table 1. Specifically, outliers were defined as observations that fall beyond 1.5 × IQR (interquartile range), where $IQR = Q3 - Q1$, and $Q3$ and $Q1$ represent the third and first quartiles, respectively. Such outliers usually indicate a file transfer workflow initiation failure. Data were then compiled into histograms and categorized by size for comparative analysis (Fig. 4, Table 1).

Alongside this manuscript, we have incorporated a repository containing all data analyses to adhere to FAIR (Findable, Accessible, Interoperable, and Reusable) data principles [20].

5 Related Work

Our literature review reveals multiple instances of software packages leveraging message queues and network data transfer within Data Acquisition (DAQ) systems. Common components across these systems typically include local RAM buffers for temporary data storage from detectors, a push/pull or publish/subscribe mechanism via sockets, and plugins for real-time data processing.

- **PvaPy:** Recent efforts established a connection between the Advanced Photon Source (APS) and the Argonne Leadership Computing Facility (ALCF) using a streaming model derived from the Experimental Physics and Industrial Control System (EPICS) [21,22]. Utilizing *PvaPy* [23], a Python interface for EPICS' pvAccess, a multi-producer, multi-consumer publish/subscribe network was constructed. This network achieved streaming rates exceeding 14 GB/s by employing multiple interconnected consumers. This work shows strong potential for integration with HPC centers, as it demonstrates high network throughput and uses a widely-adopted control system framework at beamlines across user facilities.
- **DUNE-DAQ:** The Deep Underground Neutrino Experiment (DUNE) generates neutrinos at Fermilab and detects them 800 miles away at Sanford Underground Research Facility to explore why the universe is made of matter. Their DAQ system employs *ZeroMQ* wrappers and shared memory queues for bulk data transmission from detectors, event processing, and offloading to data writer processes [24].
- **ALFA:** Developed collaboratively by the Facility for Antiproton and Ion Research (FAIR) and A Large Ion Collider Experiment (ALICE) at CERN, the *ALFA* framework utilizes *FairMQ* for its transport layer [25,26]. This layer consists of wrappers around *ZeroMQ* sockets, called Devices, which are state machines that can be arranged in various topologies to create communication channels. *ALFA* also incorporates a processing layer with support for *Apache Arrow* and *ROOT* [27].
- **ADARA:** The Accelerating Data Acquisition, Reduction, and Analysis (ADARA) system, built at Oak Ridge National Laboratory (ORNL), is another publish/subscribe system developed for real-time processing and visualization of Spallation Neutron Source (SNS) data citech17adara. The system uses a custom protocol on POSIX sockets to publish data, and supports both live and archived (persisted to disk) data streaming. The subscribers, which include the real-time visualization software Mantid and statistics/monitoring services, ingest the published data. While this system appears to be in use today [29], we cannot say for sure what the current state of the project is and if the custom protocol can handle the high data rates of modern detectors.

Although this list is not comprehensive, it underscores the diversity of existing solutions to similar challenges. Since these tools are designed with a specific DAQ system in mind (e.g., EPICS for PvaPy), using and retooling them for NCEM's DAQ would have posed a challenge. An ideal future tool would combine the best features of these systems and facilitate seamless integration with HPC centers with minimal application code changes.

6 Conclusions and Outlook

In response to the input/output (I/O) bottlenecks posed by conventional file transfer methods, this work introduced a *ZeroMQ*-based pipeline to directly transfer large experimental datasets from the NCEM facility of TMF to compute nodes at NERSC. This approach effectively bypasses large disk storage operations at both ends, facilitating on-the-fly data processing.

Our results demonstrate a significant improvement in data throughput and system predictability, achieving up to a 14-fold increase in data transfer speed compared to NCEM's file transfer workflow. Further, we upgraded NCEM's user-facing web app, *Distiller*, to enable microscopists to initiate and manage real-time jobs at NERSC from a web-based interface. These improvements reduce the turnaround time for microscopists and provides access to the new workflow without significant training overhead.

While our results confirm that streaming significantly reduces both processing delays and dependency on NERSC's shared file systems, the current implementation should be seen as a preliminary model. Its integration is tightly bound to NCEM-specific data formats and processing packages, indicating a necessity for a more universally adaptable tool that simplifies streaming to HPC facilities with minimal need for bespoke adjustments.

A more broadly applicable version of this tool should consider several key features, including but not limited to:

- *Semi-automated network management.* In our prototype implementation, the connection of various *ZeroMQ* sockets is manually configured through specific IP addresses and port numbers within a configuration file. This procedure could be streamlined by leveraging a distributed key-value store as a dynamic IP address registry. Such an approach would automate the service discovery and connection process within the wide-area network (WAN), enabling new clients to register their IP addresses and identify connection partners.
- *Decoupling of services from application code.* The current implementation also tightly binds services to NCEM-specific functionalities by subclassing the producers and consumers from our earlier file-transfer workflow. A future tool should aim for a decoupled architecture, where producer and consumer processes operate independently in separate memory spaces on the same machine. This separation would not only lower the technical threshold for adoption but also improve flexibility, allowing messages to be routed to several consumer processes for varying types of analysis.

Acknowledgments. Work at the Molecular Foundry was supported by the Office of Science, Office of Basic Energy Sciences, of the U.S. Department of Energy under Contract No. DE-AC02-05CH11231. This research used resources of the National Energy Research Scientific Computing Center (NERSC), a U.S. Department of Energy Office of Science User Facility located at Lawrence Berkeley National Laboratory, operated under Contract No. DE-AC02-05CH11231 using NERSC awards BES-ERCAP0024753 and BES-ERCAP0024754. This work was partially funded by the US Department of

Energy in the program "4D Camera Distillery: From Massive Electron Microscopy Scattering Data to Useful Information with AI/ML". We would like to thank Gatan, Inc. as well as P Denes, A Minor, J Ciston, C Ophus, J Joseph, Vamsi Vytla, and I Johnson who contributed to the development of the 4D Camera.

Disclosure of Interests. The authors have no competing interests to declare that are relevant to the content of this article.

References

1. Spurgeon, S.R., Ophus, C., et al.: Towards data-driven next-generation transmission electron microscopy. Nat. Mater. **20**(3), 274–279 (2021). https://doi.org/10.1038/s41563-020-00833-z
2. Rao, R.: Synchrotrons face a data deluge. Phys. Today **2020**(2), 0925a (2020)
3. Bard, D., et al.: LBNL Superfacility Project Report (2022). https://doi.org/10.2172/1875256. https://www.osti.gov/biblio/1875256
4. Enders, B., et al.: Cross-facility science with the superfacility project at LBNL. In: 2020 IEEE/ACM 2nd Annual Workshop on Extreme-Scale Experiment-in-the-Loop Computing (XLOOP), pp. 1–7. IEEE (2020)
5. Harris, C., Genova, A.: Distiller (2023). https://github.com/OpenChemistry/distiller
6. Ercius, P., et al.: The 4D Camera: an 87 kHz Direct Electron Detector for Scanning/Transmission Electron Microscopy (2023)
7. Hanushevsky, A.B.: Peer-to-peer computing for secure high performance data copying. Tech. rep., SLAC National Accelerator Lab., Menlo Park, CA (United States) (2002)
8. Ophus, C.: Four-dimensional scanning transmission electron microscopy (4D-STEM): from scanning nanodiffraction to ptychography and beyond. Microsc. Microanal. **25**(3), 563–582 (2019). https://doi.org/10.1017/S1431927619000497
9. Chen, Z., Jiang, Y., Shao, Y.T., Holtz, M.E., Odstrčil, M., Guizar-Sicairos, M., Hanke, I., Ganschow, S., Schlom, D.G., Muller, D.A.: Electron ptychography achieves atomic-resolution limits set by lattice vibrations. Science **372**(6544), 826–831 (2021). https://doi.org/10.1126/science.abg2533
10. Avery, P., Harris, C., Ercius, P., Genova, A., Hanwell, M.D., Zhao, Z.: Openchemistry/stempy: stempy 3.3.3 (2023). https://doi.org/10.5281/zenodo.7806318
11. Spin. https://www.nersc.gov/systems/spin/
12. Lathkar, M.: High-Performance Web Apps with fastapi: The Asynchronous Web Framework Based on Modern Python, pp. 1–309. Nanded, Maharashtra, India (2023)
13. Garg, N.: Apache kafka. Packt Publishing Birmingham, UK (2013)
14. Drake, J.D., Worsley, J.C.: Practical PostgreSQL. O'Reilly Media Inc (2002)
15. Yoo, A.B., Jette, M.A., Grondona, M.: Slurm: Simple linux utility for resource management. In: Workshop on Job Scheduling Strategies for Parallel Processing, pp. 44–60. Springer (2003)
16. Nipkow, T.: Jinja: Towards a comprehensive formal semantics for a java-like language. Proof Technology and Computation, pp. 247–277 (2003)
17. Zguide. https://zguide.zeromq.org
18. Messagepack. https://msgpack.org/

19. Battaglia, M., Contarato, D., Denes, P., Giubilato, P.: Cluster imaging with a direct detection CMOS pixel sensor in transmission electron microscopy. Nuclear Instruments & Methods in Physics Research. Section A, Accelerators, Spectrometers, Detectors and Associated Equipment **608**(2), 363–365 (2009). https://doi.org/10.1016/j.nima.2009.07.017
20. Wilkinson, M.D., et al.: The fair guiding principles for scientific data management and stewardship. Sci. Data **3**(1), 1–9 (2016)
21. Veseli, S., Hammonds, J., Henke, S., Parraga, H., Schwarz, N.: Streaming data from experimental facilities to supercomputers for real-time data processing. In: Proceedings of the SC '23 Workshops of The International Conference on High Performance Computing, Network, Storage, and Analysis. pp. 2110–2117. SC-W '23, Association for Computing Machinery, New York, NY, USA (2023). https://doi.org/10.1145/3624062.3624610
22. Dalesio, L.R., Kozubal, A., Kraimer, M.: Epics architecture. Tech. rep., Los Alamos National Lab., NM (United States) (1991)
23. Veseli, S., et al.: Pvapy: Python API for epics PV access. Proc. ICALEPCS 2015 (2015)
24. Collaboration, D.: The dune far detector vertical drift technology. In: Technical Design Report (2023)
25. Al-Turany, M., et al.: Alfa: the new Alice-fair software framework. J. Phys. Conf. Ser. **664**(7), 072001 (2015). https://doi.org/10.1088/1742-6596/664/7/072001
26. Al-Turany, M., et al.: Alfa: a framework for building distributed applications. EPJ Web Conf. **245**, 05021 (2020). https://doi.org/10.1051/epjconf/202024505021
27. Eulisse, G., Rohr, D.: The o2 Software Framework and GPU Usage in Alice Online and Offline Reconstruction in Run 3. arXiv preprint arXiv:2402.01205 (2024)
28. Shipman, G., et al.: Accelerating data acquisition, reduction, and analysis at the spallation neutron source. In: 2014 IEEE 10th International Conference on e-Science, vol. 1, pp. 223—230 (2014). https://doi.org/10.1109/eScience.2014.31
29. Kilpatrick, M., Bruhwiler, D., Carlin, E., Nagler, R., Kuhn, A., Tatulea, D., Mensmann, J., Nienhaus, M., Messmer, P., Roemer, S., et al.: Interactive Automated Bragg Peak Identification with 3D Neutron Scattering data. Tech. rep, Oak Ridge National Laboratory (ORNL), Oak Ridge, TN (United States) (2023)

Use Cases for High Performance Research Desktops

Robert Henschel[1,2(✉)], Jonas Lindemann[3], Anders Follin[3], Bernd Dammann[4], Cicada Dennis[1], and Abhinav Thota[1]

[1] Indiana University, Bloomington, IN 47408, USA
{henschel,hbrokaw,athota}@iu.edu
[2] Cendio AB, 58330 Linköping, Sweden
[3] Lund University, 22100 Lund, Sweden
{jonas.lindemann,anders.follin}@lunarc.lu.se
[4] Technical University of Denmark, 2800 Kgs Lyngby, Denmark
beda@dtu.dk

Abstract. High Performance Research Desktops are used by HPC centers and research computing organizations to lower the barrier of entry to HPC systems. These Linux desktops are deployed alongside HPC systems, leveraging the investments in HPC compute and storage infrastructure. By serving as a gateway to HPC systems they provide users with an environment to perform setup and infrastructure tasks related to the actual HPC work. Such tasks can take significant amounts of time, are vital to the successful use of HPC systems, and can benefit from a graphical desktop environment. In addition to serving as a gateway to HPC systems, High Performance Research Desktops are also used to run interactive graphical applications like MATLAB, RStudio or VMD. This paper defines the concept of High Performance Research Desktops and summarizes use cases from Indiana University, Lund University and Technical University of Denmark, which have implemented and operated such a system for more than 10 years. Based on these use cases, possible future directions are presented.

Keywords: High-Performance Computing (HPC) · Interactive Supercomputing · Research Desktop

1 Introduction

This paper employs use cases to illustrate the features of High Performance Research Desktops and to underscore the real-world impacts of enabling such use cases. The use cases are largely coming from three organizations that have been running a High Performance Research Desktop for more than ten years, Indiana University in the USA (IU), Lund University in Sweden (LU) and Technical University of Denmark (DTU).

A High Performance Research Desktop is the concept of making high performance computing and storage systems available to users through a desktop environment. It is High Performance because it leverages High Performance

Computing (HPC) compute and storage systems, and it is intended for research use as opposed to administrative or office use. For reading convenience, High Performance Research Desktops are referred to as HPC Desktops in this paper. HPC Desktops are typically deployed alongside HPC Systems, as a gateway to one or more HPC systems. However, some implementations of an HPC Desktop are not just a gateway, but also function as an environment to perform moderately parallel computational work, especially through graphical applications like MATLAB, R-Studio or similar types of applications. Users can also conveniently run visualization applications like VMD or ParaView on an HPC Desktop, without having to copy data sets or connect to remote servers. It is the goal of HPC Desktops to offer an environment that is more convenient and faster than a user's laptop or workstation. However, there will always be tasks where an HPC Desktop is not as convenient or as performant as a user's local computer [1].

HPC Desktops are deployed by a number of HPC centers and research computing organizations. Among them are the organizations represented in this paper, but also others like Purdue University [2], National Laboratory for High Performance Computing Chile [3], and the University of Chicago [4]. IU and Purdue's HPC Desktop systems were described in [5]. There are a number of remote access solutions that are used to implement HPC Desktops, such as ThinLinc [6], NoMachine [7], and FastX [8]. The authors of this paper are primarily familiar with ThinLinc. The unifying concept behind all implementations of an HPC Desktop is that users have access to a persistent Linux Desktop, and can use all the built-in tools of a desktop to organize and conduct their research. Tools such as a graphical file browser, a graphical editor and access to a graphical menu that makes it easy to launch applications. Some HPC Desktop implementations go further by providing graphical tools to interact with the batch job or launch applications remotely [9]. In short, an HPC Desktop is more than just enabling access to remote graphical applications, it is an environment where users can implement the full workflow of their computational research.

HPC Desktops are one way to enable interactive HPC. The interactive HPC community is well established and has been holding workshops and BoFs at the International Supercomputer Conference as well as the Supercomputing Conference over the last years [10]. The community has also released a state of the practice white paper recently [11]. However, interactive HPC is a much broader topic than what is discussed in that paper. This paper focuses specifically on use cases that are enabled by providing a persistent, convenient and performant HPC Desktop environment.

Section 2 outlines the technical capabilities of an HPC Desktop. It describes hardware and software features, and also focuses on the policies that are needed to make an HPC Desktop as useful as possible. Section 3 is the main content of this paper, presenting a wide variety of use cases of an HPC Desktop. Section 4 briefly lists future developments for the HPC Desktops, ranging from very tangible next steps to more speculative abstraction layers. The paper ends with a conclusion and acknowledgement section.

2 Capabilities of a High Performance Research Desktop

This section starts with explicitly spelling out the guiding principle behind all design decisions of an HPC Desktop. This guiding principle runs counter to how HPC systems are operated, but is vital for the success of HPC Desktops. The remainder of this section outlines the architecture, policies and features of an ideal HPC Desktop. An ideal setup may not have been realized in a production environment yet, but IU, LU, and DTU operate systems that implement the majority of the features outlined below.

2.1 The Guiding Principle of HPC Desktops

As briefly alluded to in the introduction, the guiding principle behind the HPC Desktop is to lower the barrier of entry to HPC systems by providing users with a convenient and stable environment that performs comparably to their laptops or desktops. This principle drives all aspects of the architecture and design of an HPC Desktop. Ideally, this means that user convenience should be considered first for all hardware, software, and policy decisions. But service providers will still need to balance operational needs, hardware availability, and demand. Moreover, these HPC Desktops are a shared resource, with multiple users sharing the same compute, storage, and software environment, which adds constraints to the usage policies. This is in stark contrast to how normal HPC systems are operated, where efficient allocation of hardware and delivering the best computational and I/O performance are considered first. By providing an HPC Desktop along side an HPC system, users are provided an environment to perform light computational and data management work outside of the HPC system, leaving the HPC system open for computationally efficient workflows.

2.2 HPC Desktops and Open OnDemand

Open OnDemand (OOD) is a widely used open-source software used to deploy web and graphical interfaces for applications [12,13]. An OOD deployment tackles many of the same use cases and scenarios that HPC Desktops address, but there are key differences. OOD also supports access to HPC storage resources in a GUI environment and other data management functions, but for computational needs, users are expected to submit jobs and launch applications on compute nodes via the OOD interface. This, in our opinion, is the major difference: while HPC Desktops can support light computational workloads as well as job submission to compute nodes, OOD only supports computational workloads on compute nodes. Using OOD, it is not possible to create a central environment where multiple applications can run on the same desktop and that users can come back to over weeks. There are pros and cons to both approaches. While it can be said that letting users do light computational work on HPC Desktops without having to submit jobs is a convenience, it also makes the service providers responsible for managing user demand and resource stability without tools designed for this purpose, like a job scheduler.

2.3 Hardware Configuration

The hardware of an HPC Desktop looks very similar to the hardware of HPC login nodes. Figure 1 shows the placement of an HPC Desktop relative to an HPC system and HPC storage infrastructure. The servers that comprise an HPC Desktop can be HPC compute nodes of the current or previous generation HPC system, with a dual CPU setup and 4 to 8 GB of memory per CPU core. In following the guiding principle, enough servers need to be available to handle the expected number of concurrently active users.

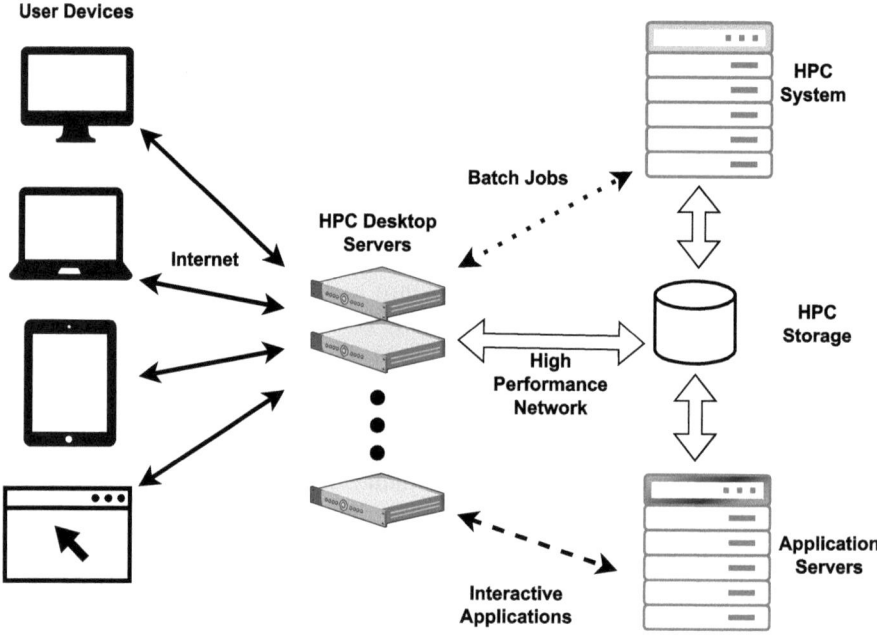

Fig. 1. Location of the HPC Desktop relative to High Performance compute and storage systems.

IU's HPC Desktop can easily handle 15 to 20 concurrent users per server, without employing application servers. Consequently, if an average of 200 active users should be supported, about 10 servers are needed for such an environment. At LU and DTU, application servers provide dedicated capacity to run computationally demanding graphical applications. This reduces the resource requirements on the desktop servers and allows for many more users per server. Those application servers may also be used for visualization applications that require dedicated GPUs, while some HPC Desktop setups handle visualization applications by running them in the GPU partition of the HPC system via the batch system. In either case, those applications can be launched from a tool like GFXLauncher. On the network, an HPC Desktop is placed in the same location as the login nodes of an HPC system and has plenty of bandwidth to HPC file systems as well as the research network and the internet.

2.4 Software Setup

The software setup of an HPC Desktop is similar to the software stack of an HPC login node. Ideally the software stack of the HPC Desktop is so similar to the software stack of HPC compute nodes that applications compiled for the HPC system can also run on the HPC Desktop, and vice versa. HPC Desktops should be able to submit jobs to the HPC system and they should mount the same file systems as HPC compute nodes and HPC login nodes so that users can work on data without having to perform data movement first. HPC Desktop servers need to have the full X11 stack installed and depending on the remote access software that is used, additional software packages, like the Xvnc server, are needed.

2.5 Customizing the User Desktop

There is a wide variety of desktop environments available, and different organizations have built their HPC Desktops on different desktop environments. Popular choices are MATE [14] and XFCE [15]. They have been chosen for their low resource requirements, compared to modern GNOME or KDE environments [16]. Among the more modern desktop environments GNOME Classic [17] has proven to be functioning well with decent resource usage. While the desktop environment can be different, it is key to customize the actual user desktop for use as an HPC Desktop. Popular customizations include modifying the application menu of the desktop environment to include shortcuts to popular applications. Another customization is to place specific icons in the "panel" and on the desktop, icons that offer shortcuts to a terminal, the file manager or help/documentation. Some institutions have developed utilities that help users with their first steps into batch system usage. Such tools are also commonly made available through desktop icons. GfxLauncher is one such tool. It is an open-source Qt-based Python application that can launch different interactive applications through the batch system using a configurable user interface. Currently, it supports launching X11-based applications, OpenGL accelerated applications (VirtualGL [18]), and Jupyter notebooks. Providing a custom desktop background in line with the organizations branding is also recommended.

2.6 Policies

Usage policies set the HPC Desktop apart from normal HPC login nodes. On an HPC Desktop, users are encouraged to perform work that may run for a long period of time, hours or days, as long as this work does not monopolize the node. There is no hog-watch setup on an HPC Desktop and CGroups is configured to prevent users from running the node out of memory and enable fair use of a shared environment.

On the IU HPC Desktop it was observed that users occasionally seem to abuse the nodes by running computational workloads not appropriate for a shared environment. However, most of the time users were not aware of the parallelism of the application that they were using. Over the last years, this occurred infrequently enough that it can be dealt with on a case by cases basis by educating the user. Monitoring scripts are in place to detect such events and notify support personnel.

HPC Desktop users can disconnect from and reconnect to their desktop session in a similar way to how screen works in an ssh environment. This feature allows users to come back to an environment for days and weeks. While it is tempting to reduce resource consumption by terminating sessions that no user is currently connected to, it is key for a convenient environment to allow users to reconnect to their sessions multiple days after they have disconnected. At IU and LU, reconnecting to a session is possible for up to 7 d. At DTU, the lifetime of a desktop session is not limited, but limits are enforced applications started from the desktop via GFXLauncher.

3 Use Cases

The use cases of this section are derived from HPC Desktops operated by IU, LU, and DTU over more than 10 years. These Desktops have attracted users from all fields of science. The use cases have been reconstructed from user interviews and from observing user support tickets. On a very high level, the use cases can be grouped into using standard desktop features to enable research workflows and using specific HPC features like the batch system. While the second ones are more interesting, the first ones should not be underestimated because they enable a convenient user environment.

3.1 Using a Graphical File Manager

The ability to use a graphical file manager is a real game changer for new users in a Linux and HPC environment. While it is true that managing files on the command line only requires learning a few commands, in practice this puts a huge burden on new users. New users usually have only ever used a graphical file manager like the MacOS Finder or the Windows File Explorer, and the concept of "running a command to perform file actions" is foreign to them. Use cases enabled by a graphical file manager include:

- Easy unpacking of archive files by selecting a file with the mouse and selecting "Extract here" from the file's context menu.
- Create an archive from a directory tree by selecting "Compress" from the directory's context menu.
- Looking up how much storage is consumed by an entire directory tree by looking at directory properties or using a disk usage analyzer tool [19]
- Moving files from one storage location to another by using "Copy and Paste" or "Drag and Drop" (for example from HOME to SCRATCH).

– File deletion, through either moving file(s) to the "Trash", or right-clicking to choose "Delete" from a pop-up menu. Having a "Trash" facility that makes it easy for users to undelete a file. This however also adds to the complexity for users to understand what files are accounted towards a user's file system quota, as large files in "Trash" can contribute to the quota.
  – Bookmarking directories in the file manager allows users to easily remember the mount points for different file system, for example HOME, SCRATCH, PROJECT etc.
  – Easily connect to "outside" storage location by using the "Connect to Server" functionality. This allows for easy data movement from Windows file shares as well as connecting to cloud storage providers.

3.2 Pre and Post Processing for HPC Jobs, Running HPC Jobs

This section lists tasks that benefit from a graphical desktop environment when preparing, submitting and managing HPC jobs. This section also lists tasks that users perform to prepare for running software on an HPC system, for example moving data sets or installing custom software packages.

  – Easy movement of files between a user's machine and the HPC Desktop. ThinLinc provides a convenient thindrives [20] mechanism for this task.
  – Download software and data sets straight to an HPC file system using a web-browser on the HPC Desktop, especially for downloads that require web authentication.
  – Long running data movement operations like rsync or moving files to a tape archive.
  – Using GfxLauncher with interactive applications, such as post processors, visualization packages and notebooks. By scheduling valuable high performance graphic nodes using the batch system with a user defined wall-time, better resource utilization is achieved. This enables users to run heavy interactive applications directly on the desktop without overloading the HPC Desktop servers. At LU, this has enabled new user groups to take advantage of HPC such as humanities (language models and 3D reconstruction in archaeology).
  – Using a graphical debugger from an interactive job with X-Forwarding to the HPC Desktop.
  – Using a graphical IDE to write, test, and debug code in an environment that mimics the destination HPC environment.
  – Running graphical HPC performance analysis tools like Vampir, MAP, the gprofng GUI [21], or NVIDIA Nsight.
  – Graphical editors to create and edit HPC batch scripts.
  – Quickly look at visualizations created by HPC jobs using an image viewer.

3.3 Non HPC Work

The HPC Desktop provides a convenient environment for running graphical applications for a long time, especially if those applications are serial or modestly parallel so that they run well in a shared environment. These applications can access data on large central file systems without having to copy the data. The ability of the user to disconnect and reconnect to an HPC Desktop over the course of days and weeks makes it easy to run an application for a long time, something that may be difficult to accomplish on a laptop. The HPC Desktop allows for sharing access to licensed software packages with a limited number of licenses. Depending on the license model, users can share the software on a central system without having to install and license the software. Some of the non-HPC tasks enabled by an HPC Desktop are:

- Long running Jupyter Notebooks or R-Studio sessions.
- Access to statistical software like SPSS, SAS, STATA (support long running stats scripts that are not parallel, but need to run for a long period of time).
- Run applications that are only licensed on central system. (shared license model for MATLAB, SPSS or Photoscan or other vended software packages)
- Visualization Software, with local or remote use of GPUs using VirtualGL.
- Run applications that operate on large data but do not require intensive CPU or excessive memory usage.

3.4 Teaching and Learning

An HPC Desktop can facilitate teaching and learning, not just for classes that require HPC systems. The obvious use case is that HPC centers and research computing organizations offer "Introduction to HPC" classes using the HPC Desktop. Students that take the class can continue to experiment and learn after class, by reconnecting to their HPC Desktop, potentially with folders and terminals still open on the desktop. This makes it much more likely that students continue using the system compared to when they connect with SSH and are presented with a "new shell" every time they connect.

Another use case is faculty members leveraging an HPC desktop in their class. Students can connect to the desktop and are presented with a pre-configured environment ready to use. This is especially relevant if the HPC Desktop offers the ability to connect via a web-based user interface. This eliminates the need for students to install an application and allows student with lower-end devices to participate equally. Another advantage of leveraging a centrally provided system is that students can get access to different software packages, for example different FORTRAN compilers or engineering applications, without having to install that software locally.

3.5 Client Server Applications

There are a number of research applications that utilize a client server compute model, where usually a graphical client application spawns a server application that handles compute intensive tasks. Example applications that have this capability include, MATLAB, COMSOL Multiphysics, ANSYS Workbench, ABAQUS CAE, and Schrödinger. The graphical client of these applications can run on an HPC Desktop and the server can run in the batch system. Since HPC

Desktops are located next to the HPC system, the client can directly communicate with the server, without having to route that communication through an SSH tunnel. This makes it a lot easier for users to utilize such client server applications, compared to running the client on a laptop and then having to manually establish an SSH tunnel to the HPC system to enable communication between client and server. Specific use cases include:

- At IU, the graphical versions of COMSOL Multiphysics and Schrödinger are available on the HPC Desktop. They can be used to perform small computations the HPC Desktop and users can send jobs to the cluster through the GUI and review results in the interface when jobs are completed. In IU's case, setting this up took some staff time to properly design and maintain the configuration files (one for each cluster to which the user is submitting jobs).
- At DTU and LU, MATLAB Parallel Server is tightly integrated into the MATLAB Desktop, that can be started from the HPC Desktop session. Via different cluster profiles, MATLAB workers can either run locally, or are dispatched to the HPC nodes.
- At IU, there are a number of users who use Jupyter Notebook or Jupyter Lab. In some cases, they need to use GPUs that are not available in IU's HPC Desktop, or they need more compute or memory resources than the shared environment of an HPC Desktop provides. Launching those notebooks in the batch system and running the web browser on the HPC Desktop is straightforward. Alternatively, X11 forwarding can be used to display a web browser running on a compute node on the HPC Desktop.

3.6 Secure Enclaves

Secure enclaves enable users to work with sensitive data sets, for example electronically protected health information, restricted research data or licensed third-party data sets with restrictive data use agreements. HPC Desktops can dramatically increase the usability of secure enclaves by providing a graphical desktop with most of the features outlined above. The specific implementation of a secure enclave depends heavily on the sensitivity of the data and the standards that the enclave needs to conform to, for example NIST 800-53/171 or FISMA. IU has used an HPC Desktop to provide researchers from multiple universities access to a secure enclave to utilize graphical statistical applications like SPSS, SAS, or RStudio.

4 Future Developments

This section speculates on future developments for the HPC Desktop. Some of the items outlined are very technical and are logical next steps to keep up with the development of technology and the evolution of Linux desktop environments. Other items are more speculative and represent a real evolution of the concept of making an HPC system accessible via a desktop metaphor.

4.1 Experiment with State of the Art Desktop Environments

Today's HPC Desktops use older or very light weight desktop environments like MATE or XFCE. The reason is that these desktops consume fewer resources, which is an important consideration for a shared environment with dozens of users per machine. However, just as the Windows and MacOS desktops have evolved over the last years, so have Linux desktop environments. Providing an HPC Desktop with Gnome 45 or the latest KDE Plasma may provide users with a more compelling environment.

4.2 Explore Deep Integration of an HPC System Into the Desktop

As outlined in Sect. 2.5, an HPC Desktop features a customized desktop that exposes some of the features of an HPC system in a user friendly way. Modern desktop environments and file browsers make it easy to develop plugins or extensions that can take customizations to the next level. A few things to explore are:

Run In Batch. When selecting the context menu of an application, offer the option to launch this application in the batch system rather than on the desktop. This can be accomplished in a number of different ways, for example by using GfxLauncher with the correct parameters or by running the application inside an interactive job. By integrating this option into the desktop environment, it becomes available for every application rather than having to provide separate icons for running the application on the desktop and in the batch system.

Recently Run Jobs. File browsers feature a Recently Opened Files section. With a plugin, the file browsers could feature a Recently Run Jobs section, that would provide a list of JobIDs and JobNames. When a job is selected, the file browser would show the location of the job script.

Move to Archive. Institutions with an HPC Desktop are very likely to also provide a long term archive for their users. Enhancing the file browser with the ability to archive a directory tree would significantly enhance the usability of such an archive and could also enforce a minimum set of metadata to be associated with the data. For example a user could select a directory to be copied to the archive and a dialog would open prompting the user for metadata, before compressing the directory tree into an archive file and moving it to the archive.

4.3 Graphical Tools for HPC Tasks

One barrier to entry in HPC is the many command line tools required to accomplish common HPC operations such as loading software modules, creating job scripts and managing running jobs. Providing a research desktop environment provides an environment where it is easy to create simple graphical user interfaces for these tasks. LUNARC has developed an LMOD browser tool, ml-browse [22], that make it easy find available software using a searchable browser interface. The GfxLauncher framework also provides a graphical job manager for monitoring and controlling running jobs. Work is also ongoing to develop a wizard for creating SLURM job scripts for common tasks.

For the Archeology department at LU a workflow was developed for running 3D reconstruction using the Metshape software, which is a graphical application with it's own batch framework. To make this workflow even easier, a graphical tool will be provided in the future to bootstrap the batch framework.

4.4 Develop a Community Around the HPC Desktop

While institutions have made their interactive tools available and have documented them on their support pages or on Github, there is no central location where "all things HPC Desktop" can be found. If such a place were to be created, it could help with:

- Share scripts and desktop customizations,
- Share experiences of what worked and didn't work when engaging users,
- Share statistics scripts and ideas for metrics.

5 Conclusion

HPC Desktops have proven successful in attracting new users to HPC systems and have broadened the user base for many institutions, including Indiana University, Lund University and Technical University of Denmark. HPC Desktops have enabled use cases that would be hard or impossible to support with traditional "ssh-only" HPC systems. HPC Desktop's unique contribution to the HPC ecosystem is to provide users with a single environment in which to perform all their computation research. This sets them apart from solutions like domain-specific science gateways or web based HPC access methods like Open OnDemand. HPC Desktops are in use by many HPC centers and research computing organizations around the world, but they are not yet a mainstream tool. Fostering a vibrant community around HPC Desktops will be instrumental in sharing best practices, innovations, and experiences, and ensuring that HPC Desktops continue to serve as an enabler of scientific discovery and innovation.

Acknowledgements. We would like to acknowledge the organizers of the Interactive and Urgent HPC BoFs and workshops at ISC and SC. We hope to leverage these events in the future to build a community around HPC Desktops. We would also like to acknowledge the many HPC centers and research computing organizations that provide an HPC Desktop or similar tool for their users.

References

1. Determine whether high performance computing can help your research (2024). https://kb.iu.edu/d/bilm
2. RCAC - Knowledge base: scholar user guide: ThinLinc (2024). https://www.rcac.purdue.edu/knowledge/scholar/accounts/login/thinlinc
3. NLHPC Laboratorio Nacional de Computacion de Alto Rendimiento. https://www.nlhpc.cl
4. University Of Chicago Basics - RCC user guide (2024). https://rcc-uchicago.github.io/user-guide/thinlinc/
5. Thota, A., et al: Research computing desktops: demystifying research computing for non-Linux users (2019). https://dl.acm.org/doi/10.1145/3332186.3332206
6. Linux remote desktop based on open-source - ThinLinc by Cendio. https://www.cendio.com
7. NoMachine. https://www.nomachine.com
8. FastX - Starnet. https://www.starnet.com/fastx
9. GfxLauncher. https://gfxlauncher-documentation.readthedocs.io/en/latest/
10. InteractiveHPC web page. https://www.interactivehpc.com
11. Reuther, A., et al.: Interactive and urgent HPC: challenges and opportunities. arXiv:2401.14550 (2024)
12. OpenOnDemand case studies. https://openondemand.org/get-involved#case-studies
13. Hudak, D.E., Johnson, D., Nicklas, J., Franz, E., McMichael, B., Gohar, B.: Open ondemand: transforming computational science through omnidisciplinary software cyberinfrastructure. In: Proceedings of the XSEDE16 Conference on Diversity, Big Data, and Science at Scale. Miami, USA (2016)
14. MATE desktop environment. https://mate-desktop.org
15. XFCE desktop environment. https://www.xfce.org
16. Desktop environments resource usage comparison. https://vermaden.wordpress.com/2022/07/12/desktop-environments-resource-usage-comparison/
17. What is GNOME classic. https://help.gnome.org/users/gnome-help/stable/gnome-classic.html
18. VirtualGL. https://www.virtualgl.org/
19. GNOME disk usage analyzer. https://community.linuxmint.com/software/view/baobab
20. Accessing local drives with ThinDrives. https://www.cendio.com/resources/docs/tag/redir_drives.html
21. gprofng GUI. http://savannah.gnu.org/projects/gprofng-gui/
22. LMOD Graphical module browser. https://github.com/lunarc/mbrowser

5th ISC HPC International Workshop on Monitoring and Operational Data Analytics (MODA24)

Preface to the 5th ISC HPC International Workshop on Monitoring and Operational Data Analytics Workshop (MODA24)

1 Objectives and Topics

After four very successful installments of the International Workshop on Monitoring and Operational Data Analytics (MODA), initiated in 2020 at ISC High Performance, we were excited to organize this year its 5th edition – MODA24.

The goal of the MODA workshop series is to provide a venue for sharing insights into current trends in MODA for HPC systems and data centers, identify potential gaps, and offer an outlook on the future of the involved fields of high-performance computing, databases, machine learning, and possible solutions. These insights will contribute to the co-design and procurement of future computing and data processing systems. The workshop is unique to the European HPC, arena being among the few to address the topic of monitoring and operational data analytics for improving HPC operations and research. Aligned with this goal, we solicited contributions presenting novel research ideas that relate to:

- Challenges, solutions, and best practices for monitoring systems at HPC and data centers. Of particular focus were operational data collection mechanisms i) covering different system levels, from building infrastructure sensor data to processing-core performance metrics, and ii) targeting different end-users, from system administrators to application developers and computational scientists.
- Effective strategies for analyzing and interpreting the collected operational data. Of particular focus are visualization approaches and machine learning-based techniques, potentially inferring knowledge of the system behavior and allowing for the realization of a proactive control loop.
- Methods, tools, and techniques for automated control of HPC systems. Such contributions might include (but were not limited to): i) use-cases that need autonomy loops and automated control and ii) instances of partial autonomy loops that need more automation and control.

2 Workshop Organization

The workshop organising and program committees consisted of academics and researchers at leading HPC sites and in industry. The reviewing of the submitted papers was balanced among the program committee members, and each paper received three or more high-quality reviews.

2.1 Organizers

Workshop Chairs

Florina M. Ciorba	University of Basel, Switzerland
Utz-Uwe Haus	HPE HPC/AI EMEA Research Lab, Switzerland
Thomas Jakobsche	University of Basel, Switzerland
Nicolas Lachiche	University of Strasbourg, France
Martin Schulz	Technische Universität München, Germany

2.2 Program Committee

Daniele Cesarini	CINECA, Italy
Ann Gentile	Sandia National Labs, USA
Thomas Ilsche	Technische Universität Dresden, Germany
Terry Jones	Oak Ridge National Laboratory, USA
Jacques-Charles Lafoucriere	CEA, France
Maxime Martinasso	CSCS, Switzerland
Diana Moise	Hewlett Packard Enterprise, Switzerland
Dirk Pleiter	KTH, Sweden / FZ Jülich, Germany
Melissa Romanus	Lawrence Berkeley National Laboratory, USA
Estela Suarez	University of Bonn / FZ Jülich, Germany
Keiji Yamamoto	RIKEN, Japan
Ales Zamuda	University of Maribor, Slovenia

3 Technical Program

MODA24 was held as an in-person half-day workshop with a balanced mix between technical paper presentations, keynote and lightning talks, and a discussion panel. The full program is available on the MODA24 website https://moda.dmi.unibas.ch/program/.

- **Keynote:** *Operating High-Performance Computers in remote and restrictive environments*, Brad Evans (Pawsey Supercomputing Research Centre, Australia)
- **Full Paper:** *An Exascale Slurm Testing and Evaluation Environment Utilizing Generated DAG Workloads*, Laslo Hunhold and Stefan Wesner (University of Cologne, Germany)
- **Short Paper:** *Challenges for monitoring and data analytics in a leadership public data repository*, Patrick Widener, Alex May, Tatiyanna Singleton and Olga Kuchar (ORNL, USA)
- **Lightning Talk:** *EMOI: CSCS Extensible Monitoring and Observability Infrastructure*, Jean-Guillaume Piccinali and Massimo Benini (CSCS, Switzerland)
- **Lightning Talk:** *How well can we predict two most important metrics for HPC jobs: runtime and queue time?*, Kevin Menear, Dmitry Duplyakin (NREL, USA) and Kadidia Konate (LBNL, USA)

- **Lightning Talk:** *Monitoring of Energy and Emissions of HPC Batch Job Using CEEMS*, Mahendra Paipuri (Centre National de la Recherche Scientifique, France)
- **Lightning Talk:** Next-Generation *Data Explanation: Bridging the Gap from Data Collection to Operational Data Analytics*, Cary Whitney (National Energy Research Scientific Computing Center, USA), Melissa Romanus, Thomas Davis and Elizabeth Bautista (LBNL, USA)

MODA24 concluded with a **panel discussion** on *MODA in multitenant and federated environments*, which included workshop speakers and one of the organizers (Utz-Uwe Haus) as moderator. This panel was highly interactive and turned into a discussion with the audience, revealing various insights into multi-tenant and federated environments.

4 Workshop Outcome

The MODA24 keynote and lightning talks, paper presentations, and panel discussion show the wide range of topics addressed, as well as the increasing importance of MODA for the HPC and data center systems and communities. At the same time, they documented the progress made since the last iteration of the workshop, showed the current state of the art, and evidenced the limitations of current solutions but also their need for reliability and stability. MODA24 further showed that key challenges still lie ahead and in particular:

- Continuous and holistic monitoring and observability of facilities, large-scale system hardware, system software, and applications are necessary to achieve data center digital twins to analyze and understand conditions of interest in relation to the location of objects (e.g. thermal hot spots).
- HPC job monitoring can reveal jobs with performance issues or inefficiencies with regards to under-utilized resources or uneven distribution of computational workload across processing units to bring efficient HPC within reach.
- HPC job-scheduling simulation is growing in importance and necessity for exploration and comparison of scheduling configurations without impacting system efficiency.
- MODA also plays an increasingly crucial role in security-related monitoring and analysis of HPC systems, such as compliance checking and system hardening (prevent a mistake/vulnerability from happening), as well as incident recording and intrusion detection (detect suspicious activities/potential attacks). Security plays an increasingly important role especially in multi-tenant HPC systems and data centers.
- The existence of a wide range of monitoring and analysis tools leads to heterogeneous software stacks that are challenging to integrate.
- Machine learning is driving the analysis of monitoring data. Unsupervised learning techniques such as automatic clustering and outlier detection can be leveraged to detect abnormal behavior even in large unlabeled datasets.

We hope that these and other aspects will figure prominently in submissions to the next edition(s) of the MODA workshop.

An Exascale Slurm Testing and Evaluation Environment Utilising Generated DAG Workloads

Laslo Hunhold[✉][iD] and Stefan Wesner[iD]

Parallel and Distributed Systems Group, University of Cologne, Cologne, Germany
{hunhold,wesner}@uni-koeln.de

Abstract. Going into the exascale era, there is an increasing demand to test and evaluate HPC tooling for such large scale computing systems. This goes beyond the aspects of scheduling performance, and also includes the development, testing and evaluation of workload manager plugins and profiling tools in the exascale. Current Slurm workload manager simulators, which are tailored for the former aspect, exhibit limitations in addressing the latter aspects.

This paper outlines the detailed steps for setting up an exascale Slurm instance with virtual nodes, enabling the simulation of 10,000 nodes on a single 8-core machine. Notably, no modifications to the source code of Slurm itself are required, ensuring straightforward portability to new releases. The paper also introduces and evaluates a software tool named WOGE (Workload Generator and Evaluator). WOGE facilitates the automatic randomised generation and accelerated execution of workloads in the form of directed acyclic job graphs (job DAGs).

To the best of the authors' knowledge, this paper represents the first comprehensive documentation on establishing a Slurm testing and evaluation environment of this scale, and the incorporation of job DAGs in this context is unparalleled in the existing literature.

Keywords: Exascale · Slurm · simulation · evaluation · testing · directed acyclic graph (DAG) · job model

1 Introduction

Supporting software, such as workload manager plugins and profiling tools, is indispensable for every HPC system. As we transition into the exascale era, this software becomes more complicated [1]. Concurrently, testing and evaluating such software becomes more challenging and costly. Examining Slurm [2], the predominant workload manager in the TOP500, we can raise the question how to address these challenges without access to a real exascale system. Existing solutions, such as Slurm simulators developed in recent years [3–6], primarily focus on the aspect of scheduling performance rather than comprehensive software integration. This emphasis sacrifices essential Slurm functionalities (e.g., job prologs/epilogs, inter-job profiling, etc.) crucial for testing and evaluating certain HPC tools. Moreover, their performance-centric approach involves profound changes to Slurm's codebase, rendering them relatively fragile. As reflected in [6], all referenced Slurm simulators, except the one in the mentioned source, are already broken, and it is likely that [6] will follow suit, given its likewise low-level modifications to the Slurm codebase.

Another critical challenge in the exascale era is the absence of historical workload data of such magnitude. The conventional approach, leveraging the parallel workloads archive [7] and utilising the SWF (Standard Workload File) format, faces limitations. Simakov et al. acknowledged this issue and transitioned to generating artificial workloads [6].

In the context of artificially generated workloads, a yet unexplored aspect is the artificial generation of directed acyclic job graphs (job DAGs) representing workloads. Unlike the prevailing literature, which often neglects job interdependencies altogether, DAGs offer a more accurate representation of the complex job interdependencies in modern workloads, partially resulting from the increased use of workflow managers in HPC.

This work delves into the detailed setup of an exascale Slurm cluster with 10,000 virtual nodes and the generation of artificial DAG workloads. The outcome is a comprehensive software tool named WOGE (Workload Generator and Evaluator), designed for the testing and evaluation of HPC tooling with artificial exascale workloads.

2 Goals

The primary objective of this work is to establish a Slurm instance on a significantly larger scale than previous simulator approaches, closely resembling a real exascale cluster. While conventional Slurm simulators primarily focus on scheduling performance, as evident in works such as [4–6], our approach aims to extend its scope to encompass observed software interaction and integration. This extension should not compromise acceleratability and must ensure easy reproducibility.

To achieve this, minimal source code modifications are pursued, acknowledging the rapidly changing and monolithic nature of Slurm's codebase. The adaptability of our proposed approach to future Slurm versions is crucial for effective evaluation, particularly in the context of Slurm software upgrades. This is in contrast to current simulator approaches heavily reliant on deep and consequently fragile Slurm source code modifications [6].

The second goal is to introduce a software utility capable of generating and expeditiously evaluating artificial yet representative exascale workloads in Slurm. Going beyond the conventional metric of scheduling performance, our utility aims to support the development, testing, and evaluation of workload manager plugins and profiling tools.

3 Methodology

Considering the absence of real data for exascale workloads [7], it becomes imperative to devise a methodology for generating random representative workloads. This entails not only the formulation of an algorithm for generating a randomised directed acyclic graph (DAG) but also the judicious selection of pertinent parameters. Utilising the DAG job model, which aligns more closely with contemporary workflow-oriented workloads, our approach involves the random parametric generation of workloads. This allows for more general assertions about the nature of the analyzed workload, establishing a foundation for characterising and artificially reproducing real workloads in turn.

3.1 Workload DAG Generation

In adopting a Directed Acyclic Graph (DAG) job model, the initial step involves the random generation of a DAG. Although a DAG is conceptually a directed graph with a strictly triangular adjacency matrix, generating one representative of an HPC workload, typically characterised by sparsity, presents a challenge.

A pragmatic approach involves grouping nodes into sets of ranks and permitting edges exclusively from one rank to its preceding rank. Algorithm 1 encapsulates this strategy, resulting in a sparsely populated DAG with only three adjustable parameters (total number of ranks, range of nodes per rank, and range of dependencies per node). The algorithm guarantees correctness by construction, as edges only exist from nodes with higher to nodes with lower node IDs, yielding a strictly upper triangular adjacency matrix for the generated DAG.

To comprehensively characterise the workload, attributes must be assigned to each job. Fundamental characteristics include the number of compute nodes required by a job and its runtime, with potentially more parameters. As each node in the job DAG represents a job, the random generation of these attributes for each node in the job DAG becomes necessary.

3.2 Parameter Choice

Determining suitable input parameters for the DAG generation algorithm and establishing ranges for job node counts and runtimes is inherently challenging. The absence of a definitive characterization of an HPC workload, coupled with variations dependent on system size and workload type, complicates this task. HPC systems dedicated to simulations, for instance, may feature large, long-running jobs arranged in a linear job graph. Conversely, systems oriented towards data processing and workflows might showcase smaller, shorter-running jobs with a more intricate graph structure.

For guidance in selecting job runtimes and node counts, we refer to two workload analyses: one conducted on NERSC's HPC systems [8] and the other on the NSF Innovative HPC program's infrastructure [9]. The former's trend

Algorithm 1: A rank-based DAG generator that also outputs the rank sets. It shall be noted here that by construction no double edges are created between nodes.

input : $r \in \mathbb{N}_0$: number of ranks
$\underline{n} \leq \overline{n} \in \mathbb{N}_1$: min./max. nodes per rank
$\underline{d} \leq \overline{d} \in \mathbb{N}_0$: min./max. deps. per node
output: $G := (V, E)$: directed acyclic graph
$R_1, \ldots, R_r$: sets of nodes of each rank

$G = (V, E) \leftarrow (\emptyset, \emptyset)$
for $i \leftarrow 1$ **to** r **do**
    $n_i \leftarrow$ DiscreteUniformRandom$(\underline{n}, \overline{n})$
    $R_i \leftarrow$ GenerateNodes(n_i)
    $V \leftarrow V \cup R_i$
    if $i > 1$ **then**
        for $j \leftarrow 1$ **to** n_i **do**
            $d \leftarrow$ Min$(n_{i-1},$ DiscreteUniformRandom$(\underline{d}, \overline{d}))$
            $D \leftarrow$ DrawDistinctRandomFrom(R_{i-1}, d)
            for $k \leftarrow 1$ **to** d **do**
                $E \leftarrow E \cup (R_i[j], D[k])$
            end
        end
    end
end

---

analysis reveals a broad spectrum of job runtimes, ranging from a few minutes to over 10 h, with a median around 30 min [8, Fig. 1]. The latter study observes a similar range of job runtimes between 1 and 9 h [9, Fig. 70], with certain short- and long-running jobs excluded from their analysis [9, Sect. 7.3].

Regarding job node counts, the NERSC study identifies a range between 1 and over 1000 nodes, depending on the cluster [8, Table 1, Fig. 2], while the NSF study notes a range between 1 and 100 nodes [9, Fig. 27, Sect. 5.2]. Despite the increase in node core counts per node in recent years, certain computations may still demand the majority of nodes, even in an exascale system [10]. Given the varied job runtimes in the referenced studies, we opt for a uniform random distribution of job runtimes between 30 min and 6 h. For job node counts, we choose a uniform distribution between 10 and 500, accommodating a diverse range of applications for a comprehensive HPC system with increasing job heterogeneity.

The DAG generator's parameters, including the number of ranks and the range of nodes per rank, are set to yield a graph that roughly represents a day's worth of work. This results in 20 ranks and a range of 1 to 20 nodes per rank.

The range for the number of dependencies per node is set between 0 and 1, producing a very sparse graph with predominantly linear structures. This choice aligns with the prevalent reality that, although HPC workflow managers tend to break up commonly observed monolithic job patterns, most jobs still do not specify explicit dependencies and remain singular, or at most, are part of a pipeline (linear graph).

Figure 1 illustrates the outcome of a randomly generated graph with these parameters, showcasing a substantial proportion of singular jobs and fragments of linear graph structures, as intended.

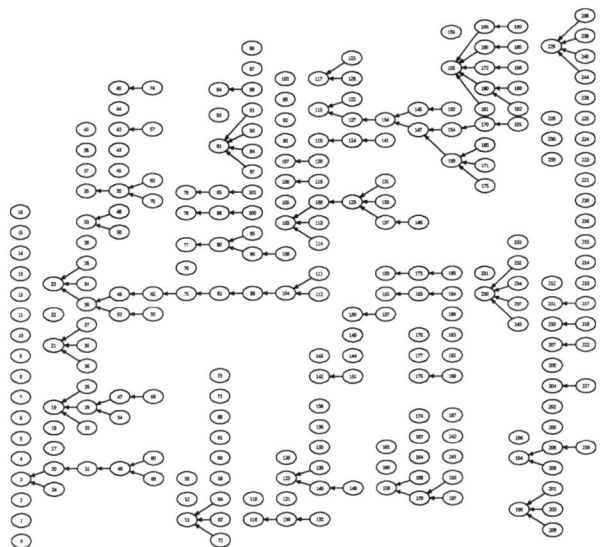

Fig. 1. Example of a seed-randomly generated graph using Algorithm 1. The graph was generated with 20 ranks, each having 1 to 20 nodes and 0 to 1 dependencies per node. Nodes are approximately grouped by their respective rank.

4 Implementation

The implementation comprises two key components. The first part entails an exascale Slurm instance featuring virtual nodes, and we elucidate the system and Slurm configuration process. The second part is a software tool interfacing with Slurm, automating the generation, submission, execution, and evaluation of workloads.

4.1 System Configuration

Our implementation is built upon Debian stable (version 12.2, bookworm), ensuring broad compatibility with Debian-derived operating systems such as Ubuntu.

MUNGE Authentication Service The initial step involves setting up the MUNGE authentication service. Install the `libmunge-dev` package, which automatically creates the unprivileged system user named "munge". This package registers and initiates the corresponding daemon while generating a MUNGE key at `/etc./munge/munge.key`. Since the entire Slurm instance operates on a single machine, there's no need to propagate the key to other machines.

Database Server To facilitate job accounting, install a MySQL server using the packages `default-mysql-server` and `libmariadb-dev-compat`. This installation registers and starts MariaDB (Debian's default MySQL server) as a service. Slurm can only access the database if granted, accomplished by creating a user via the MySQL command line:

```
create user 'slurm'@'localhost' identified by 'STORAGE_PASSWORD';
grant all on *.* to 'slurm'@'localhost';
```

Replace "STORAGE_PASSWORD" with a password of your choice.

4.2 Slurm Installation and Configuration

To scale Slurm to 10,000 nodes and beyond on a single machine, careful configuration is necessary. The following steps outline the complete setup of Slurm as a virtual exascale cluster.

Slurm Source Code Repository Due to required modifications and compile-time configurations, we cannot rely on precompiled Slurm packages provided by the operating system. Instead, we compile Slurm from source. The most flexible approach is to use the source code repository, enabling us to jump to any Slurm version.

After installing the `git` package, clone the Slurm repository at https://github.com/SchedMD/slurm.git. Checkout a specific tag, such as `slurm-23-11-0-1` (corresponding to Slurm release version 23.11.0.1), to detach from the `master` branch, avoiding intermittent breakage due to incoming developer commits.

Using the repository has the added advantage that Slurm plugins and modifications can be developed as git branches rooted in Slurm version tags. Porting to a newer Slurm version involves rebasing the branch to a new version tag, a semi-automatic process. Modifications, integrated into the build system, can be quickly installed on the system.

Slurm Build Configuration and Compilation Before automatically configuring the build system, install the build-dependency packages `gcc` (C compiler) and `libgtk2.0-dev` (optional, for `sview(1)`). Execute

```
./configure --prefix=/usr --sysconfdir=/etc --with-systemdsystemunitdir
    =/usr/lib/systemd/system --enable-multiple-slurmd
```

in the Slurm source code folder. This prepares a system-wide installation including systemd service files and allowing multiple Slurm daemons on a single machine. The next step is to run

```
make install
```

to compile and install Slurm. Afterwards, create a system user and identically named group for Slurm via

```
adduser --system --group slurm
```

and create directories reserved for the Slurm user via

```
mkdir /var/spool/slurm /var/log/slurm /run/slurm
chown slurm:slurm /var/spool/slurm /var/log/slurm /run/slurm
```

These directories will be used by Slurm to store specific runtime data. By creating separate directories, which is different from the default, we don't have to give the `slurm` user/group any more permissions than it needs. As the last step, we need to instruct systemd to automatically create the directory /run/slurm on boot, as it is otherwise deleted. We do this by creating a file /usr/lib/tmpfiles.d/slurm.conf with the following content:

```
#Type Path Mode UID GID Age Argument
d /run/slurm 0755 slurm slurm - -
```

This instructs the `systemd-tmpfiles` service to create and maintain this directory. Given we will fully automate the cluster initialization on boot later, this aspect is crucial for a reliable operation.

Slurm Configuration We now proceed to configure Slurm itself. The main configuration file is /etc./slurm.conf and needs to be identical for all nodes in the same cluster. Given we are on a single machine and all Slurm daemons access the same slurm.conf, we don't need to explicitly distribute it across our nodes. There is no default slurm.conf that we can copy to its destination. Instead Slurm installs a configurator in /usr/share/doc/slurm-*/html/configurator.html that we can use to generate a configuration file.

Unless otherwise stated, everything is kept as default. Set ClusterName to your desired cluster name. Specify SlurmctldHost as the system's hostname. Under "State Preservation" set StateSaveLocation to /var/spool/slurm/slurmctld and SlurmdSpoolDir to /var/spool/slurm/slurmd.%n (the %n is automatically replaced with the node name, a necessity given multiple Slurm daemons run on a single machine).

Opt for Pgid under "Process Tracking" to disable cgroup tracking, eliminating substantial overhead and the hard limit on our maximum node count. In the TaskPlugin section, unset Affinity and Cgroup and select None. Set JobCompType to FileTxt and JobCompLoc to /var/log/slurm/jobcomp.log.

Under "Event Logging", change `SlurmctldLogFile` to `/var/log/slurm/slurmctld.log` and `SlurmdLogFile` to `/var/log/slurm/slurmd.%n.log`. In the "Process ID Logging" section, alter `SlurmctldPidFile` to `/run/slurm/slurmctld.pid` and `SlurmdPidFile` to `/run/slurm/slurmd.%n.pid`.

Press "Submit" to generate the configuration and save it to `/etc/slurm.conf`. Open it in your editor and replace the node definitions at the end with:

```
NodeName=atom[00000-09999] NodeHostname=HOSTNAME Port=[10000-19999]
    Sockets=1 CPUs=1 CoresPerSocket=64 ThreadsPerCore=128 State=UNKNOWN
     PartitionName=part1 Nodes=ALL Default=YES MaxTime=INFINITE State=
    Up
```

Ensure to replace `HOSTNAME` with your system's hostname. This defines a cluster with 10,000 nodes. Specifically, the `CPUs`, `CoresPerSocket` and `ThreadsPerCore` settings approximately correspond to the node configuration of the current fastest supercomputer, "Frontier" (74 rack cabinets, each hosting 64 blades, and each blade consisting of 2 nodes with 64 cores per node, resulting in a total of 9472 nodes) [11].

To circumvent resource constraints intrinsic to systemd/dbus, create a file `/etc/cgroup.conf` with the single line:

```
IgnoreSystemd=yes
```

This instructs the Slurm cgroup plugin to disregard systemd, opting not to allocate cgroups via dbus, but manually instead.

Next, we modify the systemd service files to accommodate multiple Slurm daemons on one machine. Firstly, add the line `Nice=-20` to `/lib/systemd/system/slurmctld.service` below the `Type=` line. This grants the Slurm controller daemon a higher scheduling priority over other Slurm daemons and system processes.

The subsequent step involves using systemd's template service function to create a service file, facilitating the launch of each individual node. To achieve this, copy the installed service unit file `/lib/systemd/system/slurmd.service` to a new file `/lib/systemd/system/slurmd@.service`. Modify it by changing the line setting `ExecStart` to:

```
ExecStart=/usr/sbin/slurmd -N %i -D -s $SLURMD_OPTIONS
```

In essence, add the parameter "`-N %i`", an option included in our specially-configured slurmd(1) allowing the specification of which node's slurmd(1) is to be started. The "`%i`" is replaced with anything after the @-character in the service name; for example, for the service `slurmd@atom00001`, the "`%i`" is replaced with `atom00001`. This approach offers the advantage of convenient interaction and inspection for each virtual node, each assigned a systemd service when launched with the template service.

Slurm Job Accounting Configuration In addition to the core Slurm configuration, the establishment of job accounting is imperative. While the Slurm instance remains functional without it, tools like `sacct(1)` become inaccessible, notwithstanding their crucial role in certain plugins and external tools integral to a comprehensive system evaluation. The initial step involves incorporating the following lines into /etc./slurm.conf

```
AccountingStorageType=accounting_storage/slurmdbd
AccountingStorageHost=HOSTNAME
AccountingStorageUser=slurm
```

Replace HOSTNAME with your system's hostname. Subsequently, create a file /etc./slurmdbd.conf and adjust its permissions using:

```
chmod 600 /etc/slurmdbd.conf
chown slurm:slurm /etc/slurmdbd.conf
```

Fill the file with the following:

```
DbdHost=HOSTNAME
StorageHost=localhost
LogFile=/var/log/slurm/slurmdbd.log
PidFile=/var/run/slurm/slurmdbd.pid
StoragePass=STORAGE_PASSWORD
StorageType=accounting_storage/mysql
StorageUser=slurm
SlurmUser=slurm
```

Ensure to substitute HOSTNAME and STORAGE_PASSWORD with the values previously set.

Automatic Cluster Launch and Reset Considering the scale of the virtual cluster, automating its launch and reset becomes imperative. The latter entails not only stopping the Slurm daemons (controller, database, nodes) but also purging the Slurm working directories and clearing the job accounting database. The following script facilitates the cluster's launch:

```
#!/bin/sh

systemctl stop slurmctld
systemctl stop slurmdbd
rm -rf /var/spool/slurm/* /var/log/slurm/* /run/slurm/*
systemctl start slurmdbd
sleep 2
systemctl start slurmctld
printf "started slurmdbd and slurmctld\n"
for i in $(seq -f "%05g" 0 9999); do
        systemctl start slurmd@atom$i;
        printf "\rstarted atom $i/09999";
done
```

```
printf "\n"
```

Similarly, the subsequent script is suitable for resetting the cluster:

```
#!/bin/sh

for i in $(seq -f "%05g" 0 9999); do
        systemctl kill --signal=SIGKILL slurmd@atom$i;
        printf "\rstopped atom $i/09999";
done
printf "\n"
systemctl stop slurmctld
printf "stopped slurmctld\n"
systemctl stop slurmdbd
printf "stopped slurmdbd\n"
rm -rf /var/spool/slurm/* /var/log/slurm/* /run/slurm/*
printf "DROP DATABASE slurm_acct_db;\n" | mysql
```

By employing these automated launch and reset procedures, managing the virtual cluster becomes more efficient and straightforward, optimising the handling of its scale and complexity.

4.3 Workload Generator and Evaluator (WOGE)

The WOGE software tool is implemented in C99 (ISO/IEC 9899:1999), utilising the POSIX.1-2008 system API. It serves a dual purpose: firstly, generating random workloads and submitting them to Slurm, and secondly, supervising the execution of each workload while collecting diagnostic data for subsequent evaluation. This section delves into the technical design aspects in further detail.

The source code is organised into two directories: bin, designated as the output directory for compiled binaries, and src, housing the source code. The automated building process is facilitated by a portable POSIX.1-2008 makefile. This makefile is complemented by an automatic configuration shell script, configure, which dynamically adjusts the build configuration file, config.mk, to accommodate a diverse array of operating systems.

Workload Generation and Submission The workload generation in WOGE constitutes a comprehensive implementation of Sect. 3. All functions associated with the generation of directed acyclic graphs (DAGs), primarily dag_generate(), are located in src/dag.c. This is coupled with the job data structures from src/job.h in src/experiment.c to construct a holistic workload. The experiment record type serves as the repository for the complete workload specification, encapsulating both the DAG and job generation parameters.

In Slurm, the representation of this workload utilises "sleeper" jobs - jobs designed to sleep for a predetermined duration, which, in this context, corresponds to the runtime determined earlier during workload generation. Unlike only the simulation of job scheduling itself, sleeper jobs allow incorporating telemetry into the jobs themselves, enabling testing of specific plugins unfeasible with a simulated scheduler. Additionally, they facilitate the replication of prolog/epilog setups as demonstrated in [10]. Configurable jitter introduces realistic variations in job runtimes.

The generated workload is submitted using Slurm interfaces provided by `src/slurm.c`. To ensure a high API stability, Slurm command-line tools are executed through `execve(2)`, and their output is managed through a generic line-based callback function approach. Commencing with the clearance of the entire job queue using `slurm_clear_job_queue()`, sleeper jobs are individually submitted with the function `slurm_submit_sleeper_job()`. This function takes a `job_parameters` record type as input and outputs essential information about the submitted job (e.g., job ID) to a `job` record type. Upon submission to Slurm, the requested job runtime is divided by the provided speedup factor. Once all jobs are submitted, their dependencies are added using `slurm_set_job_parameter()` according to the generated DAG structure. At this juncture, the DAG is fully represented within the Slurm job queue. To minimise overhead from the job submission process, all sleeper jobs are submitted in a held state to be collectively released at a later point.

Workload Execution and Evaluation Following the submission of the workload with jobs awaiting in a held state on the cluster, the execution phase is imminent. Prior to initiation, WOGE opens the Slurm job completion log file and awaits appended lines at the end. All held jobs are concurrently released through the invocation of `slurm_release_sleeper_jobs()`. Rather than individually releasing each job internally, which would be inefficient, this is achieved through a single call to `scontrol(1)`. Upon job completion, Slurm appends comprehensive information about the job to the job completion log. This data is parsed by WOGE, marking the corresponding `job` record as finished and incorporating metadata such as eligible time, start time, end time, and more. The type and amount of collected data are configurable and extensible.

Once all jobs are completed, a separate function processes this data. This function has access to the generated workload and obtained job execution metadata. As an illustration, this version of WOGE includes a basic evaluation function measuring the total time taken to process an entire workload based on the speedup factor. However, various evaluation functions are possible. For instance, one might conduct graph analysis on the generated job DAG, correlating centrality measures of nodes with their runtime performance.

5 Evaluation

The evaluation encompasses the assessment of the Slurm environment and the WOGE software utility on a Dell Precision R7610 rack server. This system is equipped with two Intel Xeon E5-2637 v2 processors, each featuring 4 cores running at 8 threads, along with 192 GB of RAM. The operating system used for the evaluation is Debian 12.2 (bookworm). Notably, each virtual node Slurm daemon and associated processes consume approximately 16 MB of RAM. For the configured 10,000 nodes, this cumulatively accounts for 160 GB of memory usage, nearly exhausting the system's available memory.

The concurrent evaluation of both the Slurm environment and the WOGE software utility involves the generation of a one-day workload using Algorithm 1. The resulting workload is shown in Fig. 1. Job runtimes and node counts are derived using the parameters specified in Sect. 3. The observed execution time is measured across speedup factors from $\{1, 10, 20, \ldots, 200\}$, assessing both the performance consistency of the Slurm instance and the impact of accelerated execution on simulated results.

The conducted measurements, repeated 20 times for each speedup factor, are illustrated in Fig. 2. To facilitate comparison, the values are normalised by multiplying the measured times with the respective speedup factor. While the ideal scenario would manifest as a completely flat line, a slightly linear increase is observed with rising speedup factors. However, this overhead remains within the range of 0 to 3 percent relative to the non-accelerated workload runtime, which is deemed an acceptable deviation. It can be hypothesised that this marginal increase in runtime is attributed to the diminishing job runtimes versus constant scheduling times, causing the system to proportionally spend more time scheduling.

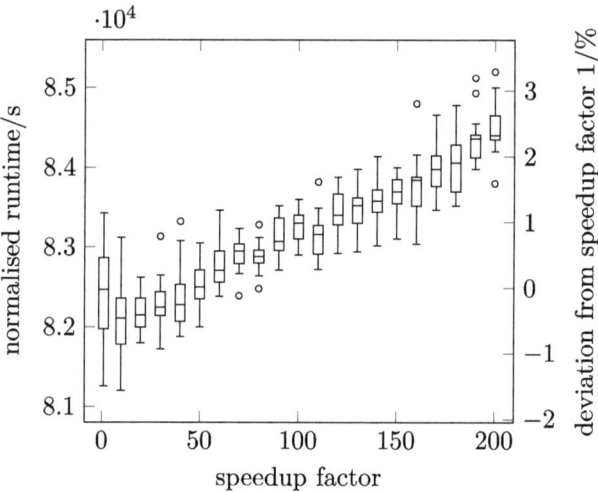

Fig. 2. The normalised runtime of the workload defined by the job DAG in Fig. 1 in relation to the speedup factor. The measurements were repeated 20 times for each speedup factor. Each job's node count and runtime were seed-randomly generated (uniformly drawn from 10 to 500 nodes and 30 min to 6 h, respectively), but remained the same across all speedup factors and runs. The normalised runtime was obtained by multiplying the measured runtime of the accelerated run with the speedup factor. The right ordinate additionally expresses the runtime deviation in relation to the median runtime of the non-accelerated runs.

6 Conclusion

In this study, we have provided a comprehensive guide on establishing an exascale Slurm instance featuring 10,000 virtual nodes or more. To the best of the authors' knowledge, these detailed instructions represent the first publication of their kind for setting up an exascale test cluster in the literature.

The objective of minimising Slurm source code modifications has been successfully realised, with the necessity limited to passing specific flags during the Slurm build system configuration. This accomplishment implies the likely longevity of the provided instructions in the foreseeable future. This stands in contrast to previous Slurm simulators, which often remained usable only until the subsequent major (or even minor) Slurm release due to their relative fragility [6].

We introduced an algorithm for the parametric generation of directed acyclic job graphs (job DAGs), marking the first instance, to the best of the authors' knowledge, of such a proposal in the context of Slurm simulation. The WOGE software utility, presented as an implementation of this workload generation method, has demonstrated its ability to be accelerated up to a factor of 200 with an acceptable measurement error of 3 percent. Utilising the Slurm command line interface instead of lower-level APIs, WOGE's Slurm interface is anticipated to remain stable and accurate in the foreseeable future. The program's flexible structure enables easy extension and adaptation for various Slurm plugin and profiling tool development and testing purposes.

Looking forward, potential extensions for WOGE include support for more intricate random distributions and graph generators, contingent on the availability of detailed exascale workload data. While this may not be immediately warranted due to the limited public data on exascale workloads, the long-term vision entails characterising and reproducing workloads based on a set of parameters. This approach would provide an opportunity to systemise the expansive and diverse forest of high-performance computing workloads.

References

1. Nikitenko, D., Voevodin, V., Zhumatiy, S.: Resolving frontier problems of mastering large- scale supercomputer complexes. In: CF '16: Proceedings of the ACM International Conference on Computing Frontiers, pp. 349–352. Association for Computing Machinery, Como, Italy (2016). https://doi.org/10.1145/2903150.2903481.
2. Yoo, A.B., Jette, M.A., Grondona, M.: SLURM: simple Linux utility for resource management. In: Feitelson, D.G., Rudolph, L., Schwiegelshohn, U. (eds.) Job Scheduling Strategies for Parallel Processing, Lecture Notes in Computer Science, pp. 44–60. Springer Berlin, Heidelberg, Seattle, WA, USA (2003). https://doi.org/10.1007/10968987_3.
3. Simakov, N.A., et al.: Slurm simulator: improving slurm scheduler performance on large HPC systems by utilization of multiple controllers and node sharing. In: PEARC '18: Proceedings of the Practice and Experience on Advanced Research Computing, pp. 1–8. Association for Computing Machinery, Pittsburgh, PA, USA (2018). https://doi.org/10.1145/3219104.3219111.

4. Simakov, N.A., et al.: A slurm simulator: implementation and parametric analysis. In: Jarvis, S., Wright, S., Hammond, S. (eds.) High Performance Computing Systems. Performance Modeling, Benchmarking, and Simulation, Lecture Notes in Computer Science, vol. 10724, pp. 197–217. Springer, Cham, Germany (2018). https://doi.org/10.1007/978-3-319-72971-8_10.
5. Chadha, M., John, J., Gerndt, M.: Extending SLURM for dynamic resource-aware adaptive batch scheduling. In: 2020 IEEE 27th International Conference on High Performance Computing, Data, and Analytics (HiPC), pp. 223–232. IEEE Computer Society, Los Alamitos, CA, USA (2020). https://doi.org/10.1109/HiPC50609.2020.00036.
6. Simakov, N.A., DeLeon, R.L., Lin, Y., Hoffmann, P.S., Mathias, W.R.: Developing accurate slurm simulator. In: PEARC '22: Practice and Experience in Advanced Research Computing, pp. 1–4. Association for Computing Machinery, Boston, MA, USA (2022). https://doi.org/10.1145/3491418.3535178.
7. Feitelson, D.G., Tsafrir, D., Krakov, D.: Experience with using the parallel workloads archive. J. Parallel Distrib. Comput. **74**(10), 2967–2982 (2014). https://doi.org/10.1016/j.jpdc.2014.06.013
8. Rodrigo Álvarez, G.P., Östberg, P.-O., Elmroth, E., Antypas, K., Gerber, R., Ramakrishnan, L.: HPC system lifetime story: workload characterization and evolutionary analyses on NERSC systems. In: Proceedings of the 24th International Symposium on High-Performance Parallel and Distributed Computing, pp. 57–60. Association for Computing Machinery, Portland, Oregon, USA (2015). https://doi.org/10.1145/2749246.2749270.
9. Simakov, N.A., et al.: A workload analysis of NSF's innovative HPC resources using XDMoD. arXiv: 1801.04306 (2018)
10. Hagerty, N., Webb, J., Melesse Vergara, V., Ezell, M.: Experiences detecting defective hardware in exascale supercomputers. In: Proceedings of the SC '23 Workshops of the International Conference on High Performance Computing, Network, Storage, and Analysis, pp. 619–626. Association for Computing Machinery, Denver, CO, USA (2023). https://doi.org/10.1145/3624062.3624134.
11. Rajaraman, V.: Frontier - World's first ExaFLOPS supercomputer. Resonance **28**(4), 567–576 (2023). https://doi.org/10.1007/s12045-023-1583-7

Challenges for Monitoring and Data Analytics in a Leadership Public Data Repository

Patrick M. Widener[✉], Alex May, Tatiyanna Singleton, and Olga Kuchar

National Center for Computational Sciences, Oak Ridge National Laboratory, Oak Ridge, TN 37831, USA
widenerpm@ornl.gov

Abstract. The availability and disposition of data has assumed increasing importance in large-scale computational science. *Data repositories* are evolving to meet new classes of requirements: compliance with government access guidelines, support for reproducibility of experimental results, and long-term availability of data products. The Constellation public data repository at the Oak Ridge Leadership Computing Facility faces these issues while being situated in one of the most productive data centers in the world. While monitoring and operational data analysis are ingrained in the operation of the OLCF's large-scale high performance computing platforms, data repositories do not have this history of support. Problems faced by Constellation range from data size (over 7 petabytes in current holdings) to analytic complexity (detailed curation is both absolutely necessary for many data sets and absolutely impossible for humans to accomplish in any practical manner) to deployment environment (OLCF storage resources are oriented toward the needs of the compute platforms). In this paper we describe some of the challenges for collecting monitoring and analytic data from a leadership public data repository. We also discuss various strategies we are pursuing in order to address these challenges, from manual data collection to plans for introducing machine learning-based curatorial techniques.

1 Introduction

Large-scale data is quickly becoming the driving force at the heart of scientific exploration. As the sizes and varieties of data in computational science have grown, the tools used to manage that data have evolved. Researchers can manage data that only they use in a variety of ways, ranging from locally attached RAID disk packs to cloud storage. *Data repositories* have emerged as critical

---

This research used resources of the Oak Ridge Leadership Computing Facility at the Oak Ridge National Laboratory, which is supported by the Office of Science of the U.S. Department of Energy under Contract No. DE-AC05-00OR22725.

data management systems for large scientific data which is shared among collaborators or with the public. The computational science carried out using large high-performance computing (HPC) machines, such as those hosted by the user facilities of the US Department of Energy (DOE), produce and consume immense quantities of such data. In fact, making data which results from taxpayer-funded research publicly available, as has been recommended by DOE [8], is only practically achievable for DOEs user facilities through the establishment of such repositories.

These repositories are deployed in the same hardware and software environment as the more mature computation-focused systems used for running large scientific applications. In many cases they share hardware and storage systems. While it is desirable to understand the behavior of repository systems in their own right, the fact of their co-location in large computing centers in DOE both reinforces the need for monitoring and analysis of their operation and complicates how that monitoring and analysis can be carried out.

In this paper we describe how the maintainers and operators of the Constellation public data repository, hosted at the Oak Ridge National Laboratory's Leadership Computing Facility, are working to meet these challenges. We discuss the system architecture of Constellation, describe current monitoring and metrics collection efforts, and provide some insight into the AI-powered analytic support which will be necessary to perform data curation at increasing scale.

2 Challenges for a Petascale Data Repository

Constellation was conceived as a long-term data storage service for published data by users and staff at OLCF. While there are now a large number of cloud storage options for "small data", even for increasingly larger values of "small", the dataset sizes addressed by Constellation are in a separate equivalence class. Constellation is biased toward datasets which comprise thousands of files or extremely large single files. For comparison, as of this writing the largest dataset managed by Constellation is 2 PB, while the largest single file size is approximately 17 TB.

As is common in many DOE and academic datacenters, users of the HPC platforms at OLCF are able to store large amounts of data for a relatively short period of time on "scratch" high-speed parallel filesystems. However, storing data for indefinite longer periods on these filesystems is not feasible for several reasons. Scratch filesystems are heavily optimized for write performance, befitting their primary purpose as persistent state storage for modeling and simulation codes running on the supercomputers to which they are attached. Space on scratch filesystems is also in heavy demand at facilities like OLCF, due to the popularity of leadership-class machines such as Frontier [9] for addressing open science problems at extreme scale. Scratch filesystems are also not equipped with advanced searching or metadata attachment mechanisms which help users to locate and examine data sets. Finally, while in practice data storage isn't usually assessed strictly on a bytes-used basis at facilities like OLCF, storage allocations for projects typically are removed when projects end. Those project lifecycles usually span 3–5 years, and scientists wishing to make data available longer-term need other options.

Constellation directly addresses these needs for OLCF. Datasets are managed on storage resources which are not in demand by production modeling and simulation jobs and which are not specifically tuned for high-speed parallel write performance. Constellation provides metadata and search services which allow external users to find and retrieve any stewarded dataset. Also, Constellation's charter is to serve as a long-term repository, allowing users to store their data without regard for project funding or associated timelines.

Constellation provides benefits over and above these needs, however. The most important is that every dataset managed by Constellation receives a *digital object identifier* (DOI) [3] from the DOE's Office of Science and Technical Information (OSTI). OSTI is the primary search tool for DOE science, technology, and engineering research and development results, and creating a DOI for each dataset provides a permanent reference which users can disseminate without fear of staleness. Additionally, trained curation staff within OLCF ensure that each dataset is tagged with metadata using widely-accepted standards, playing a critical role in making extreme-scale data more FAIR [12].

Constellation Architecture. We briefly describe the system architecture of Constellation (Fig. 1). A collection of containerized microservices takes input from a browser-based UI, which also allows users to search and select from datasets currently stewarded by Constellation. OSTI provides a REST-based API for obtaining new DOIs; UCAMS is a facility for OLCF user authentication. Data transport is handled by OLCF's installation of Globus [4], which relieves Constellation of having to manage data transfer across administrative and network boundaries and delegates both administrative and transport scalability issues to the mature Globus framework. Newly ingested datasets are staged temporarily on a parallel file system before being moved permanently to tape-based archive storage (the High Performance Storage System).

What is important to monitor? Rather than traditional system operational information, we are working to establish what things are worth monitoring from a data repository perspective. Among the questions we would like to develop leverage on are:

- *How can we quantify the impact and expense associated with operating a data repository?* Constellation operates in a DOE-funded computing facility with a well-defined mission. In order to continue providing the services of the repository, we must be able both to show that it has positive scientific impact and to justify the resources it uses. We describe our initial efforts in this regard in Sect. 3.
- *How can we better understand the data hosted by Constellation?* Answering this will enable us to address a number of legal (e.g., avoiding hosting content which is objectionable, contains sensitive data, or otherwise carries potential

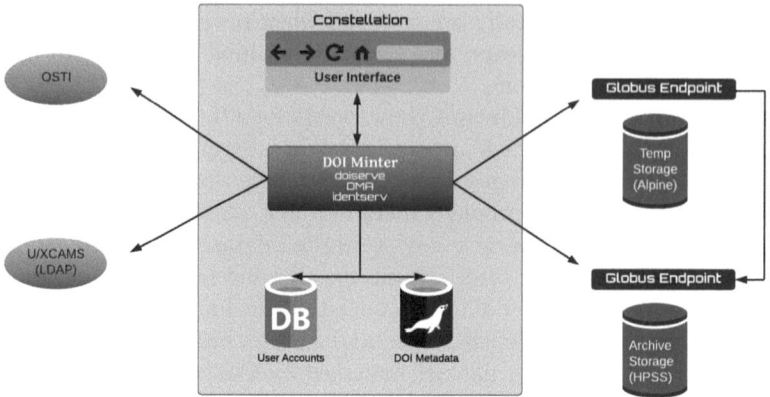

Fig. 1. An overview of the Constellation system architecture.

liability) and operational (e.g., staging data among the set of available storage resources) issues. The former is largely a curation problem, and we discuss curation issues further in Sect. 4.

3 Current Metrics Collection

There are a number of challenges in collecting metrics and monitoring information for Constellation. Monitoring work in HPC is oriented toward CPU and scheduling, neither of which is a strong concern for data repositories now (but may become more so in future as we anticipate tighter integration between data repositories and workflow management systems). Storage appliances likely to form more of the basis of data repositories like Constellation in the future will need to be instrumented appropriately. "Green datacenter" research (e.g., [6]) is increasing but still focuses strongly on cloud and not environments such as OLCF.

As an example of the monitoring we currently perform, we track requests for the various datasets Constellation stewards. These numbers are derived from a SQL database and exported manually to disk. Our analytics process is currently based on commodity "business intelligence" tools and allows us to track download information longitudinally; we have several years of this data now and can readily produce reporting about popularity of particular datasets, correlation of download requests with project timelines, and also attempted denial-of-service and intrusion attacks attempted against the browser-based UI. We intend to expand these capabilities as part of scaling our data curation processes, which we discuss next.

4 Curation: Becoming More Difficult

Data is becoming larger, more complex, and emerging from new sources and instruments (e.g., neutron scattering sources, x-ray light sources, omics facilities). A fundamental question for data repositories is how to manage and curate the volume, velocity, and variety (the three Vs) of these datasets, especially as they are now too large and complex for processing by traditional database management tools. Traditional repository infrastructures typically support common file formats; humans generally appraise and describe the datasets with a combination of basic descriptive metadata, tagging, and controlled access points. Additionally most curatorial practices are typically built around curators actively checking common data files no larger than a couple of gigabytes ("...We review as many of the files in the dataset as possible. For datasets that contain large numbers of similar files or multiple large files (e.g., >20 GB), we check a subset of the files, rather than every single file" [7].)

Science domain data curators lack appropriate tools and workflows to adequately appraise and describe extreme-scale datasets. This is not just a matter of the three V's, but also a consideration of the high costs for data movement and access [10]. We need new ways to appraise the data and have AI tools alert us to anomalies in the datasets that might otherwise go unnoticed due to their size.

Current efforts that consider data in novel ways, such as MIT's Sonification Toolkit [5] (which can render datasets as sound) are examples of innovative experimental tools that might assist in quickly alerting curators when the dataset is too large to "behold" at once. Dashboards and visualizations will need to be re-imagined to not just identify file formats but to also provide snapshots–insights into whether the data is structured or unstructured, what metadata is associated at what level, whether migration paths exist, and whether common quality-assurance issues can be identified. For example, the Renderer Tool developed at Los Alamos National Laboratory allows users to fully render a view of a hierarchical data file directly in a findable, accessible, interoperable, and reusable (FAIR) Repository [1]. Other tools such as BDBag [2] provide more integrated collections of capabilities. Additional work [10] leverages situ visualizations and workflows and can also benefit curators. Incorporating automation, rapid visualizations and real time metrics into our repositories would be invaluable to ensuring that datasets are both understandable and complement metadata facilitation.

Our group is pursuing research aimed at developing a curator's toolkit composed of discrete components, each doing one thing well: a sensitivity platform built for scale and assisted by AI to highlight files that may contain problematic data; a dashboard that extracts file formats and highlights issues that need to be reviewed more closely; automatic metadata extraction and alignment to existing controlled vocabularies. Ideally parts of this toolkit could be built into the repository itself and provide metrics and snapshots, allowing curators to highlight a dataset on ingest, and determine what needs to be reviewed at a closer level.

5 Conclusion

This work-in-progress paper has described challenges in performing monitoring and analytics associated with the Constellation leadership public data archive.

The importance of scientific data for DOE user facilities like OLCF will only increase as new DOE initiatives such as the High Performance Data Facility [11] gain momentum. The sizes of datasets managed by Constellation are also expected to continue increasing. In this environment, it will be vitally important for data repositories everywhere to monitor their activity, understand their data, and determine how best to analyze that data to help accomplish their missions. Our current work on metrics collection and advanced curation tools will give us leverage on these and other emerging issues.

References

1. Bailey, C.B., Balakirev, F.F., Balakireva, L.L.: Closing the gap between fair data repositories and hierarchical data formats. Code4Lib J. **52**, (2021)
2. Chard, K., et al.: I'll take that to go: Big data bags and minimal identifiers for exchange of large, complex datasets. In: 2016 IEEE International Conference on Big Data (Big Data), pp. 319–328 (2016)
3. DOI Foundation: DOI Handbook. https://doi.org/10.1000/182. https://www.doi.org/doi-handbook/DOI_Handbook_Final.pdf
4. Foster, I., Kesselman, C.: Globus: a metacomputing infrastructure toolkit. Int. J. Supercomput. Appl. High Perform. Comput. **11**(2), 115–128 (1997)
5. Lanier, A.: The Sound of a Sunset (2022). https://news.mit.edu/2022/sound-sunset-sonification-toolkit-0209
6. Lin, L., Chien, A.A.: Adapting datacenter capacity for greener datacenters and grid. In: Proceedings of the 14th ACM International Conference on Future Energy Systems, e-Energy 2023, Orlando, FL, USA, June 20–23, 2023, pp. 200–213. ACM (2023). https://doi.org/10.1145/3575813.3595197. https://doi.org/10.1145/3575813.3595197
7. Luong, H.Q., Fallaw, C., Schmitt, G., Braxton, S.M., Imker, H.: Responding to reality: evolving curation practices and infrastructure at the University of Illinois at Urbana-Champaign. J. eSci. Librariansh. **10**(3), (2021). https://publishing.escholarship.umassmed.edu/jeslib/article/id/449
8. Nelson, A.: Ensuring Free, Immediate, and Equitable Access to Federally Funded Research (August). https://www.whitehouse.gov/wp-content/uploads/2022/08/08-2022-OSTP-Public-access-Memo.pdf
9. Oak Ridge National Laboratory Leadership Computing Facility: Frontier. https://www.olcf.ornl.gov/olcf-resources/compute-systems/frontier/
10. Pugmire, D., et al.: Visualization as a service for scientific data. Commun. Comput. Inf. Sci. **1315**, 155–174 (2021). https://doi.org/10.1007/978-3-030-63393-6_11
11. US DOE Office of Science: U.S. Department of Energy Selects the High Performance Data Facility Lead (October). https://www.energy.gov/science/articles/us-department-energy-selects-high-performance-data-facility-lead
12. Wilkinson, M.D., et al.: The FAIR guiding principles for scientific data management and stewardship. Sci. Data **3**(1), 160018 (2016). https://doi.org/10.1038/sdata.2016.18

Fourth International Workshop on RISC-V for HPC

Preface to the Fourth International Workshop on RISC-V for HPC

1 Objectives

RISC-V is an open, community driven, Instruction Set Architecture (ISA) standard and a very diverse set of CPUs and accelerators have been, and continue to be, developed which leverage RISC-V and are suited to a range of workloads. Whilst RISC-V has become very popular already in some fields, and in late 2023 the thirteen billionth RISC-V core was shipped, to date it has yet to gain traction in HPC.

However, there are numerous potential advantages that RISC-V can provide to HPC and, assuming the significant rate of growth of this technology to date continues, as we progress further into the decade it is highly likely that RISC-V will become more relevant and widespread for high-performance workloads. Furthermore, recent advances in RISC-V are making it a more realistic proposition for these workloads, such as the recent availability of high-performance hardware built upon RISC-V.

The open and standardised nature of RISC-V means that the large and growing community can be involved in shaping the standard and tooling. This is important from two perspectives: firstly it is an opportunity for the HPC community to help shape the future of RISC-V to ensure that it is suitable for the next generation of supercomputers. Secondly, whilst there are a wide variety of RISC-V CPUs currently available, the standard nature of the tooling means that very often the same software ecosystem comprising the compiler, operating system, and libraries will run across these whilst requiring few changes.

The objective of this workshop was to bring together those already looking to popularise RISC-V in the field of HPC with the supercomputing community in general. By sharing benefits of the architecture, success stories, and techniques we aimed to further popularise the technology and increase involvement of the HPC community in RISC-V.

2 Workshop Organization

In total, there were 5 research papers submitted to the workshop, with all of these accepted. All papers underwent single-blind review and received atleast three reviews from the programme committee. In addition to the research paper presentations, the workshop began with an invited talk by Carlos Puchol who described the work being undertaken in the European PILOT project, which is developing RISC-V-based accelerators for HPC and AI workloads. Furthermore, in addition to the research component we also wanted to give the audience a view of some more mature activities going on in the RISC-V ecosystem and therefore we also had talks by Semidynamics, Codasip, and E4 Computer Engineering who are RISC-V vendors with products leveraging RISC-V. There was also a talk by a representative of the RISC-V Software Ecosystem (RISE) project, which is a collaborative effort led by industry leaders with a mission to accelerate the development of open-source software for the RISC-V architecture.

2.1 Organizers

Nick Brown	EPCC at the University of Edinburgh, UK
John Davis	Barcelona Supercomputing Centre, Spain
Michael Wong	Codeplay, Canada, Canada

2.2 Program Committee

Oliver Perks	Rivos, UK
John Leidel	Tactical Computing Labs, USA
Maurice Jamieson	EPCC at the University of Edinburgh, UK
Ruyman Reyes	Codeplay, UK
Luis Plana	Barcelona Supercomputing Centre, Spain
Joseph Lee	EPCC at the University of Edinburgh, UK
Luc Berger-Vergait	Sandia National Laboratories, USA
Teresa Cervero	Barcelona Supercomputing Centre, Spain
Chris Taylor	Tactical Computing Labs, USA

3 Outcome of the Workshop

The papers presented in these proceedings represent the state of the art in the role of RISC-V for HPC and ML workloads as of May 2024. Whilst these papers report a wide range of work in the field, there are several higher-level themes that can be observed. Firstly, RISC-V is moving very rapidly and great advances have been made since this series of workshops began at ISC in 2023. General-purpose high-performance RISC-V hardware has started to become available, and we are starting to see products built around this. Secondly, the greatest threat to a new technology is an existing solution which is *good enough*. Consequently, whilst there are specific examples of benefits that RISC-V can provide to the HPC community, for RISC-V to be adopted by HPC centres wholesale a clear and strong case must be made around how RISC-V can provide a step change in HPC capability. Thirdly, there is still work to be done in the software ecosystem to provide a complete and mature set of tooling that HPC developers would expect to have available on supercomputing systems. Nevertheless, given the popularity of the workshop it is clear that HPC is a critically important area for RISC-V and there is the potential for this rapidly growing area of technology to revolutionise the field of supercomputing in the coming decade.

Preparing to Hit the Ground Running: Adding RISC-V Support to EESSI

Julián Morillo[1](✉), Caspar Van Leeuwen[2], Bob Dröge[3],
Kenneth Hoste[4], Lara Peeters[4], Thomas Röblitz[5], and Alan O'Cais[6]

[1] Barcelona Supercomputing Center (BSC-CNS), Plaça Eusebi Güell 1-3, 08034 Barcelona, Spain
`julian.morillo@bsc.es`

[2] SURF BV, Science Park 140, 1098 XG Amsterdam, Netherlands
`caspar.vanleeuwen@surf.nl`

[3] Rijksuniversiteit Groningen, Broerstraat 5, 9712CP Groningen, Netherlands
`b.e.droge@rug.nl`

[4] Universiteit Gent, Sint Pietersnieuwstraat 25, 9000 Gent, Belgium
`{kenneth.hoste,lara.peeters}@ugent.be`

[5] University of Bergen, Museplassen 1, Bergen, Norway
`thomas.roblitz@uib.no`

[6] Universitat de Barcelona (UB), Gran Via de les Corts Catalanes 585, 08007 Barcelona, Spain
`alan.ocais@cecam.org`

Abstract. RISC-V-based high-performance processors and accelerators gain more interest for running scientific workloads. While RISC-V is already supported in Linux distributions such as Debian Sid and Ubuntu, a comprehensive stack of performance-optimized software installations is missing. For x86_64 and aarch64, EESSI already streams such software installations to any machine worldwide. Hence, we were also interested in whether one could provide such software stacks for RISC-V-based systems. The benefit would not only be that a stack with software installations optimized for RISC-V becomes easily accessible, but it would also integrate a development environment with toolchains and dependencies. This would help port more software to RISC-V, thereby increasing the platform's viability for running scientific workloads. In this paper, we describe our work on supporting the RISC-V ISA in EESSI - what issues we encountered and how we solved them. We explain our progress on implementing the core components of EESSI - CernVM-FS and Gentoo Prefix - and discuss lessons learned that could provide valuable insights for software developers porting codes to RISC-V. In summary, our experience is that researchers will soon use RISC-V...

Keywords: RISC-V · EESSI · Scientific software applications · HPC

Supported by MultiXscale EuroHPC Centre-of-Excellence, funded by the European Union, the European High-Performance Computing Joint Undertaking (JU), and countries participating in the project under grant agreement No 101093169; Grant PCI2022-134975-2 funded by MICIU/AEI/10.13039/501100011033 and by the "European Union NextGenerationEU/PRTR".

© The Author(s), under exclusive license to Springer Nature Switzerland AG 2025

1 Introduction

The development of RISC-V-based processors in the EPI initiative [24] indicates that this CPU architecture is expected to be one of the key elements in the European HPC community. One of the elements that this community would need is a viable scientific software stack. In anticipation of this, this paper focuses on supporting RISC-V-based CPU architectures in the European Environment for Scientific Software Installations (EESSI) [20,23].

The relatively young RISC-V hardware for high-performance workloads (Hifive Unmatched available since 2020) and scarcely commercially available development systems could lead to the assumption that the RISC-V software stack and system platform are highly immature and will need several additional years of development effort before complete applications can be run, benchmarked, and optimized on a RISC-V-based HPC system. However, papers such as [10] dispel this overly conservative notion. Our work shows that the platform is much more mature than expected.

To facilitate the development, testing, and use of RISC-V-based systems, this paper presents how we are adding support to EESSI, which provides a shared software stack of optimized scientific software installations that can be used on a variety of platforms. This requires supporting RISC-V in all components used in EESSI: from the software **distribution** mechanism, based on the CernVM File System (CernVM-FS) [11,15], to the **compatibility** layer, based on Gentoo Prefix [29], that ensures that the shared software stack can be used on different operating systems, to the **software** layer, where compiler toolchains and scientific software applications along with their required dependencies are installed. Our work towards supporting RISC-V on these components benefits from close collaboration with CernVM-FS and Gentoo Prefix developers.

The main contribution of the work reported in this paper is adding initial support for RISC-V to EESSI. This was achieved by the following steps/milestones:

- The CernVM-FS client was built and tested on RISC-V (Sect. 3.1).
- A dedicated CernVM-FS repository for RISC-V was created (Sect. 3.2).
- The complete EESSI compatibility layer was built for RISC-V (Sect. 4). This required (i) bootstrapping Gentoo Prefix (Sect. 4.1), (ii) installing an additional package set specific to EESSI on top of a standard Gentoo Prefix installation (Sect. 4.2), (iii) developing a controlled build environment using a RISC-V container image and Ansible [41] (Sect. 4.3), and (iv) using ReFrame [43] for running basic tests for the compatibility layer (Sect. 4.4).
- Initial software installations were performed using EasyBuild [1,32] in the EESSI software layer on top of the compatibility layer, starting with a GCC compiler toolchain (Sect. 5).

We complete the paper by reflecting on the lessons learned during the process (Sect. 6) and providing concluding remarks (Sect. 7).

2 A Shared Stack of Optimized Software Installations

2.1 European Environment for Scientific Software Installations (EESSI)

EESSI [20,23] is a community initiative aiming to provide a shared software stack of scientific software installations optimized for a wide range of system architectures.

The main goal of EESSI is to provide a collection of scientific software installations on a wide range of different platforms, including HPC clusters, cloud infrastructure, and personal workstations and laptops, without compromising the performance of that software (see Fig. 1). It allows HPC support teams to more closely collaborate on building optimized software installations. At the same time, scientists benefit from having a uniform software stack available regardless of where they want to work. Importantly, scientists get this environment without worrying about architecture-specific optimization.

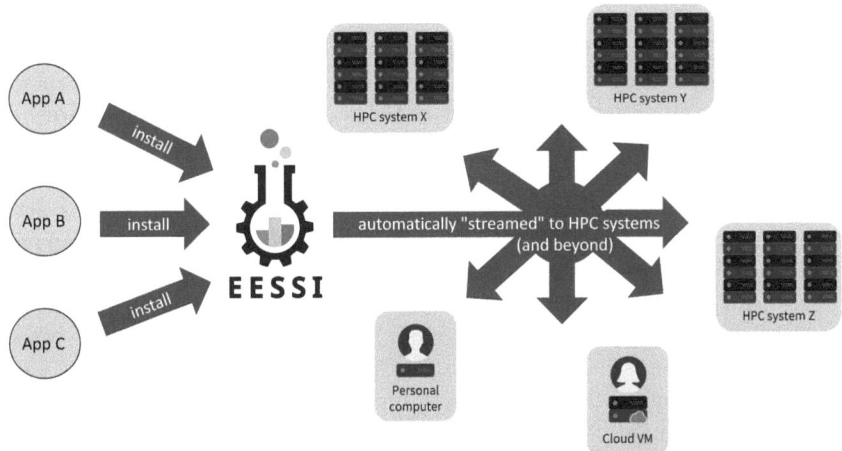

Fig. 1. Software gets added to the EESSI repository, then streamed to any end-user system that mounts the repository.

2.2 High-Level Design of EESSI

EESSI consists of 3 layers (see Fig. 2), which are constructed by leveraging various open-source software projects:

- The file system layer of EESSI uses CernVM-FS [15] to distribute the EESSI software stack to client systems.

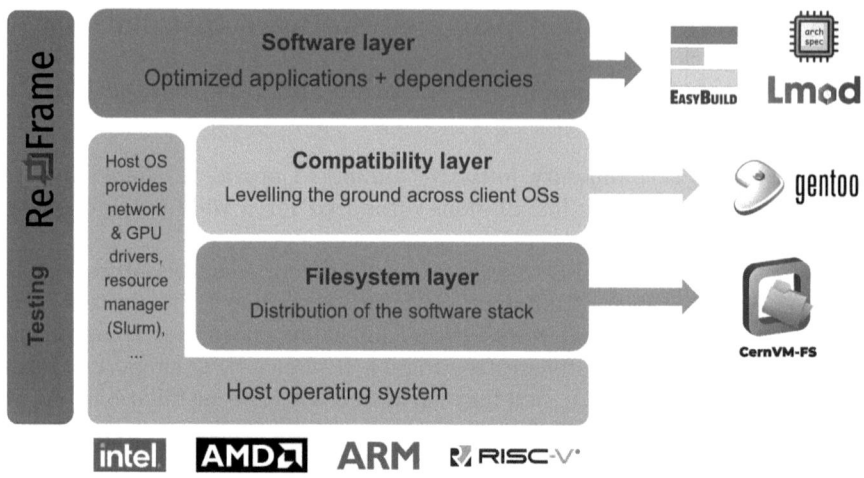

Fig. 2. EESSI's layered architecture.

- The compatibility layer levels the playing field across different versions of the Linux operating system (OS) for client systems that use the software installations provided by EESSI. It consists of a limited set of libraries and tools installed in a non-standard file system location (a "prefix"), built from source for the supported CPU families using Gentoo Prefix [29].
- The top layer of EESSI is called the software layer, which contains the actual scientific software applications and their dependencies. Building, managing, and optimizing the software installations included in the software layer is done using EasyBuild [1,32], a well-established software build and installation framework for managing (scientific) software stacks on HPC systems. Next to installing the software itself, EasyBuild also automatically generates environment module files. These files, essentially small Lua scripts, are consumed via Lmod [34], a modern implementation of the concept of environment modules that provides a user-friendly interface to end users of EESSI. The initialization script that is included in EESSI automatically detects the CPU family and micro-architecture of a client system by leveraging either archspec [8,17], a small Python library, or archdetect [7], a minimal pure bash implementation of the same concept.

Components in all three layers need to be prepared to support an additional CPU architecture such as RISC-V. This paper discusses the challenges and solutions for implementing this support per layer.

3 File System Layer

EESSI uses the CernVM File System (CernVM-FS) to distribute the software stack.

CernVM-FS is a read-only FUSE file system designed to deliver scientific software in a fast, scalable, and reliable way. Files and file metadata are downloaded on demand and efficiently cached. CernVM-FS uses standard HTTP to distribute files, which allows the exploitation of various web caches, including commercial content delivery networks. The CernVM-FS software comprises client-side software to mount "CernVM-FS repositories" and a server-side toolkit to create such distributable CernVM-FS repositories.

3.1 CernVM-FS Client for RISC-V

Before the contributions reported in this paper, there was only some experimental support for RISC-V, as stated on the CernVM-FS website [16]. Particularly, no pre-built client package for RISC-V was available. Thus, we built a CernVM-FS client from source to support RISC-V. The target platform to do that has been a SiFive Hifive Unmatched system running Ubuntu 21.04.

Initially, two of the included dependencies, namely `libressl-3.5.3` and `protobuf-2.6.1`, failed to build.

In both cases, the issue was that the `config.guess` file included failed to detect the build system type. This was because the `config.guess` copy being used was far too old (dating from 2013). The problems were resolved by adding the `autoreconf -vfi` command in the corresponding `configureHook.sh` script to generate a fresh `config.guess` file before the `configure` command was invoked.

These issues and the corresponding solution were reported to the CernVM-FS developers [18], and we opened a *Pull Request* with the needed changes [9], which was quickly merged into the main CernVM-FS development branch. The `autoreconf -vfi` is only executed if the target system is RISC-V (as requested by the CernVM-FS maintainers to merge the *pull request*), see (Listing 1.1).

Listing 1.1. Code added to `configureHook.sh` files.

```
### On RISC-V systems, we need to run autoreconf
### to detect the correct architecture
ISA=`grep isa /proc/cpuinfo | head -1 | cut -d: -f2`
echo "System ISA is: $ISA"
case "$ISA" in
*rv64*) autoreconf -vfi
esac
```

As a result of this work, CernVM-FS can now be built on RISC-V platforms *out-of-the-box*. We hope to continue collaboration with CernVM-FS developers to make CernVM-FS client available as a pre-built package.

3.2 Dedicated CernVM-FS Repository for RISC-V

Since the CernVM-FS client software is working for RISC-V, we created a dedicated repository for this CPU architecture to distribute development versions of a RISC-V EESSI stack to the community: `riscv.eessi.io`.

A corresponding page in the EESSI documentation [22] was created that will provide updated information regarding the contents of this CernVM-FS repository.

4 Compatibility Layer

The middle layer of EESSI is the **compatibility layer**, which ensures that the scientific software stack is compatible with different operating systems (different Linux distributions and even Windows via Windows Subsystem for Linux (WSL)).

It relies on Gentoo Prefix [29] by installing a limited set of Gentoo Linux packages in a non-standard location (a "prefix"), using Gentoo's package manager Portage [38]. Although it is the main component, the compatibility layer is not limited to a Gentoo Prefix installation. The complete list of components that needed some work to add RISC-V support is Gentoo Prefix installation, the EESSI package set [21], a container with Ansible [41], and ReFrame [43]. The work done on each component is explained in the following subsections.

4.1 Bootstrapping Gentoo Prefix in RISC-V

The first step to adding support in the compatibility layer of EESSI was to bootstrap a Gentoo Prefix on a RISC-V system following the instructions in Project:Prefix/Bootstrap web page [39] and considering the work in [31] that laid the groundwork. We used the same system as in Sect. 3 to do this.

The `bootstrap-prefix.sh` script already supports some RISC-V systems, but the specific architecture identifier (`riscv64-unknown-linux-gnu`) of our build machine was not known. However, a slight change to the script - as shown in Listing 1.2 - ensured that the script also works on our RISC-V system.

Listing 1.2. Patch to bootstrap-prefix.sh to catch any RISC-V tuple.

```
@@ -385,7 +385,7 @@ bootstrap_profile() {
                i*86-pc-linux-gnu)
                        profile=${profile_linux/ARCH/x86}
                        ;;
-               riscv64-pc-linux-gnu)
+               riscv64-*-linux-gnu)
                        profile=${profile_linux/ARCH/riscv}
                        profile=${profile/17.0/20.0/rv64gc/
                            lp64d}
                        ;;
```

This improvement was reported to Gentoo Prefix leading developers, who applied the patch in Listing 1.2 [14].

Next, compilation of GCC (during *Stage 2* of bootstrapping) failed with finding some header files (see Listing 1.3).

Listing 1.3. "No such file or directory" error during Stage 2 of bootstrapping.

```
...
from /home/jmorillo/gentoo/tmp/var/tmp/portage/sys-devel/gcc
   -13.2.1_p20240113-r1/work/gcc-13-20240113/libgcc/libgcc2.c
   :27:
/usr/include/stdio.h:27:10: fatal error: bits/libc-header-start.
   h: No such file or directory
   27 | #include <bits/libc-header-start.h>
      |          ^~~~~~~~~~~~~~~~~~~~~~~~~~
compilation terminated.
```

This is not caused by specifics of RISC-V systems but rather by how different Linux distributions organize architecture-dependent (header) files. On *Debian-like* distributions (our build system uses Ubuntu, which derives from Debian), this file is not directly under /usr/include but inside a directory dependent on the architecture (in our case /usr/include/riscv64-linux-gnu). When building the compiler itself, it must be told about this fact, and the Gentoo Bootstrapping process failed to do that. Fortunately, this was a previously reported *GCC bug* [12], so applying the same *patch* [44] mentioned there solved the issue (see the patch in Listing 1.4). The error and the solution were reported to Gentoo's bug-tracking system [13]. Again, they incorporated the corresponding patch to their repositories for anyone to take advantage of it (see *commits* [2,3,47,48]).

Listing 1.4. RISC-V: Add multiarch support on riscv-linux-gnu.

```
diff --git a/gcc/config/riscv/t-linux b/gcc/config/riscv/t-linux
index 216d2776a183d13ade76642b73b9bf04b0c4694e..
   a6f64f88d25c989159207cbef19778b703c95797 100644 (file)
--- a/gcc/config/riscv/t-linux
+++ b/gcc/config/riscv/t-linux
@@ -1,3 +1,5 @@
 # Only XLEN and ABI affect Linux multilib dir names, e.g. /
    lib32/ilp32d/
 MULTILIB_DIRNAMES := $(patsubst rv32%,lib32,$(patsubst rv64%,
    lib64,$(MULTILIB_DIRNAMES)))
 MULTILIB_OSDIRNAMES := $(patsubst lib%,../lib%,$(
    MULTILIB_DIRNAMES))
+
+MULTIARCH_DIRNAME := $(call if_multiarch,$(firstword $(subst -,
    ,$(target)))-linux-gnu)
```

After that, there were no more issues, and we could bootstrap Gentoo Prefix in the RISC-V architecture successfully, both on the aforementioned Hifive Unmatched and a StarFive VisionFive 2.

4.2 EESSI Package Set

On top of a standard Gentoo Prefix installation, EESSI requires a package set to be installed to provide some additional packages. This includes, for instance, some communication libraries required by OpenMPI [35], and Lmod [34] for providing an environment modules system as a user interface to the software stack.

Installing such packages on less-often-used architectures can sometimes require some effort; in Gentoo terminology, packages may not have been "keyworded" for such architectures yet, meaning that it will not even attempt to build and install them. As a first attempt to install the required packages for RISC-V, we cloned and used the package set that is usually used for the Arm CPU architecture: the full list of packages can be found in the EESSI 2023.06 RISC-V package set file [21]. Fortunately, this worked out of the box, and all packages were installed successfully on a RISC-V system.

4.3 Controlled Build Environment Using a Container and Ansible

To automate the full installation of the compatibility layer and ensure that we control the build environment, the EESSI compatibility layer is built using Ansible [41] inside a (minimal) Singularity/Apptainer [6] container.

Container images based on Debian 11 were available for the different CPU families that EESSI already supports, but Debian 11 does not support RISC-V yet. Because of this, we created a new build container recipe based on Debian Sid [4], and this is now available in the EESSI container registry on GitHub [19].

This container image could then be run using Singularity, which is available for RISC-V in the default Debian repositories in the `singularity-container` package. With this container, we can do the full installation of the compatibility layer on basically any RISC-V system, even without requiring special privileges.

While trying to run the container on a StarFive VisionFive 2 system with Singularity CE 3.10.3 we did notice that the kernel of the Debian operating system provided by StarFive (version 5.15.0-starfive) did not support SquashFS (yet). Still, we could easily work around this by first pulling in the container image and converting it to sandbox format using `singularity build --sandbox`.

Finally, it is worth mentioning that Ansible worked fine on RISC-V, and we had no problems in this regard.

4.4 Using ReFrame for Running Basic Tests

The Ansible role for installing the EESSI compatibility layer also includes a test step at the very end of the installation, which verifies that all required packages have been installed and that all customizations required for EESSI have been made. The test suite is implemented using ReFrame [43], a powerful Python framework for writing system regression tests and benchmarks. The installation of ReFrame on RISC-V worked fine, and the test step revealed only one minor issue that was entirely unrelated to RISC-V, but due to a renamed Gentoo package. This could be easily fixed, and the full test suite [42] then passed without problems.

4.5 Full Installation of the RISC-V Compatibility Layer

With all the components working correctly, a complete RISC-V compatibility layer was built in an automated way on a StarFive VisionFive 2 development board. Compared to the existing compatibility layers that EESSI provides for x86_64 and aarch64 in version 2023.06 of the stack, a few more small modifications in the customizations and configuration of the compatibility layer were done: for instance, the installation path had to be changed, the version was bumped, enforcing the installation of an older GCC version was disabled, and the linker was changed from gold to bfd. All changes can be found in a compatibility layer *pull request* [45].

The installation process was completed using these changes, and we ingested the installation to the riscv.eessi.io CernVM-FS repository. This means that the compatibility layer is now available to repository users; the examples in Listing 1.5 show how to access the compatibility layer and start a Gentoo Prefix shell.

Listing 1.5. Accessing the EESSI RISC-V repository at /cvmfs/riscv.eessi.io

```
$ ls /cvmfs/riscv.eessi.io/versions/20240307/compat/linux/
    riscv64/
bin   lib     opt     run     stage1.log   stage3.log   tmp   var
etc   lib64   reprod  sbin    stage2.log   startprefix  usr

$ /cvmfs/riscv.eessi.io/versions/20240307/compat/linux/riscv64/
    startprefix
Entering Gentoo Prefix /cvmfs/riscv.eessi.io/versions/20240307/
    compat/linux/riscv64
$ which gcc
/cvmfs/riscv.eessi.io/versions/20240307/compat/linux/riscv64/usr
    /bin/gcc
$ gcc --version
gcc (Gentoo 13.2.1_p20240210 p14) 13.2.1 20240210
```

The two RISC-V platforms used to develop both file-system and compatibility layers are Debian/Ubuntu Linux distributions. Note, however, that this does not pose any issue with accessing the EESSI RISC-V repository (Listing 1.5) from any other distribution, for example, Fedora-based. One may think that this could create additional issues due to the different package structures, but this is covered by the EESSI architecture. In any case, and as a proof of concept, we have successfully deployed the riscv.eessi.io repository in a Fedora 37 RISC-V system.

5 Software Layer

With RISC-V support in place for both the file system and compatibility layers of EESSI, we can start focusing on building the actual shared stack of installations of (scientific) software in the software layer. To this extent, we will identify fundamental applications and libraries, e.g., MPI/OpenMP and numerical libraries, relevant to the computational science domain and work on improving their support for RISC-V.

While this work has just started at the time of writing, we were able to build GCC 13.2 with EasyBuild. This is a promising first step.

5.1 Initial Step: Building GCC for RISC-V with EasyBuild

We started by trying to build and install GCC version 13.2 from source using EasyBuild, as a first step towards installing a full compiler toolchain to be employed by EasyBuild.

Initially, we ran into the same problem as we encountered during the bootstrap procedure of Gentoo Prefix when building the compatibility layer for RISC-V (see Sect. 4.1), since the patch [44] that fixes this was not included yet with GCC 13.2. A pull request [5] was opened to EasyBuild to include this patch for GCC versions 12.x and 13.x.

In addition to that, we had to make two additional changes to make the build and installation of GCC with EasyBuild on RISC-V work:

(i) The Python script that EasyBuild uses had to be updated to also add the `lib` and `lib64` subdirectories of the GCC installation to `$LIBRARY_PATH` [46]. At the time of writing, it was not fully clear to us yet why this was only required for RISC-V and not for other CPU families;
(ii) The NVPTX feature of GCC [28], which is used for GPU offloading, had to be disabled when building GCC for RISC-V.

5.2 Towards a Complete Toolchain and Software Applications

With the installation of GCC working, the next goal is to install a complete compiler toolchain that EasyBuild can use to build scientific applications and their required dependencies, which consists of a set of compilers (C, C++, Fortran), an MPI library, a BLAS/LAPACK library, and an FFT library.

More specifically, we want to install a recent version of the `foss` toolchain [27], which consists of GCC, OpenMPI [35], FlexiBLAS [26] + OpenBLAS [36], and FFTW [25]. Most (if not all) of these components should already support RISC-V.

Once we have a complete compiler toolchain in place, we will try building and installing scientific software applications (like GROMACS [30]) or benchmark tools (like HPL [33], OSU Micro Benchmarks, etc.). Other applications, already available in EESSI for different architectures (like OpenFOAM [37]), will be considered afterward. Some noteworthy examples of such software are as follows:

- BLIS
- ESPResSo
- HDF5
- LAMMPS
- LLVM

- netCDF and netCDF-Fortran
- Perl
- Python
- PyTorch
- QuantumESPRESSO
- Rust
- ScaLAPACK
- TensorFlow
- walBerla

Note that many of these software packages are known to be already working for RISC-V, so we do not expect many troubles when adding them to EESSI in such cases.

Among all this software, we aim to provide an LLVM [49] compiler installation through EESSI. Functionality in the LLVM compiler that is found to be missing will be implemented, including support for compiling Fortran software.

Applications of interest will have their performance analyzed, and the outcome of this analysis will produce co-design suggestions for compilers, runtime systems, and applications. Regular updates of these components will be added to EESSI via the `riscv.eessi.io` CernVM-FS repository and thus be available worldwide.

To finish this section, we want to stress the fact that although we have used two different RISC-V platforms for building both file-system and compatibility layers, which do not support the RISC-V RVV vector extension (basically, they do not have vector unit), this does not limit us to providing (through EESSI) vectorized versions of all the mentioned software for any specific RISC-V hardware that include this extension. In this sense, we can use QEMU [40] for developing, compiling, and testing the software, as it provides the most complete functionality among emulators and is excellent for most testing. It also allows tweaking the extensions available with `QEMU_CPU`, which is ideal. For performance measurements, however, we will need real RISC-V hardware.

5.3 Expectations and Approach for Collaboration

During the process of adding more software installations for RISC-V to the EESSI software layer, we expect to run into various (hopefully minor) problems, as a significant part of the software projects included in the EESSI software layer is probably not compatible with (or even aware of) RISC-V yet. We will engage with the developers of software projects to jointly resolve issues we observe.

Based on experiences with adding optimized software installations to EESSI for specific Arm CPU microarchitectures, we suspect that problems will arise on RISC-V with the test suites provided by some software projects.

6 Lessons Learned

As the RISC-V architecture continues to gain momentum in the realm of open-source hardware, the challenges of porting software become increasingly apparent. This paper dives into the experiences and insights gained from implementing support for RISC-V in EESSI, showing the details of the problems encountered and the solutions adopted. Sharing this information is important for the RISC-V community as most solutions can probably be applied when porting other software projects to RISC-V.

The first observation is that in projects that already support multiple CPU families (i.e. x86_64, aarch64, ppc64le) like CernVM-FS and Gentoo Prefix, it should be relatively *easy* to add riscv64 support as one already has the blueprint for needed changes (this is especially true for aarch64) and the *infrastructure* for supporting multiple architectures. In other words, whenever a problem is encountered when setting up/building in RISC-V you can always look for all necessary #ifdef, and build/configure/setup scripts for other platforms. This was the case, for example, when dealing with the error in Listing 1.3: the particular issue was already solved for other architectures that already had a correct t-linux file, so it was just a matter of applying the same solution. We think porting projects that work only in one architecture (typically x86_64) would need significantly more work, especially in the case of scientific software, where we think the porting will be more challenging (especially when considering performance).

Secondly, RISC-V already has comprehensive support in many operating systems, compilers, runtimes, and tools. The problem reported in Sect. 3.1 is an example of that: thanks to the already existent autotools support, we did not even need to *hack* the config.guess files, but just run autoreconf to have an updated (and correct) version of them. Here, we would like to highlight the importance of working with the latest versions of the involved compilers/runtimes/tools, as the RISC-V ecosystem is rapidly evolving.

From our experience, we also believe that many software packages are closer to working on RISC-V than expected. At least, this was our experience with CernVM-FS and Gentoo Prefix: we initially thought that making them work would be much more challenging, but in the end, it was a matter of solving a few minor issues.

The last comment concerns the willingness to collaborate on the RISC-V support work described in this paper, which we have seen from both CernVM-FS and Gentoo maintainers/developers, which points to high interest from the open source software community for RISC-V.

7 Conclusion

In this paper, we presented the successful history of our initial development and integration efforts toward adding RISC-V support to EESSI, a shared software stack of optimized scientific software installations. We have demonstrated a remarkable level of software readiness and maturity - paving the way to the first generation of RISC-V HPC systems that may not be so far away.

We contribute to the RISC-V software ecosystem by enabling the use of EESSI, which implies a thorough review and adaptation of all its components, i.e., the file system, compatibility, and software layers. This process included contributions to specific software projects employed by EESSI, such as CernVM-FS and Gentoo Prefix, which are now fully RISC-V capable.

A CernVM-FS repository dedicated to RISC-V (riscv.eessi.io) and accompanying documentation has been created and made available to the community.

The paper also details the problems we encountered and the solutions adopted. We think they may be of interest to the RISC-V software community. It also presents some thoughts on the experience gained throughout the process.

Overall, we have not encountered any significant roadblocks along the way, and we are confident that we will continue to make good progress as we explore adding support for RISC-V to the software layer of EESSI.

References

1. EasyBuild: building software with ease. https://easybuild.io/. Accessed 28 Feb 2024
2. 12.3.0: add 77_all_riscv_PR106271-multilib-bootstrap.patch. https://gitweb.gentoo.org/proj/gcc-patches.git/commit/?id=f373ff919da62443ca59681f219b4899e72a6f2f. Accessed 28 Feb 2024
3. 13.2.0: add 91_all_riscv_pr106271-multilib-bootstrap.patch. https://gitweb.gentoo.org/proj/gcc-patches.git/commit/?id=d5e5f9b252f00c9485c34446efc01bdd2eaaa9b1. Accessed 28 Feb 2024
4. Add Debian Sid build container with support for riscv64. https://github.com/EESSI/compatibility-layer/pull/200, opened on Mar.8, 2024
5. add multiarch support for RISC-V to all GCCcore 12.x and 13.x easyconfigs. https://github.com/easybuilders/easybuild-easyconfigs/pull/20035. Accessed 15 Mar 2024
6. APPTAINER. https://apptainer.org/. Accessed 15 Mar 2024
7. archdetect manpage. https://manpages.ubuntu.com/manpages/xenial/man1/archdetect.1.html. Accessed 12 Mar 2024
8. archspec website. https://github.com/archspec/archspec. Accessed 12 Mar 2024
9. autoreconf needed for risc-v build. https://github.com/cvmfs/cvmfs/pull/3446, opened in Nov.20, 2023
10. Bartolini, A., et al.: Monte Cimone: Paving the Road for the First Generation of RISC-V High-Performance Computers (2022)
11. Blomer, J., Ganis, G., Hardi, N., Popescu, R.: Delivering LHC software to HPC compute elements with CernVM-FS. In: Kunkel, J.M., Yokota, R., Taufer, M., Shalf, J. (eds.) ISC High Performance 2017. LNCS, vol. 10524, pp. 724–730. Springer, Cham (2017). https://doi.org/10.1007/978-3-319-67630-2_52
12. Bootstrap on RISC-V on Ubuntu 22.04 LTS: bits/libc-header-start.h: No such file or directory. https://gcc.gnu.org/bugzilla/show_bug.cgi?id=106271. Accessed 20 Feb 2024
13. d bootstrap stage 2: cannot find bits/libc-header-start.h. https://bugs.gentoo.org/890636. Accessed 20 Feb 2024
14. Catch any riscv tuple #923410. https://gitweb.gentoo.org/repo/proj/prefix.git/commit/?id=e66a8e81b12473d92c7fadb361feffb2aa127d9e. Accessed 19 Feb 2024
15. CernVM File System. https://cernvm.cern.ch/fs/. Accessed 12 Mar 2024

16. CernVM-FS: Getting Started. https://cvmfs.readthedocs.io/en/stable/cpt-quickstart.html. Accessed 13 Dec 2023
17. Culpo, M., Becker, G., Arango Gutierrez, C.E., Hoste, K., Gamblin, T.: Archspec: a library for detecting, labeling, and reasoning about microarchitectures. In: 2nd International Workshop on Containers and New Orchestration Paradigms for Isolated Environments in HPC (CANOPIE-HPC'20) (2020). https://tgamblin.github.io/pubs/archspec-canopie-hpc-2020.pdf
18. CVMFS client for RISC-V. https://github.com/cvmfs/cvmfs/issues/3441, opened in Nov.14, 2023
19. Debian Sid build container for EESSI compatibility layer. https://github.com/EESSI/compatibility-layer/pkgs/container/bootstrap-prefix/188652347?tag=debian-sid, published on Mar.8, 2024
20. Dröge, B., Holanda Rusu, V., Hoste, K., van Leeuwen, C., O'Cais, A., Röblitz, T.: EESSI: a cross-platform ready-to-use optimised scientific software stack. Softw. Pract. Exp. **53**(1), 176–210 (2023). https://doi.org/10.1002/spe.3075, https://onlinelibrary.wiley.com/doi/abs/10.1002/spe.3075
21. EESSI package set for RISC-V. https://github.com/EESSI/gentoo-overlay/blob/main/etc/portage/sets/eessi-2023.06-linux-riscv64. Accessed 11 Mar 2024
22. EESSI RISC-V development repository. http://www.eessi.io/docs/repositories/riscv.eessi.io/. Accessed 12 Mar 2024
23. EESSI website. https://www.eessi.io. Accessed 08 Mar 2024
24. European Processor Initiative. https://www.european-processor-initiative.eu. Accessed 04 Mar 2024
25. FFTW website. https://www.fftw.org/. Accessed 12 Mar 2024
26. FlexiBLAS - A BLAS and LAPACK wrapper library with runtime exchangable backends. https://www.mpi-magdeburg.mpg.de/projects/flexiblas. Accessed 12 Mar 2024
27. foss toolchain. https://docs.easybuild.io/common-toolchains/#common_toolchains_foss. Accessed 12 Mar 2024
28. GCC PTX Documentation. https://gcc.gnu.org/wiki/nvptx. Accessed 15 Mar 2024
29. Gentoo Prefix Project. https://wiki.gentoo.org/wiki/Project:Prefix, accessed: 2023-12-27
30. GROMACS website. https://www.gromacs.org/. Accessed 12 Mar 2024
31. GSoC 2022 Project Report: RISC-V support for Gentoo Prefix. https://github.com/wiredhikari/prefix_on_riscv/blob/main/docs/final_report.md. Accessed 16 Mar 2024
32. Hoste, K., Timmerman, J., Georges, A., De Weirdt, S.: EasyBuild: building software with ease. In: 2012 SC Companion: High Performance Computing, Networking Storage and Analysis, pp. 572–582 (2012). https://doi.org/10.1109/SC.Companion.2012.81
33. HPL - A Portable Implementation of the High-Performance Linpack Benchmark for Distributed-Memory Computers. https://www.netlib.org/benchmark/hpl/. Accessed 13 Mar 2024
34. Lmod: A new environment module system. https://lmod.readthedocs.io/en/latest/. Accessed 12 Mar 2024
35. Open MPI: Open Source High Performance Computing. https://www.open-mpi.org/. Accessed 12 Mar 2024
36. OpenBLAS: An optimized BLAS library. https://www.openblas.net/. Accessed 12 Mar 2024
37. OpenFOAM website. https://www.openfoam.com/. Accessed 12 Mar 2024

38. Portage package manager. https://wiki.gentoo.org/wiki/Portage. Accessed 27 Feb 2024
39. Project:prefix/bootstrap. https://wiki.gentoo.org/wiki/Project:Prefix/Bootstrap. Accessed 27 Feb 2024
40. QEMU: A generic and open source machine emulator and virtualizer. https://www.qemu.org/. Accessed 05 Apr 2024
41. Red Hat Ansible Automation Platform. https://www.ansible.com/. Accessed 12 Mar 2024
42. ReFrame test suite for EESSI compatibility layer. https://github.com/EESSI/compatibility-layer/blob/main/test/compat_layer.py, opened on Mar.15 2024
43. ReFrame website. https://reframe-hpc.readthedocs.io/. Accessed 11 Mar 2024
44. RISC-V: Add multiarch support on riscv-linux-gnu. https://gcc.gnu.org/git/gitweb.cgi?p=gcc.git;h=47f95bc4be4eb14730ab3eaaaf8f6e71fda47690. Accessed 20 Feb 2024
45. RISC-V compatibility layer 20240307 #202. https://github.com/EESSI/compatibility-layer/pull/202, opened on Mar.8, 2024
46. set $LIBRARY_PATH on RISC-V systems. https://github.com/easybuilders/easybuild-easyblocks/pull/3256. Accessed 15 Mar 2024
47. sys-devel/gcc: fix prefix riscv bootstrap for 12. https://gitweb.gentoo.org/repo/gentoo.git/commit/?id=1849c746cd35fb74c6014d1bfd2b1e287bad0a0f. Accessed 28 Feb 2024
48. sys-devel/gcc: fix prefix riscv bootstrap for 13. https://gitweb.gentoo.org/repo/gentoo.git/commit/?id=7d55c7c1d2d179894998a18dc311714e05f0d913. Accessed 28 Feb 2024
49. The LLVM Compiler Infrastructure. https://llvm.org/. Accessed 12 Mar 2024

Scaling an Augmented RISC-V Processor Design with High-Level Synthesis

Johannes Schoder[1] and H. Martin Bücker[1,2]

[1] Institute for Computer Science, Friedrich Schiller University Jena, Jena, Germany
{johannes.schoder,martin.buecker}@uni-jena.de
[2] Michael Stifel Center Jena for Data-driven and Simulation Science, Friedrich Schiller University Jena, Jena, Germany

Abstract. Motivated by major applications in machine learning, novel hardware architectures are increasingly implementing on-chip accelerators. The open architecture of the RISC-V ISA is suited to match this current trend by supporting the flexibility to add instructions for domain-specific architectures. Also, recent advances in tools for high-level synthesis reduce the required effort for the hardware design process significantly. Furthermore, program transformations rewriting a given computer code with some specified aim are a powerful software technique which, today, have not benefitted to a large extent from hardware support. The goal of this note is to analyze the potential of bringing together a custom scalable RISC-V processor design written for high-level synthesis with a particular type of program transformation on individual elementary operations. In these transformations, each scalar operation is augmented with a so-called transformed operation changing the semantics of the given program. An augmented RV32I processor design is introduced that implements not only the original operation but also its transformed operation in hardware. The new design is simulated for the AMD Alveo U50 Data Center Accelerator Card. For each scalar operation given in the original program, it enables the computation of 63 scalar transformed operations in parallel with a lower bound on the speedup of roughly 13.

Keywords: Domain-specific architecture · RISC-V · Processor design · High-level synthesis · Program transformation

1 Introduction

Program transformations take a computer program as input and generate as output another program that has some desired properties. They find applications in various areas of high-performance computing, enabling applications in science, technology, and society. In this article, we are interested in a particular program transformation that augments each scalar operation in a given program with a vector operation. This type of transformation appears in automatic differentiation [6,9,15] and is important in computational and data science. For instance, automatic differentiation is routinely used in large-scale problems involving nonlinear systems [18], minimization problems [12], sensitivity studies [14] and inverse problems [16]. It also shares marked similarities with the backbone of many algorithms in machine learning. By integrating this program transformation directly into the hardware, the user does not require specific knowledge of software tools implementing the underlying transformation rules.

However, creating a new hardware design is a tedious and complex task that often needs multiple iterations and stages in the design process. The main new contribution of this article is to provide a feasibility study assessing how the control unit and the datapath of a RISC-V processor design needs to be altered to enable the parallel computation of the original operation and its transformed operation. The processor design is built upon a prototype version of the pipelined processor design proposed by Goossens [8]. This original processor design is written for high-level synthesis suitable for AMD FPGAs. High-level synthesis significantly simplifies the design process and reduces the development time. A brief overview on using high-level synthesis for different designs is given in [10]. One of the main targets of the novel approach is to create a design that does not interfere with any execution of standard RISC-V instructions. While significant changes to the datapath and control signals of the processor design are necessary, none of these changes prohibit the execution of programs that solely execute the original operations. Our aim is to analyze how the integration of the transformed operations into hardware impacts the clock frequency and the resource usage on a current FPGA.

The structure of this article is as follows. In Sect. 2 we set the stage for the overall approach by detailing the form of a particular program transformation for which we introduce a novel RISC-V processor design in Sect. 3. A simulation of this design and resulting estimations on utilized hardware resources are reported in Sect. 4.

2 Program Transformation on the Level of Operations

Throughout this article, we are interested in the following specific program transformation which finds applications in modern machine learning workflows [6] and is also heavily used in more traditional areas of high-performance computing, including computational science and engineering [1–5]. From a conceptual point of view, the execution of any computer program written in a high-level programming language like Fortran, C or Matlab consists of a long sequence of elementary functions $\phi_i : \mathbb{R}^2 \to \mathbb{R}$. In this abstraction of running a computer code for some given input, the ith scalar operation is given by

$$v_i = \phi_i(v_j)_{j \prec i} \quad \text{with} \quad i = 1, \ldots, \ell, \tag{1}$$

where ℓ is the number of operations when executing the computer code. The notation $j \prec i$ represents a data dependence meaning that the elementary scalar functions ϕ_i stored in the intermediate scalar variables v_i are applied to a set of previously computed intermediate scalar variables $v_j \in \mathbb{R}$. To give an example, the notation includes operations ϕ_i with two input arguments such as scalar additions

$$v_i = \phi_i(v_j, v_k) = v_j + v_k, \tag{2}$$

where the values of v_j and v_k have been computed before the addition is executed.

Given such a computer code called *original program*, the program transformation considered here is carried out on the level of scalar operations. More precisely, the generated program referred to as *transformed program* not only computes all *original operations* ϕ_i of the form (1), but also the *transformed operations* given by

$$\overrightarrow{\Delta v_i} = \sum_{j \prec i} \alpha_{i,j}(v_j) \cdot \overrightarrow{\Delta v_j} \quad \text{with} \quad i = 1, \ldots, \ell. \tag{3}$$

Here, the symbol $\overrightarrow{\Delta v_i}$ is used to denote a vector of length, say p, that depends on intermediate scalar variables v_j that have previously been computed by original operations ϕ_j. Similarly, the notation $\alpha_{i,j}$ represents a scalar that may also depend on intermediate variables v_j whose values are available when the transformed operation (3) is executed. We stress that the scalar $\alpha_{i,j}$ may depend on the ith original operation ϕ_i, but is independent of v_i, the output of that original operation. If the original operation ϕ_i has two input arguments, v_j and v_k, as in (2), the notation includes transformed operations consisting of two additive terms as in

$$\overrightarrow{\Delta v_i} = \alpha_{i,j}(v_j, v_k) \cdot \overrightarrow{\Delta v_j} + \alpha_{i,k}(v_j, v_k) \cdot \overrightarrow{\Delta v_k}. \tag{4}$$

In essence, this program transformation on the level of a scalar operation augments the original program with a linear combination of vectors $\overrightarrow{\Delta v_j}$ whose coefficients $\alpha_{i,j}(v_j)_{j \prec i}$ are computed by operations accessing previously computed scalar variables v_j from arbitrary memory locations.

If the original program takes some scalar variables v_j as input, the transformed program also needs the associated vectors $\overrightarrow{\Delta v_j}$ of length p as input. Similarly, if the original program computes some scalar variables v_k as output, the transformed program also computes as output the associated vectors $\overrightarrow{\Delta v_k}$ of length p.

To the best of the authors' knowledge there is no previous work related to address the transformed equations (3) by any aspects of hardware. There is a study on applying this program transformation on assembly code [7]. In a much wider context, hardware implementations of a different program transformation are investigated; see [11] and the reference therein.

3 A RISC-V Processor Design

Throughout the novel hardware design process which is introduced in this section, a special focus is on reflecting the structure of the transformed operations of type (3) in hardware, particularly in the memory and the ALU. After discussing the design of a datapath, the following two subsections concentrate on the memory layout and the instruction encoding.

3.1 Datapath

Figure 1 shows the different pipeline stages of the new processor design implementing an adapted version of the RISC-V ISA called T-RV32I. The main building blocks of the datapath from the pipelined processor design [8] (without any transformed operations) are symbolized by dark gray boxes arranged horizontally in the middle of this figure. The red boxes on the bottom represent the necessary additions to the datapath that enable the transformed operations on vectors of length p. There are p copies of each of the three components, T-Register-File, T-ALU and T-Data Memory. These copies are called *channels* in the following. The T-Data Memory is also called T-Memory, for short.

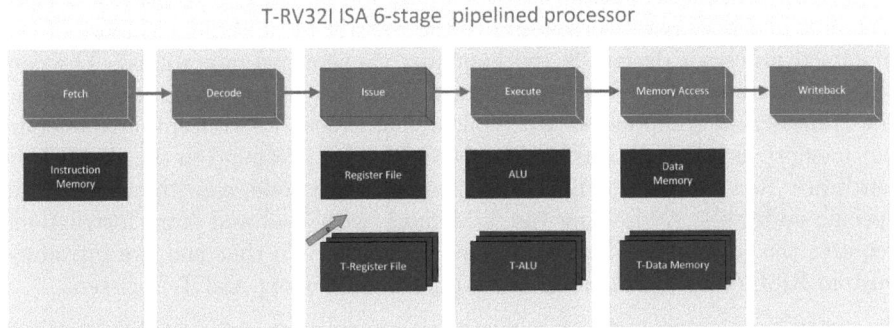

Fig. 1. T-RV32I processor design for original and transformed operations.

As the design is a prototypical implementation, the code memory and the data memory are still separated. They use the same address space, but they rely on different underlying hardware and are neither linked nor synchronized. This separation is an early-stage placeholder for future work, possibly including L1-Data Cache and L1-Instruction Cache. A key concept of the novel design is that no additional arithmetic instructions are needed for the transformed operations. So, this concept of using an adapted datapath differs from an approach using SIMD instructions, e.g., by the RISC-V standard extensions V or P [19]. The original operation is executed simultaneously with the transformed operation in hardware. In other words, every original arithmetic operation on scalar operands is always executed together with its transformed operation as a nonscalar, single, indivisible operation. That is, the instruction on the (original) general purpose path dictates the operation on the path associated with the transformed operation which is executed in parallel. Notice that the transformed operations add a substantial layer of complexity to the datapath.

Recall from Sect. 2 that the transformed operations only rely on previously computed values. This property is an important prerequisite to the new design and may limit its usefulness for transformations with a different structure. The original operations are only allowed to use values from the (original) general purpose registers from preceding processor cycles. The transformed operations, however, are allowed to operate on the content of not only the (original) general purpose registers but also the registers associated with the transformed operations from preceding cycles. Another requirement for the transformed operation is that an operation on a channel is independent from an operation on any other channel. Pipeline hazards are avoided by design, as during the stage "Issue" in the pipeline depicted in Fig. 1, there are checks determining whether any of the registers used as source registers in the current instruction are targeted as destination registers of instructions in the subsequent stages of the pipeline.

3.2 Memory Layout

Figure 2 shows how the memory is structured and partitioned in the new design. The blue and gray parts correspond to the register file and data memory of the pipelined processor design [8] (without any transformed operations). The corresponding components for the transformed operations are given in red. Again, the transformed components are replicated p times. We conceptually refer to our memory as a two-dimensional array. Columns correspond to the channels in hardware. Rows represent different variables in the code, e.g., the elements at specific addresses. Addressing the T-Memory with load and store instructions requires the selection of an address and a channel. To that end, we introduce custom RISC-V instructions for accessing the T-Memory and T-Registers.

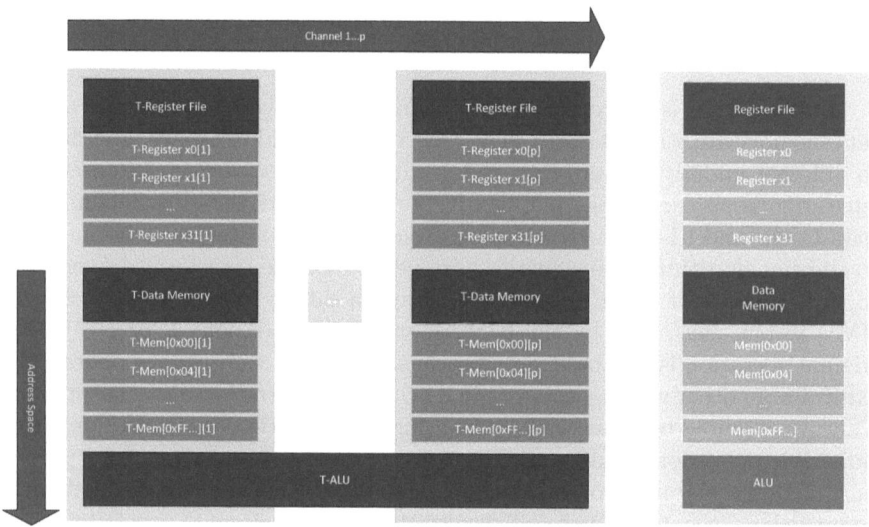

Fig. 2. Memory layout for the original and transformed operations.

3.3 Custom Instruction Encoding

Before computing a transformed operation, the respective values in the transformed memory (T-Memory) and transformed registers (T-Register) have to be set accordingly. In hardware, this can be done by setting the entries of the T-Memory at a specific channel, one at a time. To set the corresponding values in the T-Memory or the T-Register, we introduce custom RISC-V instructions to the hardware design, as the RISC-V ISA offers additional opcode encodings for free use [13], using the CUSTOM-0-type. A total of three new instructions are added to the ISA to enable the program transformation sketched in Sect. 2 in hardware. We refer to these instructions as TSW, TLW, and TMV. They represent store, load, and move instructions, respectively, and the leading character T indicates an instruction for the transformed operations. In the following summary of the instructions, the symbol T-Mem refers to the transformed memory. The symbols rs1, rs2 and rd refer to register names, either general purpose or transformed registers, depending on the context. The index of a channel falls in the range between 1 and p and is represented by channel. The abbreviation T-x[rs1][channel] represents the value stored in the T-Register rs1 in the channel with index channel, whereas x[rs1] represents the value inside the (original) general purpose register rs1. Analogously, T-Mem[x[rs1]][channel] represents the value stored in the T-Memory at the address x[rs1] in the channel channel. The following list contains more information on these custom instructions and their effects. The notation is similar to the one used in [13].

TSW: Writing a value from a general purpose register x[rs2] to the transformed memory indicated by the pair rs1 and channel.
- Instruction: TSW rs2, channel (rs1)
- Effect: T-Mem[x[rs1]][channel] = x[rs2]

TLW: Loading result information from transformed memory indicated by the pair rs1 and channel to a general purpose register x[rd].
- Instruction: TLW rd, channel (rs1)
- Effect: x[rd] = T-Mem[x[rs1]][channel]

TMV: Moving information from a general purpose register x[rs1] to a transformed register T-x[rs2][channel].
- Instruction: TMV rs2, channel (rs1)
- Effect: T-x[rs2][channel] = x[rs1]

Each of these instructions requires three parameters. For example, if the instruction TSW X0, 1 (X1) is executed, the value stored in register X0 is written to the T-Memory at channel 1 addressed by register X1.

The TSW instruction supports variable bit lengths. Similar to store instructions in the RV32I base ISA, different versions are available. The TLW and TMV instructions only support loading or moving 32 bit at once.

4 Experimental Results

In this section, we first introduce the type of transformed operations and then present the results of the high-level synthesis. Finally, we sketch validation tests of the novel approach.

4.1 Transformed Operations

For our study, automatic differentiation is selected as a common program transformation. To that end, the T-ALU is designed in such a way that the transformed operations are tailored toward the extended evaluation procedure defined in [9]. In more detail, the transformed operations that are executed in parallel to the computation of the original operations are listed in Table 1. The instructions SLL, SLLI, SRA, and SRAI do not represent arithmetic operations in the first place. Typically, they would be classified as bit-wise operations. However, in integer arithmetic, these shift operators are used for certain multiplication with or division by power-of-two numbers when executed on integer operands.

Table 1. Original and transformed operations of RISC-V integer instructions. The symbol v_k can represent an immediate value in ADDI, SUBI, SLLI, or SRAI.

Instruction	Operation	
	Original: $v_i = \phi_i(v_j)_{j \prec i}$	Transformed: $\overrightarrow{\Delta v_i} = \sum_{j \prec i} \alpha_{i,j} \cdot \overrightarrow{\Delta v_j}$
ADD, ADDI	$v_i = v_j + v_k$	$\overrightarrow{\Delta v_i} = \overrightarrow{\Delta v_j} + \overrightarrow{\Delta v_k}$
SUB, SUBI	$v_i = v_j - v_k$	$\overrightarrow{\Delta v_i} = \overrightarrow{\Delta v_j} - \overrightarrow{\Delta v_k}$
SLL, SLLI	$v_i = v_j \cdot 2^{v_k}$	$\overrightarrow{\Delta v_i} = 2^{v_k} \cdot \overrightarrow{\Delta v_j} + (\log_e 2)\, v_j\, 2^{v_k} \cdot \overrightarrow{\Delta v_k}$
SRA, SRAI	$v_i = v_j / 2^{v_k}$	$\overrightarrow{\Delta v_i} = 1/2^{v_k} \cdot \overrightarrow{\Delta v_j} - (\log_e 2)\, v_j / 2^{v_k} \cdot \overrightarrow{\Delta v_k}$

Besides these augmentations for arithmetic operations, some changes to the non-arithmetic instructions are necessary. None of these changes alter the behavior and results of the original operations. Neither do they influence the values in the original general purpose register file and the data memory. However, they add additional steps to ensure the correct execution of the transformed operations. For example, the LW instruction not only loads the content of an address in the data memory to a general purpose register, but also loads the content of all channels of an address in the T-Memory to all of the respective channels in a T-Register.

4.2 High-Level Synthesis

The C Synthesis takes the high-level synthesis code written in C as input and generates the register transfer level representation. For our synthesis, we set the memory sizes of the processor design as follows:

- Instruction Memory: 8 KB
- Data Memory: 16 KB
- T-Memory: $p \cdot 16$ KB, where p is the number of channels.

Here, all memory resources refer to block RAM on the FPGA.

As a result, an estimation of the required hardware resources on the Alveo U50DD FPGA [20] is returned. The results of the synthesis are summarized in Table 2. For the block RAM (BRAM), Digital Signal Processor slices (DSPs), Flip-Flops (FFs), and lookup tables (LUTs), the absolute numbers of required resources are shown in the columns labeled with the sign #. Additionally, the rounded percentage of the respective required resource in relation to the available resources on the Alveo U50DD is given in the column indicated by %.

Table 2. Estimated resource utilization and clock cycle time, T_c^{aug}, on the Alveo U50DD FPGA Accelerator Card after C Synthesis for varying numbers, p, of channels.

p	BRAM #	%	DSPs #	%	FFs #	%	LUTs #	%	T_c^{aug} [ns]
0	32	(1)	0	(0)	6 194	(0)	12 567	(1)	$T_c^{\text{orig}} = 2.873$
1	48	(1)	64	(1)	7 342	(0)	21 009	(2)	8.677
3	72	(2)	136	(2)	10 695	(0)	32 345	(3)	11.495
7	104	(3)	232	(3)	19 089	(1)	54 215	(6)	11.626
15	168	(6)	424	(7)	36 406	(2)	98 896	(11)	11.599
31	296	(11)	808	(13)	62 347	(3)	186 431	(21)	14.481
63	552	(20)	1 576	(26)	121 671	(6)	361 805	(41)	14.590

The largest number of channels successfully synthesized is 63. For this number of channels approximately 360 000 LUTs are used, corresponding to 41% of all LUTs which are available on this FPGA. Throughout this paper we assume that p is less than or equal to the number of channels successfully synthesized.

A significant increase of the clock cycle time is observed when the first channel is added to the design. This effect can be explained with the increased complexity of the transformed operation of the SLL, SLLI, SRA, and SRAI operations compared with the original operations; see Table 1. In hardware, the transformed operations require additional multiplications. The original operation does not require any hardware multiplication circuit, as the multiplication with or division by a multiple of two is performed by a bitwise shift.

4.3 Validation Tests

To assess the feasibility of the processor design, we automatically generate and compile test codes in the high-level language C. These test codes use random combinations of elementary operations ϕ_i. We choose the ϕ_i from the following four different types: scalar addition, scalar subtraction, left shift, and right shift. These elementary operations ϕ_i are executed on random combinations of the C data types char, short, and integer, both signed and unsigned. The test code generator offers the following parameters:

- the number of variables,
- the number of operations, and
- the number of channels for which we still use the symbol p.

This code generator is capable of producing two different code versions. The first version generates the original code that is intended to be run on the FPGA. This code also involves the necessary input for the T-Memory. Recall from Sect. 2 that if v_i is an input then the T-Memory needs the values for $\overrightarrow{\Delta v_i}$. A common situation in automatic differentiation is to initialize these p-dimensional vectors with the Cartesian unit vectors. This process is called seeding and is detailed in [9]. For that purpose, the custom instructions introduced in Sect. 3 are required. They are embedded within the C code by inline assembly statements.

The second code version produced by the generator is the result of the program transformation in software. That is, it consists of the original and transformed operations. This second version is used to validate the numerical results and compare the number of instructions with the first version.

Both code versions are compiled with the GCC compiler. An excerpt of the assembly code compiled from the first version is shown in Listing 1.1 for a single addition between two 32-bit integer numbers. Note that the excerpt is extracted from a larger program, where the seeding is included. Due to the augmented architecture of the processor design, no further instructions for the computation of the transformed operations are required.

Listing 1.1. T-RV32I assembly code for an example snippet of the first code version with 32-bit integer variables for the operation var2 = var1 + var0.

```
#var2 = var1 + var0;
lw      a4,-32(s0)
lw      a5,-28(s0)
add     a5,a4,a5
sw      a5,-36(s0)
```

In contrast to the code for the augmented processor design illustrated in the previous assembly example with four instructions, Listing 1.2 shows the equivalent second code version which computes the results of the (original and) transformed operations purely in software using $p = 2$. In this example, there are twelve assembly instructions corresponding to an increase of the number of instructions by the factor $p+1$. In other words, the augmented processor design reduces the number of required instructions by the factor $p+1$.

Listing 1.2. RV32I equivalent assembly code for an example snippet of the second code version with 32-bit integer variables for the operation var2 = var1 + var0 with two channels.

```
#ad_var2_0 = ad_var1_0 + ad_var0_0;
```

```
lw   a4,-44(s0)
lw   a5,-36(s0)
add  a5,a4,a5
sw   a5,-52(s0)
#ad_var2_1 = ad_var1_1 + ad_var0_1;
lw   a4,-48(s0)
lw   a5,-40(s0)
add  a5,a4,a5
sw   a5,-56(s0)
#var2 = var1 + var0;
lw   a4,-28(s0)
lw   a5,-24(s0)
add  a5,a4,a5
sw   a5,-32(s0)
```

We stress that this factor is even larger for shift operations, as Table 1 shows that the corresponding transformed operations need at least an additional multiplication. Thus, we model this factor as $c \cdot p + 1$, where the constant $c \geq 1$ depends on the instruction.

To quantify the execution times of the two approaches, we assume that the clock cycles per instruction executed on the original unaltered processor design, CPI^{orig}, equals the clock cycles per instruction executed on the augmented processor design, CPI^{aug}. Therefore, we use the symbol CPI to denote that quantity in both approaches. The execution time of a single combined (original and transformed) operation running on the original unaltered processor design is therefore estimated as

$$T^{\text{orig}}(p) = (c \cdot p + 1) \cdot \text{CPI} \cdot T_c^{\text{orig}},$$

where T_c^{orig} is the clock cycle time of the original processor design; see the time in the first row, $p = 0$, and the last column of Table 2. Similarly, the execution time of a single operation running on the augmented processor design is approximated by

$$T^{\text{aug}}(p) = 1 \cdot \text{CPI} \cdot T_c^{\text{aug}}(p),$$

where $T_c^{\text{aug}}(p)$ is the clock cycle time of the augmented processor design with p channels. These times are also available in the last column of this table. The resulting expected speedup is defined by

$$S(p) := \frac{T^{\text{orig}}(p)}{T^{\text{aug}}(p)} = (c \cdot p + 1) \cdot \frac{T_c^{\text{orig}}}{T_c^{\text{aug}}(p)}.$$

Recall from Table 2 that the clock cycle time $T_c^{\text{orig}} \approx 2.9\,\text{ns}$. For $p = 63$, this table indicates $T_c^{\text{aug}}(63) \approx 14.6\,\text{ns}$. So, the expected speedup is

$$S(63) \approx (c \cdot 63 + 1) \cdot 0.2$$

on the Alveo U50DD FPGA. Thus, even for $c = 1$ we expect a speedup of at least 12.8. For the different remaining values of p given in Table 2, the corresponding speedup $S(p)$ is plotted in Fig. 3, varying the constant c. This figure indicates that the speedup $S(p)$ scales with the number, p, of channels.

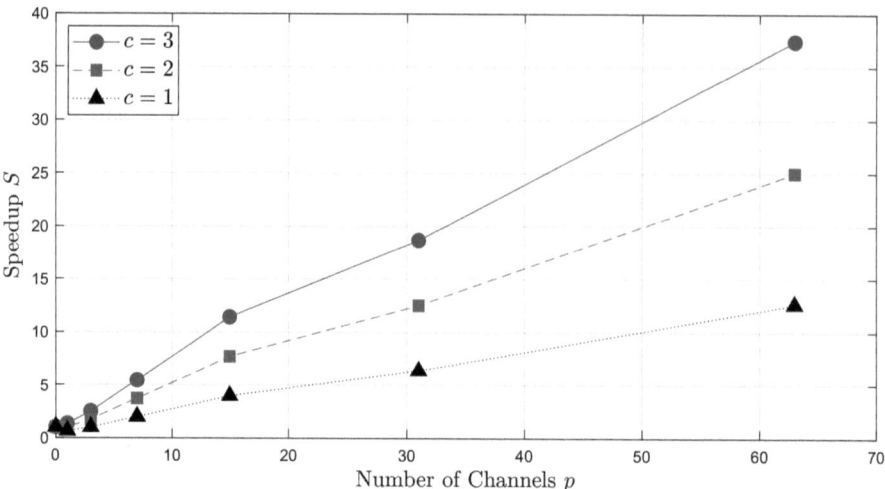

Fig. 3. Speedup as a function of the number of channels for varying constants c.

5 Concluding Remarks

This feasibility study is motivated by the increasing relevance of a specific program transformation in high-performance computing. It addresses the question whether or not it is a feasible suggestion to implement this transformation directly in hardware. To this end, a novel RISC-V processor design is introduced that augments a given pipelined processor design with the corresponding program transformation rules. These rules associate with every scalar operation of a given computer code a linear combination of vectors. The new approach, at its heart, consists of replicating register files, ALU, and data memory for each vector entry. By adapting the control unit and the datapath, it implements an augmented version of the RISC-V ISA. A simulation of the new processor design for the AMD U50 Data Center Accelerator Card shows that the novel approach is indeed promising. Although it increases not only resource usage that can be controlled by the number of vector entries but also the clock cycle time, the new approach enables an overall speedup of the intended program transformation. However, there is still room for further research. We are currently extending the approach from the ISA RV32I to RV32IMF heading further in the direction of practical applications [17].

Acknowledgements. The authors are grateful to Bernard Goossens, Université de Perpignan, France, for providing high-level synthesis code used to implement the RISC-V processor design without support for the program transformation. This case study was funded in part by the Carl Zeiss Foundation within the project "Interactive Inference."

Disclosure of Interests. The authors have no competing interests to declare that are relevant to the content of this article.

References

1. Bischof, C.H., Bücker, H.M., Hovland, P.D., Naumann, U., Utke, J. (eds.): Advances in Automatic Differentiation, LNCSE, vol. 64. Springer, Berlin (2008). https://doi.org/10.1007/978-3-540-68942-3
2. Bücker, M., Corliss, G., Naumann, U., Hovland, P., Norris, B. (eds.): Automatic Differentiation: Applications, Theory, and Implementations. LNCSE, vol. 50. Springer, Heidelberg (2006). https://doi.org/10.1007/3-540-28438-9
3. Christianson, B., Forth, S.A., Griewank, A. (eds.): Special Issue: Advances in Algorithmic Differentiation, Optimization Methods & Software, vol. 33(4–6). Taylor & Francis, New York (2018)
4. Corliss, G., Faure, C., Griewank, A., Hascoët, L., Naumann, U. (eds.): Automatic Differentiation of Algorithms. Springer, New York (2002). https://doi.org/10.1007/978-1-4613-0075-5
5. Forth, S., Hovland, P., Phipps, E., Utke, J., Walther, A. (eds.): Recent Advances in Algorithmic Differentiation, LNCSE, vol. 87. Springer, Berlin (2012). https://doi.org/10.1007/978-3-642-30023-3
6. Gebremedhin, A.H., Walther, A.: An introduction to algorithmic differentiation. WIREs Data Min. Knowl. Discov. **10**(1), e1334 (2020). https://doi.org/10.1002/widm.1334
7. Gendler, D., Naumann, U., Christianson, B.: Automatic differentiation of assembler code. In: Proceedings of the IADIS International Conference on Applied Computing, pp. 431–436. IADIS (2007)
8. Goossens, B.: Guide to Computer Processor Architecture : A RISC-V Approach, with High-Level Synthesis. Undergraduate topics in computer science, Springer, Cham, Switzerland (2023). https://doi.org/10.1007/978-3-031-18023-1
9. Griewank, A., Walther, A.: Evaluating Derivatives: Principles and Techniques of Algorithmic Differentiation. No. 105 in Other Titles in Applied Mathematics, SIAM, Philadelphia, PA, 2nd edn. (2008). https://doi.org/10.1137/1.9780898717761
10. Hoseininasab, S.S., Collange, C., Derrien, S.: Rapid prototyping of complex microarchitectures through high-level synthesis. In: Palumbo, F., Keramidas, G., Voros, N., Diniz, P.C. (eds.) Applied Reconfigurable Computing. Architectures, Tools, and Applications. ARC 2023. LNCS, vol. 14251, pp. 19–34. Springer, Cham (2023). https://doi.org/10.1007/978-3-031-42921-7_2
11. Nehmeier, M., Siegel, S., von Gudenberg, J.W.: Specification of hardware for interval arithmetic. Computing **94**(2–4), 243–255 (2012). https://doi.org/10.1007/s00607-012-0185-0
12. Heimbach, P., Hill, C., Giering, R.: An efficient exact adjoint of the parallel MIT general circulation model, generated via automatic differentiation. Futur. Gener. Comput. Syst. **21**(8), 1356–1371 (2005). https://doi.org/10.1016/j.future.2004.11.010
13. Patterson, D., Waterman, A.: The RISC-V Reader: An Open Architecture Atlas, 1st edn. Strawberry Canyon, Berkeley (2017)
14. Probst, M., Lülfesmann, M., Bücker, H.M., Behr, M., Bischof, C.H.: Sensitivity of shear rate in artificial grafts using automatic differentiation. Int. J. Numer. Meth. Fluids **62**(9), 1047–1062 (2010). https://doi.org/10.1002/fld.2061
15. Rall, L.B. (ed.): Automatic Differentiation: Techniques and Applications. LNCS, vol. 120. Springer, Heidelberg (1981). https://doi.org/10.1007/3-540-10861-0

16. Sambridge, M., Rickwood, P., Rawlinson, N., Sommacal, S.: Automatic differentiation in geophysical inverse problems. Geophys. J. Int. **170**(1), 1–8 (2007). https://doi.org/10.1111/j.1365-246X.2007.03400.x
17. Schoder, J., Bücker, H.M.: A domain-specific RISC-V processor design for accelerating automatic differentiation (2024). manuscript in preparation
18. Tijskens, E., Roose, D., Ramon, H., De Baerdemaeker, J.: Automatic differentiation for solving nonlinear partial differential equations: an efficient operator overloading approach. Numer. Algorithms **30**(3–4), 259–301 (2002). https://doi.org/10.1023/A:1020103610525
19. Waterman, A., Asanović, K., (Eds.): The RISC-V Instruction Set Manual, Volume I: User-Level ISA. RISC-V Foundation, unprivileged architecture, 20240411 edn. (2024). https://github.com/riscv/riscv-isa-manual
20. XILINX: Alveo U50 data center accelerator card data sheet. Product specification (2020), DS965 (v1.7.1)

Performance Analysis of BERT on RISC-V Processors with SIMD Units

Héctor Martínez[1], Sandra Catalán[4], Carlos García[2], Francisco D. Igual[2(✉)], Rafael Rodríguez-Sánchez[3], Adrián Castelló[5], and Enrique S. Quintana-Ortí[5]

[1] Universidad de Córdoba, Córdoba, Spain
el2mapeh@uco.es
[2] Universidad Complutense de Madrid, Madrid, Spain
{garsanca,figual}@ucm.es
[3] Universidad de Castilla-La Mancha, Ciudad Real, Spain
Rafael.Rodriguez@uclm.es
[4] Universidad Jaume I de Castellón, Castelló de la Plana, Spain
catalans@uji.es
[5] Universitat Politècnica de València, Valencia, Spain
{adcastel,quintana}@disca.upv.es

Abstract. Following the recent advances in open hardware generally, and RISC-V architectures particularly, we analyse the performance of transformer encoder inference on three low-power platforms with this type of architecture. For this purpose, we conduct a detailed profile of the inference process for two representative members of the BERT family, identifying the main bottlenecks and opportunities for optimisation on three RISC-V processors equipped with floating-point SIMD (single instruction, multiple data) units: XuanTie C906, C908, and C910.

Keywords: Deep learning · transformers · inference · multicore processors · RISC-V (RVV) · high performance · matrix multiplication

1 Introduction

Since the introduction of transformers by Vaswani et al. in 2017 [12], this type of model has garnered widespread popularity, evolving into a foundational technology in various Natural Language Processing (NLP) tasks. Particularly, transformer architectures like BERT (Bidirectional Encoder Representations from Transformers) [3] and GPT (Generative Pre-trained Transformers) [1] have achieved excellent results in language translation, summarisation, and question answering, among others. Recently, transformers have also been applied to computer vision tasks such as image classification, object detection, and segmentation [5].

Due to the sheer complexity of transformers and the enormous industry interest in generative AI (artificial intelligence), a great deal of effort is being devoted to optimising transformer *training* on virtually all types of processors and accelerators [2,7,9]. In comparison with training, *inference* incurs significantly lower computational costs. However, this second stage is usually performed on commodity CPU-based systems with stringent time limitations. Additionally, there is a cumulative impact of numerous devices –from desktop computers and laptops to smartphones and wearables– running deployed transformer-based models. The combination of these two factors accentuates the significance of analysing and optimising transformer inference.

In recent years, big data, cloud, and AI have driven the adoption of open-source software. This has allowed researchers to create an open ecosystem for industry players and technology adopters to collaborate and build upon. The RISC-V initiative and the OpenHW group are notable efforts to follow the same path for open hardware. Specifically, RISC-V is an open-source, modular instruction set architecture (ISA) that is gaining popularity due to its flexibility and suitability for integration with DL acceleration capabilities.

In this work, we target the efficient execution of transformer encoders on RISC-V processors, making the following contributions:

– We offer a detailed performance analysis of the most computationally expensive operations within the encoder, which can be leveraged to guide the optimisation of this type of computational block.
– We dissect the GEMM kernel in OpenBLAS targeting RISC-V vector extension (RVV), the basic building block of the encoder.
– We extend our study to cover the parallel scalability of the transformer block on a multi-core RISC-V platform, helping to identify optimisation challenges.
– We compare the performance of the three platforms utilised in this work, in terms of token processing throughput, normalised to the processor frequency.

2 Dissecting BERT: An Encoder-Only Transformer

In general, transformers consist of an encoder-decoder structure, though this can be adapted for specific tasks that only require one of these components. For example, transformer encoders (e.g., BERT [3] and recent vision transformers like DeIT [11]) are appropriate for classification; transformer decoders (e.g., GPT [1]) are a good option for text generation; and full transformers (e.g., T5 [10]) are preferred for translation and question answering.

In this work we focus on inference, targeting BERT because of its proven state-of-the-art performance across various NLP tasks, mostly due to its ability to capture contextual relationships within language. We emphasise that inference is usually performed on compact CPU-based systems which are subject to strong time constraints. Furthermore, the pervasive use of transformer-based models across a multitude of devices underscores the critical importance of first analysing (and subsequently optimising) transformer inference.

BERT is an encoder-only transformer that consists of an input embedding, followed by several encoder layers (hereafter, encoders), plus a final classification. The BERT model is described schematically in Fig. 1, where the actual number of encoders depends on the BERT configuration (e.g., BERT-tiny|base|large contain 2|12|24 encoder layers). Furthermore, this figure also shows that each encoder is further decomposed into a Multi-Head Attention (MHA) module and a Feed-Forward Network (FFN) module.

For inference, the input and output layers contribute little to the computational cost of the complete encoder. Therefore, in the remainder of this paper we focus on the internals of the intermediate encoders in the BERT model. The embedding layer receives an input text sentence consisting of l tokens (e.g., words), and converts that into a $d \times l$ array, where each token in the input sequence is represented as a vector of d embeddings. In batch mode, it is possible to infer b sequences simultaneously by stacking each one as a separate column of a $d \times lb$ input to the encoder. This array is denoted as the Encoder Input (E_I) in Fig. 2. The computational complexity of the transformer block is defined by the dimensions of the input (d, l, b), the number of attention heads (h) in the MHA module, and the inner/hidden dimension of the FFN module (f).

The MHA module multiplies E_I with three weight matrices –W_Q, W_K, and W_V– to obtain the *Query* (Q), *Key* (K), and *Value* (V) matrices; see the operations labelled as M1–M3 in Fig. 2. The next step splits Q, K, V into hb sub-matrices to feed the h attention heads (M4). These sub-matrices then participate in $2hb$ multiplications, labelled as M5 and M7, which are connected via a Softmax operation (M6). The output of the latter for all attention heads is concatenated (M8) into a new matrix, named as E_2, and this is multiplied by a weight matrix W_O (M9). The MHA module finally applies a layer normalisation (Lnorm, label M10) to produce matrix A_O. The FFN module takes as input A_O to compute two additional multiplications, F11 and F13, respectively involving with the weight matrices W_1 and W_2. This module also includes an intermediate GELU plus a final Lnorm (F12 and F14, respectively.)

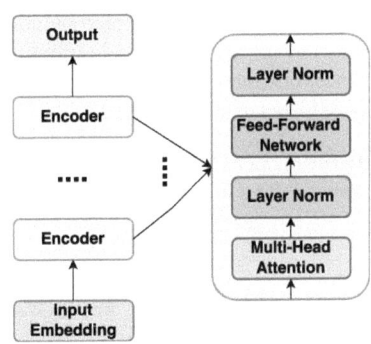

Fig. 1. BERT model.

The previous elaboration exposes that the encoder is composed of a considerable number of general matrix multiplications (GEMM) plus a few other transforms (basically, Softmax, GELU, and Lnorm). Table 1 collects all these operations, specifying the dimensions of the GEMM kernels of the form $C = A \cdot B$ using the triplet (m, n, k), where $m \times n$ correspond to the size of C, and k is the reduction axis for the product (i.e., the number of columns|rows for $A|B$).

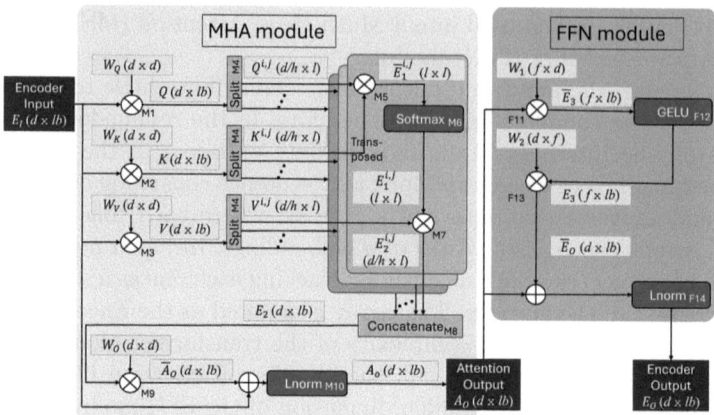

Fig. 2. Architecture of the MHA (left) and FFN (right) modules in a transformer block with h heads, operating on b sequences. The symbols "⊗" and "⊕" respectively denote matrix multiplication and summation. The notation M1–M10, F11–F14 correspond to the operations in Table 1. The multiplications in M5 and M7 are batched, with one GEMM per head and sequence.

Table 1. Left: Operations in the MHA and FNN modules. Right: Dimensions of BERT transformers employed in this work.

		m	n	k
MHA	M1-M3. $(Q, K, V) = (W_Q, W_K, W_V) \cdot E_I$	d	lb	d
	M4. $\mathsf{Split}(Q, K, V) \rightarrow$			
	$\quad (Q^{i,j}, K^{i,j}, V^{i,j})^{j=1:b}_{i=1:h}$			
	for $j = 1 : b$			
	$\quad$ for $i = 1 : h$			
	M5. $\quad \bar{E}_1^{i,j} = ((K^{i,j})^T \cdot Q^{i,j})/\sqrt{d_k}$	l	l	d/h
	M6. $\quad E_1^{i,j} = \mathsf{Softmax}\,(\bar{E}_1^{i,j})$			
	M7. $\quad E_2^{i,j} = V^{i,j} \cdot E_1^{i,j}$	d/h	l	l
	M8. $\mathsf{Concatenate}(E_2^{i,j})^{j=1:b}_{i=1:h} \rightarrow E_2$			
	M9. $\bar{A}_O = W_O \cdot E_2$	d	lb	d
	M10. $A_O = \mathsf{Lnorm}\,(\bar{A}_O + E_I)$			
FFN	F11. $\bar{E}_3 = W_1 \cdot A_O$	f	lb	d
	F12. $E_3 = \mathsf{GELU}\,(\bar{E}_3)$			
	F13. $\bar{E}_O = W_2 \cdot E_3$	d	lb	f
	F14. $E_O = \mathsf{Lnorm}\,(\bar{E}_O + A_O)$			

Param.	BERT$_B$	BERT$_L$
#Layers	12	24
d	768	1,024
h	12	16
f	3,072	4,096

3 GEMM and RISC-V

Considering the dissection of the encoder anatomy exposed in the previous section, it is clear that the final performance observed for the transformer block will heavily depend on the degree of adaptation of GEMM to the underlying architecture. The implementations of BLAS (*Basic Linear Algebra Subprograms* [4]) in general, and GEMM in particular, for RISC-V architectures with SIMD capabilities are still scarce. Currently, only OpenBLAS provides ad-hoc implementations for RISC-V with RISC-V Vector Extensions (RVV), both in versions 0.7.1 and 1.0. In the following, we provide details on the general techniques for realizing a high-performance instance of GEMM for SIMD architectures with a hierarchical memory hierarchy and its mapping to RVV, considering OpenBLAS as the reference implementation.

Virtually all GEMM realisations in open-source (e.g. BLIS, OpenBLAS) or commercial (e.g. Intel OneMKL, ARMPL) BLAS libraries follow the approach proposed by GotoBLAS2 [6] to target multi-layered memory hierarchies, SIMD units, and multi-core processors. Consider the GEMM $C = \alpha C + \beta A \cdot B$, where $C \to m \times n$, $A \to m \times k$, $B \to k \times n$, and α, β are scalars. In general, high-performance realisations of this operation follow a common high-level algorithmic strategy, depicted in Fig. 3.

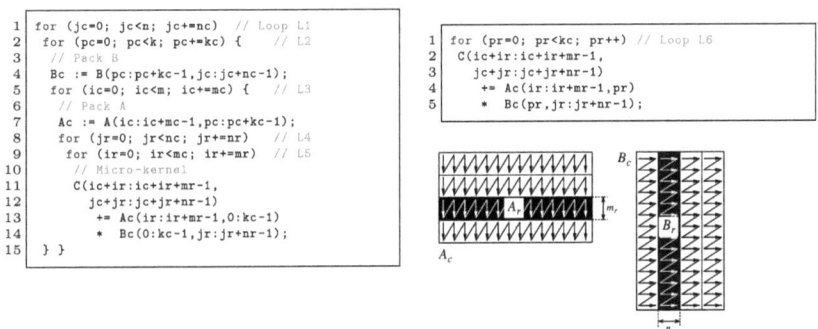

Fig. 3. Baseline high performance algorithm for GEMM. Left: blocked algorithm; Top-right: micro-kernel; Bottom-Right: Packing of input operands.

Let us consider the baseline blocked algorithm in Fig. 3(left). At a glance, the GEMM implementation is cast in terms of five nested loops labelled as L1 to L5 in the code, surrounding two packing routines (lines 4 and 7) and a so-called micro-kernel (whose code is illustrated in the top-right code) that comprises an additional loop (L6). The exploitation of the layered memory hierarchy is performed via a careful selection of the strides of the loops in the baseline blocked algorithm (values for m_c, n_c, and k_c), together with the specific placement of the packing routines of each active block of A and B. The vector (SIMD) capabilities of the underlying architecture are exclusively exploited within the micro-kernel code, that is usually vectorised (relying on the compiler auto-vectorisation capabilities or, more desirably, using vector assembly instructions or intrinsics). This micro-kernel updates an $m_r \times n_r$ micro-tile of C, proceeding as an outer product that involves one row (column) of micro-panels of A_c (B_c) at each operation. This outer product is usually cast in terms of a SAXPY ($\alpha x + y$) BLAS operation that can be easily mapped the appropriate SIMD instruction(s) of the target vector ISA (instruction set architecture). Finally, the arrangement of elements of the packed workspaces A_c and B_c enable their load into vector registers with a unit stride, favouring a proper memory bandwidth exploitation.

A proper selection of values for m_c, n_c, k_c is critical to ensure that the micro-kernel operates on data that resides close to the core, avoiding unnecessary stalls. Similarly, a proper selection of values for m_r and n_r aims to exploit the number of (vector) registers offered by the architecture, increasing performance without suffering register spilling. A proper instruction mix within the micro-kernel assures an optimal utilisation of the execution pipelines.

OpenBLAS targets these optimisation goals by implementing an assembly micro-kernel with RVV instructions targeting RVV 0.7.1 and RVV 1.0;[1] the micro-kernel used in our evaluations and provided by the manufacturers of the target cores sets $m_r = 16$, $n_r = 4$. The micro-kernel implements general optimizations (software pipelining and loop unrolling), see Listing 1.1. The code sketch constructs the body of loop L6 as a sequence of macros in order to accommodate software pipelining, and to experiment with different degrees of loop unrolling (in this case, 8). For the sake of brevity, we consider a simplified micro-kernel in which k is a multiple of 8:

- KERNEL_16x4_SETUP (Listing 1.2) configures the vector length to use, and initializes vector registers devoted to accummulation to zero.
- KERNEL_16x4_INIT (Listing 1.3) loads the first column/row of A_c and B_c, and realises their outer product by means of a coupled broadcast of individual elements of the row of B_c and a fused multiply-accumulation with each group of elements of the column of A_c by means of a vmfacc.vv (see [8] for alternatives and performance comparison on similar architectures for this operation). Finally, it proceeds by loading the corresponding elements of A_c/B_c for the next iteration.
- KERNEL_16x4_M2 (Listing 1.4) computes the accumulation for a column/row of A_c/B_c, and loads the elements for the next iteration.
- KERNEL_16x4_M1 is similar to M2 and we omit it for brevity.
- KERNEL_16x4_END (Listing 1.5) accumulates the values obtained from the outer product of the last column/row of A_c/B_c.
- KERNEL_16x4_SAVE (Listing 1.6) saves the values of the accumulators in vector registers to the final location in C, with a previous scaling by α, in a pipelined fashion.

4 Experimental Evaluation

This section characterises the inference costs of BERT-Base and BERT-Large [3], two models which are representative of transformer encoders, *on three RISC-V processors with SIMD units*.

---

[1] The differences in the micro-kernel between both versions are minimal, replacing the vle/vse instructions by their vle32/vse32 counterparts.

```
1   // Register use:
2   // t0 for k
3   // ft0-ft3,ft4-ft7,v8-v15 for B, t1-t3 for PB1
         -3
4   // v0-v3,v4-v7 for A, t4-t6 for PA1-3
5   // v16-v31 for temp C (accumulators)
6
7   asm volatile(
8   KERNEL16x4_SETUP
9
10  // Preloop
11  KERNEL16x4_I
12  KERNEL16x4_M2
13  KERNEL16x4_M1
14  KERNEL16x4_M2
15
16  "M16x4_MAINLOOP:          "
17
18  KERNEL16x4_M1
19  KERNEL16x4_M2
20  KERNEL16x4_M1
21  KERNEL16x4_M2
22  KERNEL16x4_M1
23  KERNEL16x4_M2
24  KERNEL16x4_M1
25  KERNEL16x4_M2
26
27  "addi t0, t0, -1
28  "bgtz t0, M16x4_MAINLOOP
29
30  KERNEL16x4_M1
31  KERNEL16x4_M2
32  KERNEL16x4_M1
33  KERNEL16x4_E
34
35
36  KERNEL_16x4_SAVE
37  )
```

Listing 1.1. General skeleton of the OpenBLAS SGEMM microkernel.

```
1   #define KERNEL16x4_SETUP \
2   "vsetvli  zero, zero, e32, m1"\
3   "fmv.w.x  ft11, zero         "\
4   "mv       t0,   %[BK]        "\
5
6   // Zero-out accumulators (v16-v31).
7   "vfmv.v.f v16, ft11 "\
8   "vfmv.v.f v17, ft11 "\
9   "vfmv.v.f v18, ft11 "\
10  "vfmv.v.f v19, ft11 "\
11
12  // (...) Ommitted for (v20-v27) for brevity.
13
14  "vfmv.v.f v28, ft11 "\
15  "vfmv.v.f v29, ft11 "\
16  "vfmv.v.f v30, ft11 "\
17  "vfmv.v.f v31, ft11 "\
```

Listing 1.2. Initial setup.

```
1   #define KERNEL16x4_I \
2   "addi      t1,     %[PB], 1*4 "\
3   "addi      t2,     %[PB], 2*4 "\
4   "addi      t3,     %[PB], 3*4 "\
5   // Scalar load of elem. 0 of row 0 of B (B0).
6   "flw       ft0,    (%[PB])        "\
7   // Scalar load of elem. 1 of row 0 of B (B1).
8   "flw       ft1,    (t1)           "\
9   // Scalar load of elem. 2 of row 0 of B (B2).
10  "flw       ft2,    (t2)           "\
11  // Scalar load of elem. 3 of row 0 of B (B3).
12  "flw       ft3,    (t3)           "\
13
14  "addi      t4,     %[PA], 4*4 "\
15  "addi      t5,     %[PA], 8*4 "\
16
17  // Load col. 0 of A (elems. 0-3).
18  "vle.v     v0,     (%[PA])        "\
19  // Load col. 0 of A (elems. 4-7).
20  "vle.v     v1,     (t4)           "\
21  // Load col. 0 of A (elems. 8-11).
22  "vle.v     v2,     (t5)           "\
23  // Broadcast row 0 of B (elem. 0).
24  "vfmv.v.f  v8,     ft0            "\
25  "addi      t6,     %[PA], 12*4"\
26  "addi      %[PA],  %[PA], 16*4"\
27  "addi      t4,     t4,    16*4"\
28  // Broadcast row 0 of B (elem. 1).
29  "vfmv.v.f  v9,     ft1            "\
30  "addi      t5,     t5,    16*4"\
31  // Load col. 0 of A (elems. 12-15).
32  "vle.v     v3,     (t6)           "\
33  "addi      t6,     t6,    16*4"\
34  // Broadcast row 0 of B (elem. 2).
35  "vfmv.v.f  v10,    ft2            "\
36  "addi      %[PB],  %[PB], 4*4 "\
37  // Load col. 1 of A (elems. 0-3).
38  "vle.v     v4,     (%[PA])        "\
39  "addi      %[PA],  %[PA], 16*4"\
40  // Broadcast row 0 of B (elem. 3).
41  "vfmv.v.f  v11,    ft3            "\
42  // Scale col. 0 (elems 0-3).
43  "vfmacc.vv v16,    v8,    v0  "\
44  "addi      t1,     t1,    4*4 "\
45  // Load col. 1 of A (elems. 4-7).
46  // Load elements 4-7 of col. 1 of A.
47  "vle.v     v5,     (t4)           "\
48  "addi      t4,     t4,    16*4"\
49  // Scale col. 0 (elems 4-7).
50  "vfmacc.vv v17,    v8,    v1  "\
51  "addi      t2,     t2,    4*4 "\
52  // Load col. 1 of A (elems. 8-11).
53  "vle.v     v6,     (t5)           "\
54  "addi      t5,     t5,    16*4"\
55  // Scale col. 0 (elems 8-11).
56  "vfmacc.vv v18,    v8,    v2  "\
57  "addi      t3,     t3,    4*4 "\
58  // Load col. 1 of A (elems. 12-15).
59  "vle.v     v7,     (t5)           "\
60  "addi      t6,     t6,    16*4"\
61  // Scale col. 0 (elems 12-15).
62  "vfmacc.vv v19,    v8,    v3  "\
63
64  // Complete scaling of col. 0.
65  // Complete load of row 1 of B.
66  // (...) Ommitted for brevity.
```

Listing 1.3. Update of row/col. 0 of A_c and B_c and load of row/col. 1.

4.1 Setup

In the following, we highlight the main features of the three different RISC-V processors employed for evaluation; see Table 2 for their main features.

XuantieL (XuanTie C910). We employed a Sipeed LicheePi 4a board that embeds an Alibaba T-HEAD 1520 processor integrating four XuanTie C910 cores running at 1.85 GHz. The board includes 4 GB of LPDDR4X-3733 main memory. The XuanTie C910 is a high-performance multi-core architecture targeting edge computing scenarios that require HPC vector capabilities. The processor

```
1   #define KERNEL16x4_M2 \
2   // Scale col. k by B0 (elems 0-3).
3   "vfmacc.vv  v16, v12,     v4 "\
4   // Load col. (k+1) of A (elems. 0-3).
5   "vle.v      v0,  (%[PA])        "\
6   "addi       %[PA], %[PA], 16*4"\
7   // Scale col. k by B0 (elems 4-7).
8   "vfmacc.vv  v17, v12,     v5 "\
9   // Load col. (k+1) of A (elems. 4-7).
10  "vle.v      v1,  (t4)           "\
11  "addi       t4,  t4,      16*4"\
12  // Scale col. k by B0 (elems 8-11).
13  "vfmacc.vv  v18, v12,     v6 "\
14  // Load row (k+1) of A (elems. 8-11).
15  "vle.v      v2,  (t5)           "\
16  "addi       t5,  t5,      16*4"\
17  // Scale col. k by B0 (elems 12-15).
18  "vfmacc.vv  v19, v12,     v7 "\
19  // Load elements 12-16 of col. (k+1).
20  "vle.v      v3,  (t6)           "\
21  "addi       t6,  t6,      16*4"\
22  // Scale col. k by B1 (elems 0-3).
23  "vfmacc.vv  v20, v13,     v4 "\
24  // Scalar load of elem. 0 of row 1 of B (B0).
25  "flw        ft0, (%[PB])        "\
26  // Scale col. k by B1 (elems 4-7).
27  "vfmacc.vv  v21, v13,     v5 "\
28  // Scalar load of elem. 1 of row 1 of B (B1).
29  "flw        ft1, (t1)           "\
30  // Scale col. k by B1 (elems 8-11).
31  "vfmacc.vv  v22, v13,     v6 "\
32  // Scalar load of elem. 2 of row 1 of B (B2).
33  "flw        ft2, (t2)           "\
34  // Scale col. k by B1 (elems 12-15).
35  "vfmacc.vv  v23, v13,     v7 "\
36  // Scalar load of elem. 3 of row 1 of B (B3).
37  "flw        ft3, (t3)           "\
38
39  // Complete scaling col. k by B2 and B3.
40  // Complete broadcasting row (k+1) of B (B0-B3
       ).
```

Listing 1.4. Update of row/col. k of Ac and Bc and load of row/col. $(k+1)$.

```
1   #define KERNEL16x4_E \
2   "vfmacc.vv  v16, v12, v4"\
3   "vfmacc.vv  v17, v12, v5"\
4   "vfmacc.vv  v18, v12, v6"\
5   "vfmacc.vv  v19, v12, v7"\
6
7   // Ommitted update of (v20 -v27) for brevity.
8
9   "vfmacc.vv  v28, v15, v4"\
10  "vfmacc.vv  v29, v15, v5"\
11  "vfmacc.vv  v30, v15, v6"\
12  "vfmacc.vv  v31, v15, v7"
```

Listing 1.5. Update of last row/col. of A_c/B_c.

```
1   #define KERNEL16x4_SAVE \
2   // Use v8 to store alpha.
3   "vfmv.v.f   v8,   %[ALPHA]     "\
4
5   // Load elements 0-3 of column 0 of C.
6   "vle.v      v0,   (%[C0])      "\
7   "addi       t4,   %[C0], 4*4   "\
8   // Load elements 4-7 of column 0 of C.
9   "vle.v      v1,   (%[C1])      "\
10  "addi       t5,   %[C1], 4*4   "\
11  // Load elements 8-11 of column 0 of C.
12  "vle.v      v2,   (%[C2])      "\
13  "addi       t6,   %[C2], 4*4   "\
14  // Load elements 12-15 of column 0 of C.
15  "vle.v      v3,   (%[C3])      "\
16  "addi       t3,   %[C3], 4*4   "\
17
18  // Scale elements 0-3 of col. 0.
19  "vfmacc.vv  v0,   v8, v16 "\
20  // Load elements 0-3 of column 1 of C.
21  "vle.v      v4,   (t4)         "\
22  // Scale elements 4-7 of col. 0.
23  "vfmacc.vv  v1,   v8, v20 "\
24  // Load elements 4-7 of column 1 of C.
25  "vle.v      v5,   (t5)         "\
26  // Scale elements 8-11 of col. 0.
27  "vfmacc.vv  v2,   v8, v24 "\
28  // Load elements 8-11 of column 1 of C.
29  "vle.v      v6,   (t6)         "\
30  // Scale elements 12-15 of col. 0.
31  "vfmacc.vv  v3,   v8, v28 "\
32  // Load elements 12-15 of column 1 of C.
33  "vle.v      v7,   (t3)         "\
34  // Scale elements 0-3 of col. 1.
35  "vfmacc.vv  v4,   v8, v17 "\
36  // Store elements 0-3 of column 0 of C.
37  "vse.v      v0,   (%[C0])      "\
38  "add        %[C0], %[C0], 8*4  "\
39  // Scale elements 4-7 of col. 1.
40  "vfmacc.vv  v5,   v8, v21 "\
41  // Store elements 4-7 of column 0 of C.
42  "vse.v      v1,   (%[C1])      "\
43  "add        %[C1], %[C1], 8*4  "\
44  // Scale elements 8-11 of col. 1.
45  "vfmacc.vv  v6,   v8, v25 "\
46  // Store elements 8-11 of column 0 of C.
47  "vse.v      v2,   (%[C2])      "\
48  "add        %[C2], %[C2], 8*4  "\
49  // Scale elements 12-15 of col. 1.
50  "vfmacc.vv  v7,   v8, v29 "\
51  // Store elements 12-15 of column 0 of C.
52  "vse.v      v3,   (%[C3])      "\
53  "add        %[C3], %[C3], 8*4  "\
54  // Repeat pipelined procedure for all cols. of C.
55  // (...) Omitted for brevity.
```

Listing 1.6. Final scale of accumulators by α and store to C.

adheres to the RISC-V architecture, with support for RVV version 0.7.1. Each core utilises a deep 12-stage pipeline, out-of-order, multi-issue superscalar architecture. Our core version integrates a 64-KByte, 2-way associative L1 data cache; plus a 1-MByte, 16-way associative L2 data cache (shared with the remaining cores). The hardware data prefetching was active in our setup. According to the documentation, two vector slices (pipelines) with 128-bit vector length (VLEN) are in place. With this configuration, the C910 can produce one 256-bit operation per clock cycle, and complete a 128-bit vector load/store.

XuantieM (XuanTie C908). We employed a CanMV-K230 integrating a K230 system-on-chip (SoC). The CPU subsystem in the SoC is a *"big-LITTLE"* dual-core, with two 64-bit RISC-V C908 processors working at 1.6 GHz and

800 MHz, respectively. In our study, we exclusively employ the *big* core, which supports the RVV version 1.0 on a 128-bit vector process unit, and integrates 32 KB of L1 data cache and 256 KB of L2 cache.

XuantieS (XuanTie C906). We employed a LicheeRv board from Sipeed that integrates an Allwinner D1 system-on-chip (SoC), including a single C906 core running at 1 GHz. The XuanTie C906 is a low-power core targeting IoT applications in severely power-restricted scenarios, yet it includes vector capabilities by supporting RVV version 0.7.1. The core implements a 5-stage single-issue in-order execution pipeline, with support for 128-bit vector processing. Common vector instructions require 3–4 cycles to complete in the pipeline. Our setup includes a 32-KByte, 4-way associative L1 data cache.

Table 2. Summary of the target RISC-V processors.

Name	Processor	Freq. (GHz)	#Cores	ISA (vector)	RAM (GB)	L1 (KB)	L2 (MB)
XuantieL	XuanTie C910	1.85	4	RVV 0.7.1	4.0 LPDDR4	64	1
XuantieM	XuanTie C008	1.60	1	RVV 1.0	0.5 LPDDR4	32	0.25
XuantieS	XuanTie C906	1.00	1	RVV 0.7.1	0.5 LPDDR4	32	0.25

The dimensions of the two target problems, BERT-Base ($BERT_B$) and BERT-Large ($BERT_L$), are collected in Table 1 (right). In the experiments we vary the number of tokens ($l = 128, 384$) and number of samples. Given the considerable superior memory capacity of XuantieL (4 GB) over XuantieS, XuantieM (512 MB in both cases), we set $b = 1, 32, 128$ for the former and $b = 1, 4, 8$ for the other two. Choosing a larger value for b either exhausts the memory, impeding the execution of the problem, or produces memory swapping resulting in a significant performance drop.

In our trials, each test is iterated for a minimum of 5 s. The following results correspond to average values. All computations are conducted using single precision floating point (FP32) arithmetic. Although 16-bit formats such as FP16 or BF16 are widely utilised for inference, it is noteworthy that none of the chosen processors provide hardware support for these. Nevertheless, we anticipate that a 16-bit FP performance analysis would yield similar conclusions.

4.2 Results

The plots in Fig. 4 display the average time per transformer block and the distribution of the costs for $BERT_B$ and $BERT_L$ for different numbers of tokens and samples. The results from this first experiment offer several insights *that characterise the inference performance of an encoder-only transformer on the* **RISC-V** *processors:*

– The primary contributor to execution time is the computation of six large GEMM operations, namely M1, M2, M3, M9, F11, and F13. As the values of b and/or l increase, the contribution of the two BGEMM operations (M5–M7) and, particularly, the Softmax operation becomes more prominent. The

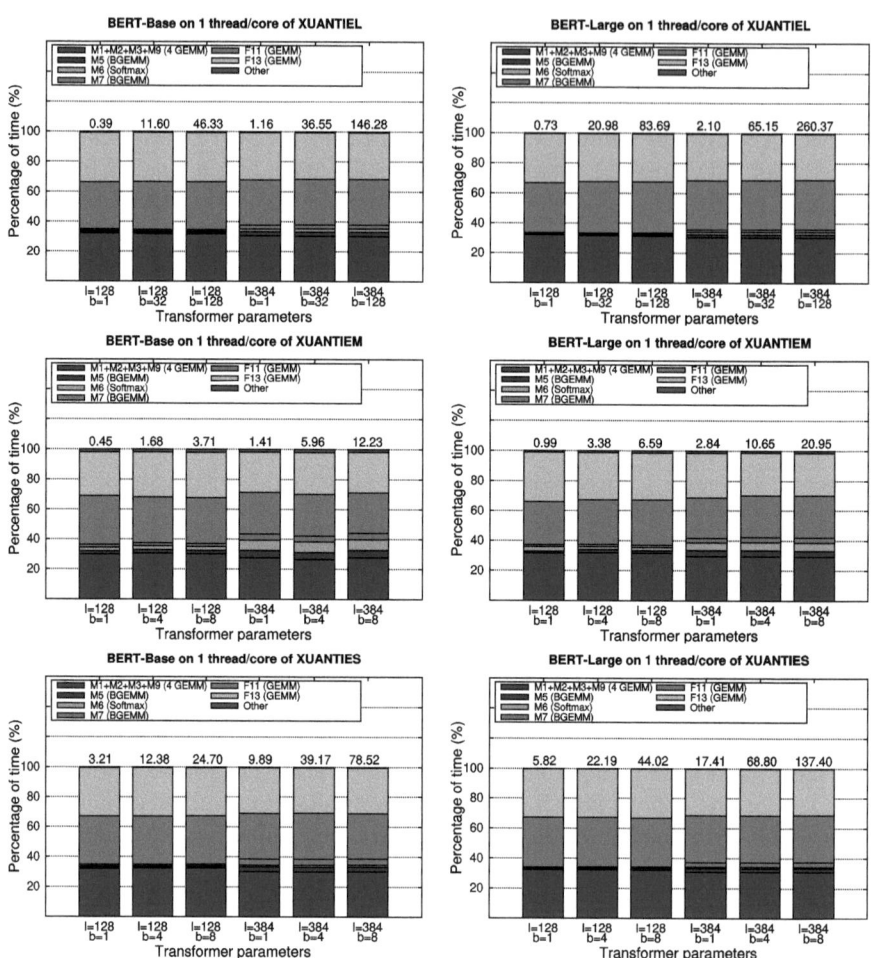

Fig. 4. Performance characterisation of BERT$_B$ (left) and BERT$_L$ (right) on the three boards targeted in this work: XUANTIEL (top), XUANTIEM (middle), and XUANTIES (bottom). The number on top of each bar display the average execution time per transformer block (in seconds).

computational cost of the remaining operations, essentially involving Lnorm with matrix addition and GELU, can be deemed negligible in all cases.
– Consistent with the cost analysis of the transformer block in Table 1, the execution time predominantly exhibits a linear growth with b. For example, in the case of BERT$_L$ executed on XUANTIEL and $l = 384$, the execution time escalates from 65.15 s at $b = 32$ to 260.37 s at $b = 128$. This progression reflects a factor of 4.0×, aligning precisely with the ratio 128/32. Table 3 offers a more detailed analysis, showing the breakdown of execution time for the distinct operations in in the transformer block. The three columns in the

middle of that table show that, when b is increased by a factor of 4 (from $b = 32$ to $b = 128$), the execution time of all the operations in the encoder grows linearly following that factor.
- The behaviour of the execution time is linear for GEMM and quadratic for BGEMM and Softmax on l, resulting in a combined global effect. To illustrate this, the three rightmost columns in Table 3 display the breakdown of the execution time, for $BERT_L$ executed on XUANTIE, setting b to 128. This experiment shows two distinct trends, depending on the type of operation. Concretely, 1) the execution time of the GEMM operations (M1+M2+M3+M9, F11, and F13) grows by a factor of 3, which is consistent with the increase from $l = 128$ to $l = 384$; 2) The execution time of BGEMM and Softmax grows by a factor of about 9, which is coherent with a quadratic increase with respect to l. The overall impact thus depends on the contribution of each operation to the transformer encoder, exposed in Fig. 4.

Table 3. Breakdown of execution time (in seconds) per operation on XUANTIE.

Operation	$BERT_L$ ($l = 384$)			$BERT_L$ $b = 128$		
	$b = 32$	$b = 128$	Ratio	$l = 128$	$l = 384$	Ratio
M1+M2+M3+M9	19.70	78.70	3.99	26.30	78.70	2.99
M5	1.39	5.46	3.93	0.65	5.46	8.36
M6	1.10	4.37	3.97	0.48	4.37	9.07
M7	1.21	4.87	4.02	0.57	4.87	8.50
F11	21.40	85.80	4.01	28.60	85.80	3.00
F13	20.00	79.70	3.99	26.60	79.70	3.00
Other	0.35	1.47	4.20	0.49	1.47	3.00
Total	65.15	260.37	4.00	83.69	260.37	3.11

As part of our performance characterisation, we also investigate the parallel scalability of the transformer encoder, discerning three types of computational components: GEMM, BGEMM, and Softmax. Figure 5 depicts the speed-up of these components for the two BERT-based encoders when operating on all four cores of the XUANTIE. The blue bars show that GEMM offers speed-ups around 3.5 for $BERT_B$ and 3.2 for $BERT_L$, which are consistent with the number of cores. The red bars depict less favourable speed-ups for BGEMM, close to 2, regardless of the transformer encoder. This poor scalability is due to the small size of the BGEMM operands. Regarding the third component, the green bars show the results for Softmax, showing a less stable behaviour, in some cases with a scalability comparable to that obtained by BGEMM and in other cases even surpassing that of GEMM. Finally, the overall scalability of the transformer encoder is very similar to that of GEMM, because this operation clearly dominates the total execution time on this particular platform (see Fig. 4).

To complete the inference characterisation of $BERT_B$ and $BERT_L$ on RISC-V processors, Fig. 6 compares the three target platforms in terms of *token processing throughput*. The comparison could have been done using the more conventional ratio *tokens per second* (i.e., $l \cdot b / Time$ in seconds), but this would be

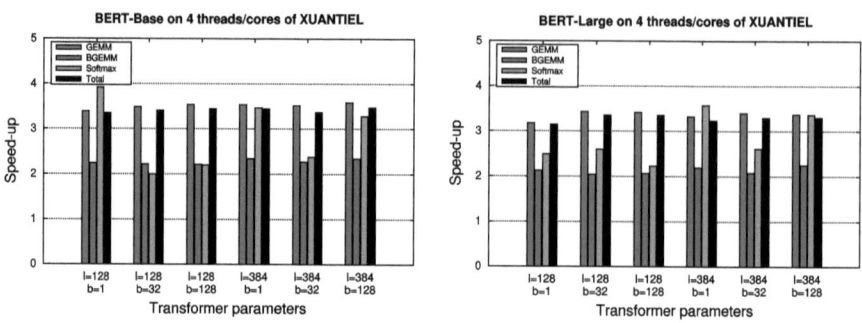

Fig. 5. Speed-up of BERT$_B$ (left) and BERT$_L$ (right) on XUANTIEL using 4 threads.

biased by the fact that the processors operate at different frequencies. To avoid this effect, we normalise the ratio to the processor frequency (f, in GHz), reporting instead $(l \cdot b)/(Time \cdot f)$. The plots reveal that the most efficient platform, according to the normalized throughput, is XUANTIEL, followed by XUANTIEM, while the least efficient is XUANTIES. In the plots some bars are missing because the experiments with large b could not be run on XUANTIES and XUANTIEM. Finally, a comparison of both transformer encoders shows that the throughput in BERT$_B$ is almost twice that of BERT$_L$, regardless of the platform. This result was expected a priori because the latter comprises more layers and these are more complex.

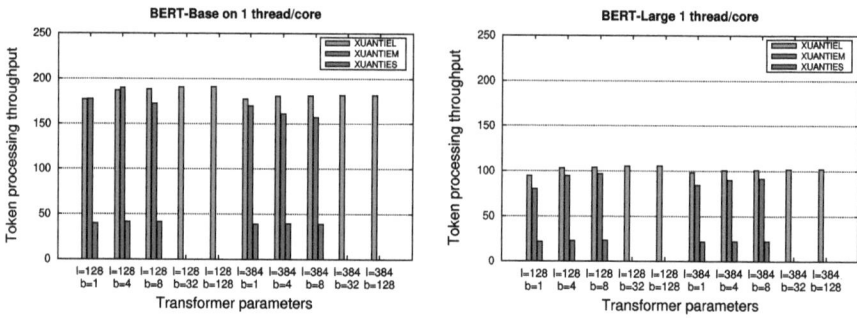

Fig. 6. Token processing throughput, normalized to processor frequency, for BERT$_B$ (left) and BERT$_L$ (right) using 1 thread.

5 Concluding Remarks

We have provided a comprehensive characterisation of two representative configurations of the inference process with the BERT Transformer, a state-of-the-art class of models for NLP tasks, on several RISC-V platforms. Through detailed experimentation and analysis, we have explored the performance and efficiency of BERT when deployed on low-power RISC-V architectures. Our findings shed light on the challenges and opportunities associated with running complex deep learning models on RISC-V platforms, which are gaining prominence as open-source hardware for running both Internet-of-Things (IoT) and high-performance computing workloads.

In our investigation, we have uncovered the impact of several aspects related to transformer execution. First, we provide a detailed breakdown of the most computationally expensive operations within the encoder, which paves the way for identifying optimisation opportunities. We have also provided a study that analyses the scalability of a multi-core RISC-V platform, which further identifies optimisation challenges. Finally, we have performed a comparison of the different platforms in terms of token processing throughput.

Acknowledgements. Research funded by projects PID2020-113656RB-C22, PID2021-126576NB-I00, PID2021-123627OB-C52, TED2021-129334B-I00, TED2021-130123B-I00 (MCIN/AEI/10.13039/5011 00011033), GVA CIPROM/2022/20, UJI-2023-04. H. M. is a POSTDOC_21_00025 fellow supported by Junta de Andalucía. S. C. is supported by grant RYC2021-033973-I, funded by MCIN/AEI/10.13039/501100011033 and the EU "NextGenerationEU"/PRTR, and UJI-2023-04, funded by UJI.

References

1. Brown, T.B., et al.: Language Models are Few-Shot Learners (2020). arxiv.org/abs/2005.14165
2. Chitty-Venkata, K.T., et al.: A survey of techniques for optimizing transformer inference. J. Syst. Archit. **144**, 102990 (2023)
3. Devlin, J., et al.: BERT: pre-training of deep bidirectional transformers for language understanding. In: Proceedings 2019 Conference of the North American Chapter of the ACL: Human Language Technologies, vol. 1, pp. 4171–4186 (2019)
4. Dongarra, J.J., Du Croz, J., Hammarling, S., Hanson, R.J.: An extended set of FORTRAN basic linear algebra subprograms. ACM Trans. Math. Softw. **14**(1), 1–17 (1988)
5. Dosovitskiy, A., et al.: An Image is Worth 16×16 Words: Transformers for Image Recognition at Scale (2021). arxiv.org/abs/2010.11929
6. Goto, K., van de Geijn, R.A.: Anatomy of high-performance matrix multiplication. ACM Trans. Math. Softw. **34**(3), 12:1-12:25 (2008)
7. Hennessy, J.L., Patterson, D.A.: A new golden age for computer architecture. Comm. ACM **62**(2), 48–60 (2019)
8. Igual, F., Piñuel, L., Catalán, S., Martínez, H., Castelló, A., Quintana-Ortí, E.: Automatic generation of micro-kernels for performance portability of matrix multiplication on RISC-V vector processors. In: Proceedings of the SC '23 Workshops of The International Conference on High Performance Computing, Network, Storage, and Analysis, pp. 1523–1532. SC-W '23, ACM, New York, NY, USA (2023)
9. Pati, S., et al.: Demystifying BERT: system design implications. In: 2022 IEEE International Symposium Workload Characterization (IISWC), pp. 296–309 (2022)

10. Raffel, C., et al.: Exploring the limits of transfer learning with a unified text-to-text transformer. J. Mach. Learn. Res. **21**(1), (2020)
11. Touvron, H., Cord, M., Jégou, H.: DeiT III: Revenge of the ViT. In: Computer Vision – ECCV 2022: 17th European Conference, Tel Aviv, Israel, October 23–27, 2022, Proceedings, Part XXIV, pp. 516–533. Springer-Verlag, Berlin, Heidelberg (2022)
12. Vaswani, A., et al.: Attention is all you need. Adv. Neural Inf. Process. Syst. **30**, 5998–6008 (2017)

Integrating RISC-V SIMT and Scalar Cores: Loosely to Tightly Coupled

Sooraj Chetput[1](✉), Anusuya Nallathambi[1](✉), Spencer Bowles[1], Justin Cambridge[1], Alex Chitsazzadeh[1], Gagan Gundala[1], Zengxiang Han[1], Johnathan Hong[1], Guilliame Hu[1], Ronit Nallagatla[1], Ansh Patel[1], Khoi Pham[1], Abinands Ramshanker[1], Htet Yan[1], FangLing Zhang[1], Zach Lagpacan[1], Clay Hughes[2], Kevin Pedretti[2], Mark Johnson[1], and Timothy G. Rogers[1]

[1] Purdue University, West Lafayette, IN 49706, USA
schetput@purdue.edu
[2] Sandia National Laboratories, Albuquerque, NM 87123, USA

Abstract. This paper investigates the integration of SIMT and scalar cores using the RISC-V based Vortex GPGPU. Initially, we detail a conventional integration with Purdue's SoCET SoC AFTx07 that follows the standard host-device CPU-GPU model found in contemporary products. Subsequently, we propose two innovative architectures designed to address control flow divergence, which impedes efficiency in parallel computing by causing threads to follow divergent execution paths. The first architecture introduces a system where threads are statically prioritized based on degrees of divergence: high-priority threads (highly divergent) are allocated to a scalar core, and lower-priority (less divergent) ones to the SIMT core, based on modifications to the Vortex GPU. Although preliminary results show improved performance for scalar core threads, the static nature of thread priority assignment results in unpredictable performance enhancements due to the scheduler's limited foresight on runtime fluctuations of thread divergence. The second architecture, currently under development, proposes a mechanism for runtime thread migration, setting a foundation for a system capable of adjusting to runtime conditions. A future, conceptual third architecture aims to dynamically assess the divergence of each thread, optimizing the integration of SIMT and scalar cores for advanced computing. This progression outlines a strategic approach to mitigate control flow divergence, promising a significant leap towards achieving higher efficiency in parallel processing systems.

Keywords: RISC-V · HPC · GPGPU · SIMT · Control Flow Divergence

1 Introduction

A Single Instruction Multiple Thread (SIMT) architecture is a model of parallel computing designed to optimize data processing by executing the same instruction across multiple threads simultaneously, each operating on different data sets. This architecture is a hallmark of General Purpose Graphics Processing Units (GPGPUs), where it significantly enhances computational efficiency and throughput for tasks amenable to parallelization. By harnessing the power of thread-level parallelism within a unified instruction stream, the SIMT model strategically merges the simplicity of single-instruction processing with the robust scalability of multi-threaded execution paradigms, offering an elegant solution to the challenges of modern computing demands and ensuring high performance in applications ranging from complex scientific simulations to real-time graphics rendering.

In this work, we explore the integration of SIMT and scalar cores within the Vortex GPGPU, revealing the potential for elevated performance and efficiency in computing applications. We leverage a specific implementation of the SIMT model, Georgia Tech's Vortex GPGPU [1–3], to explore different degrees of integration between SIMT and scalar cores. The Vortex GPGPU emobides the principles of SIMT within an open-source framework; it is based on a modified RISC-V Instruction Set Architecture (ISA), integrating custom instructions designed to optimize the SIMT stack.

The first of the three models we discuss is a loosely coupled configuration, where the Vortex GPGPU is integrated with the RISC-V based Purdue SoCET AFTx07 [14–18] microprocessor and taped-out. Such a configuration, where the CPU and GPU are connected via a bus, is prevalent in many commercial products which maximizes the utility of parallel processing.

Next, we explore two novel architectures that tightly couple the SIMT and scalar cores. The goal of these two architectures is to mitigate control flow divergence, which is found within the SIMT Stack. Control flow divergence occurs when different threads in a warp (a group of threads executed together) take different execution paths due to conditional branches. This divergence presents a significant challenge because SIMT architectures are designed to execute one instruction across all threads simultaneously. When the execution paths diverge, the SIMT pipeline handles the diverging paths sequentially rather than in parallel, negatively impacting the overall performance (see Fig. 1).

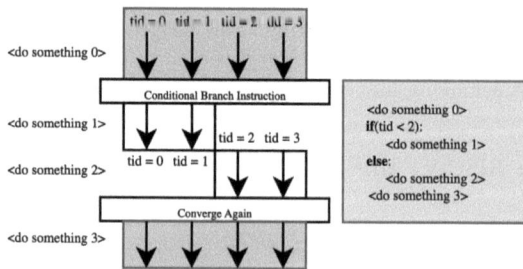

Fig. 1. Control Flow Divergence With Post-Dominator Analysis for Re-convergence

Immediate Post Dominator (IPDOM) analysis addresses this issue by identifying points in the program where divergent paths reconverge, ensuring threads execute in lock-step synchronization as much as possible. When divergence occurs, the IPDOM method serializes the execution of the divergent paths, running one path at a time while other threads wait. This method often involves executing an instruction from one path, followed by one from another path, alternating as such to prevent deadlocks that can occur due to inter-thread dependencies. The process culminates at the Immediate Post Dominator point, where threads from divergent paths can re-converge and resume execution in complete synchronization. The disadvantage of this is that SIMT lanes might be under-utilized. The concept of dynamic warp formation has been proposed to enhance SIMT lane utilization by dynamically grouping threads based on their execution paths. This method aims to create warps that can execute without divergence, maximizing the utilization of the SIMT lanes. However, implementing dynamic warp formation in hardware is challenging due to the significant overhead involved in dynamically reorganizing threads [4].

We propose tightly coupling a SIMT and scalar core, both built on the RISC-V ISA. The idea is to efficiently allocate threads based on their divergence level, directing more divergent threads to the scalar core and less divergent ones to the SIMT core. We define the highly divergent threads as *high-priority* threads and all others as *low-priority*. We introduce two architectural designs for which we implement the RTL. For each of these, the scalar core that is coupled with the SIMT execution unit is different from the host CPU.

The first architecture, V1, assigns threads based on static priority, which is assigned randomly by the software. Threads deemed to be high-priority are executed on the scalar core and low-priority threads are executed on the SIMT core. This architecture is implemented by modifying the Vortex GPU. It reveals that the threads allocated to the scalar core execute faster than those on the SIMT core in the presence of divergence and proves the possibility of using such an architecture to speed up highly divergent threads. However, the static approach is unable to determine the run-time divergence in the SIMT core, which can harm performance if the low-priority threads become highly divergent and cause congestion in the SIMT core. In order to ensure the minimum possible execution time, thread priorities need to be determined at runtime and the threads should be able to switch their execution context from the SIMT to the scalar core.

The second architecture, V2, allows for run-time thread migration from the SIMT to the scalar core. However, this version does not solve the issue of thread priority assessment based on runtime conditions, instead focusing on enabling thread migration to optimize execution. It is crucial to note that the V2 architecture is currently in the implementation phase, and as such, empirical data and performance analysis are pending. We also briefly discuss a V3 architecture design that solves the priority assessment problem in the future works section.

2 Vortex GPGPU Tapeout

In this section, we discuss the integration of the Vortex GPGPU with the RISC-V based Purdue SoCET AFTx07 SoC Chip, creating a tape-out ready chip. In this integration, tasks are allocated to the GPU by the CPU via the on-chip AHB bus, effectively following the host-device CPU-GPU model. This architecture resembles a microcontroller with augmented parallel processing capabilities.

2.1 Implementation

The SoCET design features an Advanced High-performance Bus (AHB) that interconnects several core components, including a RISC-V RV32IMCZicsrZifencei unicore Central Processing Unit (CPU), a Direct Memory Access (DMA) controller, and a memory controller [19]. Additionally, an Advanced Peripheral Bus (APB) is connected to the AHB through an AHB-APB bridge, facilitating communication with various board-level peripheral interface protocol pin drivers. The Vortex GPGPU is integrated with the AHB. This enables the Vortex GPGPU to initiate bus requests, granting it access to the local memory system. The relationship between the AFTx07, the Vortex GPGPU, and the integration modules we developed are highlighted in Fig. 2.

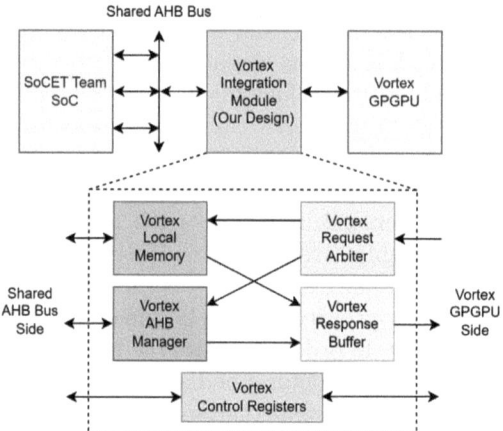

Fig. 2. Vortex GPGPU Tapeout Architecture. The SoCET Team SoC and Vortex GPGPU interface using the depicted integration modules.

2.2 Software Interface

Driver programmers are exposed to three AHB bus accessible memory-mapped control/status registers: Start Register, Start Address Register, and Status Register. The Start Register initiates GPU execution at an explicit program counter address specified by the Start Address Register. While the GPU executes, the CPU is free to do independent work, as well as poll the Status Register, which signals the completion of the GPU workload.

CPU drivers are developed to facilitate the placement of GPU programs in local or global memory and periodically poll GPU status. GPU kernel development is facilitated by using Vortex's custom instructions through C intrinsics.

2.3 Design Flow Process

The design flow process can be broken down into the front-end design and back-end design. This section will focus on the back-end implementation including synthesis and physical design to support the tapeout of the design.

We explored multiple configurations of the design varying the size of memory, the number of programmable warps, and the inclusion of a floating-point unit (FPU) to understand their impact on area and usage. We settled on four synthesized netlist configurations to pursue further for placement and routing, details of which are outlined in Table 1.

We then ran those through the physical design process, which involves partitioning the chip into smaller blocks, floor-planning the blocks on the die, placing the standard cells, building the clock tree network, and routing the wires through the chip. Each of these steps is iterative and undergoes many rounds of incremental optimization to meet power, performance, and area requirements.

Table 1. Netlist Configuration Summary

Netlist Configuration Summary				
Metrics	Config 1	Config 2	Config 3	Config 4
Cores-Threads-Warps	1–4–4	1–4–4	1–4–4	1–4–2
i-cache size	1 kB	2 kB	1 kB	1 kB
d-cache size	2 kB	4 kB	2 kB	4 kB
Shared memory	1 kB/thread	1 kB/thread	512 B/thread	1 kB/thread
Local memory	4 kB	4 kB	4 kB	4 kB
FPU	No	Yes	Yes	Yes
Area estimate	29 mm^2(Netlist)	34 mm^2(PD)	20 mm^2(Netlist)	21 mm^2(PD)

Results and Evaluation. Given the constraints from the Process Design Kit (PDK), we had to scale down the design by reducing the number of parallel warps and size of memory for the design to fit on the die. Figure 3 shows the results of taking Config 4 through the physical design flow. Looking at Fig. 4, we observe that most of the die area is being utilized by memory which has been synthesized as flip-flops due to the lack of SRAM macro cells in our PDK (Fig. 5). Figure 6 shows the total area trend for the different configurations.

2.4 Discussion

This architecture is an integration of the GPU onto an AHB bus scaled for an embedded microcontroller. This means that the bus is the performance bottleneck and limits the scalability of the design. Moreover, the size of the integrated GPU needed to be significantly reduced due to chip area limitations for the target tapeout technology available to us. This required limiting the number of concurrent threads and warps, greatly reducing the parallel capabilities of the GPU, likely limiting what applications can achieve practical execution times.

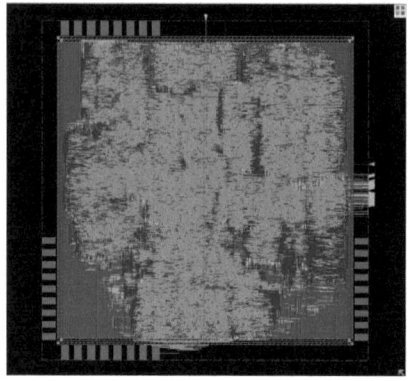

Fig. 3. SoC+Vortex Physical View

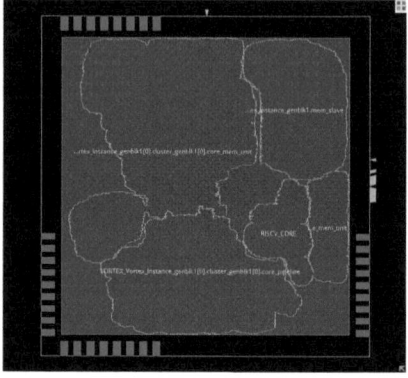

Fig. 4. SoC+Vortex Amoeba View

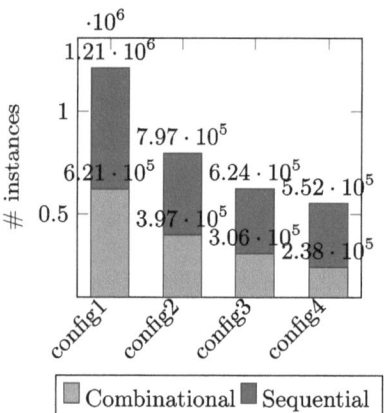

Fig. 5. No. of Instances for each Netlist Configuration

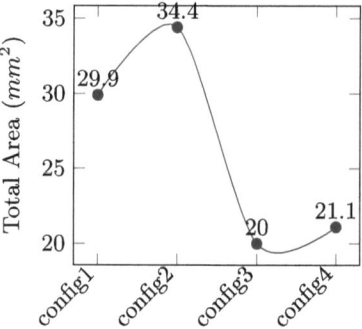

Fig. 6. Total Area for each Netlist Configuration

3 The SIMT-Scalar V1 Architecture

In this section, we discuss the V1 architecture, our initial version of the tightly integrated scalar and SIMT core designed to address control flow divergence in SIMT architectures. The V1 architecture couples the two cores at the software thread scheduler level: high-priority threads are assigned to the scalar core and low-priority threads are batched into warps and assigned to the SIMT core. The priorities of the threads are statically determined by the software.

No hardware is shared between the SIMT and the scalar core except the L1 Cache. Each core has its own bus connected to L1 through a round-robin based memory scheduler. Figure 7 shows the core and cache organization. For a cluster with N cores, N/2 cores are defined as scalar cores and the others are SIMT cores (Figs. 8, 9).

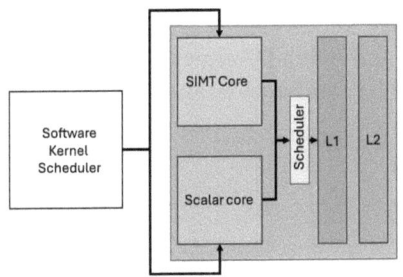

Fig. 7. SIMT-Scalar V1 Architecture

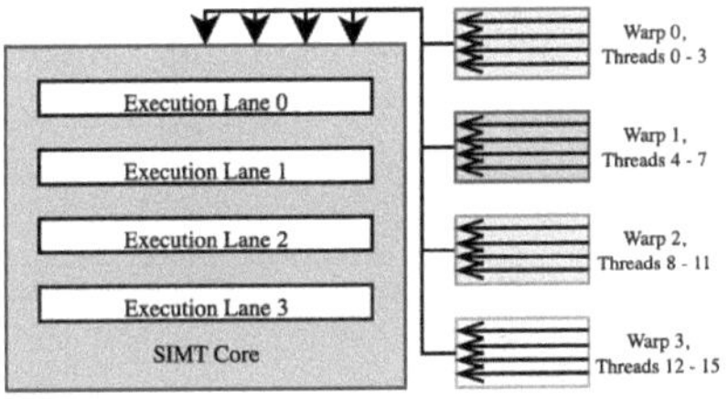

Fig. 8. SIMT Execution Lanes, Warps, and Threads

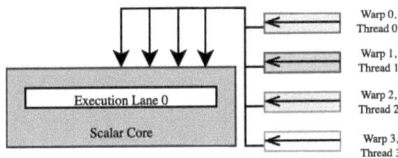

Fig. 9. Scalar Execution Lane, Scalar Threads

3.1 Scalar Core

The Vortex GPGPU's RTL is designed such that the number of warps per core and threads per warp are defined as a common parameter across the system. To create the scalar core out of the SIMT core, we modified the RTL so that the number of threads per warp can be tuned individually for each core. Setting the number of threads per warp to 1 effectively creates a scalar core. All the SIMT cores and scalar cores are assigned unique core IDs.

3.2 High Priority Thread Scheduler

The Vortex GPGPU's code base includes a software thread scheduler. The user program is compiled with the scheduler and the host CPU launches this combined binary onto the Vortex GPGPU. Once launched, the scheduler assigns the threads to the individual cores from the program's PC address. We added a custom high-priority thread scheduler to the default Vortex scheduler. The left over low-priority threads are grouped into warps and assigned to the SIMT cores by the default scheduler. Note that both the sets of threads run the same program.

3.3 Data

The Benchmarks: The benchmarks encompass custom programs that generate varying degrees of control flow divergence. The "No Divergence" program performs a straightforward vector addition. The "Low Divergence" scenario alternates between vector addition for even threads and vector subtraction for odd threads. Programs classified under "Medium" and "High Divergence" incorporate loops and intricate branching, such as nested if statements and switch statements, to induce execution path serialization.

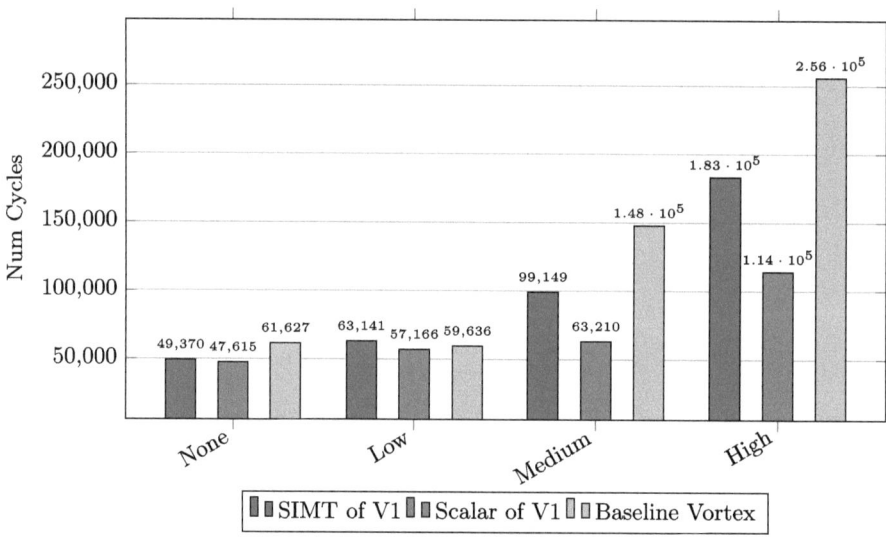

Fig. 10. Num Cycles Comparison for SIMT and Scalar Cores of V1 Architecture Across Divergence Levels vs. the Baseline Vortex.

The Benchmark Programs. This test case aims to completely randomize the control flow, results in the greatest divergence. We give this as an example test to give the reader a feel on what type of programs we used for testing.

```c
void kernel_body(int task_id, kernel_arg_t* __UNIFORM__ arg) {
    uint32_t count    = arg->task_size;
    int32_t* s0 = (int32_t*)arg->src0_addr;
    int32_t* s1 = (int32_t*)arg->src1_addr;
    int32_t* dst_ptr  = (int32_t*)arg->dst_addr;
    offset = taskID * count;

    for (uint32_t i = offset; i < offset + count; ++i) {
        if (taskID % 2 == 0) {
            if (s0[i] % 2 == 0 && s1[i] % 2 == 0)
                dstPtr[i] = s0[i] + s1[i];
            else if (s0[i] % 2 == 1 && s1[i] % 2 == 0)
                dstPtr[i] = src0Ptr[i] - s1[i];
            else if (s0[i] % 2 == 0 && s1[i] % 2 == 1)
                dstPtr[i] = s0[i] * s1[i];
            else
                dstPtr[i] = 2 * s0[i] - s1[i];
        } else {
            if (s0[i] % 2 == 1 && s1[i] % 2 == 1)
                dstPtr[i] = s0[i] + s1[i];
            else if (s0[i] % 2 == 0 && s1[i] % 2 == 0)
                dstPtr[i] = src0Ptr[i] - s1[i];
            else if (s0[i] % 2 == 0 && s1[i] % 2 == 1)
                dstPtr[i] = s0[i] * s1[i];
            else
                dstPtr[i] = 2 * s0[i] - s1[i];
        }
    }
}
```

Interpreting the Results: In our experiments, 16 threads were executed on the SIMT core in warps of four threads, while the scalar core processed four threads. The total execution time is the max(SIMT Execution Time, Scalar Execution Time) in the graph in Fig. 10. As code divergence increased, the scalar core demonstrated superior performance over the SIMT core. The scalar core consistently outperformed the SIMT core, confirming its efficacy in managing high control flow divergence.

Additionally, there is a gap in the number of cycles that the SIMT core does and the Scalar core does. This means that dynamically moving threads into the Scalar core should help bring down the total number of cycles. However, this also has limitations: when every thread diverges in a give warp, there will be no reduction in execution time even if it is moved to the Scalar core because it was always serialized even on the SIMT core. This architecture presents the greatest benefits in terms of execution time for workloads that have a moderate amount of divergence.

3.4 Discussion

There are two primary problems with the V1 design.

Assigning Priority to Threads (Problem 1): Warps that have significant thread divergence can lead to inefficient use of SIMT lanes, leading to performance degradation. Threads responsible for such divergence are best processed by the scalar core. However, the process of assigning threads to the scalar core relies on static priorities determined by the software. But, the software is not aware of the workload's runtime branch divergence patterns and fluctuations which renders the system performance effectively random and unpredictable.

Inefficient Scalar Core (Problem 2): The scalar core is a single lane version of the SIMT pipeline. Due to the design choices of an SIMT pipeline, it lacks optimizations for handling branch divergence and hazards. The thread latency of the scalar core can be improved yet by adding optimizations such as branch predictor, operand forwarding, etc.

4 The SIMT-Scalar V2 Architecture

4.1 Solving the Problems with V1

Dynamic Thread Transfer (Solving Problem 1): To solve the issue of control flow divergence, the scalar core must be equipped to intelligently prioritize divergent threads. This can be decomposed into two sub-problems: determining the divergent threads, and establishing a mechanism for migrating them from the SIMT to the scalar core.

The V2 architecture solely offers a mechanism to facilitate thread transfer during program execution. The thread priorities are still statically determined by the host CPU. For a comprehensive solution that addresses the smart thread selection, refer to the future works section.

Latency Sensitive Scalar Core (Solving Problem 2): To improve the scalar core's execution time, a simple "not-taken" branch predictor is implemented. Additionally, the multi-threaded scalar core of V1 is modified to a single threaded pipeline.

4.2 The V2 System

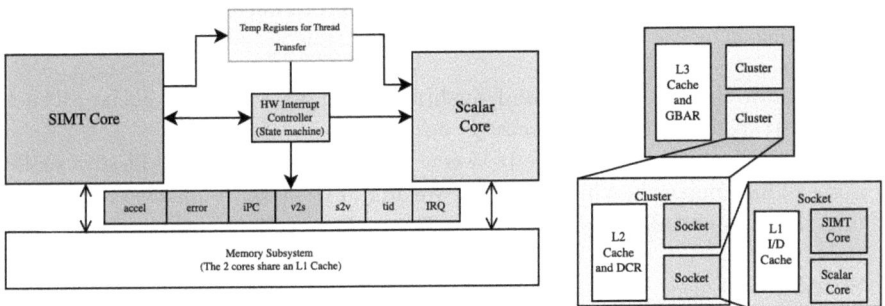

Fig. 11. V2 Architecture overview. Scalar core communicates to SIMT core via interrupts. The figure on the right demonstrates the hierarchy of the heterogeneous core.

Initiating Thread Transfer: The initial thread scheduling is orchestrated by a Kernel Scheduler on the SIMT core. Once the warps are running on the SIMT core, it signals the scalar core to start accelerating the high-priority threads.

Threads are not directly scheduled to the scalar core by the high-priority thread scheduler. The scalar core accelerates the workload by removing the divergent threads from the SIMT core. Note that the V2 arch does not define the logic for the scalar core to assess which threads are highly divergent. However, we concluded that this design would be most adaptable to future architectures where the support is provided.

Communication Between SIMT Core and Scalar Core: The scalar core's scheduler begins by waiting for a signal from the SIMT core. Upon receiving the signal, the scalar core selects the highest priority thread from the thread priority array provided by the software and communicates it to the SIMT core via doorbell registers. The doorbell registers are implemented using the Control Status Register (CSR) instructions, which are included in the original Vortex ISA.

Role of Hardware Interrupt Controller: The hardware interrupt controller detects a transfer request by looking at the "S2V" register and interrupts the warp that contains the selected thread. The interrupt service routine (ISR) copies the thread context to a temporary register file that is shared between the SIMT and Scalar Cores. These are also implemented using the CSR instructions. A custom Return from Interrupt (RTI) instruction is then used by the ISR to allow the interrupted warp to properly resume execution.

Sharing Memory Between the SIMT and Scalar Core: The shared L1 cache between the scalar and SIMT cores, as illustrated in Fig. 11, is designed to ensure efficient data transfer when threads are moved from the SIMT to the scalar core. This design decision is based on the evaluation of three potential mechanisms:

1. Utilizing a shared L2 cache and flushing the SIMT core's L1 cache at each thread transfer, which was deemed too slow.
2. Implementing cache coherence between the L1 caches of the SIMT and scalar cores. This approach, while possible, was found to be both hardware-intensive and slow, potentially leading to coherence misses in the L1 cache of the scalar core.
3. Sharing a banked L1 cache between both cores, allowing for efficient read access with minimal waiting. This option was selected as the simplest and most efficient solution.

The selected configuration ensures swift and efficient availability of data to the scalar core, facilitating the thread transfer process and improving the overall performance of the system.

A Weirdness with the Return Address. All threads are initially launched in the SIMT core, meaning that when they set their return address, they return to the SIMT core's software scheduler. However, if a thread is transferred to the Scalar core, it should instead return to the Scalar core scheduler. It is crucial not to overwrite the return address register when launching the thread on the Scalar core, as it may contain the return address for a different function called by the kernel.

To solve this, a function called "return address handler" is created, and the location (PC) of this address is written to a special purpose register before scheduling the kernels. When the kernel is launched, the return address is marked as this address stored in the hardware, and the original SIMT return address is written into another special purpose register. If a thread is transferred to the Scalar core, the new return address is also stored in a special purpose register upon thread launch. When a return is initiated from the kernel to the scheduler, the return handler function is executed. This function determines the core on which it is running—either SIMT or Scalar—and loads the correct value into the return address register before executing a jump to that address, ensuring proper return handling across both SIMT and Scalar cores.

4.3 Optimizing Scalar Core for Single Thread Latency

The average branch latency on the Vortex Pipeline is 7.09 cycles. Due to the absence of a branch predictor, the thread is stalled until the branch is resolved. To reduce the single thread latency, we are implementing a not-taken branch predictor. We will incorporate a more robust predictor in the near future.

5 Future Works

The V2 architecture implementation is currently a work in progress and will be fully benchmarked in the near future. Building on the insights gained from V2, we plan to evolve our design further into what we refer to as the V3 architecture.

Solving Thread Priority Assessment: We want to implement the scalar core such that it can make intelligent decisions on the thread it needs to pull from the SIMT core. This involves predicting thread divergence through analysis of branch history and post-dominators, allowing the scalar core to choose threads it anticipates will cause the greatest control flow divergence.

Scaling the Architecture: A natural extension of this architecture involves integrating 'm' SIMT cores with 'n' scalar cores, forming a BIG-little framework. In this setup, the scalar cores would manage the more divergent threads, while the SIMT cores would efficiently process the less divergent threads.

6 Related Works

This idea of CPU-GPU integration has resulted in a huge amount of optimization for a variety of applications [7]. For instance, query processing tasks dealing with shorter lists are better suited towards CPUs, whereas those involving lengthier lists favor GPUs [8–11].

There have been many developments towards achieving better integrated architectures. MIAOW is a GPU implementation that streamlines CPU-GPU integration by being open-source, flexible, and realistic, encouraging development and testing of advanced programming models [13]. On the other hand, there is FGPU which utilizes an open-source, configurable, and scalable GPU soft-core designed for FPGAs [12].

Finally, AMD's GCN architecture [6] employs scalar pipelines to process individual control flow instructions that are common for all the SIMT wavefronts such as function call/return address generation instructions and conditional branches. The compiler decides which instructions implement on the scalar pipeline.

7 Conclusion

Coupling a SIMT architecture with RISC-V cores in can unleash a new realm of computational efficiency and flexibility for HPC applications. This powerful combination can enhance the processing capabilities of post-exascale supercomputers by providing a customizable, open-source instruction set architecture alongside the parallel processing strength of SIMT. The result is an accelerated capacity for complex problem-solving with improved energy efficiency and the potential for more tailored computing solutions.

Building on this foundation, our research delves into the practical applications of combining SIMT and scalar cores, specifically addressing the challenges of control flow divergence. Beginning with the baseline integration of the Vortex GPGPU with the Purdue SoCET's AFTx07 SoC chip, this study laid the groundwork for examining more complex architectures aimed at improving processing efficiency. The V1 architecture, with its static thread priority assignment, shed light on the potential benefits and inherent limitations of such a system in managing divergent threads. This insight led to the development of the V2 architecture, which introduced dynamic thread transfer capabilities and scalar core optimizations designed to reduce single-thread latency and enhance overall system performance.

Looking ahead, the goal is to further refine the scalar core's ability to intelligently manage thread divergence, potentially through advanced predictive models and historical analysis. Additionally, scaling the architecture to include multiple SIMT and scalar cores presents an opportunity to create a flexible and adaptable framework capable of handling a diverse range of computing tasks.

While challenges remain, particularly in terms of dynamic thread prioritization and the scalability of the architecture, the progress made thus far provides a solid foundation for future research. As the field of parallel computing continues to advance, the insights and methodologies developed through this work will contribute to the creation of more efficient and adaptable computing architectures.

References

1. Elsabbagh, F., Asgari, B., Kim, H., Yalamanchili, S.: Vortex RISC-V GPGPU System: Extending the ISA, Synthesizing the Microarchitecture, and Modeling the Software Stack. CARRV (2019)
2. Blaise, T., et al.: Vortex: An Open Source Reconfigurable RISC-V GPGPU Accelerator for Architecture Research. Hot Chips 32 (2020)
3. Tine, B., Yalamarthy, K.P., Elsabbagh, F., Hyesoon, K.: Vortex: extending the RISC-v isa for GPGPU and 3D-Graphics. In: MICRO-54: 54th Annual IEEE/ACM International Symposium on Microarchitecture (2021). https://doi.org/10.1145/3466752.3480128
4. Fung, W.W.L., Sham, I., Yuan, G., Aamodt, T.M.: Dynamic warp formation and scheduling for efficient GPU control flow. In: 40th Annual IEEE/ACM International Symposium on Microarchitecture (MICRO 2007) (2007). https://doi.org/10.1109/micro.2007.30
5. Rhu, M., Erez, M.: The dual-path execution model for efficient GPU control flow. In: 2013 IEEE 19th International Symposium on High Performance Computer Architecture (HPCA) (2013). https://doi.org/10.1109/hpca.2013.6522352
6. White Paper | AMD GRAPHICS CORES NEXT (GCN) ARCHITECTURE (2012)
7. Vetter, J.S., Mittal, S.: Opportunities for nonvolatile memory systems in extreme-scale high-performance computing. Comput. Sci. Eng. **17**, 73–82 (2015). https://doi.org/10.1109/mcse.2015.4

8. Luk, C.-K., Hong, S., Kim, H.: Qilin: exploitng parallelism on heterogeneous multi-processors with adaptive mapping. In: Proceedings of the 42nd Annual IEEE/ACM International Symposium on Microarchitecture (2009). https://doi.org/10.1145/1669112.1669121
9. Nere, A., Franey, S., Hashmi, A., Lipasti, M.: Simulating cortical networks on heterogeneous multi-GPU systems. J. Parallel Distrib. Comput. **73**, 953–971 (2013). https://doi.org/10.1016/j.jpdc.2012.02.006
10. Shen, J., Varbanescu, A.L., Sips, H., et al.: Glinda: A frame work for accelerating imbalanced applications on heterogeneous platforms. Proc. ACM Int. Conf. Comput. Front. (2013). https://doi.org/10.1145/2482767.2482785
11. Ding, S., He, J., Yan, H., Suel, T.: Using graphics processors for high performance IR query processing. In: Proceedings of the 18th International Conference on World Wide Web (2009). https://doi.org/10.1145/1526709.1526766
12. Kadi, M.A., Janssen, B., Yudi, J., Huebner, M.: General-purpose computing with soft GPUS on FPGAS. ACM Trans. Reconf. Technol. Syst. **11**, 1–22 (2018). https://doi.org/10.1145/3173548
13. Balasubramanian, R., Gangadhar, V., Guo, Z., et al.: Miaow - an open source RTL implementation of a GPGPU. In: 2015 IEEE Symposium in Low-Power and High-Speed Chips (COOL CHIPS XVIII) (2015). https://doi.org/10.1109/coolchips.2015.7158663
14. Covey, J., Johnson, M.C.: System-on-a-chip design as a platform for teaching design and design flow integration. In: Proceedings of the 2019 on Great Lakes Symposium on VLSI, Tysons Corner, VA (2019)
15. Stevens, J.R., Skubic, J., Colter, E., Swabey, M.: Purdue microbrewer: a microcontroller generator. In: RISCV Microelectronics Conference 2017 (2017)
16. Skubic, J., Stevens, J.R., Tan, C.Y., Johnson, M., Swabey, M.: RISCV-business: a configurable, extensible RISC-V core. In: RISCV Microelectronics Conference 2017 (2017)
17. Swabey, M.A., Johnson, M.C.: Satisfying ABET criterion using an industrial microelectronic skills incubator. In: 2015 IEEE International Conference on Microelectronics Systems Education (2015)
18. https://engineering.purdue.edu/SoC-Team#chips
19. Waterman, A., Lee, Y., Patterson, D.A., Asanovi, K.: The RISC-V Instruction Set Manual Volume 1: User-Level ISA, Version 20 (2014). https://doi.org/10.21236/ada605735
20. Rhu, M., Erez, M.: The dual-path execution model for efficient GPU control flow. In: 2013 IEEE 19th International Symposium on High Performance Computer Architecture (HPCA) (2013). https://doi.org/10.1109/hpca.2013.6522352
21. NVIDIA: PTX: Parallel Thread Execution ISA version 2.3 (2010). http://developer.nvidia.com/compute/cuda

Performance Characterisation of the 64-Core SG2042 RISC-V CPU for HPC

Nick Brown[(✉)] and Maurice Jamieson

EPCC at the University of Edinburgh, 47 Potterrow, Edinburgh, UK
n.brown@epcc.ed.ac.uk

Abstract. Whilst RISC-V has grown phenomenally quickly in embedded computing, it is yet to gain significant traction in High Performance Computing (HPC). However, as we move further into the exascale era, the flexibility offered by RISC-V has the potential to be very beneficial in future supercomputers especially as the community places an increased emphasis on decarbonising its workloads. Sophon's SG2042 is the first mass produced, commodity available, high-core count RISC-V CPU designed for high performance workloads. First released in summer 2023, and at the time of writing now becoming widely available, a key question is whether this is a realistic proposition for HPC applications.

In this paper we use NASA's NAS Parallel Benchmark (NPB) suite to characterise performance of the SG2042 against other CPUs implementing the RISC-V, x86-64, and AArch64 ISAs. We find that the SG2042 consistently outperforms all other RISC-V solutions, delivering between a 2.6 and 16.7 performance improvement at the single core level. When compared against the x86-64 and AArch64 CPUs, which are commonplace for high performance workloads, we find that the SG2042 performs comparatively well with computationally bound algorithms but decreases in relative performance when the algorithms are memory bandwidth or latency bound. Based on this work, we identify that performance of the SG2042's memory subsystem is the greatest bottleneck.

Keywords: RISC-V · Sophon SG2042 · NAS Parallel Benchmark suite (NPB) · High Performance Computing (HPC)

1 Introduction

RISC-V is an open Instruction Set Architecture (ISA) that, since it was first released over a decade ago, has gained significant traction. At the time of writing it was recently announced that over 13 billion RISC-V CPU cores have been manufactured, but many of these are in embedded computing such as automotive, space, and micro-controllers. RISC-V has yet to become commonplace in High Performance Computing (HPC), but as the HPC community moves further into the exascale era and there is an increased emphasis on decarbonisation of workloads, we need to consider how to best deliver both increased performance and greater energy efficiency. To this end, there is a renewed interest in new hardware solutions and technologies built atop RISC-V have a strong potential here as they can offer specialisation whilst still providing a common software ecosystem.

Sophon's SG2042 is the first high core count commodity available RISC-V CPU designed for high performance workloads. First released in summer 2023, this mass produced, 64-core RISC-V CPU is aimed at high performance workloads. Not only does this processor provide significantly more cores that existing, SoC based, mass produced RISC-V CPUs, but furthermore the T-Head XuanTie C920 cores themselves have been designed for high performance. Consequently this new RISC-V CPU is very interesting to the HPC community and previous work [2] found that, for the RAJAPerf suite [3], it delivers a considerable performance uplift compared to existing commodity available RISC-V CPUs, but struggled to match a set of x86-based CPUs that are commonplace in HPC machines. In this paper we leverage NASA's NAS Parallel Benchmark (NPB) suite to undertake more in depth performance characterisation of the SG2042. Running this suite across CPUs that implement the RISC-V, x86-86 and AArch64 ISAs, and in the later two categories because we have selected CPUs that are used in production supercomputers, we are able to better understand the types of workloads that the SG2042 suits and where it might fall short.

2 Background

2.1 The Sophon SG2042

The Sophon SG2042 CPU is a 64-core processor running at 2 GHz and organised in clusters of four XuanTie C920 cores. Each 64-bit core, designed by T-Head, is designed for high performance workloads and adopts a 12-stage out-of-order multiple issue superscalar pipeline design [7]. Implementing the RV64GCV instruction set, the C920 has three decode, four rename/dispatch, eight issue/execute and two load/store execution units. Version 0.7.1 of the vectorisation standard extension (RVV v0.7.1) is supported [11], with a vector width of 128 bits. Each C920 core contains 64 KB of L1 instruction (I) and data (D) cache, 1 MB of L2 cache which is shared between the cluster of four cores, and 64 MB of L3 system cache which is shared by all cores in the package. The SG2042 also provides four DDR4-3200 memory controllers, and 32 lanes of PCI-E Gen4. The CPU we use for the benchmarking in this paper is contained in a Pioneer Box by Milk-V which has 128 GB of DDR4 RAM.

The SG2042's C920 core only provides RVV v0.7.1 which is not supported by mainline GCC or LLVM. To this end, T-Head have provided their own fork of the GNU compiler (XuanTie GCC) which has been optimised for their processors and supports RVV v0.7.1. It has been found [5] that GCC8.4, which is part of their 20210618 release, provides the best auto-vectorisation capability and-so this is the version we use for the benchmarking experiments undertaken in this paper. Their version of the compiler generates Vector Length Specific (VLS) RVV assembly which specifically targets the 128-bit vector width of the C920. All codes are compiled at optimisation level three, and all reported results are averaged over five runs. At the time of execution each benchmark run reported in this paper was making exclusive use of the machine.

In [2] the authors benchmarked the SG2042 using the RAJAPerf suite, however this was across a large number of individual kernels and from the results it was difficult to isolate and identify individual performance patterns. By contrast, in this paper we characterise and explore each individual benchmark of the NPB suite to better classify the performance properties of the SG2042.

2.2 NAS Parallel Benchmarks (NPB) Suite

The NAS Parallel Benchmark (NPB) suite [1] is a collection of benchmarks developed by NASA's Advanced Supercomputing (NAS) division to characterise HPC systems, especially for Computational Fluid Dynamics (CFD) applications. First released in the mid 1990s, in this paper we leverage the original eight benchmarks in the suite, which comprises five kernels and three pseudo applications. The kernels capture key algorithmic patterns that are ubiquitous throughout HPC codes and test key performance characteristics that are important across many workloads. The pseudo applications combine multiple kernels to provide more complicated workloads. All these benchmarks are configured using a variety of problem sizes known as classes. There are a variety of implementations of the suite provided by NAS, including the OpenMP and MPI versions that we use here, and throughout this paper use the official code without any modifications.

Table 1. Summary of memory behaviour for NPB benchmarks on a Xeon Platinum 8170

Benchmark	Clock ticks cache stall	Clock ticks DDR stall	Time DDR bandwidth bound
Integer Sort (IS)	35%	0%	16%
Multi Grid (MG)	34%	20%	88%
Embarrassingly Parallel (EP)	11%	0%	0%
Conjugate Gradient (CG)	19%	18%	0%
Fast Fourier Transform (FT)	13%	9%	18%
Block Tridiagonal (BT)	8%	9%	0%
LU Gauss Seidel (LU)	12%	11%	0%
Scalar Pentadiagonal (SP)	20%	21%	0%

Table 1 summarises, for each benchmark in the suite, the memory behaviour when run using OpenMP on all 26 physical cores of a Xeon Platinum 8170. The *Clock ticks cache stall* and *Clock ticks DDR stall* columns report how often the CPU was stalled on cache and main memory accesses respectively, and the *Time DDR bandwidth bound* column reports the percentage of execution time that there was a high DDR bandwidth utilisation.

The IS kernel tests indirect, random, memory accesses which it can be seen stalls a significant fraction of the CPU due to cache accesses. It can be seen that the MG kernel is heavily memory bound both in terms of time stalled on cache and main memory accesses, and also the percentage of execution time where DDR is under high utilisation. By contrast, the EP benchmark is designed to test compute performance and there are far fewer cycles stalled on memory access, and no time spent with high DDR bandwidth utilisation. CG comprises irregular memory access and nearest neighbour communication, which results in around 37% of clock ticks stalled on cache or DDR accesses, and the FT benchmark requires all-to-all communications between ranks to undertake a parallel transposition of data. For FT it can be seen that whilst there is only 22% of clock ticks stalled, which is lower than the five other kernels apart from EP, the kernel is utilising a high DDR bandwidth for 18% of the time.

The BT, LU and SP pseudo application benchmarks are more complicated than the five NPB kernels, and represent common, real-world, HPC use-cases. All three of these pseudo applications compute a finite difference solution to the 3D compressible Navier Stokes equations, where the LU benchmark solves this via a block-lower block-upper triangular approximation based upon Gauss Seidel iterative method [8]. The BT and SP benchmarks solve the same problem as LU, but base their solution on a Beam-Warming approximation. In BT the resulting equations are block-tridiagonal whereas in SP are fully diagonalised [8]. Both these systems are solved using Gaussian elimination. It can be seen from Table 1 that, out of these three pseudo applications, BT stalls the least on memory accesses and SP the most.

3 RISC-V Core Comparison

In this section we compare performance of existing commodity RISC-V solutions. Due to the difference in core counts between RISC-V CPUs, we focus here on single cores performance to understand how the XuanTie C920 core of the Sophon SG2042 performs against other widely available RISC-V cores. We compare against the U74 core [9] which is contained in the JH7200 and JH7100 SoCs of the VisionFive V2 and V1 respectively, and both of these boards contain 8 GB of DRAM. We also compare against the SiFive Freedom U740 SoC, also containing the U74 core and 16 GB of DDR, and the T-Head XuanTie C906 [7] in the AllWinner D1 SoC with 1 GB of memory.

Table 2 reports a single core performance comparison between these RISC-V technologies, for the five NPB kernels at class B, with performance reported in million operations per second (Mop/s) and a higher number is better. In italicised red is the percentage performance that a single core of this CPU delivers compared to a single C920 core found in the SG2042. It can be seen that, irrespective of the kernel, the C920 significantly out performs all other RISC-V technologies. Consistently, the U74 of the VisionFive V2 performs closest to the C920, but is still only delivering between 21% and 38% the performance of the C920. Whilst the VisionFive V1 and SiFive U740 both contain the same U74 core as the VisionFive V2, they are significantly slower and this is broadly in agreement with [2].

Table 2. Single core comparison between RISC-V technologies with performance reported in Mops/s (Higher is better) using NPB kernels running at class B. In red is the percentage performance delivered compared to the C920 core of the SG2042.

Benchmark	SG2042	VisionFive V2	VisionFive V1	SiFive U740	All Winner D1
IS	60.6	17.84 *(29%)*	6.36 *(10%)*	9.09 *(15%)*	5.41 *(9%)*
MG	1210.05	288.65 *(24%)*	72.31 *(6%)*	90.28 *(7%)*	163.19 *(13%)*
EP	31.35	12.01 *(38%)*	7.55 *(24%)*	9.08 *(29%)*	9.23 *(29%)*
CG	205.25	43.61 *(21%)*	21.96 *(11%)*	20.09 *(10%)*	12.99 *(6%)*
FT	857.64	245.99 *(29%)*	88.35 *(10%)*	116.59 *(14%)*	DNR

The C906 of the All Winner D1 is out performed by the C920 and the U74 of the V2 quite considerably. However, this is the cheapest of the SoCs considered here, and the C906 outperforms the V1 and U740 for the EP and MG benchmarks. Given the performance profile of the benchmarks reported in Table 1, this suggests that the raw compute power of the C906 is similar to that of the U74 and the memory bandwidth is greater on the All Winner D1 than the VisionFive V1 and SiFive U740. However, for those benchmarks with more complex, irregular, memory patterns such as IS and CG, the C906 seems to struggle compared to the other RISC-V cores. Incidentally, it was not possible to run the FT benchmark on the All Winner D1 due to the limited 1 GB of memory becoming exhausted.

In this section we therefore conclude that the C920 core of the SG2042 significantly outperforms all other commodity available RISC-V CPU cores. Whilst this is in agreement with [2], in this section we have compared against a wider range of RISC-V CPUs than [2] and for specific algorithmic patterns that are very commonly found in HPC codes, especially for CFD. Considering that they use the same U74 core, it is surprising that the VisionFive V2 outperforms the V1 and U740 by such a large margin, but again this is in agreement with [2,6], and one of the reasons for this is that the V2 is running at 1.5 GHz compared to 1.2 GHz for both the V1 and U740.

4 Comparing the SG2042 Against Other Architectures

In Sect. 3 we compared the performance of the SG2042's C920 core against other RISC-V commodity available CPU cores. Whilst it is interesting to explore performance against RISC-V CPUs, and indeed the C920 delivers impressive performance compared to other RISC-V hardware, to understand whether the SG2042 is a contender for HPC it is far more instructive to benchmark against CPUs of other architectures that are commonly used for HPC workloads.

Table 3. Summary of CPUs that are benchmarked in this section

CPU	ISA	Part	Base clock	Number of cores	Vector
AMD EPYC	x86-64	EPYC 7742	2.25 GHz	64	AVX2
Intel Skylake	x86-64	Xeon Platinum 8170	2.1 GHz	26	AVX512
Marvell ThunderX2	ARMv8.1	CN9980	2 GHz	32	NEON
Sophon SG2042	RV64GCV	SG2042	2 GHz	64	RVV v0.7.1

In this section we compare against CPUs of other architectures that are commonplace in HPC, and these are summarised in Table 3. The AMD EPYC is the Rome series of AMD CPUs, containing the Zen-2 micro architecture and we run this on ARCHER2, a Cray EX and the UK national supercomputer. Similarly to the SG2042, the AMD EPYC contains 64 physical cores across four NUMA regions, each with 16 cores, but has eight instead of four memory controllers and memory channels. Each core in the AMD EPYC contains 32 KB of I and D L1 cache, 512 KB of L2 cache, and there is 16 MB of L3 cache shared between four cores. Providing AVX2, the EPYC 7742 has 256-bit wide vector registers, which is double that of the SG2042, but is capable of processing two AVX-256 instructions per cycle. ARCHER2 contains 256 GB of DDR memory. We use GCC version 11.2 when compiling on ARCHER2. Simultaneous Multithreading (SMT) is disabled for our runs, which is the default configuration on ARCHER2.

We also compare against an Intel Skylake Xeon Platinum 8170, which is the same CPU used to profile the NPB benchmarks in Table 1. This Skylake-SP CPU contains 26 cores, each with 32 KB of I and D L1 cache, 1 MB of L2 cache and 1.375 MB of L3 cache (the later is shared across all cores). The Skylake supports AVX512, double and quadruple the width of the EPYC 7742 and SG2042 respectively, and each Skylake core has two FPUs. The machine we run on has 192 GB of DDR4 memory, and we use GCC version 8.4.

Lastly, we compare against the CN9980 Marvell ThunderX2 which contains 32 cores implementing the ARMv8.1 (AArch64) ISA via the Vulcan micro architecture. Each core contains 32 KB of I and D L1 cache, as well as 256 KB of L2. There is a total of 32 MB L3 cache, 1 MB per core, shared by the entire chip. NEON is supported, which provides 128 bit wide vector registers and this is interesting because it matches the vector width of the C920 core in the SG2042. Similarly to the Skylake, the Marvell ThunderX2 has two FPUs per core. This is the CPU used in Fulhame, an HPE Apollo 70 system, with 128 GB of DDR per node, we use GCC version 9.2 and SMT is also disabled in our runs.

For the performance comparison undertaken in this section, we run class C of the NASA Parallel Benchmarks and run over multiple cores of the CPUs by using the OpenMP implementations of the benchmarks [4]. Each thread is mapped to an individual physical CPU core, all reported results are averaged over five runs and all codes are built at optimisation level three.

4.1 Integer Sort (IS)

As described in Sect. 2.2, the Integer Sort (IS) benchmark is concerned with integer comparison and indirect, random, memory access performance. Figure 1 illustrates the performance results for this benchmarks across our CPUs of interested, reported in Mops/s (higher is better). It can be seen that the SG2042 performs considerably worse than all other CPUs with performance plateauing at 16 cores. By contrast, the ThunderX2 and AMD EPYC delivering similar performance until the 32 cores of the ThunderX2 are exhausted. The Skylake performs better than all the other CPUs, but is limited by its lower core count, where the ThunderX2 catches up to the Skylake at 32 cores and the EPYC outperforms it at 64 cores.

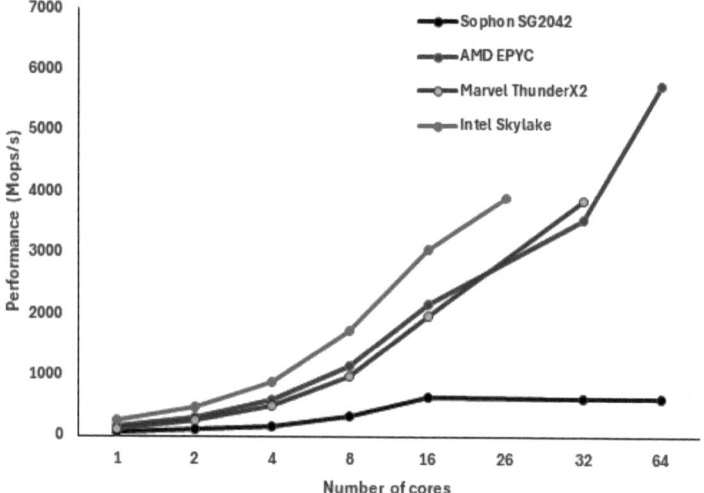

Fig. 1. IS benchmark performance (higher is better) parallelised via OpenMP

It can be seen from Fig. 1 that the SG2042 struggles significantly with this benchmark where as was seen in Table 1 the irregular, random, memory accesses result in a comparatively large number of time stalled due to cache access and DDR bandwidth utilisation is high for a small fraction of the runtime. A hypothesis is that could be due to the cache hierarchy, where the Skylake which performs the best has the largest L2 cache, 1 MB per core, compared to 256 KB (per core, 1 MB shared between four cores) for the SG2042, 256 KB for the ThunderX2 and 512 KB for the AMD EPYC. The surprise here is in the performance difference between the SG2042 and the ThunderX2, as per core they both have the same amount of L2 and L3 cache.

4.2 Multi Grid (MG)

It was illustrated in Sect. 2.2 that the Multi Grid (MG) benchmark is heavily memory bandwidth bound, and results of executing this benchmark kernel on the CPUs of interest is illustrated in Fig. 2. It can be seen that the AMD EPYC provides considerably best performance, with the Skylake and ThunderX2 delivering similar performance and both plateauing at 16 cores where memory bandwidth is likely saturated. By contrast, the SG2042 lags the other CPUs considerably, also plateauing at 16 and 32 cores but then with a performance increase at 64 cores.

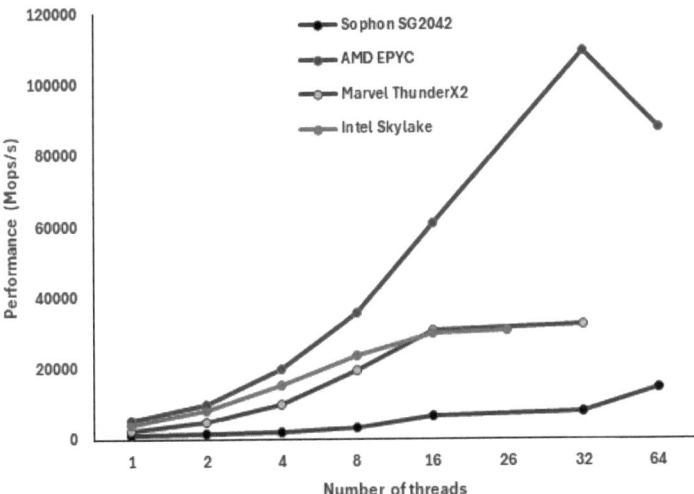

Fig. 2. MG benchmark performance (higher is better) parallelised via OpenMP

The memory configuration of the CPUs partially helps to explain the relative performance reported in Fig. 2. The AMD EPYC has 8 memory controllers and 8 memory channels, connected to DDR4-3200 memory. By contrast, the Skylake and ThunderX2 both only have 2 memory controllers and are both connected to DDR4-2666 albeit with the ThunderX2 having 8 memory channels compared to 6 memory channels in the Skylake. The SG2042 has four memory controllers and only four memory channels, connected to DDR4-3200. Whilst there are fewer memory channels on the SG2042 than the other CPUs, it also has double the memory controllers than the Skylake and ThunderX2 CPUs, and also faster memory, but lags performance compared with those CPUs. Details around the memory subsystem on the SG2042 are difficult to come by, but it is our hypothesis that the memory controllers on the SG2042 are considerably less advanced than the other CPUs considered in this section.

The behaviour of the MG benchmark also helps explain one of the anomalies of the IS benchmark performance. It was our hypothesis that the L2 and L3 cache design was in part governing performance of the SG2042 compared to other CPUs, however the ThunderX2 also has the same cache design but was faster than the SG2042 for that benchmark. However, as seen for the MG benchmark, the SG2042 is also severely memory bandwidth bound and this likely explains the gap in performance between the SG2042 and ThunderX2 for the IS benchmark.

4.3 Embarrassingly Parallel (EP)

The Embarrassingly Parallel (EP) benchmark is compute bound, and results of this on our CPUs are illustrated in Fig. 3. It can be seen that across the CPUs being tested, there are two groups; the SG2042 and ThunderX2 share very similar performance but with the SG2042's 64 cores then making a significant difference compared to the 32 cores of the ThunderX2. The EPYC and Skylake both deliver similar performance, which is greater than the SG2042 and ThunderX2, but the 26 cores of the Skylake are a disadvantage against the SG2042 which then significantly out performs the Skylake at 64 cores. The AMD EPYC performs best out of all the CPUs, especially at the larger core counts.

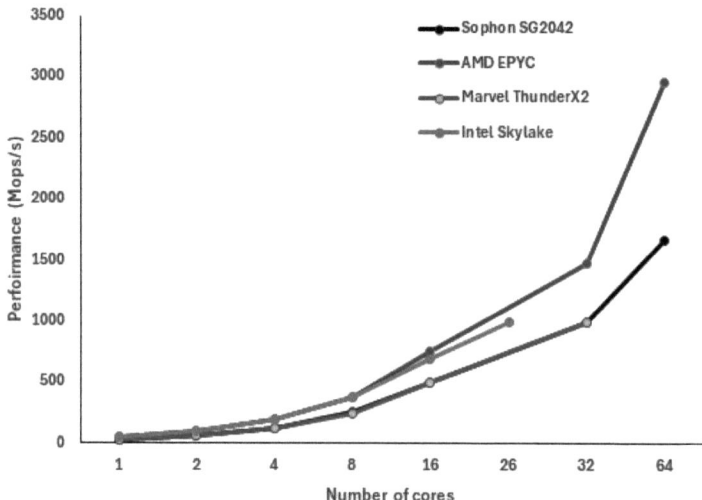

Fig. 3. EP benchmark performance (higher is better) parallelised via OpenMP

This performance behaviour is in stark contrast to the IS and MG benchmarks, and demonstrates that the SG2042 and ThunderX2 deliver very similar compute performance at the same number of cores. This makes some sense given that they both provide 128-bit vectorisation, albeit with the ThunderX2 having two FPUs per core compared to one on the SG2042. By contrast, the Skylake and AMD EPYC CPUs provides wider vectorisation, 512-bit and 256-bit respectively and this in part helps explain the performance difference between these two groups. However, given the Skylake provides AVX512, and the AMD EPYC only AVX2, and that the ThunderX2 has two FPUs per core and the SG2042 only one, clearly the GCC compiler is not able to fully vectorise the code of this benchmark and make full use of the FPUs.

Given that, at the largest number of cores each technology provides, the SG2042 performs second best for this benchmark out of all CPUs in our comparison, this demonstrates that for compute bound problems the large core count of the SG2042 is beneficial.

4.4 Conjugate Gradient (CG)

As can be seen from Table 1, the Conjugate Gradient (CG) benchmark also spends considerable time stalled on cache and DDR memory accesses, and this is because it comprises of irregular memory access and nearest neighbour communications. Figure 4 illustrates the performance of this benchmark kernel across our CPUs. Given the performance of the IS and MG benchmarks it is no surprise that the SG2042 falls short of the other technologies, but it is closer to the ThunderX2 than we had expected delivering around 50% the performance of the ThunderX2 at 32 cores.

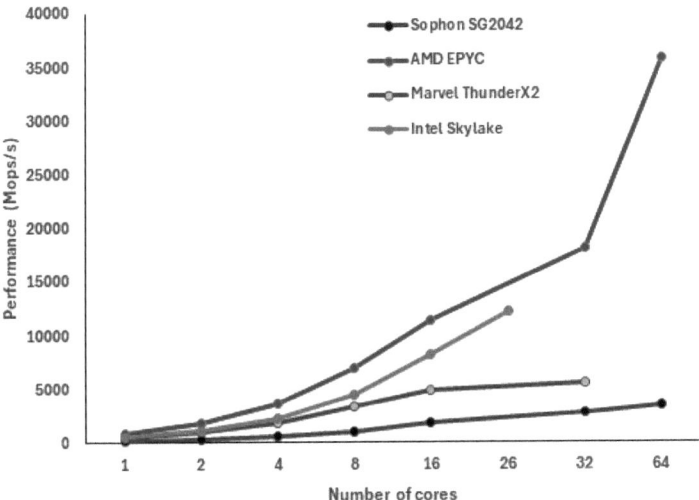

Fig. 4. CG benchmark performance (higher is better) parallelised via OpenMP

Potentially, what is making the difference here is in the size of the L3 cache, where the AMD EPYC has 16 MB L3 shared between four cores (4 MB per core), whereas the Skylake has 1.3 MB L3 cache per core shared across all cores (potentially helped by the larger 1 MB L2 cache). By contrast, both the ThunderX2 and SG2042 have the same size of 256 MB L2 and 1 MB L3 cache per core. This would help explain the performance differences, with the additional memory bandwidth limitations of the SG2042 causing additional the overhead which reduces performance further.

4.5 Fast Fourier Transform (FT)

The fast Fourier Transform (FT) benchmark requires all-to-all communication between ranks, and the performance of this benchmark can be seen in Fig. 5. As described in Table 1, for this benchmark on the Skylake there was some stalling due to cache and DDR access (13% and 9% respectively) but also for 18% of the time DDR was under high utilisation. Once again, the SG2042 is significantly slower than the other CPUs, with the ThunderX2 sitting around half way between the performance of the x86 CPUs and the SG2042 and this is likely for the same reasons explored for the CG benchmark.

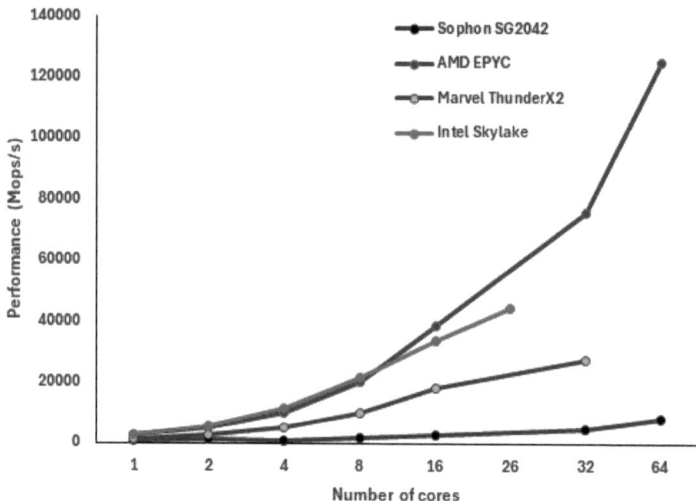

Fig. 5. FT benchmark performance (higher is better) parallelised via OpenMP

4.6 Pseudo Applications

Table 4 reports performance for the BT, LU and SP benchmarks and this is expressed as how many times faster this CPU is than the SG2042. Given the findings that the SG2042 struggles to perform when there is increased pressure on the memory subsystem, and based upon the stall numbers reported in Table 1, it was our expectation that the SG2042 would perform best for the BT benchmark and worst for the SP benchmark with the LU benchmark in between. This is broadly the case based upon the figures in Table 4, where each number reports the number of times faster than each of the other CPUs are for each pseudo application at a specific core count. It can be seen that three other CPUs significantly outperform the SG2042 for the three pseudo applications.

Table 4. For each pseudo application, the number of times faster a specific CPU is than the SG2042 at the given number of cores

Number cores	BT benchmark			LU benchmark			SP benchmark		
	EPYC	Skylake	ThunderX2	EPYC	Skylake	ThunderX2	EPYC	Skylake	ThunderX2
16	3.23	3.28	2.43	3.65	4.15	2.86	5.01	3.91	3.65
26	3.57	2.97	2.69	3.20	3.16	2.62	6.25	3.48	3.57
32	3.68	–	2.64	3.40	–	2.94	5.26	–	3.22
64	4.19	–	–	2.95	–	–	4.22	–	–

5 MPI vs OpenMP on the Sophon SG2042

In Sect. 4, the NPB benchmarks were all run using the official NAS OpenMP implementation. This is sensible given that execution is occurring within a single memory space, however a question is whether, for best performance, one should write their parallel code using OpenMP or MPI within a node. These two models are very different, where OpenMP follows a thread based approach and by default all threads share the same memory area and explicit marshalling and protection of shared memory is required. In contrast, when using MPI tasks run as independent processes which share no data and instead communicate with each other via explicit messages.

As there are both OpenMP and MPI implementations of the NPB benchmark suite, we are able to undertake a direct comparison. This is illustrated in Fig. 6 which reports the percentage performance delivered by the MPI implementation compared to the OpenMP version, for each benchmark at different numbers of cores. It can be seen that there are significant differences in performance between OpenMP and MPI for some configurations.

It can be observed, in Fig. 6, that over one or two cores the benchmarks do not benefit from MPI compared to OpenMP. However, from four cores upwards the CG and FT benchmarks run faster when using MPI than OpenMP. At 64 cores, all the MPI implementations run faster than their OpenMP counterparts. When exploring MPI against OpenMP on other architectures, MPI was always slower on the AMD EPYC and this was also true on the Skylake apart for the CG benchmark where MPI was on average two times faster than the OpenMP implementation. When profiling the CG MPI benchmark on the Skylake, it was found that clock ticks stalls due to cache reduced from 19% in the OpenMP implementation to 5.5% with the MPI version. The MPI implementation experienced no clock ticks stalled due to DDR accesses, down from 18% for the OpenMP version.

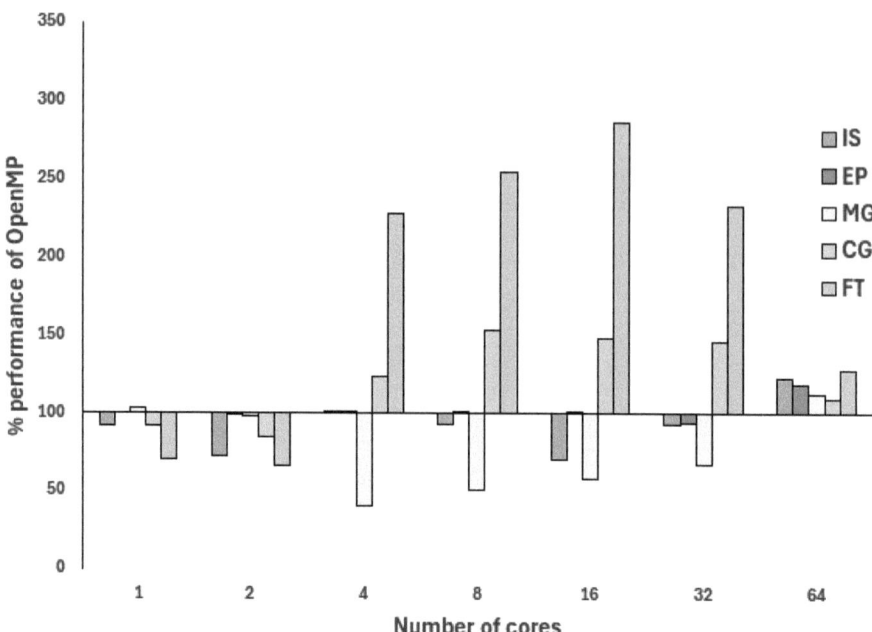

Fig. 6. Percentage performance of MPI based NPB benchmark compared to the OpenMP benchmark implementation

We surmise that the way these benchmarks are implemented means that the structure imposed by the MPI implementation tends to put less pressure on the memory subsystem when undertaking communications. For codes with heavy inter-core communication such as CG (nearest neighbour point to point) and FT (all to all collective) then this can be beneficial on the SG2042.

6 Conclusions

The Sophon SG2042 is an impressive RISC-V CPU and, using NASA's NAS Parallel Benchmark (NPB) suite, we have demonstrated that for benchmarks that closely represent ubiquitous HPC algorithms, especially in CFD, it significantly out performs existing RISC-V solutions. When compared against CPUs which implement other ISAs and whose use is widespread for high performance workloads, the Sophon SG2042 is outperformed by the AMD EPYC by between 1.77 and 15.06 times, the Intel Skylake between 0.59 and 5.98 times, and the Marvel ThunderX2 between 0.59 and 5.91 times. The SG2042 is most competitive for computationally bound codes, and its high core count ultimately out performed the Skylake and ThunderX2 for the EP benchmark. However the SG2042 CPU struggled with algorithms that are memory bandwidth or latency bound.

From this work we conclude that the memory subsystem of the SG2042 is a bottleneck, and Sophon recently announced the SG2044 which is reported to have three times the DDR memory bandwidth [10], as well as implementing RVV v1.0. This has the potential to provide a very significant performance improvement over the SG2042 for many of the benchmarks explored in this paper, and the improved memory performance will likely ameliorate the bottlenecks we have observed with the high core count continuing to deliver good computational performance. It is therefore our conclusion that the Sophon SG family of RISC-V CPUs has strong potential in HPC, and whilst the current generation SG2042 is an impressive first generation, based on announcements made by Sophon it looks likely that the SG2044 will address the key performance challenges that we have observed in this paper and make for a compelling RISC-V product family.

Acknowledgements. This work has been funded by the ExCALIBUR H&ES RISC-V testbed. This work used the ARCHER2 UK National Supercomputing Service (https://www.archer2.ac.uk). The Fulhame HPE Apollo 70 system is supplied to EPCC as part of the Catalyst UK programme. For the purpose of open access, the author has applied a Creative Commons Attribution (CC BY) licence to any Author Accepted Manuscript version arising from this submission.

References

1. Benchmarks, N.P.: NAS Parallel Benchmarks. CG and IS (2006)
2. Brown, N., Jamieson, M., Lee, J., Wang, P.: Is RISC-V ready for HPC prime-time: evaluating the 64-core sophon sg2042 RISC-V CPU. In: Proceedings of the SC'23 Workshops of The International Conference on High Performance Computing, Network, Storage, and Analysis, pp. 1566–1574 (2023)
3. Hornung, R.D., Hones, H.E.: Raja performance suite. In: Tech. rep., Lawrence Livermore National Lab.(LLNL), Livermore, CA (United States) (2017)
4. Jin, H.Q., Frumkin, M., Yan, J.: The openmp Implementation of NAS Parallel Benchmarks and Its Performance (1999)
5. Lee, J.K., Jamieson, M., Brown, N.: Backporting RISC-V vector assembly. In: International Conference on High Performance Computing, pp. 433–443. Springer (2023)
6. Lee, J.K., Jamieson, M., Brown, N., Jesus, R.: Test-driving RISC-V vector hardware for HPC. In: International Conference on High Performance Computing, pp. 419–432. Springer (2023)
7. Open xuantie c906 (2023). https://xrvm.com/cpu-details?id=4056751997003636736
8. Saphir, W., Van der Wijngaart, R.F., Woo, A., Yarrow, M.: New implementations and results for the NAS parallel benchmarks 2. In: PPSC. Citeseer (1997)
9. Sifive u74-MC core complex manual (2021). https://starfivetech.com/uploads/u74mc_core_complex_manual_21G1.pdf
10. Sophgo RISC-V Roadmap (2024). https://github.com/RISCVtestbed/riscvtestbed.github.io/blob/main/assets/files/hpcasia24/hpc_asia_wang.pdf
11. C920: Specifications (2023). https://xuantie.t-head.cn/product/xuantie/4082464366237126656

2nd International Workshop on Sustainable Supercomputing

Impact of Computational Load Balance and Power Capping on Energy Efficiency in HPC Centers

Martin Rose[1]($\boxtimes$), Jose Gracia[1], Christian Simmendinger[2], Andreas Ruopp[1], Ramil Nabiev[1], and Christoph Niethammer[1]

[1] HLRS, University of Stuttgart, Stuttgart, Germany
martin.rose@hlrs.de
[2] CoE HLRS/HPE, HPE Supercomputing EMEA, Böblingen, Germany

Abstract. In this paper we investigate the effect of power capping on the runtime and energy-to-solution for two benchmarks and seven HPC codes. We also study the impact of computational load balance on energy efficiency and we can show that power capping and improving computational load balance are independent paths that lead to increased energy efficiency in HPC centers. For some applications, we observe a minimum in energy-to-solution for a certain power cap. We estimate up to which efficiency of the computing center running compute nodes at lower power caps actually saves energy. In order to estimate how much energy can be saved by optimizing computational load balance, we present a statistical approach that uses the distribution of load balance obtained from performance analyses of many codes.

Keywords: sustainability · power capping · load balance · HPC

1 Introduction

The energy consumed in computing centers around the world increases every year due to the increasing demand for computing power and the growth of data to process. While some of the increase is driven by the availability of new technologies based on GPUs, we focus on the energy consumed in HPC applications that run on CPUs. These applications can be categorized as either being limited by the speed at which the CPU performs computations or as being limited by the speed at which the main memory can provide data to process. A single application can operate in either state, depending on the size of the dataset per CPU. Due to the complexity of the employed algorithms, applications do not perform with maximum efficiency. The efficiency can be defined in different ways, e.g., shortest time-to-solution, consumed power, or lowest energy-to-solution. There are two approaches to help improve the efficiency of applications: The common iterative approach is to analyze the performance of an application and to derive ideas for improving the source code from that analysis. Performance analysis is a time-consuming task and the reward usually reduces with every iteration while the necessary effort increases until the process comes to an end and no further improvement takes place. This first approach aims for shortest time-to-solution. In this work, we focus on computational load balance as the optimization target. A more recent approach to increase the energy efficiency of applications is to set limits to the power that a single CPU can consume. A complex and undisclosed mechanism working inside the CPU makes sure that the consumed power does not exceed the set value.

The effort to improve the efficiency of an application can be measured in funds spent on the salary of programmers for the first approach or additional system costs for the second approach. The reward can be measured in reduced spending for electricity and reduced emission of CO_2. With the availability of two approaches for improving efficiency, the question investigated in this work is whether the two approaches are mutually exclusive or if both can be applied simultaneously to the same application.

1.1 POP Performance Metrics

In the center of excellence "Performance Optimization and Productivity" (POP) a multiplicative set of metrics was developed to describe the performance of parallel HPC applications [1]. The load balance (LB) is a metric at the first level, i.e. the overall performance is directly proportional to the load balance. LB is defined as the ratio between the mean useful compute time of all MPI processes and the maximum useful compute time observed in any MPI process for a defined part of the code commonly referred to as the focus of analysis. Useful compute time is defined as the time the CPU is executing user code and not code in parallel programming runtimes like MPI or OpenMP. Performance analysis tools like Score-P [2] allow to collect LB data for each function by profiling the application during runtime. There are two reasons for LB below the optimum of 1: First, the number of instructions that each MPI process has to process can vary. Second, different MPI processes can require different numbers of cycles to process instructions due to different memory access patterns. For the duration of the POP2 project of 3 years, 10 scientists have collected performance metrics for about 140 HPC applications. The LB obtained in that effort will be used in Sect. 4.2 of this work.

1.2 Power Measurement and Control

For our study, we used the HAWK supercomputer at HLRS, which consists of 5632 compute nodes. Each node contains two AMD EPYC 7742 processors and 256 GB of main memory. The electrical power of each node is recorded every 2-3 seconds and stored in a database. The power is measured between the power supply and the mainboard, i.e., the measurement includes all components connected to the mainboard. After the completion of a compute job, the recorded power data can be retrieved for analysis. The measurement does not include the power consumed by the network switches and the cooling system.

The maximum power that each CPU in a compute node can consume is set via the AMD HSMP interface [3]. In the following, the maximum power a compute node can consume is referred to as 'power cap'. The details of the mechanisms that the CPU uses to control power consumption are unknown. One observation for all our HPC applications and benchmarks is that the CPU consumes less power when the power cap is reduced. Another observation is that the CPU does not always consume the maximum allowed power, i.e., the actual power consumption can be below the power cap.

1.3 Benchmark Applications

In order to study the energy efficiency of programs as a function of load balance, a benchmark program was written [4]. The program performs computations for a given number of elements (N) in an iterative manner. The computational work is performed by multiple threads. At the end of each iteration, a computed value is exchanged between neighbors via MPI. The next iteration can not begin before the data is received. The load balance can be controlled by the number of elements to process by each MPI process, which is reproducibly set at the start of the benchmark. The load balance is reduced due to the imbalance in the number of executed instructions among the MPI processes. The performance of the benchmark is measured in terms of processed elements per second or simply operations per second. The program uses multiple threads to perform the operations. In this work, 32 MPI processes with 4 threads each were executed on a single node of HAWK.

Two variants of the benchmark, referred to as *CPUbound* and *MEMbound*, distinguish themselves in the operations performed. *CPUbound* computes the sum of N double precision random numbers that are computed from a state of four 64-bit integers, no data from main memory is used. *MEMbound* computes the sum of values sequentially read from memory. In order to increase the pressure on the memory system and to increase the power consumption, each MPI process computes two sums from two arrays, one double precision and one long integer. This benchmark is memory bandwidth-bound.

Load balance is determined from profiling data collected with Score-P [2].

2 Related Work

In the context of HPC, the effect of power capping on performance and efficiency has been studied for various benchmarks and applications on different architectures in the past.

Haidar et al. [5] have applied a power cap to Intel KNL and determined the influence thereof on runtime and computational performance. They distinguish between CPU-bound and memory-bound applications and find that for the latter a significant reduction in consumed power can be achieved without reducing the performance of a kernel.

Krzywaniak et al. [6] have applied a power cap to Intel Xeon E5 V4 and other CPUs. Their experiments show that the Xeon E5 consumes significantly less power than what was allowed by the power cap. They also report a minimum in energy-to-solution for a certain power cap.

The computational load balance of HPC applications is a well-known metric that can be improved in an iterative process of performance analysis and code refinement that was applied in the POP project [1]. Garcia et al. [7] have developed a library that dynamically distributes CPU resources at the node level to improve the computational load balance of hybrid applications.

3 Experiments

3.1 CPUbound and MEMbound Benchmark

The two benchmarks *CPUbound* and *MEMbound* were executed with power caps of 515 W and 615 W. The values of 515 W and 615 W were chosen because HAWK nodes are operating at either of these two power caps. The non-uniform number of elements to process by each MPI process was set in a reproducible way to control the load balance. Figure 1(left) shows the power consumed by the node during the run of both benchmarks as a function of load balance for the two power caps. The power consumption of *MEMbound* is above that of *CPUbound*. Reducing the power cap from 615 W to 515 W results in a reduction of the consumed power between 90 W to 100 W for *MEMbound*. At the same time, that reduction in power cap reduces the consumed power of *CPUbound* by only 70 W. Improving load balance increases the power consumed by *MEMbound* and slightly reduces the power consumed by *CPUbound*.

The computational performance of both benchmarks (Fig. 1(right)) is obtained from the runtime and the number of benchmark-specific operations performed in that time. The performance of *MEMbound* decreases with load balance non-linearly while it decreases only slightly when the power cap is reduced. This means that the runtime changes only slightly with the power cap. The performance of *CPUbound* is proportional to the load balance for both power caps and reduces significantly with decreasing power cap. For this benchmark, the runtime depends significantly on the power cap.

After consumed power and computational performance were obtained for both benchmarks, it is possible to compute the energy per operation. Energy per operation is proportional to the energy-to-solution as the computation is completed after a fixed number of application-specific operations. Figure 2(left) shows the energy per operation for power caps of 515 W and 615 W for various values of load balance. *MEMbound* shows lower energy per operation for lower power caps while *CPUbound* shows an increase in energy per operation for decreasing power caps. Figure 2 (left) also reveals that the minimum energy per operation is at a load balance of one. Therefore, setting a power cap and optimizing load balance are two independent rewarding optimization strategies that do not make each other obsolete.

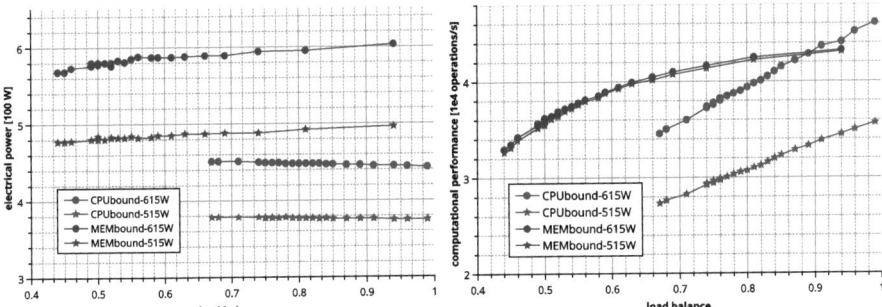

Fig. 1. Left: Electrical power of *CPUbound* and *MEMbound* benchmark for power caps of 515 W and 615 W as a function of load balance. **Right:** Computational performance of *CPUbound* and *MEMbound* benchmark for power caps of 515 W and 615 W as a function of load balance.

From the energy per operation obtained above, the factor of additional energy as a function of load balance can be computed. The factor of additional energy is defined as:

$$f_{\text{extra}}(LB) = \frac{E(LB) - E(LB=1)}{E(LB=1)} \quad (1)$$

where $E(LB)$ is the energy per operation for a given load balance. The experimental data is extrapolated by the function

$$f_{\text{extra}}(LB) = A + B * exp(-LB/C) \quad (2)$$

Figure 2 (right) shows the experimental data and the extrapolation using the parameters listed in Table 1. The parameters were determined using least squares fitting. As Eq. (2) describes the experimental data obtained for *MEMbound* well, we use the same equation to model the behavior of *CPUbound*.

Table 1. Model Parameters for Eq. (2)

parameter	CPUbound	MEMbound
A	−0.310576	−0.013913
B	3.304743	4.319171
C	0.419101	0.153815

3.2 Impact of Power Capping on Performance and Energy Consumption

The influence of the power capping on consumed power, energy-to-solution, and runtime was investigated for seven common HPC applications referred here to as

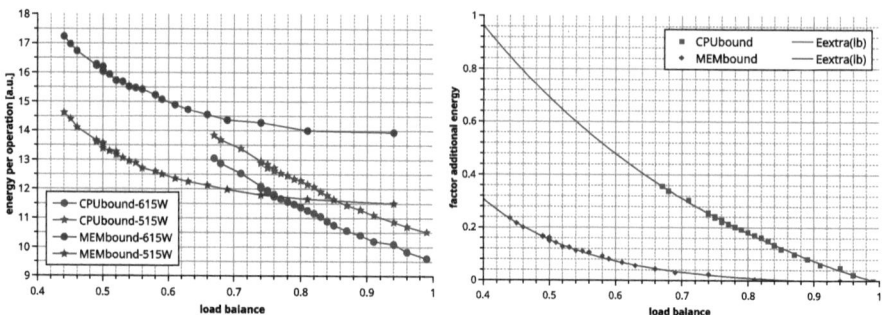

Fig. 2. Left: Energy per operation for *CPUbound* and *MEMbound* benchmark for power caps of 515 W and 615 W as a function of computational load balance. **Right:** Factor of additional energy per operation for *CPUbound* and *MEMbound* benchmark as a function of load balance.

codes A to G. The power cap of the nodes was varied between 515 W and 695 W for individual runs of the applications. Also, the core-C6 sleep state (CC6) was turned on and off. During a single run, the settings were constant. The values obtained at a certain power cap for power, energy-to-solution, and runtime were divided by the corresponding values obtained for a power cap of 615 W and CC6 off. The power cap of 615 W serves as a reference as this setting was used previously in production. The obtained data is shown for codes A and C in Fig. 3.

First of all, no significant difference was observed when turning the CC6 state on. Therefore, the effect of the CC6 state will not be discussed further in this work, all discussions refer to the experiments with CC6 off.

In the following, we will discuss the influence of the power cap on power, energy-to-solution, and runtime in order to classify the HPC applications as either memory-bound or CPU-bound.

In Fig. 3, the runtime of code A is independent of the power. This is exactly what we observed for the *MEMbound* benchmark in Sect. 3.1. Energy-to-solution and consumed power scale linearly with the power cap, which we also observe in the *MEMbound* benchmark. Energy-to-solution and consumed power have approximately the same proportionality constant in their linear dependency on the power cap. Code B behaves similarly to code A but for power caps smaller than 615 W, the runtime increases slightly. The proportionality constant for energy-to-solution is smaller than that of consumed power.

Code G deviates more from code A for power caps smaller than 615 W. The increase in runtime for small power caps is stronger than for code B. The proportionality constant for energy-to-solution is again smaller than that of consumed power. Still, the difference between energy-to-solution and consumed power is bigger than for code B. This difference could be caused by the extended runtime.

Code D behaves very similar to code G for small power caps. Data for power caps above 615 W were not collected. We conclude that the codes discussed above belong to the class of memory-bound applications because they behave like the *MEMbound* benchmark.

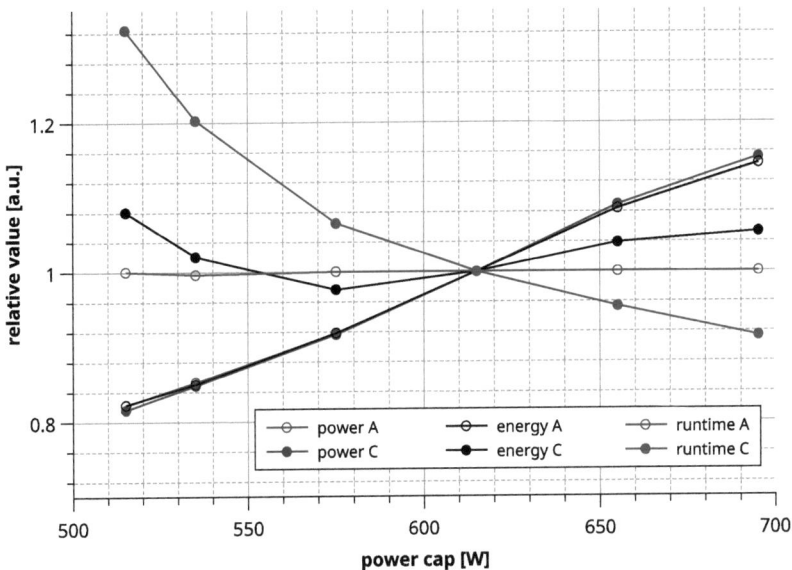

Fig. 3. Scaling of power, energy-to-solution and runtime for codes A and C.

Code C in Fig. 3 shows different behavior in runtime and energy-to-solution, which leads us to believe that this code belongs to a different class than the codes discussed before. Starting from the reference at 615 W, the runtime decreases with increasing power cap while it increases with decreasing power cap. As for all codes, the CPU manages to spend additional energy when allowed by the power cap. For this code, runtime decreases when consumed power, i.e. power cap, increases. This is the behavior of the *CPUbound* benchmark. Another remarkable observation is that the energy-to-solution shows a minimum at 575 W.

We conclude that code F belongs to the same class as code C because it shows a minimum in the energy-to-solution at 575 W and a significant increase in runtime for small power caps.

Code E shows a slight increase in runtime and a plateau in energy-to-solution for small power caps. Therefore, we conclude that this code also belongs to the second class of codes.

The scaling of the consumed power is approximately linear for all applications. This shows that the change in consumed power is indeed caused by the CPU and not by the other components on the motherboard, especially the main memory. Codes B and E show the strongest deviation from the linear behavior. At this point, we assume this behavior is due to the mechanisms used for the power management of the CPU, which are unknown to us.

From the experiments we identify two classes of codes: The first class contains codes A, B, G, and D with code A being the ideal representative of the codes investigated in this work. Codes in the first class behave like the *MEMbound* benchmark. The second class consists of codes C, F, and E where code C is the most representative of the investigated codes. These codes behave like the *CPUbound* benchmark.

4 Discussion

4.1 Energy Saving by Power Capping

The energy that can be saved by power capping depends on the application and the reference power cap. We chose the values obtained at 700 W as a reference point because this setting would be used when one expects that high power caps result in the shortest runtime. Table 2 shows relative power, relative energy-to-solution, and relative runtime for the codes of the *MEMbound* class. The first power cap for which we list the relative quantities is 615 W and the second is 515 W, i.e., the lowest power cap investigated in this work. Code D is not listed because no data was obtained for a power cap of 700 W.

Table 2. Behaviour of codes in MEMbound class

code	615 W vs. 700 W reference			515 W vs. 700 W reference		
	power [%]	energy [%]	runtime [%]	power [%]	energy [%]	runtime [%]
A	87.4	87.4	100.0	71.9	71.9	100.0
B	88.6	88.3	99.7	74.5	76.0	102.0
G	91.1	91.4	100.3	77.2	80.8	104.6

Table 3 lists relative power, relative energy-to-solution, and relative runtime for the codes of the *CPUbound* class. For each code, the values obtained at the highest power cap are the reference. The values obtained at the power cap with the lowest energy-to-solution are put into relation with the reference.

Table 3. Behaviour of codes in CPUbound class

code	power cap [W]	reference [W]	power [%]	energy [%]	runtime [%]
C	575	695	79.6	92.7	116.6
E	535	615	87.1	89.8	103.1
F	575	615	92.2	96.8	105.1

4.2 Energy Saving by Improving Load Balance

Statistical Distribution of Computational Load Balance. Now that the influence of computational load balance on the energy-to-solution is understood, the question becomes how much energy can actually be saved by improving the computational load balance of applications running in a computing center. In the following, a statistical approach to that question will be described.

The applications, the data sets they are applied to, and the users consuming CPU time in an HPC center are changing constantly over time. Therefore, optimizing the load balance of codes is a long-term task. First of all, it is necessary to understand the distribution of load balance, i.e., the fraction of codes running with load balance in a given load balance interval. The load balance determined in 115 performance assessments during the POP2 project [1] was used to produce the histogram in Fig. 4. The histogram includes codes running in various HPC centers across Europe. The performance assessments were conducted over a period of three years involving about 10 performance analysts from the project partners. The histogram shows that less than 5% of the codes have a load balance between 97.5 and 100%. The majority of codes have a load balance between 95 and 97.5%. The cumulative histogram (solid line in Fig. 4) shows what fraction of codes has a load balance below a given load balance. At the same time, this fraction of codes needs to be optimized to achieve a minimum predefined load balance for all codes.

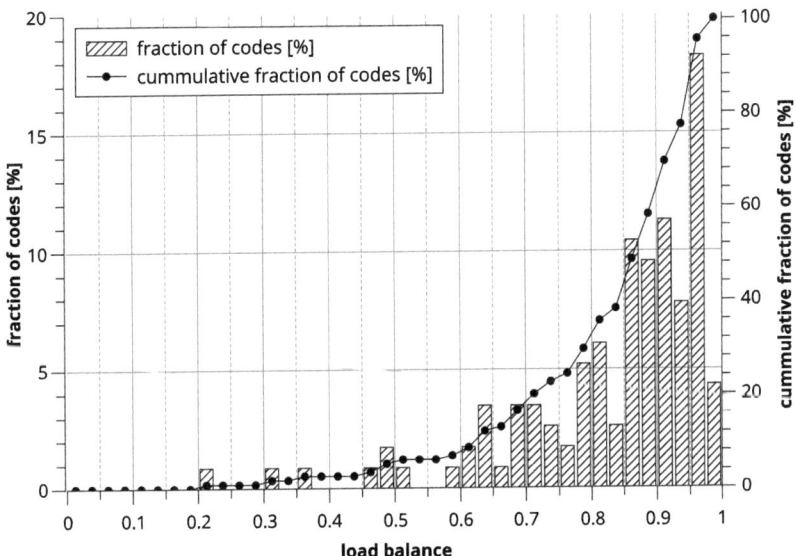

Fig. 4. Distribution of computational load balance in codes analyzed in POP2.

Statistical Model. Due to the dynamically changing workload in an HPC center, the energy saving can be estimated over a long period of time during which various different applications are executed. In order to determine the potential energy savings for a specific workload at a given time, the load balance of all codes must be determined which is a significant amount of work. The statistical approach in this work is based on the following assumptions:

- The distribution of applications with a certain load balance in a computing center is given by Fig. 4.
- All codes use an equal amount of CPU time.
- All compute nodes use equal energy E_1, independent of the executed code when the load balance is perfect.
- All codes with a load balance below LB_{min} can be optimized such that the load balance is at least LB_{min} which leads to a modified histogram.

If the load balance of all N applications is 1, the energy required to complete all runs is $E_{opt} = N * E_1$. In the unoptimized situation, where the load balance of applications is a distribution, the additional energy required to complete all runs is given by:

$$E_{add} = \sum_{i=1}^{S} E_1 * N_i * f_{\text{extra}}(LB_i) \qquad (3)$$

Where S is the number of buckets in the load balance histogram, N_i is the number of codes in bucket i with load balance LB_i. The total energy required to complete all runs in the unoptimized case is:

$$E_{tot} = E_{opt} + E_{add} \qquad (4)$$

In order to quantify the energy savings for different optimization targets, the energy efficiency is computed as:

$$H = \frac{E_{tot}}{E_{opt}} = 1 + \frac{E_{add}}{E_{opt}} \qquad (5)$$

Equation 5 has been evaluated for the distribution of load balance obtained in POP2 (Fig. 4) using $f_{\text{extra}}(LB_i)$ obtained for the *CPUbound* and *MEMbound* benchmarks. These values define the reference for the computation of the energy saving. Additionally, the model was evaluated for distributions of load balance after optimization with values of LB_{min} between 0.6 and 0.95. The obtained values for the energy efficiency are presented in Table 4. The fractional saving of energy for the optimized cases is given in brackets. The fraction of codes that must be optimized to achieve a certain LB_{min} is given in the rightmost column.

4.3 Minimum in Energy-to-Solution

As the power measurements in this work include only the energy consumed by the nodes, the question arises whether operating the nodes with the power cap

Table 4. Energy Efficiency H (Eq. 5) for various distributions of load balance

distribution	CPUbound	MEMbound	codes to optimize
POP2	1.181 (ref)	1.0653 (ref)	0%
$LB_{min} = 0.6$	1.148 (-2.8%)	1.013 (-1.8%)	7%
$LB_{min} = 0.7$	1.128 (-4.5%)	1.008 (-2.3%)	17%
$LB_{min} = 0.8$	1.097 (-7.1%)	1.003 (-2.8%)	29%
$LB_{min} = 0.9$	1.052 -11.0%)	1.000 (-3.1%)	58%
$LB_{min} = 0.95$	1.021 (-13.5%)	1.000 (-3.1%)	77%

where the minimum in energy-to-solution was observed is indeed the optimal setting for that code. As the runtime increases, the network components and infrastructure, i.e. cooling, consume extra energy. There is a point where the additionally consumed energy matches the energy saved by the compute node. We use a simple model to estimate the energy that is consumed by the computing center in addition to the energy consumed by the compute nodes. The model uses the average power of the HAWK supercomputer (2.75 MW) in the year 2021 and the corresponding energy usage efficiency (EUE) of 1.14 for the computing center (HLRS). From these values, we obtain that the computing center consumes on average 68 W additionally for each of the 5632 nodes. The underlying assumption is that the power consumed by the nodes running with an optimized power cap does not affect the average power of the supercomputer and EUE because some codes might use a higher optimized power cap while other codes might use a lower power cap than the reference value.

We choose code C to evaluate the model. Table 5 shows energy-to-solution, runtime, and node power (Pnode) for a power cap of 575 W where energy-to-solution has a minimum and for 695 W where the runtime is the shortest. The total energy (Etotal) is equal to the sum of node power and the additional power of 68 W from above multiplied by the runtime. It turns out that with a power capping of 575 W, the total energy is indeed lower than the total energy consumed with a power cap of 695 W where the runtime is the shortest. When EUE increases, the additional power per node increases. A simple analysis shows that for an EUE of 1.69, the additional power is 337 W so that the total energy is equal for both values of the power cap. In that case, the energy saved with a power cap of 575 W has been consumed by the computing center due to the longer runtime. For an EUE above 1.69 it would be more efficient to run the code with higher power caps as the shorter runtime saves energy in the computing center.

Table 5. Total energy versus power cap

power cap [W]	energy	runtime	Pnode [W]	Etotal
575	92.7%	100.0%	523	93.9%
695	100.0%	85.8%	666	100.0%

5 Conclusions

We have studied the influence of computational load balance on the performance and the energy consumption of two benchmarks where one benchmark is CPU-bound and the other is memory-bound. We were able to show that these two benchmarks respond differently to restricting the maximum power consumption and Fig. 2. While the energy per operation reduces with decreasing power for the memory-bound case, the energy per operation increases with decreasing power for the CPU-bound case. We have quantified the impact of reduced load balance on the energy required to complete a compute job. A statistical model was developed and evaluated to estimate the potential saving in energy by improving computational load balance. Our experiments show that even for perfect load balance, the application of a power cap can further reduce the energy per operation. Therefore, we investigated the effect of power caps between 515 W and 695 W on the runtime and energy-to-solution of seven HPC applications. All applications showed a behavior similar to either the CPU-bound benchmark or the memory-bound benchmark. The applications that behave like the CPU-bound benchmark show a minimum in energy-to-solution for an application-specific power cap. In order to determine whether operating a compute node with the power cap that leads to a minimum in energy-to-solution actually saves energy when considering the complete compute center, we evaluated a simple model. This analysis showed that energy is saved up to an energy usage efficiency of 1.69. Overall, we conclude that both paths, code optimization and application of power caps, are independent and rewarding actions to improve energy efficiency in compute centers.

Acknowledgement. The work presented in this paper is part of the project called "ENRICH - Energie, Nachhaltigkeit, Ressourceneffizienz in IT und Rechenzentren". The project was funded by the Ministerium für Umwelt, Klima und Energiewirtschaft Baden-Württemberg between April 1st 2021 and March 31st 2023, project number BWND21101-04.

The authors gratefully acknowledge the financial support by the Federal Ministry of Education and Research (BMBF) under the grant WindHPC (grant number 16ME0608K).

References

1. https://pop-coe.eu
2. Knüpfer, A., et al.: Score-P: a joint performance measurement run-time infrastructure for periscope, Scalasca, TAU, and Vampir. In: Brunst, H., Müller, M., Nagel, W., Resch, M. (eds) Tools for High Performance Computing 2011. Springer, Berlin, Heidelberg (2012). https://doi.org/10.1007/978-3-642-31476-6_7
3. https://github.com/amd/amd_hsmp
4. https://doi.org/10.5281/zenodo.10598397
5. Haidar, A., Jagode, H., Vaccaro, P., YarKhan, A., Tomov, S., Dongarra, J.: Investigating power capping toward energy-efficient scientific applications. Concur. Comput. Pract. Exp. **31**, e4485 (2019). https://doi.org/10.1002/cpe.4485
6. Krzywaniak, A., Proficz, J., Czarnul, P.: Analyzing energy/performance trade-offs with power capping for parallel applications on modern multi and many core processors. In: 2018 Federated Conference on Computer Science and Information Systems (FedCSIS), Poznan, Poland, pp. 339–346 (2018)
7. Garcia, M., Labarta, J., Corbalan, J.: Hints to improve automatic load balancing with LeWI for hybrid applications. J. Parallel Distrib. Comput. **74**(9), 2781–2794 (2014). https://doi.org/10.1016/j.jpdc.2014.05.004

Second International Workshop on Converged Computing on Edge, Cloud, and HPC (WOCC'24)

Preface to the International Workshop on Converged Computing on Edge, Cloud, and HPC (WOCC'24)

1 Objectives and Topics

The landscape of scientific computing is changing rapidly as complex, multi-stage pipelined workflows that combine traditional HPC computations with large-scale data analytics and AI are becoming increasingly common. Cloud computing is becoming a dominant market force, driving innovation in both hardware and the software needed to manage increasing system and workflow complexity. These next-generation workflows not only seek to improve the efficiency and scale of traditional HPC simulations, but additionally aim to apply large-scale and distributed computing to domains with high societal impact such as autonomous vehicles, precision agriculture, or smart cities. Such complex workflows are expected to require the coordinated use of supercomputers, cloud data centers, and edge-processing devices in an environment with shared characteristics. Providing a seamless environment that combines the best of these worlds leads to an era of Converged Computing.

Cloud computing technologies are gaining prevalence in HPC due to their benefits of resource dynamism, automation, reproducibility, and resilience. Similarly, HPC technologies for application performance optimization and sophisticated scheduling of complex resources are being integrated into modern cloud infrastructures. However, the convergence of HPC and cloud also raises a series of new challenges in areas of resource management, data transfers, storage, and throughput. Modern cloud and HPC frameworks provide heterogeneous resources, including processors and accelerators, diverse types of memories and storage, and network links, to match the diversity in workloads. Similarly, cloud technologies for elasticity, resilience, and multi-tenancy need to be adopted in HPC while ensuring high performance and throughput. Converged software stacks will need to provide middleware and resource management to facilitate the use of heterogeneous hardware components, improve the system utilization, and provide seamless interfaces for users and application developers.

The second International Workshop on Converged Computing on Edge, Cloud, and HPC (WOCC'24) provided the edge, HPC and cloud communities a dedicated venue for discussing challenges and research opportunities, deployment efforts, and best practices in supporting complex workflows on coordinated use of supercomputers and cloud data centers as well as edge-processing devices. The workshop encouraged interaction between participants who are developing applications, algorithms, middleware, and infrastructure for converged environments. The workshop was an ideal place for the community to define the current state of the art and identify, identify fundamental challenges and feasible future technologies and techniques. The workshop aimed to start discussion on questions, including: what changes to architecture, hardware, and middleware designs (including hardware monitoring, the operating systems, system software, and resource management) are needed? How to monitor and collect system-level metrics for utilization to identify bottlenecks to meet the different targets in performance, cost, and power budget? How to support different coupling patterns (e.g., loose or tight) between traditional scientific and big-data/AI components? What complex workflows and workloads leverage heterogeneity, elasticity, and dynamic resources provisioning?

2 Workshop Organization

All papers were submitted for double-blind review. Each paper received a minimum of 3 reviews. Double-blind peer-review was used. Papers were evaluated based on novelty, technical soundness, clarity of presentation, and impact. Five papers were accepted for technical presentation at the workshop.

Organizers

- Ivy Peng, KTH Royal Institute of Technology, Sweden
- Daniel Milroy, Lawrence Livermore National Laboratory, USA
- Valeria Cardellini, Tor Vergata University of Rome, Italy
- Tapasya Patki, Lawrence Livermore National Laboratory, USA

Technical Program Committee Members:

- Yoonho Park, IBM, USA
- Jeff Vetter, Oak Ridge National Laboratory, USA
- Daniel Ahlin, Google, Switzerland
- Claudia Misale, IBM, USA
- Jae-Seung Yeom, Lawrence Livermore National Laboratory, USA
- Rafael Tolosana-Calasanz, Universidad de Zaragoza, Spain
- Nathan Tallent, Pacific Northwest National Laboratory, USA
- Gabriele Russo Russo, Tor Vergata University of Rome, Italy
- Nina Mujkanovic, HPE, Switzerland
- Antony Chazapis, FORTH-ICS, Greece
- Jakob Luettgau, University of Tennessee Knoxville, USA
- Manolis Marazakis, FORTH-ICS, Greece

3 Outcome of the Workshop

The workshop started with a brief overview by the organizing committee followed by a keynote presentation titled "Serverless at the Convergence of Edge, Cloud and HPC: Issues and Perspectives" delivered by Valeria Cardellini. Authors of all five accepted papers were asked to present their presentations in person and Q&A sessions. An invited talk titled "Containers, HPC, and Cloud: A personal interpretation of Reinventing HPC" was delivered by Manolis Marazakis. An Invited talk titled "Cluster in the Cloud - scalable, heterogeneous compute clusters for HPC, HTC and AI in the public cloud or on-premise" was delivered by Matt Williams. The workshop ran for four hours in a half-day session.

Cluster in the Cloud—Scalable, Heterogeneous Compute Clusters for HPC, HTC and AI in the Public Cloud or On-Premise

Matt Williams[1](✉), Chris Edsall[2], Christopher Woods[1], and Sadaf Alam[1]

[1] University of Bristol, Bristol, UK
matt.williams@bristol.ac.uk
[2] University of Cambridge, Cambridge, UK

Abstract. We present Cluster in the Cloud, a free and open-source tool to create scalable, heterogeneous batch clusters on public and private cloud resources. Research workflows often require varied hardware throughout their pipeline: this may be needing a lot of RAM for one part, needing GPUs for another, or building on a particular CPU architecture; heterogeneous hardware is more and more required for research. Being able to scale heterogeneously—elastically as the work demands—is a requirement for reducing time-to-science in a cost-effective way. Clusters can be created in minutes, allowing environments to be created in response to novel research ideas or collaborations. Cluster in the Cloud provides a personal, at-scale platform for interactive and workflow based computing, AI and ML with CI/CD pipelines which are becoming more integrated into research. It has been used for published research into virology [16], carbon sequestration [13], computer science [3] and therapeutics [2] and has been deployed around the world by many universities (including Bath, Bristol, Caltech, Dublin City, RHUL and Sheffield) on public cloud and integrated into on-premise confidential computing systems.

Keywords: cloud · scalable · heterogeneous · Infrastructure-as-Code · HPC · AI · elasticity

1 Introduction

For decades, the primary mode of deployment that researchers have had to make use of large-scale compute resources has been through institutional, regional or national batch compute clusters. While the underlying hardware and the implementation of the software stacks has changed over the years, the fundamental workflow has not. This means that while there are numerous novel and innovative interfaces available to researchers, most researchers are still used to working with batch systems and have workflows that support that.

However, there is a growing demand from researchers for systems which support the flexibility that aids their research such as choice of user land tools for software compilation, choice of OS, customisable schedulers or resource management systems. On a large shared system, these are all fixed and must be balanced across the needs of all the users—needs which often are only reconsidered on a multi-year timescale.

Meanwhile, public cloud offerings have started to provide new ways to gain easy access to compute and storage solutions which researchers want to take advantage of. The downside of these platforms though, is the disconnect between the environment in which the researchers are used to running and the environments which the cloud services provide. The standard cloud interface that one is presented with upon signing up for an account is one where a high level of systems administration knowledge is required. This system administration knowledge may include networking, virtual machine configuration, port security, and subnet configuration, before finally needing to configure a batch system, all tasks which are beyond the scope of a subject matter expert. There are specialist cloud service provider interfaces available from public cloud providers for, e.g., data science workflows [9] but these tend to be single virtual machines (nodes) rather than multi-node solutions enabling high performance computing.

Many research workflows require different kinds and configurations of hardware throughout their pipeline. Whether this is simply needing a lot of RAM for a small part of the process or specifically needing GPUs for another part, heterogeneous hardware is needed to provide the best performance for their workflow, whether that's in terms of total time to solution or lowest cost. Even if not during a single pipeline step, access to varied hardware is often useful for a small research group who may have different needs or for benchmarking. All of this needs to happen in an elastically scalable fashion to provide immediate access to resources while managing costs and resource usage.

CLUSTER IN THE CLOUD is an open-source software stack designed to create a batch cluster environment—familiar to researchers—on cloud platforms and, due to the malleable and dynamic environment offered by cloud vendors, allow building personal interactive platforms on top of that. It was started in 2018 and has been used for published research projects in virology [16], global warming [13], exascale computer science [3] and medical therapeutics [2] and has been deployed around the world by many universities on public cloud (including Bath, Bristol, Caltech, Dublin City, RHUL and Sheffield) and integrated into on-premise confidential computing systems.

It builds on existing open source technologies allowing CI and CD pipelines and test-driven development of software for HPC, HTC and AI and ML use cases, as well as workflows requiring a combination of resources. In static or dedicated HPC, HTC, data analysis, AI and ML cluster environments, there is very little flexibility to compose these workflows, which is often constrained by incompatible technologies such as identity and access management (IAM), OS versions, storage and resource management and scheduling systems. The flexibility that Cluster in the Cloud provides to researchers has improved the "time to science" [4] while reducing costs associated with cloud resources. Cloud resources, particularly those offered through Cluster in the Cloud, are often not as optimised for very high-performance workloads (e.g. due to lack of compiler tuning, high-performance networks and parallel file systems) but for many research workloads, the tradeoff between the reduced compute performance and the easy of use, flexibility and improved agility of creating a new experimental environment will work in their favour.

Cluster in the Cloud has two main facets:

1. automation of the installation and setup of a batch compute cluster on public cloud or on-premise private cloud such as OpenStack (detailed in Sect. 2) and
2. a job scheduler which can automatically scale up and down heterogeneous compute resources (detailed in Sect. 3).

2 Platform Implementation

Cluster in the Cloud provides a number of automation scripts to create the infrastructure ready for a researcher to log in and start submitting jobs. This happens in three main steps:

1. setting up the static infrastructure,
2. configuring the software environment and
3. configuring the system for the specific use case including compute node configuration.

The first is handled by a suite of per-platform Terraform/OpenTofu [6,12] scripts to create a consistent baseline of virtual hardware, the second is managed by an Ansible [1] configuration which is largely cloud platform independent and the third is provided by a set of custom scripts or documented steps.

2.1 Static Infrastructure

The baseline configuration of a Cluster in the Cloud consists of just three main components:

1. a virtual network (along with a single, large subnet),
2. a virtual machine providing both a login server for end-users and management services and
3. a shared file system providing NFS.

The leading design principle constraining this design is one of reducing cost. The virtual networks generally incur no cost. The login server and management server may be combined into a small, single core, low memory virtual machine. Cloud-provided NFS servers are chosen as they incur the lowest charge while maintaining the highest compatibility with expected workloads and one is only charged for the storage volume used. The result of this is that—depending on the public cloud platform—the cost of keeping a cluster running for a month is around 30 USD. On a private cloud like OpenStack, this allows lower overhead of resources used by the potentially multiple clusters running.

The static configuration is created using Terraform/OpenTofu and once the management virtual machine is created, it uses `cloud-init` to bootstrap the system by running an `ansible-pull` playbook which then continues the rest of the automated steps. This usually takes approximately 5 minutes to complete. Cluster in the Cloud was originally designed to use Hashicorp's Terraform but after it moved to a non–open-source model, compatibility with the free software fork OpenTofu will be maintained going forwards. The static and elastically-created infrastructure is shown schematically in Fig. 1.

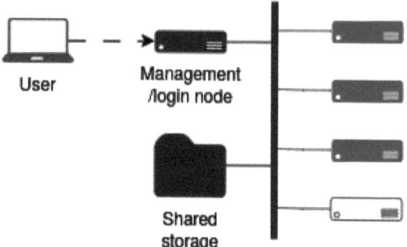

Fig. 1. Static infrastructure created by Terraform/OpenTofu in blue to the left, and elastically-created compute nodes in green to the right. (Color figure online)

2.2 Software Environment

Job Scheduler. The core component of Cluster in the Cloud is the job scheduler. This uses Slurm [7] in a simple configuration with a single partition, sharing its configuration with compute nodes via the shared file system. The main customisation that is done on the Slurm system is to allow the automatic scaling of compute nodes, described in Sect. 3.

User Management. User accounts are managed via a locally-running LDAP server. The server runs on the management node and each compute node is configured to connect to it over the local virtual network. A script to create user accounts for researchers is provided on the management server and defaults to SSH key-only logins. Since clusters are run within access-controlled tenancies and are created on a per-project basis, access is only given to the researchers working on the particular project, helping to manage the impact of any security threat, incident or vulnerability.

To allow Slurm to authenticate users across the compute nodes and management node, `munge` is used, with it configuration baked into the compute node images.

2.3 Compute Node Image Creation

A default configuration for a compute node is provided by Cluster in the Cloud to allow it to interoperate with the infrastructure and services provided. This image is automatically built during the software configuration step using PACKER [5].

The image is built on top of a standard RHEL clone (currently Rocky 9) and has built into it all the settings and configuration needed to operate as a compute node. This includes installing `slurmd`, setting the SSH configuration, installing the LDAP client, mounting the shared file system and installing the `munge` key.

Customising the Image. While users can install software that needs to be accessed by compute jobs onto the shared file system, it can be simpler, more efficient, or even necessary (for example in the case of GPU drivers) to customise the compute image directly.

Cluster in the Cloud provides a script with a hook to add custom code into the building f the compute node image, which will then take preference for any new nodes started from that point on.

2.4 Destroying a Cluster

Clusters are designed to be ephemeral, at least on the time scale of a research project. In order to control cost and manage the resources, a cluster can be destroyed in a single step using Terraform/OpenTofu, destroying all compute nodes, images, storage and virtual machines. After destruction, no charged-for resources will remain so it provides a clean break from a capacity, resource and security management perspective.

3 Elastic Scaling Implementation

The core of Cluster in the Cloud is the scalable management of compute resources in response to jobs being submitted, all built on top of Slurm's power saving system [15].

During installation of Cluster in the Cloud, the administrator configures limits on the node types available, for example they might limit the cluster to two small CPU nodes, ten large CPU nodes and four GPU nodes. The configurations for these nodes are added to the Slurm configuration along with the description of each node type (e.g. the number of cores or the amount of RAM) which are are drawn from the cloud's API. Each node is given a name derived from its canonical instance type name and a sequential number.

For each node configuration, metadata about the node is encoded into Slurm "features" including the instance type (saved as `shape`), CPU architecture and anything else that might be needed when starting the node. The presence of GPUs is encoded into the `GRES` field of a node.

Slurm allows nodes to be designated as `CLOUD` nodes which treats the node as "powered off" and subject to power saving. These nodes are still available for scheduling onto, as any other node would be. When a job is scheduled onto a node which is powered off, Slurm calls an external script to "resume" a node (`startnode`) which allows Cluster in the Cloud to hook in and interface with the cloud provider to create it. When a node is idle, Slurm will schedule it for powering off after a configurable timeout (by calling `stopnode`).

The `startnode` and `stopnode` scripts are responsible for aligning the state that Slurm is requesting with the state on the cloud platform. A custom script is provided for each of the supported cloud providers and creates an abstraction layer between Slurm's naïve "resume/suspend node" and the details of the specific cloud service. Cluster in the Cloud interprets the requests for "powering on" and "powering off" as instructions to create and destroy virtual machines. The time between submitting a job and that job starting to run on a freshly started node varies depending on the cloud provider, but benchmarks on AWS measured from 50–60.

The node configuration, creation and destruction life cycle is described below and summarised in in Fig. 2.

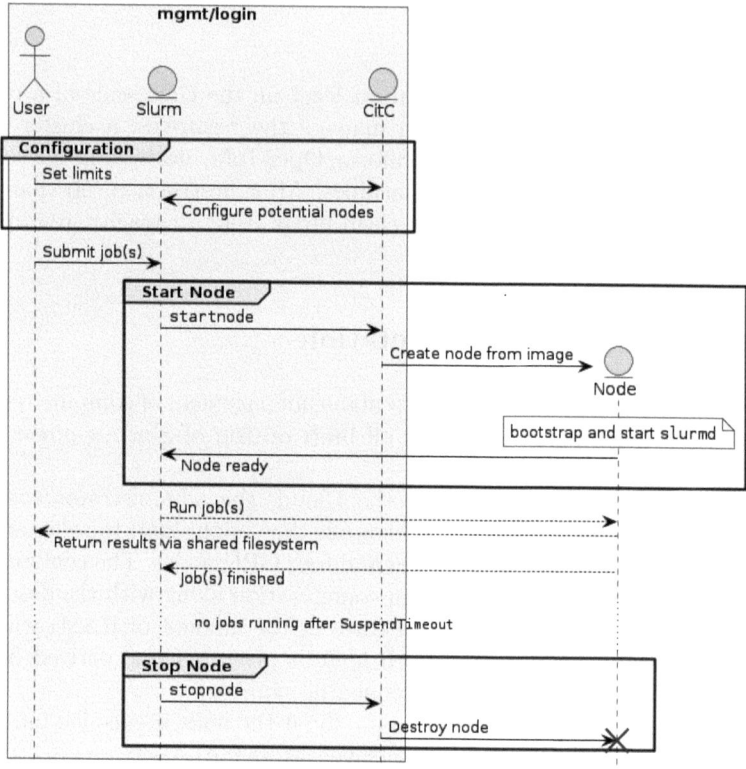

Fig. 2. The node configuration, creation and destruction life cycle.

3.1 Starting Nodes

Upon receiving a request for starting a node, startnode will first check that the node is not already running or in an intermediate (starting up or shutting down) state. In these cases it will return without performing any actions and allow Slurm to connect to the node once it has started.

The requested node name is used to query Slurm about any features that are set. The shape feature defines the instance type and the arch is used to select the correct disk image. Other details of the started node such as the virtual network to connect to, node metadata, and security groups are injected based on global system configuration.

Each node that is started is assigned an IP address by the cloud provider and is also referred to by a domain name. Once that node is destroyed, if it is restarted there is ordinarily no guarantee that it will be assigned the same IP address. This can cause an issue is there is local DNS caching on the login server, making connecting with SSH or otherwise communicating fail. To solve this, one of the checks that `startnode` does is query Slurm to see whether the node name in question has previously been registered, and if so use its previously allocated IP address when launching the virtual machine. On cloud providers which have an easy-to-use and low-cost DNS provider this step can be circumvented and directly use the central DNS with a suitably short time to live (TTL).

Node Bootstrapping. When a node starts, there are two steps that must be performed in order for the node to be able to successfully communicate with the Slurm controller:

1. set the local hostname of the node to match the node name that Slurm is expecting and
2. start the `slurmd` dæmon.

All other preparatory steps are baked into the node image as described in Sect. 2.3.

3.2 Stopping Nodes

Stopping compute nodes is a simple process of, when triggered via `stopnode`, terminating the virtual machine via the cloud interface and—if applicable—deregistering from the DNS server. Nodes become unavailable immediately and are usually completely destroyed within 30 s.

3.3 Implementation Code

The core of the code to interact with the cloud interfaces is included directly in the Ansible configuration, whereby it selects the correct implementation for the specific platform. That code, in-part, calls out to a separate Python library, `python-citc` [19].

To support this code, a cloud interface mocking library, `mebula` [18] was developed to create controlled environments in which the Python code can be unit tested before integration into Cluster in the Cloud.

4 Design Principles

Cluster in the Cloud has a number of design requirements and aims which either affect design decisions or differentiate it from other offerings available (such as AWS ParallelCluster, Azure CycleCloud, ElastiCluster, Magic Castle and RONIN). The requirements are based around who we see as the common user of a cluster like this: a researcher who is an expert in their technical field but is not a systems administrator. They will often have some support from a Research Software/Infrastructure Engineer but should be able to manage their own user space once the cluster is running. The aims are detailed below and compared with a traditional batch cluster in Table 1.

It is worth mentioning that raw compute performance is not prioritised if it were to conflict with any of the goals discussed below. Cluster in the Cloud is primarily designed for compute use cases which are loosely coupled such as parameter sweeps, embarrassingly parallel tasks, interactive work or education and will perform less well than highly-tuned on-premise resources if inter-node communication is important.

4.1 Scalable and Elastic

Being able to dynamically scale up or down as needed is one of the most powerful features that public cloud can provide. For an on-premise cluster, provisioning new hardware can easily take months, whereas on public cloud a new machine can be ready in minutes.

There is a supposed ideal that the public cloud is infinite and that one can scale up as far as one would like. However, the two limiting factors are usually 1) that there are of course limits on the available hardware, particularly for new and rare platforms and 2) there are spending rates to consider. As such, most cloud platforms apply limits to resources and so any scalability we're talking about here is working within those limits.

Within the limits applied by the cloud provider, Cluster in the Cloud is able to automatically provision new compute nodes as required by the work queue. At initial cluster creation there will be no running compute nodes and they will only be started when needed. Once the task queue is exhausted, the nodes will automatically shut down after a short timeout period.

For a traditional on-premise cluster this is not a consideration for the user as their usage fits around that of the other users and is managed via a fair-share allocation. For those running the system, however, sizing a cluster up-front requires understanding how the usage will grow with time and and opportunities to scale are rare and time-consuming. Managing a batch cluster in the cloud without scaling would result in either frequent queuing or a large opportunity for overspending on unused resources.

4.2 Heterogeneous

The need of researchers for varied hardware, either throughout a single pipeline or across different experiments demands the built-in support for heterogeneous clusters. Cluster in the Cloud supports any mixture of hardware nodes, whether varying by number of CPU cores, amount of RAM, CPU architecture or presence of accelerators. Ordinarily this is mapping directly to the "shape"/"flavor"/"instance type" that the cloud platform is providing.

As well as in principle supporting heterogeneous hardware, it can work with it in a scalable way. If a job is submitted which needs a GPU, then a GPU node will be started. If a job with high memory requirements is submitted then an appropriately sized node will be started. Similarly, if a job with low memory requirements is started then the smallest node type that can support it will be started.

4.3 Personal

Cluster in the Cloud is designed to support single user or small research group cases. Often each cluster will only be created for the duration of a single project and so can expect to last perhaps a few months or less. This allows optimisations in the design, for example not needing to maintain complex software management systems and instead prefer custom node images with the software baked in.

The benefit to the user is that they have full control over their cluster and can configure it with whatever software they like, even in ways which—under a shared cluster environment—would clash with other users.

From the perspective of an institute who would like to use Cluster in the Cloud it means that the the needs, resources and management of each person or group's cluster is segregated allowing customisation of each as their needs dictate. It also means that since it's easy to destroy and recreate a cluster, an upgrade process is not provided.

4.4 Cross-Cloud

While the original proof-of-concept was created in 2018 only to work on Oracle Cloud Infrastructure, it was redesigned in 2019 to be as cloud agnostic as possible. To date it has been ported to work on Oracle Cloud, Google Cloud, AWS, Azure and OpenStack (an open source private cloud solution).

The design primarily supports this by breaking the configuration into two layers. The custom per-platform infrastructure-as-code layer provides a common "hardware" configuration upon which a relatively consistent operating system and user land layer can be built.

This has shown to be one of the main architectural limiters in the project. Some cloud platforms will, for example, provide special extra features but if they cannot be also provided in a similar way on the other cloud providers, they will not be included in the product. While this means that certain advanced features are not accessible through Cluster in the Cloud, it provides a simplifying force on the design which aids maintainability by blocking spurious features and increasing consistency. This does have an inevitable performance penalty though as virtual machine placement, high-performance networking and parallel file systems all require some level of bespoke cloud platform integration. Introducing these features is not ruled out (see Sect. 6) but have not been prioritised thus far as high-throughput rather than tightly-coupled high-performance workloads have been the primary use case.

4.5 Familiar

The driving force behind reproducing an interface similar to that which is found in traditional batch clusters is one of familiarity. We expect the average researcher to not be able to tell the difference between connecting to a Cluster in the Cloud via SSH and connecting to their institutional cluster.

There will of course be differences, for example: partition names, software paths, data transfer speeds etc., but the core workflow and mode of interaction is designed to be as similar as possible. This means using standard UNIX accounts, providing SSH access, providing a traditional Slurm scheduler and not requiring any special configuration from the user in order to submit to the scalable or heterogeneous system.

Cluster in the Cloud deployments have been configured with interactive tools on top such as Jupyter, integrated seamlessly into the batch cluster to allow a wider range of researchers to make use of the resource.

4.6 Easy to Use

Cluster in the Cloud takes an opinionated approach to the setup that it provides, minimising the configurations that are possible. This streamlines the installation process while also aiding maintainability. The default setup has been iterated upon since the creation of the project—carefully weighting each of the other design aims detailed in this section—to provide the best experience for the standard research user. A cluster can be created from an empty cloud environment with no additional setup needed, and the user can be ready to submit in job in less than 5 min.

4.7 Optimised for Cost

A leading design constraint was that one should only pay for what they are using. This firstly leads to the core concept of scaling up and down compute resources only as needed, but secondly also guides the design of the rest of the infrastructural resources.

For a traditional on-premise cluster this is not a consideration for the user as the resource if often free-at-point-of-use and managed via a fair-share algorithm. However if they want to make use of some cloud resource then misjudging the resource requirements could result in overspend (on public cloud) or wasting resources (on private cloud).

Since the clusters are designed for personal or small group use, the expectation is that for a significant fraction of their existence, they will not be actively running jobs. For this reason, the baseline cost of keeping a cluster running, in absence of any compute nodes running is achieved by allocating as much of the remaining services to a single lightweight virtual machine holding all the management services as well as the user login interface.

Table 1. Comparison between a traditional batch cluster and Cluster in the Cloud against the design aims of the project.

	Traditional batch cluster	Cluster in the Cloud
Scalable & elastic	Fixed size dictated by the hardware purchased	Grows and shrinks as demanded
Heterogeneous	Cluster may have a mixture of hardware, but usually only a few node types	Can provide any mixture of hardware available from the provider
Personal	A shared resource which must account for many different users	Can customise the environment without affecting other users
Familiar	An environment many researchers are used to	Designed to replicate the aforementioned environment as closely as possible
Cost effective	Resources must be paid for up-front and is paid for, regardless of usage	Users only pay for compute or storage that they use

5 Work Using Cluster in the Cloud

Cluster in the Cloud has been used for a number of research projects, across many domains. One common use is for benchmarking of standard and exotic research software across hardware types [3] as it allows highly heterogeneous environments in a manageable and predictable way. Due to its encapsulation and easy of creation and destruction, it has also been used to create teaching environments, for example for giving access to GPU resources or for teaching batch computing basics.

The initial versions of Cluster in the Cloud were created in 2018 in order to support a particular research case of running cryoEM analysis pipelines for studying viral particles [14,17]. In this case, a partnership with Oracle for Research had provided cloud credits for the researcher but they had no way to effectively use them due to lack of expertise with the cloud and so Cluster in the Cloud allowed this research to happen. This work led on to similar studies in cryoEM analysis and molecular dynamics simulation pipelines for studies of nicotinic receptors [11]. Further work was then carried out from 2020 onwards into COVID-19 [4,10,16].

In other areas, it was used to study cancer radiotherapy [2] and carbon sequestration [13] where the local computing resources were either too contended or did not support the software stacks needed for the research.

6 Future Work

State Synchronisation. One fundamental split in the design is due to the fact that Slurm maintains its own understanding of the state of the system, as does the cloud provider. This means that at times—perhaps due to temporary outages, timeouts or hitting resource limits—the two states can get out of sync. The system fails safe and will not leave nodes running, but since Slurm sees nodes as persistent (by node name) while in fact they are ephemeral virtual machines, if a node fails to start then Slurm will mark it as `DOWN` and that "slot" become unavailable. If this happens repeatedly then a number of nodes may become unavailable and affect the ability of the cluster to scale. A watchdog daemon is planned which works to keep the two states in sync and allow recover of these fail states.

Parallel File Systems. By default, Cluster in the Cloud only supports simple NFS-based shared file systems in order to reduce costs. This comes at the expense of performance for compute tasks which depend on fast or highly-parallel file reading or writing. In the future, configuration could be added to enable using cloud platform's native fast parallel file systems or object stores. Work to create fast in-node distributed file systems has been started in the form of DisTRaX [8], which may be incorporated or included into Cluster in the Cloud in the future.

High-Performance Networks. When a node is started by Cluster in the Cloud it is unaware of the jobs that are going to be run on it and so it cannot take account of cluster topology for creating high-performance networks as they also might be reused immediately for a job with different requirements. Knowledge of meta-node constraints like this are in-principle possible using job submission plugins and features available in newer versions of Slurm and work is planned to find ways to incorporate this ergonomically.

Acknowledgements. The authors thank the University of Bristol for allowing time for the development of this product; to the Bristol Research Software Engineering team for architectural input and testing; and to Oracle Research, AppsBroker, AWS and Microsoft for providing engineer time to port Cluster in the Cloud to their platforms.

References

1. Ansible developers: Ansible. https://ansible.com
2. Beck, L., et al.: A novel approach to contamination suppression in transmission detectors for radiotherapy. In: IEEE Transactions on Radiation and Plasma Medical Sciences, p. 1 (2020). https://doi.org/10.1109/trpms.2020.2995059
3. Deakin, T., Poenaru, A., Lin, T., McIntosh-Smith, S.: Tracking performance portability on the yellow brick road to exascale. In: 2020 IEEE/ACM International Workshop on Performance, Portability and Productivity in HPC (P3HPC), pp. 1–13 (2020). https://doi.org/10.1109/P3HPC51967.2020.00006

4. Dommer, A., et al.: #COVIDisAirborne: AI-enabled multiscale computational microscopy of delta SARS-CoV-2 in a respiratory aerosol. Int. J. High Perform. Comput. Appl. **37**(1), 28–44 (2023). https://doi.org/10.1177/10943420221128233
5. HashiCorp: Packer. https://packer.io
6. HashiCorp: Terraform. https://terraform.io
7. Jette, M.A., Wickberg, T.: Architecture of the slurm workload manager. In: Klusáček, D., Corbalán, J., Rodrigo, G.P. (eds.) Job Scheduling Strategies for Parallel Processing, pp. 3–23. Springer Nature Switzerland, Cham (2023). https://doi.org/10.1007/978-3-031-43943-8_1
8. Mason-Williams, G.: DisTRaX. https://github.com/rosalindfranklininstitute/DisTRaX/
9. Microsoft: Data Science Virtual Machines. https://azure.microsoft.com/en-gb/products/virtual-machines/data-science-virtual-machines
10. Oliveira, A.S.F., et al.: A potential interaction between the SARS-CoV-2 spike protein and nicotinic acetylcholine receptors. Biophys. J. **120**(6), 983–993 (2021). https://doi.org/10.1016/j.bpj.2021.01.037
11. Oliveira, A.S.F., et al.: A general mechanism for signal propagation in the nicotinic acetylcholine receptor family. J. Am. Chem. Soc. **141**(51), 19953–19958 (2019). https://doi.org/10.1021/jacs.9b09055
12. OpenTofu Developers: OpenTofu. https://opentofu.org
13. Payton, R.L., Yizhuo, S., Kingdon, A., Hier-Majumder, S.: Pore Scale Modelling of Carbon Capture and Sequestration. In: AGU Fall Meeting 2019, pp. 0–2. American Geophysical Union, San Francisco, Ca, USA (2019). https://doi.org/10.1002/essoar.10502007.1, http://nora.nerc.ac.uk/id/eprint/526317/
14. Sari-Ak, D., et al.: VLP-factory and ADDomer: self-assembling virus-like particle (VLP) technologies for multiple protein and peptide epitope display. Curr. Protoc. **1**(3), e55 (2021). https://doi.org/10.1002/cpz1.55
15. Slurm Developers: Slurm Power Saving Guide (2023). https://slurm.schedmd.com/power_save.html. Accessed 19 Feb 2024
16. Toelzer, C., et al.: Free fatty acid binding pocket in the locked structure of SARS-CoV-2 spike protein. Science (2020). https://doi.org/10.1126/science.abd3255
17. Vragniau, C., et al.: Synthetic self-assembling ADDomer platform for highly efficient vaccination by genetically encoded multiepitope display. Sci. Adv. **5**(9), eaaw2853 (2019). https://doi.org/10.1126/sciadv.aaw2853
18. Williams, M.: Mebula. https://doi.org/10.5281/zenodo.4094775. https://github.com/milliams/mebula
19. Williams, M.: Python-citc. https://github.com/clusterinthecloud/python-citc/

A User-Oriented Portable, Reproducible, and Scalable Software Ecosystem

Alfio Lazzaro[1], Utz-Uwe Haus[1(✉)], Sandrine Charousset[2], and Nina Mujkanovic[1]

[1] HPE HPC/AI EMEA Research Lab, 4051 Basel, Switzerland
{alfio.lazzaro,utz-uwe.haus,nina.mujkanovic}@hpe.com
[2] EDF Lab Paris Saclay, 91120 Palaiseau, France
sandrine.charousset@edf.fr

Abstract. It is normal for scientists to perform their research on a diverse set of hardware, ranging from laptops and workstations to supercomputers and cloud resources. The standard scenario requires a mix of these resources. In this paper we describe a software ecosystem that enables users to rely on the same development environment for running their workflows across the different computational resources. We describe a modular, unified command-line interface that allows for the interaction with a user-workflow across diverse hardware platform. The software ecosystem has been successfully tested as part of the PLAN4RES EU H2020 project. It can be extended to other projects with similar requirements, so that they can benefit from the same approach for executing computational workflows.

Keywords: Computational workflows · containerized environment · supercomputing · cluster computing

1 Introduction

Scientists typical have access to a range of computing hardware for their research, from laptops and workstations (*local* resources), to supercomputers and cloud resources (*remote* resources). A standard scenario requires a mix of these hardware resources, as science projects may consist of numerous steps and methods involving multiple applications and running on various devices, from classical high performance computing (HPC) systems to cloud-based services. For example, users may carry out fast prototyping of their workflows on local resources at their disposal, then move to HPC remote resources for specific production workflows requiring more performant or specialized hardware (e.g. fast interconnects for parallel job executions, or GPUs for computation).

We note that users often prefer their local systems due to familiarity with specific operating systems (OSs), e.g. WINDOWS or MACOS, or the availability of applications not typically available on remote resources which often have a LINUX system installed, possibly with limited privileges. Pre- and post-data processing, for example, can require custom or commercial applications, where the data cannot be shared outside the user's institution due to security reasons. Conversely, data may instead be located on the remote site, and only a portion of it needed for user tests on the local machines, leaving the data closer to the computation (*edge* computing).

Cloud computing technologies have gained traction in HPC for their benefits, including resource dynamism compared to the more static approach of traditional workload managers such as Slurm and PBS, workload automation, reproducibility via virtualization, and resilience owing to their microservices approach. Supercomputers offer access to advanced HPC computing techniques and massive processing capability for grand challenges and scientific discovery. In recent years we have seen the convergence between the two spheres, as typical HPC applications such as MPI have crept into the cloud ecosystem, and HPC system vendors and sites have incorporated the notion of microservices and containerization. An overview on the differences and commonalities between cloud and supercomputers, and how to run workflows on each, can be found elsewhere [1,5,8,10,15].

This convergence and the commoditization of HPC on one side, and the growing complexity of simulation and data analysis workflows on the other, have made workflow management a necessity. The need for the efficient use of resources, as well as the increased requirements to provide constant, reliable, and reproducible results, has driven the creation of a multitude of workflow management applications, which are often domain dependant [10]. We, instead, envision a software ecosystem that enables users to rely on the same development environment (same *user-experience*) for running their workflows across local and remote resources.

In this paper, we describe a modular, unified command-line interface using containerization to enable the launching of jobs via a workload manager on a mix of hardware resources. In Sect. 2, we describe the requirements that have driven the software ecosystem development, based upon the domain-expert user's perspective (*user-oriented*). As users can integrate their specific applications in the software ecosystem as part of their favourite development workflow environment, and run seamlessly on local and remote resources, we consider this approach *portable* and *reproducible*, and it can interface with a *scalable* workload manager to carry out complex workflows. The implementation details of the software ecosystem are given in Sect. 3. The ecosystem was developed as part of the PLAN4RES EU H2020 project [3], and we present a workflow application use case in Sect. 4. Finally, concluding remarks and an outlook are given.

1.1 Related Work

Various frameworks have emerged to support user workflows from simple desktop calculations to complex activities that require large infrastructure shared by a vast community of users. Science gateways combine computational resources from grid, cloud, and supercomputers, while reducing the learning curve and barriers to entry by implementing Web and mobile applications [7]. Jupyter

Notebook has proven convenient for running workflows via a Web interface on local and remote systems. Colonnelli et al. have shown a way to execute complex distributed workflows with Jupyter, with a unified interface to Cloud and HPC for scientific applications [4]. Although these methods provide user-friendly Web interfaces out-of-the-box, they are mostly suited for scripting language applications, and not really meant for HPC execution as they lack sufficient support for the version control required for collaborative activities [14].

The EMERALD system allows to build workflows to be executed between local resources and cloud, where users can decide which computation steps should run on remote resources [13]. An abundance of studies concerning software environments that allow portable, reproducible, and scalable deployments, targeting cloud and HPC resources, exists, see for example Refs. [11,16]. Their common approach is to use software containers as execution building-blocks. We follow a similar approach, however we also provide a unified command-line interface enabling the launching of jobs via a workload manager on a diverse set of hardware and OSs.

2 Software Ecosystem Requirements

With reference to Sect. 1, we aim to design a software ecosystem that allows users to run on different computing resources with minimal burden. Here we distinguish between local and remote resources, as show in Fig. 1. In particular, local resources can have different OSs (WINDOWS, MACOS, LINUX), while we assume that remote resources are only based on LINUX for intensive and scalable computational tasks. Therefore, the goal is to have a single entry-point for the execution control of the hardware resources that integrates the local software environment, with the option of specific configurations depending on which resource is used.

We base the design requirements of the software ecosystem on a user-oriented approach, where we generalize and abstract the domain-experts software for specific hardware. The requirements were introduced during the PLAN4RES project, and generalized later on with the introduction of additional requirements, resulting in the following:

- unified control of the resources via a shell command-line interface (CLI);
- support for multiple OSs and compute systems;
- a minimal set of commands (possibly one) to interact with the resources to ensure good usability for domain-expert (non-technical) users;
- possibility to enable specific configurations via files or environment variables;
- common pre-installed components and a mechanism to add extra software to the platform as needed;
- relocation of the environment across systems with a simple drop-in replacement procedure, i.e. no installation needed and binary exchangeability;
- presumed multi-user shared environment;
- possibility to define and execute data-driven, complex workflows composed of Shell- and Python-scripts, as well as binary executables, including data transfer out of and into the storage platform.

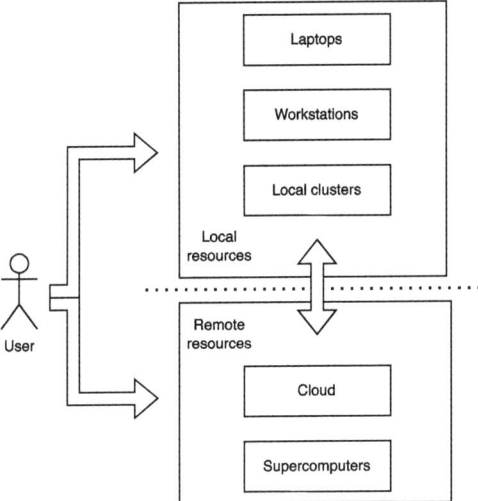

Fig. 1. User-oriented approach for running on local and remote computational resources.

The technical implementation to address these requirements is described in Sect. 3.

3 Software Ecosystem Implementation

The fundamental assumption for the software environment implementation is that all platform tools will run in a modern LINUX-based software environment, on hosts with x86_64 CPUs, where we avoid requiring LINUX-specificity by relying on topic-specific standards only, in particular POSIX. The user CLI must run in a terminal shell, which is available by default on LINUX and MACOS systems, while for WINDOWS users we suggest to use the GIT-BASH shell[1]. The scripts, data, configuration files, and application executables of the software ecosystem are organized in a specific directory structure, as described in Sect. 3.1.

To ease deployment, we create a containerized environment based on the SINGULARITY container infrastructure [6]. This container acts as *executor*, meaning that all tools are based in and operated by it. The use of containers has been proven to be a very convenient way to abstract from the underlying host OS, permitting software to run reliably when moved from one computing environment to another (assuming hardware compatibility), without having to build and configure separately [9]. This fulfills the requirement of running on a variety of hardware resources of interest.

---

[1] https://www.atlassian.com/git/tutorials/git-bash.

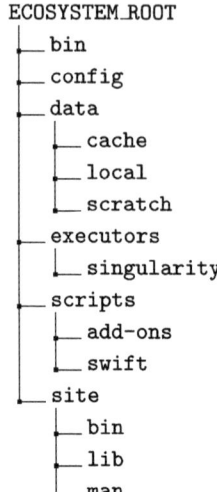

Fig. 2. Software ecosystem directory structure.

While the SINGULARITY container can run natively on a LINUX OS host, it cannot on WINDOWS or MACOS OSs[2], which is one of our requirements. For this reason, a minimal installation of a LINUX virtual machine (VM) is required. We again assume that hosts have x86_64 CPUs. We describe the container and the VM configurations in Sects. 3.2, as well as components required pre-installed, and a mechanism to add extra software to the platform as needed. Finally, in Sect. 3.3 we address the implementation requirements to define and execute data-driven, complex workflows.

3.1 Directory Structure

The software ecosystem is organized in a directory structure. The root directory, defined by the user on the computer system, needs to

- be accessible from all compute nodes that will concurrently work on the data;
- have enough space for all data and the software environment;
- satisfy POSIX file system semantics.

We refer to this directory as ECOSYSTEM_ROOT. This is also the name of an environment variable that contains the directory name, which tools can query at run-time. Inside this root directory, the directory structure shown in Fig. 2 is mandated, and can be relied upon when writing programs for use within the framework.

The ECOSYSTEM_ROOT/bin directory contains all software that is needed for workflow execution and must be in the user's search PATH so that the operating

---

[2] https://docs.sylabs.io/guides/3.8/admin-guide/installation.html#installation-on-windows-or-mac.

system can find it. This software will run the specific commands via the container available in the ECOSYSTEM_ROOT/executors directory, which includes the necessary files for building it.

The ECOSYSTEM_ROOT/config directory contains the configuration file(s), see Sect. 3.3.

All data will reside below the ECOSYSTEM_ROOT/data directory. This directory takes the role of the staging area and also the results storage area. Data cached from external sources will be stored below ECOSYSTEM_ROOT/data/cache. Local data that is specific to the user's workspace, in particular private data, should be stored below ECOSYSTEM_ROOT/data/local. The ECOSYSTEM_ROOT/data/scratch directory is used as the working directory of tools and can be used for volatile data during program runs.

The ECOSYSTEM_ROOT/scripts directory can contain more complex scripts to execute repeated tasks using executables from ECOSYSTEM_ROOT/bin.

The ECOSYSTEM_ROOT/site can be used by users to install their own local software (comparable to /usr/local on Unix systems), which already guarantees that ECOSYSTEM_ROOT/site/bin is in PATH, ECOSYSTEM_ROOT/site/lib is in LD_LIBRARY_PATH, and ECOSYSTEM_ROOT/site/man is in the MANPATH.

The directory structure can be automatically created by cloning a GIT repository, for which the created directory represents the ECOSYSTEM_ROOT path. This repository contains all scripts needed for the environment and can be shared between multiple users via the standard GIT features, like branching and forking.

3.2 Executor Environment

The execution in the platform is triggered by calling a BASH script driver in the ECOSYSTEM_ROOT/bin directory, which acts as the only *entry-point* for all users activities to be executed in the software ecosystem, including the execution on the container image with arguments designating the tool to execute. This command will parse the configuration files under ECOSYSTEM_ROOT/config and modify the environment as needed, then start the appropriate script or binary within the container environment. The driver command acts like a special shell; in fact, running it without arguments will start a shell in the container environment with all paths set up appropriately so that scripts and tools are found and can be executed

```
$ ECOSYSTEM_ROOT/bin/driver
;; Run 'driver -h' to get help.
[ENV] ~ >
```

Alternatively, the command to be executed (with its arguments) can be directly passed during the driver invocation. The configuration files are BASH shell-script fragments with default environment variables set suitable for most users, depending on the specific workflow. The users can change the values of these variables by editing the configuration files, or by exporting the values directly in the environment. For this reason, the variables are set via the syntax `VARIABLE_NAME=${VARIABLE_NAME:-DEFAULT_VALUE}`. For example, there can be multiple containers under the `ECOSYSTEM_ROOT/executors` directory that can be selected via a variable in the configuration file.

The minimal required dependencies for a LINUX host system are: the BASH shell, the GIT command, and the SINGULARITY application (we use version 3.11). We test on DEBIAN 10, UBUNTU 20.04, UBUNTU 22.04, FEDORA 35, and SUSE LINUX ENTERPRISE SERVER 15. The container image binds the host `ECOSYSTEM_ROOT` directories tree (read and write access), so that it can access all files of the ecosystem of the host system.

For the WINDOWS and MACOS host systems, we based our implementation on VAGRANT[3] and VIRTUALBOX[4] to conveniently set up a suitable VM. The VM is based on the DEBIAN 10 distribution. A `Vagrantfile` in the `ECOSYSTEM_ROOT` directory is provided for the installation of the dependencies. The user starts the VM when running the `driver` command (the `driver` will check if the VM is running, otherwise it will start it via the `vagrant up` command). Therefore there is no direct connection to the VM, making all ecosystem CLI commands independent of the host OS. We test on WINDOWS 10 21H2 and MACOS 11 and 12. The VM introduces an intermediate layer between the host system and the container image running on it. For this reason, the VM has to mount the host `ECOSYSTEM_ROOT` directories tree (described in the `Vagrantfile` and done during the provisioning of the VAGRANT VM), so that the container image can bind it. The `driver` itself will deal with the intermediate layer, so that the users will not see any difference with respect to running directly on a LINUX host system. In conclusion, the entire `ECOSYSTEM_ROOT` directory tree is shared (for reading and writing) between the Host (LINUX, WINDOWS, MACOS) and the container.

The users can build the container locally via a script available in the `ECOSYSTEM_ROOT/bin` directory, or download a pre-built version available from a given URL. Note that the build procedure will directly occur on the LINUX host or in the VM for WINDOWS and MACOS hosts. The containers include all the required packages for building the users applications such as compilers, build tools (e.g. `cmake`), Python modules, parallel libraries (e.g. `MPI`), and scientific libraries. Therefore, the container serves as a common working platform for the users, but by design does not contain the users applications. We implement the building of the pre-built container as part of a continuous-integration (CI) procedure linked to the the GIT repository of the software ecosystem. Any change of the files used for building the container pushed to the GIT repository will trigger the CI for rebuilding the container that is then stored as an artifact. In this way users can download this image and do not need to build it on their local systems. By default, the users download the containers, unless they have built a local container and set to use it in the configuration file. Then, for every execution of the `driver` there will be a check whether the local cached copy of

---

[3] https://developer.hashicorp.com/vagrant.
[4] https://www.virtualbox.org/.

the container image matches the remote one, and updates will be downloaded automatically. This check can be avoided via a configuration setting to preserve the local cached copy.

User specific software can be installed using a recipe-based *add-on* installation infrastructure. These software packages will be built and executed via the container. This procedure allows to install tools that can not be directly inserted into the container (mainly due to licensing issues). The advantage of having the add-ons not be part of the container is that users can update the container with new functionalities without the need of reinstalling them. An add-on requires a recipe file, stored under the ECOSYSTEM_ROOT/scripts/add-ons directory. The recipe is an executable script, based on makefile syntax, that supports a common set of targets, in particular install, update, status, uninstall, and help. The add-ons are installed into the directory ECOSYSTEM_ROOT/scripts/add-ons/install so that they can be executed via the driver. Binaries, libraries, and man pages are automatically added to the corresponding environment variables of the container. A user can then query the list of available add-ons via the command:

```
$ ECOSYSTEM_ROOT/bin/driver add-on
<add-on name> : <installed | not installed>

Use 'add-on <add-on name>' to install an add-on.
Use 'add-on <add-on name> help' to see a list of
    specific options per each add-on.
```

The add-ons can be parallel MPI applications, which the driver will launch through various mechanisms, such as mpiexec/mpirun commands or the srun command for the Slurm batch system.

Finally, we provide a script that can archive the entire ecosystem installed software so that it can be relocated to another system, including the possibility to store backups, or alternatively synchronize (via the rsync command) files between two locations, possibly between different users.

3.3 Workflow Execution

In this section we describe a possible user installation workflow that employs the software ecosystem described in this paper. There are 3 steps, as shown in Fig. 3: setup, configure, and run. We assume that all required dependencies mentioned at the beginning of Sect. 3 are installed on the host system. As a result of our abstraction, the same procedure is valid for local and remote resources, independently of the OS used for the local resources, with the possibility to relocate the software ecosystem across systems.

The first step (setup) is to clone the GIT repository which provides the directories tree and the default files, after which users can decide to use the remote container, which will be downloaded by calling the command:

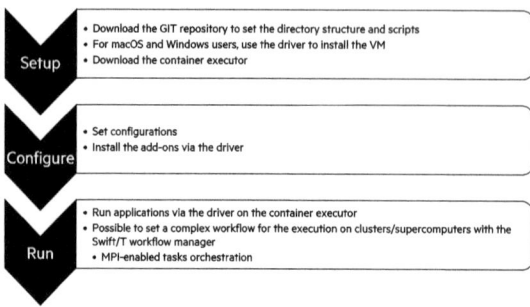

Fig. 3. Schematic example of the software ecosystem installation and usage.

```
$ ECOSYSTEM_ROOT/bin/driver -t
```

This command will download and cache the container file, and eventually test it via the installation integrity tests provided in the container. Note that every call to the `driver` command will trigger a check whether the local cached copy of the SINGULARITY image matches the one on the remote site, and will download updates automatically, unless the user enables the configuration variable to preserve the local copy.

The next step (configure) is to configure and install the proper add-ons. We again use the `driver` command, as described at the end of Sect. 3.2. Eventually, we can use the installed commands via the `driver` command, as described at the beginning of Sect. 3.2.

Finally, the user can describe complex workflows with correlated data dependencies and executions to be performed (run step). The components of the overall workflow are conceptually coupled and interact via data transfers. While it is possible to execute a complete run of the tools by executing every task individually, the true power stems from the integration of all steps into a reproducible workflow described in a documented, machine-executable workflow description. There are two approaches:

- **Manual workflows** can be constructed by explicitly using data files and scripting in a common scripting language like Shell- and Python-scripts. The users can run these scripts via the usual `driver` command.
- **Automated workflows** are defined using SWIFT/T, an MPI-oriented workflow language and runtime system [17]. Swift/T is designed to enable the execution of vast numbers of very small tasks across an MPI-enabled computing system. The tasks could be composed of Shell- and Python-scripts, as well as binary executables, all installed through the add-on procedure. This approach permits an execution model where decisions about the task execution are driven by the availability of their required input data, and where data transfers can be performed by the tool in an efficient manner adapted to the capabilities of the system, instead of being planned by the user.

4 PLAN4RES Use-case

The PLAN4RES (P4R) EU H2020 project aimed to provide a tool for optimizing and simulating the European electricity system, validating the results through real size case studies [3]. Operating the electricity system with the 2050 targeted shares of Renewable Energy Systems (RES) will only be possible and affordable if both grids and generation assets evolve towards a system designed to maximise its capacity to host such amounts of RES. This requires optimizing existing assets and new investments, while making the best use of all flexibilities, such as controllable power plants, but also storage, use of interconnections, and demand control. To achieve this, an integrated representation of the system becomes necessary, involving overcoming significant technical hurdles in the implementation and maintenance of complex models with several nested layers of structure and general and flexible algorithms for solving them, thus leading to problem sizes that grow tremendously with each level of detail modeled.

The P4R environment has been developed following the software ecosystem implementation described in this paper [12]. The main GIT repository is available on GITLAB[5]. The container executor is presented as a GIT submodule under the `executors/singularity` directory, which points to another GITLAB repository[6]. This solution allows to separate the container development versus the main P4R ecosystem. We use the GITLAB CI to build the container, which is then stored as an artifact of the repository. For convenience, the `driver` has been renamed to `p4r`. Two versions of the container are provided, containing MPICH and OpenMPI implementations, respectively. Add-ons provide users access to mathematical optimization packages [12]. The models and the solution algorithms have been implemented using the open-source *Structured Modeling System++* (SMS++)[7] package, which is provided as an add-on.

The full P4R workflow consists of the following base steps:

- access and stage data from an external source;
- run a transformation tool (a Python script, provided as add-on) on the data to convert them to a format for the following computation;
- solve the optimizations via SMS++;
- store the results of the optimizations.

A diagram of the P4R workflow is shown in Fig. 4. The workflow has been deployed both in a manual as well as an automated workflow and successfully executed on PLAN4RES partner's systems: laptops, private clusters, HPE Cray EX Supercomputers, and an AWS ParallelCluster instance[8]. Therefore, the P4R software ecosystem has been successful for providing a fast user prototyping and deployment environment for workflow execution on different hardware resources.

---

[5] https://gitlab.com/cerl/plan4res/p4r-env.
[6] https://gitlab.com/cerl/plan4res/p4r-exec-singularity.
[7] https://smspp.gitlab.io/.
[8] https://docs.aws.amazon.com/parallelcluster/.

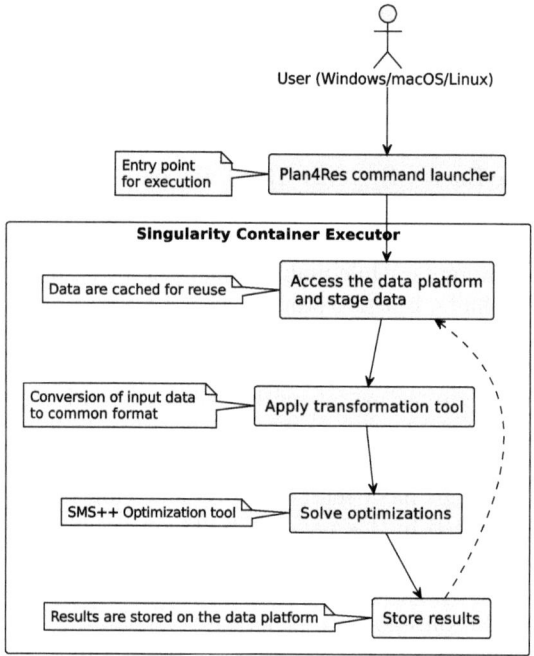

Fig. 4. Plan4Res schematic workflow.

5 Conclusion

The appearance of and convergence between such varied compute sources as HPC, cloud technologies, edge computing, novel hardware including GPUs and FPGAs in the recent years has created both opportunities as well as challenges. Users now have a more flexible, portable, and easy to deploy option via containerization, which renders the sharing and cooperation of research easier, but also introduces complexity in the workflow. In this paper we presented a software ecosystem that offers users a modular, unified command-line interface to enable the same development environment whether running their workflows on local or remote resources, thus allowing for easy deployment, letting users focus on their research instead of technological implementation specificities.

The software ecosystem has been successfully tested as part of the plan4res EU H2020 project, and was used to assess the feasibility and cost of a recently published, long-term energy scenario from the openENTRANCE EU H2020 project [2]. Currently, it is used within the openMod4Africa[9] project for case studies in Western Africa (both at the level of the whole West Africa Power Pool region, and at the level of Senegal) and Eastern Africa (for a case study at the level of the whole East Africa Power Pool and a study focused on Ethiopia). The case studies will be conducted by African experts from universities and the power

---

[9] https://openmod4africa.eu/.

pools, with the help of the European experts bringing the models. It is expected that the software ecosystem will be used by more than ten African institutions in the next two years. Another European project which will use the software ecosystem is MANOEUVRE[10]. This project has just started and is dedicated to designing transition scenarios for Europe as well as defining methodologies and providing tools for conducting the national exercises aiming at developing the National Energy and Climate Plans.

Our software ecosystem can be extended to other projects with similar requirements, such that they can benefit from the same flexible approach for executing computational workflows.

Acknowledgments. The PLAN4RES project received funding from the European Union's Horizon 2020 research and innovation programme under grant agreement No 773897.

Disclosure of Interests. The authors have no competing interests to declare that are relevant to the content of this article.

References

1. Balakrishnan, S.R., Veeramani, S., Leong, J.A., Murray, I., Sidhu, A.S.: High performance computing on the cloud via HPC+cloud software framework. In: 2016 Fifth International Conference on Eco-friendly Computing and Communication Systems (ICECCS), pp. 48–52 (2016). https://doi.org/10.1109/Eco-friendly.2016.7893240
2. Charousset, S., et al.: Best practice for performing case studies for the European energy system in transition (2023). https://doi.org/10.5281/zenodo.8288993
3. Charousset-Brignol, S., et al.: Synergistic approach of multi-energy models for a European optimal energy system management tool. Proj. Reposit. J. **9**, 113 – 116 (2021)
4. Colonnelli, I., et al.: Distributed workflows with Jupyter. Future Gener. Comput. Syst. **128**, 282–298 (2022). https://doi.org/10.1016/j.future.2021.10.007. https://www.sciencedirect.com/science/article/pii/S0167739X21003976
5. Golasowski, M., et al.: Toward the convergence of high-performance computing, cloud, and big data domains. In: HPC, Big Data, and AI Convergence Towards Exascale, pp. 1–16. CRC Press, Boca Raton (2022)
6. Kurtzer, G.M., Sochat, V., Bauer, M.W.: Singularity: scientific containers for mobility of compute. PLoS ONE **12**(5), e0177459 (2017)
7. Lawrence, K., et al.: Science gateways today and tomorrow: positive perspectives of nearly 5000 members of the research community. Concurr. Comput. Pract. Exp. **27** (2015). https://doi.org/10.1002/cpe.3526
8. Li, G., Woo, J., Lim, S.B.: HPC cloud architecture to reduce HPC workflow complexity in containerized environments. Appl. Sci. **11**(3) (2021). https://www.mdpi.com/2076-3417/11/3/923
9. Merkel, D.: Docker: lightweight linux containers for consistent development and deployment. Linux J. **2014**(239), 2 (2014)

---

[10] https://man0euvre.eu/.

10. Mujkanovic, N., Durillo, J.J., Hammer, N., Müller, T.: Survey of adaptive containerization architectures for HPC. In: Proceedings of the SC '23 Workshops of The International Conference on High Performance Computing, Network, Storage, and Analysis, SC-W 2023, pp. 165–176. Association for Computing Machinery, New York (2023). https://doi.org/10.1145/3624062.3624588
11. Piccolo, S.R., Ence, Z.E., Anderson, E.C., Chang, J.T., Bild, A.H.: Simplifying the development of portable, scalable, and reproducible workflows. eLife **10**, e71069 (2021). https://doi.org/10.7554/eLife.71069
12. PLAN4RES : Synergistic approach of multi-energy models for an european optimal energy system management tool.: deliverable D6.1 specification for the PLAN4RES platform implementation. Technical report (2019). https://www.plan4res.eu/results/deliverables/
13. Qian, H., Andresen, D.: Automate scientific workflow execution between local cluster and cloud. Int. J. Netw. Distrib. Comput. **4**, 45–54 (2016). https://doi.org/10.2991/ijndc.2016.4.1.5
14. Samuel, S., Mietchen, D.: Computational reproducibility of Jupyter notebooks from biomedical publications. GigaScience **13**, giad113 (2024). https://doi.org/10.1093/gigascience/giad113
15. Usman, S., Mehmood, R., Katib, I.: Big data and HPC convergence: the cutting edge and outlook. In: Mehmood, R., Bhaduri, B., Katib, I., Chlamtac, I. (eds.) SCITA 2017. LNICST, vol. 224, pp. 11–26. Springer, Cham (2018). https://doi.org/10.1007/978-3-319-94180-6_4
16. Vaillancourt, P., et al.: Reproducible and portable workflows for scientific computing and HPC in the cloud. In: Practice and Experience in Advanced Research Computing, PEARC 2020, pp. 311–320. Association for Computing Machinery, New York (2020). https://doi.org/10.1145/3311790.3396659
17. Wozniak, J.M., Armstrong, T.G., Wilde, M., Katz, D.S., Lusk, E., Foster, I.T.: Swift/t: large-scale application composition via distributed-memory dataflow processing. In: 2013 13th IEEE/ACM International Symposium on Cluster, Cloud, and Grid Computing, pp. 95–102 (2013). https://doi.org/10.1109/CCGrid.2013.99

Leveraging Private Container Networks for Increased User Isolation and Flexibility on HPC Clusters

Lise Jolicoeur[1,2](✉), François Diakhaté[1], and Raymond Namyst[2]

[1] CEA, DAM, DIF, 91297 Arpajon, France
{lise.jolicoeur,francois.diakhate}@cea.fr
[2] INRIA, CNRS, Bordeaux INP, LaBRI, UMR 5800, University of Bordeaux, 33400 Talence, France
raymond.namyst@u-bordeaux.fr

Abstract. To address the increasing complexity of modern scientific computing workflows, HPC clusters must be able to accommodate a wider range of workloads without compromising their efficiency in processing batches of highly parallel jobs. Cloud computing providers have a long history of leveraging all forms of virtualization to let their clients easily and securely deploy complex distributed applications and similar capabilities are now expected from HPC facilities.

In recent years, containers have been progressively adopted by HPC practitioners to facilitate the installation of applications along with their software dependencies. However little attention has been given to the use of containers with virtualized networks to securely orchestrate distributed applications on HPC resources.

In this article, we describe a way to leverage network virtualization to benefit from the flexibility and isolation typically found in a cloud environment while being as transparent and as easy to use as possible for people familiar with HPC clusters. Users are automatically isolated in their own private network which prevents unwanted network accesses and allows them to easily define network addresses so that components of a distributed workflow can reliably reach each other. We describe the implementation of this approach in the pcocc (private cloud on a compute cluster) container runtime. We evaluate both its overhead as well as its benefits for representative use-cases on a Slurm based cluster.

Keywords: Hpc · containers · cloud · VXLAN · Slurm · namespaces · PCOCC

1 Introduction

In the last decade, high performance computing has been adopted in increasingly diverse scientific domains, from climate modelling and high energy physics to genomics and AI. HPC clusters have historically focused on providing platforms optimized for compute-intensive numerical simulations, which harness the aggregate performance of a large number of nodes to perform computations in a minimal time on a fixed amount of resources using a common set of parallel programming interfaces such as MPI and OpenMP. HPC facilities have dedicated a large part of their efforts to serving this use case by providing a uniform, highly tuned software stack made of compilers, runtime systems, and libraries that users can leverage to build optimized parallel applications. However, with the increasing adoption of HPC across all scientific domains, new applications need to be able to benefit from HPC resources. As a global trend, they require a wider range of software dependencies and rely on more and more complex workflows mixing numerical simulations, AI/ML algorithms or data analysis. It is therefore becoming essential that HPC clusters provide tools that make it easier for users to deploy their own customized software stack. In contrast, cloud environments have been built from the ground up with the objective to securely run complex dynamic workloads while being shared by a very large pool of untrusted users. By providing flexibility, automation, elasticity, and scalability, cloud computing has become mainstream regarding the deployment of large-scale applications and workflows. These applications are often designed as a set of components or services, each requiring a specific runtime or software stack. Cloud providers make extensive use of hardware virtualization and containers to partition resources in a flexible and secure way as well as to facilitate application deployment by allowing the packaging of application components as shippable artifacts. The term *cloud-native* has been coined to describe applications that have been developed specifically for cloud platforms. The most popular platform for deploying these applications is Kubernetes [1], an open-source product that allows users to easily and reproducibly define and deploy their workloads on any kind of supported resource from commercial cloud offerings to self-hosted clusters or even edge devices. Kubernetes mainly supports orchestrating applications packaged as containers, a form of lightweight virtualization that operates at the level of operating system interfaces. In Linux, this capability is exposed in the form of namespaces, which allow changing the mapping of system identifiers such as PIDs, filenames, or network interfaces for a process or group of processes. By providing each application with its own virtual view of the operating system, applications can be isolated from each other and remain independent of the host system. While Kubernetes was initially primarily used to host web services, its flexibility has made it popular for running various workloads. Workflow engines enable the scheduling of complex workflows involving compute-intensive tasks on Kubernetes clusters, particularly in the AI/ML field.

While cloud and HPC have long evolved separately, there is a growing interest in bridging the gap between these two environments so that users may benefit from the best capabilities of both cloud and HPC technologies, an approach often referred to as "converged computing". In this article, we discuss how containers can help securely enable new workflows in typical HPC clusters in particular by making use of network virtualization, which is typically used in cloud settings. Indeed while HPC applications are now more and more commonly packaged in container images that can be reproducibly deployed, little attention has been given to leveraging network virtualization within an HPC environment. To our knowledge, most HPC oriented container engines, with the exception of Singularity, do not support setting up network namespaces, and little work has been published on how to expose this capability to users of an HPC cluster. We show that network virtualization can be enabled in a way that is transparent to the end user while helping orchestrating distributed applications and improving security.

2 Converged Computing

The research topics related to converged computing can be classified in three main categories: HPC in the cloud, hybrid solutions and cloud in HPC.

The first approach consists in trying to allow HPC workloads to run efficiently in the cloud, in particular using Kubernetes. Indeed, Kubernetes has quickly gained adoption among scientists wanting to leverage cloud resources for deploying computational workloads. To run efficiently, parallel HPC applications do however require specialized scheduling, resource allocation and process management which is not provided out of the box by Kubernetes. The *MPI Operator*[1] is commonly used to allow launching MPI applications on Kubernetes. To further bridge the gap with the level of support offered by HPC resource managers, multiple tools allow to easily instantiate virtual clusters within Kubernetes, in which resources are managed by an HPC scheduler such as Flux or Slurm [2,3]. Some more tightly integrate the virtual cluster to the underlying environment by delegating resource management to Kubernetes which allows the simultaneous execution of unmodified HPC and non HPC workloads [4]. Other research aims at adapting Kubernetes scheduling and placement algorithms so that it may better handle HPC workloads [5,6]. In [7], the authors present a solution to enable the scaling of HPC workloads on Kubernetes to allow for more elasticity and flexibility.

The second approach consists in creating hybrid architectures bridging cloud and HPC environments, with varying degrees of integration. For example, it can be done by offloading HPC workloads from Kubernetes to a remote HPC cluster through custom tools [8]. Another method relies on transparently converting Kubernetes-native workload specifications to Slurm commands for execution on HPC resources [9]. In [12], the authors present a proof of concept for building a Kubernetes cluster through Slurm allocations by creating Kubernetes agents on compute nodes that link back to an existing and long-standing Kubernetes control plane. The hybrid approach generally allows users to easily define their workflows through Kubernetes while still benefiting from the performance of an HPC cluster, and with minimal modification to each environment.

Finally, the third approach consists in extending HPC platforms with some capabilities more commonly available in the cloud. Many users benefit from the specialized tooling and support provided by HPC facilities and there is value in

---
[1] https://github.com/kubeflow/mpi-operator.

making it easier to deploy a wider range of workloads in this familiar environment. On-premise HPC clusters also remain a more cost-efficient platform than the cloud for many large consumers of compute resources, and some of the largest scale HPC workloads have yet to be fully supported by most cloud providers [10]. In some cases, using the cloud is not even an option that can be considered, most notably for regulatory reasons.

A noticeable step in this direction is the growing adoption of containers [11]. By allowing users to package an application along with its dependencies and deploy it on any environment, containers are a great tool to test new software, use specific versions of dependencies, and generally reduce reliance on the underlying software stack. Deploying containers on HPC environments comes with its own set of challenges: containers must run within the resource constraints set by the resource manager and being able to run a container should not provide a user with any additional privilege on the host. Moreover, containers must be quickly started on thousands of nodes without overloading the shared filesystem. As the most popular container engine, Docker, did not meet these requirements, many HPC oriented container engines were developed to better integrate containers in HPC environments [12].

3 Motivation

While containers are now commonly supported in HPC environments, they are mostly used for a very specific purpose which is to facilitate the deployment of an application, along with its dependencies, as a self-contained image that relies as little as possible on the host software stack. This explains why most of the HPC oriented container engines only make use of the mount and user namespaces to make filesystems within a container independent from the host filesystems. Other namespaces such as the PID or network namespaces are typically shared with the host. This means that, with respect to networking, processes within a container are no different from processes launched directly on the host. While common practice in HPC environments, having all processes share the same network is far from ideal both in terms of security and ease of use.

HPC clusters are typically shared by a large number of users, sometimes even from multiple institutions. When users log in interactively to a cluster, they are presented with a shell environment that resembles a shell on their personal workstation and they tend to use it similarly, forgetting that the server is shared with other users which they do not necessarily trust. A very common security issue comes from starting network applications listening on localhost without authentication on shared machines such as login nodes. The very popular Jupyter notebook server used to behave in this way by default, which was a critical issue considering that it allows to run arbitrary code once connected. Many users setup similarly insecure configurations, for example launching unauthenticated remote gdb servers or establishing SSH tunnels to private resources, forgetting that they are sharing a network with sometimes hundreds of untrusted users.

Moreover, HPC users are deploying more and more complex workflows tightly integrating parallel simulations with machine learning, data analytics, or in-situ visualization. Integrating these software components increasingly requires deploying network services within the HPC cluster. For example, workflow engines such as Fireworks[2] which are required to manage these complex workflows often store workflow state using network databases. Multiple components of a workflow may need to communicate with each other at runtime or a user may want to establish an interactive connection to a dashboard or visualization tool to monitor or even steer a computation. Even assuming that all network protocols are properly authenticated, reliably deploying network services or client-server applications is difficult on an HPC cluster with a shared network. Network daemons launched by a user cannot listen on pre-defined network ports as they may already be used by another user and the address at which they are reachable can change whenever they are started on new nodes by the scheduler for example.

One way to overcome these limitations is to leverage network namespaces to setup a dedicated network stack for containers, which is what Kubernetes does for each pod (group of tightly coupled containers). Each pod is assigned its own IP address which means there is no risk of conflict in case the same port is used by another pod on the same host. Users can also associate domain names to their services, which allows them to know in advance at which domain name and port a service will be reachable, no matter the state of the cluster or on which nodes containers are effectively deployed. Network policies can be defined to isolate traffic as needed, for example between multiple tenants.

4 A Simple Model for HPC Clusters

To take full advantage of containers and solve the issues identified above, we propose to apply a networking model loosely inspired by Kubernetes to an HPC cluster managed by Slurm. While Kubernetes and Slurm implement very different sets of features, they both share the same core capability: allocating resources on a cluster to schedule user-defined workloads.

Using Kubernetes, the main unit of scheduling is the pod which represents a set of resources on a single server in which one or more containers are executed. Containers within a pod share some of their namespaces, in particular the network namespace. Each pod thus has its own network stack, and its own IP address. Users do not normally manage individual pods. They create workload objects such as jobs or deployments which define the containers they want to run and how many times they want to run them. Kubernetes controllers then schedule the appropriate number of pods for running these workloads.

Using Slurm, the main unit of scheduling is the job, which represent a set of resources on multiple servers in which users can run one ore more steps. A step consists in the parallel execution of multiple instances of a program, within the resources allocated for a job. By making use of an HPC container engine, these programs can be run within containers.

---
[2] https://materialsproject.github.io/fireworks/.

In this work, we propose to use the concept of pods in a Slurm cluster. Mirroring the definition used in Kubernetes and other tools such as Podman, we use the term 'pod' to describe a set of namespaces, in our case PID and network, shared between multiple containers on a node. Similarly as with Kubernetes, users do not have to manage pods directly: they can submit Slurm jobs as usual and pods are automatically created when resources are allocated. Steps are then run in containers within the pod created for the job on each node. For a given job, a single pod is created per node but a node can be shared by mutliple pods if it has been allocated by multiple concurrent jobs.

The properties of Kubernetes pods were chosen to facilitate the transition from earlier types of clusters where related processes were run within the same virtual machine or bare metal operating system. These properties also help make the introduction of pods, along with network namespaces, transparent for typical HPC workloads. As processes started one a node for a job are executed within the same pod, they can interact with each other normally using either shared memory or loopback connections, but they are now isolated from processes of other jobs. Each pod is given an IP which allows it to communicate with other pods as well as with processes on the host without NAT. This allows processes in multi-node jobs to communicate normally with each other as well as with the Slurm daemons.

Kubernetes namespaces (completely unrelated to the container namespaces discussed until now) can be used to create naming scopes for group of resources such as pods as well as to define access policies between them. In a multi-tenant cluster, it is common to assign distinct namespaces to each tenant. By default Kubernetes allows unrestricted network communications between all pods and network policies are used to define filtering rules. A commonly applied policy consists in forbidding network traffic across namespaces.

In this work, as a first approach, we consider that each user of an HPC cluster is assigned its own equivalent of a namespace and we apply a default global network policy which only allows network traffic between pods belonging to the same user. Cluster administrators can also define global or per-user ingress/egress rules for communicating with addresses outside of the pod network. Support for more flexible definition of namespaces and network policies may be studied as future work.

As in Kubernetes, DNS records are created for each pod, in a subdomain associated to each namespace, or user in our current implementation. For each job, pod<n>.<jobname>.<user>.<cluster> maps to the pod on the nth node of the allocation, and <jobname>.<user>.<cluster> maps to all pod IPs. The resolver of containers started in a pod is configured to search first in their job domain, then in their namespace domain before defaulting to a set of domains configurable by cluster administrators.

HPC clusters can usually be accessed through login nodes, on which users can start interactive shells. We apply the principles described above to interactive workloads as well by automatically creating for a pod for each user when they establish their first connection to a login node. For each connection, a container is started in the pod previously created for the user and the pod is destroyed when the user no longer has any active sessions on the node. Users can also establish SSH connections to compute nodes which are allocated to them for running jobs. For each such connection, a container is created in the pod matching the most recent job on the node for the user.

5 Implementation of Pcocc Networking

The networking model described in the previous section has been implemented in pcocc (pronounced like "peacock", for private cloud on a compute cluster), a tool which allows to run virtual machines and containers in HPC clusters. While originally written as a standalone Python executable, the container engine has been recently rewritten in Rust, with one objective being to allow tighter integration with the scheduler through the use of a Slurm SPANK [13] plugin. This plugin is used to start pods by hooking into the *extern* step which is a special step that always runs as soon as nodes as allocated for a job. It then creates containers in these pods for running processes launched by each job step, either from a user specified image or from a default image. For interactive accesses, the ForceCommand directive of the OpenSSH server allows to hook SSH connections to spawn containers for each session.

Configuring network namespaces is delegated to a network daemon running on each node of the cluster. It implements a simple protocol through a local UNIX domain socket, which allows to create or teardown a network namespace for either a job or a login pod. Each namespace is provided with a single virtual Ethernet interface. In our current implementation RDMA networks are not namespaced and can be used as normal. Isolating RDMA communications is left for future work.

The main difference between the setup of pods for job or login sessions resides in how IP adresses are allocated. For jobs, a single request allows to allocate all IPs required for a job at once. The lifecycle of these IPs is tied to the lifecycle of their job which can be queried from the Slurm controller. Login sessions only allocate IPs for a single pod. Their lifecycle is tied to a lease system which the network daemon must periodically refresh to keep the allocation. The full IP allocation state is stored in etcd for high availability and for use by network daemons.

Virtual Ethernet interfaces configured for each pod are interconnected using layer 2 tunnels encapsulated by VXLAN which are configured when pods are started on a node. A unique tunnel identifier is allocated for each user which ensures that packets cannot be forwarded between pods belonging to different users. Figure 1 depicts how these tunnels are setup. Connectivity between the pod network and external nodes is provided through gateway nodes on which the network daemon setups forwarding rules based on the etcd state. It implements global and per-user filtering for connections in and out of the pod network.

As can be seen on Fig. 1 the per-job slurmstepd daemon of Slurm is put in the same network namespace as the job. This is required as this daemon provides a PMIx server that must be accessible over localhost from the job processes.

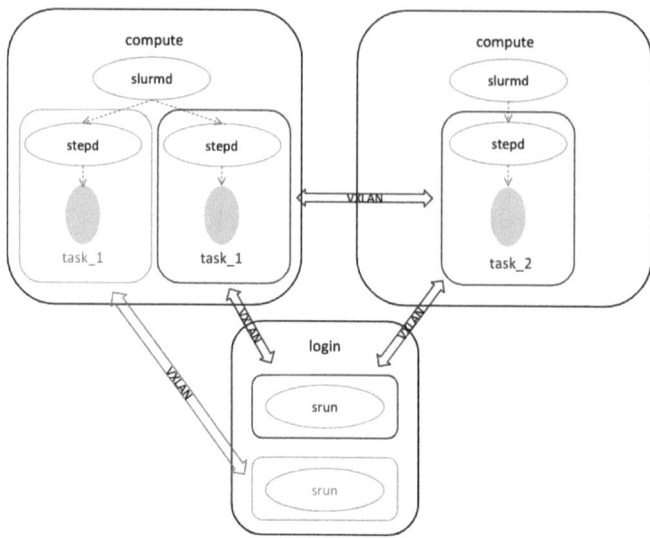

Fig. 1. Pods interconnected by VXLAN tunnels for two users executing two concurrent jobs with the Slurm srun command. Pods are depicted as colored boxes, each color representing a different user. (Color figure online)

The DNS server exposed in containers is implemented using CoreDNS. Domains are populated based on the IP allocation state stored in etcd.

This first implementation of our network model was guided by the objective of being easily deployable in an existing cluster without any disruption to non-containerized workloads. Compute nodes do not incur any additional load or complex network configuration when they are not hosting any pod and the use of an encapsulated overlay network allows some independence from the network architecture of the underlying cluster. In this work we did not leverage existing Kubernetes plugins, as custom networking logic had to be implemented in to emulate features outside the scope of the CNI and to ensure transparent operation from the point of view of Slurm. Implementing the whole network stack allowed us to more freely experiment with the design. In the future we nonetheless plan to support the CNI interface to benefit from the wide range of deployment options and features offered by Kubernetes networking solutions. In partcular, we plan to evaluate Calico which implements the container network with layer 3 routing, thus avoiding the overhead of encapsulation at the cost of a potentially more complex deployment, depending on the network layout of the cluster.

6 Performance Evaluation

To evaluate the performance of our approach, we measure the overhead of running well-known HPC benchmarks relying on MPI (HPCG and HPL) inside containers deployed by pcocc. Containerization has been shown to add negligible overhead to the execution of HPC jobs [14] when sharing the host network. However network virtualization, especially when relying on encapsulation, may increase the cost of processing each network packet and reduce application performance.

First, we focus on the overhead of using containers with virtual networks at job startup. As we want to evaluate the scalability of our approach at a larger scale, tests are run in a virtual cluster of 400 virtual machines (VMs). The VMs are organized as a typical HPC cluster managed by Slurm, each VM acting as a compute node with 6 cores.

We measure the time needed to create the networking configuration for a set of pods when launching a job. When a job is launched, each node calls the local networking daemon from the Slurm plugin and waits until the network is set up. This operation, including the call to the daemon itself, is timed and printed in the logs. For each job launch, the maximum value across all nodes is recorded as the last node to finish will also be the last one to start the MPI processes so any delay would impact the whole job execution. These maximum values are averaged across 20 executions for each job size and the results are shown at the top of Fig. 2. The total time needed to setup the network scales well with just above 800 ms needed to setup the network for a job spanning 400 nodes. Compared to the time Slurm takes to launch a job in general, which is about 300 to 500 ms in this virtual environment, we believe it is an acceptable overhead as it only doubles the time needed for smaller jobs and becomes insignificant for larger jobs as compared to the expected execution time. Next, we measure the time needed to execute a job step within an existing allocation. We use the osu_init benchmark from the OSU microbenchmark suite (v7.3) and measure the total execution time of the srun osu_init command, performed in a batch script. This test emphasizes the overhead of starting containers for each execution step, and of relying on the virtual network for performing the initial wireup of the communications between the tasks during MPI_Init. MPI_Init, which has to be called at the beginning of MPI tasks, carries out a PMIx Fence operation that exchanges messages using TCP/IP and is the most likely to be impacted by network virtualization overhead in typical MPI applications. Further communications are generally performed through RDMA which is currently shared with the host.

Performance samples are collected within a batch script which times the execution of 50 sequential steps. The bottom of Fig. 2 shows the distribution of measured times for jobs of 50 and 400 nodes in three configurations: without containers ('native'), using containers sharing the host network ('ctr') and using containers with network virtualization ('ctrnet'). The result shows that the network virtualization does not seem to impact the execution time of a step significantly, as the results for 'ctr' and 'ctrnet' stay very similar for smaller and larger job sizes. The constant gap between the native and containerized versions correspond to the container creation step, unrelated to the networking. This comforts the idea that using the container network should not significantly

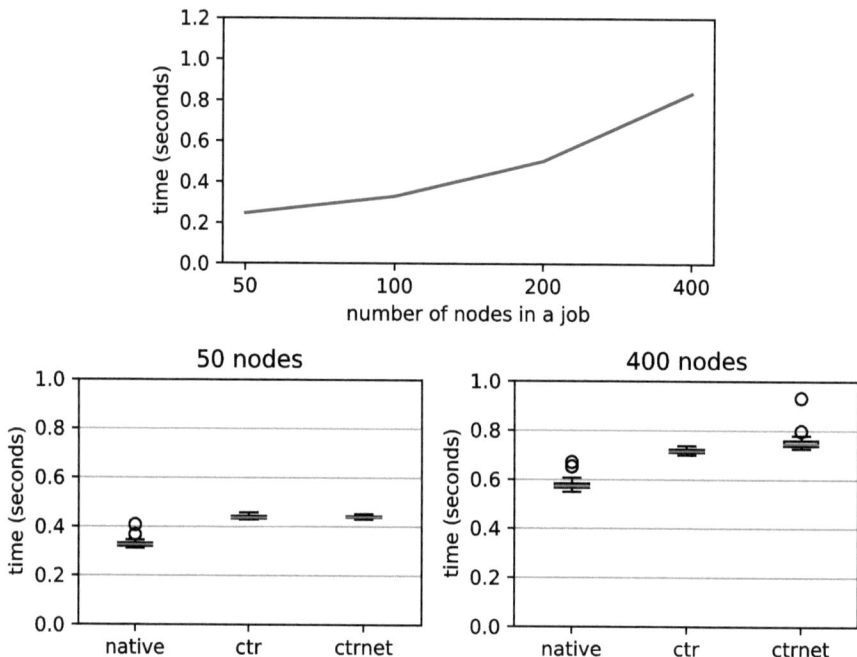

Fig. 2. (Top) Average time taken to setup the networking on a node for different job sizes. (Bottom) Execution time of a job step executing the osu_init benchmark. The nodes are virtual machines with 6 cores each.

lengthen the execution time of an MPI job, especially considering that only TCP/IP communications are affected.

Finally, we deployed our solution on bare-metal compute nodes to measure the impact of network virtualization on the execution of typical HPC workloads making full use of the underlying hadware. For this purpose, we use a compute partition composed of dual-socket Intel Xeon Gold 6148 CPUs for a total of 40 cores and 175 GB of usable memory per node. Nodes are interconnected with an EDR Infiniband network. The software environment on the cluster consists of RedHat Entreprise Linux 8.8, Slurm 23.11.1, OpenMPI 4.1.4 and PMIx v4. We chose two popular benchmarks, HPL (v2.3) [15] and HPCG (v3.1) [16], which are commonly used to assess the performance of HPC clusters for running parallel applications. We compared the results for native, containerized and containerized with network virtualization executions on 50 nodes. To ensure comparable results, all executions of a given benchmark are performed on the same set of nodes and the same software stack is deployed on the containers as on the host. The results are shown in Fig. 3. The observed differences in performance are miminal, with less than a 1% overhead for HPCG and HPL with the container network. This result is consistent with what we observed on the virtual cluster, considering that only PMIx and a few communications back to the launcher use the container network.

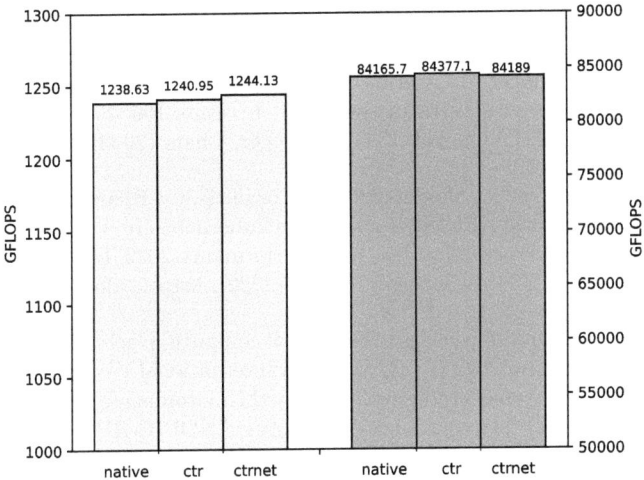

Fig. 3. Average GFLOP/s of HPCG (left) and HPL (right) on 50 nodes.

7 Conclusion

In this paper, we show how classical HPC clusters can benefit from adopting a networking model similar to that used in cloud environments. As containers have become popular to facilitate deploying complex software stacks involved in HPC workflows, we present a solution that transparently leverages network virtualization in containers to bring more flexibility and security to HPC clusters. Isolating users in their own private network prevents unwanted accesses and facilitates the deployment of services which can be reached at known ports or domain names. We evaluate the impact of our solution on application performance by timing the network creation at the beginning of a job and the execution time of typical HPC benchmarks. We find that jobs launched with virtual networks can be started in less than a second at the scale of several hundred nodes. We also observe less than 1% overhead when running common parallel benchmarks. To further confirm these results, real applications and workflows will be deployed and evaluated. In the future, we plan to evaluate alternate implementations of this model which avoid the use of encapsulation, potentially leveraging network components used in Kubernetes. We also plan to virtualize RDMA interfaces by making use of Infiniband partition keys so as to fully isolate all networks that users have access to.

Disclosure of Interests.. The authors have no competing interests to declare that are relevant to the content of this article.

References

1. Kubernetes. https://kubernetes.io/. Accessed 22 Feb 2024

2. Sochat, V., Culquicondor, A., Ojeo, A., Milroy, D.: The Flux Operator. Early access (2023). https://doi.org/10.48550/arXiv.2309.17420
3. Greneche, N., Menouer, T., Cérin, C., Richard, O.: A methodology to scale containerized hpc infrastructures in the cloud. In: Euro-Par 2022: Parallel Processing. Euro-Par 2022. LNCS, vol. 13440. Springer, Cham (2022). https://doi.org/10.1007/978-3-031-12597-3_13
4. Zervas, G., Chazapis, A., Sfakianakis, Y., Kozanitis, C., Bilas, A.: Virtual clusters: isolated, containerized HPC environments in kubernetes. In: ISC High Performance 2022 International Workshops. ISC High Performance 2022. Lecture Notes in Computer Science, vol. 13387. Springer, Cham (2022). https://doi.org/10.1007/978-3-031-23220-6_24
5. Milroy, D., et al.: One step closer to converged computing: achieving scalability with cloud-native HPC. In: 2022 IEEE/ACM 4th International Workshop on Containers and New Orchestration Paradigms for Isolated Environments in HPC (CANOPIE-HPC). IEEE (2022). https://doi.org/10.1109/CANOPIE-HPC56864.2022.00011
6. Liu, P., Guitart, J.: Fine-grained scheduling for containerized HPC workloads in kubernetes clusters. In: IEEE 24th Inernational Conference on High Performance Computing & Communications (HPCC/DSS/SmartCity/DependSys). IEEE (2022). https://doi.org/10.1109/HPCC-DSS-SmartCity-DependSys57074.2022.00068
7. Medeiros, D., Walhgren, J., Schieffer, G., Peng, I.: Kub: enabling elastic HPC workloads on containerized environments. In: 2023 IEEE 35th International Symposium on Computer Architecture and High Performance Computing (SBAC-PAD). IEEE (2023). https://doi.org/10.1109/SBAC-PAD59825.2023.00031
8. López-Huguet, S., Segrelles, J.D., Kasztelnik, M., Bubak, M., Blanquer, I.: Seamlessly managing HPC workloads through kubernetes. In: Jagode, H., Anzt, H., Juckeland, G., Ltaief, H. (eds.) ISC High Performance 2020. LNCS, vol. 12321, pp. 310–320. Springer, Cham (2020). https://doi.org/10.1007/978-3-030-59851-8_20
9. Chazapis, A., Nikolaidis, F., Marazakis, M., Bilas, A.: Running kubernetes workloads on HPC. In: ISC High Performance 2023. LNCS, vol. 13999. Springer, Cham (2023). https://doi.org/10.1007/978-3-031-40843-4_14
10. Lange, J., et al.: Evaluating the Cloud for Capability Class Leadership Workloads. ORNL/TM-2023/3083, Oak Ridge Leadership Computing Facility (2023). https://doi.org/10.2172/2000306
11. Ferlanti, E., Allen, W., Lima, E., Wang, Y., Fonner, J.: Perspectives and experiences supporting containers for research computing at the texas advanced computing center. In: Proceedings of the SC '23 Workshops of the International Conference on High Performance Computing, Network, Storage, and Analysis. ACM (2023). https://doi.org/10.1145/3624062.3624587
12. Mujkanovic, N., Durillo, J., Hammer, N., Müller, T.: Survey of adaptive containerization architectures for HPC. In: Proceedings of the SC '23 Workshops of the International Conference on High Performance Computing, Network, Storage, and Analysis. ACM (2023). https://doi.org/10.1145/3624062.3624588
13. SPANK. https://slurm.schedmd.com/spank.html. Accessed 04 Mar 2024
14. Torrez, A., Randles, T., Priedhorsky, R.: HPC container runtimes have minimal or no performance impact. In: 2019 IEEE/ACM International Workshop on Containers and New Orchestration Paradigms for Isolated Environments in HPC (CANOPIE-HPC). IEEE (2019). https://doi.org/10.1109/CANOPIE-HPC49598.2019.00010
15. HPL benchmark. https://www.netlib.org/benchmark/hpl/. Accessed 04 Mar 2024
16. HPCG benchmark. https://www.hpcg-benchmark.org. Accessed 04 Mar 2024

FLOTO: Beyond Bandwidth - A Framework for Adaptable, Multi-sensor Data Collection in Scientific Research

Alicia Esquivel Morel[1]($\boxtimes$), Mark Powers[2], Kate Keahey[3], Zack Murry[1], Tomas Javier Sitzmann[4], Jianfeng Zhou[1], and Prasad Calyam[1]

[1] University of Missouri, Columbia, MO 65201, USA
ace6qv@mail.missouri.edu
[2] Argonne National Laboratory, Lemont, IL 60439, USA
[3] University of Chicago, Chicago, IL 60637, USA
[4] University of Turin, 10095 Grugliasco, TO, Italy

Abstract. Multi-cloud environments integrated with various Internet of Things (IoT) have resulted in a diverse range of observational instruments that can be used and adapted for various use cases. An important role of these observational instruments in scientific research is to provide valuable data that can be understood and help solve practical problems. The evolution of FLOTO, an observational instrument initially designed for bandwidth measurement, has led to its adaptation for diverse multi-sensor applications. Leveraging its support for mainstream Single Board Computers (SBCs), it facilitates the deployment and operation of scientific instruments that enable data collection and sharing among different user groups. This paper explores the transition of FLOTO from its original purpose to IBIS an infrastructure management framework capable of integrating multi-sensor technologies, including environmental sensors and cameras for data acquisition and analysis. IBIS, inspired and named after the perceptive bird known for its keen eyesight, embodies the essence of a multi-sensor observational instrument designed for scientific discovery. We present a reference operation example that provides practical insights into implementing IBIS-based instruments for optimizing greenhouse environments with precision agriculture. Furthermore, we showcase how this application can be seamlessly integrated into the IBIS framework, allowing users to deploy and operate varied instruments in diverse environments. Lastly, this work provides guidelines for reproducibility, contributing to IBIS' documentation and fostering community accessibility.

Keywords: Multi-sensor data acquisition · Observational instrument · Edge computing · Reproducibility

---

Results presented in this paper were obtained using the FLOTO project (Award 2213821) supported by the National Science Foundation. This material is based upon work supported by the U.S. Department of Energy, Office of Science, under contract number DE-AC02-06CH11357.

1 Introduction

The rapid development of the Internet of Things (IoT) has revolutionized how data is collected. IoT devices can be integrated with multi-sensor and Single Board Computers (SBCs) and transformed into observational instruments for scientific exploration. In addition, these observational instruments can be integrated within multi-cloud environments, aiming researchers to gather valuable and larger numbers of data streams from a wide range of sources. Thus, enabling the connectivity between these *physical things* and the *Internet* makes it possible to remotely access any data and control this physical environment [20]. The evolution of FLOTO [18,27], a *Discovery Testbed and Observational Instrument*, initially designed for bandwidth research, has led to its adaptation for a diverse range of multi-sensor and multi-cloud applications.

FLOTO is an observational instrument that facilitates the deployment and management of widely used low-cost SBCs for large-scale data collection in field deployments. These scientific and observational instruments can be deployed for data acquisition and allow shared operation in remote areas without physical access or intervention. Furthermore, by enabling multi-tenant sharing among various applications and user groups, FLOTO aims for researchers to collaborate and unlock the full potential of the collected data. Real-time monitoring of air quality across urban landscapes, tracking movements of endangered species, or even measuring subtle fluctuations in atmospheric pressure exemplify how its capabilities can facilitate data collection for a nuanced understanding of diverse phenomena. A key question driving this research is whether FLOTO can be adapted to measure phenomena beyond its original focus on broadband. To achieve this, we propose adapting it into a flexible observational instrument. This adaptation involves seamless integration and deployment with a wider range of sensor peripherals. These peripherals could encompass environmental sensors, motion and position trackers, biometric monitors, imaging devices, and more. Additionally, it can be equipped to provide meaningful analysis of these new measurements, allowing researchers to analyze phenomena previously outside its scope.

This paper explores the evolution of FLOTO from its initial design and purpose to IBIS an adaptable platform capable of integrating multi-sensor technologies, including environmental sensors and cameras for data acquisition and analysis. IBIS, inspired and named after the perceptive bird known for its keen eyesight, embodies the essence of a multi-sensor observational instrument designed for scientific discovery. Just as the Ibis utilizes its senses to navigate its environment and gather valuable information, the IBIS instrument empowers researchers with critical insights through gathering and interpreting information from its environment. Prototype demonstration will highlight its ability to seamlessly integrate various sensor types, and effectively address diverse data collection scenarios. Finally, we illustrate IBIS' functionality in real-world settings and propose a methodology for reproducibility in "edge-to-cloud" experiments in a way that promotes community accessibility. The remainder of this paper is organized as follows: in Sect. 2, we discuss the approach and design of this edge-based observatory instrument. In Sect. 3, we present IBIS and its adaptation for an optimized greenhouse environment with precision agriculture use case. Section 4 presents application deployment and data collection. Section 5 presents the reproducibility aspect, and Sect. 6 the related work. Lastly, Sect. 7 concludes the paper and provide some insights for future work.

2 Approach

IBIS is an infrastructure management framework underlying the FLOTO project which deploys a thousand Raspberry Pi devices nationwide to measure the quality of broadband [18]. In this section, we first summarize how IBIS works, and then describe how it can be extended to support applications beyond broadband measurement, in particular applications that require combining compute capability at edge supplied by the SBCs with sensing abilities provided by a range of IoT peripherals.

2.1 IBIS: An Observational Instrument

The IBIS infrastructure [8,18] implements a general *observational instrument* pattern where a large number of *observation points* can be deployed and managed to conduct observation, and then report data resulting from this observation to a central *aggregation point* where the data can be collected, combined, and processed. In the current IBIS implementation, the observation points are implemented as single board computers (SBCs), cost-effective solutions that are lightweight enough to support large deployment scales, yet powerful enough to provide sufficient cycles for observation. The infrastructure supports easy deployment of such observation points and organization into fleets composed of hundreds of devices that can be reliably managed over time without requiring physical access to any device.

The devices are monitored and managed via a dashboard that displays device information, including device profiles, performance statistics, which applications are running on a given device, and allows operators to execute device-specific actions. To provide the actual observation function, IBIS supports the deployment of containerized *observing applications* on selected groups of devices. These applications interact with the environment to capture and report on relevant phenomena. For example, the FLOTO project applications consist of different types of broadband tests that measure and report on broadband quality at the deployment site. Each observing application generates data that represents the result of its observation. This data is then uploaded to an aggregation point by a *data uploader application* at which point it can be stored, combined, or processed.

2.2 Adapting IBIS

We point out in [18] that, like any scientific instrument, IBIS has the potential to be adapted to answer different scientific questions by varying its deployment scope, adapting it to observe diverse phenomena by coupling it with appropriate sensors or running custom applications, and using tailored data aggregation techniques. For example, instead of measuring and reporting on the quality of broadband by running broadband tests, we can observe and report on wildlife sightings similarly to what was done in [32], or use distributed learning [14] to train models locally on protected biometric data and send those models to an aggregator that combines them rather than only preserving and managing access to data. IBIS supports such adaptation by allowing the user to customize three qualities. First, a user can equip the SBCs to support the desired observational function on a hardware level. This can be done, for instance, by establishing an Ethernet connection to a router to measure broadband or attaching a camera to enable visual analysis. Second, a user needs to run an application that implements the desired observational function, e.g., runs broadband tests, performs image recognition tasks, or trains a model based on observed images. Third, a suitable data aggregator can be created to process the reported data, which can be as simple as storing it or the aggregation can involve a data processing step as in averaging gradients in learning models. The sections below discuss how IBIS supports these adaptation actions.

2.3 IBIS User Workflow

Hardware Customization. Raspberry Pi, the principal SBC that IBIS currently supports, offers a flexible peripheral connection system. The USB ports provide compatibility with familiar peripherals, while a dedicated ribbon cable port is available for dedicated camera modules. However, the true versatility lies in the General-Purpose Input/Output header (GPIO) | a 40-pin connector on all recent Raspberry Pi models. This header provides voltage and ground pins for powering circuits and general-purpose pins for two-way communication. Users can collect data from a wide range of sensors by interfacing with these pins.

Some pins even support specialized protocols like I2C, SPI, UART, and PCM, which are crucial for certain sensors to communicate effectively with the Raspberry Pi. These require a secure connection to the correct pins for proper function. The pins can be configured for peripheral-specific protocols in the OS hardware configuration file (/boot/config.txt). To simplify complex GPIO connections, Raspberry Pi offers Hardware Attached on Top (HATs), self-contained modules that stack directly onto the device, utilizing all GPIO pins. This modular approach allows for easy expansion of the Raspberry Pi's capabilities.

Adding Devices with IoT Peripherals to IBIS. The initial step in peripheral installation involves following the manufacturer's instructions for installing the device on a Raspberry Pi, e.g., plugging it into a USB port, connecting a camera cable to the camera serial port, attaching a HAT to the GPIO pins, or connecting wires to the corresponding GPIO pins. Next, the peripheral must be registered with IBIS. In principle, IBIS can support any Raspberry Pi-compatible peripherals that can be accessed via Linux device interfaces at the software level. In practice, with IoT experiencing rapid innovation and new peripherals becoming available every day, we can only provide out-of-the-box support for a limited set of such peripherals | the most common ones, covering the typical use cases | and provide instructions for users to develop their custom support to cover remaining and emergent use cases using existing drivers.

Supported interfaces currently include the Raspberry Pi camera module, access to the analog and digital I/O pins of the GPIO subsystem, and the SPI and I2C serial interfaces. To enable access via those interfaces, device operators must submit at least enough metadata so that application developers know how to access a peripheral, e.g., "device /dev/i2c-1 must be mounted into the container, and the sensor accessed at address 0x78, using a documentation link or library". To extend the scope of the system beyond these use cases, we provide documentation that allows users to extend this support. Briefly, the OS uses "device trees"—a data structure that describes the hardware components to map physical interfaces to Linux devices under /dev and load relevant kernel modules; if necessary the user can use the meta-data to specify additional device trees or parameters to load at boot (IBIS propagates this to the device's config.txt file), in addition to the information for application developers on how to access the interface once presented via the OS.

Application Development. Developing a new application consists of developing a Docker container containing an application capable of interacting with the peripheral using the information provided in the meta-data. Since IBIS itself supports primarily production capability, we recommend that this development is done on CHI@Edge [16], an edge testbed of the Chameleon project [4,17] which supports the same device and peripheral model and uses container deployment to reconfigure devices in a way similar to IBIS. After deploying the container, the user mounts the relevant interfaces from /dev (created by the OS loading device trees and kernel modules on boot) and then communicates to those interfaces using the information in meta-data, usually by leveraging standardized libraries already built into the Raspberry Pi such as the `libcamera` driver and Sense HAT libraries.

Data Collection. Lastly, the user can pair the application with a data uploader to transfer the collected data from the device to a central collection and processing point. To do this, IBIS offers an `rclone`-based default uploader application that connects to a data aggregation service currently running on the Chameleon Cloud [17] (An open experimental testbed for Computer Science funded by the National Science Foundation) and collects data from all IBIS deployments by default. Alternatively, the user can clone or modify the data uploader to connect to their own data collection facilities, such as a public cloud, or provide an upload capability more suitable to their deployment conditions (e.g., weighing power efficiency against transfer efficiency). For portability, the application is configured to honor environment variables passed to it at runtime, these variables are used to customize the operation for a particular user, such as to specify which S3 bucket to upload data to, or how often to take samples. When a job is executed on IBIS, these variables are packaged along with the containers to which they should be applied.

3 Case Study, IBIS to the Test: Optimizing Greenhouse Environments with Precision Agriculture

In this section, we showcase a use case study where we have adapted IBIS as an edge-based instrument for a specific research scenario, i.e., *precision agriculture*. This case study will explore the different IBIS components used and how they were configured to address a real-world scientific challenge. This use case study showcases IBIS by focusing on its applicability in optimizing greenhouse environments through precision agriculture.

3.1 Precise Environmental Control

Precision agriculture optimizes crop yield and growth in greenhouse production systems. These techniques, consisting of multi-sensor data collection, analysis, and decision-making systems, enable holistic control and management of crops according to the dynamics of environments, like temperature, humidity, CO_2 levels, light intensity, soil moisture, and air quality. All these factors are essential for optimal plant growth [6] and, traditionally, monitoring these parameters has been labor-intensive [5], and subject to visual observations. IBIS can simplify greenhouse management by integrating sensors that can continuously collect data on various aspects of plant health and the surrounding environments, further enhancing this application with remote sensing, and providing real-time, high-resolution data on plant parameters.

The measured plant characteristics can include plant height, leaf area index, chlorophyll content, and stress levels [24]. With the comprehensive data of plants and environments from sensors, farmers can precisely monitor and analyze plant development and health conditions across the entire greenhouse, and make optimal management decisions [29]. This enhances timely interventions to maximize yield and quality while reducing resource input. For instance, accurate measurements of soil moisture, temperature, and light intensity allow for adjustments to irrigation schedules, optimization of nutrient delivery, and mitigation of environmental stressors. Thus, these combined approaches lead to improved crop performance and resource efficiency.

3.2 Transformation to Edge and Leveraging Remote Sensing

By leveraging the IBIS infrastructure management framework as an edge-based observatory instrument, farmers can analyze data in real time and make informed decisions about irrigation, ventilation, and other environmental controls. This data-driven approach can aid farmers in cultivating diverse crops across different climates and seasons, ultimately leading to improved yields and resource efficiency. Figure 1 depicts the general architecture for leveraging sensing in greenhouse environments with precision agriculture. Adapting IBIS to leverage remote sensing involves deploying a strategic network of sensors throughout

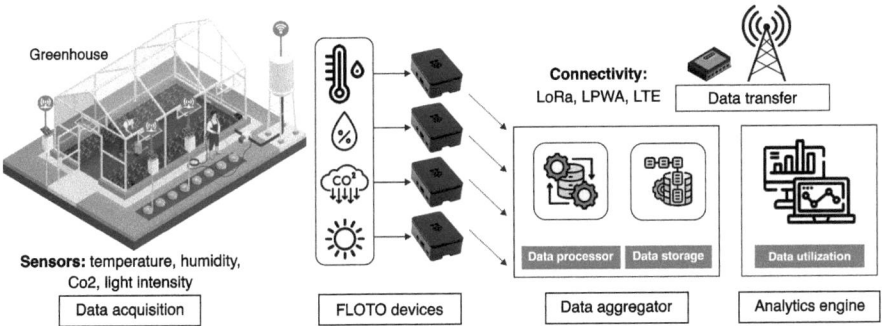

Fig. 1. General architecture for leveraging remote sensing in greenhouse environments with precision agriculture.

the greenhouse. The number and distribution of these sensors depend on several factors including greenhouse size, required spatial resolution, environmental variation, and types of measurements [25,31].

For instance, larger greenhouses may require more sensors for fine-grained measurements in different areas. Additionally, the crop type must be considered, as some crops may have specific data requirements, and sensor parameters must be selected to capture specific variables that are crucial to the crop's health and growth [23]. It is also important to capture soil moisture variations across the greenhouse, considering different locations and depths within the soil profile to run tests that can measure the moisture at different depths. This can help to correlate temperature and moisture to evaluate the utility of a sensor at one unique depth. This can aim to create plant trial setups for testing biowaste materials in organo-mineral fertilizers [26]. These sensors are connected to the IBIS devices equipped with apps for data processing and communication.

Reliable communication plays a critical role in real-time data processing and analysis. The sensor data can be transmitted through wireless communication technologies like WiFi or Zigbee, or long-range ones, like LPWAN, NB-IoT, LoRa, or LoRaWAN [2]. The application is designed to continuously collect and transmit data from the sensors to the IBIS devices and, consequently, to the data aggregator. The collected data requires filtering to remove unnecessary data points for efficient analysis, in addition to performing basic data analytics to prepare it for further processing. Sensor readings must be filtered to eliminate potentially erroneous readings. Once processed, the data is transmitted to a central analytics engine or cloud platform for in-depth analysis and storage. For example, the collected imagery data can be processed to build orthomosaic images and point cloud data of target plans, through a more holistic high-resolution spatial and spectral reflectance information of each plant, and its organs [30]. In addition, various analytics and machine learning models can be applied to extract meaningful insights and patterns. For instance, inference models can be developed to correlate plant growth parameters with environmental factors and weather predictions, optimizing irrigation scheduling, nutrient management, and pest control strategies [1]. Leveraging advanced analytics allows for further enhancement of crop productivity, resource efficiency, and sustainability.

4 Application Deployment and Data Collection

Adaptations to the Hardware. The chosen application for this prototype deployment focuses on monitoring several key environmental factors that are crucial for optimal plant growth. The initial hardware setup needs to be adapted based on the application's needs. For our prototype, illustrated in Fig. 2, we rely on the Google Coral Environmental Sensor Board board, an add-on board with sensing capabilities.

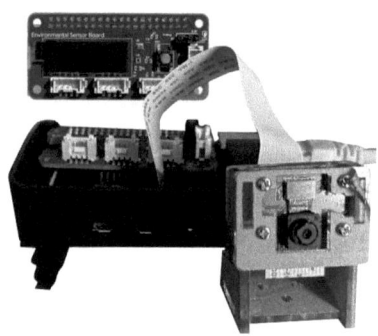

Fig. 2. IBIS hardware adaptation.

This board provides atmospheric data such as light level, barometric pressure, temperature, and humidity, and it is designed to work with the 40-pin GPIO header. In addition, we added a Raspberry Pi mini camera module with a fixed focus and the provided mount. The camera communicates through the Camera Serial Interface (CSI) with the libcamera library and Picamera2 to capture images. Continuous data collection from the Google Coral Environmental Sensor Board provides real-time updates on the environmental metrics mentioned above. Image capture with the camera is triggered at a preset interval, capturing images every 30 min. These captured images can be used to for example, to measure plants' health.

To power the device and sensors reliably, they were connected to an AC power source, with surge protectors implemented for each connection to ensure uninterrupted operation.

Challenges in Hardware Adaptation:

1. More complex peripherals for the Raspberry Pi make assumptions about the OS's inclusion and auto-detection of device trees and kernel modules, such as the "Camera Module 3" needing a very new kernel for auto-detection, or the "Coral sense HAT" which includes a custom device tree onboard in flash memory and expects the Raspberry Pi to load it automatically. Since IBIS devices do not run the Raspberry Pi OS distribution, supporting the firmware for these devices can be complex and error-prone.
2. IBIS currently uses a "one size fits all" networking model, where containers have access to a private, per-device network, and reach the outside world through NAT and the device's routing table. This makes it difficult to support experiments such as comparing Wi-Fi and Ethernet performance on the same

device or running an experiment across two devices, using one as a source, and the other as a sink for the traffic. More control of how container network traffic is mapped to the physical network interface of a device is an important feature to add.

Precision Agriculture Application. At the edge level, the application performs minimal data processing on the sensor data. Sensor readings like temperature, ambient light, and humidity can be averaged over a specific window for noise reduction before transmission. Captured images might undergo a basic resizing process to reduce storage requirements. The collected sensor data (including averaged readings for temperature and humidity) and captured images are periodically transmitted from the IBIS devices to a central server hosted on a cloud platform. On the server, the data is further analyzed using a data visualization dashboard. This dashboard displays real-time and historical trends for all collected metrics, allowing for comprehensive monitoring of environmental conditions. Captured images are stored on the server and can be manually inspected for visual signs of plant stress, such as discoloration. Additionally, software-based image analysis techniques could be explored in the future for automated stress detection. The data can be analyzed and visualized and generic analysis tools, including open-source and commercial options e.g. Grafana [3], can offer user-friendly interfaces for building dashboards.

Data Collection. The IBIS devices are programmed to collect sensor data at a user-defined frequency. A high-frequency collection rate (e.g., every minute) allows for detailed monitoring of environmental fluctuations within the greenhouse. IBIS provides a customizable data uploader container [9] that can be used in such multi-container applications. This built-in customizable data uploader container allows any data placed in this container to be uploaded to a designated cloud storage location. For this prototype, we rely on Chameleon Cloud [17] and its object store [19]. It is also important to highlight that this process can be adapted to store any other generic data from other types of sensors, and it can be easily configured to target commercial cloud back-ends.

5 Reproducibility

Our work prioritizes artifact reproducibility by employing the IBIS application store, a dedicated repository for sharing research workflows. We also consider *practical reproducibility* [15], supporting accessible, integrated, and reusable experiments, represented as a combination of hardware, experimental environment, experimental body, and data analysis. The example prototype described in this paper (gather environmental data situated within a greenhouse environment) is publicly available on the IBIS website [10]. We consider three levels of experiment reproduction within the IBIS infrastructure; first, users can achieve an **exact replication** by deploying the application provided in the public listing of our containers and applications on the IBIS dashboard, utilizing the same sensor setup (Raspberry Pi model and sensor types) within the IBIS environment and following the instructions provided in the getting started documentation [11]. This approach guarantees the most comparable results to the original experiment. In addition, the IBIS infrastructure's flexibility allows users to leverage applications while employing different compatible sensors to collect environmental data. While the core functionalities (data collection and analytics) remain the same, the specific sensor data might differ due to varying sensor characteristics. This **variation approach** can provide valuable insights into how the experiment behaves with different sensor types. Lastly, **further exploration** would be beyond replicating the experiment. Users can potentially modify the application's source code to capture additional sensor data or implement different data processing techniques within the IBIS framework. While IBIS promotes reproducibility, one potential challenge users might face is access to a Raspberry Pi and compatible sensors for an exact replication. This challenge can be overcome by emphasizing the importance of detailed and comprehensive documentation for applications and their deployment. Clear instructions, including a thorough explanation of the application's purpose and functionality, ensure clarity for users even with potentially different sensor setups. Additionally, the documentation should provide detailed descriptions of the sensor data collected and the averaging process. Guidance on how to interpret the results and potential considerations for variations in sensor setups should also be included.

6 Related Work

The convergence of multi-cloud environments and the Internet of Things (IoT) has led to a rise in observational instruments capable of collecting diverse data for various applications [12,28]. This aligns with the growing emphasis on leveraging sensor data to address real-world challenges and advance scientific research [22]. Several existing technologies address the challenge of managing large-scale deployments of devices and multi-sensors for data collection and analysis. Cloud-based platforms like AWS IoT Greengrass [13], and Azure IoT Edge [7], offer user-friendly interfaces and robust functionalities for device management, application deployment, and data integration with cloud services. However, these platforms can lead to vendor lock-in and ongoing costs. Open-source alternatives like OpenBalena [21] fleet management provide flexibility and control but do not support multi-tenancy and do not handle scalability and back-end services. We leverage this open-source fleet management and extend it with features for scaling and user experience: multi-tenant usage, ad-hoc shell commands, device collections, and a device dashboard. IBIS exemplifies a implementation of an "observational instrument", based on zero-touch installation, automated management, cloud integration, and data collection from multi-sensors.

7 Conclusions and Future Work

The Internet of Things (IoT) has revolutionized how data can be collected and processed. In addition, Single Board Computers (SBC) can be integrated with multi-sensors and transformed into observational instruments for scientific exploration. This paper presents the transition of FLOTO from its original purpose to IBIS an infrastructure management framework capable of integrating multi-sensor technologies. The seamless integration with various sensors and the ability to analyze this new data addresses a key research question: Can FLOTO be adapted to measure phenomena beyond broadband? This paper demonstrates IBIS's adaptability and effectiveness through a real-world precision agriculture application, showcasing IBIS's potential to enhance data collection methodologies. Lastly, the proposed reproducibility methodologies are based on practical reproducibility, promoting open access within the research community. Future work includes more advance sensor integration, and broaden the application scope of this work. It can include implementing advanced data analysis like Machine Learning and visualization tools. In addition, a more flexible approach that can allow control over container network traffic will be considered.

References

1. Abioye, E.A., et al.: Precision irrigation management using machine learning and digital farming solutions. AgriEngineering **4**(1), 70–103 (2022)
2. Ali, A., Hussain, T., Tantashutikun, N., Hussain, N., Cocetta, G.: Application of smart techniques, Internet of Things and data mining for resource use efficient and sustainable crop production. Agriculture **13**(2), 397 (2023)
3. Chakraborty, M., Kundan, A.P.: Grafana. In: Chakraborty, M., Kundan, A.P. (eds.) Monitoring Cloud-Native Applications, pp. 187–240. Apress, Berkeley (2021). https://doi.org/10.1007/978-1-4842-6888-9_6
4. Chameleon: Chameleon. https://www.chameleoncloud.org/. Accessed 07 Mar 2024
5. Charania, I., Li, X.: Smart farming: agriculture's shift from a labor intensive to technology native industry. Internet of Things **9**, 100142 (2020)
6. Chaudhary, D., Nayse, S., Waghmare, L.: Application of wireless sensor networks for greenhouse parameter control in precision agriculture. Int. J. Wirel. Mob. Netw. (IJWMN) **3**(1), 140–149 (2011)
7. Edge, A.I.: Build the intelligent edge. https://azure.microsoft.com/en-us/products/iot-edge. Accessed 13 Jan 2024
8. FLOTO: Floto. https://floto.cs.uchicago.edu/. Accessed 14 Feb 2024
9. FLOTO: Floto. https://github.com/UChicago-FLOTO/data_uploader. Accessed 14 Feb 2024
10. FLOTO: Floto application. https://floto.cs.uchicago.edu/applications/. Accessed 07 Mar 2024
11. FLOTO: Floto dashboard. https://portal.floto.science/dashboard/. Accessed 14 Feb 2024
12. Hassan, R., Qamar, F., Hasan, M.K., Aman, A.H.M., Ahmed, A.S.: Internet of things and its applications: a comprehensive survey. Symmetry **12**(10), 1674 (2020)
13. IoT, A.: Build intelligent IoT devices faster. https://aws.amazon.com/greengrass/. Accessed 13 Jan 2024
14. Jiang, J.C., Kantarci, B., Oktug, S., Soyata, T.: Federated learning in smart city sensing: challenges and opportunities. Sensors **20**(21), 6230 (2020)
15. Keahey, K., Anderson, J., Powers, M., Cooper, A.: Three pillars of practical reproducibility. In: 2023 IEEE 19th International Conference on e-Science (e-Science), pp. 1–6. IEEE (2023)

16. Keahey, K., et al.: Chameleon@ edge community workshop report (2021)
17. Keahey, K., et al.: Lessons learned from the chameleon testbed. In: Proceedings of the 2020 USENIX Annual Technical Conference (USENIX ATC 2020). USENIX Association (2020)
18. Keahey, K., et al.: Discovery testbed: an observational instrument for broadband research. In: 2023 IEEE 19th International Conference on e-Science (e-Science), pp. 1–4. IEEE (2023)
19. Keahey, K., et al.: Chameleon: a scalable production testbed for computer science research. In: Contemporary High Performance Computing, pp. 123–148. CRC Press (2019)
20. Kopetz, H., Steiner, W.: Internet of things. In: Real-Time Systems: Design Principles for Distributed Embedded Applications, pp. 325–341. Springer, Cham (2022)
21. OpenBalena: Open source software to manage connected IoT devices at scale. https://www.balena.io/open. Accessed 13 Jan 2024
22. Qiu, S., et al.: Multi-sensor information fusion based on machine learning for real applications in human activity recognition: state-of-the-art and research challenges. Inf. Fusion **80**, 241–265 (2022)
23. Rayhana, R., Xiao, G., Liu, Z.: Internet of Things empowered smart greenhouse farming. IEEE J. Radio Frequency Identification **4**(3), 195–211 (2020)
24. Ru, C., Hu, X., Wang, W., Ran, H., Song, T., Guo, Y.: Evaluation of the crop water stress index as an indicator for the diagnosis of grapevine water deficiency in greenhouses. Horticulturae **6**(4), 86
25. Rustia, D.J.A., Lin, C.E., Chung, J.Y., Zhuang, Y.J., Hsu, J.C., Lin, T.T.: Application of an image and environmental sensor network for automated greenhouse insect pest monitoring. J. Asia-Pacific Entomol. **23**(1), 17–28 (2020)
26. Sitzmann, T.J., Sica, P., Grignani, C., Magid, J.: Testing biowaste materials as peat replacement in organo-mineral fertilizers. Front. Sustain. Food Syst. **8**, 1330843
27. Sundaresan, S., Burnett, S., Feamster, N., De Donato, W.: {BISmark}: a testbed for deploying measurements and applications in broadband access networks. In: 2014 USENIX Annual Technical Conference (USENIX ATC 2014), pp. 383–394 (2014)
28. Vermesan, O., et al.: Internet of Things strategic research and innovation agenda. In: Internet of Things, pp. 7–151. River Publishers (2022)
29. Zhang, J., et al.: Monitoring plant diseases and pests through remote sensing technology: a review. Comput. Electron. Agric. **165**, 104943 (2019)
30. Zhou, J., Nguyen, H.T.: High-Throughput Crop Phenotyping. Springer, Cham (2021)
31. Zhou, S., Mou, H., Zhou, J., Zhou, J., Ye, H., Nguyen, H.T.: Development of an automated plant phenotyping system for evaluation of salt tolerance in soybean. Comput. Electron. Agric. **182**, 106001 (2021)
32. Zualkernan, I., Dhou, S., Judas, J., Sajun, A.R., Gomez, B.R., Hussain, L.A.: An IoT system using deep learning to classify camera trap images on the edge. Computers **11**(1), 13 (2022)

Understanding Layered Portability from HPC to Cloud in Containerized Environments

Daniel Medeiros[(✉)], Gabin Schieffer, Jacob Wahlgren, and Ivy Peng

Department of Computer Science, KTH Royal Institute of Technology, Stockholm, Sweden
{dadm,gabins,jacobwah,ivybopeng}@kth.se

Abstract. Recent development in lightweight OS-level virtualization, containers, provides a potential solution for running HPC applications on the cloud platform. In this work, we focus on the impact of different layers in a containerized environment when migrating HPC containers from a dedicated HPC system to a cloud platform. On three ARM-based platforms, including the latest Nvidia Grace CPU, we use six representative HPC applications to characterize the impact of container virtualization, host OS and kernel, and rootless and privileged container execution. Our results indicate less than 4% container overhead in DGEMM, miniMD, and XSBench, but 8%–10% overhead in FFT, HPCG, and Hypre. We also show that changing between the container execution modes results in negligible performance differences in the six applications.

Keywords: Cloud and HPC Convergence · Containers · ARM · Performance

1 Introduction

High accessibility to a wide variety of computing resources, timely access to new hardware, and cost-effectiveness motivate running HPC applications in the cloud, moving towards the convergence of HPC and Cloud [1,3,11,12,14,17]. Today, lightweight containers are replacing virtual machines (VM) to become the widely used virtualization and isolation mechanism on the cloud. Running HPC applications in a containerized environment is one main distinction from running them in bare metal on-premise HPC systems. Popular container engines on HPC systems, such as Podman [7], Singularity [10] and Charliecloud [16], are specially designed for `rootless`/unprivileged container execution while Docker, the de-facto solution on the cloud, runs containers through a `root-owned` daemon. On the convergence of HPC and cloud, one likely scenario is that a user builds an image of an HPC application from an HPC environment and deploys it on instances in a cloud environment. Therefore, the interoperability across the two environments and the associated performance impact from each layer in the dependency chain is important but not fully explored. However, despite extensive studies that have characterized and optimized the performance of HPC applications in a virtualized environment, few works have explored the portability and associated performance loss in containerized HPC applications moving between HPC and the cloud platforms [9].

The portability of containerized applications ensures that an image can be built on a host in one infrastructure and deployed on another host, likely in another infrastructure. As illustrated in Fig. 1, hardware, OS and kernel, and container engine are the three major components likely different in the two environments. Within a container, its layered architecture may also result in changes in one dependency layer cascading to subsequent layers. Although interoperability ensures that a containerized application can execute across different platforms, the combination of software in use in each layer may impact performance differently. For instance, the kernel of the host OS will be used by the containerized application, and it may consist of different versions on the building and the deployment platforms.

Besides the difference in software stacks, ARM-based processors are commonly used and offered on the cloud. Modern cloud-enhanced ARM-based processors provide extensions for security, efficient virtualization, and lower energy consumption than their x86 counterparts. However, in the HPC landscape, Fugaku is the only ARM-based supercomputer to reach the top 500 ranking during June 2020 and May 2022, while other top supercomputers are x86 based on either Intel or AMD processors.

In this work, we evaluate the impact of the differences in three layers in containerized HPC applications on the build and deployment platforms. We use six HPC applications to represent diverse CPU or Memory-intensive workloads. First, we evaluate the overhead of popular container engines in the cloud and HPC on three generations of ARM processors, including the latest Nvidia Grace Processor. Second, we evaluate the impact of changing the "OS layer" from the image when moving from the build platform to the deployment platform. Finally, the impact of switching between rootless and root-owned container engines on the deployment platform is evaluated. In summary, we made the following contributions:

– We quantify the containerization overhead in six HPC applications on three ARM processors including the Nvidia Grace CPU.
– We evaluate the impact of the changed OS layer in Docker and Podman when moving from the build to deployment platforms.
– We evaluate the impact of switching between rootless and root privileges when moving from the build to deployment platforms.

2 Background

In this work, we focus on identifying the impact of different layers in a containerized environment when migrating an HPC container between dedicated HPC systems and the cloud. In Fig. 1, we illustrate the main layers that may change when moving from one system to another. Here the hardware layer is

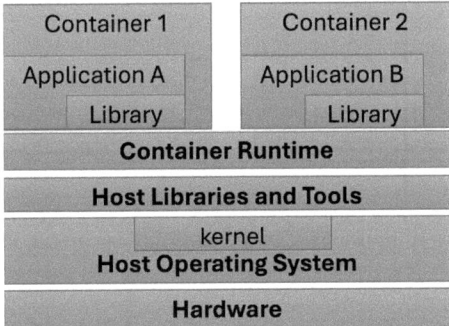

Fig. 1. A hierarchical view of different layers in a containerized environment

the lowest level and it fundamentally impacts the obtainable performance from a platform. A container shares the same Linux kernel as the host OS, but might have a different root file system and toolchain associated with the image it is running that may affect performance: the image, for example, could use `musl libc` as runtime while the host OS could use `glibc`, or different versions of compilers when building code. Finally, although standard container runtime and image specifications ensure usability from one platform to another, the specific container engine in use and its container execution mode on a host may impact performance differently.

Container Engine provides OS-level virtualization and isolation through the kernel's `namespaces` and `cgroup` in Linux. Containers are a lightweight way for managing and deploying microservices in the cloud as it does not virtualize a full guest OS for each instance of a service as required by hypervisors. On HPC systems, *rootless* container engines are popular, such as Singularity [10], Podman [7], while Docker [13] is the de-facto solution on the cloud platform. Podman has syntax compatible with Docker but does not require a privileged daemon to be running all the time as in Docker. In this work, we tackle an emerging scenario where HPC applications are migrating between native HPC systems and the cloud in portable containers. Figure 2 illustrates the main stages and platforms involved in the migration, on the target platform. There, a previously built image is downloaded and stored, converted if necessary (i.e., if an image is built on Docker and will be executed by Podman), a container is created and deployed, and then the application is ultimately executed inside the container.

Host-specific Libraries and Tools. HPC applications have high requirements to get near-hardware native performance from high-end and specialized hardware units. Vendors often provide libraries and tools that are specifically tuned to the hardware on the host platform.

Host-specific Libraries and Tools are often provided by vendors and are specifically optimized for the hardware on the host platform. These tools are crucial for achieving near-native performance of HPC applications, given

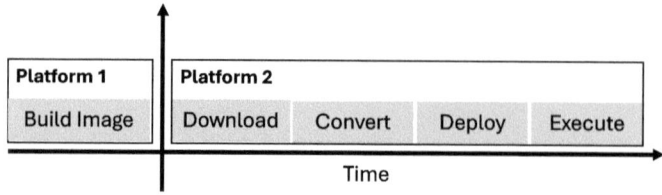

Fig. 2. The main stages of building a image on a platform and deploying it on another platform.

the stringent requirements of high-performance computing environments. For instance, when HPC applications in a container can link to the host's MPI implementation with hardware-specific optimizations, they can mitigate the performance loss due to inefficient usage of network and interconnects. Profiling tools are critical for diagnosing and optimizing applications. As processor-specific hardware performance counters often provide insights into the utilization of specific units, it is also important for HPC applications to link to the host's hardware-specific profiling capabilities.

Hardware often differentiates in Cloud and HPC environments as they deploy processors tailored for their workloads of priority. For instance, HPC platforms only use high-end multi-core processors with high computing power to meet the needs of HPC applications and x86 architecture is dominantly in use. In the Cloud environment, a high variety of processors from medium to high-end, can be chosen to different users' target on cost and performance. In recent years, ARM processors have gained increasing popularity on the cloud, represented by AWS' Graviton3 and the Ampere Altra processors.

3 Methodology

In this work, we characterize the impact of different layers in a containerized environment when migrating between the HPC system and the cloud. We identify three common changes when migrating an HPC container to the cloud environment. First, applications on HPC systems often run in bare metal, while on the cloud platform, applications are running within virtualization, and application users need to understand the overhead: not only on the main computational phase but also the deployment phase for creating and setting up a container.

The second likely change to applications that are used in dedicated HPC systems comes from the kernel of host OS and host-specific libraries, which are shared by all containers, on a deployment platform. The most common libraries used in HPC applications are the MPI library and math libraries like BLAS and FFT. Vendors often provide highly optimized libraries for a specific architecture on an HPC system. Finally, when an HPC container migrates to the cloud, unlike the rootless container execution in HPC systems, it can be executed as a privileged container execution on the cloud. Due to the difference in resource isolation mechanisms, the two container execution modes may impact applications' performance if they require specific kernel-level services.

To understand the above changes quantitatively, we design a set of experiments based on the layered architecture of a container. In particular, we control the software in use in all layers as introduced in Sect. 2 and only change a specific layer to isolate its impact. To ensure wide coverage of the study, we perform comparative studies on three platforms that feature different hardware, OS, host-specific libraries, and container engines. We also select a set of six applications with different characteristics in compute, memory access, and communication, to represent the diverse HPC workloads on HPC systems.

We first quantify the overhead of container-based virtualization. For this, we ensure that each software layer inside a container is identical to that on a platform in bare metal. Second, we use two different platforms to emulate the scenarios of changing OS kernel and host libraries layers (base image) in a containerized environment. Finally, we run HPC containers in both the rootless and privileged modes in Docker and Podman and compare the performance difference between the two modes of the same container runtime on a set of HPC applications. Table 1 summarizes the different options evaluated in each layer in this work.

Table 1. A summary of evaluated layers on the three containerized environments

Container Engine	Docker | Podman
Execution Mode	rootless | root
App Libraries	BLAS | MPI | FFT
OS	RHEL | Rocky Linux | Ubuntu | OpenSUSE
Kernel	Linux
Processor	Nvidia Grace CPU | ARM Ampere | APM X-GENE
Core	Neoverse N2 | Neoverse N1 | Cortex-A57

Hardware Infrastructure. In this work, we use three different platforms to evaluate our workloads, namely CloudLab, Pilot and Sleipner.

The Sleipner platform has the latest Nvidia Grace CPU. The node has 72 64-bit Neoverse V2 cores running at 3.4 GHz and 592 GB DRAM. The Pilot platform is based on the Altera Altra processor. Each compute node has 80 64-bit Neoverse N1 cores running at 3.0 GHz and is equipped with 526 GB DRAM and 2.4TB SSD. On CloudLab, we used the compute node with an APM X-GENE (Cortex-A57) CPU, including eight 64-bit Atlas/A57 cores running at 2.4 GHz, 64GB ECC DRAM, and 120 GB of flash memory.

Software layers mainly consists of the stack of OS and kernel, host libraries and compilers in either bare metal or a container environment. Table 2 specifies

Table 2. A summary of major software layers used in Bare Metal and Container on the three computing platforms

	Sleipner		Pilot		CloudLab	
	Host	Container	Host	Container	Host	Container
OS	RHEL 9.3	Rocky Linux 9.3	OpenSUSE 15.5	OpenSUSE 15.5	Ubuntu 22.04	Ubuntu 22.04
GCC	GCC 11.4	GCC 11.4	GCC 13.2	GCC 13.2	GCC 11.4	GCC 11.4
MPI	Open MPI 5.0.2	Open MPI 5.0.2	Open MPI 5.0.2	Open MPI 5.0.2	Open MPI 5.0.2	Open MPI 5.0.2
BLAS	OpenBLAS 0.3.26	OpenBLAS 0.3.26	OpenBLAS 0.3.26	OpenBLAS 0.3.26	OpenBLAS 0.3.26	OpenBLAS 0.3.26

the main software layers in Bare Metal and Container on the three platforms. The Sleipner platform is running Red Hat Enterprise Linux 9.3 (Kernel: 5.14.0), GCC v11.5.1 and Docker 25.0. The software stack used in the Pilot platform includes OpenSUSE 15.5 (Kernel 5.14.21) and Podman 4.7.2. while the CloudLab platform is running Ubuntu 22.04, Linux Kernel 5.14.21 and Docker 20.10.

3.1 Applications

In this work, we use six applications representative of diverse HPC workloads and algorithms. For each application, two input sizes were selected, one meant to be used at the Sleipner and Pilot platforms, and the other to be used at the Cloudlab platform. The reason for different workloads is that the Cloudlab platform is significantly older and slower than the other two, hence a similar workload input would take much longer to execute there.

DGEMM performs a double-precision matrix-matrix multiplication in the format $C = \alpha A * B + \beta C$, where A, B and C are matrices and α and β are scalars. We tested with two input sizes of 5000×5000 and 20000×20000, and five as the number of repetitions within each trial. The DGEMM benchmark we used[1] is multi-threaded through OpenMP and has no MPI support.

Hypre [6] is a library for high-performance preconditioners and solvers that help solve sparse and linear systems of equations. Hypre uses MPI as a programming model. We used the provided example of solving the convection-reaction-diffusion problem. We tested with two input problems of grid size (n) of 300 and 3000.

XSBench [20] is a proxy app of a Monte Carlo neutron transport application. The application has memory-bound characteristics. We built XSBench with MPI support and tested it with the built-in small and large problem sizes.

HPCG [4] is a Performance Conjugate Gradients benchmark that measures the performance of a system through the usage of basic operations, which includes sparse matrix-vector multiplication, global dot products, among others. We used input matrices of dimension $128 \times 128 \times 128$ and $256 \times 256 \times 256$.

---

[1] Crossroads Benchmark: https://www.lanl.gov/projects/crossroads/benchmarks-performance-analysis.php.

MiniMD is a parallel molecular dynamics mini application. It has a similar algorithm as LAMMPS (Lennard-Jones/EAM system) but has a simpler and smaller code (5000 lines vs over 200000 in the latter). Two input problems of size $64 \times 64 \times 64$ and $256 \times 256 \times 256$ are used.

fftMPI [15] is a library used to perform 2D or 3D Fast Fourier Transforms in parallel. Compared to 1D FFT, 2D and 3D FFT also include memory-bound transposes. FFT is widely used in scientific applications and signal processing. Two grids are used for evaluation: $300 \times 300 \times 300$ and $400 \times 400 \times 400$. As its names implies, fftMPI uses MPI for calculations.

Profiling. We use Linux's `perf` tool to collect hardware performance counters on data locality, memory access, and instruction pipeline. In particular, we needed to explicitly give hardware access to Docker through the usage of the feature `CAP_SYS_ADMIN` in the Sleipner platform.

4 Evaluation

In this section, we discuss three major questions regarding the usage of containers in HPC workloads. When moving towards the convergence of HPC and Cloud, one common scenario is to build the image on one platform and deploy it on another platform on the cloud.

Unless said otherwise, the execution times displayed here are the ones reported by the application (with the exception of XSBench, which does not report by default).

4.1 How Much Impact Does the Usage of a Containerized Environment for Application Deployment Cause?

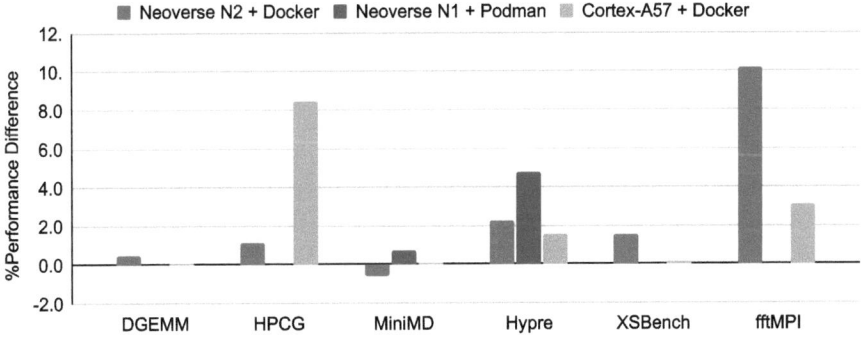

Fig. 3. Results for the six HPC applications running on three generations of ARM processor, including Nvidia Grace, ARM Ampere Altra, and APM X-GENE.

The first question deals with the overall performance of the usage of containers. Given a very similar stack between the Host OS and the Container OS, how much is the impact generated only by the isolation of process/namespaces caused by containers in terms of application execution time? Is this impact consistent in multiple ARM-based architectures?

To answer this, we designed an experiment where, in three different ARM processors, we use the same Host OS, the same Container OS for each machine and also the same software stack - this includes compilers and application libraries/dependencies. We believe that this would enable a fair comparison between the two environments. Table 2 lists the software environment in each system.

Each of the six applications listed in Sect. 3 was executed at least three times, and the plots with the performance difference data can be seen in Fig. 3. The overhead is less than 2% for non-MPI applications (DGEMM and HPCG) in the more recent platforms. Among the MPI-based applications, fftMPI is the clear outlier where the performance difference to bare metal is about 10%, while the other applications usually have less than 4%. Given that the authors were not able to execute fftMPI using the entire CPU resources of Sleipner or Pilot in a containeirized environment, but managed to do so on bare metal, we consider that there might be some interaction with the resource isolation provided by the containers and the application itself that might be causing the slowdown.

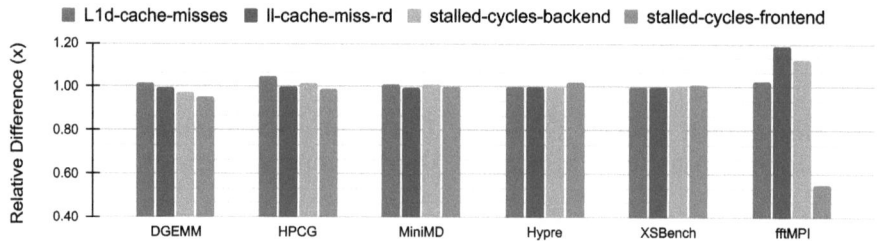

Fig. 4. The relative changes in four performance counters in six HPC applications on the Sleipner platform (Nvidia Grace) in Docker container and Bare Metal.

Furthermore, on the Sleipner platform (the Nvidia Grace processor), we further analysed performance counters that are highly related to data locality, memory access, and instruction execution pipeline, as specified in Sect. 3. Figure 4 displays the relative changes in the performance counters and, as the impact in performance execution is minimal, the results displayed over there also show very minor changes. The results show that in absolute values, we observe that the ones pertaining to the stalls and cache groups had a direct correlation with the execution time, while the SVE group didn't change significantly in its values.

Finally, another usual point when handling performance questions would be how long the Docker application itself takes to start the container. We measure both the time to execute the application using the `time` command, so this would consider the application start-up time, as well as the total time for the end-to-end process. In this case, we built an 8-layered image that amounted to roughly 1 GB in size and contained all necessary dependencies to run all the showcased applications. Figure 5 shows the collected data with the difference between such times, and overall displays that the absolute time takes usually less than 1 s, which is irrelevant if the application runs for a long time. That said, we note that it is a common practice within this field to produce very small images in a step called "multi-stage build" where a second image contains only the minimum necessary to run a certain application (the image for Alpine Linux, for example, has around 30 MB), while the compilation happens somewhere else, and we would expect this to generate even less overhead.

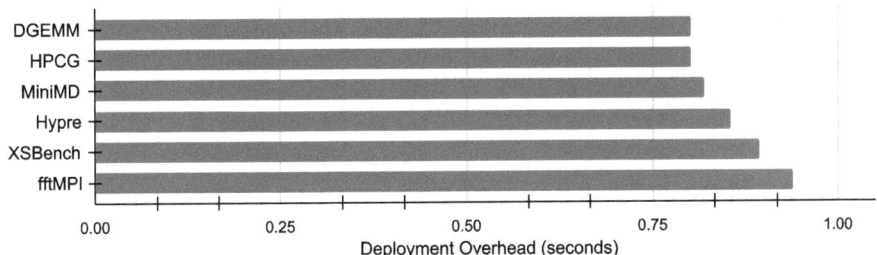

Fig. 5. The overhead of Docker container deployment on the Nvidia Grace-based platform in the six applications.

4.2 How Much Does Using a Container Base Image Different from the Host Image Affect the Application?

This is a question sometimes raised by HPC application developers and resumes to verify whether having different base images when deploying your application affects the performance even though the Linux kernel is being shared. The assumption is that the bundled packages and dependencies within the Image OS might affect performance.

The experiment design for this question involved creating a different image, with the same software stack (compilers, and application libraries), but with a different image OS than the Host OS. We design an experiment through the usage of three applications (DGEMM, HPCG and Hypre) and in two systems (Sleipner and Pilot). Instead of using Rocky Linux and OpenSUSE, as was done in the previous Section, we used Debian Trixie. The difference in performance results can be seen in Fig. 6. In practice, we see that the performance impact is between nearly 0 to a bit over 4%. In comparison to the results obtained in Q1 (where the image was roughly the same as the Host OS), we usually see a usual slowdown except for fftMPI, where apparently the layer of libraries provided by the Image OS was so different than the Host OS to the point of causing a 5% increase in speed, while in Sleipner it created a 20% slowdown.

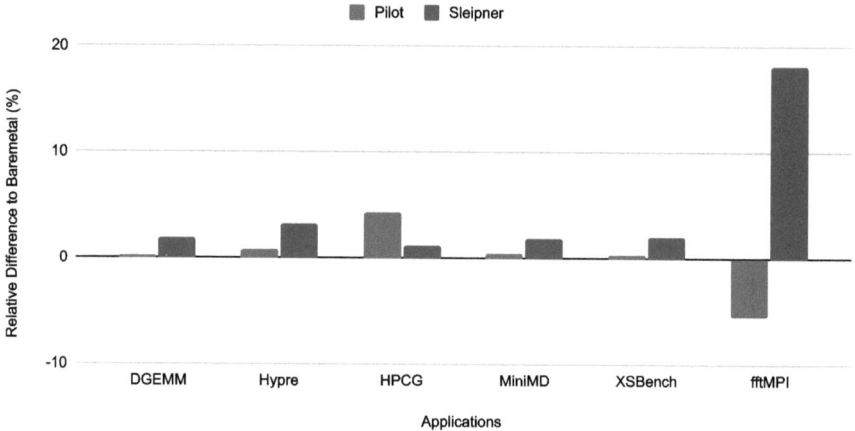

Fig. 6. Performance comparison among different images on both Nvidia Grace platform and ARM Ampere Altra.

4.3 How Much a Security-Hardened Rootless Containers Affect the Performance of Applications?

The root privileges given inside containers is a usual point raised by system administrators in HPC clusters who would rather have their containers executed in rootless mode. Docker requires that at least its daemon executes with root privileges inside the system, while Podman is usually regarded as a rootless solution.

That said, we strive to understand whether there is any impact of switching between different container engine privileges, and thus this third experiment was designed. We used our Cloudlab infrastructure, in which we have full control, to install and observe how the execution time of containers executed as root and rootless affects the overall performance in different applications. In Docker, we define a container as "root" or "rootless" depending on where the docker daemon would run. For Podman, this definition applied depending on which user would start the container (i.e., the "root" user starting the container would be considered root).

Performance results for each case can be seen in Figs. 7 and 8. In practice, while running an application in bare metal mode is slightly better than using containers, there is not any significant difference between executing different privilege modes.

5 Related Works

In virtual machines (VM), virtualization overhead was a concern in HPC applications. Cloud execution of tightly-coupled HPC workloads was previously shown to be several orders of magnitude slower than on a typical HPC cluster, and exhibited lower scalability on the cloud [8], notably due to poor performance of

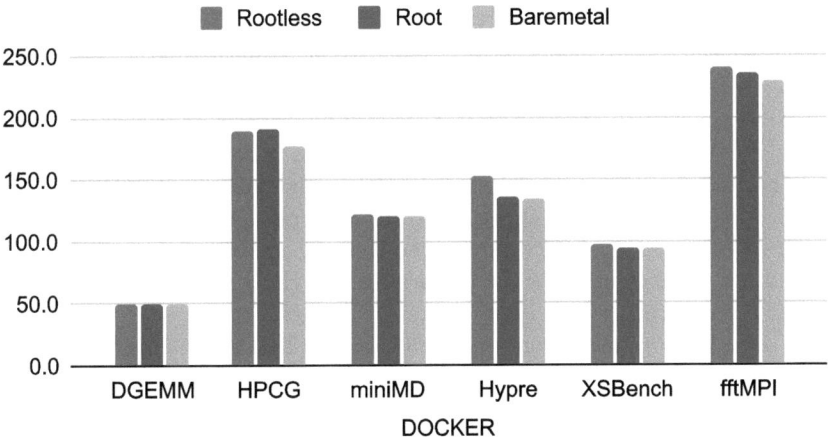

Fig. 7. The performance comparison of rootless and root container execution modes on the Cloudlab platform in Docker and Podman, respectively.

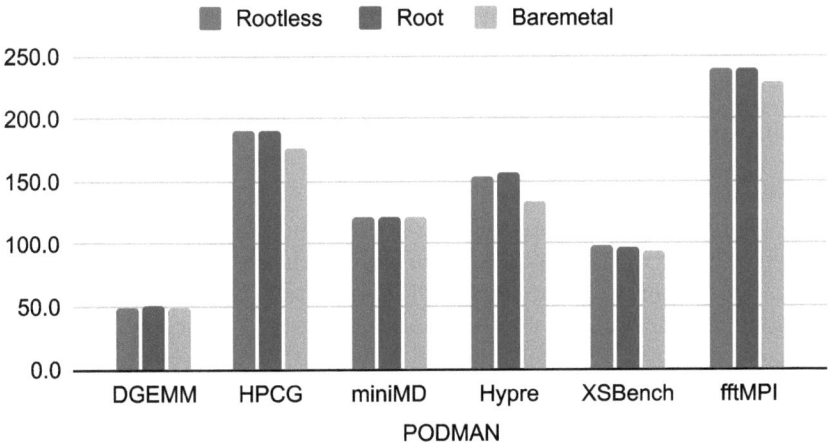

Fig. 8. The performance comparison of rootless and root container execution modes on the Cloudlab platform in Docker and Podman, respectively.

MPI collective operations [2]. The slower network interconnect in the cloud was found to be responsible for the poor performance of communication-intensive applications, this was identified to be partially due to the virtualized I/O to the network interface, that direct VM-level access could solve [5]. Regola et al. [18] identifies that virtualization has a low overhead on computing performance. However, the performance problem mostly lies in I/O overhead. Exposito et al. [5] identify that virtualized access to the NIC is still a bottleneck, but observe a low overhead in shared-memory message passing. The authors propose message-passing plus multithreading as a scalable and cost-effective solution to run HPC applications on Cloud.

On recent cloud platforms that use lightweight container-based virtualization, new optimizations are focused on improving the scalability of HPC applications. Milroy et al. [14] propose a multi-layer model to guide the porting of MPI-based HPC applications to Kubernetes using a declarative approach, along with allowing for automated MPI application lifecycle. They demonstrated strong scaling performance for a medium-scale HPC job, with 3000 MPI ranks. De Sensi [3] identify that due to the congestion-prone network on the cloud, in contrast to networks on HPC systems, co-running jobs on the cloud can cause noise and interference impacts the performance of HPC applications running on the cloud.

The portability of using containers on cloud and HPC systems has also been explored. Sindi et al. [19] proposed to leverage the portability of containers for resilience on HPC clusters. They leverage performance counter monitoring to predict the failure of the compute node and migrate a container to another node without application modification using the CRI-U tool. Younge et al. [21] also studied container portability, focusing on migrating from laptops to clouds or HPC systems. Their study used the Singularity runtime and two HPC benchmarks, HPCG and IBM on a Cray system, to pinpoint the overhead and scalability with containers.

6 Conclusions

Recent development in lightweight OS-level virtualization provides a potential solution for running HPC applications on the cloud platform, a path that was not widely adopted in the past due to the high overhead of hypervisor VM-based virtualization. In this work, we focus on the impact of changing the major layers in a containerized environment when migrating from a dedicated HPC system to the cloud platform. On the three platforms, with six representative applications, we characterized the impact of container virtualization, changed host OS and kernel, and changes in the rootless and privileged container execution. Our results indicate less than 4% container overhead in applications that are not memory intensive, but significantly higher overhead (8%–10%) in FFT, HPCG, and Hypre. We also show that changing between the container execution modes results in negligible performance differences in the six tested applications.

Acknowledgments. This research is supported by the European Commission under the Horizon project OpenCUBE (GA-101092984).

References

1. Araújo De Medeiros, D., Markidis, S., Bo Peng, I.: Libcos: enabling converged HPC and cloud data stores with MPI. In: Proceedings of the International Conference on High Performance Computing in Asia-Pacific Region, pp. 106–116 (2023)

2. Chakthranont, N., Khunphet, P., Takano, R., Ikegami, T.: Exploring the performance impact of virtualization on an HPC cloud. In: 2014 IEEE 6th International Conference on Cloud Computing Technology and Science, pp. 426–432. https://doi.org/10.1109/CloudCom.2014.71. https://ieeexplore.ieee.org/abstract/document/7037698
3. De Sensi, D., De Matteis, T., Taranov, K., Di Girolamo, S., Rahn, T., Hoefler, T.: Noise in the clouds: influence of network performance variability on application scalability. **6**(3), 1–27. https://doi.org/10.1145/3570609. https://dl.acm.org/doi/10.1145/3570609
4. Dongarra, J., Heroux, M.A., Luszczek, P.: HPCG benchmark: a new metric for ranking high performance computing systems. Knoxville, Tennessee **42** (2015)
5. Expósito, R.R., Taboada, G.L., Ramos, S., Touriño, J., Doallo, R.: Performance analysis of HPC applications in the cloud. **29**(1), 218–229. https://doi.org/10.1016/j.future.2012.06.009. https://www.sciencedirect.com/science/article/pii/S0167739X12001458
6. Falgout, R.D., Yang, U.M.: *hypre*: a library of high performance preconditioners. In: Sloot, P.M.A., Hoekstra, A.G., Tan, C.J.K., Dongarra, J.J. (eds.) ICCS 2002. LNCS, vol. 2331, pp. 632–641. Springer, Heidelberg (2002). https://doi.org/10.1007/3-540-47789-6_66
7. Gantikow, H., Walter, S., Reich, C.: Rootless containers with Podman for HPC. In: Jagode, H., Anzt, H., Juckeland, G., Ltaief, H. (eds.) ISC High Performance 2020. LNCS, vol. 12321, pp. 343–354. Springer, Cham (2020). https://doi.org/10.1007/978-3-030-59851-8_23
8. Jackson, K.R., et al.: Performance analysis of high performance computing applications on the amazon web services cloud. In: 2010 IEEE Second International Conference on Cloud Computing Technology and Science, pp. 159–168. https://doi.org/10.1109/CloudCom.2010.69. https://ieeexplore.ieee.org/document/5708447
9. Keller Tesser, R., Borin, E.: Containers in HPC: a survey. J. Supercomput. **79**(5), 5759–5827 (2023)
10. Kurtzer, G.M., Sochat, V., Bauer, M.W.: Singularity: scientific containers for mobility of compute. PLoS ONE **12**(5), e0177459 (2017)
11. Medeiros, D., Schieffer, G., Wahlgren, J., Peng, I.: A GPU-accelerated molecular docking workflow with kubernetes and apache airflow. In: Bienz, A., Weiland, M., Baboulin, M., Kruse, C. (eds.) ISC High Performance 2023. LNCS, vol. 13999, pp. 193–206. Springer, Cham (2023). https://doi.org/10.1007/978-3-031-40843-4_15
12. Medeiros, D., Wahlgren, J., Schieffer, G., Peng, I.: Kub: enabling elastic HPC workloads on containerized environments. In: 2023 IEEE 35th International Symposium on Computer Architecture and High Performance Computing (SBAC-PAD), pp. 219–229. IEEE (2023)
13. Merkel, D., et al.: Docker: lightweight Linux containers for consistent development and deployment. Linux J. **239**(2), 2 (2014)
14. Milroy, D.J., et al.: One step closer to converged computing: achieving scalability with cloud-native HPC. In: 2022 IEEE/ACM 4th International Workshop on Containers and New Orchestration Paradigms for Isolated Environments in HPC (CANOPIE-HPC), pp. 57–70. https://doi.org/10.1109/CANOPIE-HPC56864.2022.00011
15. Plimpton, S., Kohlmeyer, A., Coffman, P., Blood, P.: fftMPI, a library for performing 2D and 3D FFTs in parallel. Technical report, Sandia National Lab.(SNL-NM), Albuquerque, NM (USA) (2018)

16. Priedhorsky, R., Randles, T.: Charliecloud: unprivileged containers for user-defined software stacks in HPC. In: Proceedings of the International Conference for High Performance Computing, Networking, Storage and Analysis, pp. 1–10 (2017)
17. Reed, D., Gannon, D., Dongarra, J.: HPC forecast: cloudy and uncertain. **66**(2), 82–90. https://doi.org/10.1145/3552309. https://dl.acm.org/doi/10.1145/3552309
18. Regola, N., Ducom, J.C.: Recommendations for virtualization technologies in high performance computing. In: 2010 IEEE Second International Conference on Cloud Computing Technology and Science, pp. 409–416. https://doi.org/10.1109/CloudCom.2010.71. https://ieeexplore.ieee.org/abstract/document/5708479
19. Sindi, M., Williams, J.R.: Using container migration for HPC workloads resilience. In: 2019 IEEE High Performance Extreme Computing Conference (HPEC), pp. 1–10. IEEE (2019)
20. Tramm, J.R., Siegel, A.R., Islam, T., Schulz, M.: XSBench-the development and verification of a performance abstraction for Monte Carlo reactor analysis. The Role of Reactor Physics toward a Sustainable Future (PHYSOR) (2014)
21. Younge, A.J., Pedretti, K., Grant, R.E., Brightwell, R.: A tale of two systems: using containers to deploy HPC applications on supercomputers and clouds. In: 2017 IEEE International Conference on Cloud Computing Technology and Science (CloudCom), pp. 74–81. IEEE (2017)

8th International Workshop on In Situ Visualization (WOIV'24)

Preface to the 8th International Workshop on In Situ Visualization (WOIV'24)

1 Background and Description

Large-scale HPC simulations with their inherent I/O bottleneck have made in situ an essential approach for data analysis. In situ coupling of analysis and visualization to a live simulation circumvents writing raw data to disk. Instead, data abstracts are generated that capture much more information than otherwise possible.

The "Workshop on In Situ Visualization" series provides a venue for speakers to share practical expertise and experience with in situ visualization approaches. This 8th edition of the workshop, WOIV'24, took place as an on-site half-day workshop on May 16, 2024, co-located with ISC High Performance, after half-day workshops in 2016, 2017, 2021, 2022, and 2023 and two full-day workshops in 2018 and 2019. In 2020 we had to cancel the workshop due to the COVID-19 crisis. The goal of the workshop, in general, is to appeal to a wide-ranging audience of visualization scientists, computational scientists, and simulation developers, who have to collaborate to develop, deploy, and maintain in situ visualization approaches on HPC infrastructures.

In addition to an invited keynote talk, presentations at WOIV'24 were selected from submitted papers. These were reviewed by an international program committee comprising diverse members from academia, government, and industry and many nationalities. Each submitted paper received at least three reviews. Accepted papers were invited to present at WOIV and are published in this LNCS volume.

2 Workshop Organization

2.1 Keynote

Estelle Dirand gave the keynote speech entitled "Challenges of In Situ Processing for Energies." She presented insights and challenges faced by the energy sector. One important point she discussed is the longevity required from in situ solutions. Integration of in situ into codes is generally a time-consuming task, so choosing the right approach, and an approach that will have a long enough life, is especially important from an Industry perspective. She detailed different solutions to problems done using both Sensei and Catalyst, giving interesting insights into the challenges faced by industry researchers.

Estelle Dirand is the R&D Project Leader in Scientific Visualization at TotalEnergies. Her background is in computer science, engineering, and in situ processing.

2.2 Papers

François Mazen et al., in their paper "In Situ In Transit Hybrid Analysis with Catalyst-ADIOS2", present a workflow using Catalyst2 which combines both in situ and in transit analysis to form a complex analysis pipeline. This pipeline allows operations to be placed where they will be most effective, on the simulation nodes or on a remote resource.

Marcel Krüger et al., in their paper "InsitUE - Enabling Hybrid In-situ Visualizations through Unreal Engine and Catalyst", present a Catalyst adapter that allows data to be shared live from a Catalyst-enabled application directly to Unreal Engine.

Dennis Grieger, in his paper "Interactive In Situ Visualization", presents a pipeline composed of Sensei and Vistle, which enables interactive VR rendering of a simulation in their immersive visualization facility.

3 Organizing Committee

Workshop Chairs

James Kress	KAUST, Saudi Arabia
Francois Mazen	Kitware Europe, France

Workshop Co-organizers

Steffen Frey	University of Groningen, The Netherlands
Kenneth Moreland	Oak Ridge National Laboratory, USA
Guido Reina	University of Stuttgart, Germany
Thomas Theussl	KAUST, Saudi Arabia
Tom Vierjahn	Westphalian University of Applied Sciences, Germany

Program Committee

Andy Bauer	US Army Corps of Engineers, USA
E. Wes Bethel	San Francisco State University, USA
Jose Camata	Federal University of Juiz de Fora, Brazil
Berk Geveci	Kitware Inc., USA
Tim Gerrits	RWTH Aachen, Germany
Ingrid Hotz	Linköping University, Sweden
Shaomeng Li	National Center for Atmospheric Research, USA
Nicole Marsaglia	Lawrence Livermore National Laboratory, USA
Silvio Rizzi	Argonne National Lab, USA

Interactive in Situ Visualization

Dennis Grieger(✉)

High-Performance Computing Center Stuttgart, Nobelstraße 19, 70569 Stuttgart, Germany
dennis.grieger@hlrs.de

Abstract. To achieve interactive *in situ* visualization in immersive virtual environments, the parallel visualization tool Vistle has been coupled with the SENSEI *in situ* framework. Vistle's modular architecture, designed for distributed systems, allows *in situ*, hybrid and *in transit* workflows. A key feature is the ability to interactively configure the visualization pipeline during simulation runtime, even from within 3D virtual environments. Therefore, Vistle's *in situ* analysis runs concurrently with the simulation to apply user input to the visualization of the current simulation iteration. The trade-off is additional memory consumption.

Initial benchmarks on small-scale simulations show promising results in terms of total runtime overhead, provided the visualization pipeline has enough CPU resources to complete before the next visualization iteration is triggered.

For interactive *in situ* visualizations, remote rendering of large data objects combined with in transit visualization of smaller ones has proven to be the most effective.

Keywords: HPC · visualization · virtual reality · in situ

1 Introduction

In situ visualization improves scientific computing and visualization by analyzing large-scale simulation data directly within the computational environment where it is generated. Unlike traditional post-processing methods, *in situ* visualization integrates visualization and analysis tasks into the simulation workflow, minimizing data movement, storage requirements, and computational overhead [1]. This technique enables live exploration and analysis of simulations, providing immediate insights into complex phenomena, offering dynamic feedback loops between simulation and analysis [2] and can help debug simulations. Advancements in hardware, such as parallel computing architectures, and software, including middleware frameworks like SENSEI [3], ADIOS [4] and Catalyst [5], have propelled the adoption of *in situ* visualization across scientific disciplines [6].

The visualization of simulation data in virtual reality (VR) holds tremendous potential to allow researchers to gain new insights into complex phenomena, uncover hidden patterns in their data, and communicate their findings in more intuitive and compelling ways across a wide range of disciplines [7].VR also has the potential to enable new methods of interacting with simulations, e.g. changing boundary conditions or adapting the simulation mesh from the 3D environment.

The original version of this chapter was previously published without open access. A correction to this chapter is available at https://doi.org/10.1007/978-3-031-73716-9_35

In this paper, we present our approach of combining *in situ* visualization with interactive visualization in virtual reality environments. This is achieved by connecting simulations via the SENSEI *in situ* interface to the parallel visualization system Vistle [8, 9].

The goal is to make *in situ* visualization easier to set up and the visualization more comprehensive. Future work can build on this and implement simulation steering methods utilizing the VR environment.

2 System Description

2.1 Existing Building Blocks

The Visualization Toolkit, **VTK** [1], is a 3D computer graphics, image processing, and visualization library. VTK provides efficient data handling allowing for zero-copy integration of data arrays and flexible ownership handling.

The **SENSEI** *in situ* framework is designed to build a universal bridge between N simulation codes and M analysis tools, simplifying the coupling problem from $N \times M$ to $N + M$ combinations. It achieves this by providing abstract classes of a simulation adaptor and analysis adapters. These adaptors pass the simulation data to the analysis in the form of VTK data objects. Data transfer from the analysis to the simulation is also taken care of. Data generation and analysis is left to the concrete implementation of these adaptors [3].

Vistle [8] is a scalable tool for interactive visualization and data analysis, particularly suited for large simulation data sets and distributed computing environments.

The architecture of Vistle consists of several key components (Fig. 1) that each have their own process space:

- Modules: Vistle's functionality is provided by modules, which are specialized components responsible for performing specific tasks such as data processing, visualization or analysis. Concrete modules are for example vector to scalar conversion, slicing, isosurface or streamline calculation and rendering. These modules are MPI [11] -parallel processes but can also use OpenMP [10] for node-level parallelization. Modules have parameters, input and output ports. The ports can be connected to create a visualization pipeline. For example, the *IsoSurface* module takes a scalar field at its input port, has a parameter for the iso-value and produces the surface mesh at its output port. Data is propagated through the pipeline using shared-memory to avoid data copies between processes.
- Hub: The Hub serves as a central communication hub where data and messages are exchanged between different instances of Vistle running on distributed computing resources. The hub is running on rank zero of each cluster in a Vistle session, therefore piping all inter-cluster communication through this rank.
- Manager: The Manager is responsible for coordinating communication within an MPI-parallel instance of Vistle. It receives tasks from the hub, propagates them to the modules and reports the resulting states back.
- User interface: The user interface sends user input to the hub and displays status updates (Fig. 2).

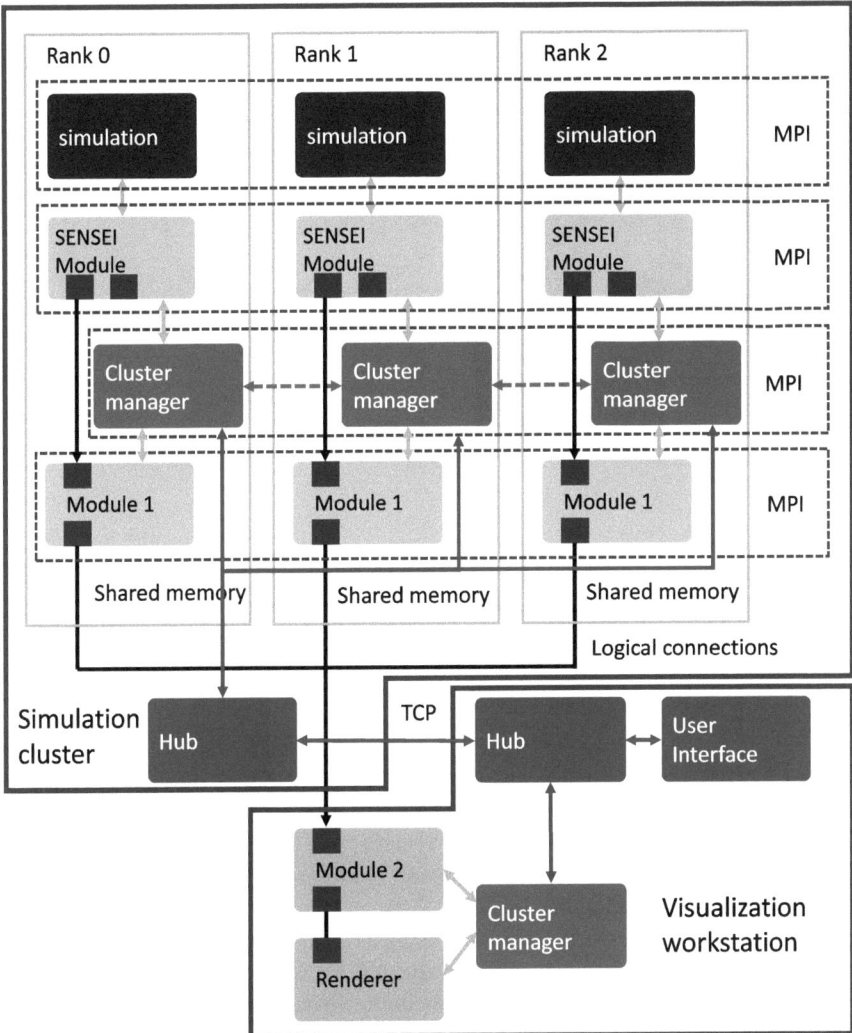

Fig. 1. Vistle's *in situ* architecture in a two-cluster setup. Modules in gray execute on the simulation cluster, teal modules on a visualization workstation, the black arrows symbolize the logical data flow between the modules. Internally this communication happens either via shared memory, symbolized by the teal arrows or via TCP if the modules are on separate clusters. Execution is orchestrated by the Hub on the visualization workstation, green arrows depict TCP control flow and data flow between clusters. Intra cluster communication is implemented with MPI as shown by blue arrows. (Color figure online)

Memory Management in Vistle. Vistle's memory management policy is that modules allocate their data in a common shared memory space. Once the object is created, it is passed on to other down-stream modules as a shared memory handle, with the promise to no longer induce changes to the object.

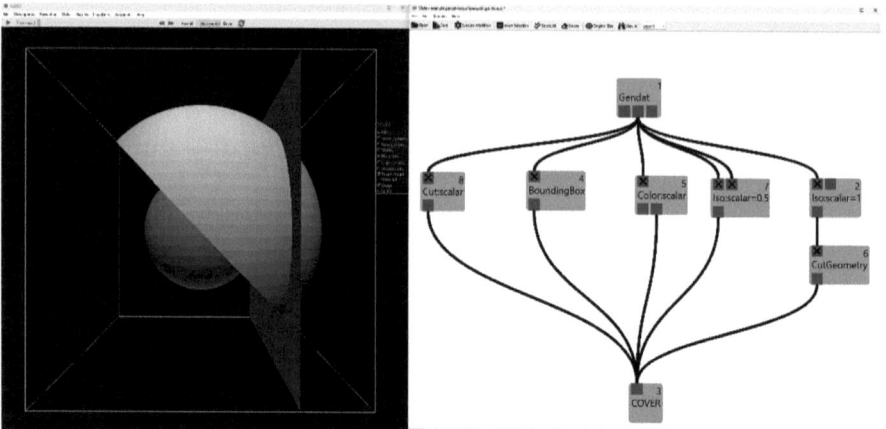

Fig. 2. Vistle's graphical user interface with pipeline (right) and results rendered in OpenCOVER (left).

An object is deleted with the last reference to its handle. Modules can cache their own and received objects to reapply their algorithms with new parameters without recalculation. For example, when the plane used to extract a slice from a grid is moved to a new location the grid does not have to be created again to calculate and draw the new slice. The caching policy can be adjusted, individually for each module, via the user interface.

OpenCOVER is a high-performance visualization tool designed for parallel rendering for multiple screens in scientific computing. OpenCOVER provides a flexible and extensible platform for building immersive visualization applications, offering support for various rendering techniques and hardware configurations. OpenCOVER is integrated in Vistle as a Vistle module. Together, Vistle and OpenCOVER enable researchers to explore complex simulation results in VR, using a variety of immersive virtual environments like head-mounted displays, power-walls or CAVEs. OpenCOVER also provides 3D interactors (Fig. 3) for various parameters of the visualization pipeline.

DisCOVERay is the remote rendering module of Vistle. It uses Embree [12] to perform raytracing on CPUs. DisCOVERay connects directly to OpenCOVER to receive viewpoints and send back the rendered images, including depth information for each pixel. OpenCOVER can overlay locally rendered objects with the images from DisCOVERay using the additional depth information. OpenCOVER also provides reprojection methods to hide latency and lower frame rates of the remotely rendered objects.

2.2 Newly Added Components

To achieve *in situ* visualization in VR a SENSEI analysis adaptor for Vistle [13] was implemented. This adaptor attaches to Vistle's shared memory space and converts the VTK objects received from the simulation to shared memory Vistle objects. This step always requires a deep copy of the underlying data arrays. In Vistle these data objects can be injected into the visualization pipeline using the newly developed SENSEI module.

Fig. 3. The HLRS CAVE running OpenCOVER with 3D interactor (red surface with spheres as handles) for streamline seed points. (Color figure online)

This module uses a dedicated thread to poll data from the SENSEI adaptor. Once all data for one simulation iteration is received the module automatically triggers the execution of itself. When executing, it sends the polled objects to the connected modules. The parameters of the module allow basic interactions with the simulation (Fig. 5, middle). Via a run/pause toggle button the simulation can be paused. Additionally, the data extraction frequency can be set to configure for which iterations data will be extracted. Iterations that do not fall in the frequency scheme will not be converted in the SENSEI adaptor, introducing minimal overhead.

The connection between the SENSEI-Vistle adapter and the Vistle SENSEI module *SenseiController* is established via a connection file that the adaptor writes at startup. The location of this file must be configured by the user via an additional module parameter. The user has to make sure that Vistle and the simulation are executed with the same MPI configuration so that shared memory is accessible to the same ranks. Once the connection is established, the adaptor asks the simulation for a list of data objects it provides. This information is propagated to the module via a shared memory message queue. The module then creates an output port for each of these data objects. The adaptor is informed by the *SenseiController* about the ports that are connected so that it only has to convert and copy these objects.

Once data is simulated and converted to Vistle objects, Vistle can transparently handle data transfer between modules running on connected clusters. This allows *in situ*, *in transit* and hybrid workflows so that resources can be optimally distributed to each pipeline stage (Fig. 4).

Most visualization frameworks (VisIt, ParaView) run all their modules in a single address space on each node [2], integrating them completely in the simulation process. Vistle on the other hand only runs a small shared memory conversion and communication

Fig. 4. Steps in the *in situ* visualization pipeline. Dark framed parts can be executed on different clusters.

library in the simulation process. All other modules in the visualization pipeline can run independently of the simulation and can be moved to different clusters. Additionally, if Vistle crashes the simulation process is not terminated.

3 Experimental Setup

The HLRS supercomputer HAWK [14] has been used in the experiments as simulation cluster. HAWK features two 64 core AMD EPYC 7702 CPUs and 256 GB of memory per node while nodes are connected via 200 Gbit/s InfiniBand. Parts of the visualization pipeline are executed on an 11-node visualization cluster that uses two 16 core Intel Xeon Gold 6134 and a Nvidia Quadro P6000 GPU per node. The visualization cluster is connected to HAWK via 25 Gbit/s Ethernet.

For qualitative testing the computational fluid dynamics code SOD2D [15] was instrumented with a SENSEI interface and used.

As a benchmark simulation the oscillator example shipped with SENSEI has been used because it is accessible for everyone to compare the results and it can be easily configured in terms of grid size, number of MPI ranks and number of threads.

3.1 SOD2D

SOD2D (**S**pectral high-**O**rder co**D**e **2** solve partial **D**ifferential equations) [15] is a computational fluid dynamics code developed at the Barcelona Supercomputing Center. The code is used here to understand the usability and qualitative impacts of interactive *in situ* runs.

The case used, simulates vortex velocities in a cube over 5000 iterations. The grid consists of 25^3 hexahedrons and is not changing over time. The simulation case requires exactly four MPI ranks and does not use other parallelization than MPI.

3.2 Oscillator

The code computes oscillators, convolved with (unnormalized) Gaussians, on a grid. The oscillators were spawned using `sample.osc`, that comes with SENSEI, as input. Execution times are measured from the first call of SENSEI's Execute function at the end of the first simulation iteration until the call to Finalize after the simulation is complete. The memory consumption measured is the maximum memory allocated during the simulation run. The grid is not changing over time so only the scalar array with one entry for every grid cell has to be processed. Figure 5 shows the used workflows and parameters. In the *in situ* run a small pipeline, consisting of four Vistle modules, is executed on the simulation cluster:

- SenseiController: receives the simulation data
- CellToVert: Cell-based data to vertex-based conversion
- IsoSurface: extraction of level set
- DisCOVERray: CPU based ray tracing renderer

DisCOVERay is then sending the rendered images to an instance of OpenCOVER on the visualization cluster.

In the *in transit* run all data is sent directly to a single node cluster. Further data processing on the visualization cluster and its possible impacts on the transmission bandwidth are not considered in this experiment. The results are compared to runs without Vistle, in which the SENSEI simulation adaptor is only checking for a connection in each iteration and then hands control back to the simulation. In the benchmark experiments every simulation iteration is visualized and the data is kept only until the next iteration has finished.

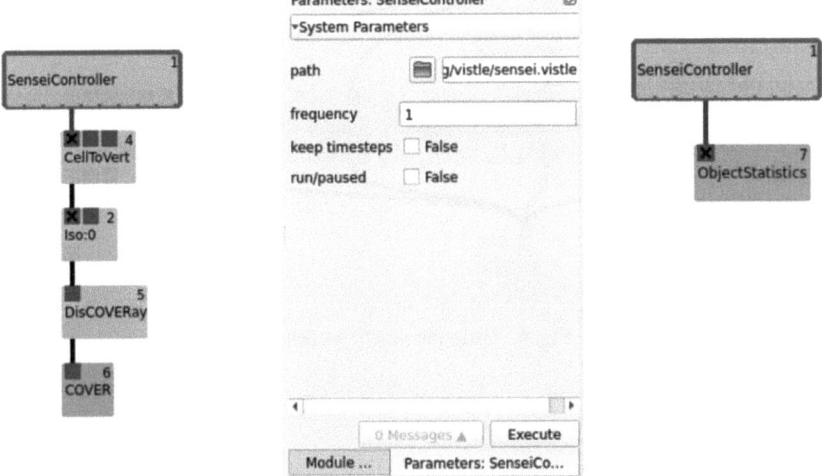

Fig. 5. Experimental pipelines for the *in situ* (left) and *in transit* (right) runs and the SENSEI module parameters (middle). Gray modules are executed on HAWK, teal modules on the visualization cluster. (Color figure online)

4 Results and Discussion

4.1 Single Cluster *in Situ* Workflows with SOD2D

For this experiment, SOD2D and the Vistle pipeline including OpenCOVER as a renderer ran on a single cluster (see Fig. 6). Our visualization cluster was chosen because the rendering step in the full in situ workflow requires GPUs and a display. The general idea of creating the analysis on the fly while the simulation is running worked quite well. Among others, iso-surface, slices and streamlines, which are most commonly used in scientific visualizations, have been tested. While it is possible to interact with the visualization in the CAVE, the visualization stutters whenever the simulation sends new data to Vistle, i.e., the visualization pipeline is triggered. This leads to frozen images in the VR environment and can make practical work impossible if processed iteration cycles are unreasonably short. This is due to OpenCOVER not being able to load incoming render-objects onto the GPU while rendering the current scene.

Due to its adaptive setup, this workflow is suitable for debugging purposes when the simulation is paused while analysis happens, but for large scale application and adequately large visualization cluster is needed.

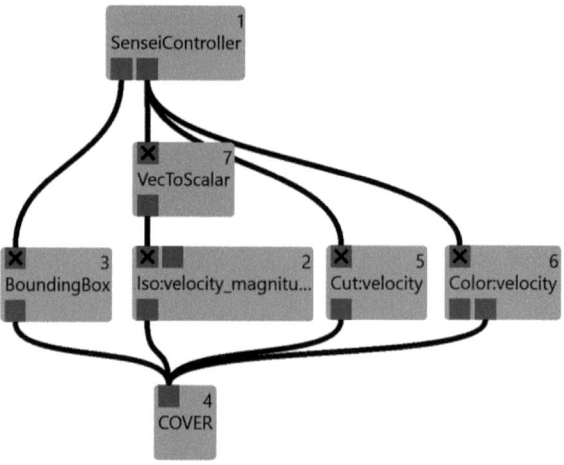

Fig. 6. Example *in situ* workflow.

4.2 Hybrid *in Transit* Workflows with SOD2D

In this experiment an instance of Vistle, running parallel to the SOD2D simulation on HAWK, is connected to an instance of Vistle on the visualization cluster. Feature extraction modules like *IsoSurface* are executed on HAWK, the render-objects are then sent through the hub on HAWK to the hub of the visualization cluster where they are propagated to the OpenCOVER module (see Fig. 7).

Advantages of the hybrid approach are that it does not require GPUs nor displays on the simulation cluster and it decouples the rendering setup from the simulation setup. This allows the simulation to run on different resources and number of ranks than the rendering. The issues with rendering freezes also occur in this setup therefore making it only suitable for analyses with low update frequency or strong data reduction.

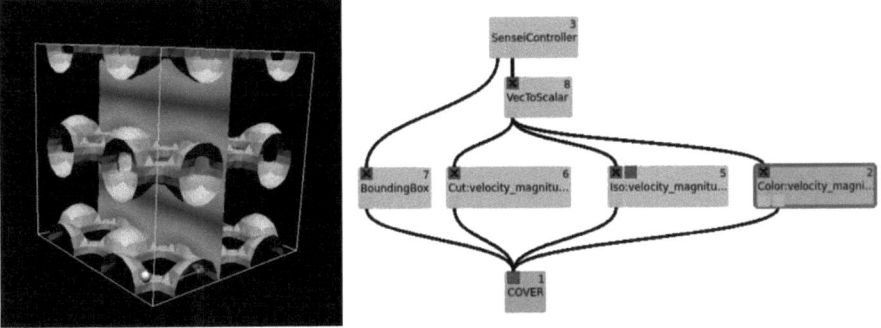

Fig. 7. *In situ* setup for the SOD2D simulation (right) and example image of the output on the visualization cluster (left).

4.3 Hybrid Remote Rendering with SOD2D

This setup is similar to the hybrid in transit workflow (see Sect. 4.2) but large render-objects like iso-surfaces are rendered on HAWK using DisCOVERay and are then super-positioned with the small ones like the bounding box in OpenCOVER on the visualization cluster.

This approach solves the stuttering during GPU upload since only the remotely rendered textures from DisCOVERay have to be uploaded on the GPU. The framerates achieved for the remotely rendered images were strongly dependent on the load induced by the simulation and the visualization pipeline, but were rarely below 20 frames per second (fps), which is not optimal for VR applications (60 fps are considered good), but usable in combination with the reprojection methods used. We found that this approach is so far the best suited for large scale interactive *in situ* visualization with Vistle.

4.4 Oscillator Benchmarks

Figure 8 shows the execution time and the memory consumption of *in situ* and *in transit* runs compared to simulation runs without Vistle. The computation time overhead in both coupled runs is increasing with the number of MPI ranks used. In the *in transit* run this is because the communication is piped through rank 0, therefore not scaling with more MPI ranks. For the *in situ* runs this is mainly due to two reasons:

- Vistle modules already use node level parallelization, therefore not scaling with more ranks per node.
- More ranks mean more MPI processes which can cause interference in the communication when overbooking CPU cores, especially since every process involved (simulation + manager + modules) can do MPI communications.

Also, once simulation iterations are executed faster than the visualization pipeline, visualization objects stack up in the pipeline causing huge memory consumption. This problem can easily be mitigated by adjusting the frequency parameter or distributing more resources to the visualization (e.g. through pinning).

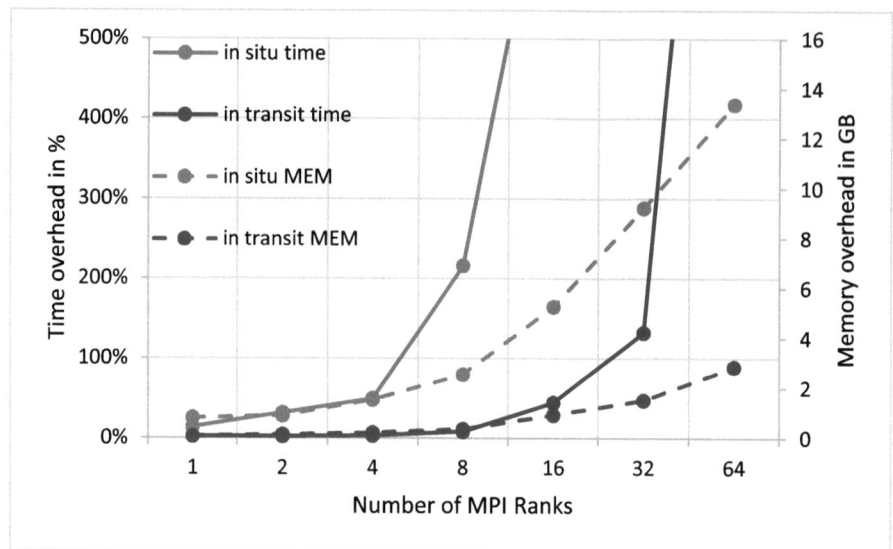

Fig. 8. Comparison of relative execution time overhead (solid) and absolute memory overhead (dashed) of the Oscillator simulation with a 64^3 vertices grid on a single 128 core node.

Since the *in transit* workflow does not scale, the following multi node experiments only compare the in situ workflow with remote rendering (see Fig. 5, left) with the baseline execution time. The results are shown in Fig. 9.

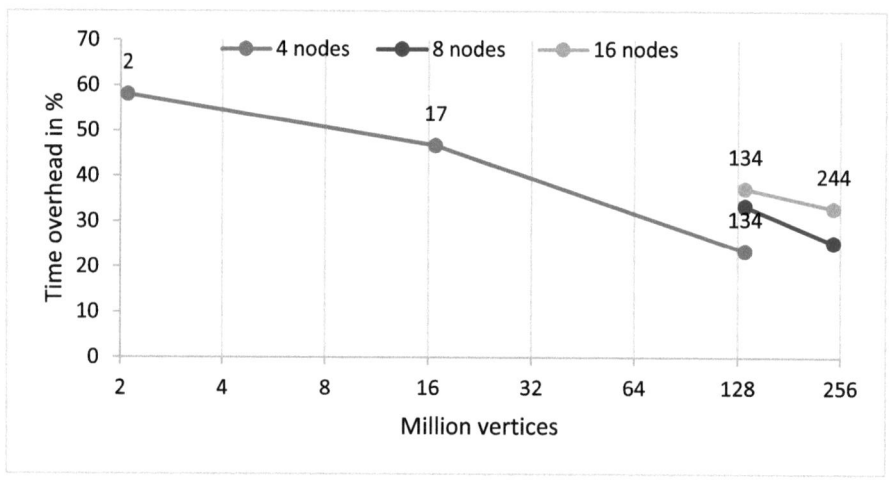

Fig. 9. Relative execution time overhead of the oscillator in situ run with remote rendering on varying gird size and number of HAWK's compute nodes. The simulation uses one MPI rank and 16 threads per node.

While the absolute overhead is mostly a comparison between the oscillator kernels and our cell to vertex base conversion followed by the iso-surface extraction the trend of decreasing overhead with larger grid sizes is promising for future application on larger simulation runs.

5 Summary

The visualization tool Vistle was extended with a SENSEI module that allows Vistle to couple with SENSEI compatible simulations. Vistle's visualization pipeline can be changed during the simulation runtime and parameterized through its VR visualization environment. First benchmarks with small simulations showed good performance as long as the visualization pipeline is given enough resources to compute within an execution interval. Since the execution interval can be configured and adapted during runtime compromises can easily be accomplished. This also applies to the computational complexity of the pipeline, which can always be reduced or shifted to another cluster. Additional memory consumption through holding the data back for interaction has to be considered when using Vistle in situ.

Qualitative experiments showed that uploading larger sized data frequently to the GPU interrupts interactivity and immersion. Hybrid *in transit* workflows with direct rendering of constant and smaller geometries on the visualization cluster and remote rendering of large updating data objects on the simulation cluster seemed to work best for large scale applications. In situ runs on a single cluster work well for simulation debugging.

The effects on larger simulations are still to be investigated. Furthermore, optimizations in the *in transit* data transfer and the memory management allowing zero-copy takeover of simulation arrays are topics for future work. Also loading new render objects while still rendering the current scene has to be implemented to significantly improve workflows without remote rendering.

Acknowledgements. This study was funded by the European Union and the European High Performance Computing Joint Undertaking in the projects EXCELLERAT (grant number 823691) and EXCELLERAT P2 (grant number 101092621).

Disclosure of Interests. The authors have no competing interests to declare that are relevant to the content of this article.

References

1. Ayachit, U., Geveci, B.: The ParaView guide: [a parallel visualization application]; updated for ParaView version 4.3. Kitware, New York (2015)
2. Whitlock, B., Favre, J.M., Meredith, J.S.: Parallel in situ coupling of simulation with a fully featured visualization system (2011). https://doi.org/10.2312/EGPGV/EGPGV11/101-109
3. Ayachit, U., Whitlock, B., Wolf, M., et al.: The SENSEI generic in situ interface, pp. 40–44 (2016). https://doi.org/10.1109/ISAV.2016.013

4. Boyuka, D.A., Lakshminarasimham, S., Zou, X., et al.: Transparent in situ data transformations in ADIOS, pp. 256–266 (2014). https://doi.org/10.1109/CCGrid.2014.73
5. ParaView Developers ParaView Documentation: Catalyst. https://docs.paraview.org/en/latest/Catalyst/index.html. Accessed 26 Feb 2024
6. Kwan-Liu, M.: In situ visualization at extreme scale: challenges and opportunities. IEEE Comput. Graph. Appl. **29**, 14–19 (2009). https://doi.org/10.1109/MCG.2009.120
7. Akpan, I.J., Shanker, M.: A comparative evaluation of the effectiveness of virtual reality, 3D visualization and 2D visual interactive simulation: an exploratory meta-analysis (2018). https://doi.org/10.1177/0037549718757039
8. Aumüller, M.: Hybrid remote visualization in immersive virtual environments with vistle (2019). https://doi.org/10.2312/pgv.20191113
9. Vistle GitHub (2024). https://github.com/vistle/vistle
10. OpenMP: The OpenMP API specification for parallel programming(2023). https://www.openmp.org. Accessed 23 Feb 2024
11. Clarke, L., Glendinning, I., Hempel, R.: The MPI message passing interface standard: working conference of the IFIP WG 10.3, 25–29 April 1994. Monte Verità. Birkhäuser Basel, Basel (1994)
12. Wald, I., Woop, S., Benthin, C., et al.: Embree. ACM Trans. Graph. **33**, 1–8 (2014). https://doi.org/10.1145/2601097.2601199
13. SENSEI GitHub: branch with Vistle analysis adaptor (2024). https://github.com/hpcdgrie/sensei
14. HLRS. HPE Apollo (Hawk) (2024). https://www.hlrs.de/de/loesungen/systeme/hpe-apollo-hawk. Accessed 22 Feb 2024
15. BSC. sod2d_gitlab: Spectral high-Order coDe 2 solve partial Differential equations (2024). https://gitlab.com/bsc_sod2d/sod2d_gitlab. Accessed 22 Feb 2024

Open Access This chapter is licensed under the terms of the Creative Commons Attribution 4.0 International License (http://creativecommons.org/licenses/by/4.0/), which permits use, sharing, adaptation, distribution and reproduction in any medium or format, as long as you give appropriate credit to the original author(s) and the source, provide a link to the Creative Commons license and indicate if changes were made.

The images or other third party material in this chapter are included in the chapter's Creative Commons license, unless indicated otherwise in a credit line to the material. If material is not included in the chapter's Creative Commons license and your intended use is not permitted by statutory regulation or exceeds the permitted use, you will need to obtain permission directly from the copyright holder.

InsitUE - Enabling Hybrid In-situ Visualizations Through Unreal Engine and Catalyst

Marcel Krüger[✉][ID], Jan Frieder Milke[ID], Torsten W. Kuhlen[ID], and Tim Gerrits[ID]

Visual Computing Institute, RWTH Aachen University, Aachen, Germany
krueger@vis.rwth-aachen.de

Abstract. In-situ, in-transit, and hybrid approaches have become well-established visualization methods over the last decades. Especially for large simulations, these paradigms enable visualization and additionally allow for early insights. While there has been a lot of research on combining these approaches with classical visualization software, only a few worked on combining in-situ/in-transit approaches with modern game engines. In this paper, we present and demonstrate *InsitUE*, a Catalyst2 compatible hybrid workflow that enables interactive real-time visualization of simulation results using Unreal Engine.

Keywords: In-situ · In-transit · Visualization Workflow · Game Engines

1 Introduction

In the last decade, commercial-off-the-shelf game engines, such as Unreal Engine (UE) [9] or Unity [28], have repeatedly proved to achieve impressive results in the production of interactive media. Their use has expanded from game development into other domains, such as television productions, architecture, and scientific research software, as these engines can provide several advantages compared to custom solutions: Most game engines are highly optimized, battle-tested solutions focusing on real-time rendering and fast interactions while treating cross-platform compatibility as a first-class requirement. Combined with the focus on accessibility, community, and development tools, they provide a strong foundation for developing scientific visualization applications [17]. However, even highly optimized engines like UE can quickly run into performance issues if not used carefully, which is especially restrictive if performance is paramount, e.g., in immersive visualization applications [15]. This can be prohibitive, especially for large datasets and simulations, making interactive visualizations with game engines no longer feasible. An established method to deal with this issue is using in-situ or in-transit paradigms that generate the visualization while the simulation is still running. Those methods allow for data reduction that makes visualizations possible and allows users to additionally get early simulation feedback. With the expected growth in simulation sizes, visualization challenges will persistently involve in-situ, in-transit, and hybrid approaches. It can be observed that recent publications aim to make these workflows easier and more accessible. Adopting common APIs, like the Catalyst API, allow for flexibly exchanging parts of the workflow as needed. While there is a lot of development concerning these workflows in the context of classical HPC-based solutions, few works consider modern game engines as part of an in-situ, in-transit, or hybrid workflow.

In this work, we present *InsitUE*, a hybrid workflow that bridges the gap between established in-situ solutions and Unreal Engine. InsitUE consists of a Catalyst2 compatible implementation enabling steerable in-situ pre-processing with minimal outward dependencies and a plugin for Unreal Engine that allows effortless interactive in-transit visualization of simulation data.

2 Related Work

The necessity and potential of in-situ/in-transit visualization are corroborated by the amount of literature, libraries, and software solutions that were published on the topic within the last decades [7,26]. Recent years saw the release of several libraries with a strong focus on making the integration of in-situ and in-transit workflows easier and more efficient for developers, such as reusing standard protocols and methods to reduce dependencies [16], infrastructure as a service approaches [25] or techniques that allow in-situ-esque processing on file-based simulation output [14]. One aspect is to make the instrumentation of simulation code as easy as possible while still remaining flexible in terms of analysis and visualization possibilities. Two prominent examples of existing approaches are the SENSEI library [5], as well as Paraview Catalyst(pre v5.8) [3]. However, they rely on the simulation developers to be familiar with VTK [27] for instrumentation and add additional dependencies, which can be prohibitive for adoption. To alleviate this issue, mesh data can also be presented by data formats that are easier to work with, such as Conduit [12] or Fides [24]. Therefore, Ascent [18] and the Catalyst2 API [4] use Conduit as the data format to pass mesh data into the in-situ library. Conduit-based APIs reduce the detailed knowledge needed, as meshes and simulation data can be described by Conduit mesh blueprints with an easier structure while reducing the dependency footprint. Catalyst2, in particular, tries to find a modular solution to in-situ workflows by defining a stable ABI and API that allows Catalyst2-enabled simulations to work with any library that implements the Catalyst2 API. During recent years, multiple implementations that fulfill the Catalyst2 API, such as Paraview Catalyst(post v5.9) [3], Adios Catalyst [21], and Ascent Catalyst [18] have emerged. While these improvements have made in-situ/in-transit processing of scientific data more accessible for developers regarding the simulation code, another important and challenging aspect of visualization is how to view and interact with the resulting data. Multiple degrees of interactivity exist when considering in-situ/in-transit workflows. One option is to write image data to disk, which can be viewed with various image viewers but offers basically no interaction; another option is to use approaches like cinema [2] that offer limited interactivity with the data through image-based methods. Lastly, tools like ParaView [1] and VisIt [8] offer interactive handling and a plethora of features but are often limited in terms of real-time performance, interaction, and responsiveness. These aspects can, however, be critical when trying to explore and experience data firsthand. Especially in immersive visualizations, these properties must be fulfilled without compromise, as cybersickness and immersion can be affected. Game engines have these requirements at their heart compared to other solutions, which are crucial for a good user experience. Consequently, it is unsurprising that game engines have gained popularity in various scientific communities to provide immersive, interactive, and engaging applications. Various works can be found that leverage game engines to visualize saved data, i.e., via the classical offline processing paradigm [10,11] or visualize simulations embedded into the engine [13]. However, both approaches are restrictive in that only the computing power of the local PC can be used, all the data has to fit into the memory, and additional infrastructure, such as HPC systems, can not be leveraged. Very little work is known that combines in-situ/in-transit workflows with game engines as visualization front-ends. One notable exception is the work by Nealey et al. [23] that presents an in-transit workflow based on SENSEI, Paraview Catalyst, and Unreal Engine. In their approach, they utilize SENSEI's in-transit capabilities to transfer data to staging nodes, which then process the data with Paraview Catalyst and extract PLY mesh geometry sent via WebSockets to Unreal Engine. While the approach enables in-transit capabilities for UE, there are four critical limitations: First, only in-transit processing is supported, requiring the complete data to be transferred to staging nodes first. Second, only mesh data can be transferred and visualized, making certain visualizations impossible, such as volume-based approaches, or dramatically increasing the amount of data for certain types, e.g., lines represented as tubes. Third, due to their connection-oriented protocol, WebSockets can be limiting when working with larger numbers of visualization clients. Lastly, the approach is only unidirectional, and no steering capabilities are part of it.

In this work, we leverage existing research and present an approach based on the Catalyst2 API and Conduit, focusing on hybrid capabilities, efficiency, and bidirectional interactivity.

3 InsitUE

The InsitUE workflow allows hybrid in-situ/in-transit visualization of simulation data, with interactive steering capabilities and flexible real-time rendering using Unreal Engine. Workflows comprise three key components that represent, on a conceptual level, the data producer, data (pre-)processor/communicator, and data visualizer. In InsitUE, the three key components are the simulation, the InsitUE Catalyst2 implementation, and the InsitUE Unreal Engine plugin. In the following section, we first provide an overview of the workflow and protocol and subsequently present the implementation of each of the three components.

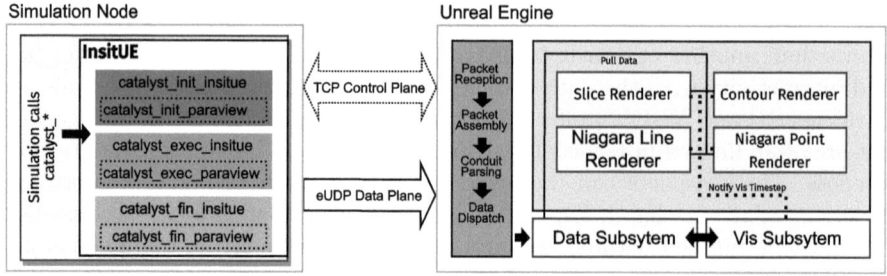

Fig. 1. InsitUE architecture: Instrumented simulation code calls the InsitUE Catalyst plugin, which optionally passes data to a Catalyst2 compatible in-situ library. The data is sent via the UDP data plane, our Unreal Engine plugin then renders the data. Optionally, data is sent back to the Catalyst plugin via the TCP control plane.

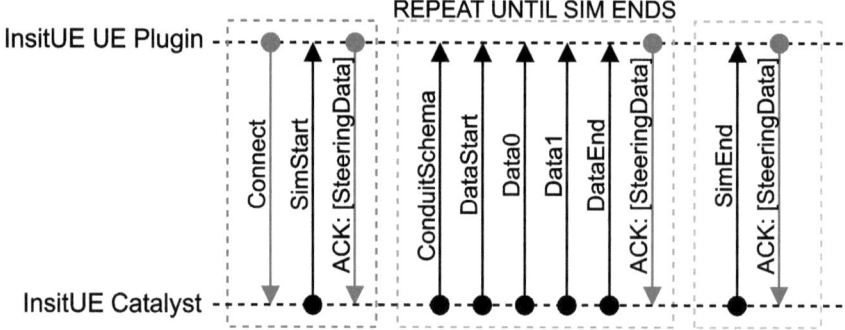

Fig. 2. Network protocol of InsitUE. UDP packets are colored in black, while the optional TCP packets are colored in purple. (Color figure online)

3.1 InsitUE Overview

On an abstract level, InsitUE follows the standard pattern of a hybrid in-situ/in-transit workflow. Data is first produced by a simulation and made available to our InsitUE data processor, which optionally performs in-situ data (pre-)processing. The data is then transferred to one or multiple visualization nodes via the network for further visualization. An overview of these three steps is represented by the Simulation Node, Network Layer, and Visualization Node in Fig. 1. Communication of InsitUE relies on two separate directional communication channels, representing one control plane and one data plane as indicated in Fig. 2. The data plane sends data from the simulation to the visualization client, while the control plane sends control data back to the simulation and is optional. In the initialization phase of the protocol, a SimStart packet is sent containing metadata, e.g., simulation name, simulation length, and other information relevant to the visualization. Afterward, data for one timestep is sent in several packets. First, the Conduit schema is sent, followed by a DataStart packet containing the size of the following byte stream. Due to possible MTU restrictions, data is sent in multiple packets containing chunks, trailed by a `DataEnd` packet. After the simulation, a `SimEnd` packet indicates the simulation's end. If the optional control plane mechanism is used, this protocol is preceded by a `Connect` from the client, and each phase is acknowledged by an `ACK` packet that optionally contains additional steering parameters for the visualization. While optional, the use of the control plane can provide important advantages: Firstly, it provides the mechanism to send data back to the simulation. The data can be either metadata or steering commands used by the simulation or the InsitUE Catalyst implementation to steer the behavior of either component. Secondly, by requiring an acknowledgment of the received data, the visualization can use the timing of this acknowledgment to influence data transmission. One option would be to acknowledge immediately after receiving the data but before visualization, which could potentially lead to data loss if the simulation progresses faster than the visualization. Another option would be to acknowledge after the data is visualized and the visualization is ready to show the next timestep, thus ensuring that no timesteps are skipped. As a last example, data acknowledgment could be tied to user input, enabling interactive human-in-the-loop workflows.

3.2 Implementation

The following paragraphs introduce the three components individually, discuss their architecture, and give a more detailed overview of their role.

Simulation. InsitUE aims to provide a flexible workflow for various simulations and simulation domains. As in-situ and in-transit workflows need access to simulation data while the simulation is still running, adding instrumentation of the simulation code is necessary. As most code instrumentation is tailored to specific software solutions, we aimed to make the workflow compatible with an already established solution. Therefore, our approach is based on the Catalyst2 API. The Catalyst2 API is an established solution implemented by various libraries, such as ParaView Catalyst [3], Adios Catalyst [21], and Ascent Catalyst [18]. Due to the small API and the stable ABI, the user can easily exchange concrete implementations. Therefore, by implementing the Catalyst2 API, Catalyst-enabled simulations can still be used in our InsitUE workflow (c.f. Sect. 4 SPH-EXA). If such an implementation does not exist, the instrumentation code can be easily added (c.f. Sect. 4 FluidX3D). Catalyst2 provides Python and Fortran bindings besides the C interface, allowing it to be compatible with most simulations.

InsitUE Catalyst. For our Catalyst implementation, we had four major requirements in mind:

(i) Compatibility with simulations previously instrumented for Catalyst2.
(ii) Interactive hybrid visualizations.
(iii) Facilitate efficient multi-node rendering.
(iv) Minimize external dependencies.

To achieve the first goal, we allow the configuration of InsitUE-specific parameters, e.g., IPs, ports, script paths, via environment variables, config files, or the Conduit node passed in the initialize phase. Configuration via config files and environment variables enables reuse of existing code. Our current implementation allows users to use TOML and YAML for config files, with an overall precedence of environment variables > config files > conduit parameters. As real-world simulations can become large, it is important to allow in-situ pre-processing of the simulation data to reduce the amount of data that needs to be transferred and processed. We utilize the Catalyst2 API for the in-situ pre-processing capabilities to support existing and future in-situ solutions. This allows us to easily embed the `catalyst_*` calls to other in-situ solutions, e.g., Paraview Catalyst and Ascent Catalyst, in InsitUE's Catalyst calls. Requirements (iii) and (iv) are crucial in determining the goal of being compatible with Unreal Engine on various systems. Unreal Engine is highly portable and can ship applications on different hardware and software environments. One critical aspect was minimizing dependencies between the simulation- and visualization environments while maintaining efficiency. While HPC environments provide possibilities to utilize highly efficient solutions, e.g., UCX, RDMA, MPI, the premise of availability quickly changes when considering non-HPC consumer environments. InsitUE aims to support various devices, from phones and tablets to multi-node rendering systems. As Unreal Engine already supports these systems, developing InsitUE's Unreal Engine Plugin with compatible dependencies is critical. Thus, existing approaches based on the aforementioned protocols are prohibitively hard to use or infeasible. These requirements led us to use custom TCP/UDP-based socket communication combined with Conduit as the data format for communicating between the Catalyst and the Unreal Engine plugin. TCP is used for the control plane, while a custom protocol on top of UDP that supports out-of-order deliveries is used for the data plane. In our current implementation, the custom protocol defines a packet as having Opcodes describing the packet type, a sender ID, a sequence number, and a chunk number followed by data.

InsitUE Unreal Engine Plugin. The InsitUE plugin for UE provides three key components:

(i) Process network communication between InsitUE's Catalyst component and Unreal Engine.
(ii) Manage data and state of the visualization.
(iii) Provide mappings between Conduit mesh blueprints and UE render components.
(iv) Provide system control UI and visualization utilities.

The network component is based on UE-native TCP and UDP sockets, which are platform-agnostic and integrate nicely with UE-native data types. The data plane component runs in a parallel thread and continuously accepts incoming packets. Chunked data packets are sorted and reassembled once they are complete. Data packets are marked as complete once the Conduit schema, data begin, data end, and all data packets are received. Reassembled packets are parsed into their Conduit representation and handed to the data subsystem for further processing. Two singleton systems in the plugin handle data and state management, namely the `DataSubsytem` and `VisSubsytem`. The `DataSubstem` stores simulation metadata, such as the minimum and maximum timestep available, the number of timesteps buffered, and the ring buffer implementation that stores individual timesteps as Conduit nodes. The data subsystem provides data to render components on request. On the other hand, the visualization's state is managed by the central `VisSubsytem`, which manages properties such as visualized timesteps and playback speed. Additionally, it synchronizes different render components and notifies them of changes in the visualization, e.g., that a different timestep should be visualized, and manages back-channeling of steering commands into the simulation. Render components in InsitUE represent components that utilize Unreal Engine rendering functionality to visualize the received data. They utilize modern and highly efficient rendering systems to provide interactive real-time visualizations.

In our current implementation, we provide render components to map triangle meshes, points, and lines directly: The mesh render component utilizes UE's procedural mesh capabilities to render triangle meshes defined by Conduit mesh blueprints, updating meshes during runtime based on connectivity and vertex attributes. Vertex attributes can be updated on the GPU if the topology does not change, while changes require rebuilding. It supports rendering vertex and cell attributes with arbitrary color transfer functions. While vertex attributes can be directly mapped to the mesh via shaders, for cell attributes, vertex duplication is used for shared vertices. The point render component builds upon UE's Niagara particle system to efficiently render points based on their Conduit representation. Once initialized, the particles remain on the GPU, and only position and attribute changes are sent. The visual representation of points, e.g., size, color mappings, etc., are implemented as custom GPU components in the Niagara system to take advantage of GPU parallelization. Line rendering is also implemented with Niagara to visualize lines and polylines efficiently. The line renderer parses the vertex positions and connectivity information encoded in the Conduit mesh blueprint, to generate a representation compatible with our Niagara line system. The system supports rendering lines in different styles and generates geometry, color mappings, etc., on the GPU, such that only vertex positions and connectivity are uploaded to VRAM. Support for volume data, non-triangle polyhedra meshes, etc., is planned and partially prototyped. Lastly, the InsitUE Unreal Engine plugin provides system control capabilities through UI elements (c.f. Fig. 3) that show the current state of the simulation and visualization, as well as interaction utilities such as gizmos that can be used during runtime. The UE plugin is designed to enable an easy workflow for developers, all components are modeled as UE native classes, that can be used from the comfort of the UE Editor. Developers effortlessly add in-transit capabilities to their projects by adding the components to their Unreal Engine scene and setting Ports, IPs, Conduit property names, etc., through the editor's user interface.

4 Results

To demonstrate the potential of InsitUE, we integrated it into two existing open-source scientific simulation solutions. To showcase the bidirectional capabilities, we provide direct and hybrid visualization of simulation data and interactive steering of the in-situ pipeline. We used Unreal Engine 5.3 and a forked Conduit version for the following use cases based on version v0.8.7. Paraview Catalyst was used for in-situ processing, which was compiled against our forked Conduit version to maintain compatibility. Visualization was performed on a Windows 10 Desktop PC with an Intel i9-13900KF, 64GB DDR5 RAM, and an NVIDIA GeForce RTX 4090.

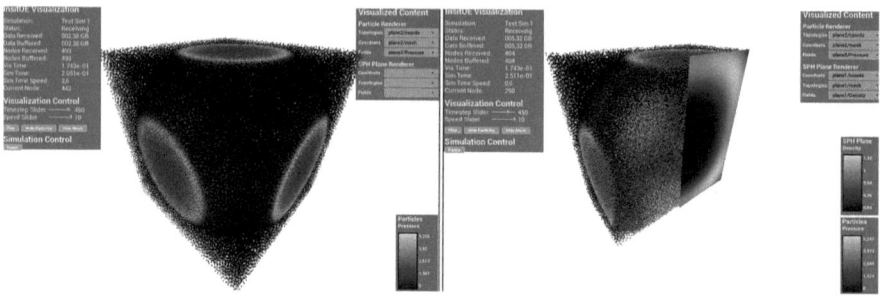

Fig. 3. Left: Visualization of SPH particles with their respective color-mapped pressure values. Right: An in-situ calculated SPHInterpolationPlane is additionally visualized.

SPH-EXA. The *SPH-EXA* [6] mini-app[1] is a framework for efficient simulation of Smoothed Particles Hydrodynamics(SPH) written in C++ to simulate multidimensional fluids based on particle movement and is part of *SPEChpc 2021 Benchmark Suites for Modern HPC Systems* [20]. The repository provides a Catalyst adaptor implementation and simulation code instrumentation that can be enabled, so no changes are required. The simulation comprised 216,000 particles in a cubic domain that simulated a spherical shock blast. The simulation ran as a parallel CPU-based simulation on an Ubuntu 22.04 128-core E7-8860 server with 1TB DDR4 RAM and no hyperthreading. Positions and pressure values of all SPH particles are sent to our InsitUE plugin to enable in-transit visualization. SPH particles were rendered with the point renderer component, and pressure was color-mapped via the Veridis color map. In a second configuration, the density was calculated via Paraview's SPHPlaneInterpolator function and visualized alongside half of the particles. The visualization ran consistently at the maximum fps of 120, and users could interactively control the camera, changing the playback speed of buffered timesteps and the ability to pause the visualization and/or simulation. The resulting visualization can be seen in Fig. 3.

---

[1] SPH-EXA code available at https://github.com/unibas-dmi-hpc/SPH-EXA.

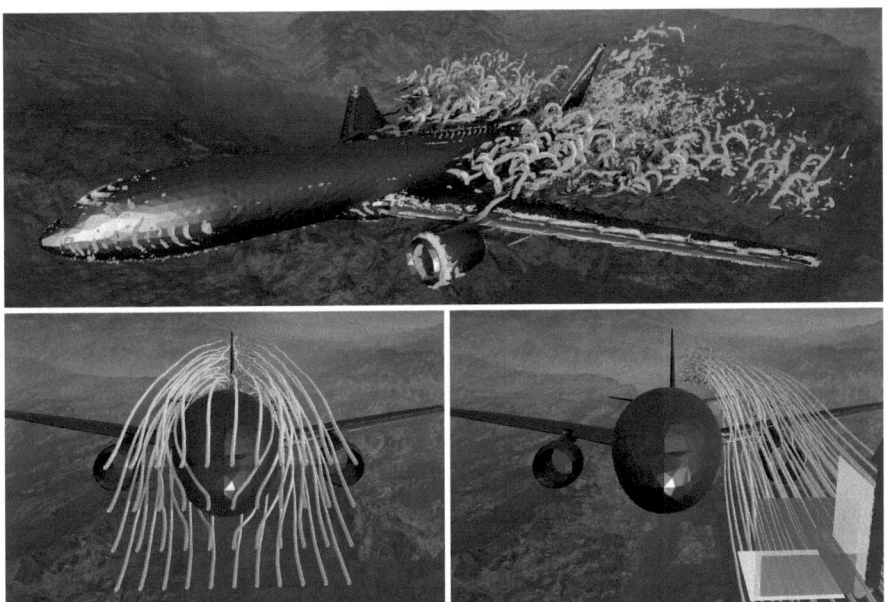

Fig. 4. FluidX3D results visualized in Unreal Engine. Top: Isosurface of Q-Criterion with velocity magnitude color mapped. Bottom left: Streamtracer on velocity field with magnitude color mapped. Bottom right: Streamlines after the seedpoint was changed.

FluidX3D. *FluidX3D*[2] [19] is an efficient C++ implementation to simulate computational fluid dynamics using a Lattice Boltzmann method (LBM) solver. The simulation code was forked and instrumented with standard Catalyst2 API calls. The simulation ran on an Ubuntu 22.04 Desktop PC with an Intel(R) Core(TM) i9-10900X CPU@3.70GHz, 64GB DDR4 RAM, and NVIDIA GeForce RTX 3090. For this showcase, we disabled FluidX3D's built-in visualizations and used GPU readbacks to pass field data to InsitUE. The simulation computes velocities on the NASA Common Research Model on a $424 \times 636 \times 141$ grid, resulting in a 436 MB vector field per timestep passed to our InsitUE Catalyst implementation with zero-copy. To demonstrate the hybrid visualization capabilities, we used Catalyst-Paraview for in-situ processing to extract streamlines and an iso-contour of the Q-Criterion, an indicator of vortical flow within the field. Sending streamlines and derived attributes such as vector magnitude and vorticity, or the contoured mesh, reduced the data size to ∼5 MB and ∼45 MB, respectively. Figure 4 shows the interactive application, where additional scenic elements were added using Unreal Engine features to increase the scene's realism. The InsitUE plugin's line and mesh render visualized the streamlines and contours, with Veridis color mapping representing the magnitude of the velocities. To demonstrate the ability to steer the in-situ visualization via InsitUE, the

---

[2] FluidX3D code available at https://github.com/ProjectPhysX/FluidX3D.

user can change the position and scale of the streamtracer source interactively in the application via the provided gizmo to change the streamtracer properties in the Paraview Catalyst pipeline. The visualization ran consistently at the maximum fps of 120 while allowing the user to control the hybrid visualization interactively.

5 Discussion and Limitations

The presented results are based on an early version of InsitUE still under active development. One critical aspect is the current implementation of the network component. While UDP has inherent shortcomings concerning reliability, i.e., packet loss and out-of-order delivery, the possibility of using UDP broadcasting has significant advantages. One concrete outlook is to utilize InsitUE on display infrastructure driven by a high number of rendering instances (>40). While TCP guarantees reliable packet delivery, it cannot broadcast packets to multiple clients without sending individual packets. This results in a reduced network throughput that can impair the overall performance. In our current implementation, we made UDP more robust by adding support for out-of-order delivery of packets. Lost packets, however, do not get retransmitted, which leads to the discard of incomplete packets. While this effect is contained to individual timesteps, it would still cause disruptive behavior, especially if network conditions are more challenging. Therefore, we plan to extend the robustness of our UDP implementation by adding packet resubmission capabilities. While several reliable UDP implementations exist, no implementation currently fulfills our requirements. Support for efficient broadcasting is especially hard to find. This will also allow us to use UDP for the control plane. In our current implementation, we chose TCP as control packets must be reliably transmitted. Lost control packets could otherwise lead to the complete halt of the simulation. Lastly, no tests using multi-node simulation setups have been performed yet. The catalyst component, network protocol, and UE plugin are also designed to handle simulation data originating from multiple simulations. Performance depends on many variables, such as the amount and kind of work done in-situ, the amount of data sent in-transit, network hardware, simulation size, etc.; therefore, we did not provide benchmarking results for the simulation side as representative cases are hard to find. As InsitUE works on the Conduit byte streams passed as part of the Catalyst2 API, any overhead will mainly arise due to network throughput. In case in-situ pre-processing is used, the processing overhead for this is inherent and can either improve in-transit performance if data reduction is performed or worsen it if data is augmented. The presented results are performed on data sizes that can be considered small in the context of in-situ/in-transit visualization. As all example cases run at the maximum frame rate of 120FPS at 4K resolution, the presented examples are not indicative of the performance limits. Further testing on larger datasets has yet to be performed to better understand the possibilities and limitations regarding the size of the data that can be visualized.

6 Conclusion and Future Work

Game engines such as Unreal Engine show great potential to be used as foundations for modern visualization tasks. Key features such as the focus on performance, platform independence, and accessibility allow visualization developers to focus on the presentation and interaction of data. The rising complexity of simulations, however, poses a serious challenge when considering the use of game engines. The primary constraints are the computational complexity of modern simulations and the size of the data. Existing in-situ/in-transit and hybrid workflows have been proven to excel in these kinds of tasks, but they are often designed around HPC workflows. In this paper, we presented and demonstrated InsitUE. InsitUE utilizes standard in-situ/in-transit practices such as Catalyst2 and Conduit while minimizing outward dependencies on our Unreal Engine plugin. This results in a steerable hybrid workflow that allows real-time rendering of simulation data in Unreal Engine. The next steps for InsitUE include the development of efficient multi-node workflows in terms of simulation and visualization. Additionally, we aim to increase the interactivity of InsitUE workflows even further through two approaches: On one hand, we plan to extend capabilities to steer more facets of the in-situ processing as well as the simulation itself; on the other hand, we plan to incorporate VTK [27]/VTM-m [22] into our Unreal Engine plugin, which allows further client-sided processing of visualization data. Lastly, we aim to integrate the InsitUE workflow into immersive visualization environments, combining the advantages of in-situ/in-transit workflows with the possibilities that virtual reality can provide. Overall, we believe that InsitUE has an exciting outlook and will be a key component of future development in our visualization lab.

Acknowledgments. The authors gratefully acknowledge the German Federal Ministry of Education and Research (BMBF) and the NRW state government for supporting this work/project as part of the NHR funding.

References

1. Ahrens, J., Geveci, B., Law, C.: Visualization Handbook, chap. In: ParaView: An End-User Tool for Large Data Visualization. Elsevier Inc., Burlington (2005)
2. Ahrens, J., Jourdain, S., O'Leary, P., Patchett, J., Rogers, D.H., Petersen, M.: An image-based approach to extreme scale in situ visualization and analysis. In: Proceedings of the International Conference for High Performance Computing, Networking, Storage and Analysis, SC 2014. IEEE (2014)
3. Ayachit, U., et al.: Paraview catalyst: enabling in situ data analysis and visualization. In: ISAV 2015. Association for Computing Machinery, New York (2015)
4. Ayachit, U., et al.: Catalyst revised: rethinking the paraview in situ analysis and visualization API. In: Jagode, H., Anzt, H., Ltaief, H., Luszczek, P. (eds.) ISC High Performance 2021. LNCS, vol. 12761, pp. 484–494. Springer, Cham (2021). https://doi.org/10.1007/978-3-030-90539-2_33
5. Ayachit, U., et al.: The sensei generic in situ interface. In: 2016 Second Workshop on In Situ Infrastructures for Enabling Extreme-Scale Analysis and Visualization (ISAV) (2016)

6. Cavelan, A., Cabezón, R.M., Grabarczyk, M., Ciorba, F.M.: A smoothed particle hydrodynamics mini-app for exascale. In: PASC 2020. Association for Computing Machinery, New York (2020)
7. Childs, H., Bennett, J., Garth, C., Hentschel, B.: In situ visualization for computational science. IEEE Comput. Graph. Appl. **39**(6) (2019)
8. Childs, H., et al.: Visit: an end-user tool for visualizing and analyzing very large data. In: High Performance Visualization–Enabling Extreme-Scale Scientific Insight (2012)
9. Epic Games: Unreal Engine. https://www.unrealengine.com
10. Gandel, L., Jomier, J.: Rendering VTK into unity (2020). https://www.kitware.com/rendering-vtk-into-unity/. Accessed 06 Mar 2024
11. Gold, L., et al.: Visualizing planetary spectroscopy through immersive on-site rendering. In: 2021 IEEE Virtual Reality and 3D User Interfaces (VR), pp. 428–437. IEEE (2021)
12. Harrison, C., Larsen, M., Ryujin, B.S., Kunen, A., Capps, A., Privitera, J.: Conduit: a successful strategy for describing and sharing data in situ. In: 2022 IEEE/ACM International Workshop on In Situ Infrastructures for Enabling Extreme-Scale Analysis and Visualization (ISAV). IEEE (2022)
13. Harwood, A.R., Wenisch, P., Revell, A.J.: A real-time modelling and simulation platform for virtual engineering design and analysis. In: Proceedings of 6th European Conference on Computational Mechanics (ECCM 6) and 7th European Conference on Computational Fluid Dynamics (ECFD 7) (2018)
14. Kress, J., Holst, G., Dasari, H.P., Afzal, S., Hoteit, I., Theußl, T.: Inshimtu – a lightweight in situ visualization "Shim". In: Bienz, A., Weiland, M., Baboulin, M., Kruse, C. (eds.) High Performance Computing. ISC High Performance 2023. LNCS, vol. 13999, pp. 257–268. Springer, Cham (2023). https://doi.org/10.1007/978-3-031-40843-4_19
15. Krüger, M., Li, Q., Kuhlen, T.W., Gerrits, T.: A case study on providing immersive visualization for neuronal network data using cots soft- and hardware. In: 2023 IEEE Conference on Virtual Reality and 3D User Interfaces Abstracts and Workshops (VRW) (2023)
16. Krüger, M., et al.: Insite: a pipeline enabling in-transit visualization and analysis for neuronal network simulations. In: Anzt, H., Bienz, A., Luszczek, P., Baboulin, M. (eds.) High Performance Computing. LNCS, vol. 13387, pp. 295–305. Springer, Cham (2022). https://doi.org/10.1007/978-3-031-23220-6_20
17. Krüger, M., Gilbert, D., Kuhlen, T.W., Gerrits, T.: Game engines for immersive visualization: using unreal engine beyond entertainment. In: PRESENCE: Virtual and Augmented Reality, pp. 1–50 (2024). https://doi.org/10.1162/pres_a_00416
18. Larsen, M., Brugger, E., Childs, H., Harrison, C.: Ascent: a flyweight in situ library for exascale simulations. In: Childs, H., Bennett, J.C., Garth, C. (eds.) In Situ Visualization for Computational Science. MATHVISUAL, pp. 255–279. Springer, Cham (2022). https://doi.org/10.1007/978-3-030-81627-8_12
19. Lehmann, M.: Computational study of microplastic transport at the water-air interface with a memory-optimized lattice Boltzmann method. Ph.D. thesis, Bayreuth (2023)
20. Li, J., et al.: SPEChpc 2021 benchmark suites for modern HPC systems. In: Companion of the 2022 ACM/SPEC International Conference on Performance Engineering (2022)
21. Mazen, F., Givord, L., Gueunet, C.: Catalyst-ADIOS2: in transit analysis for numerical simulations using catalyst 2 API. In: Bienz, A., Weiland, M., Baboulin,

M., Kruse, C. (eds.) High Performance Computing. LNCS, vol. 13999, pp. 269–276. Springer, Cham (2023). https://doi.org/10.1007/978-3-031-40843-4_20
22. Moreland, K., et al.: VTK-M: accelerating the visualization toolkit for massively threaded architectures. IEEE Comput. Graph. Appl. **36**(3) (2016)
23. Nealey, I., Ferrier, N., Insley, J.A., Mateevitsi, V.A., Rizzi, S., Schulze, J.: Sort-last in-transit data visualization with sensei, catalyst, and unreal engine. In: 2022 IEEE 12th Symposium on Large Data Analysis and Visualization (LDAV). IEEE (2022)
24. Pugmire, D., et al.: Fides: a general purpose data model library for streaming data. In: Jagode, H., Anzt, H., Ltaief, H., Luszczek, P. (eds.) ISC High Performance 2021. LNCS, vol. 12761, pp. 495–507. Springer, Cham (2021). https://doi.org/10.1007/978-3-030-90539-2_34
25. Ramesh, S., Childs, H., Malony, A.: Serviz: a shared in situ visualization service. In: SC22: International Conference for High Performance Computing, Networking, Storage and Analysis. IEEE (2022)
26. Rivi, M., Calori, L., Muscianisi, G., Slavnic, V.: In-situ visualization: state-of-the-art and some use cases. PRACE White Paper (2012)
27. Schroeder, W., Martin, K., Lorensen, B.: The Visualization Toolkit, 4th edn. Kitware. New York (2006)
28. Unity Technologies: Unity. https://www.unity.com

In Situ in Transit Hybrid Analysis with Catalyst-ADIOS2

François Mazen(✉), Louis Gombert, Lucas Givord,
and Charles Gueunet

Kitware Europe, Villeurbanne, France
{francois.mazen,louis.gombert,lucas.givord,charles.gueunet}@kitware.com

Abstract. In this short paper, we present an innovative approach to limit the required bandwidth when transferring data during in transit analysis. This approach is called *hybrid* because it combines existing in situ and in transit solutions. It leverages the stable ABI of Catalyst version 2 and the Catalyst-ADIOS2 implementation to seamlessly switch from in situ, in transit and hybrid analysis without modifying the numerical simulation code. The typical use case is to perform data reduction in situ then generate a visualization in transit on the reduced data. This approach makes the numerical simulation workflows very flexible depending on the size of the data, the available computing resources or the analysis type. Our experiment with this hybrid approach, reducing data before sending it, demonstrated large cost reductions for some visualization pipelines compared to in situ and in transit solutions. The implementation is available under an open source permissive license to be usable broadly in any scientific community.

Keywords: in situ · in transit · Catalyst · ADIOS2 · visualization · ParaView

1 Context

In situ analysis is a technique to perform data exploration and visualization during the execution of a numerical simulation, in order to reduce I/O bottleneck [1]. This technique is de facto standard when a simulation operates with large data and during several time steps. In transit analysis is an extension of in situ analysis by moving the data to a dedicated node for analysis. This circumvents many drawbacks of in situ analysis like reducing the simulation halt time, and performing analysis on dedicated visualization nodes [2]. These visualization nodes could use dedicated hardware like powerful GPUs which are not necessarily available on the nodes running the numerical simulation. However, in transit analysis requires moving the dataset over the network to reach the end point where the analysis will be performed. Thus, in transit technique is not scalable, especially when reaching exascale. In this case, the simulation output data are so large that it is nearly impossible to transfer the data in an acceptable amount of time. Thus, the data transfer becomes the bottleneck.

Many numerical simulations mitigate the data transfer problem by computing data reduction at the end of a step. For example, OpenFOAM could generate specific data reduction [3]. Some simulation codes could embed visualization routines like in DualSPHysics [4] which leverage the Visualization ToolKit (VTK) to perform isosurface extraction on-the-fly. However these solutions lack flexibility because the scientists are limited by the available features made available through simulation codes.

Kress et al. [5] identified several situations where the Visualization Cost Efficiency Factor (VCEF) is not sufficient to achieve cost savings. In particular, the case where the transfer cost is bigger than executing the visualization in-line.

2 In Situ and in Transit Hybrid Analysis

In order to benefit from in transit analysis while reducing the cost of data transfer, we developed a combination of in situ and in transit technologies. Catalyst version 2 is a recent standard to instrument numerical simulation code in a portable way thanks to its stable Application Binary Interface (ABI) [6]. As Catalyst is just a protocol to exchange data, there are several implementations or backends available. Catalyst can also work with externally managed data pointers, which allow sharing data between the simulation and the visualization software without performing any copy. The reference implementation is Catalyst-ParaView, where the data are internally transformed to VTK data objects and processed through a ParaView python analysis pipeline. Another Catalyst implementation is Catalyst-ADIOS2 [2] which uses the efficient data movement capabilities of ADIOS2 [7] to perform in transit analysis. Catalyst uses Conduit Blueprint as the backbone of data description across the various backends.

Our hybrid approach combines both of these Catalyst implementations. The data are first reduced in situ thanks to the Catalyst-ParaView implementation on the simulation nodes, then the reduced data are passed to the Catalyst-ADIOS2 implementation to be moved and then replayed with the Catalyst-ADIOS2 Replay mechanism on the visualization nodes. This replay executable then passes the reduced data to a Catalyst-ParaView implementation inside of the Visualization Cluster to perform the final analysis with dedicated resources, for example using GPUs. Unlike classic in situ, this last analysis part on the visualization cluster does not block the running simulation on the simulation cluster.

In this configuration, the numerical simulation code does not have to change because the entry point is still the Catalyst-ADIOS2 implementation on the simulation side. Our work was to upgrade the Catalyst-ADIOS2 project to orchestrate the combination of data reduction then data movement, as described in Fig. 1.

This approach compels the numerical simulation user to prepare two pipelines to be executed by the Catalyst-ParaView libraries. The first pipeline is for the data reduction in situ and the second one is for the final analysis on the reduced

484   F. Mazen et al.

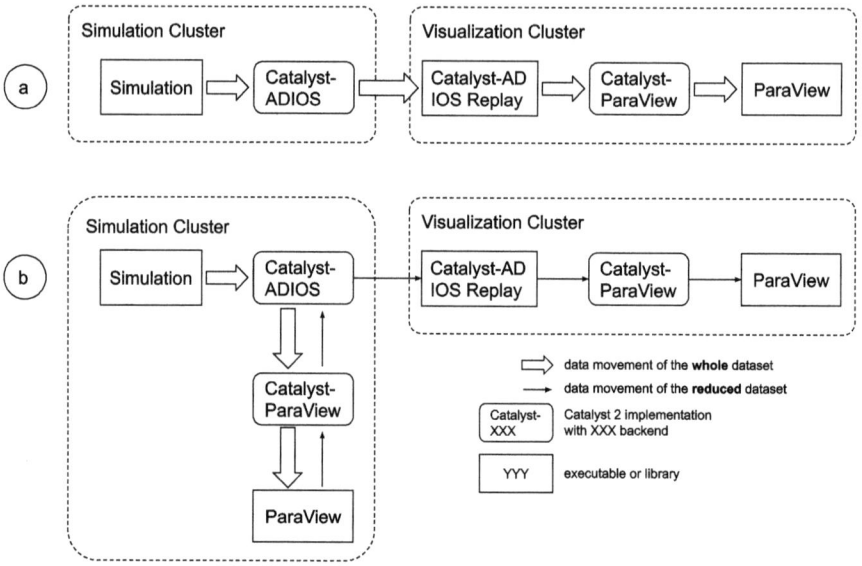

Fig. 1. Comparison of data flow between in transit solution with Catalyst-ADIOS2 (a) and our new hybrid in situ in transit approach (b), where only reduced data are sent over the network.

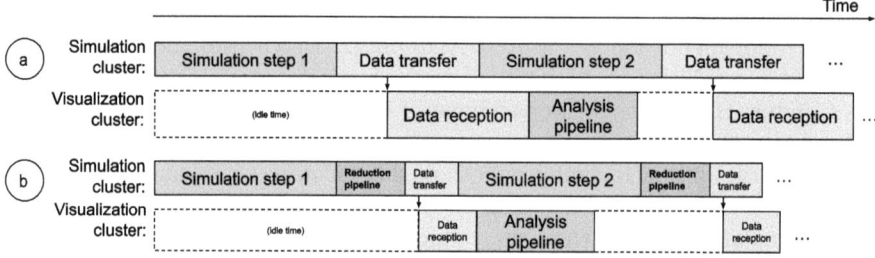

Fig. 2. Schematic timeline comparison of in transit analysis (a) and our new hybrid in situ in transit approach (b). Performance gain is expected when data reduction time and reduced data transfer time (b) is less than full data transfer time (a).

data on the simulation cluster. Thanks to the stable ABI of Catalyst version 2, the numerical simulation code does not depend on the chosen Catalyst backend. The Catalyst-ParaView and ParaView versions could have different configurations and be optimized for their running hardware. In a typical situation where the simulation cluster contains only CPUs, the ParaView instance used by the numerical simulation nodes would have to use all the available CPU-cores power with SMP backend like TBB or OpenMP, with headless and/or offscreen rendering using EGL or OSMesa. On the other hand, the ParaView instance on the Visualization cluster would leverage the GPU capabilities with dedicated rendering backends like NVidia IndeX [8].

In practice, we had to face two technical challenges. The first one was to load the Catalyst-ParaView implementation inside the Catalyst-ADIOS2 library to perform the data reduction using ParaView algorithms. The goal was to let the simulation use the same implementation of Catalyst, such as we did for the in transit case introduced in [2]. The second challenge was to get the output of the ParaView data reduction pipeline back to the Catalyst-ADIOS2 library. For this, we had to improve the existing *simulation steering* mechanism of Catalyst-ParaView by creating a new Steering Extractor filter. The output of this extractor is serialized as a conduit node and sent back to Catalyst-ADIOS2 which ordered the execution of the reduction pipeline. Then, the reduced data is passed to ADIOS2 to be sent over the network to the visualization cluster. The process is entirely handled by the Catalyst-ADIOS2 library which requires very little code modification of the simulation.

The final implementation is publicly available under a permissive open source license at the Kitware's public Gitlab instance [9].

3 Use Case and Benchmark

It has been demonstrated before [5] that some simulation workflows benefit from in transit compared to in line visualization. As depicted in Fig. 2, in situations where the visualization pipeline takes less time to execute than a simulation step, in transit saves time compared to in line. In the latter case, the time taken by the data transfer from the simulation cluster to the visualization cluster is shorter than the time it would take to perform the visualization in line. This is usually the case for visualization pipelines that involve computation-heavy algorithms such as isocontouring or volume rendering. However, cost savings are harder to achieve with larger data where the transfer time is important. Our approach is aimed to help saving costs in these situations by performing a data reduction in the simulation cluster before sending the data. Typically, this reduction can be a simple slice on the simulation data, or another type of dimension reduction. This in line reduction does not requires full simulation data movement, leveraging Catalyst's ability to manipulate pointers to data managed externally by the simulation.

For our benchmark, we considered that the visualization pipeline has two separable steps: data reduction (size, dimensionality, clustering, number of fields) and visualization of the reduced data. Compared to in transit analysis, we can achieve cost savings if the in line data reduction takes less time than sending the whole data through ADIOS2. All in all, the hybrid workflow is interesting to save costs for simulations that output data large enough to notice the synchronous transfer time, which takes resources on both clusters, and where the visualization is complex and heavy enough to justify using separate nodes for visualization.

To evaluate our solution, we used the Livermore Unstructured Lagrangian Explicit Shock Hydrodynamics (LULESH) simulation code [10] which solves a simple Sedov blast problem, and written to run on multi-node cluster. We introduce two different pipelines: one performing a slice on the 3D data showing the wavefront of the blast, and another one transforming the unstructured mesh to a smaller one with a regular structure, on which we perform volume rendering to show the shock wave propagation. The result of those is shown Fig. 3.

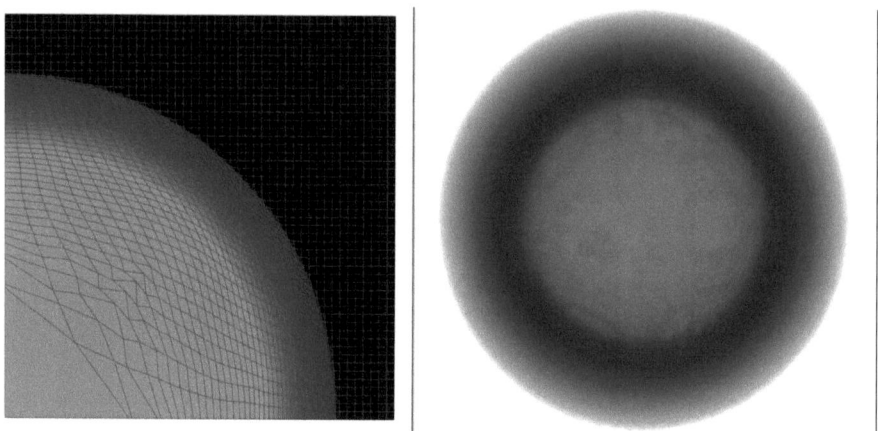

Fig. 3. Results of the 'slice' (left) and 'resampled volume' (right) hybrid rendering pipelines for timestep 1662 for a reduced 50^3 cell simulation mesh

Our testbed involves a single machine using a 16 core-12th Gen Intel i9 CPU and 128 GB of RAM. We run the LULESH simulation over several dozen time steps with a data size of 220^3, around 10 million cells. The *slice* reduction pipeline reduces the data transferred between the simulation and visualization cluster from 220^3 cells to 220^2, while the *resampling* one transfers a 30^3 structure for volume rendering. These reduction pipelines also filter out the variable fields that will not be used for visualization in order to decrease the amount of data transferred. On our test machine, we allocated 8 processes to run the simulation and another 8 to run the visualization. Due to current technical limitation in Catalyst-ADIOS2 with empty MPI rank, the *slice* pipeline was run on a single core. Data transfer between the two virtual clusters happens using a network socket, using the Sustainable Staging Transport (SST) ADIOS2 [7] engine. On a real HPC setting, this engine can take advantage of faster RDMA network interconnects.

In order to verify our hypothesis that our hybrid approach saves time overall over in transit analysis, we measured the time taken by each MPI rank at each timestep to process the simulation, perform the reduction and send the data using ADIOS2. We compared our hybrid pipeline to the equivalent pipeline performed in transit. The results presented Fig. 4 and Table 1 show the time taken by each pipeline for each of these steps averaged for all timesteps. In the case of the *slice* pipeline, the data transfer time becomes negligible in the hybrid case, and the data reduction takes more than ten times less time than the full data transfer in the in transit case. For the volume rendering pipeline involving a data size reduction using resampling, the reduction is 3.7 times faster than full dataset transfer. In both cases, our approach saved computation time (16% and 22%) on the simulation cluster compared to classic in transit analysis.

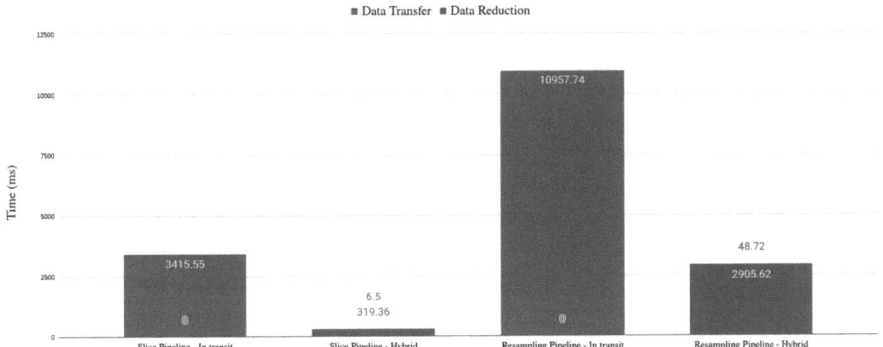

Fig. 4. Comparison of the time taken by data reduction and data transfer for both pipelines on the simulation cluster in average by timestep, for the hybrid and the in transit cases.

Table 1. Averaged compute time of time steps in milliseconds for different parts of the in transit and hybrid analysis.

	Slice Pipeline		*Resampling* Pipeline	
	In Transit	Hybrid	In Transit	Hybrid
Simulation Time (ms)	15860	15835	33539	31677
Reduction Time (ms)	0	319	0	2905
Data Transfer Time (ms)	3415	6.56	10957	48.7
Total Time (ms)	19275	16161	44497	34632
Total Gain		16.16%		22.17%

For reproducibility purpose, the code used for the experiment is available under a permissive open source license at [11].

4 Limitations and Perspectives

Beside the experimentation which validated our approach to improve the performance of large simulations, we encountered several limitations.

First, the scientists have to prepare two pipelines, one for the data reduction and one for the visualization. In situ analysis is notability known for forcing the user to anticipate the shape of the generated data before the simulation, which is sometime impossible. Some techniques have been proposed to circumvent this issue, for example by optimizing the camera placement based on the entropy of the dataset [12].

In our experiment, we reduced the size of the data via resampling to image which reduced the accuracy of the result. Hence, this approach should be evaluated and adapted to the expected analysis results. For example, if the goal is to check the general shape of the result then aggressive dimension reduction would be a good strategy. However for high accuracy results, the data reduction should be choosen and tuned carefully to not introduce any quality loss.

Another limitation is that the workflow adds a new processing block, the Catalyst-ParaView in situ processing, which limits the range of supported dataset and field types. In practice, only scalar fields and explicit topologies are supported by the framework so far, due to the current capabilities of Catalyst-ADIOS2 and Catalyst-ParaView dataset serialization.

The communication between the modules are done via the Catalyst API. Thanks to the strict ABI compatibility, the user can tune the data reduction library, currently the ParaView library, for the simulation cluster. For example, it could use an OSMesa implementation of ParaView in order to run on CPU nodes only, without forcing to use costly GPUs. As a perspective, we could envision to replace this part by some AI enhanced routines to speed-up the data reduction, without changing other processing blocks in the workflow.

Similarly, the end points could be any processing type. In our benchmark, we used the classic picture generation method to validate the correctness of the results, but we could imagine to perform advanced processing like super-resolutions of the data, Machine Learning training with the reduced dataset or specific rendering techniques which require dedicated hardware like powerful GPUs or FPGAs.

Another interesting perspective is to use the data reduction to extract region of interest in the dataset, or compute data clustering for urgent decision making [13]. The flexibility of the python pipeline of Catalyst would allow advanced detection of relevant parts to send in transit. A typical use case have been described in the Inshimtu introduction [14] where the region of interest of the Chapala cyclone is dynamically extracted in situ.

5 Conclusion

In this paper, we introduced a novel hybrid approach to address the cost of data transfer that can happen when using in transit analysis at scale. The data is first reduced in line, then the reduced data is sent over the network to the rendering nodes. Simple data reduction like resampling to a smaller dataset or discarding unused field shows very large performance gain. The innovative key point of this approach is to leverage the stable ABI of Catalyst version 2. It means that the simulation code would likely not be modified to benefit the hybrid approach, and that the flexible python pipeline does not limit the type of data reduction to perform. Finally, our approach demonstrates that the in transit analysis could be scalable by controlling the amount of transferred data in a flexible way. The proposed solution is freely available under a permissive open source license to foster reproducibility and broad adoption [9].

References

1. Bauer, A.C., et al.: In situ methods, infrastructures, and applications on high performance computing platforms. Comput. Graph. Forum **35**(3), 577–597 (2016)
2. Mazen, F., Givord, L., Gueunet, C.: Catalyst-ADIOS2: in transit analysis for numerical simulations using catalyst 2 API. In: Bienz, A., Weiland, M., Baboulin, M., Kruse, C. (eds.) High Performance Computing. ISC High Performance 2023. LNCS, vol. 13999, pp. 269–276. Springer, Cham (2023). https://doi.org/10.1007/978-3-031-40843-4_20
3. Greenshields, C.: OpenFOAM v11 User Guide 2023, The OpenFOAM Foundation, London, UK. https://doc.cfd.direct/openfoam/user-guide-v11
4. Domínguez, J.M., et al.: DualSPHysics: from fluid dynamics to multiphysics problems. Comput. Particle Mech. 1–29 (2021). https://doi.org/10.1007/s40571-021-00404-2
5. Kress, J., et al.: Opportunities for cost savings with in-transit visualization. In: Sadayappan, P., Chamberlain, B.L., Juckeland, G., Ltaief, H. (eds.) ISC High Performance 2020. LNCS, vol. 12151, pp. 146–165. Springer, Cham (2020). https://doi.org/10.1007/978-3-030-50743-5_8
6. Ayachit, U., et al.: Catalyst revised: rethinking the paraview in situ analysis and visualization API. In: Jagode, H., Anzt, H., Ltaief, H., Luszczek, P. (eds.) ISC High Performance 2021. LNCS, vol. 12761, pp. 484–494. Springer, Cham (2021). https://doi.org/10.1007/978-3-030-90539-2_33
7. Godoy, W.F., et al.: ADIOS 2: the adaptable input output system. A framework for high-performance data management. SoftwareX **12**, 100561 (2020). https://doi.org/10.1016/j.softx.2020.100561
8. Schneider, E., et al.: NVIDIA IndeX accelerated computing for visualizing Cholla's galactic winds. Parallel Comput. **107**, 102809 (2021). https://doi.org/10.1016/j.parco.2021.102809. ISSN 0167-8191
9. https://gitlab.kitware.com/paraview/adioscatalyst
10. Karlin, I., et al.: LULESH 2.0 Updates and , pp. 1–9, LLNL-TR-641973 (2013)
11. https://gitlab.kitware.com/keu-public/lulesh-adios-catalyst/-/tree/hybrid?ref_type=heads
12. Marsaglia, N., Majumder, M., Childs, H.: A trigger-based approach for optimizing camera placement over time. In: 2022 IEEE/ACM International Workshop on In Situ Infrastructures for Enabling Extreme-Scale Analysis and Visualization (ISAV), Dallas, TX, USA, pp. 14–19 (2022). https://doi.org/10.1109/ISAV56555.2022.00008
13. Flatken, M., et al.: VESTEC: visual exploration and sampling toolkit for extreme computing. IEEE Access **11**, 87805–87834 (2023). https://doi.org/10.1109/ACCESS.2023.3301177
14. https://www.kitware.com/cyclone-chapala-simulation-with-paraview-catalyst-through-kaust-imshimtu-library/

Correction to: Interactive in Situ Visualization

Dennis Grieger

Correction to:
Chapter 32 in: M. Weiland et al. (Eds.): *High Performance Computing*, **LNCS 15058,**
https://doi.org/10.1007/978-3-031-73716-9_32

The chapter "Interactive in Situ Visualization", written by Dennis Grieger, was originally published without open access. Following the authors' decision to opt for open access, the copyright of the chapter changed on 28 January 2025 to © The Author(s) 2025 and the chapter is now distributed under the terms of the Creative Commons Attribution 4.0 International License (https://creativecommons.org/licenses/by/4.0/), which permits use, sharing, adaptation, distribution and reproduction in any medium or format, as long as you give appropriate credit to the original author(s) and the source, provide a link to the Creative Commons licence and indicate if changes were made. The images or other third party material in this chapter are included in the chapter's Creative Commons licence, unless indicated otherwise in a credit line to the material. If material is not included in the chapter's Creative Commons licence and your intended use is not permitted by statutory regulation or exceeds the permitted use, you will need to obtain permission directly from the copyright holder.

Open Access This chapter is licensed under the terms of the Creative Commons Attribution 4.0 International License (http://creativecommons.org/licenses/by/4.0/), which permits use, sharing, adaptation, distribution and reproduction in any medium or format, as long as you give appropriate credit to the original author(s) and the source, provide a link to the Creative Commons license and indicate if changes were made.

The images or other third party material in this chapter are included in the chapter's Creative Commons license, unless indicated otherwise in a credit line to the material. If material is not included in the chapter's Creative Commons license and your intended use is not permitted by statutory regulation or exceeds the permitted use, you will need to obtain permission directly from the copyright holder.

The updated version of this chapter can be found at
https://doi.org/10.1007/978-3-031-73716-9_32

Author Index

A
Abdurakhmanov, I. B.   102
Acar, Mustafa Orkun   141
Alam, Sadaf   389
Antonio, N. W.   102
Anzt, Hartwig   127

B
Bard, Deborah J.   243
Bauinger, Christoph   79
Besnard, Jean-Baptiste   213
Bischof, Christian   5, 31
Blesel, Michael   5
Bowles, Spencer   339
Brown, Nick   354
Bücker, H. Martin   312

C
Calyam, Prasad   427
Cambridge, Justin   339
Carrier, John   185
Cascajo, Alberto   213
Castelló, Adrián   325
Catalán, Sandra   325
Charousset, Sandrine   402
Chetput, Sooraj   339
Chitsazzadeh, Alex   339
Cytowski, M.   102

D
Dammann, Bernd   257
Dasca, Guerau   17
Delorme, Yann T.   154
Dennis, Cicada   257
Diakhaté, François   415
Ding, Zhaohui   154
Dobrev, Plamen   115
Dröge, Bob   297

E
Edsall, Chris   389
Enders, Bjoern   243
Endo, Toshio   231
Ercius, Peter   243

F
Follin, Anders   257

G
García, Carlos   325
Gasulla, Marta Garcia   31
Genovese, Luigi   79
Gerrits, Tim   469
Givord, Lucas   482
Gombert, Louis   482
Gracia, Jose   371
Grieger, Dennis   457
Gueunet, Charles   482
Gundala, Gagan   339
Güney, Fatma   141

H
Han, Zengxiang   339
Harris, Chris   243
Haus, Utz-Uwe   402
Heldmann, Tim   5
Hennecke, Michael   185
Henschel, Robert   257
Hong, Johnathan   339
Hoste, Kenneth   297
Hu, Guilliame   339
Hughes, Clay   339
Hunhold, Laslo   273

I
Igual, Francisco D.   325
Iwainsky, Christan   31

J

Jamieson, Maurice 354
Jammer, Tim 5
Jenke, Joachim 45
Johnson, Mark 339
Jolicoeur, Lise 415

K

Kadyrov, A. S. 102
Kashi, Aditya 127
Kato, Jun 231
Keahey, Kate 427
Kreutzer, Sebastian 31
Krüger, Marcel 469
Kuchar, Olga 287
Kuhlen, Torsten W. 469
Kuhn, Michael 5
Kulkarni, Dhruva 127
Kunkel, Julian 199

L

Lagpacan, Zach 339
Lazzaro, Alfio 402
Lin, Paul T. 127
Lindemann, Jonas 257

M

Martínez, Héctor 325
Mathias, Gerald 115
May, Alex 287
Mazen, François 482
Medeiros, Daniel 439
Milke, Jan Frieder 469
Minami, Shohei 231
Miwa, Masahiro 231
Moore, Joseph 185
Morel, Alicia Esquivel 427
Morillo, Julián 297
Mujkanovic, Nina 402
Müller, Matthias S. 45
Munera, Adrian 17
Murry, Zack 427

N

Nabiev, Ramil 371
Nallagatla, Ronit 339
Nallathambi, Anusuya 339
Namyst, Raymond 415
Nayak, Pratik 127

Nguyen, Van Man 59
Niethammer, Christoph 371
Nolte, Hendrik 199
Nomura, Akihiro 231

O

O'Cais, Alan 297
Oganezov, Alexander 185
Ohtsuji, Hiroki 231
Oraji, Yussur Mustafa 45

P

Patel, Ansh 339
Pätzold, Cornelius 45
Pedretti, Kevin 339
Peeters, Lara 297
Peng, Ivy 439
Pham, Khoi 339
Powers, Mark 427

Q

Quentin, Lars 199
Quiñones, Eduardo 17
Quintana-Ortí, Enrique S. 325

R

Ramshanker, Abinands 339
Röblitz, Thomas 297
Rodríguez-Sánchez, Rafael 325
Rogers, Timothy G. 339
Rose, Martin 371
Royuela, Sara 17
Ruhela, Dhani 173
Ruopp, Andreas 371

S

Saillard, Emmanuelle 59
Sakamoto, Ryuichi 231
Scheinberg, Aaron 127
Schieffer, Gabin 439
Schoder, Johannes 312
Schwitanski, Simon 45
Sergent, Marc 59
Serra, Josep Pocurull 31
Shende, Sameer 213
Simmendinger, Christian 371
Singleton, Tatiyanna 287
Sitzmann, Tomas Javier 427
Soumagne, Jerome 185

Author Index

T
Tarraf, Ahmad 213
Thibault, Samuel 59
Thota, Abhinav 257

U
Unat, Didem 141

V
Van Leeuwen, Caspar 297
Vinayagame, Radjasouria 59

W
Wahlgren, Jacob 439
Wasserman, Mark 154

Welborn, Samuel S. 243
Wesner, Stefan 273
Widener, Patrick M. 287
Williams, Matt 389
Woods, Christopher 389

Y
Yan, Htet 339
Yoshida, Eiji 231
Yuki, Tomoya 231

Z
Zameret, Alon 154
Zhang, FangLing 339
Zhou, Jianfeng 427

MIX
Papier aus verantwortungsvollen Quellen
Paper from responsible sources
FSC® C105338

If you have any concerns about our products,
you can contact us on
ProductSafety@springernature.com

In case Publisher is established outside the EU,
the EU authorized representative is:
**Springer Nature Customer Service Center GmbH
Europaplatz 3, 69115 Heidelberg, Germany**

Printed by Libri Plureos GmbH
in Hamburg, Germany